CALIFORNIA

AN INTERPRETIVE HISTORY

McGraw-Hill

A Division of The **McGraw·Hill** Companies

CALIFORNIA:

An Interpretive History

2 3 4 5 6 7 8 9 0   DOC   DOC   9 0 9 8

ISBN 0-07-052411-4

This book was set in Times Roman by Graphic World.
The editors were Lyn Uhl and Elaine Rosenberg;
the production supervisors were Denise L. Puryear and Paula Keller.
The cover was designed by Karen K. Quigley.
Cover photo: Darrell Gulin/Tony Stone.
Project supervision was done by The Total Book.
R. R. Donnelley & Sons Company was printer and binder.

Library of Congress Cataloging-in-Publication Data

Rawls, James J.
    California: an interpretive history / James J. Rawls, Walton
  Bean.—7th ed.
      p.   cm.
    Includes bibliographical references and indexes.
    ISBN 0-07-052411-4
    1. California—History.   I. Bean, Walton. II. Title.
  F861.R38   1997
  979.4—dc21   96-40054
  http://www.mhhe.com

CALIFORNIA

AN INTERPRETIVE HISTORY

SEVENTH EDITION

James J. Rawls
Instructor of History
Diablo Valley College

Walton Bean
Late Professor of History
University of California, Berkeley

Boston, Massachusetts   Burr Ridge, Illinois   Dubuque, Iowa
Madison, Wisconsin   New York, New York   San Francisco, California   St. Louis, Missouri

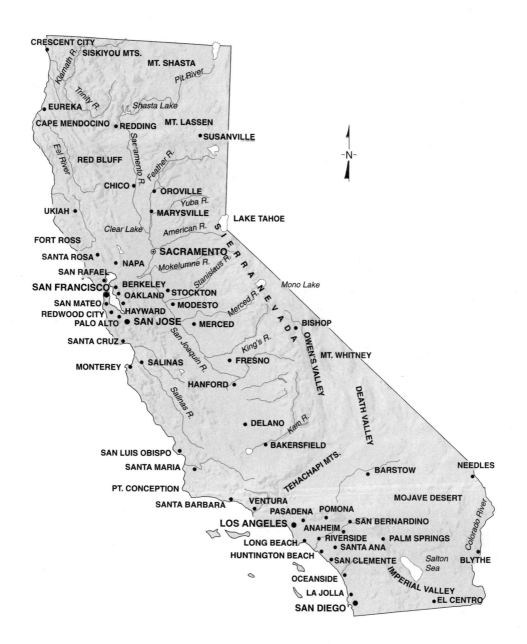

ABOUT THE AUTHORS

JAMES J. RAWLS, an instructor of history at Diablo Valley College, received his B.A. in history from Stanford University. He was awarded an M.A. and Ph.D. in history from the University of California, Berkeley, completing his doctoral dissertation under the guidance of Walton Bean. Dr. Rawls also has taught California history as a visiting associate professor at the University of California, Berkeley. He serves as the Reviews Editor of *California History,* the journal of the California Historical Society. He is the author of *Indians of California: The Changing Image* and *Chief Red Fox is Dead: A History of Native Americans since 1945,* coauthor of *Land of Liberty: A United States History,* and editor of *New Directions in California History: A Book of Readings.* His articles and reviews have appeared in such publications as *Journal of American History, Pacific Historical Review,* and *American Indian Quarterly.*

The late WALTON BEAN was, for more than 35 years, a member of the University of California, Berkeley, faculty where he taught undergraduate courses in California history and graduate courses in California and twentieth-century United States history. His highly acclaimed book, *Boss Ruef's San Francisco,* won the Commonwealth Club of California's gold medal and the annual prize of the Pacific Coast Branch of the American Historical Association. Dr. Bean also served as Asia Foundation Professor of American History at the University of Karachi from 1956 to 1958. He received his A.B. and M.A. from the University of Southern California and was awarded his Ph.D. from the University of California, Berkeley.

For Linda

CONTENTS

PREFACE

California is more than just another state. It is also a dream, a fantasy, a state of mind. This California of our collective imagination draws its power from universal human needs. Founded on expectation and hope, it promises to fulfill our deepest longings for opportunity and success, sunshine and beauty, health and long life, freedom, and even a foretaste of the future.

Two of the logical consequences of this dream-like image of California have been growth and diversity. Throughout its history, the Golden State has attracted from across the country and around the world millions of newcomers pursuing the California dream. Today California is by far the most populous state in the union and the most ethnically diverse.

For many Californians, the dream has been realized. California is the nation's wealthiest state, ranking first in industrial and agricultural production. It leads in high technology and is home to the nation's entertainment industry. If California were a separate country, it would rank seventh among the nations of the world in gross domestic product.

Other Californians have found the dream denied. Running through the state's history is a bitter strain of conflict. On its way to greatness, California has been burdened by a legacy of racism and nativism, episodes of discrimination and exclusion, a sometimes violent struggle between labor and capital, and an intense contest over the state's land and water resources.

First published thirty years ago, *California: An Interpretive History* has become the standard in the field. The seventh edition retains all the strengths of the earlier editions. It provides a comprehensive survey of the state's cultural and social affairs, along with an account of its political and economic history; it appraises the state's virtues and accomplishments, as well as its faults and failures. Original interpretations are offered of California's most controversial and persistent problems. Each chapter opens with a brief introductory section, previewing the material to be covered.

In the new edition, Chapters 1 and 2 have been substantially revised as have the last several chapters. New material has been added on recent political, economic, and social history. Minor revisions have been made elsewhere to highlight items of importance, including new sections on "Native Resistance" in Chapter 4, "Depression and Deportation" in Chapter 26, and "Entertainment" in Chapter 36. Greater emphasis throughout has been placed on the history of ethnic minorities and women. New maps, graphs, photographs, and other illustrations have been added, and the Selected Bibliographies at the end of each chapter have been updated. Readers seeking further bibliographical information are referred to Doyce B. Nunis, Jr., and Gloria R. Lothrop (eds.), *A Guide to the History of California* (1989).

Grateful acknowledgment is made for permission to quote from the following, previously published material: Joan Didion, *Slouching towards Bethlehem* (New York: Farrar, Straus & Giroux, 1968); Gerald Haslam, *Coming of Age in California* (Walnut Creek: Devil Mountain Books, 1990); Maxine Hong Kingston, *The Woman Warrior: Memoirs of a Girlhood among Ghosts* (New York: Knopf, 1976); and Ishmael Reed, *Yellow Back Radio Broke-Down* (New York: Doubleday, 1969).

I have benefited from the advice and assistance of many individuals in the preparation of this book. My greatest debt is to Eugene C. Lee, former director of the Institute of Governmental Studies at the University of California, Berkeley, who generously has read and commented on the new material in the latter chapters of this edition. I also acknowledge the assistance of Ted K. Bradshaw, the late James D. Hart, Todd LaPorte, and James J. Parsons, all of the University of California, Berkeley.

Others who have contributed to the book's improvement are Art R. Aurano, Antelope Valley College; Jacqueline R. Braitman, University of California, Los Angeles; Gregg M. Campbell, California State University, Sacramento; Kathryn Wiler Dabelow, Pasadena City College; Raymond F. Dasmann, University of California, Santa Cruz; David Eakins, San Jose State University; Robert Fricke, West Valley College; Gerald Haslam, California State University, Sonoma; Robert V. Hine, University of California, Riverside; James D. Houston, University of California, Santa Cruz; William King, Mt. San Antonio College; Dan Krieger, California Polytechnic State University, San Luis Obispo; Gary F. Kurutz, California State Library; Ward M. McAfee, California State University, San Bernardino; Shirley Ann Moore, California State University, Sacramento; Spencer C. Olin, Jr., University of California, Irvine; Donald H. Pflueger, California State Polytechnic University, Pomona; Allan Schoenherr, Fullerton College; Ray Stafanson, Chabot College; James Steidel, Canada College; Mark S. Still, College of San Mateo; Gregory H. Tilles, Diablo Valley College; Bonnie N. Trask, Fresno City College; Jules Tygiel, San Francisco State University; James C. Williams, California History Center, DeAnza College; Jerry Williams, California State University, Chico; and Charles Wollenberg, Vista College.

My students at Diablo Valley College have continued to share with me their enthusiasm for California history, and to them I am especially grateful.

James J. Rawls

CALIFORNIA
AN INTERPRETIVE HISTORY

CHAPTER ONE

Introduction: Geography and History

California is a notoriously extraordinary place. Its natural charms are of mythic proportions—the grandeur of Yosemite, the dark mystery of the redwoods, the incomparable coastline, the sun-drenched skies. These qualities have contributed mightily to the dreamlike image of California that resides in our collective imagination. Yet these qualities—and many more—also have played an important role in the historical development of California.

THE ORIGINS OF CALIFORNIA

No one knows for sure how California came to be. Stories and theories abound, but there is no consensus about the origins of this remarkable place.

The earliest attempts to account for the origination of California were made by the first peoples to live in the area. The Indians of California developed a wide variety of creation stories, each with its own unique features and cast of characters. Widely differing versions of creation flourished even within individual communities. The native people recognized the unlikelihood of agreement on matters of such importance: "This is how we tell it; they tell it differently."

Likewise, earth scientists today do not agree on the origins of California. The most widely accepted notion is the theory of plate tectonics. Tectonics is the study of forces deep within the earth that give shape to surface features such as mountains and ocean basins. According to this theory, the earth's crust and upper mantle consist of about 20 enormous plates that are in continual motion. The plates lurch and grind against one another, moving at the rate of a few inches a year. (Why the plates are moving is one of the least understood and most debated parts of the theory.) The largest of the plates is the Pacific Plate, underlying about two-thirds of the Pacific Ocean. The Pacific Plate's collision with the North American Plate is at the heart of the plate tectonics theory of the creation of California.

"For an extremely large percentage of the history of the world, there was no California," writes John McPhee, author of *Assembling California* (1993). According to McPhee, the western edge of the North American continent once was far inland, about where the Rocky Mountains are today. California began to emerge as the easternmost part of the state "rose" out of the primordial sea, carrying upward ancient ocean-floor sediments. Then, over millions of years, other parts of California began to assemble, a piece at a time. Fragments of the earth's crust arrived individually and in massive conglomerates, joining or "docking" themselves to the continent and creating what became California.

The main event was the collision of the eastward-moving Pacific Plate and the westward-moving North American Plate. As the plates collided, the Pacific Plate descended or "subducted" beneath the continent's edge. The leading edge of the Pacific Plate plunged deep into the earth and began to melt. The resultant molten rock eventually cooled to form the granite core of the Sierra Nevada mountains. Erosion later removed the surface rock, uncovering the granite below. With the weight of the overburden removed, the mountains became uplifted along deep cracks or "faults." In the enormous heat generated by subduction, metal-rich compounds dissolved into solutions and were injected into the fissures of the rocks being formed above. Different combinations of minerals at different levels precipitated to form deposits of copper, lead, tungsten, silver, and gold.

Subsequent dockings of Pacific Plate material doubled the width of California. Geologists have identified rocks in this material that came from the entire Pacific basin, encompassing origins stretching over half the surface of the earth. Thus, imbedded in the physical structure of California was a powerful metaphor for the later cultural and ethnic diversity of what became the Golden State.

As the Sierra Nevada rose in the interior, the western edge of the continental plate nosed out along the ocean floor. Sedimentary rocks and ocean-crust material were churned up and piled in great confusion along the continent's edge, forming a low-lying range of mountains along the California coast. Between the newly formed Coast Ranges and the Sierra Nevada lay a deep trough that slowly filled with volcanic debris and sediments eroded from the surrounding mountains. After more than 100 million years of accumulated fill, this intermontane trough became the great Central Valley.

For reasons that are not entirely clear, the relative movements of the Pacific and North American plates changed dramatically about 30 million years ago. The process of collision and subduction ended. Instead, the two plates began sliding past each other in a lateral motion. The boundary between the two plates became a half-mile-wide collection of deep ruptures called the San Andreas Fault zone. Land to the west of the fault began moving northwestward at the rate of a couple of inches per year. This lateral motion was smooth and continuous far beneath the surface where the earth was relatively pliable, but the rigid materials near the surface tended to lock and resist the inexorable movement. Whenever a sudden unlocking released accumulated stress along the fault, earthquakes shook the surface.

California has experienced thousands of earthquakes throughout its history. Most have been unremarkable. Accounts of devastating temblors appear in the

The San Andreas Fault cuts through California from Imperial County in the south to Mendocino County in the north. Where streams cross the San Andreas, as here in the Carrizo Plain, their beds have been abruptly displaced by lateral movement along the fault. (*Photograph by R. E. Wallace. Courtesy of the U.S. Geological Survey.*)

stories of California Indians, in the earliest records of European settlers, and in the memories of countless Californians alive today. California falls into the highest seismic risk category in the nation; the frequency of earthquakes in the state is 10 times higher than for the world as a whole.

The lateral movement of the Pacific Plate has been like a conveyor belt through the heartland of California. Much of the land to the west of the San Andreas Fault—including the sites of San Diego, Los Angeles, Santa Barbara, San Luis Obispo, and Monterey—once was located hundreds of miles to the south along the coast of Mexico. In another 30 million years, it will be hundreds of miles to the north. The stresses of this lateral movement have bent entire mountain ranges and opened "pull-apart" depressions such as the Napa and Sonoma valleys.

The final sculpting of California occurred during the Pleistocene Epoch, beginning less than 2 million years ago, when great sheets of ice covered much of the northern hemisphere. Changing sea levels altered the Pacific coastline and opened a bridge of land between the continents of Asia and North America. Glaciers in the Sierra Nevada spread and retreated half a dozen times, carving the sheer walls of Yosemite and other U-shaped mountain valleys. Between the succeeding glaciations, freshwater lakes filled the interior valleys and deposited rich layers of fertile soil. Roaming the grassy plains of California were shaggy camels, mastodons, imperial mammoths, and saber-toothed cats (later designated the state fossil, *Smilodon californicus*).

REGIONAL DIVERSITY

California is huge—the third largest of the states, after Alaska and Texas. It extends over nearly 10° of latitude, with a coastline of 1264 miles, and its land surface is almost exactly 100 million acres. Within this vast area are a greater range of land forms, a greater variety of habitats, and more species of plants and animals than in any area of comparable size in all of North America. The profusion of varying landscapes offers some of the world's most inspiring adventures in scenery and some of its finest opportunities for recreation. Altitudes vary from 14,495 feet at the top of Mt. Whitney, the highest point in the United States outside Alaska, to 282 feet below sea level at Badwater in Death Valley, the lowest point in the country, although these two points are only 80 miles apart.

Mountains cover most of the surface of California. The largest range is the Sierra Nevada, occupying one-fifth of the total area of the state. It extends more than 400 miles along California's eastern border and contains many snow-capped peaks over 13,000 feet. This massive barrier isolated the Native American cultures of California for thousands of years; it also impeded European American settlement and posed an immense challenge to the builders of the transcontinental railroad in the nineteenth century. Several modern highways through the range—including those that cross Tioga, Sonora, and Ebbetts passes—are routinely closed in the winter still today.

The eastern side of the Sierra Nevada rises steeply, whereas the western side has a more gentle slope. Forests of pine, fir, and cedar cover the lower elevations. The gold discovered in California in 1848 was eroded from rock outcroppings in the High Sierra and deposited in stream banks and ancient riverbeds of the western foothills.

Beyond the eastern slope of the Sierra is a portion of the Great Basin region, a desolate area of mountains and high desert valleys. Here lies Owens Valley, celebrated by author Mary Austin as "the land of little rain" and scene of one of the most bitter water disputes in California history. Farther east are the White Mountains where grow the bristlecone pines (*Pinus longaeva*), the world's oldest living organisms. Some of these trees have lived for more than 4600 years.

To the north of the Sierra Nevada is a mountainous region that includes the southern tip of the Klamath Mountains and the Cascades. This region's tortured terrain has made it one of the least settled areas of the state. Within the Cascades are Mt. Lassen (10,457 feet), a volcanic peak that last erupted in 1921, and Mt. Shasta (14,162 feet). To the east of the Cascades lies the rugged Modoc Plateau, a forbidding region almost completely covered with lava flows and igneous rocks extruded through vents in the earth's surface. In the northwest corner of the state are the Klamath Mountains through which the free-flowing waters of the Klamath and Trinity rivers have cut deep and twisting gorges as they rush to the sea.

The major landform provinces of California. The most striking characteristic of California geography is its diversity.

The Coast Ranges extend from Cape Mendocino in the north to Point Conception in the south. Consisting of uplifted sedimentary material, much of which has been metamorphosed, the Coast Ranges average less than 4000 feet in height. Most settlement has been in the lowlands between individual ridges, with the greatest concentration of population in the San Francisco Bay area, the only real break in the coastal mountains. Regarded as one of the world's finest natural harbors, San Francisco Bay became the gateway to the state's interior in the nineteenth and twentieth centuries.

On the seaward slopes of the northern Coast Ranges are forests of coast redwoods, the state tree of California, greatly diminished by more than a century of commercial logging. Among the coast redwoods (*Sequoia sempervirens*) are the tallest trees in the world, some having reached a height of more than 360 feet. The Sierra redwoods (*Sequoiadendron giganteum*), also known as "big trees," have the largest mass of any living thing on earth.

Lying between the Coast Ranges and the Sierra Nevada is the Central Valley, the most productive agricultural region in California. More than 400 miles long and about 50 miles wide, the Central Valley is really two valleys in one. In the north is the Sacramento Valley, drained by the southward flowing Sacramento River; the San Joaquin Valley lies to the south and is drained by the northward flowing San Joaquin River. Runoff from the Sierra foothills flows into tributaries of the two river systems which join in the Sacramento–San Joaquin Delta before reaching San Francisco Bay.

Bunchgrass prairies and oak woodlands once covered the valley floor and great tule marshes extended over the floodplain. Beavers in the inland streams first lured European Americans across the continent to California in the 1820s. Overhead is the Pacific flyway, a heavily traveled route for migrating birds. (More than 500 species of birds have been documented in California.) Beneath the surface lie rich deposits of oil and natural gas, created millions of years ago from the remains of marine plants and animals. Irrigated cropland today covers most of the valley and produces more agricultural products than any comparable region in the world.

At the southern end of the Central Valley is yet another group of mountains, the Transverse Ranges, familiar to travelers driving over the "grapevine" along Interstate 5. These ranges stretch along an east-west axis for about 250 miles and extend offshore to form the Santa Barbara Channel Islands. South of the Transverse Ranges lie the Peninsular Ranges, a northern extension of the mountainous spine of the Baja California peninsula. Settlement in the region has centered on the coastal plain at Los Angeles and San Diego. The Los Angeles Basin, the largest lowland area in California that directly fronts the ocean, became the most populous region in the state in the early twentieth century. Population spread steadily into the surrounding San Bernardino, San Gabriel, and San Fernando valleys.

The eastern half of southern California is a large desert triangle—a vast expanse of sandy valleys, dried lake beds, and short ranges of rugged mountains. The largest desert in California is the Mojave, covering about 25,000 square miles; the most notorious is Death Valley, an inferno described by one observer as "the very manifestation of a Medieval hell." To the south is the Colorado Desert, a depression that extends to the Gulf of California.

The southern deserts were as much a barrier to overland migration to California in the eighteenth century as the steep eastern face of the Sierra Nevada was in the nineteenth. These formidable obstacles—coupled with California's extreme geographic remoteness from Europe and even from the original Spanish and British colonial settlements in the western hemisphere—meant that European settlement of California began remarkably late. The Spanish founded their first settlement on the Pacific coast in 1519, at Panama. Not until 1769, two and a half centuries later, did they found their first settlement in Alta California at San Diego. Throughout the Spanish and Mexican periods the difficulty of getting to California prevented any substantial numbers of settlers from going there, and despite the American conquest and the tremendous lure of the gold discovery, that difficulty continued to retard its growth until, and even after, the opening of the first transcontinental railroad in 1869,

THE CLIMATES OF CALIFORNIA

Once the barriers of geographic remoteness had been overcome, the unique and gentle climates of California became a greater attraction than gold had been. As geographer James J. Parsons has pointed out, "It so happens that California's arbitrarily conceived boundaries outline the only area of winter rain and summer drought in North America." Except on the northwest coast, where the average annual precipitation ranges up to nearly 110 inches (at Monumental in Del Norte County), rainfall in California ordinarily occurs only between late October and early May. In the state as a whole, the average yearly precipitation is 23.88 inches; however, throughout the late spring, the entire summer, and the early autumn there is very seldom any precipitation at all.

The dry summers of California made agriculture exceedingly difficult before the development of irrigation on a vast scale in the American period. The uniqueness of the climate then gave the state a virtual monopoly on the production of many valuable agricultural crops, and the invention of the refrigerated railway car made it possible to market them throughout the country. Climate also was a vital factor in the location of other major industries in California, notably the production of motion pictures and aircraft.

Within the common pattern of summer drought, California's climatic conditions vary widely. Indeed, the climates of California are as diverse as those of southern Ireland and the northern Sahara.

California has four of the five major types of climate found around the world (only the hot and rainy tropical climate is not represented). Most common is the Mediterranean climate zone with its relatively warm, dry summers and mild winters. Even within this zone, however, are important variations. Along the coast, marine air and fog keep temperatures more moderate than in the Central Valley where summers generally are hot and cloudless. An intermediate version of the Mediterranean climate is found in the Coast Ranges and the foothills of the Sierra Nevada. Similar variations are found around the shores of the Mediterranean, in central Chile, and on the southern tip of Africa.

Semiarid or steppe climates encompass much of the San Joaquin Valley and the fringes of the Mojave Desert. Rainfall here is less than in the Mediterranean zone. A cooler version occurs in a narrow coastal strip from Los Angeles to

CLIMATE ZONES

- Mediterranean
- Semi-arid or Steppe
- Desert
- Microthermal or Alpine

The climates of California. Climatic variations in California are greater than in any comparable area in the United States.

San Diego. Notable for its sunny summers, pleasant winters, and little rain, this and the Mediterranean climate zone are what best qualify California for inclusion in the nation's booming "Sunbelt." The air pollution that has plagued the region in the twentieth century—casting a noxious pall over sunny California—is the result of a sunlight-activated chemical reaction among pollutants trapped by a combination of onshore winds, interior mountains, and temperature inversions (in which cooler marine air is trapped beneath warmer air above).

Desert climates cover the southeastern third of the state, east of the Sierra Nevada and Peninsular ranges. Cut off by mountains from moisture-laden Pacific storms, this region receives very little rain. Summer temperatures are the highest in the state, averaging over 100°F in July in Death Valley. The southwestern part of the San Joaquin Valley also is in a desert climate zone. Similar climates are found in the Sahara and the deserts of Australia.

The microthermal climates of California are much like those found in the Alps where summers are short and cool and winters are vigorous. Average temperatures in the coldest month are below freezing at the higher elevations of the Sierra, the Modoc Plateau, and the Klamath Mountains. Most of California's water originates in these higher elevations as winter snowpack and spring runoff. About three-fourths of the annual precipitation occurs in the mountainous northern third of the state, whereas today 80 percent of the water demand (mostly for agriculture) occurs in the southern two-thirds.

California's rich natural resources—its many varieties of forests and soils, its gold, oil, and other minerals—have all contributed vitally to its economic development. So has water for irrigation and power, though moving water from where it naturally occurs to where demand has been created is one of the state's greatest challenges.

SELECTED BIBLIOGRAPHY

On the geologic evolution of California, see John McPhee, *Assembling California* (1993); Rod Redfern, *The Making of a Continent* (1983); and R. M. Norris and R. W. Webb, *Geology of California* (1976). Among the many collections of Native American accounts, see especially Julian Lang (ed.), *Ararapikva: Creation Stories* (1993), and C. Hart Merriam (ed.), *The Dawn of the World* (1993). The definitive guide to California's natural diversity is Allan A. Schoenherr, *A Natural History of California* (1992). See also Philip L. Fradkin, *The Seven States of California* (1995); Michael Barbour, et al., *California's Changing Landscape* (1993); and Elna Bakker, *An Island Called California* (1984). James J. Parsons's "The Uniqueness of California," *American Quarterly*, VII (Spring 1955), pp. 45–55, is a good introduction to the effects of California's geography on its history. Geographical, historical, and political maps are contained in David Hornbeck, *California Patterns: A Geographical and Historical Atlas* (1983); Crane S. Miller and Richard S. Hyslop, *California: The Geography of Diversity* (1983); Michael W. Donley et al., *Atlas of California* (1979); Warren A. Beck and Ynez D. Haase, *Historical Atlas of California* (1974) and *Historical Atlas of the American West* (1989); and Robert D. Durrenberger, *Patterns on the Land* (1960).

CHAPTER TWO

The Original Californians

"In the beginning there was no sun, no moon, no stars. All was dark, and everywhere there was only water." So begins a creation story told by the Maidu Indians of California.

According to the traditional beliefs of many of the state's native people, the California Indians were created and have lived forever in their ancestral homeland. Anthropologists, however, believe that the aboriginal population of California descended from ancient peoples who crossed into North America from Asia over the land bridge connecting the two continents during the glaciations of the late Pleistocene Epoch.

Whatever the origins of the first Californians, the archaeological record reveals a process of dynamic change and adaptation during thousands of years of human occupation. At the time of first European contact in the sixteenth century, native people were living in each of the diverse regions of California. Because their technology did not include metal implements, the California Indians represented a survival of the stone age. But the causes and the meaning of this fact have been much misunderstood, largely because of the persistence of rather primitive ideas about the nature of primitive people, and particularly the persistence of racism— the belief that some races are biologically, morally, and intellectually inferior to others, and the use of this belief to justify the oppression of some races by others. Among competent ethnologists, the race theories underlying this pattern of thought have long been discredited.

The survival of a stone age culture in California was not the result of any hereditary biological limitations on the potential of the Indians as a race. They had been geographically and culturally isolated. The vast expanse of oceans, mountains, and deserts had sheltered California from foreign stimulation as well as from foreign conquest, and even within California the Indian groups were so settled that they had little contact with each other. On the positive side, California supported a much larger number of Indians than did any other region of comparable size in North America north of Mexico. The California Indians had made a successful adaptation to their environment, and they had learned to live without destroying each other.

FOOD AND POPULATION

The nature and extent of the food supply deeply influenced the culture of the Indians of California, and determined the size of their population. Most of them lived entirely by hunting, fishing, and gathering. Agriculture was practiced only in the southernmost portion, particularly among the Cahuilla, and in the extreme southeastern portion along the lower Colorado River. But the natural sources of food were remarkably diverse and often ingeniously obtained. The greatest staple was the acorn, which because of its high fat content has a higher caloric value than wheat. When washed free of tannic acid, acorn flour was made into porridge or bread. In many desert areas, mesquite pods took the place of acorns. Deer and small game were generally available. Insects were a widely accepted source of nutriment. Fish were abundant in the streams, notably salmon in the northwest. Fish and meat were often dried. Along the coast, shellfish were consumed in quantities, and many shell mounds as much as 30 feet high, which accumulated as heaps of kitchen refuse over periods of 3000 years, provide important archaeological clues to Indian life.

The term "Digger" as applied to the California Indians is a pejorative misnomer, based on the mistaken idea that they lived largely by grubbing up roots. American pioneer immigrants, seeing Indian women busy with digging sticks, were unaware that they wanted root fibers for basketmaking more often than for food. The diet of the California tribes did include certain roots and bulbs, but perhaps the real reason the Digger legend persisted was that it was easier to deprive the Indians of their lands and their lives if it could be believed that they were only miserable and subhuman creatures anyway.

The most distinctive method used in preparing food was the process of leaching the tannic acid from acorn flour. The flour, produced by pounding husked acorns with a stone mortar and pestle, was winnowed by tossing in a shallow basket. Then it was spread out in a sandy, shallow depression or basin and repeatedly doused with water to wash away the acid. Bread might then be baked in an earth oven, but much more commonly the flour was placed in a basket with water brought to a boil by dropping in hot stones. This produced a gruel or porridge, which was eaten either plain or flavored with berries, grass seeds, nuts, or bits of meat or fish.

The cooking basket might be caulked with pitch or tar, but it was often so tightly woven that it would hold boiling water without caulking. As this suggests, the California Indians were remarkably skilled in basketmaking. In this art they had no equals anywhere in the world, either in the utility of the product or in the beauty of the designs. They had developed basketry to such a point that pottery making was hardly necessary and was confined mainly to the southern region, which was influenced by southwestern Indian culture.

Hunting was mainly with the bow, which was often backed with sinew for extra strength. Arrows were cleverly feathered, and the heads were made of obsidian,

A Pomo gift basket, decorated with shell disks and covered with yellow, green, blue, white, and red feathers in geometric design. (*Courtesy of the Smithsonian Institution.*)

which is sharper than flint and more readily shaped by flaking. Knives were also of obsidian. Fishing was done with nets or hooks; with harpoons, particularly for salmon; or with poison, accomplished by throwing buckeyes into small pools at the edge of a stream.

The hunting and fishing were done mainly by men, the gathering of plant foods and the cooking by women. Work activities, however, occasionally overlapped. Men sometimes aided in the collecting of plant foods (such as knocking acorns from oak limbs) and women hunted and trapped small game. In general, everyone worked hard, and the division of labor was fair and effective. The picture of the Indians as lazy is the result of the demoralization that set in after the coming of the white man, who treated Indians as if they were inferior beings and seemed intent on proving that they were.

California Indians engaged in a wide variety of proto-agricultural practices to manage their resources and enhance the yield of potential food sources. They practiced periodic burning of groundcover to replenish the soil, pruned plants and trees, and culled animal and insect populations. In addition, the Mojaves and the Yumas practiced agriculture to the extent of planting corn, bean, and pumpkin seeds in the mud left by the annual floodwaters along the lower Colorado; farther west, agriculture existed among the Cahuilla. But with such partial exceptions, the Indian agriculture of the American southwest did not spread into California. One essential explanation of this is that the aboriginal California Indian population was in a Malthusian equilibrium. The natural food supply was moderately abundant and fairly well assured. The attempt to divert labor from hunting and gathering to the unfamiliar and risky techniques of agriculture would have produced a net loss from the disruption of the existing system.

The actual number of persons supported by this system in California, before the coming of the Spaniards, can never be precisely determined, but a reasonable estimate is that there were at least 300,000 Indians within the present boundaries of the state when the first Spanish settlement was founded in 1769. There have been extremely wide variations among the estimates of the aboriginal population of North America as a whole, but Indian population density in California before European contact was much greater than the average for other areas in what is now the United States.

ASPECTS OF MATERIAL CULTURE

Dwellings were generally simple, often conical or dome-shaped, except in the northwest, where they were often solid-frame structures built of redwood planks and in rectangular form. In central California, poles and brush were the most common building materials, and many houses were built partly underground or banked with earth for insulation.

The sweat house, or *temescal,* was a distinctive institution, and its use was generally confined to men. An open fire, not steam, was used to produce heat, and as the upper part of the *temescal* would fill with smoke, the men would lie on the floor. Then, while still perspiring freely, they would rush to a nearby stream or lake and plunge into the water. In central California this was done as a means of keeping clean as well as healthy; a ritually purifying act. Women and children generally

Interior of a *temescal* in central California. (*Courtesy of the Bancroft Library.*)

were expected to do their bathing less ceremoniously, and in the early morning before the men were awake. The *temescal* also had some of the aspects of a men's club, and in some tribes the older boys and men customarily gambled, worked, and slept there.

The most common type of boat was the *tule balsa,* a raft made of reeds bound into a boatlike shape. Seagoing dugout canoes, carved from half a redwood trunk, were used in the northwest; the Chumash of the Santa Barbara Channel region also made seaworthy canoes, though of plank rather than dugout construction.

Men ordinarily wore no clothing at all; the standard garment for women was a knee-length skirt. This was made of plant fibers or skins. In the latter case the lower part was slit into fringes for decoration and freedom of movement. Women also wore beautifully decorated round basketry caps. When the weather forced a degree of protection from cold, both sexes wore blankets and robes made of furs. The sea otter was most prized, but deer and rabbit skins were more common. Foul weather gear also included short trousers, buckskin shirts, and jackets. Ritual costumes, worn only on special occasions, were elaborately constructed and included feather headdresses, feathered capes, shell necklaces, and earrings. Body painting and tattooing also were practiced by many California Indians.

LOCATION, LINGUISTIC GROUPS, TRIBES

The pattern of availability of plant and animal foods, and the complete reliance upon them, tended to determine not only the number of people in a community, but also its location. The California Indians lived in settled villages of about 100 to 500 inhabitants, usually groups of kindred families; the location of these communities was determined very precisely by the availability of food and water.

Another culture-determining factor was the variety of languages. Language barriers combined with the localized nature of food supplies to intensify isolation and provincialism. Of the five main language stocks in California, four were common to other parts of North America, suggesting that there had been a vast jumble of migrations in very ancient times, before the mixture hardened. These five main stocks were subdivided into 21 language families, which in turn were subdivided into numerous dialects, most of which were mutually unintelligible. Indian California was the region of greatest linguistic diversity in the world, excepting, according to some scholars, only the Sudan and New Guinea.

Typically, California Indians knew that they had been born and would die in a little town on the bank of a certain stream and that the land in the immediate vicinity belonged to their people. Just across certain hills, on another stream, were other people whom they might visit and with whom, if they could converse, they might intermarry, but on whose proprietary rights they should not infringe. Trade routes crisscrossed California and the exchange of goods was common. Inland tribes, for instance, traded obsidian and deerskins to coast dwellers for shell beads, dried fish, and sea otter pelts.

Anthropologists have attempted various definitions of the "tribe" in California. It may be considered a body of people who occupied a distinct territory and shared a similar culture; on this basis there are over 100 such tribes. Anthropologist Lowell J. Bean has described them as "non-political, ethnic nationalities." California tribes did not generally have centralized governmental structures but consisted of several independent units often identified as "tribelets." Each tribelet included a group of neighboring villages, perhaps with a principal village and three or four smaller ones. Tribelet populations ranged from several hundred to several thousand individuals; territorial boundaries were vigorously defended.

Elsewhere in North America a tribe was ordinarily a nation with a strong and militant national consciousness. With the exception of the Mojaves and the Yumas on the southeastern margin, no such breadth of organization or political consciousness existed among the California Indians. The village community was usually the highest political unit. It is easy to see why the California Indians found it difficult to organize effective resistance to a handful of Spaniards, let alone to a horde of Anglo-Americans.

SOCIAL CULTURE

The most extraordinary diversity prevailed not only among the languages spoken but also in nearly all other aspects of culture. Elements of culture occurring only in part of California, most of them only in a small part, greatly outnumbered those that were universal. Anthropologists have divided California into six major, geographically distinct "culture areas," within which residents shared common traits, such as dress, housing, manufacturing methods, and other routine activities. These six areas are commonly identified as the southern, central, northwestern, northeastern, Great Basin, and Colorado River culture areas. The northwest culture area had many of the characteristics of the tribes to the north of it, and the culture patterns of the Colorado River area bore some resemblance to those of tribes to the east. The central culture area was the most distinctively "Californian." Even within these broad subdivisions, there was great diversity. Meaningful generalizations can be made about California Indian culture only if it is understood that there were exceptions to almost every general statement.

Except for the tribes along the Colorado River, the California Indians generally were peaceable and unaggressive. Yet ethnographic and historic resources indicate that wars were not uncommon. The causes of armed conflict included trespassing, poaching, the abduction of women, and competition for rare resources. Wars seldom were very lengthy, but they could be deadly. The chief of a tribe was not necessarily the military leader, unless he had given some special evidence of military skill. More common than warfare were feuds involving persons and families rather than tribes. Murder was the prime cause, and ordinarily the victim's relatives could be propitiated by some sort of payment for their loss. Even when an intertribal offense led to a small battle, one side would often pay the other to prevent further attacks. If a series of reprisals occurred, it might end with each side compensating the other for the damages.

Social classes hardly existed, except in the northwest, where there was the greatest interest in acquiring wealth and personal property and where slavery, based

CULTURE AREAS

S - Southern
C - Central
NW - Northwestern
NE - Northeastern
GB - Great Basin
CR - Colorado River

The tribal boundaries within each of the culture areas changed over time. The boundaries depicted here are based on the earliest evidence available for each group. (*From* Indians of California: The Changing Image *by James J. Rawls. Copyright 1984 by the University of Oklahoma Press.*)

on debt, was commonly practiced. Indians in other areas were not uninterested in wealth, however. Gambling was widespread. Money was in the form of strings of beads made of dentalium shells or clam shells.

The family was by far the most important social institution, and in general a highly effective one. Marriage was a formal and honored institution that established

A Hupa woman with shell necklace, apron, and basket hat, as photographed near the Klamath River in the early 1900s. (*Courtesy of the Huntington Library, San Marino.*)

a lifelong relationship of mutual commitment; divorce was often difficult and prostitution was unknown. In the central region a kinship taboo forbade conversation with one's mother in law. One interpretation sometimes placed on this custom, however, is erroneous: It actually resulted not from a fear of meddling by the spouse's parents, but rather from great respect for them.

Women played an essential role in all native cultures. Female elders passed on knowledge, both practical and esoteric, that was necessary for the continued functioning of the tribal unit. In addition to gathering and processing much of the food supply, women also were responsible for constructing and maintaining storage facilities. In the central region, women built thatched granaries 15 feet high to store surplus acorns. Women also participated in ritual activities and could gain status through their skill in dancing and singing. Among the Cupeño of the southern region, women sang "enemy songs" in which they chastised villagers who were not conforming to group norms. Along the southern coast, Chumash women often ruled one or more villages. In the northwestern culture area, women served as spiritual leaders.

Religious leadership was combined with the medical profession in the person of the shaman, who was believed to be in direct communication with the supernatural world. Illness was thought to be caused by foreign disease objects in the body, and the shaman claimed the power both to introduce such objects and to remove them, usually by sucking them out. Also included in the religious leadership of most tribes were priests and ritualists. Priests maintained the balanced order of proper behavior and enjoyed considerable political, legal, and economic authority. Ritualists conducted the activities necessary for religious ceremonies. Ceremonial observances were everywhere associated with adolescence and with mourning, and there were many first-fruit, first-salmon, and acorn-harvest festivals.

There were widespread religious cults. The shamans did not usually dominate these loosely organized associations, although they might assume a certain degree of local leadership in explaining their rites. In the southern culture area the *toloache,* or jimson-weed cult, was prevalent. A drink made from the narcotic jimson weed was used to induce sacred visions as part of the initiation ceremonies. Among the Gabrielino and Juaneño this cult was much elaborated, and related to belief in a deity called Chinigchinich. In central California the Kuksu cult placed more emphasis on esoteric rites that included dancers impersonating several deities. The "world-renewal" cult was a major aspect of religious life on the northwest coast. Its rites were designed to renew abundant food supplies and to prevent calamities.

California Indians believed that all of nature was interconnected and was suffused with a sacred power. Human beings were to respect that power by following carefully prescribed guidelines in even the most routine of daily activities. Killing an animal, drinking from a spring, or entering a cave was to be accompanied by a ritual act, however simple, as a sign of respect and acknowledgment. As Native American historian Edward D. Castillo (Cahuilla/Luiseño) has written, "The religious beliefs and traditions of the Indians of California teach that the blessings of a rich land and a mild climate are gifts from the Creator. The Indians show their love and respect for the Creator—and for all of creation—by carefully managing the land for future generations and by living in harmony with the natural environment."

The religious ideas of the California Indians were, and are, more elaborate than commonly supposed. Their view that the universe is diminishing in quality and quantity bears a striking similarity to the concept of entropy central to modern physics. Likewise, their belief that a prehuman race inhabited the earth is an interesting foreshadowing of the idea of evolution. Some of the beliefs of the Spanish missionaries, such as the idea that human beings were sinful and fallen creatures, were essentially foreign to Indian religious beliefs.

The California Indians had no system of writing, beyond the use of designs and symbols in the decoration of rocks, or in groundpainting as a part of religious ceremony and instruction in the southern region. The highly stylized rock paintings of the Chumash were among the most spectacular and elaborate of any created in the United States. Yet the Indians of California were prehistoric in that they left no written records. In this sense, we speak of California as having been first "discovered" by the Spaniards, and of its "history" as having begun at that time.

SELECTED BIBLIOGRAPHY

For the general reader and student the best introductory volumes are Joseph L. Chartkoff and Kerry Kona Chartkoff, *The Archaeology of California* (1984); Michael J. Moratto, *California Archaeology* (1984); Robert F. Heizer and Albert B. Elsasser, *The Natural World of the California Indians* (1980); Heizer and Mary Ann Whipple (eds.), *The California Indians, a Source Book* (1971); and Theodora Kroeber, *Ishi in Two Worlds* (1961). The most complete reference is Heizer (ed.), *California* (1978), a volume in the Smithsonian Institution's *Handbook of North American Indians.* A summary account of precontact culture appears in Lowell J. Bean, "Indians of California," *California History,* LXXI (Fall 1992), pp. 302–323, part of a special issue devoted to the topic. See also James J. Rawls, *Indians of California* (1984).

The best estimate of the number of Indians in California before the coming of the Spaniards appears in Sherburne F. Cook, *The Population of the California Indians, 1769–1970* (1976). On the proto-agricultural activities of the California Indians, see Thomas C. Blackburn and Marion K. Anderson (eds.), *Before the Wilderness: Environmental Management by Native Californians* (1993), and Henry T. Lewis, *Patterns of Indian Burning in California* (1973). Among the many volumes on the history of individual cultures are William McCawley, *The First Angelinos* (1996); Bean (ed.), *The Ohlone Past and Present* (1995); and Bean, *Mukat's People: The Cahuilla Indians of Southern California* (1972). Other useful volumes include Malcolm Margolin (ed.), *The Way We Lived* (1993); Bean (ed.), *California Indian Shamanism* (1992); Bean and Sylvia Brakke Vane (eds.), *Ethnology of the Alta California Indians* (1991); Heizer and Elsasser (eds.), *A Bibliography of California Indians* (1977); and Campbell Grant, *The Rock Paintings of the Chumash* (1965).

CHAPTER THREE

Discovery, Exploration, and Founding

The story of Spanish California is one of great color and fascination, even though the Spaniards themselves were disappointed in it and, in general, regarded it as one of the least important of their colonies.

THE FINDING AND NAMING OF CALIFORNIA

Hernán Cortés, the conqueror of the Aztec empire in central Mexico, was also chiefly responsible for discovering the lower part of what the Spanish ultimately called "the Californias." In his urge to explore northwestward from the lands of the Aztecs, Cortés was following the lure of various tales of magnificent wealth. Spaniards of his time put their trust in the ancient and medieval legends of the Terrestrial Paradise and the Amazon Island, and in such American Indian tales as those of the Seven Cities and of El Dorado, "the Gilded Man," a king whose subjects covered him with gold dust every morning and washed it off every night. In 1533 Cortés dispatched the expedition that discovered lower California, first assumed to be an island rather than a peninsula.

All the early Spanish exploring expeditions involved extreme hardships, and several ended in complete disaster. In some cases only fragmentary records of them exist. Many details are uncertain, and one of these is the identity of the explorer who first applied the name, California.

For centuries the derivation of the name was even more uncertain than the question of who first applied it. In 1862, however, Edward Everett Hale discovered what is undoubtedly the correct explanation. Hale was a Boston Unitarian minister and writer, otherwise best known for his story, "The Man without a Country." In the course of his wide readings he came across an old Spanish novel, *Las Sergas de Esplandián (The Exploits of Esplandián)*, written about 1500 by Garcí Ordóñez de Montalvo. In it there were several references to an Amazon island called California.

Montalvo's *Sergas de Esplandián* was a sequel to his translation into Spanish of the Portuguese novel, *Amadís de Gaula*. It was an inferior sequel; as Hale remarked, the *Sergas* was deservedly forgotten for 300 years, and its role as the source of the name of California was thus forgotten with it. In the early years of the sixteenth century, however, Montalvo's story went through several editions, and there can be little doubt that Cortés and his captains, if they had not read it, had at least heard it described. In 1524, in a letter to the king, Cortés reported his expectation of finding an island of Amazons a few days' sail to the northwest.

Amadís of Gaul had been the late-medieval ideal of the perfect knight. Montalvo's Esplandián was introduced as the son of Amadís. In the course of a siege of Constantinople in which father and son were leading the defense of the city against a motley army of pagans, there suddenly appeared among the besiegers a certain Calafía, queen of California. This, wrote Montalvo, was an island "on the right hand of the Indies" and "very near to the terrestrial paradise." It was inhabited by black women "without any men among them, because they were accustomed to live after the manner of Amazons." Their weapons were of gold, "for in all the island there is no other metal." In California "there were many griffins, on account of the great ruggedness of the country." When the griffins were young, "the women went out with traps to take them to their caves, and brought them up there. And being themselves quite a match for the griffins, they fed them with the men whom they took prisoners, and with the boys to whom they gave birth." For battle, these monstrous birds were trained to seize men from the ground and drop them from great heights. Later the Amazon queen converted to Christianity, married a relative of Esplandián, and returned with him to California. "What happened after that," wrote Montalvo, "I must be excused from telling." The reader may doubt that the marriage was an entirely happy one.

It may have been in derision that Spanish explorers gave to a barren and hostile place the name of the fabled land of gold they had hoped to find. An alternative explanation is that to Spanish soldiers of the time of Cortés the "California" of contemporary parlance would in itself have been a highly opprobrious name, directly suitable for a land of desolation and terror—a land in which women were the soldiers and in which women despised men and set griffins on them.

Because California's actual history has so often resembled romantic fiction, it is not entirely inappropriate that it got its name from a novel.

CABRILLO AND THE DISCOVERY OF ALTA CALIFORNIA

The evidence that Spanish explorers first sighted Upper (or Alta) California by land, near its southeast corner, is not quite substantial enough to take the traditional honor of discovery away from Juan Rodríguez Cabrillo, who first sighted it from the sea in 1542. The main purpose of Cabrillo's expedition, sent out under the orders of the viceroy of New Spain, was to search for the long-rumored though mythical Strait of Anián, later sought by the English under the name of the northwest passage. For more than two centuries the dream of a water route to Asia through North America would continue to lure the explorers of several nations.

Cabrillo sailed from the port of Navidad on the west coast of Mexico on June 27, 1542. His two small ships, the *San Salvador* and the *Victoria,* were poorly built, manned by conscripts, and wretchedly provisioned. On September 28 he discovered and entered the fine harbor of San Diego. His name for it was San Miguel, but this and the names of all the other points he discovered were changed by later explorers, particularly by Vizcaíno.

After spending 6 days at San Diego, the little vessels made a series of anchorages at Santa Catalina Island, San Pedro, and Santa Monica, and then at Ventura and several other points along the Santa Barbara Channel. They could make no landings north of Point Conception because of the powerful northwest winds. Cabrillo decided to spend the winter in the harbor of an offshore island. Although Cabrillo's men had established generally friendly relations with the Indians on the mainland, they had serious problems with the Indians on the island. On about Christmas Eve, 1542, a shore party was attacked by the islanders. In an attempt to rescue his men, Cabrillo fell and broke his arm or leg. The wound became infected, and the captain died on January 3, 1543. It was long believed that Cabrillo's anchorage and death occurred on San Miguel Island, but recent research by historian Harry Kelsey indicates that these events probably transpired far to the south on Santa Catalina Island.

In obedience to Cabrillo's dying wish, and in spite of their pitiful hardships, his men agreed to continue their explorations under the leadership of the chief pilot, Bartolomé Ferrelo. Before they turned back on March 1, they had actually reached a point off the coast of southern Oregon, but again they could find no new anchorages. In April they reached their home port of Navidad, nearly starved and desperately sick with scurvy. They had found no straits and no rich cities, and they could hardly have appreciated the future value of what they did find. But it is clear that the discoverers of Upper California were men of admirable courage and extraordinary devotion to duty.

FRANCIS DRAKE AND NOVA ALBION

More than a generation elapsed between the Cabrillo expedition and the next landing by Europeans on the coast of Upper California. This was the visit of Francis Drake and the *Golden Hind* in 1579. It occurred by accident in the course of a 3-year voyage around the world, a voyage intended partly to open up English trade with the Moluccas and partly to "anoy" the king of Spain in "his Indyes" by engaging in what the English regarded as privateering and the Spaniards regarded as piracy. In this period Queen Elizabeth suspected King Philip of complicity in a series of plots on her life, and relations between England and Spain were seldom very far short of outright war. Another and incidental purpose of the voyage was to search for the northwest passage.

Nearly a year and a half after he sailed from England, Drake had to make an emergency landing on the coast of California to careen and repair his ship. The *Golden Hind,* originally named the *Pelican,* was a vessel of only 100 tons burden, and by this time she was carrying about 30 tons of captured Spanish treasure, mostly silver. The seams in her hull had begun to open. On June 17, 1579, Drake found "a convenient and fit harborough" where he stayed for 5 weeks. It is probable that this occurred on the Point Reyes Peninsula at what is now called Drake's Bay, although the location of the landing has long been in dispute. Only Drake's Bay has the "white bancks and cliffes" whose resemblance to the cliffs on the English Channel contributed to Drake's naming the place Nova Albion, or New England.

The Indians were the feature of the visit that Drake's men found most interesting, and to which their accounts of it devoted the greatest detail. From the descriptions of the houses, the feathered baskets, the ceremonies, and the language of these Indians, anthropologists have clearly identified them as the Coast Miwok, whose country included Point Reyes in present-day Marin County. Drake's men assumed, incorrectly, that the Indians in placing a feathered crown on Drake's head were turning over the sovereignty of their country to him. The Indians also cried pitifully and tore their cheeks with their fingernails until the blood ran, and the English supposed this to be a kind of sacrifice to them as gods. The facts are that these were the mourning practices of the Coast Miwok and that the Indians undoubtedly regarded the Englishmen as relatives who had returned from the dead. Historian Arthur Quinn has interpreted this early encounter as a dark prophecy of

An artist's conception of California's Coast Miwok Indians greeting Francis Drake in 1579. Note especially the central figures lacerating their cheeks and, in the background, the setting up of the plate of brass. (*Courtesy of the Bancroft Library.*)

the future course of Indian-white relations in California: "It *was* dead generations the natives saw wade onto Point Reyes, dead generations of their people. But it was future death, not past. . . . The mournful wailing of the women held a deeper truth than anyone at that time knew."

In claiming the country for Queen Elizabeth, Drake erected a plate of brass with a chiseled inscription and a hole for a sixpence bearing Her Majesty's picture. In 1937 the University of California announced the finding of this plate and later placed it on display in the Bancroft Library. Experts at Columbia University made tests on the plate in 1938 and pronounced it genuine. However, new tests made in the mid-1970s at the Lawrence Berkeley Laboratory and at Oxford University used the far more sophisticated testing techniques developed in the interim, and the modern researchers concluded that it was "unreasonable to continue to believe in the authenticity of the plate." Analysis of the trace elements found in the metal corresponded to brass of the twentieth century rather than the sixteenth, and x-ray diffraction tests revealed that the brass was produced by a modern rolling process unknown at the time of Drake. Nevertheless the plate remains on display in the Bancroft, and the controversy over its authenticity continues.

The main significance of the voyage of the *Golden Hind* was that it was the second ship to sail around the world, the first English ship to do so, and the first ship of any nation to make the entire voyage under one commander (Magellan had been killed in the Philippines). Drake's title of knighthood, granted after his return, was a modest recognition of so great an achievement. The significance of his landing in California, however, has sometimes been misunderstood and exaggerated.

THE MANILA GALLEON AND THE CALIFORNIA COAST

The Philippine islands were added to the Spanish colonial empire by a gradual process of conquest beginning in 1565, and they were governed as a part of the viceroyalty of New Spain until the end of Spanish control in Mexico. By the time of the Drake expedition the Spaniards had already established a profitable trade route between Mexico and the Philippines, and for many decades Spanish interest in the coast of California was largely the result of the fact that the ships from Manila sailed past it, with their rich cargoes from the orient, on the last leg of their long trans-Pacific voyage to Acapulco.

Manila was a very convenient gathering point for luxury goods from many parts of east Asia, to be exchanged for silver and gold from the mines of Mexico, and the trade became so large that merchants in Spain were in danger of losing their Mexican markets. Under the prevailing mercantilistic system that discriminated against the colonies in favor of the mother country, the king decreed in 1593 that the Manila galleons must be limited to one a year, and their cargoes to a value of 250,000 pesos. Nevertheless the profits were extremely high, and because cargoes were now concentrated in a single annual voyage, there was great temptation to crowd extra goods into space that should have been reserved for food and water. The voyage from Manila usually took 6 or 7 months, during which the crews suffered horribly from starvation, thirst, and scurvy. They also had to fear English pirates, ever since the forays of Drake. There was, it seemed, a growing need for a port on the California coast where the annual Manila galleon could get fresh food and water and perhaps an escort vessel.

The Spanish authorities entrusted the galleon of 1595 to the Portuguese merchant-adventurer Sebastián Rodríguez Cermeño, on condition that the voyage should include an exploration of the California coast in search of the best site for a port of call. After an especially harrowing passage across the Pacific, Cermeño sighted land somewhere north of Cape Mendocino. There his ship, the *San Agustín,* was nearly wrecked by a storm, and several of the officers took every step short of mutiny in an effort to persuade him to give up the projected explorations. He refused, and on November 6, rounding Point Reyes, he anchored in Drake's Bay, which he called the Bay of San Francisco.

On shore, the Spaniards assembled a launch that had been brought along for use in exploring coastal areas. This little vessel was to be their salvation, for on November 30 a great gale from the southeast, the direction in which the bay is completely exposed, drove the *San Agustín* aground. The breakers pounded it to pieces in a few hours and strewed its cargo, provisions, and timbers along the beach. To the amazement and outrage of his crew, not even this disaster persuaded Cermeño to abandon his interest in exploration. With 70 men crowded into the open launch, the *San Buenaventura,* he found excuses for many landings, and although he sailed past the Golden Gate without seeing it, he described many other points with remarkable accuracy considering his difficulties.

VIZCAÍNO AND MONTEREY

Cermeño had found no new harbor that was safe, and the viceregal government doubted the thoroughness and accuracy of his charts. The further search for a good harbor in northern California was now entrusted, after long negotiations, to another *adelantado,* or merchant-adventurer, Sebastian Vizcaíno. On the understanding that he would be rewarded with various concessions including the future command of one of the Manila ships, Vizcaíno invested a considerable amount of his own capital in an elaborate expedition in 1602. Setting out from Acapulco with two ships and a launch, he permanently renamed many of the places along the California coast, and on December 16 he entered a bay that he named for the viceroy, the conde de Monterey. Vizcaíno announced himself as the discoverer of this bay, although he was not. Cermeño had seen it 7 years earlier, and his description of it, though not detailed, was actually far less misleading than that of Vizcaíno, who made absurdly exaggerated claims for its value as a harbor.

Vizcaíno seems to have feared that if he did not return with a favorable report, he would not receive the rewards he hoped for. The result was that he described the bay to the viceroy not only as having an abundance of fine timber for shipbuilding, but as being "sheltered from all winds"—a claim that can only be described as positively fraudulent, because the bay actually includes no proper harbor at all.

Viceroy Monterey, pleased with the idea that a fine port would bear his name, awarded Vizcaíno the command of the next Manila galleon. Shortly afterward, however, Monterey was promoted to the viceroyalty of Peru. His successor as viceroy of New Spain, the marqué de Montesclaros, completely distrusted Vizcaíno, revoked the award of the galleon, and went so far as to have the expedition's map maker convicted of forgery and hanged.

Montesclaros ridiculed and blocked the whole project of a California port of call. He pointed out, correctly, that when the galleons sighted California, they had only a few days' voyage left, because the strong prevailing winds and currents along the coast almost always bore them swiftly southward. In this judgment, history vindicated him, for even after Upper California was finally settled more than a century and a half later, the annual ships from Manila almost never stopped there.

The lapse of 60 years between Cabrillo and Vizcaíno, and of another 167 years between Vizcaíno and actual Spanish settlement of California, emphasizes the utter isolation of California and the low regard in which the Spaniards held it. California was a place that should have contained gold, but apparently did not; a place where a strait should have been, but was not; a barren and dangerous coast that a ship sailed past once a year. Getting to it from Mexico was far more trouble than it was worth. Just as the winds and currents made the southward voyage brief and easy, they made the northward voyage long, difficult, and sometimes impossible. Land travel seemed even more forbidding. Lower California was on the very rim of Christendom during the whole of the Spanish colonial period in America, which lasted more than three centuries, and for all but the last half century of that period, Upper California remained beyond the rim.

SPAIN'S INDIAN POLICIES

New Spain lacked the manpower for the settlement of its remote and unprofitable northern frontiers. When the colonization of these areas finally came, it was largely through an ingenious plan intended to transform the Indians into colonists by the use of that remarkable institution, the Spanish mission.

The Spanish attitudes toward the Indians grew from an interesting blend of religious, economic, military, and political motives. The Indians were officially regarded not only as subjects of the Spanish monarchy with rights to its protection, but also as human beings with souls to be saved. Their Most Catholic Majesties, the Spanish monarchs, made frequent references to their duty of Christianization, and the missionaries were untiring in their efforts to carry it out. There were others, however, who were primarily interested in the Indians because they could be made to labor for the profit of their conquerors. In return for the salvation of their souls, the Indians were required to contribute the labor of their bodies.

The most essential key to the Spanish colonial plan, however, was that Indians were to be made Spanish—in religion, in language, and in the gradual intermixture of blood. They were to be required to work; they were also to be permitted to live (if they survived the epidemics of smallpox and typhus). These views were quite different from those of the English colonists; there was no comparable plan for assimilating the Indian into the Anglo-American scheme of things, and displacement or extermination was almost the only alternative. As for racial intermarriage, the Anglo-Americans were usually intolerant of it. They were generally able to secure wives of English descent, whereas the Spanish American colonies were extremely unattractive to Spanish women.

THE MISSION AS A FRONTIER INSTITUTION

As a method of advancing and consolidating a frontier, the mission had its roots in the long struggle against the Mohammedan Moors in Spain. The cross and the sword had moved forward together, in forcible conversion of the infidel. In Spanish America, each mission had a small guard of soldiers, and there was usually a larger garrison at a *presidio,* or military post, nearby. Cooperation between padres and soldiers was seldom cordial, but it was always indispensable. The missionaries were typically men of tremendous courage and faith, but, with the exception of those who actively sought martyrdom, they were usually aware that the strength of their own personalities had to be supplemented by the soldiers' weapons, even though they were constantly anxious lest the soldiers corrupt the Indian neophytes, or apprentices to Christianity. Throughout the Spanish empire, as historian Harry Crosby has observed, "missions were the crux of the conquest." Mission practices were everywhere directed toward the same goal: "the abolition of any pre-Christian practices, religious or secular, that were considered impediments to conversion or to integration with the greater Spanish economy."

The mission, thus, was not only a church but also an agricultural *pueblo,* or town, in which hundreds or even thousands of Indians were concentrated. There were cultivated fields, gardens, orchards, and vineyards, often fenced with nearly impenetrable hedges of prickly pear, and watered from irrigation ditches with stone dams. At a little distance, each mission had its *rancho,* and, eventually, large herds of cattle.

Theoretically every mission was temporary. If the plan had worked as the Spanish government hoped, each mission would have been "secularized" 10 years after its founding. That is, the pueblo would receive a grant of 4 square leagues of land; the fields, town lots, and other property would be parceled out among the Indians; and community government would pass to native officials who had been trained for the purpose. The mission church would be turned over to parish priests, known as "secular" clergy, as distinct from the missionaries, who were called "regular" clergy, because they were under the regulations and vows of a particular order. The missionaries were then supposed to begin their work all over again farther on, in a continuous process of frontier expansion.

In practice, however, the schedule was never met. Most missions continued for decades, and some for more than a century. Although the Laws of the Indies provided that mission Indians should receive real training for self-government, in practice they received little or none. The missionary fathers made the basic mistake of regarding the Indians as children whose minds were incapable of development

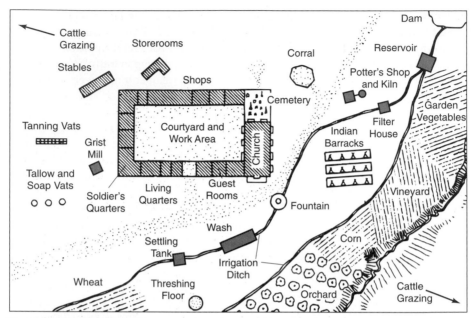

Generalized plan of a mission compound on the Spanish colonial frontier. (*Adapted from* California Patterns: A Geographical and Historical Atlas *by David Hornbeck. Copyright 1983 by the Mayfield Publishing Company.*)

beyond the child's level. They turned them into helpless dependents and kept them in that condition. Every detail of work, play, clothing, and even the choice of a mate, was rigidly controlled. So far as possible the missionaries kept their charges from contact with any Europeans but themselves and did not prepare them to take a place in any kind of society but that of the mission. When secularization finally came, the whole community simply disintegrated.

There are many viewpoints concerning the effect of mission life itself on Indian morale. The Spanish missionaries often spoke of the "temporal and spiritual conquest" of new provinces. The phrase is apt. Very often, no real conversion took place after the Indians' own gods were destroyed. One skeptical California ranch owner, Antonio María Osio, doubted that Indians in the missions ever adopted a true Christianity "simply because they had been sprinkled with baptismal water." Religious instruction consisted primarily of endless repetitions of ritual passages. In the end, many Indians were spiritually as well as physically conquered, their spirit broken.

Spain had entrusted the frontier regions of northwestern Mexico to the black-robed missionaries of the Society of Jesus in 1591. A century later the Jesuit frontier had been extended northwestward on the mainland as far as the country of the Pimas, and Father Eusebio Kino had begun the building of the missions in Pimería Alta—northern Sonora and southern Arizona. Kino rediscovered the forgotten fact that Baja

California was a peninsula and not an island and persuaded his superiors to establish the first of the missions on the peninsula in 1697. But in 1767 the king issued an order expelling the Jesuits from all the Spanish dominions. Charles III of Spain had become convinced that the Jesuits were involved in plots against the interests of the crown.

GÁLVEZ AND THE PLAN FOR ALTA CALIFORNIA

The expulsion of the Jesuits from New Spain was entrusted to Visitor-General José de Gálvez, who turned the Baja California missions over to military administrators under Captain Gaspar de Portolá, and then to the Franciscans under Father Junípero Serra. The names of these three remarkable men soon became important in the story of the founding of Alta California.

Gálvez was the most effective visitor-general in the history of New Spain, though not the first. The *visita* was a distinctively Spanish administrative technique for investigations and reorganizations, and a *visitador-general* was a special deputy of the king, with extraordinary powers overlapping and sometimes transcending those of the viceroy.

The *visita* of Gálvez, which began in 1765, was primarily intended to reform the finances and increase the revenues of New Spain as a part of the energetic attempts to reorganize the Spanish government under Charles III after the expensive and disastrous Seven Years War. The expulsion of the Jesuits was an added assignment. But the consolidation of the northwestern frontier and its extension to Alta California were Gálvez's own projects, and seem to have been the result of his intense personal ambitions. He had risen from rather humble origins, and although he was a brilliant, forceful, and generally successful administrator, he was also unusually vain, selfish, ruthless, deceitful, and unstable. It was, indeed, because of Gálvez's possession of this very combination of qualities that the occupation of San Diego and Monterey, long considered and periodically given up as hopeless, actually materialized. New Spain had been decaying, and he now made it appear to be flourishing and expanding. This was the sort of achievement which, along with others, later led to his being made Minister of the Indies.

Gálvez proposed a scheme for the consolidation and development of the whole of the far northwest under a vast new governmental unit to be called a *commandancy-general,* and to include the areas of Sinaloa, Sonora, Chihuahua, and the Californias. To justify this plan, he made use of the old and perennial fear that some other European power would establish itself on the Pacific coast and menace New Spain from the north. It was long believed that the Spanish colonization of Upper California occurred because of a diplomatic report that Russia was about to move in the direction of Monterey. The truth was that Gálvez's plan was already well advanced when this absurdly exaggerated report reached him, and that he merely added it to the rumors he himself had been spreading about various alleged intentions of the English and the Dutch. Another argument used by Gálvez in support of his plans was that the development of Alta California would ultimately provide a great source of royal revenue, although, as it turned out, the result was an annual deficit during most of the period of Spanish rule.

Gálvez ordered the founding of the new port of San Blas on the coast of Mexico several hundred miles northwest of Acapulco as a naval and supply base for the Californias. In 1768 Gálvez sailed from San Blas for Baja California, where he completed the planning of the "sacred expedition" that would colonize Alta California in the following year. The various divisions of this expedition, two by land and three by sea, were to be launched from the peninsula.

The mainland approach was blocked by Indian rebellions in Sonora. These had been going on unchecked for many years, but Gálvez was sure that a determined military campaign could quickly suppress them. That campaign, however, proved to be as maddeningly unsuccessful and frustrating as a number of its predecessors had been. Once, while visiting Sonora, Gálvez actually suffered a temporary attack of insanity. He had been increasingly given to the belief that he received divine instructions, and now for a brief time he was convinced that he was God himself. At one moment he proposed to reduce the Indians to submission by importing 600 Guatemalan apes as soldiers.

From the viewpoint of the United States, it is fortunate that the Spaniards occupied Alta California when they did. Tenuous as that occupation was, it may ultimately have forestalled the acquisition of the territory by some nation strong enough to have delayed or even prevented its later acquisition by the United States. But at the time and under the circumstances in which it was undertaken, the Spanish occupation of Alta California was impractical and unnecessary, and largely a result of the mental instability of Gálvez, who conceived and ordered it.

THE FRANCISCANS AND FATHER SERRA

A handful of Spanish officers and missionaries and a scarcely larger number of mestizo and mulatto soldiers and sailors carried out the founding of the colony of Alta California under fantastic difficulties. The military men and the missionaries had quite different ideas of what they were doing and why, and they were often at cross-purposes. But their joint achievement is an impressive tribute to human courage in the face of adversity.

St. Francis of Assisi had founded the Order of Friars Minor, oldest and largest of his orders, in the thirteenth century. The Franciscans were the first missionaries in the new world, where their work began with Columbus's second voyage and continued vigorously in many parts of Spanish America through the later period when the Jesuits and other orders shared the missionary field. The name of Gray Friars was sometimes given to the Franciscans because their robes were woven of white and black wool; the color of their habit was still gray at the time of the founding of Alta California, though later it was changed to brown.

The decision to entrust the California missions to the Franciscans was the result of the belief that they were not only more obedient to the vows of poverty than were the Jesuits, but also less disposed to subordinate the interests of their country to those of their order. This had become the prevailing opinion in the Spanish government. It was inaccurate, and it was unfair to both the orders concerned. Certainly the relations between the Franciscans and the governmental officials in

Father Junípero Serra
(1713–1784), founder of the
first nine missions in Alta
California. (*Courtesy of the
Bancroft Library.*)

California were to include a long series of sharp disputes. Father Junípero Serra, in particular, vigorously subordinated everything to his conception of religious duty.

Father Junípero, the first and most famous of the missionaries in Alta California, was a Spanish farmer's son, born in the village of Petra on the island of Majorca in 1713. The family name Serra is the Catalonian form of the Castilian word *sierra*. Upon joining the Franciscan order, Miguel, as he was originally called, exercised the privilege of choosing a name by which he wished to be known "in religion." Junípero had been the name of one of St. Francis's closest companions, whose devotion was said to have inspired the founder to wish "that I had a whole forest of such Junipers."

Serra became a professor of philosophy at the University of Majorca, but at the age of 35 he determined to give up this quiet and relatively comfortable position for the strenuous life of a foreign missionary. He also hoped for martyrdom, as had St. Francis himself, although in neither case was this hope fulfilled. According to Father Francisco Palóu, Serra's former pupil and later companion, assistant, and biographer, Serra once spoke of martyrdom as the true "gold and silver of the Indies" for which they would search.

As prospective missionaries, Serra, Palóu, and Juan Crespí, another of Serra's former students, were first assigned to the apostolic College of San Fernando in Mexico City. This establishment was both a headquarters for Franciscan missionaries in New Spain and a special training center to accustom them to privation, fatigue, mortification, and penance.

In manifestations of zeal, no one excelled Serra. Upon his arrival in Mexico he had chosen to walk all the way from Vera Cruz to the capital. Early in the course of the journey he suffered an insect bite that became infected. He neglected medical care for it, and his leg and foot remained swollen and ulcerous for the rest of his life, a condition that he alternately ignored and regarded as a blessing. While delivering missionary sermons he would sometimes scourge his own shoulders with a chain, or, holding a cross in one hand, beat his breast with a stone held in the other, or burn his bared chest with lighted candles. He slept on a narrow bed made only of hard wooden boards. He kept a thong of sharp-pointed iron links hanging on the wall beside the bed for scourging himself when thoughts that he regarded as sinful came in the night. St. Francis had practiced mortification of the flesh, and it was not uncommon among the missionaries of Serra's time, although regulations of the apostolic college provided that it should never go so far as to be permanently incapacitating.

After an impressive record in missionary work in the Sierra Gorda and other parts of Mexico, Serra became father-president of the missions in Baja California, and then of the prospective new missions in Alta California. At the time of his appointment to the latter post, he was 55 years old. He held it until his death in 1784 at the age of 70. As father-president of Alta California, Serra founded the province's first nine missions. Throughout his life he was a vigorous, hard-driving man, never turning back from a task he had begun, always demanding the full measure of work from others as well as from himself. In physical stature, Serra was short, not more than 5 feet 2 or 3 inches in height—but in courage and determination, he was a giant.

THE SACRED EXPEDITION

Supplies and men for the first missions and presidios to be founded in Alta California came in part from the peninsula and in part from the mainland by way of San Blas. The Pious Fund of the Californias, transferred from the custody of the Jesuits to that of the Franciscans, was extended to the new ventures in the north, and Gálvez and Serra agreed that church furniture, ornaments, vestments, and utensils, as well as livestock and other supplies, were to be drawn from the Baja California missions.

As was customary in founding new establishments, a number of Christianized Indians from the peninsula were taken along with the expedition in order to serve as, so to speak, bellwethers for the new flock. In addition to soldiers from the garrison at Loreto under Captain Fernando Rivera y Moncada, 25 Catalonian volunteers, light infantry under Lieutenant Pedro Fages, were detached from their previous assignment to the campaign in Sonora. There were also several blacksmiths, cooks, and carpenters, along with Miguel Costansó, military engineer and cartographer, and Dr. Pedro Prat, army surgeon of French ancestry.

The expedition as a whole was under the command of Capt. Gaspar de Portolá. When settlements had been established at San Diego and Monterey, Portolá and Rivera were to return to duty on the peninsula, leaving Lieutenant Fages in charge of the military and civil government of the new colony.

Three ships were provided for the expedition, the *San Carlos,* the *San Antonio,* and the *San José,* all less than 200 tons, and all hastily and imperfectly constructed under the difficulties that still hampered shipbuilding on the Pacific coast. All three vessels reached Baja California from San Blas in leaky condition, even before the beginning of the longer voyage, and all three had to be careened and repaired. Visitor-General Gálvez personally superintended the repairs and the loading of the flagship, the *San Carlos,* and carried some of the mission furniture on board with his own hands. When the vessel sailed from La Paz, on January 9, 1769, he accompanied it in a launch to see her round Cape San Lucas. The *San Antonio,* a smaller supply ship, sailed from Cape San Lucas on February 15. The third vessel, the *San José,* was lost with all on board somewhere on her way toward San Diego.

Of the two land parties, the first was under Captain Rivera, with 27 *cuirassiers.* On the frontier the cuirass was a sleeveless jacket of tough leather, made by quilting several thicknesses of deerskin or sheepskin, and usually arrowproof. Father Crespí, chaplain and diarist of the expedition, noted quite accurately that these *soldados de cuera,* or leather-jacket soldiers, were the best light cavalry in the world and were equally skilled as cowboys. Driving a large herd of cattle, horses, and mules, this party set out from the northernmost Spanish outpost in Baja California on March 24.

The second land contingent, including Portolá and Serra, left the same point on May 15. Following the trail made by Rivera, and less encumbered with livestock, it could move somewhat more rapidly, but the journey over deserts and gullies was a hard one. When Serra's ulcerated leg threatened to disable him completely, he asked a muleteer to treat it as he would a sore foot on one of his animals. The muleteer's poultice of mud and herbs had an almost miraculous effect, and Serra was able to continue, much relieved.

The first objective of the whole expedition was the founding of a presidio and a mission at San Diego as a way station for the journey to Monterey. The *San Antonio* was first to arrive at San Diego, on April 11, after a relatively easy voyage of 54 days. The *San Carlos,* although she had started a month earlier, did not arrive until nearly 3 weeks later, after 110 days at sea. The effects of scurvy had advanced so far that no one was able to lower a boat, and the men on shore had to board it in order to do so. The first Spanish settlement in Alta California was a sail-tent hospital. Doctor Prat was himself so ill that he could be of little help to the others. He later became insane.

The first land party, under Rivera, arrived on May 14, and Rivera ordered the tents moved several miles northward to the foot of the hill where the presidio would later be built. Portolá rode in a little ahead of his men on June 29, and Serra and the others reached the stricken camp on July 1. Of about 300 men in the various branches of the sacred expedition of 1769, not more than half survived to reach San Diego, many died of scurvy there, and for months half the survivors were too sick to travel farther. All but a handful of the Christianized Indians who had been brought with the land contingents had died or deserted; the military officers had felt compelled to deny them rations from the dwindling food supplies.

Of the sailors, 38 had died. The *San Antonio,* with a truly skeleton crew of eight men, had to be sent back to San Blas to bring new supplies for the whole expedition and new crews for both ships. The *San Carlos* was left at anchor in the bay with two men on board to keep it from being stripped by the Indians. The whole situation was stark and desperate. Nevertheless, 2 weeks after his arrival at San Diego, Portolá set out toward his main objective, the legendary harbor of Monterey, taking with him Rivera, Fages, Costansó, Father Crespí, and nearly all the others who were still able to travel, leaving Serra at San Diego to care for the more than 50 invalids.

On the way north the expedition felt several earthquakes near the river called the Santa Ana, or *Río de los Temblores.* Four days later the *Río de Porciúncula,* site of the future pueblo of Los Angeles, was named by Crespí for the day of its discovery and crossing, August 2. This was the day of the festival of Our Lady the Queen of the Angels, one of many titles of the Virgin Mary. For Franciscans, in particular, an important shrine of the Virgin was the chapel of Porciúncula, near Assisi, where St. Francis had worshipped.

Continuing northwestward on a route that would become El Camino Real (The King's Highway), remarkably close at most points to the route of the modern Highway 101, the expedition eventually reached the shore of the Bay at Monterey. Portolá, however, failed to recognize the bay for he could see nothing resembling the fine harbor, praised by Vizcaíno and subjected in the interim to 167 years of idealized imagination. Moreover, Portolá and his half-starved men had managed to convince themselves that they would find the *San José,* with abundant food supplies, riding at anchor in that harbor.

After a few days' search the party pushed on northward along the coast. At the end of October they reached Point San Pedro and looked across the Gulf of the Farallons toward Point Reyes and Drake's Bay, which to them was Cermeño's Bay of San Francisco. Although Point Reyes was 40 miles away and they could not be sure of its identity from that distance, they saw enough to increase their fears that they must have passed Monterey without finding it. Sergeant José Ortega understood some Indians to be trying to tell him that a ship was anchored somewhere to the north. Heading a party of scouts, Ortega found his advance blocked by a vast and unknown bay, which he sighted, probably on November 1, 1769, from the top of the ridge between the present cities of Pacifica and Millbrae. Historians long supposed that he also found the Golden Gate at this time, but this is untrue. It was not until a year later that Pedro Fages, scouting northward along the east bay shore, became the first Spanish explorer to see the narrow gap between the peninsulas. Navigators had failed for centuries to see it from the ocean, assuming that Drake probably did not. Part of the explanation lies in the fogs that so often shroud the Golden Gate, and part in the fact that Angel Island and the Berkeley hills lie behind it in such a position as to give, from any distance at sea, the impression of a continuous coastline.

Neither Portolá nor anyone else in the expedition seems to have regarded the discovery of the great bay as anything but an obstacle, except for Father Crespí, who wrote in his diary: "It is a very large and fine harbor, such that not only all the navy of our Most Catholic Majesty but those of all Europe could take shelter in it."

Considering how long Spaniards had been searching for the Strait of Anián, it is surprising that no one speculated that it might now have been discovered, but for weeks the attention of these men had been desperately concentrated on the search for a harbor with a ship in it, and food on the ship. An attempt was made to get around the bay, and Ortega and his scouts got just around the southern end of it, but on November 11 the whole expedition gave up and turned back the way it had come. The group arrived back in San Diego on January 24, 1770.

Nothing encouraging had happened at San Diego during their absence. Serra had founded the mission of San Diego de Alcalá at a temporary location in a hut on Presidio Hill, on July 16, 1769, but there was not yet a single convert. One Indian baby was offered for baptism, but Serra's joy turned to grief when the Indians suddenly snatched it from his arms and ran off before the ceremony could be completed. Yet nothing, it seemed, could discourage the indomitable father-president.

On February 10, 1770, Portolá sent Rivera and 40 men on the long journey back to Baja California for supplies. A month later, when there was still no sign of the *San José* or of the return of the *San Antonio,* Portolá announced that if no relief came by March 19, the feast of St. Joseph, the patron of the expedition, he and his men would march south the next morning. Serra and Crespí protested, refused to turn back, and arranged that they would be taken on board the *San Carlos,* still anchored in the bay, to await the coming of a supply ship. After 9 days of prayer, the *San Antonio* was sighted on the very afternoon of March 19. The danger of abandonment had passed.

Portolá now sent the *San Antonio,* carrying Serra, Costansó, and Fages, on to Monterey. Portolá himself set out for the north again by land, with 12 soldiers, leaving 8 to guard San Diego. This time, at last, Portolá fully realized that what he had previously seen of the harbor of Monterey was all there was of it—at best a roadstead with no shelter from the north wind. But he had his orders, and so a presidio of poles and earth was constructed at Monterey and a mission, San Carlos Borromeo, was built nearby under the direction of Serra. Both were formally established on June 3, 1770. Leaving Fages in charge of the government of Alta California, Portolá then sailed for Mexico.

There was great formal rejoicing in Mexico City over the establishment of the new province, even though the reports of Portolá to the visitor-general and the viceroy were more candid than they cared to hear. Portolá was of the opinion that if the Russians wanted Alta California, which he doubted, they should be allowed to have it as a punishment for their aggressive designs.

SELECTED BIBLIOGRAPHY

Harry Kelsey is the author of several works on the discovery and early exploration of California: "Mapping the California Coast," *Arizona and the West,* XXVI (Winter 1984), pp. 307–324; "Finding the Way Home," *Western Historical Quarterly,* XVII (April 1986), pp. 145–164; and *Juan Rodríguez Cabrillo* (1986). See also Nancy Lemke, *Cabrillo* (1991). The classics in the field are Henry R. Wagner's *Spanish Voyages to the Northwest Coast of America in the Sixteenth Century* (1929), and *Juan Rodríguez Cabrillo* (1941). See also W. Michael Mathes, "Apocryphal Tales of the Island of California and Strait of Anián," *California History,* LXII (Spring 1983), pp 52–59; and Jack D. Forbes, "Melchor Díaz and the Discovery of Alta California," *Pacific Historical Review,* XXVII (November 1958), pp. 351–358.

A translation of the parts of Montalvo's *Las Sergas de Esplandián* relating to Queen Califía, with commentary, may be found in Edward Everett Hale, *The Queen of California* (reprinted in 1945). See also Donald C. Cutter, "Sources of the Name 'California,'" *Arizona and the West,* III (Autumn 1961), pp. 233–243, and Dora B. Polk, *The Island of California* (1991).

Arthur Quinn's *Broken Shore* (1981) includes a lyrical account of the landing of Francis Drake in California. Warren L. Hanna's *Lost Harbour* (1979) is a convenient guide to the maze of arguments over Drake's landing spot. Hanna concludes that the evidence is insufficient to warrant a final judgment. See also Norman J. Thrower (ed.), *Sir Francis Drake and the Famous Voyage, 1577–1580* (1984), and John Sugden, *Sir Francis Drake* (1991). On the controversy over Drake's plate, see James D. Hart, *The Plate of Brass Reexamined* (1977), and the response by Robert H. Power, "A Plate of Brass 'By Me . . . C.G. Francis Drake,'" *California History,* LVII (Summer 1978), pp. 172–185, followed by Hart, *The Plate of Brass Reexamined: A Supplementary Report* (1979).

William L. Schurz chronicled *The Manila Galleon* (1939). On the Cermeño expedition, see Wagner, "The Voyage to California of Sebastián Rodríguez Cermeño in 1595," *California Historical Society Quarterly,* III (April 1924), pp. 3–24. Mathes, *Vizcaíno and Spanish Expansion in the Pacific Ocean, 1580–1630* (1968), considerably enhances Vizcaíno's reputation and the significance of his explorations.

Colin M. MacLachlan, *Spain's Empire in the New World* (1988), offers a new analysis of theory and practice in the Spanish empire. The mission system appears in a favorable light in Herbert E. Bolton, "The Mission as a Frontier Institution in the Spanish American Colonies," in his *Wider Horizons in American History* (1939). For a survey of the literature see John Francis Bannon, "The Mission as a Frontier Institution: Sixty Years of Interest and Research," *Western Historical Quarterly,* X (July 1979), pp. 302–322.

Harry W. Crosby, *Antigua California* (1994), Herbert I. Priestly, *José de Gálvez* (1916), and Charles E. Chapman, *The Founding of Spanish California* (1916), deal with the backgrounds of the colonization of Alta California. Robert Browning (ed.), *The Discovery of San Francisco Bay* (1992) and Frank M. Stanger and Alan K. Brown, *Who Discovered the Golden Gate?* (1969) are illuminating. Accounts of the sacred expedition include Herbert E. Bolton, *Fray Juan Crespí* (1927); Priestley, *Description of California by Pedro Fages* (1937); Douglas S. Watson, *The Spanish Occupation of California* (1934); and two accounts of Gaspar de Portolá by Fernando B. Companys (1983) and Josep Carner-Ribalta (1992).

Maynard Geiger, *The Life and Times of Fray Junípero Serra* (two volumes, 1959), is a work of urbane scholarship, in welcome contrast to the defensive tone of Zephyrin Engelhardt, *The Missions and Missionaries of California* (four volumes, 1908–1915). More recent biographies of Serra include those by Don De Nevi and Noel F. Moholy (1985) and Martin J. Morgado (1991). See also Iris H. W. Engstrand, *Serra's San Diego* (1982), and the startling speculations in Janie L. Gustafson, "Never to Turn Back: Three Years in the Life of Junípero Serra," Ph.D. thesis, Graduate Theological Union, Berkeley (1986).

CHAPTER FOUR

Outposts of a Dying Empire

The Spanish occupation of Alta California now consisted of two pinpoints on the coast, 450 miles apart. In 1771 Serra moved the mission of San Carlos Borromeo from Monterey to the Carmel River. This mission became Serra's headquarters for the arduous struggle to establish the others. Ultimately there would be 21 missions in Alta California, 9 of them founded during his lifetime, but at the beginning only Serra himself foresaw such a degree of success. Differences of opinion between Serra and Governor Fages deepened into a feud. Repeatedly Fages vetoed Serra's requests for new missions because there were not enough soldiers to protect them.

BUCARELI, ANZA, AND THE FOUNDING OF SAN FRANCISCO

Visitor-General Gálvez returned to Spain in 1771, and a new viceroy, Antonio de Bucareli, arrived in the same year. At first Bucareli was too busy with other duties to take much interest in Gálvez's new colony. In 1773, however, he turned his attention to it, and for several years he gave it enough care and support to bring it through its precarious infancy. Again the fear of foreign encroachments reinforced Spanish interest in California, the English now rivaling the Russians as objects of concern. The voyages of Captain James Cook in the 1770s indicated a renewed English interest in the Pacific.

In 1773 Serra made a journey to Mexico City to plead for more support for new missions and the removal of Lieutenant Fages as governor of Alta California. Bucareli replaced Fages with Captain Rivera, although this would soon involve Serra in more disputes with the new governor than with the old one.

About the same time, Captain Juan Bautista de Anza submitted a proposal for an expedition to open a land route from northern Sonora to Monterey. With eager encouragement from Serra, Viceroy Bucareli resolved not only to adopt Anza's project of a new land route to Monterey, but also to empower him to extend Spanish settlement to the strategic bay of San Francisco. Anza was an ideal leader for the project. The opening of a trail from Sonora to Alta California had been the dream of his family for three generations. He led two expeditions to California, one to explore the trail and the other to bring settlers, including some for the new San Francisco site.

On the first of these expeditions Anza rode out from Tubac, a presidio south of Tucson, in January of 1774. One of the men with Anza was Father Francisco Garcés. This remarkable Franciscan had already traveled through the Colorado River region and had won the confidence of Salvador Palma, chief of the Yumas. The goodwill of the Yumas was a vital factor in the success of Anza's expeditions. Ferried across the Colorado River with the aid of the Yumas and their tule rafts, Anza and his men struck out westward across the sand dunes of the Colorado Desert, became lost, and finally struggled back to the river after 10 days. After leaving much of their baggage with Chief Palma, they traveled southward to get around the dunes, turned west again, and on March 22, 1774, they reached the Mission of San Gabriel, founded 3 years earlier. Continuing to Monterey, and returning the way he had come, Anza reached Tubac in May, and a few months later went to Mexico City to make a full report to the viceroy.

Encouraged by the opening of the new route from Sonora to California, Bucareli promoted Anza to the rank of lieutenant colonel, and planned new expeditions for 1775. An expedition to explore San Francisco Bay began under Captain Miguel Manrique, but this commander lost his mind a few days after leaving San Blas and had to be put ashore. He had left several loaded pistols about his cabin, and one of these accidentally exploded, wounding his successor, Lieutenant Juan Manuel de Ayala. The lateness of Spanish settlement of upper California can be vividly seen in the fact that this unfortunate pistol shot occurred within a few days of "the shot heard round the world," fired at Lexington, Massachusetts, on April 19, 1775, and signaling the beginning of the American Revolutionary War.

On August 5 a launch made at Monterey and piloted by Ayala's sailing master, José Cañizares, became the first Spanish vessel to enter the Golden Gate, known to the Spaniards merely as *La Boca,* or the mouth. Ayala's ship, the *San Carlos,* sailed through the next day. His wound confined him to his cabin, but the crew spent several weeks in making a thorough exploration of the arms of the bay with the launch. The names of Angel Island and of Alcatraz, the *Isla de los Alcatraces,* or island of the pelicans, date from the Ayala expedition, although the name of Alcatraz was then applied to the island now called Yerba Buena.

The second Anza expedition also began in 1775 and was responsible for the founding of the presidio and mission at San Francisco in the following year. Except for Anza's own small escort, this expedition consisted almost entirely of settlers who would remain in California as *pobladores,* or populators. There were about 30 soldier-colonists and their families and 4 civilian settlers and their families, recruited mainly in Sinaloa. The need for *married* soldiers in California came from both the need for future citizens for the province and the desire to reduce the difficulties with the Indians repeatedly caused by soldiers who were either unmarried or living far from their families in Mexico. In 1773, for example, three soldiers at San Diego had been accused of raping two Indian girls and murdering one of them. Sent to Mexico for trial, the soldiers were spared their lives but were sentenced to spend the rest of their lives as citizens of California, a somewhat paradoxical verdict reflecting the evil reputation the new colony had in Mexico.

The time when people would want to go to California was far in the future; only those in the direst poverty were willing to go, and then only on the promise of the government to outfit them completely and to pay all their expenses for years to come. Upon Anza's warning to Viceroy Bucareli, however, all such payments were in the form of clothing, food, equipment, and supplies, and not in cash, which might have been gambled away immediately.

With the second Anza expedition went a large herd of cattle and horses to serve as breeding stock. Following his previous route, Anza reached San Gabriel in January 1776. There he learned that the Indians had attacked and destroyed the mission at San Diego in the previous November, killing Father Luis Jayme and two soldiers and mutilating the body of Father Jayme.

Governor Rivera had only 70 soldiers in the whole province, scattered among five missions and two presidios. He was on his way from Monterey to San Diego to punish the offenders, and Anza was induced to join forces with him for that purpose. Their arrival at San Diego, coinciding with those of a supply ship for San Blas and a small land force sent up from the peninsula, completely overawed the Indians; however, Rivera was excommunicated by the padres for entering the improvised church to seize an Indian chief who had sought the right of asylum, but who was suspected of being the main instigator of the revolt.

In March, Anza's party of colonists reached Monterey, and Anza himself proceeded to the San Francisco peninsula to choose the sites for the new presidio and mission. Governor Rivera, in spite of orders from the viceroy, had done nothing to prepare for the founding of San Francisco and was in fact bitterly opposed to it. He was now 65 years old and had repeatedly requested retirement. He was still a captain, and part of his irritation at this time was undoubtedly the result of his belief that Anza, who was only 41, had gained promotion to a higher rank for services no greater than his own. It was Rivera, after all, who had led the first overland party of Spanish colonists into California. A few years later, during the Yuma massacre, he would be killed while leading the last one, at the age of 70.

For the site of the new presidio, Anza chose a point near the northernmost tip of the San Francisco peninsula. The whole northern part of the peninsula consisted largely of sand dunes, but about 3 miles to the southeast of the presidio site Anza found a little oasis on a creek, and here, on March 29, 1776, he marked the site of the mission. He named the creek *Laguna de Nuestra Señora de los Dolores* because March 29 in the religious calendar was the Friday of Sorrows, referring to Our Lady of Sorrows, the Virgin Mary. From this there later arose the popular name of Mission Dolores for what was officially the Mission of San Francisco de Asís.

Various obstacles, including some set up by Governor Rivera, delayed the actual founding of the new establishments for several months. In the meantime Anza

○ - **Mission**
□ - **Pueblo**
△ - **Presidio**

SAN FRANCISCO SOLANO DE SONOMA (1823)
SAN RAFAEL ARCÁNGEL (1817)
PRESIDIO DE SAN FRANCISCO
SAN FRANCISCO DE ASÍS (1776)
SAN JOSÉ DE GUADALUPE (1797)
SANTA CLARA DE ASÍS (1777)
PUEBLO DE SAN JOSÉ (1777)
SANTA CRUZ (1791)
VILLA DE BRANCIFORTE
SAN JUAN BAUISTA (1797)
PRESIDIO DE MONTEREY
SAN CARLOS BORROMEO (1770)
NUESTRA SEÑORA DE LA SOLEDAD (1791)
SAN ANTONIO DE PADUA (1771)
SAN MIGUEL ARCÁNGEL (1777)
SAN LUIS OBISPO DE TOLOSA (1772)
LA PURÍSIMA CONCEPCIÓN (1787)
SANTA INÉS (1804)
SANTA BARBARA (1782)
PRESIDIO DE SANTA BARBARA
SAN BUENAVENTURA (1782)
SAN FERNANDO REY DE ESPAÑA (1771)
SAN GABRIEL ARCÁNGEL (1771)
PUEBLO DE NUESTRA SEÑORA LA REINA DE LOS ANGELES DEL RÍO DE PORCIÚNCULA
SAN JUAN CAPISTRANO (1776)
SAN LUIS REY DE FRANCIA (1798)
SAN DIEGO DE ALCALA (1769)
PRESIDIO DE SAN DIEGO

Spanish California. (*From* Indians of California: The Changing Image *by James J. Rawls. Copyright 1984 by the University of Oklahoma Press.*)

departed for Mexico and left Lt. José Moraga in charge of the new colonists. On June 27, 1776, a group of 193 persons, mostly soldier-settlers and their families, arrived at the site of the San Francisco mission. The presidio was formally established under the command of Moraga on September 17, and Father Palóu formally opened the mission on October 9.

NEVE AND THE PUEBLOS OF SAN JOSÉ AND LOS ANGELES

The year 1776 was a time not only of Spanish colonial expansion, but also of re-organization. José de Gálvez, having become Minister of the Indies in the royal government of Madrid, authorized a plan to reorganize the higher administration of the frontiers of New Spain. In 1776 the entire group of frontier provinces from Sinaloa, Sonora, and the Californias to New Mexico and Texas was detached from the control of the viceroy at Mexico City and placed under a commandant-general of the "Interior Provinces" with headquarters at Arispe in Sonora.

Within the Californias there was also bureaucratic change. Alta California was now regarded as more important than Baja California, and this was reflected in the reorganization of their joint government in 1776. Felipe de Neve was now appointed governor of both the Californias, with headquarters at Monterey, where he arrived to replace Rivera early in 1777. Neve was another army officer, and probably the best administrator among the Spanish governors of California. In his *reglamento* of 1779, revising and enlarging an earlier decree of Viceroy Bucareli, Neve established the code of law that remained in effect until the end of Spanish rule. Father-President Serra found Governor Neve even more determined than his predecessors to maintain the authority of the government over that of the missionaries. The governors had been so instructed, because it was the policy of the entire Spanish government at this time to treat the church as essentially an arm of the state.

Neve also had been ordered to try to solve the food supply problems of the presidios by establishing agricultural towns or pueblos. With the establishment of secular farming communities, one in the north and one in the south, Neve hoped that the military and civil establishment would no longer have to depend for food either upon the missions or upon the expensive and hazardous supply line from San Blas. In November 1777 he collected 14 men and their families from the presidios of Monterey and San Francisco and settled them at the new pueblo of San José de Guadalupe, the first town to be founded in Spanish Alta California.

In the same year Neve made a personal survey of possible locations for a southern pueblo. He chose a point near the *Río de Porciúncula,* about 9 miles southwest of the mission of San Gabriel. There was no harbor, and no navigable river, but that was of no importance for a small agricultural community. Neve set September 4, 1781, as the date for the founding of the pueblo, and it has served as the official birthday ever since. Its name was to be *El Pueblo de Nuestra Señora la Reina de los Angeles del Río de Porciúncula,* or the Town of Our Lady the Queen of the Angels by the River of Porciúncula. That this would soon be abbreviated was rather obviously inevitable, but the part of it to be chosen by popular usage was a matter of accident. It might have been *Porciúncula,* which, because it means "little portion," would be more than a little incongruous today. It turned out to be *Los Angeles,* or rather, in the Spanish and Mexican periods, usually simply *Angeles.* The modern American expression, "the City of the Angels," often imagined to be a translation of the name, is inaccurate.

It is ironic that San Francisco and Los Angeles, hardly the least materialistic and self-indulgent of modern cities, were named, respectively, for the ascetic St. Francis of Assisi and for the Virgin Mary.

Like the San Francisco colonists, the Los Angeles *pobladores* were drawn from the poorest classes of Sinaloa, people to whom any change offered some hope of improvement. Neve asked for 24 experienced farmers, but it proved impossible to obtain that many. Early in 1781, 12 settlers and their families were sent north. The Los Angeles settlers and their dependents, 46 persons in all, arrived at San Gabriel mission in August. Their origins, as historian Hubert Howe Bancroft puts it, were a mixture of Indian and Negro with here and there a trace of Spanish. Indeed, about half the founding families were of partial African ancestry; one mulatto settler, Francisco Reyes, served as alcalde (chief administrative officer) of the pueblo in the 1790s. The San José colonists were ahead of those in Los Angeles, not only in priority of founding, but also in educational matters. Of the nine heads of families now at San José, there was one who could read and write.

One of the most persistent problems at these remote outposts of empire was the scarcity of Spanish-speaking women. The few women who were willing to come were the wives of soldiers, government officials, and early pueblo settlers. Women who were widowed often found employment as *llaveras* (keepers of the keys) at the missions. Eulalia Arrila de Pérez, the *llavera* at San Gabriel, supervised the padres' kitchen, oversaw the laundry, and managed the wine presses and other small manufactures. "It was I," she later recalled, "who made the chocolate, the oil, the candy, the lemonade. I made so much lemonade that some of it was even bottled and sent to Spain."

NATIVE RESISTANCE

The Indians of California responded to missionization in a wide variety of ways. Some joined the missions out of curiosity; others came because they viewed the missionaries as shamanlike intermediaries to the spirit world. Many California Indians, however, resisted all efforts at missionization.

Passive resistance in the missions included noncooperation, work slowdowns, and the destruction of tools and equipment. Fugitivism was a constant problem. Thus, one of the principal duties of soldiers garrisoned at the missions was to track down and bring back runaways. Indians also resisted the missionaries' attempts at conversion. According to Antonio María Osio, it was customary at Mission San José for Indians to receive a dozen or more lashes after Sunday mass for any offenses they had committed during the week. Then, as a sign of submission, the chastened Indians were expected to kiss the missionary's hand. Osio reported that one new recruit refused to follow the custom, saying to the startled priest: "Father, take your Christianity. I don't want it anymore because I am returning to my land."

Active resistance to missionization included short-lived revolts, occasional attempts to murder individual missionaries, and raids on mission herds by mission fugitives and unconverted Indians. The first violent attack occurred at San Diego on August 15, 1769, within a month of the mission's founding. Six years later came the killing of Father Jayme when the Indians again attacked the San Diego mission.

The most successful instance of violent resistance occurred on the California side of the Colorado River where two settlements were founded in Yuma territory

Eulalia Arrila de Pérez served as the *llavera,* or keeper of the keys, at Mission San Gabriel in the 1820s and early 1830s. (*Courtesy of the Security Pacific Collection, Los Angeles Public Library.*)

in 1780. Over the protests of the padres, both establishments along the Colorado were peculiar mixtures of mission, presidio, and pueblo. In June 1781 Captain Rivera and his party of married soldiers reached the Colorado on their way to California. Some went ahead to San Gabriel, but about half the party including Rivera camped on the eastern bank of the river to rest. Their cattle destroyed part of the Indians' supply of mesquite beans, and Rivera's men generally succeeded in antagonizing the Yumas even more than the Spaniards at the new missions had done. The Yumas, whose location on the Colorado River was so strategic, were more capable of armed resistance than other California tribes. On July 17 the Yumas destroyed both missions and the next day crossed the river to surprise and kill Rivera and all his soldiers. The women and children with the Spaniards were captured. Altogether, 30 soldiers and 4 padres, including Garcés, were put to death. Captain Don Fernando Rivera y Moncada, the weary and irascible old veteran who had felt condemned to interminable service in some of the most difficult roles ever demanded of a soldier or a colonial administrator, was released from duty at last.

From the Spanish point of view, the Yuma massacre was a terrible disaster. Some of the captives were later ransomed, but no serious attempt was made to punish the

Yumas or to reopen the Colorado River route. The Anza Trail remained cut off until the 1820s, and in the meantime there was virtually no land communication at all between Mexico and California.

For the next 40 years, from the Yuma massacre in 1781 to the final collapse of Spanish rule over Mexico in 1821, New Spain made little effort to strengthen its outposts in Alta California. There, as elsewhere, the overextended Spanish colonial empire was on the defensive and crumbling. The mission system continued to expand, but it did not succeed in turning the Indians into genuine colonists. Other than the native Indians, there were about 600 persons in Alta California in 1781, and about five times as many in 1821, but the increase was almost entirely from the birth of descendants of the earlier colonists rather than from the arrival of new ones. The numbers of cattle and horses grew much more rapidly, and a fourth institution, the private rancho, began to develop along with the presidios, missions, and pueblos. Nellie Van de Grift Sánchez and other writers have called Spanish California an "Arcadia." Like that isolated mountain kingdom in ancient Greece, it was quiet, simple, and pastoral (at least for the colonial elite). But life for all was by no means as ideal as this analogy would imply.

THE IMPACT OF THE MISSIONS

Following Serra's death in 1784 his longtime companion Francisco Palóu served briefly as father-president. The following year Fermín Francisco de Lasuén became head of the Alta California missions and served as father-president from 1785 to 1803. It was Lasuén who supervised the building of the beautiful churches, several of which are extant, that replaced the rude structures of Serra's time. Under Lasuén each mission developed into a kind of polytechnical school, teaching the Indians to do fine leather work, operate tile factories and carpentry shops, and even do mural painting. During his tenure as father-president the number of missions doubled, from 9 to 18, and their Indian population more than doubled, rising to about 20,000, nearly as large as it ever became.

Early visitors to Spanish California often described in detail the operations of the missions and their impact on the Indians. In 1786 the comte de La Pérouse, a European nobleman engaged in a global voyage of scientific exploration for the French government, visited Monterey. The two vessels under La Pérouse were the first ships, other than those of the Spanish themselves, to visit Alta California since the voyage of Drake more than two centuries earlier. The French visitor had the highest admiration for the character of the missionaries—"these men, truly apostolic, who have abandoned the idle life of a cloister to give themselves up to fatigues, cares, and anxieties of every kind." But he doubted that they were accomplishing anything of permanent value. Under their theocratic system the Indian was "too much a child, too much a slave, too little a man." In the resorting to stocks, irons, and the lash, and in the use of soldiers to hunt down those who tried to escape, La Pérouse found a distressing resemblance to the slave plantations he had seen in Santo Domingo.

Indians at Mission San Carlos Borromeo in Carmel lined up in rigid formation for the visit of La Pérouse in 1786. From a 1791 watercolor copy of the lost original painting made at the occasion. (*Courtesy of the Museo Naval, Madrid.*)

Five years after La Pérouse's visit, Monterey welcomed another scientific exploring expedition, this time Spanish, under the command of Alejandro Malaspina. In the crew of one of Malaspina's ships, incidentally, was the first Anglo-American who came to California and stayed—one John Green, a sailor from Boston who died of dropsy a few hours after the expedition arrived at Monterey in 1791. Malaspina's impression of the mission system was in considerable contrast to that of La Pérouse. He denounced the "ridiculous inventions of many foreign authors, who, confusing at times the system with the abuses and ignoring always the primary object of such establishments, have painted all our missions in America as horrible and oppressive." There was no doubt in Malaspina's mind that the missionaries in California had accomplished a great good. The Spanish priests had brought to the Indians "the end of a thousand local wars that were destroying them, social beginnings, a pure and holy religion, safe and healthy foods," and a variety of other blessings.

The question of whether the Indians in the California missions were exploited and wretched or contented and appreciative has long been a matter of debate. It has been said that "the preponderant testimony" describes the mission Indians as happy and well-adjusted, preferring mission life to their previous freedom and grateful for close supervision, hard work, colorful rituals, and the salvation of their souls. This is, to say the least, an extremely questionable conclusion. The bulk of the evidence has been the writings of the missionaries, who naturally tended to believe what they deeply yearned to believe about a matter so vital to their consciences. It is significant that the padres always applied the term "neophytes," or apprentices in Christianity, even to Indians who had been born in the missions and spent their entire lives there. The belief that any group of human adults could be happy under a system that treated them as if they were hopelessly retarded children was a very questionable one indeed.

The Spanish divided the colonial population, at the missions and elsewhere, into two main groups, the "rationals" and the "irrationals." The *gente de razón,* the people of reason, included all who were not full-blooded Indians. This idea of "civilized" or "rational" persons was also used interchangeably with "whites." Any admixture of white ancestry, mestizo or mulatto, was counted as white, and also qualified a person as rational. This distinction was itself irrational. In essence it was a distinction between human and subhuman. Among the rationals, the very few "pureblooded Spaniards" were at the top of the colonial heap, and degrees of admixture often effectively determined social status.

The best evidence of how the Indians actually felt about the missions would be the testimony of the Indians themselves, and unfortunately very few of them had any opportunity to get their testimony into the historical record. One who did was Victoria, an Indian girl who grew up in the Mission of San Gabriel and later married the "Scotch *paisano,*" Hugo Reid. It should be noted that it was Reid who recorded his wife's recollections and that his non-Catholic background, along with his status as the recipient of a rancho grant carved out of San Gabriel mission lands, gave him a viewpoint that was particularly hostile to the missionaries. The Franciscan historian Father Zephyrin Englehardt described Hugo Reid as "that embittered Scotchman" who "lied about religious matters."

Nevertheless, it is clear that Victoria regarded life in the mission as a life of misery, humiliation, and terror. The alliance of the padres and the soldiers, she told her husband bitterly, had turned even Indian leaders like her own father into humble, confused, awkward, and shamefaced men. She could not entirely understand why her people, the Gabrielino, who had once given good accounts of themselves in occasional battles with neighboring tribes, had offered so little resistance to the Spaniards; however, she remembered how the soldiers, armed with muskets, had come to her village when she was 6 years old and taken its people to the mission. At first the Indians had been filled with surprise and astonishment; then a strange lethargy set in. They were told to fear a hell that was lacking in their own religion. Corporal punishment, also, was something that had been unknown to them before.

One stark episode that Victoria remembered from her mission childhood occurred when an Indian woman who had a miscarriage was charged with infanticide and punished by having her head shaved, by being flogged every day for 15 days, by wearing irons on her feet for 3 months, and by "having to appear every Sunday in church, on the steps leading up to the altar, with a hideous painted wooden child in her arms." This took place while San Gabriel was under the regime of Father José María Zalvidea, a particularly stern disciplinarian. In Hugo Reid's opinion, Zalvidea "must . . . have considered whipping as meat and drink to [the Indians], for they had it morning, noon and night."

Like Serra, Zalvidea was as stern with himself as with his Indian wards. He often lashed his own shoulders and back, and under his coarse robe he always wore a belt with iron points pressing into his flesh. He made San Gabriel "the Pride of the Missions," and yet to a man of his faith, pride was the first of the seven deadly sins. Perhaps this conflict was one of the things that unbalanced his mind; he later suffered a nervous breakdown and was transferred to San Juan Capistrano for hospitalization.

Also from the history of the San Gabriel mission we have the testimony of a 24-year-old female shaman named Toypurina. In 1785, she participated in a conspiracy of neophytes and unconverted Indians to destroy the mission. Like other shamans and native leaders, Toypurina likely regarded the missionaries as a threat to her traditional status and authority. When questioned about her role in planning the revolt, Toypurina expressed the anger that she and many of her people felt toward the Spanish colonizers: "I hate the padres and all of you, for living here on my native soil, for trespassing upon the land of my forefathers."

A more positive view of mission life comes from a manuscript written by Pablo Tac, a mission Indian born at San Luis Rey. Tac and another Luiseño youth were taken to Rome by a missionary in 1833. In his manuscript, deposited in the Vatican Library, Tac expressed thanks to God for the coming of the missionaries to California and made no reference to native resistance. He did observe, however, that thousands of his people died as "a result of a sickness that came to California" and that many left "for the woods" rather than submit to Spanish domination.

The most revealing evidence of the impact of the missions on the California Indians was recorded in the mission registers. There one finds a terrifying death rate, caused primarily by diseases for which the Indians lacked immunity. Confinement within the adobe walls of the missions also deprived the Indians of the degree of sanitation they had enjoyed in their own villages from their *temescáls* and their practice of occasionally burning their old dwellings and building new ones. Concentration of Indians in large numbers at the missions, the changes in diet, and the imposition of an alien discipline and regimentation all contributed to the high death rate. The mission registers also revealed a surprising variation in experience from mission to mission. Indians at the Santa Cruz mission, for example, survived an average of $8\frac{1}{2}$ years after conversion, whereas those at San Luis Obispo survived more than twice as long. The infant mortality rate, also erratic, was generally high: more than half the Indians born in the missions died before their fifth birthday. During the entire mission period, the native population from San Francisco Bay to San Diego fell from 72,000 to 18,000—a decline of over 75 percent.

The debate over the impact of the missions on the California Indians has been revived in recent years by the movement to have Junípero Serra declared a saint. The canonization process began in 1934 on the 150th anniversary of Serra's death. Thousands of documents on Serra and the missions were assembled by church historians, and in 1985 Pope John Paul II declared Serra to be "venerable," the first step toward sainthood. Three years later the pope elevated Serra to the second step, declaring him "beatific." Supporters of the Serra cause rejoiced that the church at last "recognized the extraordinary holiness of this man who was the founder of civilization in California." Opponents denounced the move. Some described Serra as a "sadist" and a "fanatic," while one critic of the mission system complained that the canonization of Serra "would be another insensitive reminder of past oppression and maltreatment."

ATTEMPTS AT REINFORCEMENT

At the end of the eighteenth century Spain began to experience a long series of international difficulties in which it would gradually drift from humiliation into utter disaster. In 1790, in a treaty with England, Spain was forced to give up its claims to exclusive rights on the Pacific coast north of California. George Vancouver was appointed as a British commissioner to work out details of the application of the treaty, and in 1792 and the following year he visited several points in California, with special interest in the presidios. The fourth and last of these, at Santa Barbara, had been established in 1782. Vancouver was amazed at their weakness. At the time of his visits there were two cannons at the presidio of San Francisco, neither of them serviceable, and three at San Diego, none of them even mounted. Santa Barbara had two cannons, and Monterey eight. The Spanish authorities, worried because the extent of this weakness would now be known to the British government, made plans to try to strengthen their feeble hold on the province.

In 1796 the viceroy, the marqués de Branciforte, and the governor, Diego de Borica, made plans for a new type of pueblo to be colonized by retired soldiers and their families. These ex-soldiers not only would be self-supporting but would provide a ready reserve in case of foreign incursions. The attempt to carry out this project illustrated the able planning that so often characterized Spanish colonial administration, and the typical frustration of such planning by hopeless difficulties.

The site of the new pueblo, to be called the Villa de Branciforte, adjoined the lands of the Mission Santa Cruz—to the bitter objections of the padres. The funds available for founding the new town were sadly inadequate. Not a single ex-soldier could be found in Mexico who would go there voluntarily, and nearly all the colonists who finally arrived in 1797 were men convicted of petty crimes, now sentenced to live in a Spanish version of Botany Bay. It is not surprising that the Villa de Branciforte did not flourish, although it struggled along for many years as a collection of huts. Such was the last attempt under Spanish rule to found any new civil or military establishment in California, with the exception of a few cattle ranchos on lands granted mainly to noncommissioned officers retired from garrison duty.

A dismal impression of Spanish prospects in California must remain, even though Governor Diego de Borica, a jovial Basque who was an early California booster, did his best to brighten the picture in a number of his reports. "This is a great country," he wrote soon after his arrival at Monterey, "the most peaceful and quiet country in the world; one lives better here than in the most cultured court of Europe." Toward the end of his governorship (1794–1800), Borica was still interlarding his reports with such glowing remarks as, "To live much, and without care, come to Monterey." But in view of the fact that ill health was causing him to beg for retirement, as Rivera and Neve had done before him, we must suspect that his continued praise of life in California may have been designed to help in finding a willing and competent replacement. This was not easy. The governorship of California was not one of the more desirable posts in the Spanish colonial service.

EXPLORATION OF THE CENTRAL VALLEY

Spanish settlement in Alta California was confined to a thin coastal strip. Except for the two short-lived establishments on the Colorado which were wiped out by the Yumas, the farthest-inland Spanish settlement was Mission Soledad—only 30 miles from the sea. Following the discovery of the Central Valley by Pedro Fages during his exploration of the northeastern reaches of San Francisco Bay in 1772, there were periodic efforts to find places suitable for missions in various parts of the great interior region.

No missions were actually founded there, however, and the purposes of most of the Spanish expeditions into the valley were no more than those of pursuing escaped neophytes, punishing occasional raiders, and recovering stolen cattle and horses. The frequent raids on the livestock of the coastal settlements were carried on mainly by Indians who had once lived in the coastal areas but had fled to the interior to avoid missionization.

The outstanding figure among Spanish explorers of the Central Valley was Lt. Gabriel Moraga. His father, José, the first commandant of the Presidio of San Francisco, had brought Gabriel to California as a boy with the second Anza expedition. Between 1805 and 1817 the younger Moraga led a large number of expeditions into the great valley. He was responsible for such names as those of *El Río de Nuestra Señora de la Merced,* the River of Our Lady of Mercy; *El Río de Los Santos Reyes,* the River of the Holy Kings; the San Joaquin and Sacramento rivers; *Mariposa,* from the many butterflies seen there in 1806; and *Calavares,* a place of skulls.

THE COMING OF THE RUSSIANS

In the early nineteenth century the Spanish claim of exclusive rights to settlement in California was challenged by the establishment of a Russian fur trading outpost north of San Francisco. Count Nikolai Petrovich Rezanov, an official of the Russian-American Fur Company, visited San Francisco in the spring of 1806. He came seeking supplies to relieve the danger of starvation in the Russian colony at Sitka, and incidentally investigating the possibilities of the fur trade in northern California itself. The Spaniards were aware that the Russian position in the Pacific northwest was almost as weak as their own, and they were concerned lest it be strengthened. Trade between Spanish colonies and foreigners

The Legacy of Spain and Mexico in the United States (1994) and Doyce B. Nunis, Jr. (ed.), *Southern California's Spanish Heritage* (1992).

Bernard E. Bobb, *The Viceregency of Antonio Maria Bucareli* (1962), includes a description of Bucareli's policies toward California. Herbert E. Bolton, *Anza's California Expeditions* (five volumes, 1930), exhaustively chronicles the two expeditions and the founding of San Francisco; the first volume was published separately as *Outpost of Empire* (1931). See also Harlan Hague, *The Road to California* (1978); Theodore E. Treutlein, *San Francisco Bay* (1968); John Galvin (ed.), *The First Spanish Entry into San Francisco Bay, 1775* (1971); and Edwin A. Beilharz, *Felipe de Neve* (1971). Documents on the founding of Los Angeles were included in the Historical Society of Southern California's annual publication of 1931, the year of the sesquicentennial.

The first two volumes of the *History of California,* written by Henry L. Oak [also included as volumes XVIII (1884) and XIX (1885) of *The Works of Hubert Howe Bancroft*] are a compendium of detailed information. The many books that dwell on the romantic aspects include Nellie Van de Grift Sánchez, *Spanish Arcadia* (1929), and Irving B. Richman, *California under Spain and Mexico* (1911).

Leon G. Campbell, "The Spanish Presidio in Alta California during the Mission Period, 1769–1784," *Journal of the West,* XVI (October 1977), pp. 63–77, and Richard S. Whitehead, "Alta California's Four Fortresses," *Southern California Quarterly,* LXV (Spring 1983), pp. 67–94, are brief summaries, while Max L. Moorhead, *The Presidio* (1975), offers a more extensive analysis but excludes the Californias. Joseph P. Sánchez, *Spanish Bluecoats* (1991) describes the Catalonian soldiers who served on the northern frontier.

"Spanish Explorations of California's Central Valley" is the subject of Donald C. Cutter's Ph.D. thesis, University of California, Berkeley (1950).

The literature on the impact of the missions on the Indians is extensive. Among the best recent accounts are Robert H. Jackson and Edward Castillo, *Indians, Franciscans, and Spanish Colonization* (1995); Randall Milliken, *A Time of Little Choice* (1995); Jackson, *Indian Population Decline* (1994); and Castillo (ed.), *Native American Perspectives on the Hispanic Colonization of Alta California* (1991). The most damning account of the missions appears in Rupert Costo and Jeannette Henry Costo (eds.), *The Missions of California: A Legacy of Genocide* (1987). Earlier critiques appear in Sherburne F. Cook, *The Conflict between the California Indian and White Civilization,* Part II (1943); and "Historical Demography," in Robert F. Heizer (ed.), *California* (1978), pp. 91–98. Francis F. Guest, "An Examination of the Thesis of S. F. Cook on the Forced Conversion of Indians in the California Missions," *Southern California Quarterly,* LXI (Spring 1979), pp. 1–78, and "Cultural Perspectives on California Mission Life," ibid., LXV (Spring 1983), pp. 1–66, offer a more positive view. See also his *Hispanic California Revisited* (1996) and *Fermin Francisco de Lasúen* (1973). For an analysis of the importance of Indian labor, see the corresponding chapter in Robert Archibald, *The Economic Aspects of the California Missions* (1978).

George Phillips suggests that the California Indians were far from passive in their response to the missions; see his *Indians and Intruders in Central California, 1769–1848* (1993). A neglected aspect of the period has been examined by Albert L. Hurtado in "Sexuality in California's Franciscan Missions," *California History,* LXXI (Fall 1992), pp. 370–385. On the controversy over the missions' founder, see James A. Sandos, "Junípero Serra's Canonization and the Historical Record," *American Historical Review,* XCIII (December 1988), pp. 1253–1269. For the views of foreign visitors, see Malcolm Margolin (ed.), *Monterey in 1786: The Journals of Jean Francois de La Pérouse* (1989); Donald C. Cutter, *Malaspina in California*

(1960) and *California in 1792* (1990); and Francis J. Weber, "The California Missions and Their Visitors," *The Americas,* XXIV (1968), pp. 319–336.

Accounts of the coming of the Russians include T. C. Russel (ed.), *The Rezanov Voyage to Nueva California in 1806* (1926); *Langsdorff's Narrative of the Rezanov Voyage* (1927); and "The Russians in California," *California Historical Society Quarterly,* XII (September 1933). See also James R. Gibson, *Imperial Russia in Frontier America* (1976), and P. A. Tikhmenev, *A History of the Russian-American Company* (1978).

CHAPTER FIVE

A Marginal Province of a Troubled Republic

As one of the most isolated and least valued of all the colonial possessions of Spain, California had grown used to being neglected. The independent nation of Mexico, periodically torn with revolutionary disturbances and established as a republic after a brief and tragic interlude under the "empire" of Agustín Iturbide, was even less able than Spain had been to concern itself seriously or effectively with the distant northern region.

GOVERNMENT AND POLITICS IN THEORY AND PRACTICE

The most influential framers of the Federal Constitution of the United Mexican States, adopted in 1824, were liberal idealists who modeled their country's new organic law in part on that of the United States of America. But there were great differences between the political, economic, and social backgrounds of the two countries. In Mexico, not even the upper class had acquired any substantial experience in self-government under Spanish colonial rule, and only a tiny fraction of the people were literate and prosperous enough to take an informed part in public affairs. Nevertheless, on paper the constitution of 1824 guaranteed both complete political equality and complete racial equality. Not only were Indians entitled to vote and to hold office, but like all other citizens they were supposed to enjoy full freedom of person and property.

The liberal Mexican constitution makers of 1824 dreamed of developing a civil society and a prosperous economy in which republican government and equal rights for all people could become more than empty phrases. As applied to the remote province of California, these vague hopes led to several new policies. Governors of California were now authorized to permit freer trade with foreigners, subject only to import duties, to move toward secularization of the missions, and to increase rancho land grants, including grants to foreigners willing to be naturalized and to accept Roman Catholicism.

Under the first Mexican constitution, California was only a territory, not a state, although it was promoted to the rank of a "department" under the constitution of 1836 and the laws of 1837. Governors were appointed by the government of Mexico. There was a provincial legislative branch, of sorts, in the form of an elected *diputación,* but in practice it functioned only occasionally when the governor chose to convene it, and then merely as an advisory rather than a legislative body. In effect, the governor not only acted as the civil and military executive but also controlled the provincial lawmaking process, and he exercised nearly all the judicial authority in the more important matters. The general government of California remained what it had been under Spain, a petty military despotism. Control from Mexico City, however, was greatly weakened because the government could provide few soldiers of any sort, and one competent or reliable, for service in California; it lacked the money to pay them.

During California's Mexican period, one important substitute for a system of checks and balances did arise: the comic-opera "revolution," a political device characterized by bombastic "pronouncements," chesslike marches and counter-marches, and noisy but bloodless artillery duels, just out of range, in which both sides retrieved each other's cannonballs and fired them back.

As the power of the Mexican governors and the Franciscan missionaries weakened, the real authority in California, insofar as there was any, gravitated into the hands of a small group of *ranchero* families, mostly California-born. The fact that these families were so closely intermarried was one reason that there was so little actual killing in battles between revolutionary factions. There was too much risk of killing a brother-in-law.

The main political motives of the leaders of this little ranchero oligarchy were, first, the hope of taking over from the missions their lands, their cattle, and their skillful cowboys and, second, the desire for political power and glory. In their struggles to achieve these objectives, the *californios* were badly divided by per-sonal, factional, and sectional disputes. In the rivalry be-tween *norteños* and *sureños,* such northern California leaders as Juan Bautista Alvarado, Mariano Guadalupe Vallejo, and José Castro were aligned against southern California politicos like José Antonio Carrillo, Pío Pico, and Juan Bandini. Confronted by the restless ambitions of these volatile native sons of California, governors sent up from Mexico had an increasingly difficult time.

Josiah Royce later maintained that the bloodless revolution, given the lim-itations of its social and historical context, was really a comparatively civ-ilized method of settling internal political differences. Government by mock revolution had serious defects, however, and one of these was that the result-ing decisions were likely to be temporary. In one 5-year period, from 1831 to 1836, Mexican California had 11 distinct gubernatorial administrations, not counting 3 men who were appointed to the governorship by Mexico but whom the Californians did not permit to take office. By contrast, there had been only 10 governors in the whole period of more than half a century of Spanish rule.

THE SECULARIZATION PROBLEM

By far the most important political issue in the province during the 1820s and 1830s was the question of the secularization of the missions, or rather, and more realistically, the question of who was to profit from the acquisition of their lands and herds. This troublesome problem so far overshadowed all others that the whole story of the political and quasi-military events can best be understood in connection with it.

As early as 1749, by royal order, the Spanish government had made an attempt to secularize the missions of Mexico—that is, to turn the properties over to the Indians and to replace the missionaries with secular parish clergy. This attempt was abandoned largely because there were not enough secular priests available.

When Mexico gained its independence in 1821, the California missionaries were alarmed. Most of the missionaries were Spaniards, and as such they were targets for the hostility of Mexican revolutionary nationalists. For centuries the creoles had hated the *gachupines*. A "creole," or *criollo,* was a person who had been born in the Spanish American colonies; sometimes the word meant a person of entirely European ancestry; sometimes it was used without regard to racial origin. The Mexican word "*gachupines,*" meaning men born in Spain, had originally meant "those who wear spurs," and it implied, usually correctly, that the Spanish-born regarded themselves as superior beings.

For centuries the Spanish church had been an integral part of Spain's authoritarian system of colonial control. Inevitably, republican theories were often anticlerical. Such theories, however, were often rationalizations for avarice. There was rising criticism of the missions for their temporal wealth and for their exploitation of the Indians. Unfortunately these were the same privileges that many an eloquent anticlerical wanted to appropriate for himself.

The padres argued that the mission Indians were not ready for secularization, and this was certainly true. That the missions had failed to make them ready after more than half a century and showed no signs of ever making them ready were facts that the missionaries blamed on the alleged inherent defects of the Indians rather than on the defects of the mission system or on their own desire to perpetuate it.

Meanwhile the Indians themselves were becoming increasingly restive. In 1824 during a concerted rebellion they briefly took over control of the missions at Santa Barbara, Santa Inés, and La Purísima Concepción, with some loss of life and much property damage. Soldiers crushed the insurrection after a battle in which there were many Indian casualties. In 1829 an Indian named Estanislao, after the Polish Saint Stanislaus, became the leader of a large band of Miwoks in the San Joaquin Valley. He issued a ringing challenge to the Mexican authorities: "We are rising in revolt. . . . We have no fear of the soldiers, for even now they are very few, mere boys . . . not even sharpshooters." Near the river that was later named after him, "Stanislaus" and his followers fought a battle with 100 soldiers and militiamen under Lt. Mariano Vallejo. This and other campaigns completely failed to subjugate the Miwoks. Until the end of the Mexican period they would continue to block Mexican settlement of the San Joaquin Valley and to raid ranches in the coastal areas to obtain horses.

FROM ECHEANDÍA TO FIGUEROA

The first governor of California under the Mexican republican constitution, or more precisely and officially the first *jefe político superior* and *comandante general militar,* was José María Echeandía, a lieutenant colonel of engineers. He arrived in 1825 with instructions to proceed cautiously and gradually toward ultimate secularization; however, though he drafted various plans for this eventuality, a number of formidable difficulties stood in the way. The missions were still the chief source of supplies for the presidios. Cash revenues for the territorial government depended on duties levied on the goods imported in exchange for Californian cowhides and tallow, and the missions were still the chief producers of the hides and tallow.

To add to the governor's troubles, he was in poor health and spent much time in San Diego to escape the fogs of the north. In 1829 the unpaid soldiers at Monterey revolted under the leadership of an ex-convict who was living in California as a part of his sentence. The revolt was suppressed after a bloodless "battle" near Santa Barbara, but later in the same year, in deep discouragement, Echeandía submitted his resignation.

Early in 1830 a conservative and proclerical "centralist" faction gained control of the government in Mexico. Its appointee as governor of California was a reactionary politician and army officer, Lt. Col. Manuel Victoria, a vigorous opponent of secularization and a stern believer in the virtues of military authority. Shortly before the centralist coup, the previous Mexican regime had appointed the radical republican José María Padrés as governor, but before he could take office his appointment was superseded by Victoria's. Padrés remained in California in his earlier position of adjutant inspector of troops. He despised both the personality and the ideas of the man who would now hold the higher office. Padrés was not only a bitter critic of the missions, but also a man of considerable ability and personal magnetism, and several young Californians, including Vallejo and Alvarado, became his disciples. He taught them, as Bancroft put it, "to theorize eloquently on the rights of man, the wrongs of the neophytes, and the tyranny of the missionaries."

Shortly before Victoria arrived at Monterey, Padrés induced the outgoing Governor Echeandía to issue an order for general secularization. When Victoria reached the capital early in 1831, he promptly suspended this decree and soon afterward proclaimed a number of repressive measures. For opposition to his policies he banished several prominent men, including Padrés, and imprisoned several more. The result was an insurrection in southern California, led by José Antonio Carrillo and ex-Governor Echeandía.

When a small force under Governor Victoria met the rebels north of Cahuenga Pass, near Los Angeles, on December 4, 1831, hostilities might have been confined to the verbal level if the governor had not made a slurring remark about the fighting qualities of his own men. One of his aides, Lt. Romualdo Pacheco, was so goaded by this sarcasm that he drew his saber and rode out ahead of the governor's troops. On the rebel side, young José María Ávila was burning with resentment at having been imprisoned in Los Angeles for sedition. He suddenly charged at Pacheco and killed him with a pistol, then spurred toward Victoria and wounded him with a lance thrust. A soldier shot Ávila with a musket, and Victoria, though badly wounded, killed Ávila with his sword. Forty-three years later a son and namesake of Romualdo Pacheco, born a month before his father's death, would become one of the American governors of California.

By provoking actual bloodshed, Governor Victoria had violated the rules of the California political game. He was packed off to Mexico on the next ship, and there was a chaotic scramble for power. For about a year the south was ruled by Echeandía and the north by Agustín Zamorano. (Zamorano is better known for having imported California's first printing press, used mainly for the publication of official documents.)

The ouster of Governor Victoria was a deathblow to the mission system. Although the conservative faction was still precariously in power in Mexico City, it recognized the need to conciliate the rebellious Californians by permitting secularization of the missions and by appointing a governor who could be trusted to carry it out in the fairest way possible. The man selected was Brevet Brigadier General José Figueroa, governor from early in 1833 until his death in 1835.

FIGUEROA AND SECULARIZATION

In terms of both ability and character, Figueroa was far the best of all the officials sent up by the Mexican republic. The tragedy was that no governor could have arranged the assignments of the mission lands to private ownership in an orderly and satisfactory manner under the conditions that existed.

In August 1833 the Mexican Congress adopted an immediate general secularization law which was extremely vague about procedures for carrying it out. It soon appeared, however, that this law was largely the work of that vocal champion of freedom for the Indians, José María Padrés, and that Padrés had also engineered the Mexican government's approval of an ambitious "colonization" scheme under which he and a group of his Mexican friends were to take over the lands of the missions. His close associate José María Híjar was to be not only the "director of colonization" but also the new governor of the territory.

A substantial number of colonists actually arrived from Mexico to occupy their new estates. Governor Figueroa, however, had already appointed the administrators, or *comisionados,* who were to supervise the disposal of mission lands, and his appointees were all Californians. A notable example was Mariano Guadalupe Vallejo, appointed by Figueroa as not only the administrator of the Sonoma mission and grantee of the Petaluma rancho, but also the military commander of the whole northern frontier district. When Vallejo, Alvarado, and other former Californian admirers of Padrés heard that among his colonists there were 21 prospective mission administrators from Mexico, and when they recalled that there were just 21 missions, their feelings toward their erstwhile intellectual leader underwent a sharp and sudden change. Fortunately, from their point of view, the credentials of Padrés and Híjar were canceled from Mexico City in another of the kaleidoscopic shifts of Mexican politics.

Figueroa's proclamation of August 9, 1834, defined the general terms under which the process of secularization was to be conducted over the next 2 years. Half the property was supposed to go to the Indians, and the law forbade them to dispose of it, but these provisions were not effectively carried out. Some Indians tried to make a living by farming their small allotments of land near the mission buildings, but none of them retained these lands more than a few years. Many never realized that they were supposed to have been given any land at all. The law attempted to limit the killing of cattle, but as the time of secularization approached, the missionaries slaughtered much of the stock in order to salvage, from the sale of the hides, as much wealth as possible for the Pious Fund. As a result, the missions were surrounded with thousands of skinned carcasses rotting in the sun.

For several years the morale of the padres had been declining. Many of them were old men who had lived so long in the missions that they regarded them as their only homes. Some, on the other hand, looked forward to relief from their responsibilities. Shortly before secularization one padre wrote that there was "hardly anything of the religious left in me. . . . I made the vows of a Friar Minor; instead I must manage temporalities, sow grain, raise sheep, horses, and cows. . . . These things are as disagreeable as thorns . . . , and they rob me of time, tranquility, and health both of soul and body."

Because there were no secular parish priests to replace them, the Franciscans remained at the mission churches to continue their religious duties. For a time many of the neophytes remained huddled around the padres, whereas some left the coastal area to find homes with alien tribes in the interior. Indians who had been trained as *vaqueros,* or cattle wranglers, became laborers on the private ranchos into which the mission lands were gradually subdivided. Still others were able to gain a living as laborers in the towns.

The padres had predicted accurately the fate that was in store for the mission Indians when secularization came. As Father-President Durán pointed out, the Indians living in the pueblo of Los Angeles were forced to labor for the merest pittances and were subjected to frightful punishments for their trivial misdeeds; they were given no security of any kind and were in every way "far more wretched and oppressed than those in the missions."

ALVARADO AND PROVINCIAL AUTONOMY

Figueroa was deeply disturbed by the failure of his secularization policies to protect the legal and moral rights of the Indians. In any event, his efforts were cut short when, in the fall of 1835, he died of an apoplectic stroke. His passing removed a brake from the rapacity of the mission administrators and their friends and relatives, and again plunged California into noisy "revolutionary" struggles for control of the governorship. After the brief terms of José Castro and Nicolas Gutiérrez as acting governors, Mexico sent up a new champion of centralism, Col. Mariano Chico, who repeated most of the blunders of Governor Victoria and lasted only 3 months before he too was expelled.

Juan Bautista Alvarado, the clever and eloquent young president of the *diputación,* now emerged as the hero of the Californians, particularly the northerners. With the aid of about 30 riflemen led by Isaac Graham, a Tennessee backwoodsman who had come to California to operate a whisky distillery, Alvarado seized control of Monterey and deported most of the Mexican officials. On November 7, 1836, California was proclaimed "a free and sovereign State," until Mexico should repudiate centralism and restore the principles of the federalist constitution of 1824. Alvarado became provisional governor, and Vallejo, already in charge of the northern frontier, now became the military commander of the whole California department. Vallejo was Alvarado's uncle, though only 2 years his senior and also less than 30 years old.

As one of his first official actions, Alvarado proclaimed that the capital of California would continue at his native Monterey. (An act of the Mexican Congress in 1835 had promoted Los Angeles from a pueblo to a city and ordered the capital transferred there.) Alvarado, however, was forced to placate the southerners by permitting them to choose a subgovernor with considerable regional authority. Even if Mexico had not had its hands full with the Texan War of Independence, it would probably have been disposed to compromise with Alvarado by appointing him as the legal governor of California under the Mexican republic. He accepted this arrangement in 1837 and continued to hold the office for 5 years.

In the period before the last fragments of the mission holdings passed into private hands at the end of 1845, the administration of these properties grew steadily more corrupt, incompetent, and generally disgraceful. In 1839 Alvarado made a belated and perfunctory effort at reform by appointing a visitor-general of missions, the naturalized Englishman William E. P. Hartnell; however, Hartnell's efforts were futile, partly because mission administrators, such as Vallejo for San Rafael and Sonoma, and Pío Pico for San Luis Rey, had too much power in their respective districts. When Hartnell tried to make changes in some of Vallejo's plans for San Rafael, Vallejo actually arrested him.

Alvarado and Vallejo soon fell to quarreling with each other, and by 1842 they were both so disillusioned with the anarchic state of affairs in the province that they willingly turned over the political and military commands to the last governor from Mexico, Brigadier General Manuel Micheltorena. He was an amiable man, but his administration was no better than those of most of his predecessors. The army of 300 soldiers he brought with him consisted almost entirely of ex-convicts. Because they failed to receive their pay (as usual), they obtained food and other items by a highly informal process of foraging, to the outrage of the local population. Alvarado and José Castro led still another revolt, and there was a new "battle of Cahuenga Pass" in February 1845. It was a repetition of the encounter on almost the same spot in 1831, except that this time the only casualties were a horse and a mule, but it was enough to induce Governor Micheltorena to follow the examples of Governors Victoria, Chico, and Guitíerrez by departing for Mexico, along with his ragged and thieving soldiers.

This marked the failure of the last attempt to reestablish any more than nominal Mexican control over California. Pío Pico assumed the governorship with

Los Angeles as the capital, but having no influence much farther north than Santa Barbara he had to compromise with the *norteños* by recognizing José Castro as military commandant. This gave Castro the de facto control of the Monterey customs house and consequently of most of the governmental income. This arrangement, made on the eve of the Mexican War, left the province as weak and divided as it had ever been.

THE HEYDAY OF THE RANCHEROS

Throughout the Mexican period the potential resources of California remained not only underdeveloped but largely unsuspected. The most substantial economic activity was cattle raising, and the chief commercial products were hides and tallow for export. The local processing of these commodities went no farther than the staking out of the hides to dry in the sun and rendering of the fat into tallow by melting it in kettles, after which it was poured for storage into bags called *botas,* made out of whole hides.

After the missions disintegrated, there was virtually no manufacturing. Rawhide was used as a local makeshift for all sorts of purposes, but the manufacture of hides into shoes and other leather products was done in New England. Even the simple processes of making soap and candles out of the tallow were done in Chile or Peru. The missions, for their own use, had made such things as coarse woolen blankets, crude shoes, the leather parts of saddles, soap, candles, and coarse pottery. They had also developed irrigated agriculture to the point of producing a remarkable variety of grains, vegetables, and fruits, and some wine and brandy. All these skills disappeared after secularization. The diet of the rancheros and their families consisted largely of fresh or dried beef. Not even milk was widely used, and little or no butter or flour was produced. Even such ordinary articles as brooms had to be imported.

There were about 20 private rancho land grants during the Spanish regime, and about 500 during the Mexican period, of which the great majority were made after secularization and especially by Governors Alvarado, Micheltorena, and Pico. Under the liberal Mexican colonization provisions of 1824 and 1828, the maximum legal limit for a private rancho grant in California was 11 square leagues—about 50,000 acres, or 76 square miles. Not even this generous limit was always applied, because in many cases several different grants were made to the same individuals.

In a ranching country where a dozen acres of grassland might be required to pasture a single cow through the long, dry summer season, such vast grants were not regarded as too large, and minor discrepancies in boundary measurements were of no importance. The boundaries were laid out without the aid of surveying instruments, and the methods of measuring distance ranged between pure guesswork and laying out lengths of a lasso from the back of a horse. As corners of the grant, the *diseño,* or map, might show markers no more permanent than a pile of stones or a clump of cactus. The whole process was accomplished with an easy informality which was very convenient at the time but which would later contribute to the maddening and almost endless confusion of efforts to establish land titles in American courts.

The Lugo family on their rancho in southern California in the 1880s. (*Courtesy of the Seaver Center for Western History Research, Natural History Museum of Los Angeles County.*)

Except for a few grants in the Sacramento Valley, held mainly by naturalized foreigners, the ranchos were located where the missions had been, in a narrow strip along the coast. Cattle were driven on the hoof to the *matanzas,* or slaughterings, as near as possible to the coastal points where the hides and tallow were stored to await the foreign trading ships. Other than the horse and the mule, the only form of land transportation was the lumbering, springless, spine-jarring *carreta,* an oxcart with wheels sliced from a big log. Excellent horses, however, were so numerous that they were allowed to run and graze freely, dragging lassos for easy catching. Walking was a lost art. It was much easier to catch a passing horse, ride it where one wished to go, and turn it loose again. To Richard Henry Dana, all Californians in the 1830s seemed to be centaurs, and John Bidwell, in 1846, heard a local proverb to the effect that no Californian with a claim to any trace of Spanish blood would do any work that could not be done on horseback.

Some of the most skillful riders were the daughters of the rancheros. California girls usually rode with ease by the time they were 6 to 8 years old. "I never saw ladies in the East," proclaimed one incredulous visitor, "who could approach the poorest of the Spanish ladies whom I have yet seen ride." Women also became owners and administrators of ranchos, holding about 4 percent of the lands granted by the Mexican government as well as properties acquired through inheritance. Among the ranchera elite was Apolinaria Lorenzano, the unmarried owner of three ranchos. Rancheras supervised their vast estates in a manner similar to that of their male counterparts. They presided over large households and supervised Indian workers who tended their vast herds and fields.

On the typical California rancho there were between 20 and several hundred Indian workers, perhaps 4000 in all. This work force included former mission Indians and new recruits gathered by the ranch owners. In return for their labor, the Indians usually received nothing more than shelter, food, and clothing. Although the Indian laborers were nominally free, in practice they were bound in a state of peonage for as long as the ranchero cared to hold them. Rancho society was essentially feudal; the rancheros ruled as lords on their great landed estates, while the Indians who tended the fields and herds served as serfs.

The plentitude of cheap Indian labor also contributed to the ranchero's reluctance to work. A recurring phrase in conversation was *"poco tiempo,"* or "too little time," meaning that there was not time enough today to do anything that could be done tomorrow. In the pursuit of pleasure, however, the Californians showed more vigor. There was prodigal hospitality in the entertainment of strangers, and singing and dancing were passions with Californians of all ages. Favorite dances were the *fandango,* the *jota,* the *borrego,* the *jarabe,* the *bamba,* and the somewhat more dignified *contradanza.* The *bamba* required a señorita to perform its lively and intricate steps with a full glass of water on her head. In one of the easier variations, while constantly tapping the floor with her feet, she had to step into a silken hobble, raise it to her knees, lower it again, and give two or three whirls, all

Fandango. A romanticized view of life on a California rancho, painted by Charles Christian Nahl in 1873. (© *Courtesy of the Crocker Art Museum, Sacramento.*)

The classic description of the hide and tallow trade was written by Richard Henry Dana in *Two Years before the Mast.* Though it is usually thought of as a portrayal of life at sea and as a tract intended to reform the working conditions of seamen, much of the book was devoted to Dana's observations ashore in California; the crew, in the employ of Bryant and Sturgis, spent most of the 2-year voyage in collecting hides along the California coast.

The Danas of Cambridge were one of the oldest and most distinguished families of New England. As a Harvard undergraduate, Richard Henry had suffered a temporary breakdown of his eyesight, attributed to a case of measles. At the age of 19, in 1834, he signed on as a common sailor for the long voyage to California in the hope that it would improve his health, a purpose which it seems to have accomplished remarkably well almost from the time the ship left Boston harbor.

The outward-bound cargo of "everything under the sun" was quickly disposed of at Monterey, where boatloads of eager purchasers were rowed out to the ship as if it were a floating department store. Dana's pride in his New England heritage was reinforced by what he saw of the Californians, "an idle, thriftless people" who could "make nothing for themselves." The country abounded in grapes, he wrote, "yet they buy, at a great price, bad wine made in Boston and brought round by us, and retail it among themselves at a real (12½ cents) by the small wine glass." Their cowhides, "which they value at two dollars in money, they barter for something which costs seventy-five cents in Boston; and buy shoes (as like as not made from their own hides, which have been carried twice around Cape Horn) at three and four dollars, and 'chicken-skin boots' at fifteen dollars a pair."

Loading the hides was a strenuous operation. Most of the hide depositories had inadequate harbors and the ship had to be anchored as much as 3 miles offshore. A hide would spoil if it got wet, and each one, stiff and heavy and as broad as the arms could reach, had to be tossed up and balanced on the sailor's head so that he could wade through the surf and put it into a swaying small boat.

The hide and tallow trade was significant not only because it influenced the economic history of New England and of early California, but also because it increased the interest of Americans in a distant region with which for many years it formed almost their only contact. *Two Years before the Mast,* published in 1840, brought Americans the same message that Captain Shaler's journal had carried more than three decades earlier, but Dana's message was more substantial and convincing. "In the hands of an enterprising people," he wrote, "what a country this might be!"

THE BEAVER TRAPPERS

Just as American seagoing commerce with California had begun in the quest for the skin of the sea otter, so the history of overland contact had its beginnings in the search for beaver pelts. The trapper was the spearhead of the American land-ward advance, particularly in the far west; the first American overland expedition to California was conducted in 1826 by a young beaver hunter named Jedediah Strong Smith. It was he who deserved the title of "the Pathfinder," a title bestowed in later years upon a more publicized and less authentic hero, John C. Frémont. Smith set out with 17 men to traverse the unexplored desert region between the Great Salt Lake and California. His objectives were the opening of a virgin beaver country and the establishment of a place of deposit on the Pacific for the furs of this new empire. On November 27, 1826, Smith and his men reached San Gabriel Mission, then at the height of its temporal prosperity. From Father José Bernardo Sánchez, the jovial successor of the gloomy Zalvidea, the Americans received a full measure of hospitality which they remained to enjoy for several weeks.

In the words of his biographer, Dale L. Morgan, Jedediah Smith was "an unlikely sort of hero for the brawling West of his time, that West about which it has been said that God took care to stay on his own side of the Missouri River." The "mountain men" have been portrayed in stereotype as murderous brawlers, given to drunken orgies at their periodic rendezvous. Actually, though there were many such men among them, the personalities and backgrounds of the trappers were remarkably diverse. Smith was a quiet young man who never used tobacco or profanity, partook of wine or brandy only sparingly, and was deeply imbued with a Calvinist religious faith.

In December, Smith journeyed to San Diego in the hope of securing Governor Echeandía's permission to travel in California, but the governor, lacking a full realization of the unlimited energies of American business enterprise, found it difficult to believe that Smith was not a spy. He was inclined to send Smith and his men to Mexico for trial, but he compromised and ordered them to leave California by the way they had come.

Smith chose to define "California" as being merely the coastal strip of missions and presidios. Thus he felt that he had complied with the governor's orders when, in January 1827, he moved northwestward across the Tehachapis into the San Joaquin Valley. This he found to be a trapper's paradise, and he had accumulated a large number of pelts by the time he reached the river known thereafter as the American. Late in May, apparently by the way of the north fork of the Stanislaus River and Ebbetts Pass, Smith accomplished the first recorded crossing of the Sierra and reached his headquarters in northern Utah on July 3.

Within 10 days he was on his way back to California with 18 men, but his luck was worse than in the previous year. At the Colorado crossing the Mojaves attacked the party and killed 10 of its members. In September the survivors reached the camp of the first expedition in the northern San Joaquin Valley, but when Smith sought assistance at the Mission San José, about 15 miles north of the pueblo of the same name, Father Narciso Durán arrested him, and only released him to go to Monterey for another conference with Echeandía. The governor was even more disposed than before to make Smith stand trial for illegal entry into the province, but uncertainty about the consequences of such strong action led to a renewal of permission for the trappers to depart. Early in 1828 they made the first recorded journey by land up to the northwestern coast of California into Oregon. There the Umpquas killed most of the men. With only two others, Smith finally reached the Hudson's Bay Company headquarters at Fort Vancouver. Three years later he was killed by Comanches on the Santé Fé Trail.

While Smith was pioneering the routes between the Great Salt Lake and California, other adventurous American trappers and traders had been making their way from Missouri into New Mexico. The most notable of these was James Ohio Pattie, who pressed on from Santa Fé to California by way of the Gila Valley. Pattie's father, Sylvester, was a product of the Kentucky and Missouri frontiers and had taken his son with him to the southwest. The younger Pattie proved to be a very enterprising but intensely conceited and hot-headed boy. In the fall of 1826 he and a party of other fur hunters trapped along the Gila River to the Colorado. Moving northward, they got into a quarrel and then a bloody battle with the Mojaves. In warfare with the Indians, Pattie and his companions committed atrocities as vicious as those of the so-called savages. It is probable that the reason the Mojaves attacked the 1827 expedition of Jedediah Smith, although they had been peaceful during his previous journey through their country, was that they had had dealings with the Pattie expedition in the meantime.

When Pattie returned to Santa Fé, the governor of New Mexico confiscated all his furs because they had been gathered in Mexican territory without a license. Undaunted, he set out again along the Gila in the fall of 1827, this time in a group under the command of his father. At San Diego Governor Echeandía, already irritated by the unauthorized incursions of Jedediah Smith, put these new intruders in jail, where Sylvester Pattie died.

At this time an epidemic broke out in the northern missions. According to James Ohio Pattie's own account, he had fortunately brought along a supply of "smallpox vaccine," and he was released in order to undertake a vaccination tour, immunizing more than 20,000 persons, mostly Indians, as far north as Fort Ross. In historical fact the epidemic was of measles, not smallpox, and the "vaccination" fantasy was one of the many tall tales that later appeared in *The Personal Narrative of James O. Pattie*. The editor of that remarkable volume, and also, to an unknown extent, the writer of it, was Timothy Flint, an author of many works about the west in which fact and fiction were seldom clearly distinguishable. *The Personal Narrative,* first published in 1831, was the original "western," the prototype of uncounted thousands of writings that have since fed the public appetite for the vicarious enjoyment of adventure and violence.

Other trappers soon improved upon the routes of Smith and Pattie. The expeditions of Ewing Young and William Wolfskill blazed trails from Taos and Sante Fé to Los Angeles. In 1833 Joseph Reddeford Walker, a fur trapper from Tennessee and Missouri, made the first westward crossing through the center of the Sierra Nevada. Walker's expedition from the Rockies to California was a branch of the operations of Captain Benjamin Bonneville, who was on a 2-year furlough from the United States Army. Ostensibly, this leave was granted so that Bonneville could engage in the fur business, but one purpose of it may have been the encouragement of explorations, of potential military value, in Mexican territory. Walker's men discovered what was later the main wagon-train route through central Nevada, along the Humboldt River, which they called more appropriately the Barren. Though their trail over "the dark and deathlike wall" of the Sierra is partly a matter of speculation, it probably lay somewhere between the headwaters of the East Walker River and those of the Tuolumne. They have often been credited with being the first white people to see the Yosemite Valley. Cold, hunger, and exhaustion dulled their appreciation of it that day in the fall of 1833, and indeed some historians have maintained that what they really saw was Hetch Hetchy Valley.

EARLY SETTLERS

The first foreigners to settle permanently in Spanish California did so by accident. In 1814 John Gilroy, a Scottish sailor on an English ship, was left at Monterey because of sickness. He married a daughter of the Ortegas, acquired a part of their lands, and lived to see a flourishing American town, bearing his name, on the site of his rancho. Like so many holders of Mexican titles, however, he would finally lose his property to American land lawyers and squatters.

The first American settler in California, or rather the first one around whose name any substantial body of fact and legend has gathered, was Joseph Chapman, sometimes called "the unwilling pirate." A member of the Bouchard expedition, he was captured at Monterey in 1818 but claimed that Bouchard had shanghaied him in Honolulu. In any case, his skills as a millwright and boatbuilder soon made him a welcome and useful resident.

The next few years saw the arrival of several remarkable Yankees who came as traders and remained to gather a great share of the profits of merchandising into their own hands. William Goodwin Dana and Alfred Robinson at Santa Barbara and Abel Stearns at Los Angeles became the chief merchants of their communities and, partly by marriage, large landowners as well; Thomas O. Larkin became the most important merchant in Monterey.

William G. Dana arrived at Santa Barbara from Boston in 1826. Although he was a relative of the more famous Richard Henry, there was no direct reference to him in *Two Years before the Mast,* and this has given rise to much interesting speculation. It was said that Richard refused to see William at the time of his visit to Santa Barbara. The reason, apparently, lay in the story of William's eager espousal of the Roman Catholic faith, of Mexican citizenship, and of young Josefa Carrillo of Santa Barbara, with no more regret than that the formalities of naturalization delayed the marriage for 2 years (by which time the bride was 16 years old). It seems probable that Richard, so much more bound to the Calvinist religion, the inherited patriotism, and the racial pride of the family, had his kinsman in mind when he wrote that certain Americans in California had "left their consciences at Cape Horn."

Don Abel Stearns was also the bearer of an old and distinguished Massachusetts family name. He went first to Mexico and had already become naturalized when he arrived in California in 1829. As a prosperous trader in hides and liquors he was as flagrant a smuggler as most of his competitors, and yet in 1836 he was appointed *síndico,* or fiscal agent, of the village. Nicknamed *Cara de Caballo,* or Horseface, he was a homely man even before he acquired a scar about the mouth, left by the knife of a disgruntled customer in his store. Nevertheless, his appearance did not prevent his marriage to beautiful Doña Maria Francisca Paula

Arcadia Bandini, and with the added influence of his wife's relatives he began to acquire the estates that soon made him the largest landowner and cattleman and the wealthiest citizen of southern California. He had no children, which was most unusual among those who married "native daughters." Don Guillermo and Doña Josefa Dana, for example, had 21.

The title of "don," derived from the Latin *dominus,* or "lord," was applied in Mexican California to almost any man of more or less substantial means, particularly a landowner. In baptism and naturalization a foreign first name was officially changed to its Spanish equivalent. In polite address this might also be done unofficially, as in the case of Don Tomás Larkin, one of the few foreign residents who managed to rise to positions of wealth and importance in California without embracing Roman Catholicism, Mexican nationality, and a native daughter.

Thomas Oliver Larkin, another Massachusetts Yankee, came to Monterey in 1832 at the suggestion of his half-brother, John Cooper, who was already engaged in trade there. One of Larkin's fellow passengers on the long voyage around the Horn was Rachel Hobson Holmes, on her way to join her husband at Hilo. There she discovered that she was a widow, and a few months later Larkin proposed to her by correspondence. A civil marriage ceremony between two non-Catholic foreigners would have been questioned by the Mexican authorities, and consequently the ceremony was performed on board a ship off the Santa Barbara coast. Mrs. Larkin was the first American woman to live in California.

Larkin opened a general store at Monterey, and his business as an intermediary between ranchers and traders was soon flourishing remarkably. Larkin had, as Bancroft put it, "no inconvenient veneration for the revenue laws," and he offered a tempting charge-account system. The chief officials of the province, among others, became heavily indebted to him. He did a thriving business in redwood lumber, largely for export to the Hawaiian Islands and Mexico. And in his designs for his own home, the customs house, and other buildings, he established the "Monterey style" of architecture.

All these early American immigrants had come by sea and taken up residence in the coastal strip. In addition, there were those who came overland and settled mainly in the interior. The first important settler in this American overland migration was "Dr." John Marsh. Still another son of Massachusetts, Marsh had graduated from Harvard with the class of 1823. Later he "read medicine" under an army surgeon stationed in Minnesota, but the surgeon died before Marsh had completed the program of study. Marsh then sold guns to the Sioux in violation of federal law, and in flight from a warrant for his arrest on this charge he emigrated to Los Angeles in 1836. He was destitute, and to earn money he secured permission to practice medicine. For credentials he offered his Harvard bachelor of arts diploma, correctly suspecting that he was the only person in the town who could read the Latin in which the diploma was printed. Because his fees were paid almost entirely in cowhides, his little adobe soon resembled a warehouse rather than a medical office. After a few months, in order to purchase a ranch, he sold his stock of hides for $500 and accepted Roman Catholicism and naturalization.

Sutter's Fort. (*Courtesy of the Bancroft Library.*)

Marsh was now a morose and greedy man, determined to acquire wealth in compensation for his many disappointments. In 1837 he bought a huge tract near the Sacramento–San Joaquin Delta at the foot of Mount Diablo. Marsh made it the first successful rancho in the great Central Valley. This he accomplished largely by taking payment in cattle for his medical services throughout the northern California settlements. He customarily exacted a fee of 50 head.

Two years after Marsh settled in the region of the San Joaquin Delta, John Sutter arrived with his ambitious designs for the Sacramento Valley. Sutter, originally Johann August Suter, was a German Swiss, and in the history of the American movement overland into California he and his New Helvetia were to play a significant role.

Sutter, like Marsh, was a fugitive from tragedy and from justice. In Switzerland he had been married only 1 day before the birth of his first son, and the marriage was unhappy even though it finally produced five children. Sutter always lived extravagantly, and in 1834, faced with debtor's prison after the failure of his dry goods business, he deserted his family and absconded to America. After interludes in St. Louis and Santa Fé, he went with a trapping expedition to Oregon, and then by ship to Honolulu, Sitka, Yerba Buena, and Monterey, where he arrived in July 1839. In the meantime his powers of romantic imagination had made him "Captain" Sutter, formerly of "the Royal Swiss Guard of France." In Oregon he had heard of the Sacramento Valley, and there he now sought the wide-open spaces where people could plan things as they would like them to be.

The quarrel between Governor Alvarado and Comandante Vallejo was at its height, and Alvarado thought he saw a chance to use Sutter, and his grandiose colonization scheme, as a check upon Vallejo's power and pretensions. With the governor's blessing, Sutter selected a tract on the Sacramento River at its junction with the American. After 1 year, the minimum period of legal residence, the glamorous newcomer received not only Mexican citizenship and a grant of 11 square leagues but also the status of a regional official. He was authorized "to represent in the Establishment of New Helvetia all the laws of the country, to function as political authority and dispenser of justice, in order to prevent the robberies committed by adventurers from the United States, to stop the invasion of savage Indians and the hunting and trapping by companies from the Columbia." Beginning with beaver pelts and wild-grape brandy, Sutter went on to establish a cattle ranch and farm, using the labor of Indians and vagabond foreigners and succeeding remarkably, for a time, in obtaining credit. In 1841, for example, when the Russian-American Fur Company abandoned Fort Ross, Sutter's note for $30,000 secured the purchase of its implements and livestock with only $2000 paid down. Several cannons from Ross strengthened the defenses of Sutter's own fort. That establishment would soon be a focal point for early American overland migration.

COVERED WAGONS, 1841 TO 1846

The first organized group to cross the Rockies for the purpose of settlement in California was the Bidwell-Bartleson party of 1841. The previous year, John Marsh had written a letter to some friends in the neighborhood of Independence, Missouri, praising the lands and climate of California and minimizing the difficulty of getting there. Lured by this and other rosy testimonials, more than 500 persons organized a Western Emigration Society and pledged to assemble near Independence in the following spring. During the winter, however, Missouri newspapers circulated stories that painted a sharply different picture. One of these concerned the harsh treatment accorded some Americans at Monterey during the "Graham affair" in 1840. Isaac Graham and his band of American riflemen had participated in Alvarado's little revolution of 1836. They later complained that Governor Alvarado was not sufficiently grateful to them. "I was insulted at every turn," Alvarado told Alfred Robinson, "by the drunken followers of Graham." The alcoholic boastings of Graham's men led to rumors that they were plotting a Texan-style revolution. As a result, in April 1840 Graham and 38 other foreigners, mostly Americans, were arrested, packed into Monterey's one-celled jail, and then sent to Mexico. Later they were set free.

In Missouri, however, the news of the episode so discouraged the members of the Western Emigration Society that only one of the original signers appeared at the appointed place in May 1841. This was John Bidwell, a young former schoolteacher. In addition to Bidwell, 68 new prospects appeared. John Bartleson was elected captain, solely because he insisted that otherwise he would not go. As Bidwell later put it, very generously, Bartleson "was not the best man for the position," but "he had seven or eight men with him, and we did not want the party diminished."

No one in the group had ever been west, and their only maps were ridiculously inaccurate. When the time came to leave the Oregon Trail and strike out across the Great Basin for California, about half the emigrants prudently decided to go on to

Oregon, and several others turned back toward Missouri. The rest managed to find the Humboldt River, but had to abandon their wagons. Near the Humboldt Sink, Bartleson and eight other men took the best horses, deserted the party, and rushed on ahead. They failed to find a pass and returned shamefacedly, begging a share of the little food that remained. Bidwell quietly readmitted them to the group. It did not need to be said that he and not Bartleson was now the captain. At the end of October, miraculously, they found their way over the Sierra and down to the Stanislaus, and on November 4, 1841, they arrived at Marsh's ranch.

The miserly Marsh demanded high prices for supplies. By contrast, when Bidwell visited Sutter's Fort a few weeks later, he was cordially welcomed, as nearly all newcomers were. Sutter was the emigrant's benefactor and friend, New Helvetia was to be the headquarters for several rescue parties sent to help stranded travelers over the Sierra. On the other hand, legend has somewhat exaggerated Sutter's generosity. He saw the early American migrants as potential assets to his colonial establishment—as workers for his increasingly varied enterprises and as ultimate buyers of some of the vast lands he had received for the asking.

In the fall of 1841 an emigrant party including William Workman, John Rowland, and Benjamin D. Wilson traveled from Santa Fé to Los Angeles. In 1843 Lansford W. Hastings, a frontier lawyer with filibustering ambitions, led a group into California from Oregon. Several of its members, including Hastings, had the perverted desire to shoot down an Indian, and the unprovoked murders they committed in the upper Sacramento Valley stored up trouble for them and for future pioneers. The Stephens-Townsend-Murphy party, coming from Missouri in 1844, was the first to succeed in getting wagons over the Sierra, and also the first to make use of what would later be the main route, the Donner Pass, though that name was not acquired until the tragedy that was to follow 2 years later.

The year 1845 saw the beginning of a somewhat more substantial annual migration. Reports from Thomas O. Larkin, John Marsh, and John C. Frémont were stirring up interest in California. Lansford W. Hastings, through speech making and the publication of his dangerously misleading *Emigrant's Guide,* was pursuing his dream of leading hordes of Americans to the western paradise, and hoping that their gratitude would make him a new Sam Houston, president of a Pacific republic or governor of a new American state. The largest emigrant party of 1845, the Grigsby-Ide group, had more than 100 members, and the total for the year was more than 250 persons. More than twice as many came in 1846.

The worse-than-worthless advice of Lansford W. Hastings was a cause of dangerous delays for many of them, and it led the Donner party into the worst disaster in the history of the California Trail. The Donner party was organized at Springfield, Illinois. It passed through Independence on time, in May, but instead of taking the established route by way of Fort Hall, north of the Great Salt Lake, it followed "Hastings' Cutoff" to the south of it. Winter set in early. On November 2 the main party decided to rest overnight only a few miles short of the Sierra summit. That night a snowstorm blocked the pass. Most of the party was snowed in near Donner Lake until February, and many survived only by eating the flesh of the dead. Of 87 persons in the original group, 40 perished. There was heroism as well as horror. James Reed left the party to bring back provisions and returned leading a relief expedition from Sutter's Fort. During his absence, the family of Patrick and Margaret Breen took in two of Reed's children and cared for them along with their own seven children. When rescuers arrived, Tamsen Donner refused to leave her husband, George, who was too weak to travel. Their three daughters were saved, but George and Tamsen died.

Alfred Robinson had written to Larkin urging all possible efforts to publicize California, so that "the American population will be sufficiently large to play the Texas game." But California before the gold rush was less attractive to American settlers than either Texas or Oregon; the emigrants to California were primarily interested in trying to advance their own fortunes rather than their country's, and many were so discouraged that they drifted north to Oregon or back to "the States." Nevertheless, overland emigration would undoubtedly have made a change to American sovereignty inevitable in a few years. It had not yet accomplished this by 1846, but other related historical forces had been set in motion.

SELECTED BIBLIOGRAPHY

Adele Ogden's *The California Sea Otter Trade* (1937) is the best treatment of its subject. Significant memoirs are William Shaler, "Journal of a Voyage from China to the North-Western Coast of America Made in 1804," *American Register . . . for 1808,* pp. 136–175, edited and with an introduction by Lindley Bynum (1935), and Richard Cleveland, *Narrative of Voyages and Commercial Enterprises* (1842). See also Magdalen Coughlin, "Boston Smugglers on the Coast," *California Historical Society Quarterly,* XLVI (June 1967), pp. 99–120. The hide and tallow trade is best described in Richard Henry Dana, *Two Years before the Mast* (1840, with many reprintings); Alfred Robinson, *Life in California* (1846); and Doyce B. Nunis, Jr. (ed.), *The California Diary of Faxon Dean Atherton, 1836–1839* (1964).

The story of the beaver trappers and traders is told in Richard Batman, *James Ohio Pattie's West* (1986), and James Clyman, *Journal of a Mountain Man,* edited by Linda M. Hasselstrom (1984). Robert G. Cleland's *This Reckless Breed of Men: The Trappers and Fur Traders of the Southwest* (1952) is readable and reliable. Dale L. Morgan's *Jedediah Smith and the Opening of the West* (1953) is a brilliant biography; the journal of Harrison Rogers is in Harrison C. Dale (ed.), *The Ashley Smith Explorations and the Discovery of a Central Route to the Pacific, 1822–1829* (1941). See also David J. Weber, *The Californios versus Jedediah Smith* (1990). The Walker expedition is recorded in Bill Gilbert, *Westering Man* (1983); *The Adventures of Zenas Leonard,* edited by John C. Ewers (1959); and *The Life and Adventures of George Nidever,* edited by William H. Ellison (1937). LeRoy R. Hafen (ed.), *The Mountain Men and the Fur Trade of the Far West* (10 volumes, 1971), provides 300 biographical sketches.

On American and other immigrants to California before 1849, both by sea and by land, an indispensable source is the "Pioneer Register," an alphabetical biographical dictionary appended to volumes II–V of the Bancroft *History of California.* A group portrait appears in Charles B. Churchill, *Adventurers and Prophets: American Autobiographers in Mexican California, 1829–1847* (1995). The story of the most prominent Anglo-American in the province is well told in Harlan Hague and David J. Langum, *Thomas O. Larkin* (1990). *The Larkin Papers,* edited by George P. Hammond (10 volumes, 1951–1964), also has references to a remarkable number of persons. *John Marsh, Pioneer* (1930), and his biographer, George D. Lyman, were both medical men with far-ranging interests. James P. Zollinger's *Sutter, the Man and His Empire* (1939) and Richard Dillon's *Fool's Gold: The Decline and Fall of Captain John Sutter of California* (1967) are good biographies. *Sutter's Own Story,* edited by Erwin G. Gudde (1936), is his story as he told it orally to Bancroft. Crucial to an understanding of current scholarship are the critical essays in Kenneth N. Owens (ed.), *John Sutter and a Wider West* (1994) and Allan R. Ottley (ed.), *John A. Sutter's Last Days* (1986).

Good accounts of 'the overland migration are in John D. Unruh, Jr., *The Plains Across: The Overland Emigrants and the Trans-Mississippi West, 1848–60* (1979); George R. Stewart, *The California Trail* (1962); and Irving Stone, *Men to Match My Mountains: The Opening of the Far West, 1840–1900* (1956). Rockwell D. Hunt's *John Bidwell* (1942) is a useful biography. There were many memoirs, including Bidwell's *A Journey to California in 1841* (1842) and *Josiah Belden, 1841 California Pioneer,* edited by Doyce B. Nunis, Jr. (1962). For a biography of the founder of Stockton, see James Shebl's lively *Weber!* (1993). On the Donner tragedy, see George R. Stewart, *Ordeal by Hunger* (1936); Jeannette G. Maino, *Left Hand Turn: A Story of the Donner Party Women* (1987); Joseph A. King, *Winter of Entrapment* (1994); Kristin Johnson, *Unfortunate Emigrants* (1996); and Donald L. Hardesty, *The Archaeology of the Donner Party* (1997).

A well-balanced view of this period may be found in John A. Hawgood, "The Pattern of Yankee Infiltration in Mexican Alta California, 1821–1846," *Pacific Historical Review,* XXVII (February 1958), pp. 27–38. See also David J. Langum, *Law and Community on the Mexican California Frontier: Anglo-American Expatriates and the Clash of Legal Traditions, 1821–1846* (1987).

CHAPTER SEVEN

The American Conquest

The United States in 1846 declared war on Mexico, and during the course of that war American military forces occupied California. At war's end in 1848, the two nations negotiated a treaty in which Mexico ceded California and other borderland provinces to the United States. These events constitute a watershed in California history: the Mexican War and subsequent transfer of title stand as the great discontinuity in the state's history.

OVERTURES, DIPLOMATIC AND UNDIPLOMATIC

Official American efforts to acquire California had an inauspicious beginning in 1835, as an extension of President Andrew Jackson's plans for the purchase of Texas. These schemes originated largely in the fertile brain of Colonel Anthony Butler, an old friend of Jackson's, to whom the president had unwisely entrusted the ministry to Mexico. Butler disgraced himself and his government by letting it be known in Mexico City that he expected to purchase the republic's northern territories by buying some of its political leaders. When Butler later tried to implicate Jackson in his schemes for bribery, Old Hickory denounced him as a liar.

President Jackson was interested in California mainly because the acquisition of San Francisco Bay, as a port for American commerce and whaling in the Pacific, might reconcile the north to the annexation of Texas as a slave state. Jackson in 1837 unsuccessfully offered $3.5 million for Mexican recognition of a southwestern boundary of the United States extending along the Rio Grande and thence westward to the Pacific along the 38th parallel. He was unaware that this line would have left the entrance to San Francisco Bay about 12 miles south of the border.

The panic of 1837 began a few weeks after the inauguration of Martin Van Buren, Jackson's chosen successor. Van Buren's single term as president was one long period of depression in which the Treasury was in no condition to provide for purchasing new territory. With economic recovery in the 1840s, the United States began to assert its manifest destiny to extend its borders to the Pacific. Early in the John Tyler administration, Daniel Webster as secretary of state and Waddy Thompson as minister to Mexico advocated a plan to secure California in exchange for cancellation of American financial claims against the Mexican government. But again, as in the Anthony Butler episode, an American blunder raised an outcry in Mexico City that made any peaceful cession of territory to the United States politically impossible.

Early in September 1842, Commodore Thomas ap Catesby Jones, commander of the American Pacific squadron, received a false report at Callao, Peru, that the United States and Mexico were at war and that Mexico intended to cede California to Great Britain rather than see it fall into American hands. Admiral Thomas and his British Pacific squadron had just left Callao, reportedly under sealed orders from England. Jones, who had received instructions in Washington a year earlier to act quickly in just such an eventuality, promptly sailed for California in what he supposed to be a race with Thomas. He anchored at Monterey on October 18 and on the next day demanded the peaceful surrender of the port and the district. This was concluded on the 20th, the American flag was raised, and Jones proclaimed California under armed but courteous and benevolent American occupation. This proclamation remained in force only 1 day. On the 21st, when Jones landed in person and examined the latest official communications from Mexico, he realized that he had been completely and regrettably misinformed.

Commodore Jones sent a letter of explanation to Governor Micheltorena who was then in southern California. On receiving the news of the seizure, Micheltorena advised Jones to come to him at Los Angeles. There he received the commodore and his explanations with courtesy and hospitality, but sent reports to Mexico City in an entirely different tone. The Mexican government conveyed an angry protest to Washington demanding extreme punishment for Jones, but although the United States disavowed his actions, he suffered only a temporary removal from his command.

As the Jones incident clearly shows, American suspicions of the designs of Great Britain on California played a large part in American thinking, and incidentally provided a very useful rationalization of American designs. The fact was that Her Majesty's government had no intention whatever of trying to acquire California. There were outward appearances of a designing nature, however, quite sufficient to provide fuel for American fears. In 1839, for example, a London publisher brought out the first book in English entirely devoted to California. This was Alexander Forbes's *History of Upper and Lower California* which advocated a plan for the British colonization of vast tracts of land in California. In 1841 Sir George Simpson of the Hudson's Bay Company visited California and concluded quite correctly that some native Californians were so afraid of American control that they would welcome a British protectorate. Sir George's enthusiasm for such a development was obvious, and Americans had no way of knowing that the British government did not support his views.

The French, also, had some degree of interest in California dating all the way back to the visit of the comte de La Pérouse. In 1842 the French agent Eugène

Duflot de Mofras reported that California was certain to pass to some power other than Mexico, and soon. French hopes were faint, based on little more than the idea that Mexico might prefer to see California in the friendly hands of a Latin and Catholic nation, rather than under Anglo-Saxon Protestants. The weakness of Mexican control of California had been so apparent to any observer for so long that a spate of foreign designs was inevitable.

PLANS OF THE POLK ADMINISTRATION

James K. Polk of Tennessee was a political disciple of Andrew Jackson, who lived to congratulate him on his inauguration as President in March 1845. Polk, like his mentor, was always ready to believe any rumors of fell designs on the part of the British. Polk also shared some of the anti-British views of Senator Thomas Hart Benton of Missouri, powerful chairman of the Senate military affairs committee. Benton firmly though incorrectly believed that perfidious Albion had intended to acquire California ever since Drake claimed and named New Albion in 1579.

On coming into office, President Polk confided to Secretary of the Navy George Bancroft that the acquisition of California would be one of his most cherished goals. Within the month of Polk's inauguration, Governor Micheltorena and his *cholo* troops were virtually deported from California, and this ended the last desperate effort to assert any effective control over the province from Mexico City. When the news of this development reached the east coast in June 1845, a chorus of newspaper editorials began to call for American acquisition.

During this same period, Polk received reports from Mexico City of the startling proposal of a young Irish priest named Eugene McNamara to bring 2000 families, 10,000 colonists altogether, to a grant of 3000 square leagues in California. McNamara gained the approval of the archbishop of Mexico, and addressed a burning appeal to the Mexican president in which he warned that "before another year the Californias will form a part of the American Nation. Their Catholic institutions will become the prey of the Methodist wolves; and the whole country will be inundated with these cruel invaders." The McNamara scheme was wildly impracticable, but many Americans regarded it with true alarm as being somehow simultaneously a British and a popish plot.

Having determined to acquire California, Polk would have preferred to purchase it. He sent John Slidell on an ill-fated mission to Mexico with an offer of as much as $40 million for Upper California and New Mexico. "Money," said Slidell's instructions, "would be no object when compared with the value of this acquisition." This was Polk's own view, but he was well aware that the prospects of success were dim, and therefore he put an alternative plan into operation simultaneously. This involved secret instructions to Thomas O. Larkin, consul at Monterey since the previous year, to try to persuade the Californians to secede from Mexico and seek American protection.

Larkin had been highly successful in his business pursuits in California, but he had not become a *californio*. He also took great pride in the fact that his were the first children born in California of parents who had both been born in the United

States. He had been reporting to Washington every suspicion and rumor of sinister British intentions toward California, and in some instances he seems to have exaggerated his reports beyond what he himself believed, so great was his yearning for American annexation at this time. On October 17, 1845, a secret dispatch signed by James Buchanan, the secretary of state, appointed Larkin "confidential agent in California." He was instructed to warn the Californians against any attempt to bring them under the jurisdiction of "Foreign Governments." Further, he was to "arouse in their bosoms that love of liberty and independence so natural to the American Continent." Should California assert and maintain her independence, Buchanan wrote to Larkin, "we shall render her all the kind offices in our power as a Sister Republic."

The plan had real possibilities. Larkin was on friendly terms with officials at Monterey, whom he had supplied for years with most of their provisions and merchandise. The government had reached a state of truly insufferable confusion, and almost everyone admitted the need for some decisive change. Since the departure of Micheltorena, the capital and the assembly had been at Los Angeles under Don Pío Pico as governor, while the customs and the treasury remained at Monterey, with Col. José Castro as military commander. Mariano Guadalupe Vallejo was frankly reconciled to American annexation because he considered it both inevitable and preferable to the alternatives. Colonel Castro, though he bristled at any suggestion of American military force, was confidentially circulating a plan for "declaring California independent in 1847–1848, as soon as a sufficient number of foreigners should arrive." Larkin also enlisted the cooperation of Jacob P. Leese of Sonoma, Don Abel Stearns of Los Angeles, and J. J. Warner from near San Diego, and all three became not only active in the scheme, but also convinced that it would work.

The promising Polk-Larkin plan for winning the province by peaceful conciliation of the *paisanos* was impeded by resentment of the blustering actions of Capt. John C. Frémont in California in March 1846. A few weeks later the scheme was entirely nullified by the Bear Flag Revolt—in which Frémont also had a part—and by the outbreak of the Mexican War.

JOHN CHARLES FRÉMONT

Frémont was one of the most controversial figures not only in the history of California but in the history of the United States. His mother, the young wife of a wealthy and elderly citizen of Richmond, had run away with a young French émigré. In Virginia a divorce could only be obtained from the state legislature, which refused to pass the necessary act. Frémont's parents lived together as husband and wife until the death of the father, which occurred when John Charles was 5 years old. The circumstances of his birth seem to have given him, as in the analogous case of Alexander Hamilton, a feeling of extraordinary need to establish his place in the world. He was like the young Hamilton, too, in that his promising qualities attracted the sympathy of influential men who helped him gain an education. But there was also a side of Frémont's personality that

John Charles Frémont
(1813–1890), an impulsive
participant in the Bear Flag
Revolt. (*Courtesy of the
Bancroft Library.*)

made him impulsive, unstable, and erratic throughout his life. He was ever the impatient opportunist and adventurer, and there was hardly a single action of his whole career that did not produce some troublesome set of complications, and interminable disagreement among biographers and historians about his motives and conduct.

As a lieutenant in the Corps of Topographical Engineers, Frémont met Senator Thomas Hart Benton, who inspired the younger man with his own fiery enthusiasm for the vast possibilities of westward exploration and expansion and with his dream of extending American territory to the Pacific. At Benton's home Frémont met the Senator's daughter Jessie, an extraordinary girl of 16 whose great intellectual gifts had been developed by her father's intensive and devoted tutoring. Frémont and Jessie were secretly married a few months later, and after stormy protests Benton was reconciled to the marriage. Frémont gained a brilliant and beautiful wife and a brilliant and influential father-in-law, and both became his invaluable though highly possessive allies.

Frémont then led a series of western exploring and scientific expeditions, authorized by Congress at the prompting of Senator Benton. The first of these followed the Oregon Trail as far as South Pass in the Rockies. The final report of this expedition—combining Frémont's own genius for publicity with his wife's sparkling literary style—was widely circulated and established Frémont as a national hero.

His second expedition, in 1843 and 1844, proceeded to Oregon, then south along the eastern side of the Cascades and the Sierra Nevada, and across the Sierra into

California by way of Carson Pass. There was a temporary flurry over Frémont's setting out with a howitzer, which the War Department had specifically ordered him not to take on the grounds that the expedition was supposed to be scientific and not military. It had to be explained that Jessie Frémont had intercepted this dispatch and had taken it upon herself to suppress it, but her father defended this action successfully in the Senate.

With the second expedition already well publicized, the Frémonts' collaborative prose soon described it in even more fascinating terms than the first. Understandably the report was another best-seller and became the most widely read description of the far west.

In Washington, D.C., in the spring of 1845, Frémont became convinced that war with Mexico was imminent, that his third expedition should be prepared for military rather than merely scientific activities, and that with it he should play an important role in conquering California. In this idea he received some private encouragement from Senator Benton and from Secretary of the Navy Bancroft. There is no evidence, however, that Frémont received authorization for military operations in Mexican territory either from President Polk or from the War Department. Nevertheless he recruited 60 armed men, all expert marksmen, and arrived in California in December 1845. Early in 1846 Frémont appeared at Monterey. He had come, he said, merely to survey a route to the Pacific, and his men were not soldiers. Colonel Castro, however, peremptorily ordered Frémont and his armed force out of California. In angry and headstrong defiance, Frémont entrenched his men on Hawk's Peak (now Frémont Peak) in the Gabilán Mountains overlooking the Salinas Valley and raised the American flag. Castro called for volunteers and raised a force of about 200. Larkin mediated, and Frémont, after 3 days on his mountaintop, retreated to the Sacramento Valley. Obviously playing for time, he moved slowly northward—"slowly and growlingly," as he put it in a letter to his wife.

On May 9, 1846, he was overtaken near Klamath Lake in southern Oregon by Lieutenant Archibald H. Gillespie of the Marine Corps, who had come to California disguised as a merchant traveling for his health, under instructions from Polk and Buchanan to cooperate as a secret agent with Larkin in the plan of peaceful persuasion. Gillespie, like Frémont, was a rash and high-spirited young man. Arriving in California in April, he had heard reports that war with Mexico was imminent, and these reports he brought to Frémont along with a packet of letters from Senator Benton. The two young officers seem to have convinced each other that the plan for peaceful conciliation was now out of date, that bold initiative was called for, and that Frémont's force should return to California prepared for military action.

Whether Gillespie brought Frémont any secret official authorization to proceed in this way has been hotly debated. There is no reliable documentary evidence for this claim. Frémont probably acted, as he had already acted several weeks earlier at Hawk's Peak, on his own imagination of what the interests of the United States required him to do under particular circumstances. Thus, his own ambitions and impulses had free rein.

THE BEAR FLAG REVOLT

In the meantime, a crop of frightening rumors had circulated among the American immigrants recently settled in the Sacramento and Napa valleys. Frémont and his men had spread some of these rumors on their way northward. In particular, it was falsely reported that Colonel Castro would soon follow up his expulsion of Frémont with an expulsion of all the American settlers.

The origins of the Bear Flag Revolt were confused, and the evidence, especially on Frémont's part in it, is often contradictory. The American settlers in the area were a miscellaneous group of people in a very insecure situation. Nearly all of them were rough pioneers. Some were roving hunters and trappers, or runaway sailors. Most were squatters who probably believed the rumors that they would soon be attacked and driven out of California. Emboldened by the return of Frémont, on June 10 a group under the rough-and-ready Ezekiel Merritt began the revolt by seizing a herd of horses intended for Castro's militia. Some further and more formal action was needed, lest the rebels remain merely horse thieves. Thus on the morning of Sunday, June 14, a party of more than 30 armed settlers descended upon the village of Sonoma.

There were no longer any soldiers at this former military post, and Colonel Vallejo was no longer on active duty, but the filibusters surrounded his home and informed him that he was a prisoner of war. He invited the leaders in to explain what war he was a prisoner of, and when this proved a difficult question, he brought out bottles of *aguardiente* to aid in the discussion. Ezekiel Merritt, William Knight, and Robert Semple had entered first. The rest waited outside for several hours and then elected John Grigsby to go in and investigate. After another interval, they sent in William B. Ide, who, according to his own account, found the previous commissioners befuddled by Vallejo's brandy. Ide, a teetotaler, finally arranged the terms of capitulation, with Jacob P. Leese, Vallejo's brother-in-law, acting as translator.

Colonel Vallejo was probably the most widely respected citizen of California. He had no objection to being arrested because as an advocate of American annexation he was thus relieved of his embarrassing trust as a Mexican officer. The sensible course would now have been to parole him, and he was given some assurance that this would be done, but instead he was taken under arrest to Sutter's Fort. Frémont, who now placed the fort virtually under his own command, committed the foolish outrage of ordering Vallejo into a cell, where he was imprisoned for 2 months. Frémont, feeling that Castro had humiliated him, now acted as if it were Castro and not Vallejo who was his prisoner. He sternly reprimanded Sutter for trying to make Vallejo's bare cell more comfortable.

At Sonoma, Ide and his associates declared themselves a republic and devised a flag. It was a piece of white cotton cloth, with a star and a stripe. In the upper left-hand corner a large lone star, obviously suggesting an analogy with the history of Texas, was painted in red. To the right of the star, and facing it, was what was intended as a grizzly bear, passant. Under these emblems, "CALIFORNIA REPUBLIC" was lettered in black ink. A broad stripe of red flannel, made from an article of used clothing variously recalled as either a petticoat or a man's shirt, was sewn along the bottom of the cotton. This was the original of the banner which the California Legislature adopted in 1911 as the state flag and which since then must be flown over all state buildings.

In later years Ide and Frémont made rival claims, both considerably exaggerated, for credit in the matter of the Bear Flag Revolt. Frémont's connection with the beginning of it was highly equivocal and opportunistic. He helped to foment the rebellion by encouraging the American settlers to goad the *californios* into attacking them so that he and his men could come to their defense. Castro sent about 50 men northward across San Francisco Bay to try to retake Sonoma. On June 24, there was a skirmish north of San Rafael, later magnified into the "battle of Olompali." In the entire "Bear Flag war," two Americans and five or six *californios* were killed.

Frémont, having now assumed command of the Bear Flaggers and having infor-mally merged his force with theirs, crossed from the Marin peninsula on July 1. Entering the long-ungarrisoned little ruin of the San Francisco presidio, he spiked its 10 old Spanish guns. This was a typically Frémontian act—dashing in appearance but superfluous in reality. Those venerable cannons had been cast in Lima about 1625, and for at least 40 years they had been incapable of firing so much as a salute. In a more notable and enduring achievement, described in his *Memoirs,* Frémont gave the entrance to the bay "the name of Chrysopylae, or Golden Gate, for the same reasons that the harbor of Constantinople was called Chryoceros, or Golden Horn."

Frémont joined a Fourth of July celebration at Sonoma, and the next day he more or less formally organized the "California battalion" of American volunteers, with himself in command and Lieutenant Gillespie as adjutant. On the 7th, however, Commodore Sloat raised the American flag at Monterey. It was raised at Yerba Buena and Sonoma on the 9th, and replaced the Bear Flag at Sutter's Fort on the 11th. The life of the Bear Flag "republic," a rather romantic and later fantastically romanticized period of a little less than a month, was thus ended.

By instigating the filibustering activities known as the Bear Flag Revolt, and by participating in them, Frémont actually accomplished only two things. One was an unnecessary embitterment of feelings between Americans and *californios,* in viola-tion of the United States government's policy and best interests. The other was an enhancement of his own somewhat spurious popular reputation as a patriot and hero.

THE MEXICAN WAR AND CALIFORNIA

The causes of the Mexican War were complex and are still disputed. Only a brief sketch of its general background is necessary here. In the 10 years since the establishment of the Republic of Texas in 1836, Mexico had never recognized it as independent. In February 1845 the American Congress passed a joint resolution inviting Texas to join the American Union. Mexico regarded the prospective American annexation of Texas as a hostile act and broke off diplomatic relations with the United States, threatening war but not declaring it. President Herrera prudently feared that a war would not only fail to regain Texas but also lose

California and New Mexico. He hinted that he would receive an American minister. After Slidell had reached Mexico City, Herrera changed his mind, but the report that he had even considered receiving an American negotiator led to his overthrow by General Paredes.

Mexico was particularly bitter at the claim of Texas that its southern boundary was the Rio Grande, rather than the Nueces River, some distance to the north. On April 7, 1846, President Polk learned of Mexico's refusal to receive Slidell. The next day General Zachary Taylor was ordered to cross the Nueces and occupy the disputed zone. Soon several Americans were killed in skirmishes with Mexican troops. With this news in hand, Polk asked Congress to declare that a state of war existed by hostile action of Mexico. Congress did so, and Polk signed the declaration on May 13, 1846.

Several months earlier, Secretary of the Navy Bancroft had instructed Commodore John D. Sloat of the Pacific squadron that in the event of war with Mexico he was to occupy such ports in California as he considered necessary for the establishment of American authority in the province. In June, at Mazatlán, Sloat received definite but still unofficial reports that the United States and Mexico were at war. On July 2 he anchored at Monterey, but hesitated lest he repeat the embarrassing mistake of Commodore Jones. He offered to fire a salute to the Mexican flag, an honor which the port authorities declined because they lacked the powder to return it. The presidio at Monterey had three guns, all of different caliber, and the California navy consisted of one small vessel with no guns.

After 5 days' delay, Sloat made up for his hesitancy on July 7 by issuing a proclamation which went so far as to declare that "henceforward California will be a portion of the United States." Although he came "in arms with a powerful force," it was not as an enemy to the people of California but "as their best friend." He painted a glowing picture of the benefits that would follow, including greater political freedom and stability, honest and efficient administration, and "a great increase in the value of real estate."

On July 23, Sloat, who had been in ill health for some time, turned over his command to Commodore Robert F. Stockton, and the tone of the occupation changed sharply. Stockton, like Frémont and Gillespie, was eager to distinguish himself by vigorous action. As one of his first acts after assuming command, Stockton mustered the "California Battalion of Mounted Riflemen" into United States service (apparently the naval service, though this has never really been clear), commissioning Frémont as major and Gillespie as captain. Stockton then issued a new, bombastic, and offensive proclamation to the people, drawn up with the advice of Frémont and Gillespie. Colonel Castro at Santa Clara and Governor Pío Pico at Los Angeles announced that resistance was hopeless, and both left for Mexico. In August, Los Angeles was occupied without resistance. Stockton was now able to announce that California was "entirely free from Mexican dominion," but he irritated the Angeleños by unnecessarily ordering martial law, and then made the further mistake of leaving Gillespie in charge with a small garrison.

The inhabitants of Los Angeles were not accustomed to strict maintenance of order, and Gillespie's rules were oppressive and arbitrary. The order for a curfew, for example, was highly unrealistic. When some of the more disorderly elements behaved with their customary exuberance, Gillespie began to treat them as rebels before they had actually thought of rebellion. They soon thought of it, and Captain José María Flores and several other officers led a revolt that spread rapidly throughout southern California.

On September 24 Gillespie was besieged on Fort Hill near the Los Angeles plaza, but his courier managed to get through to inform Stockton at San Francisco. Soon afterward Gillespie surrendered under terms that permitted him to march his men to San Pedro for embarkation. At San Pedro, however, they met a relief force of marines and sailors who had arrived from San Francisco, and who now joined them for a march back toward Los Angeles. The march was hot and dusty and by foot because the rebels had rounded up all the horses in the region.

About 15 miles inland, at Domínguez Rancho on October 8, the Americans encountered a force led by José Antonio Carrillo, well-mounted and equipped with a surprisingly effective cannon. This had long been used to fire salutes at the Los Angeles plaza on festive occasions. Before the town's surrender to Stockton it had been buried in the garden of Señora Inocencia Reyes. Dug up and lashed to the running gear of a wagon, it proved a deadly weapon, and the "battle of the Old Woman's Gun" was a brilliant victory for the *californios*. The Americans suffered a number of casualties and withdrew to San Pedro, leaving Los Angeles in rebel hands for 3 months more.

In June, at Fort Leavenworth, General Stephen Watts Kearny had received instructions from the secretary of war to occupy New Mexico and then proceed to California to organize a military and civil government there. Kearny occupied Santa Fé without resistance and set out for California with 300 dragoons. On the way, unfortunately, he met Kit Carson, whom Stockton had sent eastward in August with the premature news that California was peacefully and firmly in American hands. Kearny sent most of his force back and continued with only about 100 men. When they reached southern California, they had come 2000 miles in one of the longest and most difficult marches in American Army history. They were exhausted and half-starved, and most of their mounts had been worn out and replaced with mules or unbroken horses.

Several hours before dawn on December 6, Kearny was encamped near the Indian village of San Pascual, about 35 miles northeast of San Diego, when he learned that a rebel detachment was in the village. Kit Carson assured him that the Californians were cowards who would not and could not fight. Hoping to capture the rebels' horses, Kearny roused his men for an immediate advance in the darkness, cold, and fog. The wretched mounts of the dragoons moved with widely varying speeds, and the rebels, under Andrés Pico, lured them into a pursuit until they were widely strung out, then suddenly turned to attack them.

The American cavalry sabers were hopelessly ineffective against the Californian lances, wielded by men whom Kearny well described as "admirably mounted and the very best riders in the world; hardly one that is not fit for the circus." Practically all the casualties were on the American side—22 killed, including several officers, and 16 wounded, including Kearny himself.

Andrés Pico (1810–1876), commander of the *californios* at the battle of San Pascual. (*Courtesy of the
Seaver Center for Western History
Research, Natural History Museum
of Los Angeles County.*)

In spite of their impressive achievements on the battlefield, the rebels were
weakened by the usual chronic dissensions, by a shortage of powder, and by their
gradual abandonment of hope that they could hold out until Mexico should be
victorious over the United States in the main theaters of war. A joint force under
Stockton and Kearny recaptured Los Angeles on January 10, 1847, after minor
skirmishes.

Flores now fled to Sonora, and Andrés Pico chose to surrender the rebel forces
to Frémont, who had reached the San Fernando Valley from the north. Frémont was
flattered at being the officer who now received the final surrender, and by the terms
of the Capitulation of Cahuenga on January 13, 1847, he extended full pardon to all
the rebels. The surrender at Cahuenga ended organized resistance to the American
occupation. It also marked the beginning of a series of bitter disputes over the
question of who was now in command and who was authorized to act as military
and civil governor.

Commodore Stockton still considered himself in charge, and before sailing for
further operations on the west coast of Mexico, he appointed Frémont his successor
as governor of California. General Kearny refused to recognize this appointment
and regarded Frémont as under his own command. Frémont was able to persuade
himself that authority he had received from a commodore in the Navy should
prevail over the orders of a brigadier general in the Army who was now his own

immediate superior. On this basis Frémont rashly assumed the powers of governor and repeatedly defied military orders from General Kearny.

Frémont's defiance of authority led to the feeling among most of his brother officers that if Kearny had ordered a court-martial in California, Frémont might have been shot. Instead the court-martial of Frémont was conducted in Washington, D.C. During the proceedings Frémont, and Benton as his counsel, did everything they could to impugn Kearny's integrity and destroy his reputation. Nevertheless, in January 1848 Frémont was found guilty of disobedience of orders and sentenced to dismissal from the service. President Polk approved the verdict but remitted the penalty. Bitterly, Frémont refused this executive clemency and resigned his commission. Popular opinion generally supported Frémont. In the eyes of the American people in the 1840s, insubordination was not a very serious offense.

In later years John Frémont was one of the first two senators from California, temporarily a millionaire from the mineral proceeds of his Mariposa land grant, the first candidate of the Republican party for the presidency in 1856, and temporarily a major general in the Civil War. Nevertheless Jessie Benton Frémont once told one of his aides: "Oh, if my husband had only been more positive! But he never did assert himself enough. That was his great fault."

The war with Mexico was concluded on February 2, 1848, with the signing of the Treaty of Guadalupe Hidalgo in which Mexico ceded California and other territories to the United States. Only 9 days earlier gold had been discovered in the foothills of the Sierra Nevada, an event unknown to the signers of the treaty. Knowledge of the discovery could have made little difference in the negotiations in any event. Mexico had been overrun by American troops and was in no position to quibble over terms of peace, even though California would now be considerably more valuable than it had yet appeared to be.

SELECTED BIBLIOGRAPHY

Neal Harlow, *California Conquered: War and Peace on the Pacific, 1846–1850* (1982), analyzes American interest in California and the reasons for the American victory. Norman A. Graebner, "The Mexican War: A Study in Causation," *Pacific Historical Review,* XLIX (August 1980), pp. 405–426, concludes that force was necessary for the United States to accomplish its designs on California. For a broad overview see Jack K. Bauer, *The Mexican War, 1846–1848* (1993).

Earlier American projects for peaceful acquisition are described by Robert Glass Cleland in "The Early Sentiment for the Annexation of California," *Southwestern Historical Quarterly,* XVIII (1914–1915), pp. 40, 121–161, 231–260; George P. Hammond (ed.), *The Larkin Papers,* volumes III and IV; John A. Hawgood (ed.), *First and Last Consul: Thomas Oliver Larkin* (1970); Harlan Hague and David J. Langum, *Thomas O. Larkin* (1990); Graebner, *Empire on the Pacific* (1955); and Frederick Merk, *Manifest Destiny and Mission in American History* (1963). See especially A. Brooke Caruso, *The Mexican Spy Company: United States Covert Operations in Mexico, 1845–1848* (1991). On rival aspirations, see Merk, *The Monroe Doctrine and American Expansionism, 1843–1849* (1966); E. D. Adams, "British Interest in California," *American Historical Review,* XIV (July 1909), pp. 744–763; Gene A. Smith, "The War That Wasn't: Thomas ap Catesby Jones's Seizure of Monterey," *California History,*

LXVI (June 1987), pp. 104–114; and Russell M. Posner, "A British Consular Agent in California: The Reports of James A. Forbes, 1843–1846," *Southern California Quarterly,* LIII (June 1971), pp. 101–112.

The first major biography of Frémont, by Allan Nevins, was generally sympathetic. The first edition of this work bore the title *Frémont, the West's Greatest Adventurer* (two volumes, 1928), but the title was later changed to *Frémont: Pathmarker of the West* (rather than "Pathfinder," which had been used in the long subtitle of the original edition). Bernard De Voto, in *The Year of Decision, 1846* (1942), deplored all adulation of Frémont, past, present, and future. But Irving Stone, with the license of the novelist, exalted Jessie and her husband in *Immortal Wife* (1944); a more balanced appraisal appears in Pamela Herr, *Jessie Benton Frémont* (1987). See also Pamela Herr and Mary Lee Spence (eds.), *The Letters of Jessie Benton Frémont* (1993). Dwight L. Clarke, in *Stephen Watts Kearny, Soldier of the West* (1961), sought to rescue Kearny from the "historical eclipse" to which he was consigned by Frémont and his admirers. See also Kenneth M. Johnson, *The Frémont Court Martial* (1968). Ferol Egan's *Frémont* (1977) is lively and engaging, but Andrew Rolle's *John Charles Frémont* (1991) is more analytical. Mary Lee Spence and Donald Jackson (eds.), *The Expeditions of John Charles Frémont* (3 volumes, 1970–1984), make the original documents available.

See also Fred B. Rogers, *William Brown Ide, Bear Flagger* (1962); Werner H. Marti, *Messenger of Destiny* (1960), on Archibald Gillespie; and John A. Hawgood, "John C. Frémont and the Bear Flag Revolution," *Southern California Quarterly,* XLIX (June 1962), pp. 67–96. The conclusion of the war and its continuing legacy is described in Richard Griswold del Castillo, *The Treaty of Guadalupe Hidalgo* (1990).

CHAPTER EIGHT

The Gold Rush

It is ironic but understandable that the Spaniards, who had found so much gold in other parts of the hemisphere, failed entirely to find the vast treasure of the Sierra Nevada. They had seen little reason to explore the approaches to the Sierra, and even less reason to settle there, and the local Indians, if they noticed any gold, had no interest in it. During the Mexican period a minor discovery was made in 1842 at Placerita Creek, about 35 miles northwest of Los Angeles. The first gold ever sent from California to the United States Mint came from that area, but the placers there were of trifling importance, received little attention, and were soon played out.

MARSHALL'S DISCOVERY AT SUTTER'S MILL

The crucial discovery was the result, although the accidental and indirect result, of an American's ingenuity. James Wilson Marshall was a moody and somewhat eccentric master carpenter who had come from Missouri to Oregon in 1844 and then south to California in 1845. In August 1847 Marshall contracted with John A. Sutter to build a sawmill in the foothills in order to provide lumber both for Sutter's own use and for sale to immigrants. Marshall chose a site on the south fork of the American River, where there was an abundance of timber and a flow of water that looked ideal for diversion into a millrace. The site was about 45 travel miles east-northeast of Sutter's Fort, at a place called Coloma from the Indian name Culloomah, or "beautiful vale." With a crew including several Mormons and a number of Indian laborers, construction proceeded remarkably well. In January it appeared that the tailrace needed to be further deepened and its bottom cleared of obstructions. It was while Marshall was inspecting the progress of this work that on January 24, 1848, he saw a glittering particle, caught behind a stone beneath the water. The tailrace was, in effect, a sluice cut through a sandbar at a bend of the river, and if Marshall had actually been searching for placer gold, he could hardly have hit upon a better way of finding it.

With his glittering discovery, Marshall rode down to New Helvetia. There, behind a locked door, Sutter put the samples to several tests in the light of what he knew of the properties of the metal and what he could learn from the *American Encyclopedia.* When Sutter concluded that "It's gold—at least twenty-three-carat gold," Marshall got into such a state of feverish excitement that he insisted on riding back to Coloma in the rain in the middle of the night—the first victim of the gold mania. Sutter's behavior was somewhat less erratic; his primary concern was that the discovery would endanger the completion of his sawmill. At Coloma he persuaded the workers to continue with their task and to confine their prospecting to Sundays.

Efforts to keep the news from spreading were in vain. For example, one of the children of Mrs. Wimmer, the cook at Coloma, talked of the discovery to a teamster; then, to save her boy from being ridiculed as a liar, the good woman showed the teamster some nuggets. Sutter himself made an agreement with some Indians for a lease on the land around Coloma. In dispatching a messenger to Colonel Richard B. Mason, the military governor at Monterey, asking for validation of this agreement, Sutter not only revealed the discovery but sent along 6 ounces of gold to prove it.

Although the news leaked out quickly enough, it attracted very little attention for several months. There had been idle rumors of gold ever since the expeditions of Drake and Vizcaíno. None had actually been found until the trivial Placerita discovery of 1842, and this suggested that although there was some gold in California, there was not enough to make it worth digging. Brief news reports of gold near New Helvetia, written with obvious lack of conviction, appeared in the two little weekly newspapers of San Francisco—one item in the *Californian* on March 15, 1848, and another in the *California Star* 10 days later—without creating any notable excitement.

THE FORTY-EIGHTERS

The gold fever did not begin to be epidemic until May 12. On that day, in San Francisco, the mania that would eventually spread over the whole world was touched off deliberately and for purposes of revenue by the enterprising merchant, manipulator, real estate speculator, and Mormon elder, Samuel Brannan.

Brannan had arrived in 1846 as the leader of the California Mormons. A remarkably vigorous young man of Irish ancestry, articulate, ingenious, and highly opportunistic, he began his career as a molder of opinion and emotion by editing a journal published in New York for the Mormons of the Atlantic seaboard. When the leaders at Nauvoo, Illinois, determined in 1845 that the Latter-Day Saints should "flee out of Babylon," Elder Brannan, then 26 years old, was delegated to lead a party of more than 200 by ship around the Horn to California. They sailed from New York in the ship *Brooklyn* on February 4, 1846. As a flight from the sovereignty of the United States, this migration was frustrated by the Mexican War. When the *Brooklyn* anchored in San Francisco Bay, on July 31, 1846, it found itself alongside the *U.S.S. Portsmouth,* whose commander, Captain John B. Montgomery, had landed on the 9th to raise the American flag over Yerba Buena.

View of San Francisco, 1847. Note that Montgomery Street was then at the bay shore. (*Courtesy of the Bancroft Library.*)

The arrival of the Brannan party tripled the population of that village. The first buildings had been erected there in 1835 when William A. Richardson, an English deserter from a whaler, had put up a shanty of rough boards. Early in 1847, Lieutenant Washington Allon Bartlett of the *Portsmouth* changed the name of Yerba Buena to San Francisco. Otherwise, the town's history had not yet been very eventful. No one there was as yet especially prosperous, with the exception of Samuel Brannan, who was already its leading citizen.

Brannan engaged in an assortment of business activities and investments, flagrantly putting Mormon funds to his own use and profit. Charged with embezzlement, he was the defendant in one of the first jury trials ever held in California, but the jury disagreed. He continued to gather in the tithes and to decide what should be done with the proceeds. When Brigham Young sent down a deputation from Salt Lake City to bring back "the Lord's money," Brannan said that he would turn over the money when he got a receipt signed by the Lord. Finally Brannan's superiors in Utah "disfellowshipped," or excommunicated, him, though for some time he denied the validity of this proceeding.

One of Brannan's enterprises was a general store at Sutter's Fort. In March 1848, after customers at this store had begun to offer gold in payment for whisky and other commodities, Brannan became aware of the reality of the discovery and of the uses to which he could put it. He spent the next several weeks in quietly purchasing every article of merchandise he could get hold of in northern California that would be in demand by gold seekers, then moving these articles to his store at New Helvetia. Then, on May 12, he came down to San Francisco, waved a bottle of gold dust in one hand and his hat in the other, and shouted

"Gold! Gold! Gold from the American River!" When samples of gold reached Monterey, on June 20, Alcalde Colton recorded that "the blacksmith dropped his hammer, the carpenter his plane, the mason his trowel, the baker his loaf, and the tapster his bottle. All were off for the mines, some on horses, some on carts, and some on crutches, and one went on a litter."

The symptoms of the craze which the sight of gold now began to produce in many men have often been described, but perhaps never more vividly than by James H. Carson:

> I looked on for a moment; a frenzy seized my soul; unbidden my legs performed some entirely new movements of polka steps—I took several—houses were too small for me to stay in; I was soon in the street in search of necessary outfits; piles of gold rose up before me at every step; castles of marble dazzling the eye with their rich appliances; thousands of slaves bowing to my beck and call; myriads of fair virgins contending with each other for my love—were among the fancies of my fevered imagination. The Rothschilds, Girards, and Astors appeared to be but poor people; in short, I had a very violent attack of the gold fever.

Within a short time nearly every town in California lost a majority of its population. On May 29 the *San Francisco Californian* complained that "The whole country, from San Francisco to Los Angeles, and from the sea shore to the base of the Sierra Nevadas, resounds with the sordid cry of gold, GOLD, GOLD! while the field is left half-planted, the house half-built, and everything neglected but the manufacture of shovels and pickaxes." The paper also announced that it was suspending publication; it had no choice, in view of the departure of its staff, subscribers, and advertisers. A few days later the *California Star* also suspended for the same reason.

Even the California Indians did not remain immune to the lure of gold. Colonel Mason estimated in 1848 that more than half the gold diggers in the California mines were Indians. At first, many Indian miners worked as laborers for white Californians, often in a state of peonage similar to their status on the Mexican ranchos. Others labored as independent agents and traded their gold to white merchants for a variety of goods. As hostilities between Indians and whites increased, the number of Indian miners in the goldfields declined rapidly.

Soldiers and sailors deserted by the hundreds. Colonel Mason reported that he was powerless to stop desertions, especially after a soldier on a 3 weeks' furlough found $1500 worth of gold, more than his Army pay for 5 years. Mason toured the diggings in July. Some Mormon miners asked him whether they must turn over to Sam Brannan the tithes of their findings which he was soliciting from them, to which the governor replied that they were required to pay as long as they were fools enough to do so.

During the summer months the contagion began to spread to Hawaii, Oregon, and Utah, and in the fall to Mexico, Peru, and Chile. Altogether probably about 6000 gold seekers came to California from these areas in 1848. The main gold rush from "the States" did not begin until the year of the discovery was almost over.

THE FORTY-NINERS

In September 1848, Lieutenant Edward F. Beale arrived in Washington with reports and also with some actual specimens of gold, sent by Larkin. This led to many newspaper comments and to fairly wide discussion, but as yet few planned to leave for California. The spread of the gold craze over the whole country came after the sending of President Polk's annual message to Congress on December 5. Polk welcomed the news as a justification of his policies in acquiring the Mexican cession. In evidence, the president appended Colonel Mason's report of his personal tour of the diggings, in which Mason asserted that there was enough gold "in the country drained by the Sacramento and San Joaquin Rivers" to pay the cost of the Mexican War "a hundred times over." Two days later Lieutenant Lucien Loeser arrived at the capital with a tea caddy crammed with 230 ounces of gold. Placed on display at the War Department, this soon drew excited crowds.

The mania for sudden wealth now pervaded all classes, and the urge to be off to the goldfields stimulated many related industries. One of these was the hasty publication of alleged guidebooks of varying degrees of fraudulence, most of them derived, at best, largely from Mason's report, along with some fragments of the writings of Larkin, Frémont, and Lansford W. Hastings. One such opus, published in New York in December 1848, was *The Emigrant's Guide to the Gold Mines . . . ,* 30 pages long and selling for 25 cents, or 12½ cents without the map; the latter alternative was the better buy, because the map was entirely worthless. Another item, of 1849 vintage, was *The Digger's Handbook and Truth about California* by one D. L. Sydney. In penciled insertions on the title page of a surviving copy of this work, some disillusioned purchaser identified the author's initials, D. L., as "Damn Liar."

There were three main routes to the goldfields: by way of the Isthmus of Panama, around Cape Horn, or overland. The sea routes drew the heavy traffic in the first months of the great rush in the winter and early spring of 1849 because they were open all year round, although in the long run more than twice as many gold seekers would go to California by land as by sea. Before 1849 the Cape Horn route had been the most traveled one, but it covered a distance of about 18,000 nautical miles and took 5 to 8 months, and thus the Panama shortcut suddenly became attractive to thousands who feared that all the gold might be gone before they could arrive to claim their share of it.

Moreover, it happened that a new passenger service on the Panama route was just becoming available. Three 1000-ton paddle-wheel steamers were built for the run from Panama to California and Oregon. The first of these, the *California,* left New York in October 1848. When she arrived in Panama in January, she found 700 Americans clamoring to get aboard. They had traveled by ship to Chagres, by small boat up the fever-infested Chagres River, and by mule the rest of the way across the isthmus. The *California*'s rated capacity was not more than 250. After days of intensive ticket scalping, the *California* sailed with about 400 on board. During most of 1849, because of delays at Panama, the average time from New York to San Francisco by this route was 3 to 5 months, though by 1850 increased service in the Pacific had reduced it to 6 to 8 weeks.

Overland routes to California, 1849. (*Adapted from California Patterns: A Geographical and Historical Atlas by David Hornbeck. Copyright 1983 by the Mayfield Publishing Company.*)

Of the Argonauts who chose to travel around the Horn, many were organized in joint stock companies, both for the voyage and in the expectation of working together in mining operations after their arrival. These companies usually purchased old ships, which they fondly supposed they could sell in California. Actually, most of these vessels joined the fleet of several hundred hulks that were abandoned to settle gradually into the mud along the San Francisco waterfront, and nearly all the companies disintegrated into smaller groups more suitable for prospecting. The removal from service of the hundreds of obsolete old vessels, at the same time that the gold rush was stimulating the building of the clipper ships, made the early 1850s the golden age of the American merchant marine. The new California clippers were designed to carry premium freight at maximum speed. They were much less important for carrying passengers, who found them highly uncomfortable. In 1851 the maiden voyage of Donald McKay's *Flying Cloud* set a record of 89 days from New York to San Francisco, a record which held for over a century. (The record was beaten in 1989 when an ultralight racing yacht, *Thursday's Child,* using computerized weather maps and high-tech equipment, made the voyage in just under 81 days.)

A majority of the forty-niners traveled overland, especially those from the Ohio and Mississippi valleys. The main route was the California Trail, by way of the Platte, South Pass, and Humboldt. This route was already well-established by the earlier emigrants, but for each person who followed it in 1848 there were 50 in 1849, some of them in wagon trains miles long. Between the Rockies and the Sierra the loss of oxen and horses was dreadful because the great trek used up all the grass within easy reach of the trail. By the time they reached the 40 miles of unbroken desert southwest of the Humboldt Sink, many were no longer concerned to save their property, but only their lives, and the trail was littered with an almost incredible miscellany of discarded articles. There was very little danger from hostile Indians at this time, but there was a major epidemic of Asiatic cholera. The disease was not only agonizing and usually fatal but also peculiarly terrifying because medical science had not yet discovered that it was transmitted mainly through the contamination of drinking water, and those who tended the sick or came anywhere near them imagined that the ghastly affliction might be spread in various other ways.

Besides the three main arteries of travel, a number of alternate routes attracted smaller contingents. Some crossed the isthmus by way of Nicaragua rather than Panama. There were several fairly important southern trails, not only across Texas and New Mexico, but also across old Mexico. A number of forty-niners branched off from the main California Trail by going southwest from Salt Lake to southern California, and for some who rashly attempted a shortcut from this route Death Valley earned its name. Others turned north of the Sierra and into the upper end of the Sacramento Valley by way of the Pit River. This roundabout way, known as Lassen's Cutoff, was as outrageously misnamed as Hastings' Cutoff, and in general Peter Lassen and Lansford Hastings were about equally incompetent as guides. The majority chose a direct route through the central Sierra, though many were frightened by the reputation of Donner Pass and instead used Carson Pass about 20 miles south of Lake Tahoe.

Near the end of 1849 the "long tom" appeared as an enlargement and a considerable improvement of the rocker. The tom was usually about 12 feet long, stationary, and placed where a stream of water could be run through it from a ditch or a wooden flume. This eliminated both the pouring of water and the rocking of the cradle. About a year later the long tom evolved into a sluice, a whole series of riffle boxes fitted together into a continuous string, sometimes as much as several hundred feet in length. This device, though commonly employed even in ancient times, seems to have been reinvented in California. In an important related development, a wing dam was built part way across a stream to divert a flow of water into a sluice; sometimes an entire river was dammed and turned aside to expose the pay dirt in a section of the streambed. The reason such relatively efficient methods were so slow in appearing was that they required fairly large groups of men to work together, and in the first 2 years the miners were so intensely individualistic that the industry was still at most a small-business operation.

The final separation of gold from the sand and other dross was often accomplished by the use of mercury, or quicksilver, which has the property of amalgamating with gold. When this amalgam is heated in a closed vessel, the mercury vaporizes. Thus separated from the gold, the mercury can also be recovered, as soon as it cools again from vapor to liquid. Fortunately, quicksilver had been found in 1845 at New Almaden in the hills a few miles south of San José. (For later advances in mining technology, see Chapter 13.)

MINING CAMP LAW

The primary concern of the early California miners with legal problems was in the regulation of mining claims. Because the mining camps had sprung up beyond the reach of any established law, they had to adopt their own regulations. Practically none of the land in the gold region had passed into private hands, and the rights of the Indians were ignored. California was in the midst of a peculiarly awkward transition from Mexican to American sovereignty. Congress had not provided for the extension of American territorial government to any part of the Mexican cession, and even if it had, there was no federal mining law that would have been relevant to the California mining camps, because no precious metal had ever been discovered before on public lands of the United States.

In devising their own mining codes the Argonauts were acting in a tradition of American frontier self-government that went all the way back to the Mayflower Compact. In each camp there was a mass meeting to organize a "mining district" and elect a committee to draw up a set of regulations. Eventually more than 500 camps adopted such codes. Each code defined the permissible size of a claim and required that it be continuously worked if it was to remain valid. Thus the title was merely usufructuary, not a title to ownership of the land but merely to the use of it for mining purposes. Each district elected a recorder, variously called an arbitrator or chairman, and often its only officer. His duties were to keep the register of claims and to settle disputes arising from charges of claim jumping, sometimes with the assistance of a panel of arbitrators chosen by the contestants.

As described thus far, the plan was highly reasonable and highly democratic. A far less admirable aspect of the codes was that many of them included "restrictive covenants" barring Mexicans, Asians, or other foreigners. Still other problems of the mining camps arose from the extemporized administration of criminal justice, the resort to lynching and vigilantism. But racial oppression directed against foreigners and Indians in early American California and extralegal methods for the punishment of crime are the subjects of other chapters.

THE HISTORICAL SIGNIFICANCE OF THE GOLD RUSH

The traditional view of this remarkable migration describes it as the most fortunate as well as the most significant factor in the whole of California's history. It can be cogently argued, however, that in the long run the state would have been better off if it had contained no gold at all, that because of its other advantages it would eventually have become just as populous and prosperous, and that in the meantime its social evolution would have been not only more gradual, but also far more orderly and civilized.

Obviously the lure of sudden wealth brought an early and rapid influx of population. At the end of 1848 about 6000 miners had obtained about $10 million worth of gold. In 1849 the amount produced was two or three times as large, but there were more than 40,000 miners to share in it, and thus the individual miner's average daily return declined radically. In 1852, the peak year, the output was about $80 million and the number of miners about 100,000. During the 100 years after the beginning of the gold rush, the output of California gold totaled about $2 billion. All the gold produced in a century was worth less than the value of 1 year's agricultural output of the state in the 1960s, and much of the gold was ultimately destined to be put back into the ground, in the Treasury Department's hoard at Fort Knox.

It may be granted that if there had been no gold discovery, Oregon would probably have been ready for admission as a state before California was. The first transcontinental railroad might have been built to Oregon. But if California's first transcontinental railroad had been built later, it might have been in the hands of a somewhat less rapacious group of men and it might have obtained less of a stranglehold on the state's economy and politics.

What sort of people did the gold rush bring to California? Bancroft's famous description is interestingly balanced: "the toiling farmer, whose mortgage loomed above the growing family, the briefless lawyer, the starving student, the quack, the idler, the harlot, the gambler, the hen-pecked husband, the disgraced; with many earnest, enterprising, honest men and devoted women." The women were few, however, and, in general, the notion that the Argonauts came to California as pioneers and commonwealth builders is a myth. The great majority of them came in the hope that they could quickly plunder California of its treasure and return to their homes. Many of the forty-niners were young married men hoping to make enough to return to their wives and children with financial security. Most of those who remained in California did so because they failed to accumulate even enough

Hope and grim determination are in evidence in this rare daguerreotype showing a woman in the diggings at Auburn Ravine in 1852. (*Courtesy of the California State Library.*)

to get them back home. On the whole they were unsuccessful, disillusioned, embittered men.

Women accounted for only about 2 percent of the California-bound Argonauts in 1849, but within a decade they made up half of some wagon trains. Most women on the overland trail maintained traditional roles, doing the "women's work" of cooking and washing and tending the children. Once in California, however, they were able to break the bonds of domesticity and to enjoy a greater freedom than they had known back home. This emerging independence was registered in a divorce rate that was the highest in the nation. Women on the California frontier also became proprietors of a variety of enterprises, and some even adopted unorthodox clothing as a symbol of their liberation from prior constraints. "I commenced my new business in my ordinary long dress," wrote Eliza Farnham about her days as a pioneer farmer in Santa Cruz, "but its extreme inconvenience induced me, after the second day, to try the suit I had worn at home in gymnastic exercises. . . . When I had once put it on, I could never get back into skirts during working hours."

Women remained a rarity in most gold-rush communities. They represented about one-twelfth of the state's population according to the census of 1850, increased only to one-third in 1880, and did not equal the number of men until 1900.

The hard labor, the shockingly inflated prices, and the prevalence of sickness and of home sickness all added to the widespread sense of desperation that so many gold-rush diaries record. Often there were efforts to find relief in a desperate kind of humor, as in the naming of such camps as Hell's Delight, Gouge Eye, Poker Flat, Devil's Retreat, Murderers' Bar, Poverty Hill, and Gomorrah, and in the organization of the Ancient and Honorable Order of E Clampus Vitus, or "the Clampers." The derivation of the name of this miner's fraternal society is unknown; there are no records of its early meetings, it is said, because they were devoted so largely to hard drinking that no one was ever in condition to keep minutes, or able the next day to recall what had happened. In general, however, there was tragedy rather than humor or romance in the drinking, gambling, and vice in which many miners sought escape from the hardships and anxieties of "seeing the elephant," as the experience of mining came to be called.

The gold rush was the product of a kind of mass hysteria, and it set a tone and created a state of mind in which greed predominated and disorder and violence were all too frequent.

SELECTED BIBLIOGRAPHY

J. S. Holliday's *The World Rushed in: The California Gold Rush Experience* (1981) is a combination of biography and epic narrative. Other good general accounts include Paula Mitchell Marks, *Precious Dust* (1994); Donald Dale Jackson, *Gold Dust* (1980); and John W. Caughey, *Gold Is the Cornerstone* (1948), reissued as *The California Gold Rush* (1975). Rodman W. Paul, *California Gold* (1947), stresses the technological, economic, and legal aspects; see also his later work, *Mining Frontiers of the Far West, 1848–1880* (1963). For a comparative analysis of the gold rushes in California and Australia, see David Goodman, *Gold Seeking* (1994).

On the discovery itself see Theressa Gay, *James Marshall, Discoverer of California Gold* (1967), and Rodman W. Paul (ed.), *The California Gold Discovery* (1966). Paul Bailey, *Sam Brannan and the California Mormons* (1953), deals with Brannan's role. Barry L. Dutka, "New York Discovers Gold in California," *California History,* LXIII (Fall 1984), pp. 313–319, and Ralph P. Bieber, "California Gold Mania," *Mississippi Valley Historical Review,* XXXV (June 1948), pp. 3–28, describe the excitement in the east. E. Gould Buffum, *Six Months in the Gold Mines* (1850), and James H. Carson, *Early Recollections of the Mines* (1852), describe the days of '48.

Two indispensable guides to the wealth of gold-rush documents are Gary F. Kurutz (ed.), *The California Gold Rush: A Descriptive Bibliography* (1996), and Robert H. Becker (ed.), *The Plains and the Rockies: A Bibliography of Narratives* (1982). The most comprehensive survey is Unruh, cited in Chapter 6, but see also Mary Gordon (ed.), *Overland to California with the Pioneer Line* (1983); George R. Stewart, *The California Trail* (1962); and Ralph Bieber, *Southern Trails to California in 1849* (1937). The diet of the forty-niners is examined in Joseph R. Conlin, *Bacon, Beans, and Galantine Truffles* (1985). David Rich Lewis,

"Argonauts and the Overland Trail Experience: Method and Theory," *Western Historical Quarterly,* XVI (July 1985), pp. 285–306, offers a systematic content analysis of diaries kept by men on the way west. Mortality on the overland trail is the subject of Robert W. Carter, "'Sometimes When I Hear the Winds Sigh,'" *California History,* LXXIV (Summer 1995), pp. 146–161.

Several recent studies have focused on the role of women in the great migration: John Mack Faragher, *Women and Men on the Overland Trail* (1979); Sandra Myers, *Ho for California!* (1980); Lillian Schlissel, *Women's Diaries of the Westward Journey* (1982); Ruth B. Moynihan (ed.), *So Much to Be Done* (1990); and JoAnn Levy, *They Saw the Elephant: Women in the California Gold Rush* (1990). A special issue of the *Pacific Historical Review,* LXI (November 1992), is devoted to western women's history.

John H. Kemble, *The Panama Route, 1848–1869* (1943), and Bayard Taylor, *El Dorado, or Adventures in the Path of Empire* (2 volumes, 1850), deal with the isthmian approach. Oscar Lewis, *Sea Routes to the Gold Fields* (1949), and James P. Delgado, *To California by Sea* (1990), also include Cape Horn.

Some of the best descriptions of life in the diggings are in *The Shirley Letters from the California Mines, 1851–1852* (1949); Frank Marryat, *Mountains and Molehills* (1855, 1962); Sarah Royce, *A Frontier Lady* (1932); Josiah Royce, *California . . . A Study of American Character* (1886, 1948); and Charles H. Shinn, *Mining Camps* (1885, 1948). Hubert Howe Bancroft's social history of the gold rush is *California Inter Pocula* (1888). Views of the darker side include George Payson, *Golden Dreams and Leaden Realities* (1853), and Hinton R. Helper, *The Land of Gold: Reality versus Fiction* (1855).

On aspects of legal history see John P. Reid, *Law for the Elephant: Property and Social Behavior on the Overland Trail* (1980), and John Umbeck, "The California Gold Rush: A Study of Emerging Property Rights," *Explorations in Economic History,* XIV (July 1977), pp. 197–226.

CHAPTER NINE

A New State and Frontier Politics

The Congress of the United States, deadlocked over the future of slavery in new territories, provided no legal form of government whatever for California from the end of the Mexican War in 1848 until its admission into the Union on September 9, 1850. During this period the confused conditions of the gold rush intensified the confusion that resulted from California's undetermined and very peculiar legal and political status.

MILITARY GOVERNMENTS

From the outbreak of the war until the ratification of the treaty of peace, California was governed under the customs of international law which provided that in conquered territory under military occupation the previous system of local law remain in effect with such modifications as the military commander considered necessary. Thus the American commanders were also ex officio governors; however, there was much uncertainty about their legal status, powers, and responsibilities. Further confusion arose from the changes of personnel. The "governorship" of California passed from Commodore Sloat to Commodore Stockton to Colonel Frémont to General Kearny to Colonel Mason—five governors in the first 10 months of American occupation.

The prevailing system of local government in Mexican California, which the American military governors necessarily adopted, was based on the powers of the alcalde, an office derived from the Arabian and Moorish *Al-Cadi*, or village judge. The duties of the alcalde were many and remarkably varied, and his jurisdiction was ill-defined and unclear. He performed the functions of mayor, sheriff, and judge, often arresting a person, presiding over the trial, passing sentence, and enforcing the sentence. The partriarchal aspects of the office and the absence of the separation of powers were shocking to many Americans. Walter Colton, appointed and later elected as the first American alcalde of Monterey in 1846, wrote that "such an absolute disposal of questions affecting property and personal liberty never ought to be confided to one man. There is not a judge on the bench in England or the United States whose power is so absolute as that of the alcalde of Monterey."

From the beginning the American military governors assumed that the ultimate annexation of California to the United States was a foregone conclusion. This view was strengthened in March 1847 by the arrival of Colonel J. D. Stevenson's regiment of New York Volunteers, recruited with the understanding that they would be disbanded in California at the end of the war and would thus provide not merely a garrison but a body of permanent American settlers.

The Treaty of Guadalupe Hidalgo was ratified in May 1848, and the official news of the ratification reached California on August 6. Thereafter, military government had to be continued de facto, with no other legal basis than the law of necessity. Even before the end of the technical state of war, there were many protests against "the inefficient mongrel military rule," as a writer in the *California Star* described it, and against alcalde rule.

THE CONSTITUTIONAL CONVENTION AND ITS PROBLEMS

With the news of the ratification of the treaty, the question of how California was supposed to be governed became extraordinarily difficult and embarrassing. Congress could not agree on any system of civil government for California. All such plans bogged down in the national political struggle which had raged since the introduction of Representative David Wilmot's proposal that slavery be forbidden in any territory acquired from Mexico.

General Bennet Riley succeeded Colonel Mason as "civil" governor in April 1849. Late in May he received news that Congress had again adjourned without agreement on a territorial organization for California, and on June 3 he issued a call for a constitutional convention to meet at Monterey on September 1. He had no real authority to do this, but it was a wise and necessary solution of the problem. It was also consistent with the attitude of President Zachary Taylor, a southern Unionist who felt that California might help to break the congressional deadlock over the territorial expansion of slavery if it would confront the rest of the country with an accomplished fact, by drawing up a state constitution that would settle the explosive issue so far as California was concerned.

The president could make this suggestion only informally and unofficially because all the legal authority in the matter lay with Congress. Under the normal procedure, patterned roughly on that of the Northwest Ordinance, Congress would first have established a territorial government; then, when the territory had enough inhabitants, Congress would have passed an "enabling act," authorizing an elected convention (or sometimes the territorial legislature) to prepare a constitution and submit it for congressional approval with the admission of the state. All but four new states, since the original thirteen, had evolved through the territorial stage in this way. California would skip that stage entirely—as Vermont, Kentucky, Maine, and Texas had done—but under circumstances that differed from those prevailing in any of them.

President Taylor sent T. Butler King of Georgia as his personal and confidential emissary to California. In the sweltering summer of 1849, King traveled throughout the mining regions, urging the busy miners to take an interest in the forthcoming elections of delegates to the convention. The steamer on which King had arrived from Panama also carried another politician of even greater importance to California's future. This was William M. Gwin of Tennessee, a Democrat who had served one term in Congress. Early in March 1849, after Congress had adjourned with no solution of the California tangle, Gwin realized that California would soon form its own state government. He left Washington with the announced intention of assisting in that process and then of returning as one of the first United States senators from the new state. He achieved both of these ambitions. Obviously, not all of California's golden opportunities were in its mines.

Early in September the convention assembled at Monterey, in Colton Hall, a substantial building that the first American alcalde had erected as a town hall and schoolhouse. Of the 48 delegates who attended, 37 were from the northern districts. The constitutional convention of 1849, however, was not mainly a convention of forty-niners. A large majority of the delegates had been in California more than 3 years. Eight were native Californians, of whom the most important were Mariano Guadalupe Vallejo of Sonoma and José Antonio Carrillo of Los Angeles. Of the Americans, a substantially larger number had come from northern states than from southern. About half the members were less than 35 years old. The 14 lawyers formed the largest single occupational group. One delegate, B. F. Moore, from Florida and San Joaquin gave his occupation as "elegant leisure."

General Riley's proclamation had left open the question of whether the new government should be that of a state or of a territory, and this was one of the first questions the convention settled. On a motion introduced by Gwin, who could not become a senator from a territory, the vote was decisively for a state government, even though every southern California delegate who was present voted otherwise. The landowners of what would soon be the southern "cow counties" were well aware that the taxation of ranch land would be the main source of early state revenues, because the miners, though now a large majority of the citizens, generally owned no land on which to pay taxes. The administrative expenses of a territory, on the other hand, would have been paid by the federal government. Naturally the southern Californians would have preferred that alternative, but they were hopelessly outnumbered. Carrillo proposed a compromise by which the part of California north of San Luis Obispo would be a state and the southern part a territory, but the idea was not seriously considered.

To the surprise of many, the question of slavery was easily decided by a unanimous vote. However, the overwhelming sentiment for the exclusion of slavery from California was not based on humanitarian considerations. The question had come to a head in the mines when Colonel Thomas Jefferson Green and a group of other Texans had appeared at Rose's Bar on the Yuba River with a number of black slaves. Green and his fellow Texans appropriated a large number of claims and set their slaves to working them. The Argonauts, whether from the north or from the south, were sensitive on the matter of the dignity of hard manual labor, or rather of their particular form of it; they were outraged at the imputation that gold mining was work appropriate for black slaves. On Sunday, July 29, a mass meeting resolved "that no slave or Negro should own claims or even work in the mines," and served notice that the slaves must be out of the district by the next morning. Three days later the same miners elected William E. Shannon as their delegate to the convention at Monterey. It was Shannon who introduced the provision that "Neither slavery nor involuntary servitude, unless for the punishment of crimes, shall ever be tolerated in this state."

A few of the members of the convention held liberal views on racial matters, but the majority did not. This was clear in the debates on a proposal to exclude free blacks, as well as slaves, from California—debates that brought forth angry feelings. The proposal to exclude free blacks was introduced by M. M. McCarver from Kentucky and Sacramento. Many owners of slaves, he said, were planning to bring them to California and free them there on condition that they work in the mines as indentured servants. Moreover, McCarver asserted, free blacks were "idle in their habits, difficult to be governed by laws, thriftless and uneducated," and their presence in California would be an evil "greater than that of slavery itself." At one point the exclusion clause was actually adopted, and it would have remained in the document except for a growing fear that Congress might consider it in violation of the federal Constitution and therefore reject the California constitution as a whole. Blacks were citizens in some of the states in the north, and the federal Constitution declared that citizens of each state should be "entitled to all privileges and immunities of citizens in the several states." The overriding consideration was the fear of anything that might delay the full establishment of "a proper form of state government" and its full national recognition.

At this time the power to deny suffrage on the ground of race was still within the constitutional authority of a state. Here, the chief complication was that the former Mexican citizens of California had the right to become American citizens under the treaty of peace. Most Mexican Californians had some degree of Indian ancestry, and Mexican law had not formally denied suffrage to Indians. In an uneasy compromise the California constitution extended the suffrage only to white male citizens, but authorized the state legislature by a two-thirds vote to extend it to Indians or the descendants of Indians. That the legislature would do this was most unlikely.

The problem that gave the convention most trouble was the question of the eastern boundary. Should this be based on the Sierra Nevada and the Colorado River, or should there be a much larger California extending several hundred miles farther east? The convention's committee on boundaries proposed the Sierra–Colorado River line. Gwin, supported by Henry W. Halleck, secretary of state under Mason and Riley and delegate from Monterey, favored the much larger unit, with a boundary east of the Great Salt Lake. The convention, changing its mind repeatedly, almost broke up over this question. As usual, the delegates were primarily concerned with the possible reactions in Washington, D.C. Some argued that Congress might reject the constitution and postpone the admission of California if its boundaries were too large. Others argued the opposite. In the end the decision was for the present boundaries of California: on the north, the 42nd parallel; on the east, the 120th meridian southward to its juncture with the 39th parallel (a point in Lake Tahoe); thence in a straight southeasterly line to the intersection of the 35th parallel and the Colorado River; then down the middle of the channel of that river to the Mexican border, at the point where the Gila flows into the Colorado.

California was the first American state to include in its constitution a provision for the separate property of married women. All property of the wife, owned by her before marriage or acquired afterward by gift or otherwise, should remain her property. Such had been the law in Mexican California, and the Americans were under some obligation to preserve it— but an argument offered by Halleck was probably more effective. He advised all his fellow bachelors to vote for this section because it would attract not only prospective wives, but *wealthy* prospective wives, to California. In vain did some of the married delegates protest that nature had made men the protectors of women and that the constitution should not tamper with this relationship.

For public education, California made the usual provisions of a frontier state. That is, it announced its acceptance of the land grants that the federal government customarily made to new states for the support of public schools and for a "seminary of learning," or university. Robert Semple, president of the convention, exuberantly asked his colleagues: "Why should we send our sons to Europe to finish their education? If we have the means here we can procure the necessary talent; we can bring the President of Oxford University here by offering a sufficient salary." But even if Oxford had had an official with the title of president, the University of California could not easily have attracted him, even 20 years later when that institution was actually opened. Until the twentieth century it would remain small and isolated.

The great seal of the state of California was adopted at the 1849 constitutional convention in Monterey.

Some other uninformed statements were also made in the convention, as when a delegate objected to the phrase "a jury of his peers" on the ground that there was no house of peers in democratic America. But in general the convention did a fairly creditable job under difficult circumstances. It is true that not much of the constitution of 1849 was original. A majority of its provisions were taken from the constitution of Iowa; much of the rest of it came from the constitution of New York.

The design accepted for the state seal, on the other hand, was quite original and distinctive, if somewhat cluttered. Minerva, the Roman goddess of political wisdom and of handicrafts and the guardian of cities, appears in the foreground. At her feet crouches a grizzly bear feeding on bunches of grapes. A miner works with rocker and bowl, ships ply San Francisco Bay, and the snowy peaks of the Sierra Nevada are seen in the distance. The Greek motto "Eureka" and 31 stars, the last one for the new state of California, are at the top of the design.

One point of dissension was raised: Mariano Vallejo objected to the bear. It reminded him of the indignities he had suffered in the Bear Flag Revolt, and he proposed that it be removed from the seal unless it were shown as secured by a lasso in the hands of a *vaquero*. In the end he accepted the assurances of Anglo-American delegates that this particular bear signified no offense to the native Californians.

THE FIRST LEGISLATURE

A month after the convention adjourned, the first state officials were elected on November 13, 1849, the same day on which the constitution was ratified by a light vote, 12,061 in favor and 811 against. Peter H. Burnett was elected governor, and John McDougal lieutenant governor. On December 15 the legislature began to assemble at the first state capital, San José. In joint session of the two houses, it elected Frémont and Gwin as United States senators; Frémont had the larger number of votes, but a drawing by lot gave him the short term, ending March 3, 1851, whereas Gwin drew the term extending 4 years longer.

The permanent location of the state capital was left open to future bids from rival towns, in order to ensure that land and buildings would be provided without cost to the state government. The fact that California had not yet been admitted to the Union made the prospects of obtaining state funds uncertain, and because the first legislature failed to establish a permanent location, the capital was hawked about in a most undignified manner. Within 5 years the seat of government would be moved from San José to Vallejo, back to San José, back to Vallejo, to Sacramento, back to Vallejo, to Benicia, and at last, in 1854, permanently to Sacramento.

The first state legislature of California, though not a very distinguished body, did not entirely deserve the name that it acquired, "the legislature of a thousand drinks." The appellation seems to have grown out of a phrase repeatedly used by Thomas Jefferson Green. That irrepressible political adventurer from Texas, unabashed when the miners excluded him and his slaves from the Yuba diggings, had secured election as state senator from Sacramento. Moreover, he became chairman of the senate finance committee and was seeking election to one of the four new major-generalcies of the state militia. A number of the candidates for various offices to be filled by the legislature maintained bars from which they dispensed hospitality to the members in the hope of receiving their votes in return. At the end of each day's session, at least until the one that elected him as a militia commander, Green loudly invited the legislators to have "a thousand drinks" at his expense; journalists could not resist the temptation to apply the phrase as a description of the legislature generally.

THE ADMISSION OF CALIFORNIA TO THE UNION

Congress nearly rejected the new government of California. The new state's admission would upset the equal balance in the number of free and slave states and in the number of their United States senators, a balance that had long given the south a veto against federal laws inimical to its "peculiar institution." In the great debates in the national capital, southern senators demanded an extension of the Missouri Compromise line of 36°30′ to the Pacific coast. This line would have bisected California just south of Monterey, and the portion to the south of it would have been organized as a territory open to slavery. The "great compromise" proposed, instead, that California be admitted as a free state, as its people desired, but that the territories of Utah and New Mexico be organized without the ban of the Wilmot Proviso against slavery. Daniel Webster, in his famous speech in the Senate on March 7, argued for this solution and tried to allay the protest of northern abolitionists and opponents of the expansion of slavery. Slavery, he said, had been perpetuated mainly for its usefulness in the production of cotton. Nature itself had excluded slavery from California and New Mexico by making their lands so arid that cotton could never be grown there, "and I would not take pains uselessly to reaffirm an ordinance of nature nor to re-enact the will of God." Webster could hardly have foreseen that with the help of irrigation California would one day produce more cotton than any other state but Texas.

At last, when the south had been further mollified by a stringent new law regulating the return of slaves who had escaped into northern states, the "omnibus" provisions of the great compromise were approved. The president signed the bill for the admission of California on September 9, 1850. The news reached San Francisco on October 18 and was celebrated with colorful parades, but the new state government had already been operating for nearly a year, exactly as if it had been authorized by Congress. Californians were showing a strong disposition to take things into their own hands.

THE FEUD BETWEEN BRODERICK AND GWIN

Under the constitution of 1849, elections of governors and other state officials were held every 2 years, in the odd-numbered years. The Democrats won virtually every important election in California in the 1850s except the state elections of 1855, which they lost largely because of the bitter rivalry between the two main Democratic leaders—one of the most sensationally destructive rivalries in American political history.

MOVEMENTS FOR STATE DIVISION

The early historians who believed that Broderick's opposition to the territorial expansion of slavery, rather than his desire for political power, was his most significant motive were probably committing an error of emphasis. The same historians tended to see a proslavery conspiracy in the demands of southern California for separation from the rest of the state during the 1850s. Later historians, such as William Henry Ellison, argued that this was simply and completely an error of fact. It was true that the southern counties of California repeatedly sought permission to secede from the northern ones, Ellison concluded, but the slavery question did not have anything to do with these efforts except that many imagined that it did. The real cause of the movement was the grievance of southern California against too much taxation and too little representation. Recent research by historian Ward McAfee has revealed that the advocates of state division were actually driven by a complex set of motives.

The fears expressed by the southern California delegates in the convention of 1849, to the effect that their part of the state would have to pay an unfair share of taxes, proved to have been extremely well founded. In 1852 Governor McDougal conceded that the 6 cow counties of southern California, with a population of 6000, paid $42,000 in property taxes, while the 12 mining counties, with a population of nearly 120,000, paid only $21,000. A state law exempted from taxation all mining claims on "United States lands," where the great majority of the claims were located. This was one of the innumerable statutes of the 1850s that conferred special favors on the mining interests.

Gradually the justice of southern California's grievance became recognized throughout the state, and in 1859 the legislature approved a plan introduced by Assemblyman Andrés Pico. This provided that the part of California south of 35°45' (the northern boundary of San Luis Obispo County) should become the territory of Colorado. The voters of that region also approved the plan, but coming as it did on the eve of the Civil War, it had no chance of passage in the national capital. Most members of Congress, ignorant of affairs on the remote Pacific coast, could not be dissuaded from the belief that the measure was simply another dangerous aggravation of the slavery issue.

CALIFORNIA AND THE CIVIL WAR

The amount of pro-Confederate sentiment in California was grossly exaggerated during the war—by those who felt and cherished it, by those who feared it, and by those who, for their own political and personal reasons, wished to make it appear greater than it was. Most histories have reflected the contemporary exaggeration. Actually, less than 7 percent of the population of California in 1860 had come from the seceded states and there was never any genuine danger that California would desert the Union cause.

Disloyal conspiracies did exist in California, but they were on a small scale. There were clandestine pro-Confederate societies like the Knights of the Golden Circle, the Knights of the Columbian Star, and the Committee of Thirty, but they had only a fraction of the membership that wild rumor attributed to them. There were various dreams of seizing federal arsenals and gold shipments, and there was one romantic but futile attempt to put a conspiracy into actual operation. A group of Southern sympathizers secretly armed the small schooner *Chapman* at San Francisco in the hope of capturing a Pacific Mail steamer to use as a privateer under a Confederate letter of marque. Federal authorities knew of the plot almost from its beginning, and they seized the *Chapman* as she was weighing anchor.

The elections and the trends in party politics gave ample evidence that California was safe for the Union. In the state campaigns of 1861 the Republicans and the Union Democrats repudiated the right of secession and pledged the support of California for the war, and their candidates, running on these strongly Unionist platforms, polled together more than two-thirds of the votes. In the California elections of 1861, the continuing Democratic schism enabled the Republicans to elect their first governor, Leland Stanford, by a substantial plurality. By 1864, although the Democrats were reunited in support of the Union, the Republicans had been very successful in branding all Democrats as disloyal, and consequently a large majority of Californians voted for the reelection of Lincoln. The Republicans called themselves the Union party from 1863 to 1867.

Because it was never necessary for anyone to "save California for the Union," it is absurd to say that anyone did; however, this honor has been variously claimed for Reverend Thomas Starr King, Colonel Edward D. Baker, Governor Stanford, and others. King was a much beloved Unitarian minister, called to San Francisco from Boston in 1860. He was a captivating orator, and in several lecture tours he spoke for the Union and particularly for contributions to the work of the Sanitary Commission, the "Red Cross of the Civil War." Partly as a result of his efforts, California contributed more than a fourth of the amount that the commission received in the entire country. Colonel Baker, a close personal friend of Abraham Lincoln, was one of the leading organizers of the Republican party in California.

California's military participation in the Civil War was very limited. The federal government did not favor the use of California volunteers in the main theaters of the war because their transportation was too expensive, and the draft was never enforced in California for the same reason. General Don Andrés Pico, victor of San Pasqual and the signer of the Treaty of Cahuenga with Frémont, was deeply hurt by the rejection of his offer to raise a regiment of native Californian cavalry. About 500 young Californians, including several native ones, offered their services to Massachusetts if that state would pay the cost of their organization and transportation. It did so, and the "California Battalion," as part of the 2nd Massachusetts Cavalry, took part in more than 50 engagements, mainly in Virginia. About 16,000 volunteers enlisted in California during the war, but they were used mainly for local garrison duty, for guarding the overland mail routes, or for policing Indians in the northwest. A "California Column" was sent to New Mexico in 1862 to repel a Confederate invasion of the territory, but the enemy withdrew before a battle could be fought, and many members of the column left it to join a local mining rush.

SELECTED BIBLIOGRAPHY

Theodore Grivas, *Military Governments in California, 1846–1850* (1962), does much to dispel the confusion that has surrounded that subject. The official *Report of the Debates in the Convention of California* (1850) was well prepared by J. Ross Browne. David Alan Johnson, *Founding the Far West* (1992), analyzes the motives and ideological intentions of the members of the constitutional convention; but see also Cardinal Goodwin, *The Establishment of State Government in California, 1846–1850* (1914). Also valuable are William H. Ellison, *A Self-Governing Dominion: California, 1849–1860* (1950); Woodrow J. Hansen, *The Search for Authority in California* (1960); and William E. Franklin, "Peter H. Burnett and the Provisional Government Movement," *California Historical Society Quarterly,* XL (June 1961), pp. 123–136. Donald C. Briggs's *Conquer and Colonize: Stevenson's Regiment and California* (1977) is a thorough account which emphasizes the positive contributions of Stevenson's men. Important memoirs are Walter Colton, *Three Years in California* (1850); Samuel H. Willey, *The Transition Period of California* (1901); William H. Ellison (ed.), "Memoirs of Hon. William M. Gwin," *California Historical Society Quarterly,* XXI (1940), pp. 1–26, 157–184, 256–277, 344–367; and Charles A. Barker (ed.), *Memoirs of Elisha Oscar Crosby* (1945).

On the admission of California see Ronald C. Woolsey, "A Southern Dilemma: Slavery and the California Statehood Issue in 1850—A Reconsideration, *Southern California Quarterly,* LXV (Summer 1983), pp. 123–144. Robert G. Cowan's *The Admission of the 31st State by the 31st Congress* (1962) is an annotated bibliography of the congressional speeches.

The Broderick-Gwin feud may be traced in Arthur Quinn, *The Rivals* (1994); James O'Meara, *Broderick and Gwin* (1881); Thomas, *Between Two Empires . . . William McKendree Gwin* (1969); David A. Williams, *David C. Broderick: A Political Portrait* (1969); and A. Russell Buchanan, *David S. Terry* (1956). On the American party, see Peyton Hurt, "The Rise and Fall of the 'Know Nothings' in California," *California Historical Society Quarterly,* IX (March and June 1930), pp. 16–49, 99–128.

The state division movement is covered in William H. Ellison, *A Self-Governing Dominion,* and the Pacific Republic idea in Joseph Ellison, *California and the Nation.* For a more recent view see Ward M. McAfee, "California's House Divided," *Civil War History,* XXXIII (June 1987), pp. 115–130. See also Ronald C. Woolsey, "Disunion or Dissent?" *Southern California Quarterly,* LXVI (Fall 1984), pp. 185–206, and "The Politics of a Lost Cause," *California History,* LXIX (Winter 1991), pp. 372–383.

Gerald Stanley is the author of several important articles on politics before and during the Civil War: "Racism and the Early Republican Party: The 1856 Presidential Election in California," *Pacific Historical Review,* XLIII (May 1974), pp. 171–187; "Slavery and the Origins of the Republican Party in California," *Southern California Quarterly,* LX (Spring 1978), pp. 1–16; "The Slavery Issue and Election in California, 1860," *Mid-America,* LXII (January 1980), pp. 35–46; "Civil War Politics in California," *Southern California Quarterly,* LXIV (Summer 1982), pp. 115–132. See also Robert J. Chandler, "Friends in Time of Need: Republicans and Black Civil Rights in California during the Civil War Era," *Arizona and the West,* XXIV (Winter 1982), pp. 319–340. Older studies include George T. Clark, *Leland Stanford* (1931); Earl Pomeroy, "California, 1846–1860," *California Historical Society Quarterly,* XXXII (December 1953), pp. 291–302; Benjamin F. Gilbert, *The Governors of California* (1965); Royce D. Delmatier et al., *The Rumble of California Politics* (1965); and Norman E. Tutorow, *Leland Stanford* (1970).

Benjamin F. Gilbert's "California and the Civil War, a Bibliographical Essay," *California Historical Society Quarterly,* XL (December 1961), pp. 289–307, is very useful. See also his "The Confederate Minority in California," ibid., XX (June 1941), pp. 154–170. On California contributions to the war effort, see Tom Generous, "Over the River Jordan: California Volunteers in Utah during the Civil War," *California History,* LXIII (Summer 1984), pp. 200–211; Darlis A. Miller, *The California Column in New Mexico* (1982); Robert Monzingo, *Thomas Starr King* (1991); Richard H. Peterson, "The United States Sanitary Commission and Thomas Starr King in California, 1861–1864," *California History,* LXXII (Winter 1993/1994), pp. 324–337; Russell M. Posner, "Thomas Starr King and the Mercy Million," *California Historical Society Quarterly,* XLIII (December 1964), pp. 291–308; Aurora Hunt, *The Army of the Pacific* (1951); and Oscar Lewis, *The War in the Far West* (1961).

CHAPTER TEN

Crime and Punishment

One of the most striking and significant evidences of the chronic social disorganization in post-gold-rush California was the outbreak of a rash of "vigilance committees." Most historical treatments of these bodies have condoned their actions, and many have even glorified them. The present account takes a different view.

THE NATURE OF VIGILANTISM

Richard Henry Dana, in the chapter that he added to his *Two Years before the Mast* after his return visit to California in 1859, described San Francisco as having been rescued from

> its season of heaven-defying crime, violence, and blood . . . and handed back to soberness, morality, and good government, by that peculiar invention of Anglo-Saxon Republican America, the solemn awe-inspiring Vigilance Committee of the most grave and responsible citizens, the last resort of the thinking and the good, taken to only when vice, fraud, and ruffianism have entrenched themselves behind the forms of law, suffrage, and the ballot.

Several historians, writing in the same tone of defensive righteousness, have perpetuated the racist notion that vigilantism was one of the evidences of Anglo-Saxon superiority, a proof of American ingenuity in adapting self-government to the special conditions of the frontier.

The truth is, first, that vigilantism was not a superior institution and, second, that there was nothing exclusively Anglo-Saxon about it, except perhaps the use of the rope instead of the bullet. *Vigilante* is a Spanish word meaning lookout or a guard, and the first "committee of vigilance" in California was organized in Los Angeles in 1836. This "*junta defensora de la seguridad pública*" seized a man and a woman from the custody of the alcaldes and shot them for the murder of the woman's husband.

The true and great contributions of "Anglo-Saxon" jurisprudence have been on the side of the due process of law, whereas the methods of the vigilance committees were parodies of due process. Their methods were generally more organized and elaborate than those of mere lynch mobs, but the "committees" did not hold their "trials" in open court. They acted in anger and in haste. They did not consider motions for change of venue. Witnesses for the defendants were usually afraid to testify, or even to appear. The committees often resorted to hanging because they had no way of enforcing a sentence of long-term imprisonment. And there was no provision for appeal or for executive clemency.

Taking the law into one's own hands, particularly after regular courts had been established, was itself a criminal action. Yet, remarkably enough, the early American historians of California almost unanimously applauded it. Even the idealistic philosopher Josiah Royce, in spite of his personal detestation of violence and bullying, strongly praised "popular justice" as exercised by the vigilance committees of San Francisco. Hubert Howe Bancroft indulged in the most elaborate defenses and rationalizations of "popular tribunals" on such grounds as the sacred right of revolution. He maintained that the vigilantes were "the people," and that the people (especially the self-appointed "best" people) were above all law. These apologistic viewpoints have too often gone unchallenged.

The motives of the vigilantes were complex and remain a matter of dispute. Some joined the vigilance movement for reasons of economic self-interest. Others were moved by unconscious forces deep in their psyche. People who form lynch mobs and vigilance committees are themselves often inwardly tortured by assorted feelings of guilt. Samuel Brannan, who did more than anyone else to instigate vigilantism in San Francisco, was building the first great California fortune on money that he had diverted from church property and tithes to his personal use and profit. Apostate though he was, he was not unaffected by the knowledge that his former church regarded him as the supreme example of the corrupting influence of money on the human soul. Clearly, Brannan was subconsciously seeking freedom from his own guilt in arrogating to himself the punishment of others.

The emotion of guilt is essentially the fear of punishment. Gratification in inflicting pain, humiliation, and even death and destruction upon someone else results from the subconscious, irrational feeling that thereby one somehow achieves escape from punishment, or even assures one's own survival. In varying degrees and circumstances the latent existence of this sadistic pattern is universal among human beings. Because it is the least admirable of human traits, and also because rational recognition of it defeats its hidden irrational purpose, people resort to extreme sanctimoniousness in order to disguise it, in their own minds most of all. This element accounts for the strange air of righteous solemnity often noted in a number of the public ceremonies sponsored by the San Francisco committees of vigilance.The rank and file of these organizations included a substantial contingent of the worst and most guilty, who joined for the conscious purpose of saving themselves from hanging. But the leadership included some of the "best" men, many of whom joined for more subtle and obscure, but not entirely differ-

"Hounds" attacking Chileans in San Francisco, July 15, 1849. (*Courtesy of the Bancroft Library.*)

ent, reasons. Vigilantism was a manifestation of moral self-delusion and self-righteous sadism.

THE "HOUNDS" IN SAN FRANCISCO

Congress left California almost literally lawless from 1846 to 1850. Within this vacuum there began to appear, in San Francisco, a form of organized lawlessness and terrorism. When Colonel Stevenson's regiment of New York Volunteers was disbanded, a group of its members led by Lieutenant Sam Roberts formed an organization called the Regulators, or more commonly, the Hounds, allegedly dedicated to maintaining public order, and especially devoted to hounding Latinos and other "foreigners" out of California. Alcalde Leavenworth tried to use them as deputy policemen, but he could not control them. They held drunken parades and levied tribute, bullied merchants by day and looted foreign settlements by night. In the evening of July 15, 1849, they paraded to an attack upon Little Chile, a tent community at the foot of Telegraph Hill, where some of them murdered a mother and criminally assaulted her daughter.

The next morning Sam Brannan addressed a crowd from the roof of the alcalde's little office on the Plaza. A counterorganization called the Law and Order party was formed and its members deputized, a charitable fund for the Chileans was collected, and by sunset Roberts and 18 other Hounds had been caught and imprisoned in a ship in the bay.

Nine men were more or less legally convicted of crimes, but the penalty was banishment, and this proved unenforceable. Many of the Hounds continued their depredations, though no longer openly. In such activities they were joined by some of the "Sydney Ducks," ex-convicts or escaped convicts from Australia. The Australian immigrants were thus given a bad name that most of them did not deserve.

THE SAN FRANCISCO COMMITTEE OF 1851

The beating and robbery of C. J. Jansen, a prominent merchant, in his shop in the heart of town on February 19, 1851, produced another outburst of popular excitement. Two Australians, Berdue and Windred, were arrested and mistakenly identified by Jansen as the men who had assaulted and robbed him. A mob incited by Brannan was preparing to seize and hang the two prisoners without a trial when a young merchant named William Tell Coleman managed to catch the ear of the crowd and to persuade it to organize a "people's court." This procedure, with Coleman acting as prosecutor, resulted in a hung jury. The two men were then returned to the jurisdiction of the regular authorities.

On May 4, 1851, there occurred the fifth and greatest in a series of fires that had repeatedly devastated the city. The fact that this fifth fire occurred on the anniversary of the second one intensified the growing suspicion that all the fires were incendiary, set by Hounds and Sydney Ducks in revenge and defiance and to facilitate looting. Loot was found hidden in the "Sydney Town" district and criminals were thought to be emboldened by the failure to hang the supposed robbers of Jansen. A volunteer night patrol was organized, and on Sunday, June 8, the *Alta California* published a proposal for a "committee of safety" or "committee of vigilance." That afternoon a meeting in Sam Brannan's office determined to call a larger meeting of other responsible citizens, and on June 9, in Brannan's building, that meeting adopted a constitution for the first San Francisco "Committee of Vigilance."

The very next evening, taps on a fire bell summoned the committee to pass judgment on John Jenkins, who had been caught stealing a small safe and was dragged to the committee's headquarters instead of the police station. Jenkins was insolent and threatened that his friends were organizing to rescue him and destroy the committee. The decisive moment came when William A. Howard, a sea captain, cried, "Gentlemen, as I understand it, we came here to hang somebody." Coleman opposed hanging a man at night and suggested waiting until dawn, when Jenkins would "rise with the sun." But Brannan secured the approval of the crowd in the Plaza, and there, from a beam at the south end of the "Old Adobe," Jenkins was hanged by moonlight. Thus, the committee began its work by hanging the first criminal it appre-

The execution of John Jenkins on the night of June 10, 1851, by the San Francisco Committee of Vigilance. (*Courtesy of the Bancroft Library.*)

hended, within a few hours after his crime, and for a rather petty robbery rather than a murder.

A coroner's inquest into the death of Jenkins identified nine vigilantes as parties to it, but the committee made their arrests impractical by releasing the names of all its members. In July, the committee chanced to apprehend James Stuart, an Australian who had escaped from jail at Marysville while awaiting trial for the murder of a sheriff. After securing a highly picaresque confession from Stuart, the committee hanged him, and in August it also hanged two other Sydney Ducks, McKenzie and Whittaker, whom Stuart's confessions had implicated in various robberies. Before its extrajudicial activities ended in September, the vigilance committee of 1851 had made nearly 90 arrests. Besides its four hangings, it had whipped 1 man, sentenced 28 to deportation, remanded 15 to the authorities for trial, and released 41.

The roster shows that along with Brannan the founders and early members of the vigilance committee of 1851 were predominantly commission merchants and sea captains—two groups who disliked government, courts, lawyers, and politicians as forces that threatened interference with their own freedom of action. It was a peculiar base on which to rest a claim that the leading vigilantes were "the best citizens" of the community, but this claim was made, and has been periodically repeated ever since. It is significant that no lawyers whatever were members of the

Committee of Vigilance. The committee would not have welcomed their membership, even had they wished to join it.

STATEWIDE VIGILANCE

San Francisco's example inspired the formation of several local vigilance committees in other towns and an increase of less formal lynching in the mining communities. Of dozens of such cases, perhaps the most infamous was the hanging of the Mexican woman Juanita by a mob of miners at Downieville on July 5, 1851. They had gathered to hear a Fourth of July oration by United States Senator John B. Weller and afterward had celebrated far into the night. In the early hours of the morning Juanita killed one of them with a knife. The friends of her victim, one Joseph Cannon, asserted the theory that he had not intended to harm her and that his purpose in entering her cabin was only to apologize to her for having broken her door down, which had happened only because he was intoxicated.

Within a few hours Juanita was brought to "trial" by what one observer, David P. Barstow, called "the hungriest, craziest, wildest mob that ever I saw anywhere." After saying that she would defend herself again in the same way under the same circumstances, Juanita adjusted her own noose and stepped from the improvised scaffold. Barstow was certain that "the hanging of the woman was murder. No jury in the world, on any principle of self-defense or protection of life and property, would ever have convicted her."

In the riotous cow town of Los Angeles in the 1850s there were more executions, both legal and extralegal, than in the much larger city of San Francisco. It was sometimes difficult to distinguish the legal executions from the lynchings in Los Angeles because of the tendency of the constituted authorities to authorize vigilantism. In 1851, the mayor and the city council created a vigilance committee by formal action. Among those it hanged were three men charged with the murder of Major General J. H. Bean of the California militia. One of the men hanged was later proved innocent. In 1854, Mayor Stephen C. Foster dispersed a mob bent on lynching the gambler and killer Dave Brown by promising that if the regular authorities did not succeed in convicting and executing him, he would resign as mayor and join the vigilantes. When Brown's lawyers secured a stay of execution, Mayor Foster kept his promise, directed the lynching, and resumed his office after it was over.

The most famous case in the southern mines occurred at Columbia on October 10, 1855. This was the hanging of John S. Barclay for killing an intoxicated man who had laid violent hands on Barclay's wife. There was a mock trial in which only the prosecutor, a local political idol who had just been elected to the state senate, was permitted to speak at any length. The drunken viciousness of the mob, the extreme courage of the sheriff in risking his life to try to take the prisoner away from it, and the fact that by that time the legal courts in the area were well organized, produced some local reaction against lynching in general.

THE SAN FRANCISCO COMMITTEE OF 1856

The revival of the vigilance committee in San Francisco in 1856 was in part a result of the subconscious and irrational motivations that were characteristic of vigilante behavior in general. Interacting with these psychological aspects, however, were economic, political, and even ethnic and religious factors. The committee of 1856 was dominated by the city's leading merchants, who wished to bring about great reductions in their taxes by discrediting the city government as corrupt and wasteful and by taking control of it themselves. The city had been governed mainly by the Democratic organization headed by David C. Broderick. Many of Broderick's followers were Irish Catholics, and many of them were particular objects of vigilante hostility.

The immediate cause of the revival of the vigilance movement was the shooting of James King of William, the anti-Catholic editor of the *Daily Evening Bulletin,* by the politician James P. Casey, on May 14, 1856. James King had added the name of William, his father, to distinguish him from other James Kings in the District of Columbia, where he was born. His editorship of the *Bulletin* was a sort of journalistic vigilantism. The pen, he felt, could be mightier than the rope or the whip; the printing press, a mightier punisher of evil than the gallows. He denounced the Tammany-style political machine of David C. Broderick and accused him of having imported James P. Casey from New York City as an expert ballot-box stuffer. Casey was elected a county supervisor in an election widely denounced as corrupt. King published in the *Bulletin* the fact that Casey had served a term in the New York state penitentiary at Sing Sing.

A great many people had come from the older parts of the country to escape their pasts, so many that it was often considered a necessary convention in California that a person's past was nobody's business. A popular song of the period was

Oh, what was your name in the States?
Was it Thompson or Johnson or Bates?
Did you murder your wife and flee for your life?
Oh, what was your name in the States?

King's exposure of his prison record deeply disturbed Casey and made him almost incoherent. He threatened King in the *Bulletin* office and shot him on the street an hour later.

The shooting of King became interrelated in the public mind with the earlier killing of General William H. Richardson by the gambler Charles Cora. Richardson, then serving as United States marshal, had become extremely angry when Cora and his mistress, the wealthy Arabella Ryan, keeper of a notorious house of prostitution, attracted attention by sitting directly behind Richardson and his wife in a box at the opening of a new theater. The next evening Richardson, clearly intoxicated, accosted Cora on the street and drew a derringer pistol. Cora drew his own derringer and fired a fatal shot. Cora's first trial ended in a hung jury, and he was in jail awaiting a second trial when the shooting of James King of William occurred.

On the day that King was shot, a group of former members of the vigilance committee of 1851 determined to reactivate the movement, under the leadership of William Tell Coleman, now the most respected of the group. The committee began to collect arms and to form a military unit. On the other hand, a number of prominent citizens formed the Law and Order party, denouncing the vigilantes and adopting the name of the organization of 1849, which had taken all its actions against the Hounds in full cooperation with the legal authorities. Among the Law and Order leaders were Mayor Van Ness, Sheriff Scannell, and General William Tecumseh Sherman, whom the governor of the state had recently appointed commander of the San Francisco district of the California militia.

On May 16 Governor J. Neely Johnson came down from Sacramento to confer with Coleman. Few state executives have ever been more bitterly denounced than Johnson was for his role in these conferences and in the events that followed them. He was only 28 years old at the time—California in the 1850s was a young man's country—and he was in an extremely explosive situation. In his discussion with Coleman he believed that he had secured a promise that the vigilantes would not attack the jail to seize Cora and Casey. Coleman later maintained that he had merely promised to give notice before moving to seize the two men and that a condition even of this promise was that the governor guarantee "*an immediate trial and instant execution*" by the public authorities. Four days after the shooting, 2500 armed vigilantes advanced on the county jail and removed Cora and Casey to the committee's headquarters. The sheriff's 150 deputies made no attempt to resist, and

Fort Gunnybags. From a contemporary letter sheet. (*Courtesy of the California Historical Society.*)

T.C.BOYD.

Published by the NOISY CARRIER'S BOOK AND STATIONERY CO., 87 Battery Street, San Francisco.

The tone of most earlier historical treatments of the vigilantes was set by three important and influential accounts, all written about the same time. Charles H. Shinn, in his *Mining Camps* (1885), accepted very uncritically the reminiscences of the participants whom he interviewed. Josiah Royce, in *California, from the Conquest in 1846 to the Second Vigilance Committee in San Francisco* (1886), was more critical of the miners, but praised the San Francisco committees. Hubert Howe Bancroft, in *Popular Tribunals* (2 volumes, 1887), defended some of the rural tribunals and was positively worshipful of the urban ones; his views reflected the feelings of most San Francisco businesspeople, of whom Bancroft was one.

Mary Floyd Williams edited the *Papers of the San Francisco Committee of Vigilance of 1851* (1919). Her *History of the San Francisco Committee of Vigilance of 1851* (1921) is scholarly in details but generally very admiring. George R. Stewart, *Committee of Vigilance, Revolution in San Francisco, 1851* (1964), is also sympathetic. The highly laudatory spirit of *"The Lion of the Vigilantes:" William T. Coleman and the Life of Old San Francisco* (1939), by James A. B. Scherer, is well-suggested by its title, taken from Robert Louis Stevenson. Also generally favorable is Roger Olmsted, "San Francisco and the Vigilante Style," *The American West*, VII (January and March 1972).

Critical treatments of vigilantism are in Ethel May Tinneman, "The Opposition to the San Francisco Vigilance Committee in 1856," M.A. thesis, University of California, Berkeley (1941); William H. Ellison, *A Self-Governing Dominion, California, 1849–1860* (1950); A. Russell Buchanan, *David S. Terry of California, Dueling Judge* (1959); John W. Caughey, *Their Majesties, the Mob* (1960); and Roger W. Lotchin, *San Francisco, 1846–1856: From Hamlet to Modern City* (1974). Doyce B. Nunis, Jr. (ed.), *The San Francisco Vigilance Committee of 1856: Three Views* (1971), includes an excellent historical introduction and bibliographical essay.

The "official response" to the problem of crime and punishment is described in Shelley Bookspan, *A Germ of Goodness: The California State Prison System, 1851–1944* (1992).

CHAPTER ELEVEN

Racial Oppression and Economic Conflict

In the years after the gold rush a large majority of the American citizens of California cherished a fixed belief in the innate superiority of "whites" over other races. They also believed that Protestant Christians were better people than the followers of other religious faiths and that persons of Anglo-American nativity were innately superior to those of other national origins.

Of the fears, the hatreds, and the various kinds of intolerance that accompanied this set of opinions, the deepest were probably associated with the idea of racial superiority. In part, this was because that idea was very closely associated with economic group interest; equally important, however, were the essentially irrational aspects of racial fears and hatreds.

TREATMENT OF MEXICAN MINERS

As Americans poured into the mining districts of California in 1849 and 1850, they found themselves in competition with substantial numbers of foreigners. The most numerous of these were Mexicans from the state of Sonora, as the naming of one of the largest towns in the southern mines attested. Feelings of hostility left over from the Mexican War were intensified because many of the Sonorans were experienced miners, skillful in locating good claims. Others were peons brought to California in labor gangs to work the claims of their wealthier Mexican masters. Americans feared that foreigners were removing too much of the readily available gold and that there would soon be none left. Mining camp codes, enforced by vigilance committees and soon ratified by the state legislature, excluded Mexicans and Asians from many of the diggings.

Further evidence of antiforeign sentiment appeared when the California Legislature of 1850 enacted a foreign miners' license tax. Introduced by Senator Thomas Jefferson Green, the act required miners who were not citizens of the United States to pay a fee of $20 a month. This levy was so high that the Mexicans, upon whom most of the burden would fall, were unable or unwilling to pay it, and a mass meeting in the town of Sonora announced their refusal. Hundreds of armed American miners, including many veterans wearing their old Mexican War uniforms, then gathered at Sonora to aid the collectors of the tax and to prevent Mexicans from mining without a license.

At this time there were about 15,000 Mexicans in the "southern mines"—Calaveras, Tuolumne, and Mariposa counties. Under the pressures of the tax and of threats of violence, about 10,000 left the region in the summer of 1850, most of them to return to Mexico. Although the Treaty of Guadalupe Hidalgo provided that Mexican citizens of California who chose to remain there for a year became American citizens automatically, many Americans, in ignorance or defiance of this provision, lumped all "Mexicans" together, and many native Californians were driven from the mines along with the Mexican nationals, in fear of their lives and with bitterness in their hearts. Their protests had little or no political effect. On the other hand, the protests of American merchants in the mining districts, who had lost so many customers, were strong enough to carry considerable weight in the legislature, especially when it became clear that the nearly prohibitive tax was bringing in only a small amount of revenue. The tax was repealed in 1851, but it was soon reenacted in more moderate form.

LAND-TITLE TROUBLES

Among the circumstances that made for lawlessness and violence in early American California, one of the most important was the confused condition of the ownership of land. Not until 1851 did the United States government determine its general policy toward the confirmation of titles to the vast lands that had been granted under Mexico; after the determination of the policy, many more years were required to secure actual approval of claims.

American laws required that land titles be defined exactly and clearly, and by American standards the Mexican system was incredibly lax and vague. In California, the Mexican authorities failed to provide the grantees with adequate evidence of their titles or to keep adequate records in the archives. Maps, when there were any, were very sketchy, for professional surveyors were seldom available. The frequent use of the expression "a little more or less" (*poco más ó menos*) after any measure of distance was typical of the Mexican grant system. There were several legal requirements, such as that a grant had to have been approved by the territorial assembly and to have been occupied; very seldom, however, had all the requirements been fulfilled.

There were more than 500 ranchos in Alta California in 1846, but more than 800 claims were filed in the American courts, many of them covering portions of ranchos. The claims covered nearly all the valley lands of the coastal region as far north as the Russian River and a number of large tracts in the Sacramento and northern San Joaquin valleys.

The Treaty of Guadalupe Hidalgo promised that "property of every kind" belonging to Mexicans in the ceded territories should be "inviolably respected," but

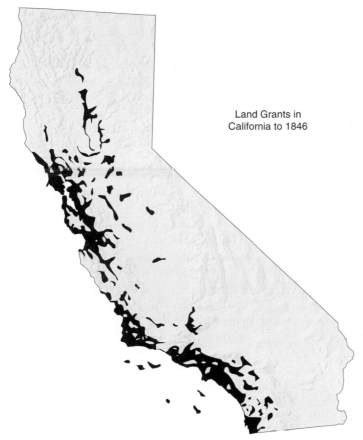

Land Grants in
California to 1846

The dark areas on the map show the grants that were confirmed by the
United States. (*From* Land in California *by W. W. Robinson. Copyright
1948 by the University of California Press.*)

American settlers generally believed that all the lands in California were now, or
ought to be, United States public lands by right of conquest. Americans were
accustomed to occupy tracts on the federal public lands before they were surveyed
and opened to settlement, and then to be permitted to buy the land at the minimum
price. The American settlers of California could not believe that a few hundred
Mexican grantees would be permitted to monopolize some 13 million acres of land,
little of it visibly improved and much of it entirely unoccupied.

Most of the claims did not represent lands that had been long in the possession
of old California families as their homes. In fact a majority of the grants were dated
within the last 5 years before the American conquest, and it was accurately
suspected that some of those claimed to have been made under Mexican governors
had been signed by them after the forced expirations of their terms of office, and
antedated. There were many multiple grants. The various claims of the Pico family

totaled 532,000 acres, and those of the De la Guerra and Carrillo families more than 300,000 each. Moreover, large-scale speculation had begun. Thomas Larkin, for example, had purchased several claims totaling nearly 200,000 acres.

Governor Richard B. Mason had instructed his secretary of state, Captain Henry Halleck, to make a study of California land titles. In a report completed early in 1849, Halleck pointed out that most of the Mexican claims were imperfect and asserted that many of them were fraudulent. This report had the effect of encouraging the views of those who were known to themselves as "settlers" and less favorably described as "squatters." Their vigorous opinions produced several episodes of violence, of which the most tragic was the "squatter riot" at Sacramento in the summer of 1850.

The town was located on land granted to Sutter by Alvarado, a grant that would eventually be upheld. Several thousand settlers, refusing to recognize the validity of this title, had squatted on vacant lots owned by purchasers from Sutter. After sheriff's deputies began to destroy the squatter's houses and fences, there was a meeting to collect money for a legal defense fund. James McClatchy, later the founder of the city's leading journalistic family, told this meeting that "If the speculators want to fight, I am for giving them battle. . . . Let us put up all the fences pulled down and also put up [hang] all the men who pull them down." He was arrested for trying to carry out at least a part of his threat. On August 13, when an armed band moved to rescue McClatchy from the riverboat that served as a jail, Mayor Harden Bigelow gathered a crowd of citizens, and in a clash at 4th and J Streets the city assessor and three squatters were killed and the mayor was wounded. The next day another battle led to the death of Sheriff Joseph McKinney and several others on both sides.

In the meantime the secretary of the interior had appointed a brilliant young attorney, William Carey Jones, to make another investigation. Jones had married a sister of Jessie Benton Frémont, and the views of California land titles that he embodied in his report in March 1850 coincided with the opinions of his father-in-law, Senator Benton, and also with those of John C. Frémont, his brother-in-law and client, who had had the good fortune to purchase the only Mexican grant on which large amounts of gold were subsequently discovered. The Jones report maintained that the grants were mostly "perfect titles . . . , and those which were not perfect— that is, which lack some formality, or some *evidence* of completeness, have the same *equity* as those which are perfect." Thus Jones recommended a very liberal policy toward the Mexican grants. Naturally the claimants praised this report and the settlers denounced it.

THE ACT OF 1851 AND THE LAND COMMISSION

The act that determined the policy of the United States toward the land claims in California was introduced by Senator William M. Gwin, chief political spokesman for the American settlers. His bill provided for the appointment by the president of a board of three commissioners. This board was to decide the validity of all claims to land under Mexican titles. All the lands of the rejected claims were to be regarded as public lands. Both the claimant and the United States had the right of appeal to the federal district court and then to the United States Supreme Court. Critics of this plan argued that it would have the effect of confiscating the lands of the grantees in California, and thus of violating the treaty with Mexico; every title would be treated as a fraud against the United States until its holder had established it in three different courts, one of them the Supreme Court, located 3000 miles away.

The land commission held its hearings from January 1852 to March 1856. All its sessions were held in San Francisco except for one brief term at Los Angeles. Of the more than 800 cases presented to it, all but a few were appealed to the district court, and 99 were appealed to the Supreme Court. Ultimately 604 claims, involving nearly 9 million acres, were confirmed, while 209 claims, involving about 4 million acres, were rejected. Some of the cases dragged on in the courts for several decades, and the *average* length of time required to secure evidence of ownership was *17 years* from the time of submitting a claim to the board.

By the time a grant was confirmed, its original holder was usually bankrupt. The litigation required for an American title under the system established by the Gwin act was long and ruinously expensive. Although the alleged excessiveness of the lawyers' fees has often been exaggerated, there were dozens of instances in which grantees were ruined while their attorneys became rich, especially by taking part of the fees in land, holding the land as a speculation, and ultimately winning the case. If grantees tried to sell part of their land to pay the costs of litigation, they could get only a low price because they did not yet have a secure title. If grantees finally managed to establish their title in court, they often found their land occupied by settlers who refused to get off.

The impoverishment of the old land-owning families of California evoked expressions of intense bitterness. Apolinaria Lorenzano, once the proud owner of three ranchos, mourned the loss of her lands: "I find myself in the greatest poverty, living by the favor of God and from handouts." Another ranchera, María Amparo Ruiz Burton, traveled to Washington, D.C., to lobby Congress on behalf of the claims of the dispossessed grantees. Burton also attempted to present her case to the general public through *The Squatter and the Don* (1885), a novel filled with a sense of loss and betrayal. "Land is not considered private property until the title to it is confirmed and patented," she wrote. "As the proceedings to obtain a patent might consume years, almost a lifetime, the result is that the [grantees] are virtually despoiled of their lands. . . ."

One of the most striking of the land grant cases was that of John C. Frémont's claim to Las Mariposas, the only Mexican grant in the mother lode region. Consisting of a sizable part of the present Mariposa County, this grant had been made to Juan B. Alvarado by Governor Micheltorena in 1844. Far from having fulfilled the requirement of occupancy, Alvarado had not even seen the place when in 1847 he sold it to Frémont for $3000. Gold was discovered on it in the spring of 1849—so much gold, in fact, that it became known as the "$10 million" grant. The district court ruled the claim invalid on the ground that the

The Chinese almost always considered it useless and unwise to try to defend themselves against any action, even including violence and robbery, directed against them by Americans. This was true even before a peculiar decision of the state supreme court rendered them still more helpless. A state law of 1850 forbade blacks and Indians to testify in court, either "in favor of, or against a white man." In *People v. Hall* in 1854, Chief Justice Hugh C. Murray (who was 29 years old) pronounced the doctrine that the Chinese were legally Indians, because both were probably descended from the same Asiatic ancestors. Thus nonwhites (and whites also) were denied legal protection from any outrage at the hands of a white person if the only witnesses were black, Chinese, or Indian.

In the meantime another legal weapon against the Chinese had been found in the federal law which had provided since 1790 that only "free white persons" could be naturalized. This provision was a deep flaw in the application of American ideals of democracy. In California, the provision was used in a remarkable number of laws as an excuse for other forms of discrimination. This shabby device would continue to be employed for nearly 100 years. Its use would end only when discrimination on the ground of race was finally stricken from the federal naturalization statutes in 1952. In California, state laws directed against "aliens ineligible to citizenship," as a euphemism for aliens of nonwhite ancestry, began to appear in 1855 when the legislature sought to impose a head tax of $50 on all immigrants "who cannot become citizens." This was soon declared unconstitutional because the state could not tax immigration, but another state law of 1855 made ineligibility for citizenship the main definition of those to whom the foreign miners' license tax applied, and thus ensured the enforcement of the tax more specifically against the Chinese.

Fortunately, the Chinese were a people who had developed a remarkable adaptability during many centuries of oppression in China itself. Their sufferings, however, and those of all the other racial minorities, were overshadowed by the disasters that befell the California Indians.

THE "INDIAN QUESTION"

Since the 1820s the federal government had followed a "removal policy" as its general solution of "the Indian problem." A "permanent Indian frontier" had been created along the eastern edge of the Great Plains. By a long series of treaties the Indian nations or tribes of the eastern and central parts of the country had been induced to move west of this line to new lands which the American government promised to reserve for them in perpetuity. But this process had scarcely been completed when in the 1840s the extension of the American boundary to the Pacific made the line obsolete. A new federal policy for the Indians of the west had to be devised.

In 1850 Congress passed an act authorizing three Indian agents, or commissioners, to negotiate a series of treaties with the California tribes. The commissioners were Redick McKee, George W. Barbour, and Dr. Oliver M. Wozencraft. They negotiated 18 treaties affecting 139 tribes or bands. In each of the treaties the natives acknowledged the jurisdiction of the United States, agreed to refrain from

Unratified treaty lands, 1851–1852. (*From* Indians of California: The Changing Image *by James J. Rawls. Copyright 1984 by the University of Oklahoma Press.*)

hostilities, and ceded to the federal government all claims to the territory they had held. In return the commissioners promised the Indians provisions, cattle, and large tracts of land to be set apart for reservations. The proposed reservations totaled 11,700 square miles, or 7,488,000 acres. This was about 7½ percent of the entire land area of the state. Moreover, although Congress had appropriated only $50,000 for the work of the commissioners, they let contracts totaling nearly $1 million for provisions and cattle, on the theory that, as they reported to Washington, "it is *cheaper* to feed the whole flock for a *year* than to fight them for a *week.*"

The federal commissioners overreached themselves, and, unfortunately, their plan failed. Only a small fraction of the California Indians moved even temporarily to the proposed reservations. Opponents of the plan believed it intolerable that vast tracts of rich land within the state should be made the exclusive domain of Indians, and the state legislature recommended that the federal

Biddy Mason (1818–1891), an early Los Angeles philanthropist. "The open hand is blessed," she once said, "for it gives in abundance, even as it receives." (*Courtesy of UCLA Special Collections.*)

for about 1 percent of the state's total population. They remained concentrated in the major cities where they found their employment opportunities routinely restricted by racial discrimination. Many worked in menial occupations in the lowest ranks of the service and food industries; others were able to overcome discrimination and achieve success as independent business entrepreneurs. Biddy Mason was a black woman who arrived in southern California in 1851 as a slave, obtained her freedom 5 years later, became a successful midwife and nurse, invested in Los Angeles real estate, and established herself as a local philanthropist. Unfortunately, Mason's success was exceptional rather than typical of the experiences of California's earliest black residents.

SELECTED BIBLIOGRAPHY

Practitioners of the "new western history" have emphasized the importance of racial and ethnic minorities. See especially Patricia Nelson Limerick, *Legacy of Conquest* (1987); Richard White, *It's Your Misfortune and None of My Own* (1991); Limerick (ed.), *Trails: Toward a New Western History* (1992); and Sucheng Chan, Douglas Henry Daniels, Mario T. Garcia, and Terry P. Wilson (eds.), *Peoples of Color in the American West* (1994). On the changing status of ethnic minorities in California, see R. F. Heizer and A. J. Almquist, *The Other Californians* (1971); Tomás Almaguer, *Racial Fault Lines: The Historical Origins of White Supremacy in California* (1995); and Lisbeth Haas, *Conquests and Historical Identities in California, 1769–1936* (1995).

On Mexican Americans, see the special issue of *California History,* LXXIV (Fall 1995), edited by Richard A. Garcia; Leonard M. Pitt, *The Decline of the Californios* (1966); M. Colette Standart, "The Sonoran Migration to California, 1848–1856," *Southern California Quarterly,* LVIII (Fall 1976), pp. 333–358; and R. H. Morefield, "Mexicans in the California Mines, 1848–53," *California Historical Society Quarterly,* XXXV (1956), pp. 37–46. See also Richard H. Peterson, "Anti-Mexican Nativism in California, 1848–1853" *Southern California Quarterly,* LXII (Winter 1980), pp. 309–328.

Joseph Ellison, *California and the Nation, 1850–1869* (1927); W. W. Robinson, *Land in California* (1948); and William H. Ellison, *A Self-Governing Dominion* (1950), included well-balanced treatments of the Mexican-grant problems. See also Robert H. Becker, *Diseños of California Ranchos* (1964) and *Designs on the Land* (1969). Paul W. Gates, in "The Adjudication of Spanish-Mexican Land Claims in California," *Huntington Library Quarterly,* XXI (May 1958), pp. 213–236, and "California's Embattled Settlers," *California Historical Society Quarterly,* XLI (June 1962), pp. 99–130, concluded that it was the settlers, rather than the grantees, who were most unfairly treated. Many of Gates's articles have been collected in his *Land and Law in California* (1994). The role of Henry Halleck is examined in Beverly E. Bastian, "'I Heartily Regret that I Ever Touched a Title in California,'" *California History,* LXXII (Winter 1993/1994), pp. 310–323.

On the Chinese, see Sucheng Chan, *Asian Californians* (1991) and *Asian Americans* (1991); Gunther Barth, *Bitter Strength* (1964); "The Chinese in California," *California History,* LVII (Spring 1978), special issue; S. C. Miller, *The Unwelcome Immigrant* (1970); A. P. Saxton, *The Indispensable Enemy* (1971); Sandy Lydon, *Chinese Gold* (1985); Rodman W. Paul, "The Origin of the Chinese Issue in California," *Mississippi Valley Historical Review,* XXV (1938), pp. 181–196; and Stanford M. Lyman, *The Asian in the West* (1970).

On the Indians, see James J. Rawls, *Indians of California* (1984) and "Gold Diggers: Indian Miners in the California Gold Rush," *California Historical Quarterly,* LV (Spring 1976), pp. 28–45; Theodora Kroeber, *Ishi in Two Worlds* (1962); Benjamin D. Wilson's report in John W. Caughey (ed.), *The Indians of Southern California in 1852* (1952); Richard Dillon, *Burnt-Out Fires* (1973); Gregory A. Reed, *An Historical Geography Analysis of the Modoc Indian War* (1991); and George H. Phillips, *Chiefs and Challengers* (1975); "Indians in Los Angeles," *Pacific Historical Review,* XLIX (August 1980), pp. 427–452, and *The Enduring Struggle: Indians in California History* (1981). *The Population of the California Indians,*

1769–1970 (1976), by Sherburne F. Cook, deals with the decline in numbers. Two recent works provide additional insight into Indian-white relations in northern California: Albert L. Hurtado, *Indian Survival on the California Frontier* (1988), and Lynwood Carranco andEstle Beard, *Genocide and Vendetta* (1981). The founder of the reservations, Edward Fitzgerald Beale, is the subject of three biographies: Stephen Bonsal (1912), Carl Briggs and Clyde Trudell (1983), and Gerald Thompson (1983). Thompson's account is the most comprehensive. Other recent accounts of the reservation system appear in Ray Raphael, *Little White Father* (1993), and Phillips, *Indians and Indian Agents: The Origins of the Reservation System in California, 1849–1852* (1997). See also Valerie Sherer Mathes, "Indian Philanthropy in California," *Arizona and the West,* XXV (Summer 1983), pp. 153–166; Byron Nelson, *Our Home Forever* (1988); and Todd Benson, "The Consequences of Reservation Life," *Pacific Historical Review,* LX (1991), pp. 221–244.

Rudolph M. Lapp is the author of several important studies of blacks during this period: *Blacks in Gold Rush California* (1977), *Archy Lee* (1969), and *Afro-Americans in California* (1987). Other general accounts include B. Gordon Wheeler, *Black California* (1993); Kenneth G. Goode, *California's Black Pioneers* (1974); and Delilah Beasley, *The Negro Trail Blazers of California* (1919). More specialized treatments appear in William E. Franklin, "The Archy Case," *Pacific Historical Review,* XXXII (1963), pp. 137–154; J. A. Fisher, "The Struggle for Negro Testimony," *Southern California Quarterly,* LI (1969), pp. 313–324; Dolores Hayden, "Biddy Mason's Los Angeles, 1856–1891," *California History,* LXVIII (Fall 1989), pp. 100–115; and Shirley Ann Wilson Moore (ed.), "African Americans in California," ibid., LXXV (Fall 1996), special issue.

CHAPTER TWELVE

Culture and Anarchy

The society of gold-rush California was not the typical society of the older American agrarian frontier. The wealth produced by the gold rush meant that there were many who could afford the good things of life. The demand was primarily for material luxuries, but it included cultural satisfactions as well, for the gold rush had drawn a remarkable number of educated men. Moreover, the great distance from the eastern sources of cultural amenities had a hothouse effect on their local production.

On the other hand, the new culture, being so precocious, was inevitably awkward and crude. The new Californians themselves were predominantly youthful, and overwhelmingly male. Half the forty-niners were between the ages of 20 and 30, and a man of 45 was likely to be described as "the old gentleman." This society made up so largely of young men was peculiarly rough and boisterous.

NEWSPAPERS AND LITERARY MAGAZINES

The most immediate demand of most Americans for the printed word, after, perhaps, their Bibles, was in the form of the newspaper, and the attempt to meet this need had begun soon after the American occupation. The first issue of California's first newspaper, the weekly *Californian,* appeared at Monterey on August 15, 1846, about 5 weeks after Commodore Sloat's landing. To publish it, the naval chaplain Walter Colton went into partnership with the tall frontiersman Robert Semple, whom Colton described as "true with the rifle, ready with his pen and quick at the type case." In a dusty storeroom they found a battered Ramage press, made in Boston many years earlier. Agustín V. Zamorano, a Mexican official, had imported it to Monterey in 1834. "The press was old enough to be preserved as a curiosity," Colton recalled, and "the types were all rusty. . . . It was only by scouring that the letters could be made to show their faces." There was a barrel of ink but no paper, and the early issues came out on sheets intended for cigar wrappings, about

12 inches by 8 inches. Half in English and half in Spanish, the *Californian* appeared each week until May of 1847 when Semple moved it to San Francisco and sold it. Its first rival, established by Sam Brannan, was the weekly *California Star,* which had been appearing regularly at San Francisco since January 9, 1847. It was printed in a loft above a gristmill.

At that stage in the development of California journalism, it was not surprising that 4 months passed between the great gold discovery and the recognition of its importance by the two tiny newspapers, and that Edward C. Kemble, the young editor of the *Star* in 1848, missed one of the greatest news stories of the century and had to spend the rest of his life trying to explain his oversight. After the suspension of the two little San Francisco weeklies during the early months of the gold mania, Kemble became the owner of both of them. The result of this merger was the *Alta California.* First published under that title in January 1849, it became the first California daily a year later, and survived for 41 years more. In many respects it was the most important of all of California's early newspapers.

There were soon literally hundreds of newspapers. Throughout the mining districts almost every boomtown had its paper, some with such names as the *Nevada City Miner's Spy Glass* and the *Downieville Old Oaken Bucket* (though in picturesqueness of title none could match *Satan's Bassoon,* published briefly in San Francisco). Most of the mining-district papers, of course, were ephemeral, partly because of the mobility of their subscribers.

The gold that poured into San Francisco multiplied the wealth of "the city" in many forms. No one made a fortune in journalism in this period, but that was largely because so many tried. In the 10 years after the gold discovery 132 periodicals were started in San Francisco alone, and the total number of their proprietors, editors, and reporters was more than 1000. They were printed in six different languages and represented eight religious denominations and seven political parties. In 1859 there were 12 San Francisco dailies, most notably the *Alta,* the *Herald,* the *Call,* and the *Bulletin.*

Poetry, short stories, and other literary pieces often appeared in the early newspapers, for no other frontier has ever inspired so many of its people to write. The scenes of California, and the experiences of getting there and living there, were so often extraordinary and dramatic that they cried out for description. A literary weekly, the *Golden Era,* flourished from the first day of its publication in 1852 and soon had more subscribers than any other paper on the Pacific coast. Much of its success was due to the enthusiasm of one of its young editors, Rollin M. Daggett, who traveled through the mining districts to sell subscriptions and also wrote many of the sketches describing the miners' lives. Though it paid nothing for poetry and only $5 a column for prose, nearly every writer who achieved any reputation in early American California found in it the opportunity for literary apprenticeship. Bret Harte worked on its staff, first as a typesetter and then as a columnist, and it was in the *Era* that he published his first successful story, "M'liss."

The tone of the *Golden Era* was informal to the point of breeziness, and this gave it a popular appeal that enabled it to outlast a number of competitors, including several that aspired to higher literary levels. One of these was *Hutchings'*

Illustrated California Magazine, published for 5 years beginning in 1856. Its founder, James M. Hutchings, was an Englishman who had worked in the mines before establishing himself as a writer with his *Miner's Ten Commandments* (leading off with "Thou shalt have no other claim than one"). Printed on a single sheet, this new decalogue sold nearly 100,000 copies.

WRITERS OF THE FIFTIES

Of all the early accounts of life in the mining camps of the gold-rush period, the best were the letters written by a remarkably observant young woman, Louise Amelia Knapp Smith Clapp, who signed herself "Dame Shirley." Her husband, Dr. Fayette Clapp, practiced medicine in 1851 and 1852 at Rich Bar and then at Indian Bar on the north fork of the Feather River, and while living with him there she wrote 23 letters to her sister in the east. "I take pains to describe things as I see them," she wrote, "hoping that thus you will obtain an idea of life in the mines *as it is.*" During much of her sojourn she was the only woman in camp, and she invited her sister to imagine spending a winter in a place where there were "no fresh books, no shopping, calling, nor gossiping little tea-drinkings . . . no latest fashions, no daily mail (we have an express once a month), no promenades, no rides or drives; no vegetables but potatoes and onions, no milk, no eggs, no *nothing.*"

The "Shirley letters" were first published in 1854 in *The Pioneer,* a lively but unfortunately short-lived San Francisco literary monthly. This same journal also served to popularize the writings of the first of the far-western humorists, Lieutenant George H. Derby of the U.S. Army topographical engineers, otherwise known as "John Phoenix." Assigned to duty in California, Derby wrote humorous sketches for the *Alta* under his alternate pseudonym of "Squibob" ("a Hebrew word, signifying 'There you go, with your eye out'"). His first really important literary opportunity came when his friend John J. Ames, editor of the weekly *San Diego Herald,* the Democratic organ in the district, left Derby in charge of the paper for several weeks. "John Phoenix" burlesqued everything in the *Herald*'s news and editorial columns, and among other delightful outrages switched its political support to the Whigs. Then he described editorially, and in advance, the fight that might be expected to occur when the powerfully built and vengeful Ames should return to San Diego: "We held [him] down over the press by our nose (which we had inserted between his teeth for that purpose)" and, "while our hair was engaged in holding one of his hands," struck off a fair copy of the *Herald*'s advertisements on the back of his shirt. Actually, Ames appreciated this most famous joke of early California as much as anyone did, and a few years later he edited the first collection of his friend's *Phoenixiana* in book form. Almost as important as Derby's own writings in the history of American humor were the many stories that were told about him, one being that before introducing his bride to his mother he told each that the other was deaf and then let them shout at each other for half an hour.

Alonzo Delano, or "Old Block," also wrote many humorous sketches, collected into a book called *Chips from the Old Block,* which sold nearly 15,000 copies in

California. He was famous for his prodigious nose; in fact he once asked a passing stranger to brush a mosquito from the end of that protuberance, because "You are nearer to it than I am." For eastern readers, on the other hand, he wrote one of the most realistic accounts of the gold rush, *Life on the Plains and among the Diggings.*

It is significant that the best writers of the far west in these years of hazard and hardship were people who had suffered intense personal tragedies in their earlier lives. Shirley was an orphan, Phoenix's father was an eccentric who deserted the family, and Old Block's wife died young, leaving him to care for two invalid children. That Phoenix and Block were humorists may be explained in considerable part by the fact that people often laugh because they are afraid they will cry. Mark Twain would write in his old age that "Everything human is pathetic. The secret source of humor is not joy but sorrow."

Tragedy also haunted the life of John Rollin Ridge, or "Yellow Bird." That he was half Indian might not in itself have made his life too difficult, for his father was a wealthy Cherokee chief. But when John was 12 years old, he witnessed the bloody knife murder of his father by a group of Cherokees who hated him for signing a treaty under which they had given up their lands. A decade later Ridge appeared in gold-rush San Francisco and began to write poems under the name of Yellow Bird, a literal translation of his Indian name.

Ridge's main literary achievement was the creation of California's greatest legend in his book called *The Life and Adventures of Joaquín Murieta, Celebrated California Bandit,* published in 1854. Of the many crimes committed in various parts of the state in the early fifties, some of the most notorious were attributed to five men, all known as "Joaquín." The Joaquíns had five different surnames, one of which was believed to be Murieta. In 1853 the state legislature passed an act authorizing Captain Harry Love, a former Texan, to recruit a band of mounted rangers at state expense for the capture of any or all of the five Joaquíns; Governor Bigler, about to seek reelection, personally offered $1000 reward for any of them. The rangers returned from their forays with a head pickled in a jar of alcohol and collected the reward, although there was no reliable identification, and one of the rangers later boasted in a saloon that one pickled head was as good as another.

Such was the vague and dubious factual background from which John Rollin Ridge constructed his narrative. One of the threads he wove into it was the Robin Hood legend. Another thread was obviously suggested by one of the Shirley letters, describing the whipping of a Mexican by the vigilance committee of Indian Bar and the victim's oath of deadly vengeance against his tormenters. This man now became "Joaquín Murieta," and as Joaquín carried out his oath of revenge, always with his knife, Yellow Bird may have been vicariously avenging himself against the murderers of his father. Through Joaquín's guerrilla attacks upon the *gringos,* Ridge may also have vicariously redressed some of the grievances of his own people.

BRET HARTE

Francis Brett Harte had been sending poems to the papers under the name of "Bret" for several years before he came to California as a boy of 17, in 1854. Legend has exaggerated his subsequent experience and knowledge of the California mining camps, just as his famous stories created a romanticized picture of mining life which came to be accepted as more genuine than the reality.

Having followed a married sister to the town of Union, now Arcata, Harte became the printer's devil and then the junior editor of the town's weekly paper, the *Northern Californian.* In February 1860, a gang of local scoundrels sneaked into the Indian village on Gunther's Island in Humboldt Bay one morning before dawn and perpetrated the most contemptible racist massacre in the history of the state. With hatchets and axes they killed 60 Indians, mostly women and children. Harte bitterly denounced the murders in an article headed "Indiscriminate Massacre of Indians—Women and Children Butchered." Threats against his life soon became so menacing that he left Arcata by steamer for San Francisco, but he had already demonstrated his personal courage beyond question.

In San Francisco, not long after this episode, Jessie Benton Frémont read some of Harte's work in the *Golden Era,* invited him to her home, and introduced him to her literary and political friends. Frémont also used her influence to get Harte a federal patronage appointment as a clerk in the surveyor general's office and then a better position in the branch mint. These jobs allowed him time for writing while assuring him of an income. For several years his poems and stories about California were mostly romantic tales of Spanish colonial days.

The writing that gave Harte an enduring place in the history of literature was done in less than 3 years while he served as the first editor and the most important contributor of *The Overland Monthly,* founded in 1868 in San Francisco. Up to this time Harte had regarded the American period in California with a kind of genteel contempt. In one of his early articles, he had called the 1850s "a hard, ugly, unwashed, vulgar, and lawless era." By 1868, however, Harte was convinced that the time had come to enshrine the gold rush in romantic fiction, and for the early issues of *The Overland* he wrote his best stories. "The Luck of Roaring Camp" is concerned with the death of the camp prostitute in childbirth and the adoption of the baby by the miners. In "The Outcasts of Poker Flat" a gambler and a prostitute sacrifice their own lives in attempts to save their companions, trapped by a snowstorm. In "Tennessee's Partner," after a miner has gone to the dogs and been hanged for robbery, his partner claims the body for burial and soon afterward dies of grief and loneliness.

Harte's most famous poem, usually known as "The Heathen Chinee," though its original title was "Plain Language from Truthful James," appeared in *The Overland* in 1870 and hilariously tells of how a pair of gamblers were outcheated in a card game by the bland and wily Ah Sin. Harte was unhappy when this poem, which he regarded as a trifling little burlesque, became the most widely known of all his writings, and because he detested racial persecution, he was further troubled when the climactic line, "We are ruined by Chinese cheap labor," had the serious side effect of popularizing an anti-Chinese slogan. Unintentionally, he had made a major contribution to the anti-Asian stereotype in America.

Some of Miller's poems were not entirely without literary merit. This is the most that can reasonably be said for them, but they were probably as important as the poetic efforts of any of his contemporaries on the Pacific coast, even though aspiring poets were very numerous. When Bret Harte compiled an anthology of California poetry in 1866, there were so many outraged protests from poets whose work had not been included that he felt compelled to bring out another volume.

Many of the aspirants were women, and the most talented of these was Ina Coolbirth. She had had a miserable early life, which she seldom talked about. Born Josephine Smith, she was the daughter of a younger brother of the Prophet of the Mormon church. Her father died when she was a child, and her mother left the church when the Prophet announced the doctrine of polygamy. Ina suffered through an unhappy early marriage and a deeply distressing divorce in Los Angeles, and came to San Francisco about 1865. Harte engaged her as one of his coeditors of *The Overland Monthly,* and she became a good friend of several of California's male writers, though the thought of remarriage was too painful for her to consider. Her gentle verses were an escape from sadness through pleasure in such things as flowers, birds, and the wind. For more than 20 years she was a librarian in the Oakland public library, and some of the happiest moments of her life began when a ragged boy named Jack London asked her whether she could suggest anything for him to read. She was also a foster mother, in the more literal sense, to Joaquin Miller's daughter Cali-Shasta, and to two nieces.

Quite a different sort of poet was Adah Isaacs Menken, who bared her emotions in her passionate poems as she bared her body on the stage, in flesh colored tights and strapped onto the back of a horse, in a more or less dramatized version of Byron's "Mazeppa."

CHURCHES AND SCHOOLS

The first Protestant congregation in San Francisco was organized in November 1848, when it was necessary to include Methodists, Baptists, Presbyterians, Congregationalists, Episcopalians, and Mormons in a community church in order to pay the salary of one chaplain, Timothy Dwight Hunt. "There was sweet pleasure in our unity in diversity," Hunt recalled, with a twinge of regret that the unity could not endure. As wealth rapidly increased and the city's population gradually became a little more settled, eight major Protestant denominations were soon going their separate ways to heaven. By 1852 San Francisco had at least 30 places of worship, including 22 Protestant, 6 Roman Catholic, and 2 Jewish. Throughout the mining camp towns, earnest evangelists were spreading the gospel, though unfortunately their ministrations were usually least successful with those most obviously in need of redemption.

The Roman Catholic church in California, which had fallen into utter decay during the last years under Mexico, experienced a remarkable development as a result of the gold rush. In 1846 there were only 13 priests in the whole of Alta California, most of them almost starving. By the early fifties there were more than 100, and their work was being very generously supported. In 1852 it became appropriate to appoint the first archbishop of San Francisco, Joseph S. Alemany.

In contrast with the earnest concern for religious education on the part of the churches, the state government failed miserably to make adequate provision for public schools. Not until 1851 did the legislature pass a law authorizing local communities to establish public schools at their own expense, and not until the following year did it provide any state financial support. California's first public high schools, in San Francisco and Sacramento, were not established until 1856. Superintendent of Public Instruction Andrew Jackson Moulder reported that in the 5 years before 1858 California had spent $754,000 on its prisons, and little more than a third of that amount for public education—an expenditure of nearly $2000 for each convict, and $9 for each child. Scarcely more than a fourth of the children of school age were attending public schools, usually for less than 6 months of the year.

The gross dereliction on the part of the state government, reflecting the selfishness and irresponsibility of the majority of its citizens and their elected representatives, afforded a special opportunity for the private efforts of a devoted few. Various private schools and academies came into existence, most of them church-supported, but it is doubtful that any real collegiate instruction began before the sixties. By 1866, largely through the efforts of John Swett as state superintendent, several new laws had been passed expanding educational opportunity. For white children, though not for others, something like a decent public elementary school system was established, but even this existed only in the larger towns. Such was the limited state of educational progress a full 20 years after the American occupation of California.

SELECTED BIBLIOGRAPHY

Any account of the subject of this chapter must be indebted to Franklin Walker's excellent volume, *San Francisco's Literary Frontier* (1939). Also useful are Gerald Haslam (ed.), *Many Californias* (1991); Kevin Starr, *Americans and the California Dream* (1973); and the chapter "Culture and Anarchy on the Pacific Coast," in Louis B. Wright's *Culture on the Moving Frontier* (1955).

The status of California women is suggested in several recent works: Robert L. Griswold, *Family and Divorce in California, 1850–1890* (1982); Bonnie L. Ford, "Women, Marriage, and Divorce in California, 1849–1872," Ph.D. thesis, University of California, Davis (1985); Jacqueline Barnhart, *The Fair but Frail: Prostitutes in San Francisco, 1849–1900* (1986); and Ida Rae Igli (ed.), *No Rooms of Their Own* (1991).

On pioneer journalism, see Barbara Cloud, *The Business of Newspapers on the Western Frontier* (1992). *A History of California Newspapers, 1846–1858*, by Edward C. Kemble, first published in 1858, and edited by Helen Harding Bretnor (1962), is still useful. See also John Bruce, *Gaudy Century* (1948); Emerson Daggett (ed.), *Frontier Journalism* (vol. II, 1939), in the WPA *History of Journalism in San Francisco;* John D. Carter, "The San Francisco *Bulletin,* 1855–1865," Ph.D. thesis, University of California, Berkeley (1941); and William B. Rice, *The Los Angeles Star, 1851–1864* (1947).

The best edition of *The Shirley Letters from the California Mines* is by Carl I. Wheat (1949); see also Rodman W. Paul, "In Search of 'Dame Shirley,'" *Pacific Historical Review,* XXXIII (May 1964), pp. 127–146. George R. Stewart's *John Phoenix, Esq.: The Veritable Squibob* (1937) is an engaging biography, as is James W. Parins's *John Rollin Ridge* (1991).

George R. Stewart, *Bret Harte* (1931), is thorough and critical. See also Richard O'Connor, *Bret Harte* (1966), and Gary Scharnhorst (ed.), *Bret Harte's California* (1990). Materials on Mark Twain's western period include Nigey Lennon, *Mark Twain in California* (1982); Edgar M. Branch, *The Literary Apprenticeship of Mark Twain* (1950); Ivan Benson, *Mark Twain's Western Years* (1938); Henry Nash Smith (ed.), *Mark Twain of the Enterprise* (1957); and Bernard Taper (ed.), *Mark Twain's San Francisco* (1963). Richard A. Dwyer and Richard E. Lingenfelter, *Dan De Quille: The Washoe Giant* (1992) and James J. Rawls (ed.), *Dan De Quille of the Big Bonanza* (1980) include accounts of the rivalry of Mark Twain and De Quille. Martin S. Peterson, *Joaquin Miller* (1937), deals with the poet's life, work, and literary reputation. See also James W. Parins, *John Rollin Ridge* (1991); Hector H. Lee, "The Reverberant Joaquín Murieta in California Legendry," *Pacific Historian,* XXV (Fall 1981), pp. 38–47; and M. M. Marberry, *Splendid Poseur: Joaquin Miller* (1953). *Ina Coolbirth* (1973), by Josephine D. Rhodehamel and Raymund F. Wood, is a biography of California's first poet laureate.

On the churches, see Carl Guarneri and David Alvarez (eds.), *Religion and Society in the American West* (1987), and Sandra S. Frankiel, *California's Spiritual Frontiers* (1989). Other recent works include Laurie F. Maffly-Kipp, *Religion and Society in Frontier California* (1994); Michael Engh, *Frontier Faiths: Church, Temple, and Synagogue in Los Angeles, 1846–1888* (1991); and the multivolume series, *The Religious Contours of California,* edited by Phillip E. Hammond and Ninian Smart. On the schools, see Irving G. Hendrick, *California Education* (1980); John E. Baur, *Growing Up with California: A History of California's Children* (1978); W. W. Ferrier, *Ninety Years of Education in California, 1846–1936* (1937); David F. Ferris, *Judge Marvin and the Founding of the California Public School System* (1962); James E. Myers, "The Educational Work of Andrew Jackson Moulder," Ph.D. thesis, University of California, Berkeley (1961); and Nicholas C. Polos, *John Swett: California's Frontier Schoolmaster* (1978).

CHAPTER THIRTEEN

A Frontier Economy

Early in 1848 California's population other than Indians was less than 15,000. According to the federal census of 1850 it was about 93,000, but this census had a number of notorious defects, the most glaring of which was that all the returns for San Francisco, Contra Costa, and Santa Clara counties were lost. The state took its own census in 1852 and counted 223,856. For 1860 the regular census figure was more than 380,000, and for 1870 more than 560,000. Because the small proportion of women made California's birthrate lower than its death rate, immigration was obviously responsible for the remarkable growth in population. And in these years the search for economic opportunity was by far the most important force in bringing newcomers to California.

Throughout the period between the gold rush of forty-nine and the completion of the transcontinental railroad 20 years later, the mining of precious metals dominated the state's economy. The gold output gradually declined after the peak years of the early 1850s, but the rich silver mines of the Comstock lode in western Nevada began to produce enormous new wealth in 1859, and the development of the Comstock was essentially a California enterprise.

GOLD MINING

"The miners are beginning to discover," said the *Alta California* in the autumn of 1851, "that they are engaged in a science and a profession, and not in a mere adventure." Within a few years the gold in the beds and banks of the streams and in surface outcroppings of quartz was inevitably depleted. Rich deposits of the metal lay far below the surface in solid rock or deep in the gravelly hillsides, but mining them required the use of engineering techniques that demanded heavy equipment and substantial amounts of capital.

In extracting gold from solid rock, through processes variously described as quartz, vein, or lode mining, the auriferous rock taken from a mine shaft or tunnel had to be crushed to a fine powder. After an assortment of ingenious contraptions had proved worthless, better results were obtained with more traditional devices, of which the most important was the stamp mill. Dating at least as far back as the sixteenth century in Europe, this was essentially a large mechanized version of the mortar and pestle.

Another machine important in quartz mining was a mule-powered contrivance developed in Spanish America and called an *arrastre,* usually anglicized as "arrastra." A mule, plodding around a circular track, moved a horizontal shaft extending from a central post that served as a pivot, and heavy abrasive stones attached to the shaft were thus dragged over the gold-bearing material.

It was difficult to grind the ore fine enough, and often less than half the gold actually contained in the crushed rock could be separated from it by quicksilver amalgamation. Part of the loss occurred because some of the gold was encased in metallic sulfides on which the mercury would not act. After about 1860, treatment of the heated mixture by chlorine gas to break down the sulfides increased the yield considerably. Sometimes the pulverized rock, mixed with water, was made to flow over coarse blankets so that fine particles of gold were caught in the cloth. The legend of the golden fleece had probably originated in the application of this method to sheepskin in ancient times.

Another major source of gold lay in the "Tertiary gravels." During the Tertiary geologic era a great river flowed through the region of the northern mines, laying down an immense bed of gravel containing scattered flakes of gold. Later when the whole region was thrust up to become part of the Sierra Nevada, new rivers—the Feather, the Yuba, the Bear, and the American—began to flow transversely through the bed of

Hydraulicking. (*Courtesy of the Bancroft Library.*)

the older one. Much of that bed, however, was now on hilltops and hillsides which had since been gradually covered over with debris. Access to these gravel deposits came with the introduction of hydraulic mining, in which an entire hillside could be washed loose by directing powerful streams of water against it. For this purpose, in 1853, a former sailmaker named Anthony Chabot constructed a canvas hose, and a Connecticut Yankee named Edward E. Matteson invented a tapered nozzle of sheet iron. Thus "hydraulicking" was born. As the placers gave out and the river-mining communities declined, hydraulic towns like Dutch Flat, Iowa Hill, and Gold Run sprang up and flourished.

Part of the financing required by the expensive quartz and hydraulic operations came from joint-stock companies organized by working miners, but for men of small capital the chances for profit steadily declined. Many of those who remained in the industry were employed by increasingly large corporations, which tended to hire Americans as specialists in management and the handling of equipment and machinery, while employing Chinese and Mexicans for less-skilled labor. About 100,000 men were still engaged in gold mining in California in 1861, but by 1873 there were less than 30,000, of whom three-fifths were Chinese.

Whatever techniques might be devised, the supply of gold was not inexhaustible. After hitting a record level of more than $80 million for 1852, the state's gold production decreased year by year until 1865, when it was less than $18 million. At that point it became stabilized, continuing to average about $17 million a year until the turn of the century.

THE BEGINNINGS OF BANKING

Few of the citizens of California in the early American period understood the nature and importance of banks as institutions for the lending and investment of money in business and industrial enterprise. To most Californians, as to most Americans in the years since the disastrous nationwide panic of 1837, "bank" was a hated word, for it seemed to mean primarily a corporation enjoying the special legal privilege of printing and issuing notes that circulated as paper money.

This privilege had, indeed, been much abused in the older states. Most of the paper money in circulation throughout the country had been issued by hundreds of separate banking corporations chartered by special acts of state legislatures. The notes of these so-called state banks were unregulated either by government or by specie reserves, and many people had been swindled by receiving payment in such depreciated paper.

William M. Gwin was one of these, and in the tradition of Jacksonian democracy he had led the crusade against paper money in the California constitutional convention of 1849. The result was a provision similar to those included in nearly every other new state constitution adopted between the panic of 1837 and the Civil War: "The Legislature shall have no power to pass any act granting any charter for banking purposes." In California the presence of gold in great quantities made possible its use as the dominant medium of exchange, and for many decades even large financial transactions in California were likely to be conducted in piles of gold coins, especially the $20 gold pieces known as double eagles.

Thus the state's constitutional ban against the issuance of bank notes as paper money caused relatively little trouble. But in a growing economy the need for savings, lending, and investment institutions was so great that their existence was inevitable. The main effect of the state's provisions against chartering banks was simply to confine the banking business to entirely private concerns, without any particular legal sanction and without any public regulation. In the early mining camps banking arrangements were often very simple; saloonkeepers often doubled as bankers. For many years after the gold rush a great deal of the banking was done as a sideline by firms engaged in other businesses, notably express companies, real estate brokers, and merchandisers of all sorts.

Under the circumstances, the wonder is that banking failures and defalcations were not more frequent than they were. In the early 1850s, flush times and fantastic rates of interest made the lending of money immediately profitable. But a panic began in 1855, touched off by the collapse of the San Francisco branch of a St. Louis express and banking concern. The panic spread quickly, bringing ruin to several other banking agencies. Adams & Company had been weakened by ruthless competition from Wells, Fargo, the western branch of the powerful American Express. When Adams & Company went down in the California panic of 1855, there was such a run on the offices of Wells, Fargo that even this giant of early western finance had to resort to a temporary suspension of payments. Economic revival came slowly, until the great treasure of the Comstock lode brought a new era of financial growth.

THE FIRST COMSTOCK SILVER BOOM, 1859–1864

Between the Washoe and Carson valleys, a little less than 40 miles due east of Donner Pass and about 20 miles east of the California state line, stood a barren-looking mountain known in the 1850s as Sun Peak. Deep in the mountain, later named Mount Davidson, and coming to the surface on its eastern side, lay the world's richest deposits of silver, mixed with lesser deposits of gold. Eventually $400 million worth of the two metals, largely silver, would be taken from this great lode before its permanent decline in the early 1880s, and for a time the city that mushroomed around the entrances to the mine shafts would be larger than any in the far west except San Francisco and Salt Lake City.

Beginning as early as 1850, placers in a canyon at the base of the mountain yielded moderate amounts of gold, but the flakes were hard to separate from a wretched "blue stuff." This the prospectors threw aside, cursing it because it clogged the riffle bars in their gold rockers. First to establish that the blue stuff was silver ore and to discover some of the outcroppings of the lode far up near the head of the canyon were Ethan Allen Grosh and Hoseah Ballou Grosh, sons of a Pennsylvania minister.

In 1857 both of the Grosh brothers died and their secret was temporarily lost. However, a sheepherder and prospector named Henry Tompkins Paige Comstock, known as "Old Pancake" from his chief article of diet, had learned enough from the Groshes to suspect that they had made some great strike. His frantic efforts to locate it for himself were unsuccessful, and in 1859 the lode was discovered anew by the Irish prospectors Patrick McLaughlin and Peter O'Riley. Comstock was in no sense the real discoverer, but by means of bluster and bluff he was able to fool McLaughlin, O'Riley, and the other miners then in the district into believing that he had established some sort of title to the land. Thus, for no better reason than his capacity for bragging and deceit, his name became immortalized in the name of the lode.

Another local prospector was James Fennimore, a drunken teamster who had fled from a murder charge in California and changed his name to Finney and who was known in the Washoe regions as "Old Virginia" from his habit of boasting about the state of his birth. One night, the story goes, he fell and broke a whiskey bottle. Rising unsteadily to his knee, he said, "I baptize this ground Virginia Town." For a time the place was known as Virginia, and later as Virginia City.

The circumstances of the naming of the Comstock lode and of its local metropolis are not inappropriate to the general tenor of their history—a fantastic narrative in which the dissolute, selfish, and dishonest aspects of human nature were all too apparent. These qualities, on the other hand, were alloyed with considerable amounts of ingenuity, courage, and hard work.

Interest continued to center on the gold content of the lode until July 1859, when some ore samples taken over the Sierra to Nevada City were assayed at nearly $3200 a ton in silver, and about half as much in gold. Soon the great rush of fifty-niners from California to Washoe was on, reversing the direction of the rush of forty-nine. To the amazement of the Comstock miners, one of the hardest problems came from the unprecedented size of the veins. Removal of the ore created chambers too vast to be supported by any known method of timbering, and disastrous cave-ins threatened to shut down one of the richest mines until a young German engineer, Philip Deidesheimer, saved the situation by inventing the process of "square sets." These were made of timbers 4 to 6 feet long framed together in a series of interlocked cribs resembling a honeycomb.

The Comstock soon demanded large aggregations of capital for its mines and ore-processing mills, and San Francisco bankers, along with thousands of small investors, rushed to outbid each other for shares in the bonanza. Virginia City saloons provided not only whiskey but great quantities of oysters and champagne, and tickets to see such visiting luminaries as Adah Isaacs Menken were sold for as much as $100.

Several mines paid huge returns for several years, but there were many fraudulent sales of stock in properties with no real access to the lode, and the richer mines became entangled in a maze of litigation. In 1864, when a number of the largest ones had run into *borrascas* and were levying assessments on their stockholders instead of paying dividends, the inflated market for silver stocks collapsed and their total value shrank by more than half. The Comstock had come to the end of its first boom, though it was destined for another and larger one a few years later. (See Chapter 15.)

AGRICULTURE

As in several other parts of the American far west, cattle ranching was second to mining in the economic life of the frontier period. But agriculture in the sense of the cultivation of the soil, as distinct from grazing, was far less important. The California missions had once produced a variety of grains and fruits for local consumption, but after the missions were secularized, these activities had almost disappeared except for a little grape growing for the purpose of making wine or brandy. Cultivation can barely be said to have existed at all in California during the last years under Mexico, and even after the gold rush its advance was slow and sparse. The insecurity of land titles, the lure of quicker wealth in other activities, and the unfamiliarity of such peculiar farming conditions as the rainless summers all served to retard agricultural development. The food supply of the Argonauts was largely imported; the main exception was California beef, salted or driven to the mining camps on the hoof.

In 1846 there had been about 400,000 cattle in Alta California, worth about $4 a head. At the end of 1849 the price reached $500 a head at Sacramento, and for years afterward it was more than $50. Large herds were driven overland from the lower Mississippi valley and the southwest, thus increasing the stock and, to a degree, improving the breeds. In 1860 the number of cattle in the state was more than 3 million, but 2 years of disastrous drought, from 1862 to 1864, nearly wiped out the herds and the industry. The great drought marked the transition from the "age of grass" to an age of grain, and wheat now replaced beef as the state's most important agricultural product.

Fruit and vegetable production in the early American era were significant mainly in confirming some of the extraordinary potentialities of California soils and climate, and thus foreshadowing the tremendous developments of the future. One of the most important pioneers in the dissemination of knowledge in this field was not a farmer, but a Yankee merchant who became the state's leading agricultural publicist and lobbyist. This was James Lloyd LaFayette Warren, who came to Sacramento from Boston in 1849, engaged in general merchandising, and then specialized in seeds, nursery stock, and agricultural implements. He sponsored the exhibitions that grew directly into the California state fair, and in 1854 he secured the establishment of the State Agricultural Society. He also founded the *California Farmer,* the state's first agricultural periodical.

EARLY MANUFACTURES

The needs of the miners for great quantities of lumber made sawmills the foremost branch of manufacturing in the early period of statehood. Wooden sluices and flumes were indispensable in the more advanced states of placer and hydraulic mining, as were heavy timbers in the underground operations of the quartz and silver mines. Moreover, construction in the towns was generally of wood, as was fencing in the rural areas. To meet these demands a raw material of splendid quality and supposedly inexhaustible quantity was available in the redwoods. In 1860 Mendocino County produced 35 million feet of lumber, mostly redwood, and Humboldt and Santa Cruz counties milled 30 and 10 million feet, respectively.

Flour milling grew and flourished along with the increasing production of wheat. The development of mills for the making of coarse woolen cloth was similarly interrelated with the spread of sheep raising, while tanneries and the making of heavy leather goods were encouraged by the plentiful supply of cowhides. Another important infant industry was the making of wagons and carriages, of which the outstanding shops were those of John Studebaker at Placerville and Phineas Banning at Wilmington. Claus Spreckels and William T. Coleman emerged as leaders in the refining of sugar-cane from the Pacific islands. In iron manufactures the leading establishment was the Union Iron Works at San Francisco, founded in 1849 and using imported iron. The absence of any important deposits of either iron or coal in California, shortages of labor and capital, and the lack of a regional population large enough to make an adequate market were among deterrents to the growth of manufacturing in the state.

TRANSPORTATION

Before the railroads came, the movement of freight and passengers by water was considerably easier than their movement by land. Consequently the first major arteries of inland trade and transportation in American California were the routes of the paddlewheel steamers on San Francisco Bay and on the larger rivers of the Central Valley—between San Francisco and the most important commercial towns of the interior, Sacramento, Stockton, and Marysville. After dozens of small compa-nies had entered the business, overcompetition and rate wars led in 1854 to the con-solidation of most of them into the California Steam Navigation Company, which came to enjoy a virtual monopoly of the bay and river traffic. On land, the develop-ment of stagecoach lines soon replaced the "pack mule express," and in 1854 five-sixths of the local stage lines were integrated into the California Stage Company, which could then offer regular service over routes totaling more than 1500 miles.

The Overland California Mail Act, passed by Congress in 1857, provided subsidies in the form of mail contracts and thus made possible the opening of overland stagecoach service between St. Louis and San Francisco in the following year. The postmaster general awarded the contract to the Overland Mail Company, headed by John Butterfield of New York, which was able to establish within 12 months a stage line 2800 miles long, employing nearly 1000 people, and providing 24-day service betweeen San Francisco and the Mississippi River. In the meantime, there had been spectacular but unsuccessful experiments with camel caravans over the southern route to California and with the pony express over the central one. The pony express, though highly colorful, failed to make any substantial profits during its 18 months of operation and came to an end in October 1861 with the opening of the first transcontinental telegraph line.

SELECTED BIBLIOGRAPHY

Doris M. Wright's "The Making of Cosmopolitan California . . . 1848–1870," *California Histor-ical Society Quarterly,* XIX–XX (December 1940 and March 1941), pp. 65–79, 323–343, is a detailed study of the varied components in the growth of population. Georges Sabagh, "A Critical Analysis of California Population Statistics . . . 1850–1870," M.A. thesis, University of California, Berkeley (1943), points out the defects of the census figures. See, however, Dennis E. Harris, "The California Census of 1852: A Note of Caution and Encouragement," *Pacific Historian,* XXVIII (Summer 1984), pp. 58–64.

Gold mining in the 1850s and 1860s is described in Rodman W. Paul, *California Gold* (1947), and John W. Caughey, *The California Gold Rush* (1975). The rise of the hydraulic method is described in Sherwood D. Burgess, *The Water King, Anthony Chabot* (1992) and the first chapter of Robert L. Kelley, *Gold vs. Grain* (1959). See also David J. St. Clair, "New Almaden and California Quicksilver in the Pacific Rim Economy," *California History*, LXXIII (Winter 1994/1995), pp. 278–295. Social and economic change in the post-gold-rush period is the subject of three recent studies: Ralph Mann, *After the Gold Rush: Society in Grass Valley and Nevada City, 1849–1870* (1982); Rodman Paul, "After the Gold Rush, San Francisco and Portland," *Pacific Historical Review*, LI (February 1982), pp. 1–22; and Lary M. Dilsaver, "From Boom to Bust: Post Gold Rush Patterns of Adjustment in a California Mining Region," Ph.D. thesis, Louisiana State University (1982).

Roger Charles Lister, *Bank Behavior, Regulation, and Economic Development: California, 1860–1910* (1993) is an excellent introduction. Ira B. Cross, in *Financing an Empire: History of Banking in California* (4 volumes, 1927) and in "Californians and Hard Money," *California Folklore Quarterly*, IV (July 1945), pp. 270–277, also treats these complex matters with clarity. A special issue of the *Journal of the West*, XXIII (April 1984), edited by Larry Schweikart, is devoted to "Banking in the West." See also Lynne P. Doti and Larry Schweikart, *Banking in the American West* (1992).

The most widely read account of the early years of the Comstock lode was in Mark Twain's *Roughing It*. More serious treatments include George D. Lyman, *The Saga of the Comstock* (1934), and Grant H. Smith, *History of the Comstock Lode* (1943). California and Nevada mining are placed in broader context in Rodman W. Paul, *Mining Frontiers of the Far West, 1848–1880* (1963); Richard H. Peterson, *The Bonanza Kings* (1977) and *Bonanza Rich* (1991); and Mark Wyman, *Hard-Rock Epic* (1979).

On cattle ranching, see Robert G. Cleland, *The Cattle on a Thousand Hills* (1941); John W. Caughey, "Don Benito Wilson," *Huntington Library Quarterly*, II (April 1939), pp. 285–300; and James M. Jensen, "Cattle Drives from the Ranchos to the Gold Fields of California," *Arizona and the West*, II (Winter 1960), pp. 341–352. On the development of California agriculture, see Lawrence J. Jelinek, *Harvest Empire* (1979); Frank Adams, "The Historical Background," in *California Agriculture* (1946), edited by Claude B. Hutchison; Walton Bean, "James Warren and the Beginnings of Agricultural Institutions in California," *Pacific Historical Review*, XIII (December 1944), pp. 361–375; Paul W. Gates, *California Ranchos and Farms, 1846–1862* (1947); and Gerald L. Prescott, "Farm Gentry vs. the Grangers: Conflict in Rural America," *California Historical Quarterly*, LVI (Winter 1977/78), pp. 328–345. Especially useful is Richard J. Orsi (compiler), *A List of References for the History of Agriculture in California* (1974).

The economic material in the *History of California*, volume VII, 1860–1890, by Frances Fuller Victor and William Nemos (*Bancroft's Works*, volume XXIV, 1890), is fairly comprehensive, though undigested. A valuable study of lumbering is H. Brett Melendy, "One Hundred Years of the Redwood Lumber Industry, 1850–1950," Ph.D. thesis, Stanford University (1952).

On transportation within the state, see Jerry MacMullen, *Paddlewheel Days in California* (1944), and Oscar O. Winther, *Express and Stagecoach Days in California* (1936). On the overland operations, see LeRoy R. Hafen, *The Overland Mail, 1849–1869* (1926); Roscoe P. Conkling and Margaret B. Conkling, *The Butterfield Overland Mail, 1857–1869* (3 volumes, 1948); Edward Hungerford, *Wells, Fargo* (1949); J. V. Frederick, *Ben Holladay, the Stagecoach King* (1940); W. Turrentine Jackson, *Wagon Roads West* (1952) and "Wells, Fargo Staging over the Sierra," *California Historical Society Quarterly*, XLIX (June 1970), pp. 99–134; Harlan D. Fowler, *Camels to California* (1950); and Raymond W. Settle and Mary Settle, *Saddle and Spurs: The Pony Express Saga* (1955).

CHAPTER FOURTEEN

Building the Central Pacific Railroad

For 20 years after the gold rush, Americans in California felt extremely remote from the people of the older states, as indeed they were. For many, the dream of a transcontinental railroad symbolized all sorts of hopes for better things.

In the older parts of the country, talk of a transcontinental railroad had begun at least as early as 1832. The first proposal to receive a serious hearing before Congress came in 1845 from Asa Whitney, a New York merchant who had made a large fortune in trade with China and who saw a Pacific railroad as a great new artery of American and European trade with the orient.

Throughout the 1850s, with the intensification of sectional bitterness, southerners feared that a northern or central railroad would develop new free states, and argued that a southern route, which did not have to cross the great barriers of the Rockies and the Sierra Nevada, could be built much more economically and quickly. Northerners, on the other hand, were adamant against a railroad that would aid the expansion of slaveholding. Congress could agree only on a provision for surveys of all the possible routes. These surveys, published in 1855 in 13 fat volumes of *Pacific Railroad Reports,* concluded only that five different transcontinental routes were feasible.

JUDAH AND THE CONCEPTION OF THE CENTRAL PACIFIC

Credit for the specific plan that led to the building of the first transcontinental railroad belongs mainly to Theodore D. Judah, a brilliant young construction engineer. Judah in his twenties had established a reputation as an engineering genius through such feats as the building of the Niagara Gorge Railroad in New York. In 1854, when he was 28, the promoters of the Sacramento Valley Railroad brought him to California to build their line from Sacramento to Folsom, the first railroad on the Pacific coast.

Judah soon became so fanatically devoted to the idea of a central route for the first transcontinental railroad that a number of his listeners questioned his sanity on the subject, particularly those who had had the experience of crossing the Sierra Nevada. But the idea, with its promise of an end to California's isolation, became increasingly popular, and in 1859 the state legislature approved a Pacific Railroad Convention to drum up interest in the railroad project. When this body met in San Francisco, it delegated Judah to carry its views to Washington, D.C.; however, although he lobbied skillfully and impressively, the sectional deadlock still prevented action.

In 1860 Judah made an intensive search for the best crossing of the Sierra. Daniel W. Strong, a druggist in the prosperous hydraulic-mining town of Dutch Flat, pointed out that Dutch Flat was located on a natural ramp, a long and unbroken ridge extending upward toward Emigrant Gap and Donner Pass. Judah observed that because the slope of this ridge was so gradual and continuous, it would be possible for a railroad to reach the summit elevation of about 7000 feet in a distance of little more than 70 miles from the valley floor with a maximum grade of only 105 feet to a mile. Tremendously excited by this discovery, Judah sat at the counter of Strong's drugstore and drew up tentative articles of association for the Central Pacific Railroad of California.

Judah, Strong, and a number of citizens of Dutch Flat and the neighboring towns were able to muster about a third of the money that would have to be paid down in order to form a corporation. Full of confidence, Judah hurried to San Francisco to secure the remainder, but to his disappointment and disgust not one of the large capitalists in the city would invest in the project. Until Congress acted, they said, construction of the railroad could not begin, and they estimated that after its beginning, 12 to 20 years would pass before its completion. Their money was bringing large and immediate returns in far safer enterprises.

ENTER THE FOUR "ASSOCIATES"

In his appeals to the San Francisco financiers, Judah had made the tactical error of including an appeal to their public spirit and long-range vision. He turned next to the merchants of Sacramento, and with them he made no such blunder. Instead he planned his arguments in order to put all the emphasis on the possibilities of large and early returns on very modest initial investments: with a concrete proposal before it, Congress would offer cash subsidies that would pay for the construction; operating income need not wait for completion of the transcontinental line, or even of the line within California; the profitable freighting business between Sacramento and the Comstock could very soon be captured for the Dutch Flat route, simply by building a good wagon road over Donner Pass to the head of construction of the Central Pacific as it advanced into the mountains.

One evening in the autumn of 1860, in a room over the hardware store of Huntington & Hopkins in Sacramento, a group of merchants assembled to hear Judah's plea. Among those present were Collis P. Huntington, Leland Stanford, Charles Crocker, and Mark Hopkins. Because these men were destined to be the "Big Four," the "railroad kings," of California and of most of the American far west, and thus to acquire not only fantastic wealth but also enormous economic and political power, their backgrounds are of considerable interest.

Mark Hopkins, Collis P. Huntington, Theodore Judah, Leland Stanford, Charles Crocker. (*Courtesy of the Bancroft Library.*)

All of them had come from middle- or lower-middle-class families, and though all were prosperous by 1860, none, as yet, was rich. Collis P. Huntington, the son of a miserly tinker in a small town in Connecticut, had become self-supporting at the age of 14 and a successful traveling salesman a year later. At 21 he was operating his own store at Oneonta, New York. In 1849, with a capital of $1200, he joined the gold rush. Buying and selling food and other supplies while waiting for steamer connections in Panama, he tripled his capital. In California, one day's work in the mines convinced him that mining was not his occupation, and instead he opened a store in Sacramento. Leland Stanford, son of an innkeeper in rural New York, had studied law in an office in Albany and practiced in Wisconsin before also the Central Pacific's chief legal counsel, and he did not resign from that position while he was serving as a supreme court justice.

DIFFICULTIES, AND THE DEATH OF JUDAH

Actual construction of the railroad began on January 8, 1863, after Governor (and railroad president) Stanford had thrown the first shovelful of earth in the presence of a crowd assembled near the levee at the foot of K Street in Sacramento. But in spite of the support already promised by the federal government, a tangle of problems held back the early progress of construction and threatened the very life of the project. Costs were heavy. Iron rails and locomotives had to be bought in the east at wartime prices and transported to Sacramento by sea at wartime freight rates. Cash was short, for each 40-mile unit of construction had to be completed before the federal subsidy on it was forthcoming, and interests hostile to the railroad did everything they could to discourage private investors from lending it money. The Pacific Mail Steamship Company, the California Steam Navigation Company, Wells, Fargo & Company, the California Stage Company, and the Sacramento Valley Railroad, as well as all the California bankers who had money invested in one or more of these enterprises, naturally anticipated that the building of the Central Pacific would injure them, and they joined in denouncing it. A pamphlet called *The Great Dutch Flat Swindle* charged that the promoters were not genuinely interested in a transcontinental railroad at all, but merely in the profits of a wagon road to Washoe and in the collection of subsidies.

The Central Pacific's own chief engineer had reason to know that these charges were not entirely unfounded as they applied to the motives of the "associates" at this time. Feeling that his own personal honor was involved, Judah was now bitterly at odds with the four men who were in control. The differences were those between a man primarily interested in the construction of a great railroad and four men primarily concerned with making enormous profits. When these four awarded the construction contracts to Charles Crocker and Company, a dummy concern owned by themselves, Judah protested as strongly as he could. At last he broke with them completely. In October 1863 he sailed for New York, having accepted $100,000 for his interest in the Central Pacific, but taking with him options to buy out Huntington, Stanford, Crocker, and Hopkins for $100,000 each if he could persuade the Vanderbilts or other eastern capitalists to back him.

At this point the Sacramento four were discouraged and willing, as Charles Crocker put it, to "take a clean shirt and get out," but Judah contracted yellow fever in Panama and died on November 2, shortly after his arrival in New York. His death was a major tragedy. If he had lived and if his hopes for a reorganization of the Central Pacific under his own leadership had been fulfilled, the history of California might have been very different.

In order to begin collecting the larger subsidies for building in the Sierra Nevada, the Big Four maintained that the "western base" of the mountains was located only 7 miles east of Sacramento. On the plea that without the higher initial subsidies the whole project might have to be abandoned—and with the aid of some ingenious testimony by the California state geologist and the state surveyor general—the federal government was persuaded to accept this remarkable claim, and the base of the Sierra Nevada was thus moved a considerable distance westward into the Sacramento Valley. The Big Four were now men who could move mountains. They felt no gratitude toward Judah and did not even name a crossroads station in his honor. When at last something like a suitable monument to Judah was erected at Sacramento in 1930, the initiative came not from the railroad's management but from the American Society of Civil Engineers.

SOLVING THE PROBLEMS OF CONSTRUCTION

By 1865 the initial shortage of cash had been overcome. Federal, state, and county subsidies had built up the Central Pacific's treasury, and freight and passenger revenues began to come in with the completion of the early sections of track. Moreover, the money paid out for construction was being paid to Charles Crocker and Company on terms that assured very generous profits to that company's backers, the Big Four. At the outset Crocker knew nothing whatever about the building of a railroad, but in view of the remarkable profits to be gained from that activity, under contracts made without the inconvenience of competitive bidding, he was more than willing to learn.

A shortage of labor now replaced the shortage of cash as the most chronic problem holding back the rate of construction. California white workers demanded high wages, and many of them accepted jobs only in order to get a free ride for part

Chinese workers replacing a trestle with earth fill. (*Courtesy of the Bancroft Library.*)

are sympathetic biographies. *Collis Potter Huntington* (2 volumes, 1954), by Cerinda W. Evans, is extremely, earnestly, and naïvely apologistic. The recent availability of *The Collis P. Huntington Papers, 1856–1901* (1978) on microfilm is likely to stimulate additional research. See also "Railroads in California and the Far West," a special issue of *California History,* LXX (Spring 1991), edited by Richard J. Orsi. (Additional sources are listed in the bibliography for Chapter 19.)

CHAPTER FIFTEEN

The "Terrible Seventies"

By a cruel paradox, the completion of the first transcontinental railroad not only failed to bring California the expected surge of prosperity, but also marked the beginning of a deep and general depression that continued through the whole of the next decade. A frustrated and embittered populace blamed its disappointments and sufferings on the railroad and on the Chinese. Thus the difficulties of a long period of economic distress were aggravated by racial antagonism and political upheaval.

THE ONSET OF DEPRESSION

One of the many unexpected and unfavorable effects that the completion of the Pacific railroad had on the economy of California was that it suddenly exposed its merchants and manufacturers to intense competition from those of the eastern cities. Until 1869 the bulk of the commerce of California and of most other parts of the far west had come by water to San Francisco. Now the San Francisco merchants, already overstocked in anticipation of new demand, instead found the market glutted with new goods shipped in by rail. As for the hope that the goods exchanged between Europe and the orient would be transshipped by rail across North America and thus help to enrich California's great seaport, most of that trade now passed instead through the Suez Canal, opened in the same year as the Pacific railroad. Nor did land values rise as expected. California speculators had so overinflated the prices of land in anticipation of a boom that the actual completion of the Central Pacific caused a reaction and a decline in real estate values, rather than an advance.

After many years of labor shortage there was now an oversupply and chronic unemployment. In 1868 various labor organizations had been strong enough to secure the passage of a state law providing for an 8-hour day in public works contracts, and unions had been able to persuade many private employers to agree to the same policy. In order to roll back this advance on the part of labor, certain employers in San Francisco carried on a nationwide propaganda campaign designed to bring as many new workers as possible to California and thus to weaken labor's bargaining power. At the same time, Chinese immigration increased sharply, encouraged by the Burlingame Treaty of 1868, and the completion of the railroad released about 12,000 Chinese construction workers, nearly all of whom drifted back to crowd the California labor market.

When the panic of 1873 struck the national economy as a whole, it intensified the depression that had begun in California 4 years earlier.

TRANSPORTATION MONOPOLY

When the first transcontinental railroad was opened, the Big Four did not believe that freight and passenger revenues would ever provide the large and guaranteed profits that they had received from construction subsidies. Thus they made efforts to retire from railroading with the fortunes they had already accumulated, but for several reasons they did not carry out their plans. The original reason was that they could find no buyer on terms they regarded as favorable, but there were other and more positive factors, which reconciled them to continuing in the railroad business. There were more land grants to be had, from further construction within California and from a new transcontinental line to be built on the southern route. Even more important, there was the prospect of being able to control rates and ensure profits by establishing throughout most of the far west a monopoly—of unprecedented degree and scope—over transportation, the life's blood of the regional economy.

To ensure its control over the main seaport area, the Central Pacific put together a network of local rail lines around San Francisco Bay and also gained virtually complete domination of the bay's strategic waterfronts.

In 1852 the ownership of all the waterfront and tidelands of Oakland had been granted to that infant community by the state. Oakland, in turn, had promptly granted the whole of these lands to one of its leading citizens, Horace W. Carpentier, in return for his promise to build three wharves and a schoolhouse. In 1868 Carpentier offered the railroad a controlling interest in the waterfront if it would make Oakland its main terminus on the east side of the bay. Ownership of the lands then passed to the Oakland Waterfront Company, a new corporation in which Carpentier and Leland Stanford were the main stockholders. Not until the early twentieth century would the monopoly of Oakland's waterfront be broken.

San Francisco, though it put up a bitter fight, was hardly more successful in escaping from decades of railroad domination. Most of its tidelands had remained under state ownership. In 1868, at the suggestion of ex-Governor Stanford, a state senate committee recommended that several miles of the San Francisco waterfront, including all of it that was suitable for railroad terminal facilities, be sold at nominal prices to corporations controlled by the Big Four. The *Bulletin* led other newspapers in denouncing this proposal as a breathtaking outrage, and the railroad had to be content with a mere 60 acres. But this was enough for a terminal; the Central Pacific had other means of assuring that no competing railroad would

Transportation monopoly. The principal routes of the Southern Pacific Railroad in California, 1884.

approach San Francisco for a long time to come, and it had already established political control of the state board of harbor commissioners.

While they were completing their stranglehold on the bay, the Big Four were also making plans to capture the rest of California. They bought out the promoters of the California and Oregon Railroad and began construction of the "Shasta route," extending up the Sacramento Valley and eventually to Portland. A line to run southward from the San Francisco Bay region through the coastal counties to Los Angeles and San Diego had been proposed in 1865 as the announced purpose of a Southern Pacific Railroad Company incorporated by a group of San Francisco capitalists. The Big Four acquired control of the Southern Pacific in the late sixties. In the meantime, in 1866, Congress had provided for the first southern transcontinental railroad and authorized the Southern Pacific to build its western link. Thus by gaining control of the original Southern Pacific, the chief owners of the Central Pacific not only gained control of southern California but also guaranteed themselves a long period of freedom from competition with another transcontinental route.

In 1870 the Big Four were ready to begin construction of the line to southern California—the contracts, of course, being awarded to the Contract and Finance Company. They had already decided not to build along the coast, but rather through the San Joaquin Valley, because the usable lands in the coastal counties were under private ownership, whereas the San Joaquin Valley was still largely government land where the railroad could locate its grants along its right-of-way.

In its dealings with cities and towns the railroad was equally ruthless in putting its own interests ahead of the public's. Los Angeles, though it had only about 6000 people, was the largest town in southern California and already had rail connections with the coast at San Pedro and Santa Monica. Crocker threatened to ruin Los Angeles by leaving it off the main line unless it would make the Southern Pacific a present of the Los Angeles and San Pedro Railroad, and pay a further subsidy of $600,000. In an effort to make San Bernardino an example of what could happen to towns that resisted this kind of extortion, the Southern Pacific built its division point a few miles away, thus creating the new town of Colton. For similar reasons the Central Pacific had created the "spite towns" of Lathrop, near Stockton, and Goshen, near Visalia.

By 1882 the Southern Pacific had gained full domination of the southern transcontinental line; its "Sunset Route" extended all the way from southern California to New Orleans. For many years the Big Four sought to maintain the fiction that the Central Pacific, the Southern Pacific, and a number of other lines were under separate control, but the newspapers and the public became well aware that "the railroad" was a single entity. They began to call it "the Octopus" and to think of its tracks as tentacles reaching from Oregon to Louisiana. Officially, the name Southern Pacific emerged as the name of the whole system in 1884, when the Southern Pacific Company of Kentucky was incorporated and took a lease on all property of the Central Pacific. (The name persisted until the late 1990s when the Southern Pacific was bought by the rival Union Pacific.) Kentucky was chosen for the legal corporate headquarters of the system, not because the Big Four had plans for operating there, but simply because the railroad incorporation laws of that state were among the laxest in the Union.

Monopoly of California rails would not have provided so effective a monopoly of transportation if there had been extensive competition by water. But in 1869 the Big Four bought the California Steam Navigation Company, and with it the control

The Curse of California. A cartoon from a San Francisco weekly magazine, *The Wasp,* Aug. 19, 1882. (*Courtesy of the Bancroft Library.*)

of the bulk of the river traffic. As for ocean commerce, they first made a series of rate-fixing agreements with the Pacific Mail Steamship Company and then, in 1874, organized their own steamship line, the Occidental and Oriental. By 1880 they had so weakened the formerly dominant Pacific Mail that they were able to control it also.

In no other region of the United States did a railroad enjoy such a degree of freedom from competition. Thus entrenched, the Big Four were free to adopt a system of setting freight rates according to the highest charge that the traffic would bear without completely bankrupting the shipper and thus depriving the railroad of his future business. The railroad could also favor one shipper and ruin another by quoting different rates for the same service. Often its agents would demand to examine the shipper's books and then set the rate according to what they thought the shipper could afford to pay. No railroad system in the world had a greater variety of rates—some high, some low, some published, some secret.

The railroad's power to make or break almost anyone engaged in agriculture, mining, manufacturing, or commerce, through its discriminatory freight rates, was effectively used in interrelation with the development of its control over politics.

Through its rates it could reward its friends and punish its enemies. If politicians did not have economic interests of their own which could be favored or ruined by rate manipulation, their constituents did. The railroad also corrupted politics in a variety of ways and at all levels of government: federal, state, and local. Money was paid to politicians under an assortment of disguises. An officeholder or candidate who was a lawyer might receive a secret fee or salary for unspecified "legal services." For others, there were contributions for "campaign expenses." The Southern Pacific developed a political machine far more powerful than any other in the state. California's government, as well as its economy, became a prisoner of "the railroad."

LAND MONOPOLY

Further public resentment against the railroad grew out of the fact that it had become by far the largest private landowner in the state. Railroads that became parts of the Southern Pacific system received from the federal government a total of 11,588,000 acres in California, about 11½ percent of the entire land area of the state. These railroad land grants, added to various other factors, made the ownership of California's arable land more concentrated than in any other part of the nation. "Land monopoly" was a burning issue.

The general policy of the federal government, under such laws as the Homestead Act of 1862, encouraged the ownership of land in small farm units. But in California the operation of that policy was almost entirely thwarted. According to the theory pronounced in 1893 by Frederick Jackson Turner, "the existence of an area of free land, its continuous recession, and the advance of American settlement westward, explain American development." This "Turner hypothesis" was an oversimplification even as applied to the upper Mississippi valley, the region Turner knew best. As applied to the development of California, the Turner theory of the significance of the frontier is worthless.

If public land in California was fertile or located where transportation facilities would make it possible to market its produce, such land was usually engrossed by speculators before a genuine homesteader had a chance to file on it. The government's retention of alternate sections within the limits of railroad land grants often failed to help the early settler, for by the time they were surveyed and opened the settler typically found himself outbid by a speculator. Government surveyors, private surveyors working under government contracts, and officials of the federal and state land offices acquired advance knowledge of the lands and used this knowledge for speculation on their own behalf or in collusion with others. Many of the most successful California land brokers were also surveying contractors, and thus laid the foundations of their prosperous careers.

The federal government granted more than 8 million acres of land to the state— 2 million acres as "swamp and overflow" land under an act of 1850 and more than 6 million acres for educational purposes. The state's disposition of these lands was careless, improvident, and in many cases riddled with fraud. Lands in California that had the appearance of swamps in the rainy season might actually be among the

Miller & Lux holdings in the north San Joaquin Valley. (*From* Garden of the Sun *by Wallace Smith. Copyright 1939 by Lymanhouse, Los Angeles. Courtesy of the Bancroft Library.*)

richest lands, but they were sold, mostly to large operators, at $1.25 per acre, which was refunded to the purchasers if they swore that they had spent a like amount in reclamation.

The possibilities for building up huge landholdings were spectacularly illustrated in the story of Henry Miller, who became the state's leading cattle baron. Born Heinrich Alfred Kreiser, he had arrived in New York from Germany at 19, in 1847, with no resources except his boyhood training in the care of livestock and the cutting of meat. In 1849, with the savings from his wages as a butcher's helper, he bought a ticket to California. From operating a butcher shop in San Francisco, Miller quickly branched out, buying cattle and then buying lands for pasturage. In the San Joaquin Valley, for example, he was so skillful in acquiring swamp and overflow lands that eventually he owned both banks of the San Joaquin River in a solid strip more than 100 miles long, from the area west of Modesto to the region of Madera. Through water monopoly he was able to control much of the land surrounding his own. He formed an effective partnership with Charles Lux, a tall Alsatian who was somewhat more polished than Miller and who often represented the firm's interests in San Francisco while Miller was looking after its ranches in the interior. Ultimately Miller & Lux owned more than a million acres, and Miller liked to boast that he could ride from Mexico to Oregon and sleep every night in a ranch house of his own.

The engrossment of arable land in advance of agricultural settlement and development was a chronic problem in California, and would long have remained so, even if it had not been increased and complicated by the railroad land grants. In general, the question of the wisdom and necessity of granting public lands to railroads in the American west has remained highly debatable. The legal purpose of the grants was to aid the construction of the lines, but the railroads derived their returns from them after the lines were built—often many years afterward. In California, in particular, the grants clearly proved to have been an unwise and unsound policy. They added greatly to the wealth and power of the owners of the Southern Pacific at a time when their wealth and power had already become far too great for the public good.

The expansion of the railroad network in the 1870s did have the desirable effect of encouraging the spread of agricultural settlement in the great Central Valley, but it also created a special set of land-tenure problems. Some of these may be seen in poignantly human terms in the tragic experiences of the settlers of the district of Mussel Slough, near Hanford in what is now Kings County.

The Southern Pacific had published a number of pamphlets inviting settlers to occupy lands within the limits of its grant in the southern counties of the San Joaquin Valley. The railroad had not yet acquired full legal ownership of these lands from the federal government, but its pamphlets promised that as soon as it did so, the settlers would be assured the right to buy the land they had occupied. Prices were predicted in vague and misleading terms, such as "from $2.50 upward" per acre; however, it was very clearly stated that the prices would not include the value of the settler's improvements. Mussel Slough, which carried part of the waters of the Kings River into Tulare Lake, offered possibilities for irrigation, and between 1872 and 1875 the settlers pooled their labor and constructed an elaborate system of irrigation works.

Congress repeatedly failed to appropriate enough money for the effective administration of the land offices, and this delayed the sale of the lands for many years. In 1878, after the railroad had at last acquired the titles, it addressed letters to all settlers informing them of the price of the land they occupied and that it was now for sale "to anyone." These prices ranged from $17 to $40 per acre, and the settlers charged that they included the value of their improvements, in violation of the railroad's published promises. But the federal courts upheld the railroad's contention that it was violating no specific legal contract.

Walter J. Crow and Mills D. Hart now purchased occupied lands from the Southern Pacific at about $25 per acre. The settlers charged that Crow and Hart, whom they denounced as "Buzzard and Gizzard," were dummy purchasers hired by the railroad, although this assumption was based only on the fact that they were willing to pay the railroad's price for the land. On the morning of May 11, 1880, United States Marshal Alonzo W. Poole, acting under federal court orders from San Francisco, drove out in a buggy with Crow and Hart to put them in possession of the lands they had purchased and to evict the occupants. When a group of more than 20 settlers appeared, mounted and armed, the result was the "battle of Mussel Slough," at a point about 5 miles northwest of Hanford. It is impossible to determine who fired first but seven men were killed, including Crow and Hart. Later five of the settlers were convicted of resisting a federal officer and served 8-month jail sentences. Because much of the public believed that the railroad had cruelly deceived and robbed the settlers, the prisoners were widely regarded as heroes rather than convicts. More than any other single development, the tragedy at Mussel Slough dramatized the intense popular resentment against large landholders in general and the railroad in particular.

THE COMSTOCK AND OVERSPECULATION

During the 1870s the mining industry proved to be as great a disappointment as the railroad. In this period the Comstock lode experienced its greatest boom. It produced about three times as much silver as in the previous decade, because of the unparalleled richness of the ore at the deeper levels. Yet the effect on California was not to relieve the depressed conditions of the 1870s but to make them worse. The capital of the region, badly needed in other fields, became concentrated in the speculative market for Nevada mining stocks, and the gyrations of these stocks on the San Francisco exchange infected the public with a gambling mania that became one of the most unhappy characteristics of the times. The new bonanza created enormous fortunes for a few men who controlled the richest mines and thus had inside knowledge to use in manipulating the stock market—but by this process they impoverished thousands of other investors.

The first group to attain a degree of power that justified the title of "kings of the Comstock" were certain officials of the Bank of California, who became known as the "bank ring" or "Ralston's ring." A state law of 1862 had permitted the incorporation of banks, and under this law William Chapman Ralston had organized the Bank of California in San Francisco in 1864, just as the first Comstock boom was ending. Most of the mines were in *borrasca,* and several of them were flooded. Many of the owners were in financial difficulties, and William Sharon, whom Ralston had chosen as the bank's agent in Virginia City, tempted them into heavy borrowing. Then, after a series of foreclosures, the bank came into control of a major portion of the mines and mills. These were consolidated under Sharon's management, and new machinery was installed; deeper deposits of rich ore were discovered, and millions of dollars began to pour into the vaults of the bank and the personal accounts of its officials.

With so much of the Comstock's silver behind it, the Bank of California now became and remained for several years the most highly regarded financial institution in the far west, and William Chapman Ralston was generally recognized as the leading citizen of San Francisco. Toward that city, in his own mind, his relationship became that of Lorenzo de Medici to Florence. He sponsored and controlled a panoply of enterprises—carriage, watch, and furniture factories, woolen mills, foundries, and sugar refineries, a theater, and urban and rural real estate. In his villa at Belmont he provided lavish hospitality for every famous personage who came to San Francisco. For the distinguished tourist in California an invitation to Belmont became more essential than a trip to Yosemite. When Ambassador Anson Burlingame passed through on his way to China, Ralston named a townsite after him and sold him one of its attractive lots for a future home.

It is interesting to compare the occasion when Ralston had the opportunity to have a town named after himself. The directors of the Central Pacific, in the process of creating a new community on their line in the northern San Joaquin Valley, offered to name it Ralston, partly in gratitude for a loan he had once made to Stanford. Ralston politely declined the honor—but the railroad directors insisted on bestowing it upon him less directly. They named the town Modesto. The idea that modesty was actually one of Ralston's prominent traits can only be regarded, as the directors regarded it, with some hilarity. They were well aware that it was San Francisco, and not a raw new village, which he wished to be considered as his monument.

About the time of the organization of the Bank of California, a self-trained mining engineer named Adolph Sutro conceived a brilliant and daring plan for a revolutionary method of mining the Comstock lode. Sutro proposed digging a tunnel 4 miles long into the heart of Mount Davidson to strike the center of the lode at a depth of about 1650 feet, directly under Virginia City. This was a magnificent plan, but Ralston and Sharon opposed it. If the mines became dependent on the use of his tunnel, then Sutro, not Ralston and Sharon, would rule the Comstock. Other capitalists, following the lead of the mighty Bank of California, refused to invest in the tunnel or to lend money to its promoter.

Not even a beginning was made in the actual construction of the Sutro tunnel until the autumn of 1869. In the meantime the supremacy of Ralston and Sharon was being challenged from another quarter, by the rising fortunes of a group of four Irishmen who would eventually be the wealthiest of the Comstock's kings. John W. Mackay, James G. Fair, James C. Flood, and William S. O'Brien had all been sons of poor Irish immigrants. Mackay and Fair were experts on the mines; Flood and O'Brien knew the San Francisco stock market. With inside information, shrewd guesses, and good luck, their fortunes increased steadily. In 1873 they struck the big bonanza, the very "heart of the Comstock," underlying a group of neglected mines which they had bought up and merged under the name of the Consolidated Virginia.

Ralston, whose preeminence was thus threatened, had been overextending himself in imaginative but unsound investments, such as silk mills and a large tobacco plantation near Gilroy. In 1872 he began construction of the Palace Hotel in San Francisco. With its tier-on-tier balconies around a central garden court, it required 3 years to complete and cost nearly $7 million. The Palace was a larger luxury hotel than the city could then support, and for many years most of its hundreds of rooms were usually unoccupied.

In the attempt to replenish his wealth, dangerously depleted by such prodigal ventures, Ralston resorted to a desperate gamble. Believing that the Consolidated Virginia's big bonanza must extend into the property of the neighboring Ophir mine, he set out to gain control of the Ophir by buying up a majority of its stock. This drove prices on the San Francisco exchange to ridiculous and unprecedented heights. Elias Jackson Baldwin, then the Ophir's largest stockholder, sold out to Ralston at the very peak, and was known ever after as "Lucky" Baldwin. In January 1875, information that the great bonanza did not actually extend to the Ophir led to the collapse of its stock.

On August 26, 1875, a run on the Bank of California forced Ralston to close the bank's doors. Next morning the directors asked for and received his resignation; then he went for his accustomed swim in the waters of the bay, from which his body was recovered a few hours later. Whether he died by accident or suicide is unknown.

Gripped with panic, depositors descend upon the Bank of California to make withdrawals in August 1875. (*Courtesy of the Bancroft Library.*)

The "Irish four" made Ralston's calamity their own opportunity. Mackay, Fair, Flood, and O'Brien took over several of the bank's mines and mills, consolidated them with their own combine, and established a degree of control over the Comstock that exceeded anything the bank ring had achieved. They also did everything they could to obstruct the completion of Sutro's tunnel, just as Ralston and Sharon had done. By the time the tunnel was completed, in 1879, the richest ore bodies had already been exhausted and the great days of the Comstock were over.

SELECTED BIBLIOGRAPHY

"The Terrible Seventies" is the title of a chapter in Gertrude Atherton's *California, an Intimate History* (1914). The volumes by Lewis, Daggatt, Tutorow, and Lavender, cited for the previous chapter, are also useful here. See also Henry George. "What the Railroad Will Bring Us," *The Overland Monthly,* I (October 1868), pp. 297–304; John H. Kemble, "The Big Four at Sea; the History of the Occidental and Oriental Steamship Company," *Huntington Library Quarterly,* III (April 1940), pp. 339–358; and Michael Magliari, "Populism, Steamboats, and the Octopus: Transportation Rates and Monopoly in California's Wheat Regions, 1890–1896," *Pacific Historical Review,* LVIII (November 1989), pp. 449–470.

On land monopoly, see Chapter 6, "California Latifundia," in Carey McWilliams, *California: The Great Exception* (1949), and Paul W. Gates, "The Homestead Law in an Incongruous Land System," *American Historical Review,* XLI (July 1936), pp. 652–681. Gates, "California's Agricultural College Lands," *Pacific Historical Review,* XXX (May 1961), pp. 103–122, shows the extent to which the Morrill Act facilitated land speculation. John Thompson and Edward A. Dutra, *The Tule Breakers: The Story of the California Dredge* (1983), tells how 1 million acres of wetlands were "reclaimed." Lloyd J. Mercer, "Land Grants to American Railroads: Social Cost or Social Benefit?" *Business History Review,* XLIII (Summer 1969), pp. 134–151, defends the grants. The largest speculator's defense of his own activities may be found in "Henry George Reexamined: William S. Chapman's Views on Land Speculation in Nineteenth Century California," by Gerald D. Nash, in *Agricultural History,* XXXIII (July 1959), pp. 133–137. M. Catherine Miller's *Flooding the Courtrooms: Law and the Far West* (1993) is a legal biography of Miller & Lux, whereas Edward F. Treadwell's *The Cattle King* (1931) is a laudatory "dramatized biography" of Henry Miller by a Miller & Lux attorney. *The Mussel Slough Tragedy* (1958), by James L. Brown, is a balanced account, as is the chapter on the same subject in Wallace Smith, *Garden of the Sun* (1939); see also John A. Larimore, "Legal Questions Arising from the Mussel Slough Land Dispute," *Southern California Quarterly,* LVIII (Spring 1976), pp. 75–94.

George D. Lyman, *Ralston's Ring* (1937), covers the period from 1864 to 1875. See also David Lavender, *Nothing Seemed Impossible: William C. Ralston and Early San Francisco* (1975); Dan De Quille (William Wright), *The Big Bonanza* (1876, 1947); C. B. Glasscock, *The Big Bonanza* (1931); and Robert E. Stewart, Jr., and Mary F. Stewart, *Adolph Sutro: A Biography* (1962). Oscar Lewis, *Silver Kings: the Lives and Times of Mackay, Fair, Flood and O'Brien* (1947, 1986), deals largely with their personal lives and those of their families. Marion S. Goldman, *Gold Diggers and Silver Miners* (1981), portrays women on the Comstock as entrepreneurs, not hapless victims.

CHAPTER SIXTEEN

Political Turmoil and a New Constitution

During the hard times of the 1870s, class and racial antagonisms in California increased. Opposition to the Chinese intensified, and demands for political and economic reform led to the creation of a new state constitution.

THE INCREASE OF ANTI-CHINESE SENTIMENT

During most of the 1860s, when jobs were plentiful in California, the flow of Chinese immigration was slight. At the end of that decade, however, when the beginning of a long period of hard times and unemployment coincided with a renewed upsurge of Asian immigration, many Californians demanded ever stronger measures designed not merely to exclude any further Chinese immigrants but to drive out those who had already arrived.

At the same time, the federal government—through the Burlingame Treaty, the Fourteenth Amendment, and the Civil Rights Act of 1870—positively encouraged Chinese immigration and blocked various efforts of state and local authorities to discourage it. Anson Burlingame, American minister to China, had a strong admiration for the Chinese and a strong sympathy for the Chinese imperial government. The Burlingame Treaty of 1868 provided for the right of free immigration from China. The Fourteenth Amendment to the federal Constitution, ratified in the same year, forbade any state to "deprive any person of life, liberty, or property, without due process of law" or to "deny to any person within its jurisdiction the equal protection of the laws." The federal Civil Rights Act of 1870 prohibited discrimination in the courts and discriminatory taxes against any particular group of immigrants.

Under these measures the federal courts struck down most of the varied and ingenious anti-Chinese weapons in the arsenals of California state and municipal law. For example, in 1870 when the flow of new arrivals had made the tenements of San Francisco's Chinatown even more than usually overcrowded, a new ordinance made it a misdemeanor to maintain or occupy any sleeping room with less than 500 cubic feet of air per person. But the attempt to enforce this provision soon overcrowded the jails to such a degree that the city was grossly violating its own ordinance. In some of the most important opinions that invalidated this and various other anti-Chinese statutes, Justice Stephen J. Field of the United States Supreme Court wrote masterpieces of refined but scathing sarcasm.

Much of the anti-Chinese feeling was based on essentially irrational fears, directed against an alien people who worshiped strange gods, ate strange foods, and were thought to suffer from strange diseases. But there were more substantial grounds for anxiety about the Chinese, not the least of which was that their willingness to accept low wages tended to depress the wages of American workers. It is significant that Irish Americans were in the vanguard of most of the attacks on the Chinese. A generation earlier, when large numbers of Irish had migrated to the United States after the potato famine of the 1840s, it was they who had been denounced as a menace to the living standards of American labor. Now they could enjoy the position of being the denouncers. In the 1870s the Irish and the Chinese were the two largest foreign-born groups in California, each forming more than a tenth of the population of the state. In San Francisco more than a fifth of the population was Chinese, and the Irish formed almost as large a proportion. The Irish, being white and thus eligible for naturalized citizenship, now formed a large bloc of voters, whereas the Chinese had no votes.

"Anti-coolie clubs" joined with labor unions and "eight hour leagues" in organizing anti-Chinese parades and other public demonstrations in San Francisco. "Coolie" was a word around which a great deal of emotion and confusion revolved. Its probable derivation was from *kuli,* meaning "muscle" in Tamil, a language of southern India. The British, using it to mean a hired unskilled laborer or servant, introduced the word into China, where it was approximated by two Chinese characters meaning "bitter strength." In the middle of the nineteenth century a flourishing traffic in the importation of laborers from China into South America became known as the "coolie trade." Many of these laborers had been kidnapped and were held under "labor contracts" that amounted to slavery. It was often charged that the bulk of Chinese immigration to California was a part of this same infamous coolie system, enforced by the Chinese Six Companies in San Francisco. On the other hand, these companies earnestly denied that any Chinese had come to California involuntarily and earnestly asserted that their own purposes in helping their compatriots to find jobs were wholly benevolent. The truth was somewhere between these two opposite claims.

The strongest defenders of the Chinese, apart from Christian missionary groups, were California employers, whose most common argument was that the Chinese did no harm to American labor because they performed only the hard or menial tasks that white workers did not want, such as the reclaiming of tule swamps, seasonal agricultural labor, domestic service, or laundering. The Chinese were also being employed, however, in a growing list of industries in which they were clearly in competition with whites, especially the manufacturing of cigars and shoes. Moreover, when Chinese began to be not merely workers in such factories but also

Pacific Chivalry.

This Thomas Nast cartoon first appeared in *Harper's Weekly* in 1879. It illustrates the unsympathetic attitude of many eastern journals toward California's mistreatment of the Chinese. *(Courtesy of the Bancroft Library.)*

owners of them, thus threatening to put white manufacturers out of business, a number of white employers suddenly became as anti-Chinese as the white workers had ever been.

There were several outbreaks of mob violence. The worst occurred in Los Angeles on the evening of October 24, 1871, after a white man had been killed during a dispute between two Chinese companies. With complete impunity a mob of about 500 people looted and burned the local Chinatown and killed 18 or 19 Chinese, leaving 15 of them hanging from makeshift gallows. Lesser incidents occurred sporadically throughout the 1870s in towns all the way from Chico to San Diego. California newspapers deplored these outbreaks, largely on the ground that they gave California a bad name in the eastern states and made eastern newspapers unsympathetic toward California's demands for Chinese exclusion.

THE WORKINGMEN'S PARTY OF CALIFORNIA

Unemployment, discontent with economic, social, and political conditions in general, and the idea that the Chinese were the prime cause of all difficulties combined to bring about a crisis of unrest in San Francisco in the summer and fall of 1877. The number of Chinese immigrants arriving at San Francisco in the previous year, more than 22,000, had broken all records, and the resulting situation may be compared not to a melting pot but to a pressure cooker.

For several years the unemployed of the whole state had flocked into "the city," where they gathered on street corners and vacant lots to discuss their grievances and to grow bitter at the lavish displays of wealth by some of their more fortunate fellow citizens. In the evening of July 23, 1877, there was a mass meeting on the of Nob Hill where Crocker, Stanford, and Hopkins had built their mansions, and where Crocker had built his famous "spite fence." Crocker had wished to occupy the entire block between California and Sacramento streets, but a man who owned one small lot with a house on it had refused to sell. Crocker had then surrounded three sides of the lot with a board fence 40 feet high, almost entirely shutting out the view and the sunshine from the little home. Pointing to the fence, Kearney cried that if it was not soon taken down, the working people should tear it down. Then he went on to other remarks about the outrages committed by large capitalists, the corruption of incumbent politicians, and the need for his new political party.

Fearing that Kearney's speeches would lead to more riots like those of July, the city government hastily adopted an ordinance against addressing any meeting of more than 25 persons in language suggesting violence or destruction of property. This promptly became known as the "gag law," and served mainly to increase the pressure of the discontent that it sought to repress. Under this ordinance Kearney was arrested, but in his trial in January 1878 he was acquitted on the ground that no violence had actually resulted from his words. In fact, Kearney's speeches and the hope of successful political action through his new party seem to have offered a kind of safety valve. His speeches were generally extemporaneous, and accounts of them differed widely. For example, he was charged with having said that his followers should hold a Thanksgiving Day parade if they had to march "up to their knees in blood," but it was established in court that he had said not "blood" but "mud." Whatever else he may have said, it is certain that he formed the habit of ending his speeches with: "And whatever happens, the Chinese must go!"

THE CONSTITUTION OF 1879

Demands for a new state constitution had been heard periodically since the 1850s and had increased in volume as the great depression of the 1870s lengthened and deepened. After several defeats at the polls, the calling of a new constitutional convention was finally approved by the voters in the state elections of September 5, 1877. At that time the Workingmen's Party of California was still only in its inceptive stage in San Francisco. By the following April, however, when the legislature passed an enabling act setting the elections of delegates to the convention for June 18, 1878, the party under Kearney's leadership was sufficiently well-organized to nominate a full ticket of delegates in every part of the state. Fear that the Workingmen might actually control the convention became so great among conservatives that in most districts the Republican and Democratic nominations were fused, under the label of "Non-partisan."

The convention whose delegates were elected in June of 1878 and which met at Sacramento in September was more than three times as large as the Monterey convention of 1849, with 152 delegates as compared with 48. It was in session nearly 6 months, as compared with 6 weeks. In place of an imitative, short, and concise document, it produced one that was much more original, extraordinarily long, and extremely detailed. Yet California's second constitutional convention achieved remarkably little net improvement over the first, and virtually every hope of effective reform was ultimately disappointed.

Of the 152 delegates 78 were Non-partisans, 51 Workingmen, 11 Republicans, 10 Democrats, and 2 independents. Of the Workingmen, 30 were from San Francisco, and thus the Workingmen carried the city but not the state. By occupation, 57 delegates were lawyers, mostly conservatives; 39 were farmers; 8 were merchants; and the others were scattered over a wide range reflecting the diverse skilled trades of the San Francisco work force. The conservative delegates, including some of the shrewdest lawyers and politicians in the state, could have controlled the convention easily had it not been that some of the reforms demanded by the Workingmen were also demanded by the farmers, and that, on the issues where these two groups could unite, they commanded a majority.

The economic and political discontent of the farmers in the 1870s was expressed largely through the Grange movement. The movement had gained control of several legislatures in the middle west and secured the passage of state laws for the regulation of railroad rates. More than a fourth of the delegates in the California convention were in effect representatives of the Grange movement, though they had no separate party denomination.

Railroad regulation was one objective that attracted not only the joint support of workers and farmers but the support of many business organizations as well. A law of 1876 had defined and prohibited extortion and unjust discrimination in rates and had created a state board of transportation commissioners. The railroad executives had rendered this body powerless simply by refusing to make reports to it. In an effort to make regulation a reality, the new constitution provided for a state railroad commission of three members elected to 4-year terms, with power to establish rates and to set fines and imprisonments for violations.

The farmers also demanded changes in the tax structure to decrease their excessive tax burden. With the help of the workers they secured a provision that mortgage holders must pay the tax on their portion of the equity in a farm. In the hope of fairer assessments of taxes on land, which had fallen very heavily on the farmers and very lightly on the railroad under the system of independent county assessors, a state board of equalization was created.

Corporations and especially banks were the targets of much invective in the convention. Dr. Charles C. O'Donnell, a San Francisco physician who was one of the most vociferous of the Workingmen delegates, defined a corporation as "a corrupt combination of individuals, formed together for the purpose of escaping individual responsibility for their acts." The new constitution included a number of provisions that sought to increase the accountability of bank and other corporation directors and stockholders.

The anti-Chinese article was long, elaborate, and emotional. It authorized the legislature to protect the state from "aliens, who are, or may become . . . dangerous or detrimental"; it forbade the employment of Chinese by corporations, or on public works "except in punishment for crime"; it authorized cities to restrict the occupancy of Chinese to certain districts or even to forbid their residence within city limits; and it denounced and prohibited "Asiatic coolieism" as "a form of human slavery."

The result of the convention's labors was almost the longest written constitution in the world, several times as long as the Constitution of the United States; it was ultimately exceeded in length and verbosity only by the constitutions of Louisiana and India. Virtually no one was entirely satisfied with the convention's massive product, and the public debate over its ratification was confused. Conservatives denounced it as communistic and malicious. Workers, on the other hand, were angered because it did so little that was directly in the interest of labor. The provision that "eight hours shall constitute a legal day's work on all public works" added nothing whatever to the law of 1868, which had proved to be merely a recommendation without any provision for enforcement. The strongest sentiment for ratification came from the farming areas, where the Grangers cherished dreams of lower freight rates and lower taxes. On May 7, 1879, the new constitution was adopted by a majority of less than 11,000 out of a total vote of 145,000.

THE FRUSTRATION OF REFORM

The general failure of the constitution of 1879 to produce major improvements in the state's government was most glaringly exemplified in the story of the railroad commission. Instead of establishing new rates, the commission generally adopted the existing ones, except for a lowering of freight rates on certain agricultural products of the northern Sacramento Valley, where a commissioner's farm was located. This same commissioner was permitted to buy lands, which he then sold to the treasurer of the Southern Pacific at a profit of $100,000, and another commissioner suddenly acquired a fortune for which he could not account. Largely by means of such corrupt methods, the railroad's power to control the state would continue to exceed the state's power to regulate the railroad for three decades more.

The constitutional requirement that the creditor rather than the debtor must pay the tax on the mortgaged portion of property was soon easily and almost universally evaded by raising the interest to a rate large enough to include the tax. Equally disappointing to the farmers was the general ineffectiveness of the state board of equalization. The railroad was usually able to escape from higher assessments by contesting them in the courts.

The Workingmen's party began to disintegrate soon after it reached the zenith of its power in the elections of September 3, 1879, in which the Workingmen elected the chief justice of the supreme court, 5 of the 6 associate justices, 11 senators, and 16 members of the assembly. In addition they elected the Rev. Isaac S. Kalloch, a Baptist minister and sensational pulpit orator, as mayor of San Francisco. His administration, however, was stormy, unsuccessful, and discredited. In the course of a long-continued exchange of personal insults, Kalloch was shot and wounded by Charles de Young, publisher of the *Chronicle*. Kalloch's son later shot and killed de Young and was acquitted of murder. Within a year after the adoption of the new constitution the Workingmen's party had virtually disappeared.

The constitution of 1879, though without substantial reason, was given some of the credit for the upturn in economic conditions in California in 1880, and the return of prosperity reduced the intensity of demands for political and social change.

CHINESE EXCLUSION

Another development that reduced public discontent in California was the surrender of the federal government to the state's demands for a ban on Chinese immigration. This occurred because the anti-Chinese vote in California actually came to hold the balance of power between the parties in national as well as in state politics.

Chinese immigration to the United States was so concentrated on the Pacific coast that the other states could not understand California's concern about the problem, but it became clear that California's electoral votes, along with those of Washington and Oregon, could swing the presidency to the party that made the strongest promises to exclude the Chinese. The presidential elections of 1876 and 1888 were so close that the majorities in the electoral college went to the candidates who had received the minorities of the popular votes. The popular majorities for James A. Garfield in 1880 and Grover Cleveland in 1884 were less than 25,000.

In this situation the national Republican and Democratic platforms began to rival each other in echoing Californian anti-Chinese slogans. The result was a federal law in 1882 which prohibited Chinese immigration for 10 years. In 1892 the Chinese Exclusion Act was extended for 10 years more, and in 1902 the ban was made permanent.

The exclusion law contributed to a general demographic and economic decline among the Chinese in California. Boycotts of Chinese-produced goods by white consumers reduced significantly the economic opportunities for the Chinese. By the early 1900s, there were virtually no Chinese cigar or shoe makers left. Many were relegated to the ranks of common laborers. Others found employment as farm workers. Few Chinese women lived in California at the time of exclusion, and thus the immigrant population faced extraordinary difficulties replenishing itself through natural increase. The exclusion law not only made it nearly impossible for additional Chinese to enter California, it also caused great hardships for those who were already here.

SELECTED BIBLIOGRAPHY

On the Chinese, see Sucheng Chan, *This Bittersweet Soil* (1986) and *Asian Californias* (1991); Judy Yung, *Unbound Feet* (1995); Benson Tong, *Unsubmissive Women* (1994); Charles J. McClain, *In Search of Equality* (1994); Shih-shau Henry Tsai, *The Chinese Experience in America* (1987); Stanford M. Lyman, *The Asian in the West* (1970); Howard Brett Melendy, *The Oriental Americans* (1972); Sandy Lydon, *Chinese Gold* (1985); and Raymond Lou, "The Chinese American Community of Los Angeles, 1870–1900," Ph.D. thesis, University of California, Irvine (1982).

The literature on the opposition to the Chinese is extensive: Alexander P. Saxton, *The Indispensable Enemy* (1971); Stuart C. Miller, *The Unwelcome Immigrant* (1970); Gunther Barth, *Bitter Strength* (1964); Ping Chiu, *Chinese Labor in California* (1963); Elmer C. Sandmeyer, *The Anti-Chinese Movement in California* (1939); and Mary Roberts Coolidge, *Chinese Immigration* (1909). The broader context, brilliantly analyzed, is provided by Robert W. Cherny's "Patterns of Toleration and Discrimination in San Francisco," *California History,* LXXIII

(Summer 1994), pp. 130–141. On the Los Angeles riot of 1871, consult the articles by Paul M. De Falla, *Historical Society of Southern California Quarterly,* XLII (March and June 1960), pp. 57–88, 161–185, and William R. Locklear, ibid., XLII (September 1960), pp. 239–256.

The best recent study of the Workingmen's party is Neil Larry Shumsky, *The Evolution of Political Protest and the Workingmen's Party of California* (1992). Older accounts include Ralph Kauer, "The Workingmen's Party of California," *Pacific Historical Review,* XII (September 1944), pp. 278–291; James Bryce, *The American Commonwealth,* volume II (1889); and Ira B. Cross, *A History of the Labor Movement in California* (1935). Anti-Chinese action in rural California is described in Daniel Cornford, "To Save the Republic," *California History,* LXVI (June 1987), pp. 130–142, and Michele Shover, "Chico Women," ibid., LXVII (December 1988), pp. 228–243.

James P. Walsh (ed.), *The San Francisco Irish, 1850–1876* (1978), and R. A. Burchell, *The San Francisco Irish, 1848–1880* (1980), are major contributions to our understanding of the role of the Irish in California society. Patrick J. Dowling, *California: The Irish Dream* (1989), offers a series of brief portraits of Irish immigrants.

The *Debates and Proceedings* of the 1879 constitutional convention were published in three volumes (1880). See also Carl B. Swisher, *Motivation and Political Technique in the California Constitutional Convention, 1878–1879* (1930), and Dudley T. Moorehead, "Sectionalism and the California Constitution of 1879," *Pacific Historical Review,* XII (September 1943), pp. 287–294.

On exclusion of the Chinese, see Sucheng Chan (ed.), *Entry Denied: Exclusion and the Chinese Community in America, 1882–1943* (1991); Jules Becker, *The Course of Exclusion, 1882–1924* (1991); and Lucy E. Salyer, *Laws Harsh as Tigers* (1996).

CHAPTER SEVENTEEN

Economic Growth

The increase of wealth in California in the late nineteenth and the early twentieth centuries was substantial, but it was far from being an orderly process. Neither the people of California nor those of the United States had yet learned to exert any significant degree of control over the violent fluctuations of the regional and national economies. The 1880s were relatively prosperous, but the panic of 1893 led to another depression so severe that the growth of California's population in the 1890s was a mere 22.4 percent—the lowest rate for any decade between the 1830s and 1930s. The turn of the century, however, coincided with the beginning of a new cycle in which the growth of northern California was impressive and that of southern California truly phenomenal.

THE WHEAT BONANZA

The droughts that had ruined the cattle industry in the early 1860s were followed by a series of rainy winters, and beginning with the crop year 1866–1867 the generous rainfall made possible a full discovery of the potentialities of the Sacramento and San Joaquin valleys for the growing of wheat without irrigation. It was an ideal crop for the wide, flat valley lands in a time of distant markets and a sparse rural population with limited capital, and for about 30 years, from the early 1860s until the panic of 1893, wheat was California's largest and most profitable agricultural commodity.

The largest wheat grower in the state was Dr. Hugh J. Glenn, who had a medical degree from the University of Missouri but who occupied himself after 1867 with buying land on credit until he had 55,000 acres, extending for 20 miles along the west bank of the Sacramento River, where he ultimately produced more than half a million bushels a year. His mammoth wheat ranch was in Colusa County; in 1891, after his death, his achievements were memorialized in the creation of Glenn County.

Wheat ranching was a highly speculative enterprise. It also became increasingly mechanized, and one of the most significant aspects of the age of wheat in the great Central Valley of California lay in its contributions to the development of agricultural machinery. The old walking plow known as the "foot burner," with its single plowshare, was replaced by the "Stockton gang plow," which had several shares attached to a beam, moved on wheels, and was adjustable in width and depth. In a scene made famous in Frank Norris's *The Octopus,* there were 35 such plows in echelon formation, each with 5 plowshares and drawn by 10 horses. At the Glenn Ranch plowing was often done with as many as 100 gang plows at once, each drawn by an eight-mule team. The Central Valley also produced new machines for planting, pulverizing the earth, and spreading it over the seed in one operation, as well as improvements of the earlier machines to combine the cutting and threshing of the grain. The flat land and dry summers of the valley made it possible to use the largest steam-powered "combined harvesters" in the world, machines so large and heavy that they required 36 horses to move them. The need for mechanical motive power led directly to the invention of the tractor, first used in the San Joaquin Valley with steam power in 1886. Later Benjamin Holt of Stockton and others would adapt the tractor to the internal combustion engine and develop the "caterpillar" track.

The dry farming of wheat had the peculiar disadvantages of a one-crop agricultural economy. It was a kind of soil mining, ruthlessly carried on year after year without fertilizer or rotation, and inevitably the soil was exhausted and the

A steam-powered harvester on a wheat ranch in the San Joaquin Valley. *(Courtesy of the Bancroft Library.)*

yields declined. Wheat as a dominant crop began to decline in the middle 1880s under competition from the Mississippi valley and from Russia, and it collapsed in the depression of the 1890s. The spread of irrigation had also begun to make wheat less profitable than other California farm products.

One partial compensation for the decline of wheat growing in the 1890s was the rise of sugar-beet production in the same decade, led by Claus Spreckels with his beet fields and refining plants in the Watsonville and Salinas areas and by the Oxnard brothers, Robert and Henry, in southern California.

WINES

The growing of grapes and the manufacture of the fermented juice into wine had their beginnings in California at the missions, for sacramental purposes and for the personal use of the mission fathers, but though the vines were hardy, the mission grapes and the processes of manufacture were of poor quality. Commercial production also began in southern California. Jean Louis Vignes, a most appropriately named vintner from the region of Bordeaux, brought cuttings from France to a vineyard in Los Angeles in the early 1830s, and William Wolfskill established another vineyard nearby a few years later.

After the discovery of gold the center of grape and wine production shifted to the valleys around San Francisco Bay, and in the 1850s the Hungarian exile Agoston Haraszthy began the work that made him the father of the modern California wine industry, especially at his Buena Vista estate in the Sonoma Valley. In 1861 the state legislature appointed him a commissioner to report on means of improving the industry, and in this capacity he toured the wine regions of Europe and returned with 200,000 cuttings and rooted vines, representing 1400 varieties. Meanwhile, the success of the cooperative community at Anaheim, a German wine colony southeast of Los Angeles founded in 1857, had also become an important factor in the industry's growth.

In the 1870s and 1880s the California vineyards were nearly wiped out by *Phylloxera,* a genus of tiny insects resembling aphids, and the ravages of this pest were brought under control only by gradually replanting the vineyards with resistant stocks. In spite of this and other temporary setbacks the industry flourished, largely by a process of fusing a great number of varieties of European vines and wine-making skills. Vineyards spread through the Sonoma, Napa, Santa Clara, and Livermore valleys. The climate and soils of the Central Valley were also found to be highly favorable, particularly for dessert wines, table grapes, and raisins; ultimately the greatest of all concentrations of vineyards in California would be in Fresno County. In 1900 California produced 19 million gallons of wine, more than 80 percent of the nation's output.

THE CITRUS INDUSTRY

Like the mission grape, the mission orange was not of very good quality. It was thick-skinned, pithy, and often sour. William Wolfskill and a few others operated orange groves in the Los Angeles area during the gold rush, shipping the fruit north to help combat scurvy among the miners. The significant beginnings of the California orange industry came with three new developments of the 1870s. These were the discovery that oranges grew better on lands that were slightly higher and out of the coastal fog belt, the introduction of the navel orange from Brazil, and the advent of the railroad.

In 1870 J. W. North and his associates purchased the lands of a defunct silk colony on the Rancho Jurupa near what would soon be the town of Riverside, began an irrigation canal from the Santa Ana River, and planted orange groves. Three years later members of the Riverside group obtained two of the dozen budded trees which the first American Protestant missionary at Bahia, Brazil, had sent to the Department of Agriculture at Washington. Within a remarkably short time the large, sweet, seedless Bahia navels were in production under the name of "Riverside navels." Substantial rail shipments to St. Louis and Chicago were under way before the end of the 1870s, and in the next decade, with the development of refrigerator cars, rail shipments were increased in volume and extended to the Atlantic coast. The great citrus belt of southern California was in process of rapid formation.

Use of the summer-ripening Valencia orange, along with the winter-ripening Brazilian navels, made possible a year-round output. Moreover the Valencias flourished nearer the coast, and with their increasing introduction in the early twentieth century the citrus belt extended from Santa Barbara to San Diego and from Pasadena to Riverside. Southern California became responsible for more than two-thirds of the nation's production of oranges and more than 90 percent of its lemons.

The early development of the marketing of citrus fruits involved many difficulties. The period from 1869 to the end of the century was one of serious decline in American agricultural prices because of expanding production, deflated currency, and the farmer's weak position in bargaining. Farmers seldom had enough information about the market to know what a fair price would be, and speculators took every possible advantage of their ignorance. The markets for citrus fruits and other California specialty crops were from 2000 to 3000 miles away. Sometimes the anxious shipper of a carload of fruit would receive nothing but a bill and the information that the arrival of other shipments on the same day had so glutted the market that the price received was insufficient to pay the freight and handling charges. The answer was the cooperative marketing organization, in which the California fruit growers eventually achieved considerable success.

In an effort to combat the speculators who controlled the citrus market in the early years, an Orange Growers' Protective Union of Southern California was formed in 1885. Another orange growers' union was formed in 1891 and reorganized as the Southern California Fruit Exchange in 1893. After oranges had begun to be grown in important quantities as far north as Oroville and Chico, central California growers joined the organization, and in 1905 the new name of California Fruit Growers' Exchange reflected this broadened membership. The organization was so successful that its brand name, "Sunkist," finally became

Asian workers in the 1890s picking oranges near Santa Ana. (*Courtesy of the California Historical Society.*)

almost synonymous with "California oranges and lemons" in popular usage, and in 1952 its name was officially changed to Sunkist Growers, Inc.

The nonprofit methods of the grower-owned cooperative exposed it to specious charges of being anticapitalistic. As the cooperative system took root in several other fields of agriculture, including deciduous fruits, raisins, walnuts, and dairy and poultry products, many of the private wholesalers frantically denounced the whole cooperative marketing idea as sheer communism.

On the other hand, one of the ablest leaders of the California Fruit Growers' Exchange, Charles C. Teague of Santa Paula, described it as a "federated democracy." The democracy, of course, extended only to the growers, not to the unorganized and disfranchised people who did the physical work. The citrus industry was built on cheap alien labor, in the beginning mainly Chinese and later Japanese and Mexican.

The remarkable economic achievements of the citrus growers were due in part to the fact that many of them were "gentlemen farmers," individuals who had acquired considerable capital before they were attracted to California to enter this particular industry, and therefore could generate sufficient money and credit to ensure success. They called themselves "growers" to dissociate themselves from the rustic clumsiness and ignorance which they felt to be implied by the word "farmer." In later decades California agriculture in general would become so successfully commercialized that the word "agriculture" itself would begin to be replaced by the new term "agribusiness."

THE RISE OF SOUTHERN CALIFORNIA

Through the 1870s the main movement of population into California was confined to its north central parts. From the next decade onward, however, southern California grew at a more rapid rate than did the north.

The first southern California boom, a very modest one, occurred between 1868 and 1876. After the droughts that wiped out the livestock of the region, Abel Stearns narrowly escaped the sale of his 200,000 acres of land in the San Gabriel and Santa Ana valleys for $4000 in delinquent taxes. He was saved from utter financial ruin when a group of San Francisco capitalists led by Sam Brannan purchased his ranches and began in 1868 to subdivide them into 40-acre tracts. Having bought the land at distress prices, the Brannan syndicate netted more than $2 million from this investment.

Along with the spread of the citrus industry, a special factor in this early boom was the "health rush" to southern California which began about 1870. That the climate of the area was helpful in curing tuberculosis was actually a sad delusion, but the physicians of the time encouraged thousands of invalids and their families to believe it, and southern California newspaper editors and other boosters proclaimed its truth. By 1900, after medical theory had generally abandoned the idea, its influence declined, though a myriad of other health fads continued to flourish.

The alleged health-giving properties of California's climate led one observer to assert that California was fast becoming "the land of handsome men," and David Starr Jordan pronounced with the scientific authority of a recognized biologist and educator that "California college girls, of the same age, are larger by almost every dimension than are the college girls of Massachusetts. They are taller, broader-shouldered, thicker-chested (with ten cubic inches more lung capacity), have larger biceps and calves, and a superiority of tested strength."

The superior potential of California for agriculture was also widely advertised, though the reports of squashes and melons so large they had to be picked on horseback led to counterpropaganda from other parts of the country to the effect that California farmers spent more time in exaggeration than in cultivation. A newspaper editor in Jackson, Mississippi, wrote that "California is a state of mind—exaltation is in the atmosphere. Birds of gorgeous plumage flit through the trees but they have no song. Flowers astound in size, gorgeous color, and infinite variety, but they have little perfume." If this writer had also asserted that the grapes, though beautiful, were sour, it could scarcely have been more obvious that envy was mixed with his derision.

The Southern Pacific Railroad had a vast amount of land to sell, and it took a leading part in the great campaign of advertising California. The railroad's publicity bureau had a number of able popular writers on its payroll, and in a flood of books, both fiction and nonfiction, and of magazine articles and stories, they described California's charms and embellished its romantic heritage. It was the

Southern Pacific that began the publication of the phenomenally popular *Sunset,* a magazine of western travel and living. Many independent writers contributed to this flood of publicity. The transplanted New Englander, Charles F. Lummis, editor of the monthly magazine *Land of Sunshine,* later renamed *Out West,* went so far in romanticizing southern California's past and present that for a time he was the leading cultural chauvinist of the region. Throughout the country the lure of California was becoming so strong that there was an eager market for almost anything that was written or said about it.

When the Santa Fe Railroad reached Los Angeles in 1885, it began a rate war with the Southern Pacific. For a brief time, a ticket from Kansas City to Los Angeles could be bought for $1, and the low rates, along with the attendant advertising, launched southern California as a major tourist attraction and contributed to the real estate boom that reached a climax in 1887. Real estate sales in Los Angeles County exceeded $200 million during that year as new lands were settled and brought into profitable use.

A promotional brochure published by the Southern Pacific Railroad in 1907 "boosting" the attractions of California. (*Courtesy of the California State Library, Sacramento.*)

The most colorful figure in the history of California irrigation development was Canadian-born George Chaffey, a self-educated engineering genius. The greatest of Chaffey's accomplishments was his development of irrigation in the lower Colorado River area. The region was one of the dreariest desert wastes in the world, though the soil potential was extraordinary. In 1896 the California Development Company was organized, and in 1900 it secured Chaffey's services. Below the Mexican border he found some ancient dry watercourses through which very economical canals could be built, and within a year he had completed a 70-mile canal through Mexican territory, entering California at the twin border townsites which he called Mexicali and Calexico.

One of his greatest inspirations was a new name for the Colorado Desert: the Imperial Valley. This dramatic change of name did much to change the image that had repelled settlers from the area. They began to move into it in substantial numbers, and the desert did in fact begin to turn into a kind of agricultural empire.

Chaffey left the company in 1905. Not long afterward his successors built a risky bypass canal around the diversion headgate. After torrential rains the river burst through at this weak point and poured northwestward into the Imperial Valley, turning the dry Salton Sink into the Salton Sea, covering 40 miles of the Southern Pacific's roadbed, and threatening eventually to inundate the whole region. The federal government did not intervene because the break was in Mexican territory, and the flooding continued unchecked for nearly 2 years. The Southern Pacific, after taking the opportunity to acquire control of the California Development Company, finally brought the flood under control in 1907 by dumping thousands of carloads of rock and gravel, and the development of the Imperial Valley was resumed.

ELECTRIC RAILWAYS AND URBANIZATION

The years before and after the turn of the century were the era of the street and interurban electric railway—a development that played a vital part in the urbanization and particularly in the suburbanization of American society. The building of electric railway lines tremendously facilitated the growth of metropolitan areas by making it possible for those who worked in the center of a city to live in its outskirts or suburbs in more comfortable homes built on less expensive land. Few workers were willing to spend more than a total of an hour a day in commuting; therefore, in the horse-and-buggy and horsecar era the practical maximum size of a city was little more than 12 square miles, that is, the area within a radius of 2 miles, the distance that could be traveled in 30 minutes. The trolley car, which could travel at least 5 miles in the same length of time, made it possible for the main residential area of a city to be nearly seven times as large as before—nearly 80 square miles. The interurban electric railway also did much to increase mobility, and tended to consolidate neighboring towns into a single metropolis.

The cable car had provided a colorful interlude. It was invented in San Francisco by Andrew S. Hallidie, a manufacturer of wire rope, and after the first cable line

On the left stands Collis P. Huntington (1821–1900) with his nephew Henry E. Huntington (1850–1927). In between stands a newsboy on a San Francisco sidewalk in the 1890s. (*Courtesy of the Huntington Library.*)

was built in 1873, on Clay Street, the idea spread to other cities. But the electric trolley introduced in Richmond, Virginia, in 1888 was obviously so much more efficient and economical even on steep hills that cable lines soon disappeared everywhere except in San Francisco, where a few have been retained, largely as tourist attractions and for reasons of local nostalgia.

Street and interurban electric railways reached the height of their importance between the 1890s and the beginning of the automobile age in 1919. The chief opportunities for profits for the promoters of these lines came not from operating revenues but from simultaneous speculation in the real estate which a new line could make suddenly and enormously more valuable.

San Francisco, "the city" of American California's first half century, was confined to a mere thumbnail of land only 7 miles square at the tip of a peninsula. Most of the space eventually to be occupied by the metropolis of the San Francisco Bay region was in the East Bay. These facts made a strong impression on Francis Marion "Borax" Smith, a capitalist of large imagination. In 1893, Smith began to reinvest the fortune that he had acquired in the borax business in Death Valley in a great scheme to consolidate and expand the street railway lines of the East Bay cities into the Key System, and to connect this network with San Francisco by an expanded and consolidated ferry service.

In the southern part of the state, Henry Edwards Huntington was the leading figure in interurban transportation development. Henry was the nephew of Collis P. Huntington, who had no son and who hoped that his nephew would succeed him in the leadership of the Southern Pacific Railroad. This dynastic plan was strengthened when Collis arranged the marriage of Henry to a sister of Collis's adopted daughter. In San Francisco in the 1890s Henry became vice president of the Southern Pacific, but after the death of his uncle in 1900 the hopes for his succession to the presidency of the railroad were frustrated when Edward H. Harriman of New York, who already controlled the Union Pacific, gained control of the Southern Pacific as well. This virtual merger continued until 1913 when the federal government dissolved it.

Henry E. Huntington faced the new century by moving most of his own investments and operations to southern California. In 1902 he invested most of his funds in a consolidation and expansion of the street and interurban railways of the region in and around Los Angeles under the name of the Pacific Electric Railway Company. Within a few years the Pacific Electric (PE) and its "Big Red Cars" welded 42 incorporated cities within a 35-mile radius of Los Angeles into the fastest-growing body in America. The PE became by far the largest network of its kind, with more cars than any five other interurban electric systems, and its transportation of freight as well as passengers cut so heavily into the business of the Southern Pacific in the region that after many efforts Harriman finally succeeded in buying Huntington out, at an enormous price, in 1910.

In less than a decade Huntington became wealthier than his uncle had ever been, mainly by buying great tracts of land in southern California just before announcing that new branches of the Pacific Electric would be built through them. He had separated from his first wife in the year his uncle died. He was divorced in 1906, and a few years later married his uncle's widow, thus consolidating the entire family fortune. After 1910 he retired from the more active aspects of business and devoted himself to filling his mansion at San Marino with his collection of manuscripts and rare books in the fields of English, colonial, and southwestern American literature and history. After his death in 1927 this was opened to scholars as the Huntington Library. The magnificent grounds of his estate, and his great collection of paintings, were opened to the public.

railroad

Henry E. Huntington shaped the system of transportation which, along with other forces, launched the entire region from Santa Monica to Redlands, and from San Fernando to Santa Ana, on the road to becoming the great City of Southern California.

SELECTED BIBLIOGRAPHY

Various aspects of economic development are treated in Robert G. Cleland and Osgood Hardy, *The March of Industry* (1929); Claude B. Hutchison (ed.), *California Agriculture* (1946); and Gerald D. Nash, *State Government and Economic Development* (1964).

Accounts of wheat ranching are in Wallace Smith, *Garden of the Sun* (1939), and Joseph A. McGowan, *History of the Sacramento Valley,* volumes I, II (1961). The mechanization of California agriculture is described in Walter A. Payne (ed.), *Benjamin Holt* (1983), and Robert E. Ankli and Alan L. Olmstead, "The Adoption of the Gasoline Tractor in California," *Agricultural History,* LV (July 1981), pp. 213–230. On marketing problems, see Rodman W. Paul, "The Great California Grain War, *Pacific Historical Review,* XXVII (November 1958), pp. 331–350, and "The Wheat Trade between California and the United Kingdom," *Mississippi Valley Historical Review,* XLV (December 1958), pp. 391–412. On sugar, see Thomas J. .Osborne, "Claus Spreckels and the Oxnard Brothers," *Southern California Quarterly,* LIV (Summer 1972), pp. 117–126.

On wine production, see Brian McGinty, *Strong Wine: The Life and Legend of Agoston Haraszthy* (1998); Vincent P. Carosso, *The California Wine Industry, 1830–1895* (1951); and Ralph B. Hutchinson, "The California Wine Industry," Ph.D. thesis, University of California, Los Angeles (1969).

The rise of the citrus and related industries and of cooperative marketing can be traced in a special issue of *California History,* LXXIV (Spring 1995); Richard G. Lillard, "Agricultural Statesman: Charles G. Teague of Santa Paula," ibid., LXV (March 1986), pp. 2–17; Vincent Moses, "Machines in the Garden: A Citrus Monopoly in Riverside, 1900–1936," ibid., LXI (Spring 1982), pp. 26–35; Edward J. Bachus, "Who Took the Oranges Out of Orange County?" *Southern California Quarterly,* LXIII (Summer 1981), pp. 157–174; Walter Reuther, H. J. Webber, and L. D. Batchelor (eds.), *The Citrus Industry* (1967); H. E. Erdman, "The Development and Significance of California Coöperatives, 1900–1915," *Agricultural History,* XXXII (July 1958), pp. 179–184; and Richard J. Orsi, "The Octopus Reconsidered: The Southern Pacific and Agricultural Modernization in California, 1865–1915," *California Historical Quarterly,* LIV (Fall 1975), pp. 197–220.

On the rise of southern California, see Mike Davis, *City of Quartz* (1990); Kevin Starr, *Inventing the Dream* (1985); Remi A. Nadeau, *City-makers* (1948); John E. Baur, *Health Seekers of Southern California* (1959); Glenn S. Dumke, *The Boom of the Eighties in Southern California* (1944); and Carey McWilliams, *Southern California Country* (1946). A thorough account of the promotional literature appears in Alfred Runte, "Promoting the Golden West," *California History,* LXX (Spring 1991), pp. 62–75. Frank L. Beach, "The Transformation of California, 1900–1920," Ph.D. thesis, University of California, Berkeley (1963), analyzes the great acceleration of the westward movement from the older states to California in the early twentieth century. See also Warren Thompson, *Growth and Changes in California's Population* (1955).

Irrigation developments are described in Donald J. Pisani, *To Reclaim a Divided West* (1992) and *From the Family Farm to Agribusiness* (1989); Robert Kelley, *Battling the Inland Sea* (1990);

M. Catherine Miller, *Flooding the Courtrooms* (1993); Donald Worster, "Hydraulic Society in California," *Agricultural History,* LVI (July 1982), pp. 503–515; Douglas R. Littlefield, "Water Rights during the California Gold Rush," *Western Historical Quarterly,* XIV (October 1983), pp. 415–434; and Lawrence B. Lee, "William Smythe and the Irrigation Movement: A Reconsideration" *Pacific Historical Review,* XLI (August 1972), pp. 289–311.

George W. Hilton, *The Cable Car in America* (1971), traces the cable car's rise and decline. On the great era of street and interurban electric railways, see George H. Hilton and John F. Due, *The Electric Interurban Railways in America* (1960); William D. Middleton, *The Interurban Era* (1961); Robert M. Fogelson, *The Fragmented Metropolis: Los Angeles, 1850–1930* (1967); William B. Friedricks, *Henry E. Huntington and the Creation of Southern California* (1992); and James Thorpe, *Henry Edwards Huntington* (1994).

CHAPTER EIGHTEEN

Culture and Oligarchy

In the late nineteenth century a few men with great fortunes dominated California to a degree that justifies the description of its social and political systems as oligarchic. Several of the state's major writers devoted their work largely to protests against this situation. For this as well as other reasons California was producing a remarkable portion of the country's most significant writing.

HENRY GEORGE

In the writings of Henry George, California made a striking contribution to the history of ideas. George's theories grew directly out of his personal observation of the California social environment in the late 1860s and the 1870s, and his beliefs were the responses of a sensitive man to conditions and problems that were then more particularly apparent in California than in any other part of the nation. He concluded that monopoly in land, above all, had given oligarchical power to such men as the Big Four, "who a few years ago were selling coal-oil or retailing dry goods, but who now count their fortunes by the scores of millions." George's denunciation of the "unearned increment" from the increase in the value of land and his remedy, a single tax that would confiscate private land ownership, formed a major chapter in the history of native American radicalism.

George was born in 1839 in Philadelphia. His formal education ended early, and throughout his life he insisted that formal education had little importance or value. He worked for several years as a printer before he came to San Francisco at the age of 19. His writing career began with a series of jobs as reporter or editor for newspapers in San Francisco, Oakland, and Sacramento. One day in 1870, when he was editing the *Oakland Transcript,* he sought relaxation in a ride through the foothills overlooking the bay. A passing teamster told him that the land they were crossing, part of a large unused tract, was being held for a price of $1000 per acre. "Like a flash it came upon me," he recalled in later years; here was the answer to the enigma of why progress had its twin in poverty, of why when wealth increased, poverty increased with it. As land values rose with the growth of population, the person who worked the land had to pay too much for the privilege. The noblest form of labor, the production of food, was robbed to pay a huge unearned increment to the land speculator.

George denounced the railroad as the state's largest private landowner and as the beneficiary of vast subsidies in both land and cash. In a pamphlet titled *The Subsidy Question* (1871), he turned laissez faire theories against big business, reversing the usual line of argument. George pointed out that the railroad, which dominated business in California, had grown not by free competition but by monopoly; that it had been built mainly with government money; and that subsidies were a tremendous form of governmental intervention in the workings of a free economy.

In 1871, also, George published *Our Land and Land Policy,* a pamphlet of about 100 pages in which he first outlined his general doctrine. Stressing the enormous withdrawals of public lands as grants to the railroads, he proposed that the ownership of these and all other lands should be returned to the people, by means of a single massive tax on land that would equal its rental value and thus have the effect of appropriating its ownership and income to the government. George argued that an end to private rent and to speculation in land would bring an end to industrial depressions and maldistribution of wealth, would free business from all other forms of taxation, and indeed would cure virtually all the ills of society.

George's doctrine appeared in elaborated form in 1879 in his *Progress and Poverty,* which became one of the phenomenal best-sellers of all time. By the turn of the century there were more than 5 million copies of his writings in circulation, and their influence abroad, particularly in England, was at least as great as in the United States. He popularized what had been well called the dismal science of economics in words that often had not only the qualities of poetry but the fervor of religion. The single tax, he wrote, would bring "the Golden Age . . . , the culmination of Christianity—the city of God with its walls of jasper and its gates of pearl."

By later standards some of his ideas were illiberal. One of his early editorials justified lynching; he was opposed to labor organizations and to strikes; and he was extremely hostile to the Chinese. George's single-tax dogma was a naïve and emotional panacea. Yet the idea and the man who advanced it still command respect for their part in stimulating popular thought about the problems of society.

AMBROSE BIERCE

Another major literary product of California journalism was Ambrose Gwinett ("Almighty God") Bierce, also known as "Bitter Bierce" and "The Wickedest Man in San Francisco." Though quite as vigorous as Henry George in criticizing things as they were, Bierce claimed to despise reform and reformers—one of the many paradoxes that characterized his personality.

The son of Marcus Aurelius Bierce, an unprosperous farmer who fathered 13 children and gave every one of them a name beginning with "A," Ambrose was born in a backwoods portion of southeastern Ohio. The economic and emotional hardships of his early life contributed much to his permanent embitterment. In Bierce's parody, the saccharine opening lines of "The Old Oaken Bucket,"

How dear to this heart are the scenes of my childhood,
When fond recollection presents them to view . . . ,

were soured into

With what anguish of mind I remember my childhood,
Recalled in the light of a knowledge since gained;
The malarious farm, the wet, fungus grown wildwood,
The chills then contracted that since have remained.

Bierce welcomed the Civil War as an escape from his family, but 4 years of bloody action did nothing to sweeten his temperament. After the war he came to the far west, and in 1868 he took over the writing of a column called "The Town Crier" in the *San Francisco News Letter.* In later years Bierce became the much-feared literary dictator of the Pacific coast with his columns in the San Francisco *Argonaut,* then in the *Wasp,* and finally, after 1887, in young William Randolph Hearst's *Examiner.* Bierce's short stories have often been compared to those of Edgar Allan Poe, but where Poe often resorted to the supernatural, the weird events in Bierce's narratives always had some sardonic but ostensibly rational explanation at the end. His best stories were those collected in *Tales of Soldiers and Civilians,* later published as *In the Midst of Life.*

In *The Devil's Dictionary,* Bierce defined "birth" as "The first and direst of all disasters," and he often argued that suicide was not only a right but almost a duty. And although the circumstances of Bierce's own demise have remained a mystery, it is clear that in 1913 when he planned to join the army of Pancho Villa as an "observer," he was seeking a death which he did not quite wish to inflict by his own hand. "Goodbye," he wrote to his niece, "if you hear of my being stood up against a Mexican stone wall and shot to rags please know that I think it a pretty good way to depart this life. It beats old age, disease, or falling down the cellar stairs. To be a Gringo in Mexico—ah, that is euthanasia!" Bierce was a deeply tortured man, never fully aware of the causes of his misery.

FRANK NORRIS

In contrast with Bierce, who regarded childhood as a disaster and the rest of life as not much better, Frank Norris attributed to his childhood much of his great enthusiasm for both real and fictional experience. The gifted novelist, Norris once wrote, was the man who retained the dramatizing imagination of a boy.

Benjamin Franklin Norris, Jr., was born in Chicago in 1870 of able and energetic parents. When Frank was 14, the family moved to San Francisco. At 17 he was sent to Paris to study art, but when he began to write stories instead, his father maintained that he was wasting his time and summoned him home. At 20 he enrolled in the University of California and spent 4 years there. Having disliked the stylistic conformity which his English professors at Berkeley demanded, he spent a fifth collegiate year in a creative writing course at Harvard, where he worked on two stories of San Francisco, *McTeague* and *Vandover and the Brute.*

Much influenced by the works of Émile Zola, *McTeague* was the first important contribution to naturalism by an American writer. Its hero is a charlatan dentist, McTeague, who marries Trina, a girl who has won $5000 in a lottery; however, her cousin and jilted suitor takes revenge by informing the authorities that the dentist is practicing without a license. The novel became a study of the degeneration of Trina into miserliness and of McTeague into sadistic brutality. *Vandover and the Brute* has the same basic theme—a man's deterioration into the beast within him. In the end, Vandover's downward path goes so far that he actually becomes a victim of lycanthropy, the delusion that he is a wolf.

Norris soon discovered that the naturalism of these works was too undiluted to permit the publication of either of them as a first novel at a time when the American reading public still demanded that fiction be highly romanticized. In search of further training and experience as a writer he joined the editorial staff of the San Francisco *Wave,* hoping that some New York publisher might recognize his talent. The hope was fulfilled. S. S. McClure, who kept an eye on the San Francisco journals for new writers, telegraphed an offer to employ Norris as a regular writer. The publication of *McTeague* followed a few months later, in 1899.

Much encouraged, Norris conceived one of the most ambitious projects in the history of American literature, a trilogy to be called the *Epic of the Wheat.* The first part would describe the growing of the wheat in California, the second its distribution by the board of trade or "pit" in Chicago, and the third its consumption in a famine-stricken village in Europe. Each of the three novels would have a central episode based on an actual occurrence, and the first, *The Octopus, a Story of California,* would center upon the battle of Mussel Slough. But Norris was not concerned with precise accuracy of historical detail; his intention was to tell the truth in what he regarded as a larger sense, including the greatest possible element of dramatic impact. Although in the course of this research he did apparently visit the town of Tulare, the Bonneville of *The Octopus,* he spent much more time on a 10,000-acre wheat ranch near Hollister, so that the locale described in the novel was not actually that of the San Joaquin Valley in 1880 but rather of a coastal valley in 1899, and the wheat growers were not the small farmers of the actual episode, but large ranchers. Consolidating his California, Norris also transplanted a mission and a sleepy old Mexican town, based on San Juan Bautista, across the Coast Range and into a story in which they had had no actual part.

The Octopus also included a number of more basic inconsistencies. As a "novel with a purpose," *The Octopus* departed from Norris's goal of naturalistic objectivity and became in many of its passages a propagandistic tract for reform of the trusts. Norris was perceptibly influenced by the writers whom he met in the offices of *McClure's Magazine* and who would soon launch the muckraking movement. Theodore Roosevelt read *The Octopus* as a tract and remarked to a friend that apparently "conditions were worse in California than elsewhere." *The Octopus* was and will remain one of the most important of American novels.

Although Norris often wrote mystical praises of "the People," that is, the lower and lower-middle classes, he was a snob, with strong biases of both class and race. He was anti-Asian and anti-Semitic, and an admirer of Kipling's Anglo-Saxonism as well as of his literary style. Like most major writers, Norris was as contradictory and complicated as life itself, and he loved life to a degree that made his early death at 32, of appendicitis, peculiarly sad. *The Pit,* based on an actual attempt to corner the wheat market at Chicago, had degenerated into a conventional love story, and was appearing serially in the *Saturday Evening Post* when he died. He had not begun the writing of *The Wolf,* the projected third volume.

JACK LONDON

Few men have risen to success through greater difficulties than did Jack London. He was an unwanted and illegitimate child, born in San Francisco in 1876, presumably the son of William H. Chaney, an itinerant Irish astrologer who denied paternity and whom he never saw. His mother secured a name for him by marrying John London, a kindly widower who gave his stepson what little feeling of stability there was in his earliest years. The boy grew up on the Oakland waterfront. At 15 he was an oyster pirate, at 17 he went to sea on one of the last seal-hunting voyages out of San Francisco Bay, and at 18, in 1894, he traveled to the east coast and back as a member of the California contingent of Coxey's army of unemployed. One of his hobo acquaintances introduced him to the *Communist Manifesto,* and his left-wing socialist opinions solidified after he returned to Oakland and experienced a series of cruelly hard and low-paying jobs, in which he worked for 60 hours a week in a jute mill, in a hand laundry, and at shoveling coal. For years he signed many of his letters "Yours for the Revolution."

After a few months at Oakland High School and a semester at the University of California, he joined the Klondike gold rush in 1897. He discovered no gold but he collected a great deal of material for the stories through which he hoped to make a living. His first publisher, the *Overland Monthly,* offered him $5 for a story of 5000 words, and when even this small payment was slow in coming, he visited the office of the magazine and collected the amount in small change from the pockets of the assistant editor and the business manager, by threat of physical violence. But success came soon afterward. In 1900 S. S. McClure discovered London, as he had discovered Norris, and published London's first book, a collection of stories called *Son of the Wolf.* Within a few years London was the highest-paid, best-known, and most popular writer in the world, displacing his hero Rudyard Kipling in the possession of these honors.

The Call of the Wild (1903), the most famous of London's many stories of the far north, concerned a dog that was kidnapped in California and taken to Alaska where he reverted to savagery and ran with a wolf pack. There were several partly autobiographical novels, including *Martin Eden* (1909) and *John Barleycorn* (1913). And there were several novels or other works of socialist propaganda, the most important of which was *The Iron Heel* (1907). This story was especially striking in that it predicted the rise of fascism.

London's social and political ideas were an amalgam of Darwin, Spencer, Marx, and Nietzsche. As his attempt to cross Marx's proletarianism with Nietzsche's Superman suggests, London's professions of socialism were out of tune with his own strongest feelings. His best writing was concerned not with hopes of an idealized collectivist society, but rather with the opposite theme of the triumph of some individual man or beast over more ordinary members of the respective species in some contest of wild and primordial violence. London's racism, moreover, was more extreme than either Kipling's or Norris's.

London was too emotionally insecure to be capable of happy marriage or of any other stable personal relationship. His second wife, Charmian Kittredge, lived in mortal terror that some other woman would take him away from her as easily as she had seduced him from his first wife, Bessie Maddern. Hoping to find security in a magnificent house, London spent more than $90,000 on a mansion of stone in Sonoma County, but shortly before he was to have moved into it the interior of the house was destroyed by fire. There could be no doubt that the fire had been set deliberately, and the loss was intensified by the pain of speculating on the identity of the person who had hated him enough to do such a devilish thing to him. The alcoholism that had endangered his health for many years became progressively worse, and in 1916, at 40 and in great pain from uremia, he ended his life, perhaps inadvertently, with an overdose of morphine. His career had symbolized the elemental power of humanity to struggle against tragedy and heartbreak, a struggle that was no less admirable because in his case the odds were too heavy to be overcome.

HISTORIOGRAPHY

Well before the end of the nineteenth century, California witnessed the carrying out of a truly remarkable project for the writing of its history, a project which in its unbounded ambitiousness was characteristic of the state itself. One day in 1859 Hubert Howe Bancroft, the most successful bookseller in San Francisco and in the whole of the west, happened to place together all the items in his store that dealt with the Pacific coast. Such was the nucleus of the incomparable Bancroft Library. From collecting books, and later manuscripts, Bancroft progressed to the idea of bringing together the history that was in them. Calculating at one point that it would take him 400 years to read the whole of his collection, let alone to write a history from it, and being of a practical turn of mind, he employed a staff of assistants when the actual research and writing project began in 1871. The ablest of these was Henry L. Oak, a young graduate of Dartmouth College who was originally employed as librarian and who had no more formal training as a historian or experience as a writer than did Bancroft himself.

Few things even in California have grown as the Bancroft project grew. *Bancroft's Works,* published between 1882 and 1890, filled 39 fat and closely packed volumes. Bancroft himself was substantially the author of about one-fourth of these books. The others were written, as well as researched, by his assistants. In all these *Works,* however, Bancroft most unwisely and unfortunately represented himself as the sole author; the assistants received no credit except in the thirty-ninth

Hubert Howe Bancroft
(1832–1918), pioneer California
historian and bibliophile. His
collection of books and
manuscripts became the core of
the Bancroft Library at the
University of California, Berkeley.
*(Courtesy of the California
Historical Society.)*

volume, called *Literary Industries,* in which Bancroft described the process of authorship in a most inadequate and misleading way.

The five volumes on the general history of California to 1848 were written by (Henry L. Oak. As a whole they were superior to the two volumes on the period 1848 to 1890 written mainly by two of Bancroft's other assistants, William Nemos and Frances Fuller Victor. And a comparison of Oak's writings with the volumes on California that were actually written by Bancroft (*California, Pastoral, California Inter Pocula,* and *Popular Tribunals*) makes it clear that Oak was a better historian than his employer. When Henry Oak, having become a brooding invalid after 20 years of hard and anonymous labor, wrote an ineffectual protest, Bancroft replied: "I doubt that authors are in the habit of giving their employees any credit at all." In making this statement Bancroft was quite unaware of its impropriety and irrelevance. Why later historians have failed to give proper credit to Oak for the authorship of the best volumes in the Bancroft history of California is harder to explain.

In the process of marketing the mammoth series, also, Bancroft resorted to devices that were highly questionable, though he himself did not consider them so. Many purchasers of the series, who signed up at the beginning, were not told what a large number of volumes they were contracting to buy. When the *Works* first began to appear, Leland Stanford had generously subscribed for 40 sets, under the impression that a full set would consist of five or six volumes. But after receiving and paying for 40 copies of each volume of the *Works* through the twenty-third one, he canceled his subscription in an acid letter.

Finally, when the *Works* were followed in the early 1890s by the *Chronicles of the Builders of the Commonwealth,* and when it became known that in these enormously expensive vanity publications the length and tone of each biography was determined by the number of thousands of dollars subscribed by the biographee, there was a blast of public criticism that damaged Bancroft's reputation. Collis P. Huntington had subscribed a large sum for the glowing 110-page biography of him that appeared in the *Chronicles.* On the other hand, the biography of Leland Stanford, which had been fully prepared for publication, was omitted from the set because Stanford refused to make payment.

When the wealthy land-title lawyer Theodore H. Hittell wrote his own *History of California,* which was published in four volumes between 1885 and 1897, the extreme public criticisms of a number of Bancroft's methods had misled Hittell into supposing that there could be no value in any of *Bancroft's Works,* and he refused to consult them. Hittell's history was a good one; it could have been still better if he had not made this unfortunate misjudgment.

Not long after Josiah Royce had become a junior member of the philosophy department at Harvard, the publisher of a projected series of volumes on "American Commonwealths" selected him, as one of the most promising young men who had come to the east out of California, to write a volume on his native state. Royce obtained permission to use the Bancroft library, already by far the largest and best collection of sources in the west. He also received much helpful advice from Henry Oak. Royce's *California, from the Conquest in 1846 to the Second Vigilance Committee in San Francisco, a Study of American Character* (1886) took the form of an effort to establish the validity of the Hegelian dialectic of order and disorder, authority and freedom.

LORDS OF THE PRESS

In the later decades of the nineteenth century and the early years of the twentieth, journalism in California's metropolis of San Francisco differed from that of the frontier days in that there came to be a smaller number of larger newspapers, owned and controlled by a few wealthy men.

Of the major San Francisco dailies destined to survive into the twentieth century the oldest were the *Evening Bulletin,* founded in 1855, and the *Morning Call,* which dated from 1856. But these were ultimately outstripped in circulation and influence by two morning papers: the *Examiner,* which began as the weekly *Democratic Press* in 1863, and the *Chronicle,* founded as the *Daily Dramatic Chronicle* in 1865 by the brothers Charles and M. H. de Young.

One of the most striking developments in the whole colorful history of American newspapers was the rise of William Randolph Hearst, who was born in San Francisco in 1863 and took over the ownership and control of the *Examiner* in 1887, when he was less than 24 years old. George Hearst, his father, had bought the paper a few years earlier to advance his political ambitions. In January 1887, a Democratic majority in the California legislature elected George Hearst to the United States Senate, and it was on March 4, the day he took his seat in Washington, that he made the gift of the *San Francisco Examiner* to his son.

A few months earlier, William Randolph Hearst had been expelled from Harvard at the end of his junior year for indulging in an obscene expression of contempt for his professors. Since then he had worked as a reporter for Joseph Pulitzer's *New York World* in order to study Pulitzer's methods. These he would soon apply to the moribund little *Examiner* with many elaborations of his own and with spectacular results. Young Hearst quickly expanded the *Examiner* from four pages to eight, banished advertising from the front page in favor of headlines followed by sensational stories of crime and corruption, and brought in many special features for the reader's amusement. The term "yellow journalism" has its origin when Hearst hired away from Pulitzer the cartoonist of a popular early comic strip called "the Yellow Kid."

Hearst went to unusual lengths with the "arranged story": if the news that actually happened was not lively enough, he manufactured news that was. At the *Examiner*'s expense a young couple were married in a balloon, and even, according to the *Examiner*, spent their honeymoon there—"up in the clouds." The real secret of Hearst's success was in his genius for spectacular entertainment. "The public," he wrote in an editorial in 1896, "is even more fond of entertainment than it is of information," and this philosophy of journalism became increasingly important in later years when he acquired an unprecedented number of newspapers in many cities, including the largest cities in the country. He maintained extraordinarily close control over the news and editorial policies of all his papers, and thus he had a greater influence on what was printed and read in America than any other man before or since.

No other California newspaper publisher acquired national influence comparable to Hearst's, but within the state there were several figures of regional importance. In Sacramento the history of the *Bee* became synonymous with that of the McClatchy family, from the time when James McClatchy became editor in 1857, the year the *Bee* was founded. McClatchy had come from Ireland as a boy, and he brought an Irishman's hatred of land monopoly to his leadership of the squatters in the gold-rush period and then to the *Bee*'s editorial columns. At his death in 1883 the control of the paper passed to his son Charles ("C.K."), who was its fighting editor for nearly 50 years. The most important figure in southern California was Harrison Gray Otis, a native of Ohio who arrived in Los Angeles in 1882 and began his long career as editor and publisher of the *Los Angeles Times*. From the beginning, Otis was an unabashed booster of his adopted city. Praised by some as a visionary and damned by others as a reactionary, Otis's influence on the political, economic, and cultural development of the region was unparalleled.

THE ARTS AND ARCHITECTURE

The outstanding painter of pioneer life in California was Charles Christian Nahl. Born into a family that had achieved artistic distinction in Germany for six

Sunday Morning in the Mines. Painted by Charles Christian Nahl in 1872. (© *Courtesy of the Crocker Art Museum, Sacramento, California.*)

generations, Nahl came to California in 1850 and was soon the leading producer of lithographs for letter sheets, the famous souvenir stationery on which the miners wrote home the news from the goldfields. After Judge E. B. Crocker became his patron in 1867, Nahl was able to devote the greater part of his time to his work in oils, and a number of his paintings were included in the Crocker Art Gallery in Sacramento. Probably the best of these, and certainly the best known, was his *Sunday Morning in the Mines,* which appears badly overcrowded in small reproductions, but less so in the original, a canvas 9 feet long and 6 feet high.

Thomas A. Ayres became famous as the first artist to portray Yosemite Valley. In 1855 Ayers was a member of the first tourist party ever to enter the valley; in five days he produced five drawings, one of which, *The High Falls,* has scarcely been excelled among the thousands of later efforts. Albert Bierstadt and Thomas Hill were among the many who later painted the Yosemite and other California landscapes.

The most intriguing work of Hill, however, was his attempt to provide the ultimate commemoration of the transcontinental railroad in his *Driving the Last Spike.* Leland Stanford had commissioned this painting and promised $50,000 for it; such, at least, was Hill's impression, but after the artist had spent 4 years at work on the huge and elaborate canvas, Stanford refused to buy it and denied that he had ordered it. His most vocal objection was that some 70 officials of the Union and Central Pacific railroads were in the massive picture, very few of whom had actually been present at the scene; even Judah, who had died 6 years previously,

Driving the Last Spike. This controversial canvas, painted by Thomas Hill between 1887 and 1891, contains over 400 figures, including 70 recognizable portraits. *(Courtesy of the California State Railroad Museum, Sacramento.)*

was included. In somewhat the same mood in which he broke relations with Hubert Howe Bancroft, Stanford stood four-square against contractual imposture, and in favor of historical accuracy. It was also true, however, that relatives of Charles Crocker strongly objected to the prominent position occupied by Stanford at the center of Hill's picture, and that Stanford's repudiation of the painting tended to restore the peace in the railroad family.

Scottish-born William Keith, whose active career extended from the 1860s until his death in 1911, attained greater prestige than any other California artist. His early paintings of the Sierra country were done with almost photographic realism, but his maturity and his success came when, much to the disappointment of his close friend John Muir, he turned from the high mountains to pastoral landscapes of the foothills, done with a highly mystical quality.

The best California sculptor of the period was probably Ralph Stackpole, whose busts of several well-known San Franciscans were excellent portraits in stone. Greater popular acclaim, however, went to the attitudinized athletic figures by Douglas Tilden, such as the five men operating an antique drill press in the sculpture created for the "Mechanics' Monument" at Market and Bush Streets in San Francisco.

In the field of music, San Francisco had heard its first grand opera as early as February 12, 1851, when the Pellegrini opera troupe presented Bellini's *La Sonnambula*

A photograph by A. J. Russell of the jubilant scene at Promontory, May 10, 1869. Note the contrast with Hill's idealized painting on the previous page. *(Courtesy of the Oakland Museum.)*

at the Adelphi Theater. But throughout the nineteenth century, traveling performers from the east continued to outshine the local talent, both in music and in drama.

In architecture, regional developments were somewhat more distinctive. "California mission architecture" has as much interest for the history of mythmaking as for the history of architecture. Charming legends to the contrary, the roof tiles were not shaped on the thighs of Indian women, and the designs for the California mission buildings added little to the older Mexican models. As for the so-called Monterey colonial style, introduced by Thomas Larkin in the 1830s, it was adapted from buildings he had seen in Massachusetts and North Carolina, and nothing about it was either Spanish-colonial or Mexican-republican except the use of adobe as the handiest material for the walls. Nevertheless, in the early twentieth century, "mission revival" and Monterey colonial buildings formed the basis of an important regional architectural tradition.

The availability of redwood in the American period gave San Francisco in the late nineteenth century a larger proportion of wood frame residential buildings than any other city in the nation. Redwood became so common that there were many attempts to use paint to disguise it as stone, and the wooden house of David D. Colton on Nob Hill was even painted to simulate an Italian marble palace. Even so, the Colton house was a less offensive monument to conspicuous and meretricious waste than were the neighboring mansions of Crocker, Stanford, and the rest.

Postcard showing California Street cable car and Stanford and Hopkins mansions on Nob Hill. *(Courtesy of the Bancroft Library.)*

Beauty was regarded as deriving from ornamentation rather than from any genuine architectural function, and there was a profusion of jigsaw carpentry on porches and of ironwork on mansard roofs. In the construction of public buildings the era is notorious for the tendency of architects to try to build monuments to themselves rather than design structures that would effectively serve the purposes for which they were intended.

SCHOOLS, COLLEGES, AND UNIVERSITIES

The development of a sense of public responsibility for education in California in the nineteenth century was slow, lagging far behind the growth of the state's economic resources and population. Not until 1874 did the state adopt compulsory education, and even then, although it applied only to the elementary level, the law was bitterly opposed on the grounds that it was an arrogation of new power by the government. As for public secondary education, there were only 16 high schools in the state in 1879, and several of them were wiped out by the provision of the new constitution that denied state tax funds to high schools on the ground that the primary and grammar schools were still inadequately supported—which was all too true.

The movement to establish kindergartens in California was led by Emma Marwedel, a German-born educator who opened the state's first kindergarten in Los Angeles in 1870. One of her former pupils, Kate Douglas Wiggin, taught the first free kindergarten classes in a slum district of San Francisco in 1878. To raise money for her school, Wiggin wrote *The Birds' Christmas Carol* (1887), a popular and moving account of an ethereal child. Later she achieved national fame as author of the even more popular *Rebecca of Sunnybrook Farm* (1903).

elementary teachers. In 1900 these institutions enrolled about half the women then pursuing higher education. The oldest women's college in the west was opened as a young ladies' seminary in Oakland in 1871 by Dr. and Mrs. Cyrus T. Mills and chartered as Mills College in 1885. Most of the other collegiate institutions in California were coeducational, but the status of women in higher education remained precarious. When enrollment of female undergraduates at Stanford University exceeded expectations, Jane Lathrop Stanford issued an edict in 1899 strictly limiting their admission: "I mean literally *never* in the future history of Leland Stanford Junior University can the number of female students at any one time exceed 500." Several decades would pass before university trustees voted to lift the limit on female admissions.

SELECTED BIBLIOGRAPHY

On several aspects of this chapter see Kevin Starr, *Americans and the California Dream, 1850–1915* (1973).

Henry George is the subject of biographies by Steven Cord (1965, 1984) and Charles A. Barker (1955). The best treatments of Bierce are Paul Fatout (1951) and Richard Saunders (1985). Important writings on Frank Norris include the biography by Franklin Walker (1932) and the studies by Ernest L. Marchand (1942), Warren French (1962), Donald Pizer (1966), and Robert D. Lundy, "The Making of *McTeague* and *The Octopus*," Ph.D. thesis, University of California, Berkeley (1956). See also Joseph R. McElrath (ed.), *Frank Norris: A Descriptive Bibliography* (1992) and the special issue of *American Literary Realism, 1870–1910*, XI (Autumn 1978). On the treatment of the battle of Mussel Slough by Norris and others, see the articles by Irving McKee, *Pacific Historical Review*, XVII (February 1948), pp. 19–28, and James Lorin Brown, ibid., XXVI (November 1957), pp. 373–376.

Jack London has attracted a wealth of biographers: Earle Labor (1994), Carolyn Johnston (1984), Joan Hedrick (1982), John Perry (1981), Andrew Sinclair (1977), Richard O'Connor (1964), Joan London (1939), and Irving Stone (1938).

On historiography see John W. Caughey, *Hubert Howe Bancroft* (1946); Harry Clark, *A Venture in History* (1973); Robert W. Righter, "Theodore H. Hittell and Hubert H. Bancroft," *California Historical Quarterly*, L (June 1971), pp. 101–110, and Robert V. Hine, *Josiah Royce* (1991).

Much information on both major and minor literary figures may be found in Franklin Walker, *San Francisco's Literary Frontier* (1939), *A Literary History of Southern California* (1950), and *The Seacoast of Bohemia* (1966); Lawrence Clark Powell, *California Classics* (1971); and Gerald Haslam (ed.), *Many Californias* (1991). Robert Louis Stevenson left some lively vignettes of his sojourn in California; all are included in James D. Hart (ed.), *From Scotland to Silverado* (1966).

On the press, see John P. Young, *Journalism in California* (1915); John Roberts Bruce, *Gaudy Century* (1948); and *History of Journalism in San Francisco* (1939–1941), by the California Writers' Program of the WPA. Of the several biographies of Hearst, those by Cora B. Older (1936) and John K. Winkler (1928, 1955) were almost as indulgent toward their subject as were his own parents; the best general treatments are W. A. Swanberg, *Citizen Hearst* (1961), and Judith Robinson, *The Hearsts* (1991). James R. Wotherspoon, "The San Francisco *Argonaut*, 1877–1907," Ph.D. thesis, University of California, Berkeley (1962), deals with the most important of the weeklies. On Los Angeles journalism, see Richard Connelly Miller, "Otis and His *Times,*" Ph.D. thesis, University of California, Berkeley (1961), and Edwin Bingham, *Charles F. Lummis* (1955). See also Sherilyn Cox Bennion, *Equal to the Occasion* (1990), an account of women editors in the nineteenth century.

Edna Milton Hughes, *Artists in California, 1786–1940* (1986), lists over 6000 California artists, while Jeanne Van Nostrand, *The First Hundred Years of Painting in California, 1775–1875* (1980), describes in more depth the work of 80 major artists. See also Eugene Neuhaus, "Charles Christian Nahl, the Painter of California Pioneer Life," *California Historical Society Quarterly,* XV (December 1936), pp. 295–305, and *William Keith, the Man and the Artist* (1938). A special issue of *California History,* LXXI (Spring 1992), is devoted to California art in the nineteenth century.

Harold Kirker's *California's Architectural Frontier* (1960) and *Old Forms on a New Land* (1991) are important social histories, as is Sally Woodbridge's *California Architecture* (1988).

William Warren Ferrier, *Ninety Years of Education in California, 1846–1936* (1937), is valuable for the early decades, though less so for the period after 1900. See also Judith Rosenberg Raftery, *Land of Fair Promise: Politics and Reform in Los Angeles Schools, 1885–1941* (1992); Irving G. Hendrick, *California Education* (1980); and Doyce B. Nunis, Jr., "Kate Douglas Wiggin: Pioneer in California Kindergarten Education," *California Historical Society Quarterly* (December 1962), pp. 291–307. On higher education see Gunther Barth, *California's Practical Period* (1994); John R. Thelin, "California and the Colleges," *California Historical Quarterly,* LVI (Summer and Fall 1977), pp. 140–163, 230–249; Verne A. Stadtman, *The University of California, 1868–1968* (1970); Edward M. Burns, *David Starr Jordan* (1953); Gunther W. Nigel, *Iron Will: The Life and Letters of June Stanford* (1985); and Andrew Rolle, *Occidental College* (1986).

CHAPTER NINETEEN

Politics in the Era of Railroad Domination

The last third of the nineteenth century was an age of unparalleled corruption in American public life. The leaders of huge corporations dominated not only the American economy, but also American politics; and they tended to despise the politicians, many of whom they easily corrupted, and also to feel contempt for government itself. In no state was politics more subservient to big business than in California, for in no other state, as James Bryce remarked, were politics and the economy "so much at the mercy of one powerful corporation." In California the Southern Pacific represented the greatest accumulation of wealth. It was the largest landowner, it was the largest employer of labor, and its rail system was the longest in the nation.

The degree of railroad domination in California has sometimes been exaggerated, and this has led some historians to minimize it to the extent of calling it a mere legend. Historian William Deverell, for instance, recently surveyed a half-century of hostility directed at the Southern Pacific and questioned "whether there actually was an all-powerful, monolithic railroad corporation." It is true, of course, that railroad control was far from complete, but in general it was highly effective. The power of the Southern Pacific was not a monolith, nor was it a myth.

When the government of California began its attempts to regulate the Southern Pacific in the 1870s, the railroad responded by intensifying its control of the state government. The more corrupt methods by which the railroad intervened in politics were kept as secret as possible, but the workings of the Southern Pacific's "invisible government" could not always be kept invisible, and they were starkly revealed in such episodes as the publication of the "Colton letters" and the "Dear Pard" letters, the struggle of Los Angeles for a free harbor, and the railroad's attempt to escape from the payment of its debt to the United States.

THE COLTON LETTERS

For 4 years before his sudden death in 1878, David D. Colton had been the confidential manager of the railroad's political interests in California, while Collis P. Huntington was serving the same function in Washington, D.C. Colton was highly skilled in the shadier methods of influencing politicians. He amassed a fortune by performing this type of confidential service in exchange for opportunities to share in the profits of enterprises which would benefit from the special political privileges he could obtain. Collis P. Huntington in 1874 had persuaded his partners to approve an agreement under which Colton was permitted to acquire a large amount of railroad stock on credit. The new associate often used the expression "we five" in his letters to Huntington, though some of the newspapers described the group more accurately as "the Big Four and a Half."

When Colton died, his widow received only a little more than half a million dollars in the settlement of his estate. Not long afterward when some of the details of the estate of Mark Hopkins were made public and Mrs. Colton noticed that some of Hopkins's shares of stock were quoted as having a far higher cash value than she had been allowed for her husband's identical shares, she concluded that the railroad leaders had cheated her. When they coldly refused a more favorable settlement, she sued the Big Four for $4 million. In 1883, in the course of the trial, her attorneys suddenly introduced as evidence several hundred letters that had been exchanged between Colton and Huntington in the years between 1874 and 1878.

In explicit detail these letters revealed Colton's activities in influencing the elections, reelections, and votes of members of the California Legislature and the California congressional delegation, and Huntington's similar activities with members of Congress in the east. There were innumerable references to payments of money without vouchers and discussions of the amounts which particular legislators and legislative measures might be expected to cost. In one letter, for example, Huntington had written that "It costs money to fix things . . . I believe with $200,000 I can pass our bill, but that it is not worth this much to us." In another instance he wrote that "the boys are very hungry, and it will cost us considerable to be saved."

The state supreme court, in the case of *Ellen M. Colton v. Leland Stanford et al.,* refused to award Mrs. Colton a larger settlement. But the damage to the Southern Pacific's reputation was far greater than the value of the widow's highest demands. For decades afterward the railroad's opponents could and did cite the Colton letters whenever they wished to denounce the Southern Pacific for corrupting politics. Moreover, a widespread public reaction was that the Big Four were men who would defraud a partner's widow—a more serious moral offense to some people than the payment of money for the votes of politicians.

THE HUNTINGTON-STANFORD FEUD

Collis P. Huntington's contempt for people who sought public office, which was extremely apparent throughout his letters to Colton, bore a significant relation to his feelings toward Leland Stanford. For many years Huntington had resented the degree to which Stanford received the lion's share of public attention while he, Huntington, did most of the hard work of managing the railroad's affairs. In 1885, when Stanford secured election to the United States Senate, Huntington was deeply angered. The honor had been promised to Aaron A. Sargent, a close friend of Huntington's who had rendered many years of faithful service to the railroad's interests in both houses of Congress.

When the founding of a memorial university was announced, Huntington felt that Stanford's vanity had become completely unendurable, and he made plans to deflate it. At an annual meeting of stockholders in 1890 Huntington announced that he would support Stanford's election to a second term as senator only on condition that he himself be elected to the presidency of the railroad, which Stanford had held for 30 years. Then, after assuming the presidency, Huntington publicly stated that unlike his predecessor he would never "use this great corporation to advance my personal ambition at the expense of its owners, or put my hands in the treasury to defeat the people's choice, and thereby put myself into positions that should be filled by others."

Enemies of the Southern Pacific had often charged that large amounts of railroad money were spent by the railroad to secure Stanford's election and reelection by the California Legislature as United States senator. Now the charge was directly corroborated by the president of the railroad itself. Huntington threw his open denunciation in Stanford's face with no more warning than either of them had had from Ellen Colton. In the next few hours Stanford's friends saw him age 10 years, and his death in 1893 was undoubtedly hastened by Huntington's carefully laid plan to destroy him.

Beginning in 1892 and continuing for several years afterward, Stanford's former private secretary, J. M. Bassett, published in the *San Francisco Report* at weekly intervals a series of letters which he addressed to Huntington. These letters, opening with the salutation "Dear Pard," were intended to injure Huntington as Stanford had been injured. They were filled with charges of the wholesale corruption of national, state, and local officials by the railroad, and though they had little effect in penetrating the thick skin of Collis P. Huntington, they added significantly to a growing mass of public evidence.

LOS ANGELES FIGHTS FOR A FREE HARBOR

In another of his early actions as the new president of the Southern Pacific, Huntington reversed Stanford's policy toward the location of a modern deep-water harbor for Los Angeles. Senator Stanford had supported proposals for federal aid in the construction of a breakwater at San Pedro. Huntington decided that the harbor must be built at Santa Monica because he was able to purchase enough land there to ensure that the Southern Pacific could dominate the harbor by preventing any competing railroad from gaining access to it. Huntington saw no reason why the railroad should have less control over the future port of Los Angeles than it had long exerted over the port of San Francisco. But Los Angeles, though it had only

50,000 people in the early 1890s, felt the stirrings of its future growth and power and determined to fight for a harbor that would be at least relatively free of Southern Pacific control.

In 1891 a board of Army engineers reported that San Pedro Bay was the best site in the region for the construction of a breakwater and thus for the creation of a great harbor. But the next year, Huntington served blunt notice that he would use all his influence in Congress to block any appropriation for the San Pedro project. Los Angeles rebelled, and its chamber of commerce was able to enlist some powerful allies in the fight. Harrison Gray Otis and the *Times,* the owners of the new Terminal Island Railroad, and Democratic Senator Stephen White led the opposition. Huntington's supporters in Congress argued that the government should not spend money for a harbor at San Pedro when "private enterprise"—that is, Mr. Huntington—was willing to undertake the cost of construction nearby; however, it was well known that Huntington expected to persuade Congress to pay for a still larger breakwater at Santa Monica.

In 1896 Congress passed an appropriation for whatever site a new board of engineers should approve. When this report again favored San Pedro, Huntington secured 2 more years of delay. But at last, in April 1899, the first bargeload of rock was dumped to begin construction of the breakwater at San Pedro. In later years the breakwater would be extended eastward to protect the combined harbor of San Pedro and Long Beach; and Los Angeles would become one of the world's great seaports, as well as one of its great cities.

THE FUNDING BILL

The original construction of the Central Pacific had been made possible by federal loans of nearly $28 million payable in 30 years. No payment of interest was required until the full maturity of the loans. Simple interest at 6 percent added more than $50 million to the total obligation that was legally payable by the year 1899. In the 1870s, though the Big Four began to vote themselves huge dividends, they set aside nothing for the ultimate payment of the railroad's debt to the government. Instead, they propounded a long series of ingenious and specious arguments for its cancellation.

Congress in 1878 passed a law requiring the Central Pacific to create a sinking fund of 25 percent of the net earnings of the parts of its rail lines that had been built with federal aid. Huntington denounced the legislators who voted for the new law as "communists." But the railroad, by manipulating both traffic and bookkeeping so as to credit as little as possible of its earnings to the original "bond-aided" portions of the lines, kept the sinking fund to a small fraction of its total debt to the government. In the 1890s Huntington advanced a series of proposals for a funding plan to delay payment for 50 or 100 years, at the extremely low interest rate of $\frac{1}{2}$ of 1 percent. In California this aroused more opposition than any other measure in the long history of public resentment against the railroad, and Adolph Sutro and William Randolph Hearst led a chorus of denunciation of it as a plot to escape the debt entirely.

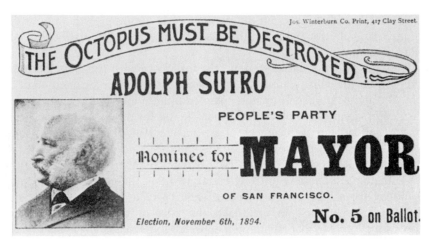

A handbill from Adolph Sutro's antirailroad mayoral campaign in 1894. *(Courtesy of the Sutro Library, San Francisco.)*

Adolph Sutro had sold all his stock in his Comstock tunnel as soon as it was completed. With the million dollars salvaged from that venture, he had moved to San Francisco, and there, by buying land whenever the local market for it reached the bottom of one of its periodic depressions, had become the owner of one-twelfth of the city's entire area. Seal Rocks, the Cliff House, the gardens of his home, and other adjoining portions of his great estate were opened to the public as a park. When the Market Street Railway Company, a Southern Pacific subsidiary, took over the trolley line to this park and refused to continue a low round-trip fare, Sutro built his own parallel line and declared himself the defender of the people against the greed of the Octopus. In 1894 Sutro was elected mayor of San Francisco as the candidate of the People's Party. Sutro won the nomination and the election, partly because his many philanthropies had made him a popular figure, but also because he organized a series of mass meetings to denounce Huntington's funding plan.

William Randolph Hearst also threw the full weight of the *San Francisco Examiner* into the battle against the funding plan, and in 1894 the *Examiner* obtained more than 200,000 signatures on petitions against it. In 1896, when the crucial vote in Congress was approaching, Hearst sent Ambrose Bierce and the cartoonist Homer Davenport to Washington, D.C. For more than 20 years Bierce's opinions of the Southern Pacific leadership had been typified by his frequent printed references to "£eland $tanford," and his articles on the funding bill were as merciless as anything in his long career of journalistic mayhem. His most effective dispatch reported a conversation on the steps of the national Capitol in which Huntington asked him to name his price for stopping his attacks and Bierce replied that his price was the railroad's full debt to the government, payable to the United States Treasury. At the same time, Davenport was making Huntington the villain of some of his most famous cartoons.

HIGHWAYMAN HUNTINGTON TO THE VOTERS OF CALIFORNIA:

"Hand Over Your Honor, Manhood and Independence, and Be Quick About It."

First published in the *San Francisco Examiner* in 1898, this cartoon was typical of Homer Davenport's attacks on the political power of the Southern Pacific. *(Courtesy of the Bancroft Library.)*

In the face of Huntington's claim that failure to adopt his funding plan would bankrupt the whole Southern Pacific system the rebellious California Legislature adopted a resolution urging the federal government not only to foreclose but to assume the ownership and operation of the railroad if necessary. When the funding bill was finally voted down in Congress in January 1897, popular opinion in California was so overjoyed that Democratic Governor James H. Budd proclaimed Saturday, January 16, a public holiday in celebration. Two years later a compromise agreement was reached, and under its terms the railroad completed the payment of its entire debt to the federal government by 1909.

THE SOUTHERN PACIFIC MACHINE

The Los Angeles harbor fight and the funding battle were almost the only major political defeats that the railroad suffered before 1910. These two defeats occurred during the hard times of the 1890s, when public discontent was at a maximum, and they were in considerable part the results of personality conflicts in which the increasing tactlessness and ruthlessness of the aging Collis P. Huntington infuriated other large operators. Moreover, these two issues involved the national government. In purely state and local matters, attempts to break the grip of the railroad's political machine brought only a long succession of humiliating failures for nearly half a century.

By the 1890s the head of the railroad's political department, who was also its chief legal counsel, had become a much more important official than the governor;

in fact he usually had the power to name the governor, or any other public officer in California. Under his direction there was a railroad political manager in every county in the state. This manager might be the Republican boss in a Republican county or the Democratic boss in a Democratic county; in doubtful counties he was merely the railroad boss, with whom both Republican and Democratic bosses had to deal.

A system of political alliance with the other public utility corporations was an important factor in the railroad's power over local political bosses. The railroad itself was then the only statewide public utility, but the political interests of local street railway, gas, light, and telephone companies were similar to its own if on a smaller scale. The railroad and the other utilities were the private business corporations that could profit most directly from special favors granted by government agencies, and consequently they joined in furnishing the bulk of the money that corrupted state and local politics. This alliance came to be known in California as "the associated villainies."

To place all the blame upon the railroad and other utility corporations, however, ignores the fact that they could not have corrupted the state if so many of its citizens had not been corruptible. When lawyers who were not already on the railroad's payroll were elected to the state legislature, they were likely to receive a letter from the law department of the Southern Pacific stating that the railroad wished to retain an outstanding attorney from their region during a period which happened to coincide with that of the coming session at Sacramento. A retainer fee was enclosed, and the privileged nature of the attorney-client relationship protected the secrecy of the transaction.

Of all the agencies of state government, the railroad was most careful to control the bank commission. Bankers who gave aid and comfort to the railroad's enemies could suddenly find themselves in disastrous trouble with this board of commissioners. Consequently, businesspeople or farmers who displeased the railroad by denouncing its rates, or by voting against its candidates, would suddenly find themselves unable to obtain further loans from their bank.

Another effective form of influence was the free pass. It cost relatively little, and it reached people who would have resisted more obvious forms of bribery. Instead of being considered a bribe, the railroad pass was a status symbol. The person who held it felt allied with the successful and powerful leaders of society against the ignorant and envious rabble. The constitution of 1879 specifically forbade free passes for state officeholders, but the provision was never enforced.

Many of the smaller newspapers were subsidized not only with advertising contracts but with regular and secret monthly stipends. Larger publishers such as Harrison Gray Otis, M. H. de Young, and John D. Spreckels were far too wealthy to be influenced by trifling financial considerations. But each of these three men had perennial hopes of going to the United States Senate, and though they often joined in attacks on the railroad, there were also many occasions when each of them tempered his criticism of the Southern Pacific because of his own political ambitions.

Not even the courts were immune from the railroad's influence. Justices of the federal and state supreme courts traveled on passes. Most of the judges of the federal district and circuit courts in San Francisco were appointed at the instance of California senators who spoke with the railroad's voice. Justice Stephen J. Field, great and brilliant "craftsman of the law," was a personal associate of the Big Four, owed his position in the United States Supreme Court to their influence, and rendered them invaluable service by writing many of the opinions through which the highest Court long protected the railroad and other corporations from effective government regulation.

As for the judiciary at the state level, the machine controlled the election of judges, and one of the regular duties of a county boss was to provide the railroad with secret annotated lists of veniremen to aid its attorneys in impaneling sympathetic juries.

WILLIAM F. HERRIN

Among the important sources of the railroad's power was its ability to enlist the most talented lawyers in its service. One such person was William F. Herrin, who headed the Southern Pacific's legal and political departments from 1893 to 1910. It was under Herrin that the railroad's political machine in California reached its highest level of efficiency.

Herrin in 1889 had won a national reputation when, as special counsel, he aided a United States attorney in defending a federal marshal, David Neagle, against a murder charge. The case grew out of the earlier and equally sensational legal battle in which Sarah Althea Hill had claimed that she was the legal wife of Senator William Sharon under the terms of a "contract marriage," and that she was thus entitled to a large part of his enormous fortune. During the court proceedings Sharon died, and his alleged widow married one of her attorneys, David S. Terry, former chief justice of the California Supreme Court. United States Justice Stephen J. Field, while on federal circuit court duty in San Francisco, ruled that Mrs. Terry had not been Sharon's wife and had no valid claim on the Sharon estate. Both the Terrys had brought weapons into the courtroom, and both of them threatened Field's wife.

At the time of Justice Field's next visit to California, United States Marshal Neagle was assigned as his bodyguard, and when, in a railway station in Lathrop, Terry approached Field and struck him, Neagle shot Terry dead. *In re Neagle* became one of the great cases in the history of American federal-state relations. No federal law had authorized Neagle's assignment as bodyguard or his action in killing Terry; but the United States Supreme Court ruled that these had been "fairly and properly inferable" from the Constitution. It was one of the broadest interpretations yet given to the implied powers of the national government.

Herrin was the attorney who contributed most to the preparation of the case for Neagle in the circuit court proceedings at San Francisco. Collis P. Huntington, deeply impressed with Herrin's talents, chose him, as he had once chosen David D. Colton, to be the railroad's western political manager.

From his office in the Southern Pacific's headquarters at Fourth and Townsend streets in San Francisco, Herrin not only directed all the company's manifold ibid., XXVII (August 1958), pp. 281–298; Eric F. Petersen, "The End of an Era: California's Gubernatorial Election of 1894," ibid., XXXVIII (May 1969), pp. 141–156; John T. McGreevy, "Farmers, Nationalists, and the Origins of California Populism," ibid., LVIII (November 1989), pp. 471–495; David B. Griffiths, "Anti-Monopoly Movements in California, 1873–1898," *Southern California Quarterly,* LII (June 1970), pp. 93–121; and Michael P. Rogin and John L. Shover, *Political Change in California* (1970).

CHAPTER TWENTY

Labor and Capital

The period of the late nineteenth and early twentieth centuries was not only an age of business domination; it was also a time of working-class organization. Unions increased in strength and challenged, often unsuccessfully, the powers of corporate America. Radical organizations appealed to the discontented and called for fundamental economic and political change. In California, as Carey McWilliams once observed, the struggle between labor and capital was one of total engagement.

BACKGROUNDS OF THE CALIFORNIA LABOR MOVEMENT

The first large-scale labor movement in the state, the Workingmen's party of 1877 to 1880, contributed very little to the development of modern labor organization. Denis Kearney was ignorant of the principles of trade unionism, and with minor exceptions the Workingmen's party received no support from the few small unions then in existence in California. California legislation in the interest of labor also remained very limited. A state bureau of labor statistics was established in 1883, but laws providing on paper for the mechanics' lien and for an 8-hour day on government work lacked provisions essential for their enforcement.

Throughout the country attempts at effective labor organization suffered from labor's chronic disunity and confusion of aims. One great dispute was over the question of whether labor should avoid organized political action and confine itself to "pure and simple" or "bread and butter" unionism, that is, to collective bargaining with employers for strictly economic goals. Another basic disagreement concerned the form of organization. The oldest and most conservative plan was that of craft unionism, in which each skilled trade in a city had its own local union, reaching out toward federation with other locals in the same craft on a state and national basis, and also toward city, state, and national federations of the unions of the various crafts. This idea produced the body that would ultimately evolve into American labor's most important one, the American Federation of Labor.

between strikers on the one hand and strikebreakers and the police on the other led to hundreds of injuries and four deaths. Again, as in 1877 when the apparent use of the police on the side of the business community had led the "workingmen" to form a new political party, so in 1901 the assignment of the police to protect strikebreakers led to the organization of the new Union Labor party of San Francisco. For a time that party actually gained control of the city government. During its first 6 years of existence, however, it was controlled by an opportunistic and corrupt political boss, Abraham Ruef, and thus it became significant mainly for its part in the extreme corruption of California party politics, which would at last produce major attempts at political reform in the city and the state.

San Francisco women also participated in union organizing in the early 1900s. Most women workers remained concentrated in low-paying positions, often working in dangerous or unsanitary conditions. In 1901 several hundred waitresses, demanding higher wages, fought a bitter strike that closed nearly 200 San Francisco restaurants. The city's female laundry workers struck 6 years later, as did women who worked at the Ghirardelli chocolate factory. One of the largest strikes came in 1919 when 1300 female telephone operators went on strike, demanding and winning the right to bargain collectively.

TRIUMPH OF THE OPEN SHOP IN LOS ANGELES

In the same turn-of-the-century period when the idea of the closed shop was coming as near to acceptance in San Francisco as anywhere else in America, Los Angeles was becoming the country's leading citadel of the open shop, based on precisely the opposite principle, under which employers refused to make agreements requiring union membership of their employees and even refused to bargain with unions at all.

This remarkable polarization of institutional patterns in the two cities was one of the many extreme contrasts between them. The population of southern California remained relatively sparse and rural before 1900, and because industry was still on a trifling scale in Los Angeles several decades after it had begun to flourish in San Francisco, unions in Los Angeles were less deeply rooted. But of all the factors impeding union growth in southern California the most remarkable and effective was the personality of Harrison Gray Otis, publisher of the *Los Angeles Times*. With a great fortune built on a highly profitable newspaper and on vast real estate investments in California and Mexico, Otis made himself the leader of the most intransigent group of organized employers to be found anywhere in the United States.

Otis believed that men of wealth, in their wisdom and genius, were the only men to be trusted with economic or political power. A related part of his thinking was that the military plan of social organization was an excellent system. The good soldier never struck and never boycotted. This feeling provided much of the emotional force behind Otis's crusade for the open shop, which he rationalized as "industrial freedom"—the freedom of workers not to join a union and the freedom of employers to discharge them if they did. Otis often said that he favored the "closed shop," by what he regarded as the only proper definition of it: closed to union members.

In 1890 Otis precipitated the first major conflict between employers and unions in Los Angeles, with the intention of destroying the printers' union, the oldest union in the city. Printers, as Otis pointed out, were the only workers in southern California who were still getting boom-time wages. The boom of the 1880s having collapsed, a wage cut was in order. But instead of negotiating a new agreement Otis announced a 20 percent cut, locked his union printers out, and refused to discuss a compromise. Before doing this he had formed an association with the publishers of the other three Los Angeles dailies, and had arranged to bring in nonunion printers from San Diego and elsewhere. He paid these strikebreakers the previous union wages—until the strike collapsed. Other unions helped the printers by contributing funds and by joining in a boycott of the *Times* and its advertisers. This boycott was a failure, but it tended to solidify the Los Angeles labor movement for the years of struggle that lay ahead.

The employers who were most antagonistic to unions formed an Employers' Association under the leadership of Otis. They also established an Independent Labor Bureau to carry on a wide campaign of advertising in the east, promising jobs at high wages for nonunion workers. The Merchants' and Manufacturers' Association of Los Angeles, originally formed in the 1890s to promote commercial and industrial enterprise, was at first outwardly neutral in Otis's war with the unions, but in 1903 the M&M announced that it would unite with employers injured by boycotts, which it branded as "unAmerican, unjust, unwarranted, and illegal." Soon afterward, however, it launched a boycott policy of its own—against employers who negotiated with unions. Bank loans were withheld and orders were transferred to other companies. The M&M's boycott was more effective than any that union labor ever attempted.

At this time the drive for the open shop was becoming a national movement. A major slogan of this movement was "The Right to Work," the title of a widely discussed article by Ray Stannard Baker which expressed sympathy for the "scab" miners in a recent Pennsylvania coal strike. The National Association of Manufacturers declared against recognition of labor unions in 1903, and its president founded a Citizens' Industrial Association of America. This body, in turn, fostered local Citizens' Alliances in which the public was invited to join with employers in fighting organized labor. In Los Angeles the Citizens' Alliance soon recruited the country's largest per capita membership, with heavy financial support from Otis, Henry E. Huntington, and others.

The struggle reached a crisis in 1910, when organized labor took the offensive in a drive for effective unionization of the Los Angeles metal trades. In the spring the metal trades employers of San Francisco agreed to an 8-hour day but warned that they could not long continue it unless their competitors in Los Angeles were unionized and forced to accept the same terms. Consequently, union organizers and funds from San Francisco suddenly strengthened the metal trades unions of Los Angeles to such a degree that they were able to begin a strike of 1500 workers

The Los Angeles Times building following the dynamite bombing of October 1, 1910. *(Courtesy of the California Historical Society Ticor Collection, Department of Special Collections, University of Southern California Library.)*

on June 1, 1910, the largest strike the city had ever witnessed. The employers refused to negotiate, and the battle attracted national attention because the whole future of the open shop was clearly at stake in the city where it was strongest. The *Times* outdid itself in denouncing the assault on "the cradle of industrial freedom," and organized labor and its sympathizers throughout the country denounced the *Times* as the nation's leading symbol of union smashing.

Before dawn on the morning of October 1, while the strike was still in full swing, a tremendous explosion destroyed the *Times* building, killed 20 men, and injured 17 others. Immediately the open-shop forces attributed this "crime of the century," as the *Times* called it, to a dynamite bomb planted by union labor's agents. Labor's partisans, on the other hand, charged that the cause was a leaking gas main, typical of the "fire-trap" in which Otis had compelled his employees to work. Unhappily the truth was that a dynamite bomb had been used and that certain individual union officials were guilty of planning the outrage.

The tragedy of the *Times* was a part of a nationwide struggle between the International Association of Bridge and Structural Iron Workers and the large employers in the field. In 1906 the employers began a belligerent campaign to destroy the power of the Iron Workers and succeeded in establishing the open shop throughout the industry in all large cities except Chicago and San Francisco. Driven to desperation, the union's national leaders secretly resorted to terrorism, and over a period of several years dozens of nonunion construction projects in a number of cities were damaged by explosions of dynamite, though until the *Times* bombing none of these had resulted in loss of life.

William J. Burns, head of a private detective agency, was already investigating some of the lesser incidents when he was employed by the mayor of Los Angeles to investigate the *Times* disaster. In April 1911 Burns arrested Ortie McManigal, a professional dynamiter, who confessed his own part in the bombing campaign and described its planning by officials of the union at their national headquarters in Indianapolis. Union secretary John J. McNamara, his brother James B. McNamara, and McManigal were then brought to Los Angeles to be tried for complicity in the bombing of the *Times*.

Samuel Gompers, president of the American Federation of Labor (AFL), staked his prestige and that of the AFL on the belief that the charges against the McNamara brothers were a frame-up, and Clarence Darrow, one of the country's ablest trial lawyers, was employed for the defense. But on December 1, 1911, the millions of Americans who believed the McNamara brothers to be the innocent victims of an employer conspiracy were stunned by their confession of guilt. The evidence against them was overwhelming, and Darrow advised his clients to plead guilty in order to save their lives.

The McNamaras' confession demoralized American labor, emboldened employers, and intensified the bitterness between the two sides. In Los Angeles the result was 30 more years of dominance for the open shop.

AGRICULTURAL LABOR: UNORGANIZED AND DISFRANCHISED

Historically, the family farm has been the institution most typical of American agriculture. Only a fourth of those gainfully employed in farming in the United States have been wage workers, and these have been "hired men" attached more or less permanently to one farm and living with the family that owned it. In California, however, more than two-thirds of the total number of persons engaged in agriculture have been wage laborers, the majority of them alien, nonwhite, and migratory. California's "peculiar institution," comparable in some ways to southern black slavery, has been seasonal migratory agricultural labor in which the worker lacked the protection offered in other fields by labor unions and by the right to vote.

Several circumstances contributed to this situation: the persistence of large units of land ownership in California, specialization in a particular seasonal crop, as opposed to the year-round operations of the "general farm" more common in the middle west and the availability, in each successive generation, of some new supply of cheap labor drawn from some supposedly inferior race—first the Indians, then the Chinese, and later the Japanese, Hindustanis, Mexicans, and Filipinos.

cific Historical Review, XVII (February, 1948), pp. 37–42; Paul F. Brissenden, *The I.W.W.* (1919, 1957); and Carleton H. Parker, *The Casual Laborer in America* (1920). General accounts of the IWW are Patrick Renshaw, *The Wobblies* (1967); Melvyn Dubofsky, *We Shall Be All* (1969); and Joseph R. Conlin, *Bread and Roses Too* (1969).

Mitchell Slobodek's *A Selective Bibliography of California Labor History* (1964) is thorough and well-annotated.

CHAPTER TWENTY-ONE

The Roots of Reform

The forces that contributed to the reform impulse in California in the early twentieth century were many and varied, but the statewide reform coalition that finally achieved a breakthrough in the state elections of 1910 had its immediate origins in developments in the cities of San Francisco and Los Angeles.

BOSS RUEF AND THE UNION LABOR PARTY

Throughout the United States, as Lord Bryce remarked in *The American Commonwealth,* the government of cities was a conspicuous failure of American democracy. This had been true in varying degrees since the early days of New York's Tammany Hall, but the problem had become worse in the age of industrialization and urbanization between the Civil War and the rise of the progressive movement in the early twentieth century. Cities, corporations, and labor unions grew so rapidly that government and law could not keep up with them. One result was an increase in the importance of the city boss as an extralegal figure who could furnish a bridge between the lagging institutions of politics and the urgent demands of the expanding conglomerations of economic power. The boss served as a broker in a corrupt system of alliances between big business and politics that menaced democracy in cities throughout the nation.

Cosmopolitan San Francisco might have been expected to produce as the most famous of its bosses a figure as colorful as the city itself. Abraham Ruef was the only son of a moderately wealthy San Francisco family of French Jewish origin. He was a man of unusual culture and brilliant intelligence, heightened by a good university and legal education. After graduating from the University of California in Berkeley and from its law school in San Francisco, he entered politics as an idealistic young reformer. But his ideals began to decline when he attended his first Republican county convention, an experience that impressed him with the apparently hopeless realities of machine rule. Surrendering to opportunism, he became the Republican subboss for a district in the northern part of the city. There, at the grassroots level, he learned to bestow the many services and favors that typical nineteenth-century American city bosses and their machines exchanged for the gratitude and the votes of poor and immigrant families—from gifts of turkeys at Christmas to help with naturalization papers.

At the turn of the century the mayor of San Francisco was the reform Democrat James D. Phelan. Son of one of the city's leading bankers, Phelan was also a millionaire banker in his own right, and as a public officeholder he was above the temptations to corruption that afflicted persons of lesser integrity and inferior financial independence. Ordinarily Phelan held fairly liberal views on a number of economic and social issues, including the rights of organized labor, but during the great strike in the summer of 1901 his wealthy friends persuaded him to order city police to ride on the drays beside "scab" teamsters, thus using the police themselves as virtual strikebreakers.

This led to an angry outcry that if the power of government was thus to be used for the destruction of unions, then union members must enter politics and elect a government of their own; with this intention a group calling itself the Union Labor Party of San Francisco was organized in September. The philosophy and strategy of American craft unionism were generally opposed to any such movement, and not a single important official of any of the larger San Francisco unions would associate with the new party. It might have died at birth had it not acquired a foster father: Abraham Ruef perceived that he could use it for his own purposes, though he had no genuine interest whatever in labor unions except his interest in their members' votes for candidates he controlled.

Because Mayor Phelan had angered conservatives by refusing to call for state troops to put down the strike almost as much as he had angered labor by his use of city police, his renomination was impossible. The Democratic and Republican nominees for mayor were colorless men. For the Union Labor candidacy, on the other hand, Ruef chose his friend Eugene E. Schmitz, president of the musicians' union. Schmitz was of German-Irish descent and of Roman Catholic faith, and in San Francisco this combination of ethnic and religious factors appealed to such an extraordinarily high percentage of the electorate that it was an essential source of Schmitz's political success, and consequently of Ruef's as well. Schmitz was a tall, handsome, distinguished-looking, commanding figure of a man, and also a model husband and father. "The psychology of the mass of the voters," Ruef told Schmitz, "is like that of a crowd of small boys," to whom such qualities had a deep emotional appeal.

Schmitz was elected mayor in 1901, 1903, and 1905. In the first two of these elections the Union Labor ticket gained only a few seats on the 18-member board of supervisors, the legislative branch of the city-and-county government. But in 1905, to Ruef's own surprise, every one of his 18 Union Labor nominees for the board of supervisors was elected. Voting machines were used for the first time, and nearly all of Schmitz's admirers, fearing to invalidate their votes among the complicated battery of levers, took the easy course of pulling down one lever for the straight party ticket.

Most of the new city fathers were obscure men who knew little about the nature of their office except the popular belief that supervisors customarily received bribes. They suspected, quite accurately, that Ruef received large payments from public utility corporations. In vain he pointed out to them that as a lawyer who held no public office he could quite legally receive such payments as attorney's fees, but that payments to them, as public officials, would be bribery. The new supervisors concluded that although this fine distinction might be law, it was not justice. They demanded that Ruef share his fees with them if he expected them to vote for the measures his corporate clients desired.

Several transactions of this kind were carried out in 1906. For example, the United Railroads of San Francisco, the largest street railway company, asked for a special ordinance permitting it to convert all its remaining cable car lines to overhead electric trolleys. The company paid an attorney's fee of $200,000 to Ruef; he divided $85,000 among the supervisors, and the ordinance was passed. The Pacific Gas and Electric Company (PG&E) paid Ruef $20,000; of this sum he paid $13,250 to the supervisors and thereby persuaded them not to make a drastic reduction in the gas rate. There were other corrupt arrangements involving telephone and water companies.

THE SAN FRANCISCO GRAFT PROSECUTION

Such instances of corruption were by no means unprecedented, either in San Francisco or in other large American cities of the time. What was really extraordinary about them was that through some very unusual circumstances they became known to the public in complete detail. The year 1906 brought two crucial events in San Francisco's history: One was the disastrous earthquake and fire, in April, and the other, in October, was the announcement of the beginning of what turned out to be the most persistent graft prosecution in the history of any city in the United States.

The earthquake which rocked San Francisco at 5:14 in the morning of April 18 was so severe that it caused a number of deaths and injuries within the first few moments. But San Franciscans, anxious to counteract the idea that a similar catastrophe could ever destroy their city again, have always correctly insisted that the greatest damage was done not by the earthquake—over which human beings had no conceivable control—but rather by the subsequent fire, whose recurrence a better-planned water system could render impossible. The initial shock, which started more than 50 separate fires almost immediately by breaking gas connections and chimneys and overturning stoves, also shattered most of the flimsy water mains and left the fire fighters helpless. The fires, merging into one vast, continuous conflagration and raging for 3 days and 2 nights, destroyed the greater part of the city. Early estimates of the loss of life put the figure at about 450. More recent research has indicated that as many as 3000 people may have been killed in the disaster and property valued at $1 billion was destroyed.

The painful difficulties of the struggle to build a new city on the ruins of the old made San Franciscans less tolerant of corruption in their city government and

The San Francisco business community had enthusiastically supported the prosecution at its beginning, when it had appeared to be directed against corrupt politicians, especially "Union Labor" politicians. But when these men were promised immunity as a reward for furnishing the evidence on which a number of the city's best-known business executives were indicted, the business community's enthusiasm for the prosecution rapidly cooled. In the city elections of 1909 the prosecution was voted out of office in favor of an administration that would discontinue the graft cases.

The San Francisco graft prosecution aroused a deeper and more sustained indignation in the rest of the state than it did in the city itself, and thus it contributed to the growing statewide demands for political reform.

THE GOOD GOVERNMENT MOVEMENT IN LOS ANGELES

The Southern Pacific machine dominated Los Angeles politics at the turn of the century, but opposition to it was building up in almost every sector of political opinion from the right to the left.

Harrison Gray Otis, leader of the city's conservative employers, believed that nothing could possibly contribute as much to the growth, improvement, and prosperity of the community as did the leadership of vigorous individuals like himself. Therefore, as he saw it, the general welfare required that there be no unnecessary restraints upon such persons in the free exercise of their talents for acquiring the wealth that was their incentive and reward. But the railroad had become just such a restraint upon free enterprise, and Otis opposed its bureaucratic power almost as much as he feared and detested labor unions, or even socialism.

As distinct from the conservatives, like Otis, who had a chronic distrust of government and feared that any political change would open the door to unionism and radicalism, there were various groups of reformers who placed their faith in the improvement and strengthening of government. These groups were divided into political and moral reformers on the one hand, and social and economic reformers on the other.

The political and moral reformers included prominent businesspeople, lawyers, and journalists who shared the conservatives' belief in the supreme importance of business enterprise, but also believed that much could be accomplished by bringing "business efficiency" and "business integrity" into politics. The social and economic reformers believed not merely that government should become more honest and more efficient, but that it should be used to effect deeper and broader improvements in the workings of society. They included socialists and persons impressed by the writings of Henry George and Edward Bellamy or by the social gospel then being preached in many churches. To an extraordinary degree, union labor in Los Angeles had also been driven into alliance with such groups as a result of the extreme tactics of Otis and his associates.

In the face of this diversity among the opponents of the railroad machine in Los Angeles, it was very difficult to assemble a strong coalition of reformers, but this was accomplished, largely through the remarkable talents of Dr. John Randolph

Haynes. Since his arrival in 1887, Haynes had combined the most successful medical practice in Los Angeles with the building of a fortune in real estate—a combination of achievements that won him the respect of some of the most conservative of the business community. Largely through Haynes's charm and prestige, and through a Direct Legislation League that he headed, Los Angeles was persuaded to adopt the initiative, the referendum, and the recall in its new charter of 1903.

This was the first provision for the recall in any governmental unit in the world and the first adoption of the initiative and the referendum by a city. In 1904, moreover, Los Angeles put the recall to use for the first time in history. A Good Government League, in which Dr. Haynes was prominent, organized a successful campaign to recall City Councilman J. R. Davenport for voting to award the public printing contracts to the *Los Angeles Times* when several other bids had been much lower.

This episode ended any possibility of support from Otis for the political reformers, and thereafter the *Times* never spoke of the Good Government League except to denounce and ridicule its leaders as "the Goo-Goos." But the opposition of the *Times* served to increase the support for reform on the part of Otis's newspaper rival and personal enemy, Edwin T. Earl, publisher of the *Los Angeles Express*. Earl was not only a publisher but also the state's largest lemon grower and consequently an opponent of the Southern Pacific, whose freight rates on lemons were among its most piratical exactions.

In the spring of 1906 Earl hired a young journalist named Edward A. Dickson and authorized him to begin a series of editorials in the *Express* denouncing the railroad machine for its control of the Los Angeles city council. Soon afterward Dickson joined with three young lawyers, Meyer Lissner, Russ Avery, and Marshall Stimson, in organizing a Non-Partisan Committee of One Hundred, and in the city election of 1906 the reform candidates nominated by this group won almost every important office except the mayoralty.

THE LINCOLN-ROOSEVELT LEAGUE

All the leaders and nearly all the members of the Los Angeles "Non-Partisan" group were in fact Republicans. Many were businesspeople who favored political and moral as distinct from social and economic reform. For decades most people in business had been Republicans, whereas city workers had usually been Democrats. In the early twentieth century, reform-minded Republicans in California were deeply concerned lest the Democrats gain leadership of the reform movement in general and thus capture the state government.

The Republican state convention at Santa Cruz in September 1906 made it even more obvious than usual that the California Republican party machinery was subservient to the railroad and its allies. Abe Ruef, who had just reached the height of his power, controlled every member of the large San Francisco delegation and could thus choose the nominee for governor. To secure the nomination of the railroad's candidate, James N. Gillett, William F. Herrin gave Ruef $14,000 "to pay

The Shame of California. Photograph from the *San Francisco Call,* Sept. 10, 1906. Abe Ruef is seated in the center. The future governor, James N. Gillett, stands behind him. Justice Frederick W. Henshaw of the state supreme court stands at the far left. Congressman Joseph R. Knowland at the far right.

the expenses of the delegates." On the evening after the convention adjourned there was a testimonial banquet at which a photograph was taken, showing Ruef seated at the center of a long table with Gillett standing behind him, his hand on Ruef's shoulder in a gesture of affectionate gratitude. Justices of the state supreme and appellate courts, indebted to Ruef for their renominations, were included in the group. Along with such machine stalwarts was Walter Parker, Herrin's lieutenant in Los Angeles. For years afterward this picture was widely reprinted with such captions as "The Shame of California" and "Herrin's Cabinet."

The announcement of the beginning of the San Francisco graft prosecution in October 1906, discrediting Ruef and the nominees of the Santa Cruz convention along with him, gave the Democrats an extraordinary opportunity to win the governorship and most of the other state offices. They had a strong antirailroad platform, and their candidate for governor, Theodore A. Bell, was a vigorous young man with a good reform record as district attorney of Napa County. The Democrats' chances, however, were sabotaged by the ambitious machinations of William Randolph Hearst in his attempts to gain the Democratic nomination for the presidency. In an effort to show the national Democratic party that it could not do without him, Hearst in 1906 was sponsoring a third-party movement called the Independence League, in New York, California, and a few other states. The league's ticket in California, with San Francisco district attorney William H. Langdon as the candidate for governor, took enough votes from Bell and the Democrats to give the election to Gillett and the Republicans.

In December 1906 Dr. Haynes again displayed his talent for encouraging broad coalition among reformers by organizing a dinner at the California Club in Los Angeles with Lincoln Steffens as the principal speaker and Edward Dickson and Meyer Lissner among the guests. Steffens urged the Los Angeles reformers to extend to the state level the efforts that had brought important successes in the recent city elections.

A few weeks later Dickson went to Sacramento as correspondent for the *Los Angeles Express* at the session of the state legislature beginning in January 1907. The chance assignment of adjoining desks in the press row to Dickson and to

Chester H. Rowell, editor of the *Fresno Morning Republican,* became one of the most important circumstances leading to the movement that would free the Republican party and the state government from the Southern Pacific Railroad.

Dickson and Rowell had never met before, but as they exchanged impressions of the 1907 legislature, which was hardly less subservient to the railroad than the Santa Cruz convention had been, the two journalists discovered that they shared a burning disgust with the condition of California politics. They agreed to join in an attempt to organize a reform movement and sent out the call for a new organization in letters to reform-minded Republicans, especially newspaper publishers and editors, throughout the state.

A southern California group met in Los Angeles on May 21, 1907, adopted Dickson's suggestion of the name of "Lincoln Republicans," and drew up an "emancipation proclamation," which announced as its first objective "the emancipation of the Republican Party in California from domination by the Political Bureau of the Southern Pacific Railroad Company and allied interests." Other proposals were the direct primary; the initiative, referendum, and recall; effective regulation of railroad and other utility rates; the outlawing of racetrack gambling; conservation of forests; a workers' compensation act; a minimum wage law for women; and woman suffrage.

On August 1 a larger statewide group met in Oakland and adopted the official name of "the League of Lincoln-Roosevelt Republican Clubs." This hyphenated title was the result of a significant compromise with the desire of Francis J. Heney to change the name to "the Roosevelt League." Heney was an intense admirer of Theodore Roosevelt and particularly of that aspect of his views which led the President to denounce as "malefactors of great wealth" such men as E. H. Harriman, head of the Southern Pacific. Roosevelt's national leadership was an important source of inspiration to progressive Republicans in California, but at Dickson's insistence the name of Lincoln was also retained and included to appeal to Republicans of more traditional views.

In 1908 the reformers were able to elect enough members of the legislature to make possible the enactment of a direct primary law in the 1909 session. It soon became clear that in 1910, with the nominations of party candidates taken away from machine-controlled conventions and given directly to the voters, the league might gain control not only of the state Republican party organization, but also of the entire state government, particularly if it could find a very strong candidate for governor to head its ticket.

At first it was supposed that the candidate would be Heney, whose leadership of the San Francisco graft prosecution was making him the state's best-known reformer. But in November 1908, early in the trial of Ruef, Heney was shot and almost fatally wounded by a man whose earlier criminal record Heney had exposed while questioning him as a prospective juror. Whether Heney would make a full recovery was uncertain for several months, and when he did return to the fray, his personality was more extreme and irascible than ever. Many Republicans regarded Heney as "too radical" and particularly resented his open dislike and distrust of all businessmen. Moreover, Heney was a registered Democrat.

discriminatory practices in which the Southern Pacific had indulged for so many decades. In the vanguard of the demand for this reform were groups of shippers and merchants, who wanted to stabilize their businesses. Another measure assigned the commission the power to regulate the rates charged by all other public utilities, except those that were municipally owned. The graft prosecution in San Francisco had more than demonstrated the inadequacy of local regulation of utilities, and officials of several utility corporations favored the new law. The two 1911 laws provided California with what was probably the most comprehensive system of public utility regulation in the country.

Both measures passed by unanimous votes in both houses. Railroad regulation, in particular, was so long overdue in 1911 that not even the railroad attorneys and lobbyists tried to oppose it. Officials of the Southern Pacific found themselves glad to escape from such costly nuisances as the payment of secret rebates to favored shippers within the state, notably several oil companies. After the new system had been in operation a few months, William F. Herrin made a remarkable address to the California Bar Association in which he concluded that "I think no railroad manager would agree to dispense with government regulation at the cost of returning to the old conditions."

GOVERNMENTAL EFFICIENCY AND FINANCE

Many progressive reformers believed that the principles of scientific management, then in vogue in private enterprise, must be introduced into government. They proceeded to develop California's first coherent system of supervision over state finances, largely under the leadership of John Francis Neylan, a dynamic young newspaper reporter who had attracted Johnson's attention while covering the 1910 campaign for the *San Francisco Bulletin*. Neylan proposed the creation of a new agency to be called the State Board of Control, and at the age of 26 he was appointed its first chairman. Under this board California had its first comprehensive budget and its first general inventory of state property. The board exposed graft, regained embezzled money, and secured the removal of 16 corrupt officials.

Taxation in California had undergone a major reorganization in 1910, mainly as a result of the desire of business leaders for a more orderly system. Since 1879 all property taxes had been collected by county boards of assessment under the loose supervision of a state board of equalization. Under the act of 1910 a state tax on the gross incomes of corporations was created, and property taxes were to be paid only to county and local governments. The new state taxes on corporation incomes were set at very moderate levels.

The Bank Act of 1909 was another example of the influence of private economic groups on reform in the progressive era and of the desire of many such groups to use the power of government to bring greater orderliness into their own activities and thus increase their profits and reduce their losses. The act was drawn up mainly by a committee of the California Bankers Association and remained the state's fundamental banking law until the 1930s. It created the office of state superintendent of banks, whose duties would include periodic examination of the financial soundness of the banks.

"MORE DEMOCRACY"

The progressives' view of human nature reflected an Emersonian optimism about humanity's innate capacity for good, and therefore they had a strong faith in the political abilities of "the people." Most of the leading California Republican progressives, though they regarded themselves as patrician reformers, also had a strong faith in democracy as against the conservative emphasis on "representative" government. Thus the heart of their reform program lay in a group of devices for increasing the power of the voters.

Foremost among these devices was a state constitutional amendment providing two methods of direct participation by the people in the lawmaking process: The initiative enabled the voters to enact laws or constitutional amendments that had presumably been blocked by legislators' unresponsiveness to popular demands; the referendum empowered the people to veto acts of the legislature. A petition signed by 8 percent of the number of voters in an immediately preceding gubernatorial election could place an initiative proposal on the ballot; a referendum required 5 percent. Some of the progressives would have preferred a fixed number of signatures, perhaps 30,000. They pointed out that under the percentage system, with future increases in the state's population, the gathering of an ever-increasing number of signatures would become too difficult and expensive for reform groups and practicable only for large special interests. But this warning, which would prove distressingly valid in later years, went unheeded in 1911.

The recall of public officials, the second major proposal that Governor Johnson urged upon the legislature, was much more hotly contested, especially because it included the recall of judges. The conservative minority argued that this would interfere with the impartiality of court decisions by requiring judges to "keep their ears to the ground," but Johnson replied that this was better than keeping their ears to the railroad tracks.

Several other measures were also designed to give more power to the voters and to decrease the power of "party bosses." For example, the "party column" and the "party circle," which had encouraged voting a straight party ticket, were eliminated from the ballot.

"NONPARTISANSHIP" AND CROSS-FILING

The corruption of political parties in California by machine rule had been so extreme that the Johnson progressives mistakenly blamed much of the evil on the party system itself. Consequently, they tried to bring about the virtual destruction of political parties in the state, and although they did not quite succeed in doing this, their efforts had the effect of ensuring that the two-party system would remain extraordinarily weak in California for almost half a century to come.

"Freak" Legislation?

This cartoon provided editorial support for the minimum wage law and other legislation proposed by the progressives, 1911–1913. Note especially the startled reaction of "Plutocracy" in the lower left-hand corner. *(Courtesy of Special Collections, University Research Library, UCLA.)*

opposed any minimum wage laws whatever, for the same reason that it opposed compulsory arbitration—that the setting of terms by government boards might weaken and even replace union bargaining. The minimum wage, labor feared, would become the maximum. The 1911 legislature adopted an 8-hour day for women, excluding farm labor and the canning and packing industries, but it did not seriously consider a minimum wage. No state had such a law until Massachusetts adopted the first one in 1912. Katherine Philips Edson of Los Angeles, president of the California Federation of Women's Clubs, led the movement that secured the passage of a California minimum wage law for women and children in 1913.

Records of the bureau of labor statistics showed that a third of the women workers in California were being paid less than 15 cents an hour, and Katherine Edson and other advocates of the new law argued that this condition was a menace to the women's health and morals. An industrial welfare commission was to administer the act, and Governor Johnson, who had joined in pressing for passage of the law, appointed Edson as the commission's executive officer. Edson long had believed that the state should assume a larger responsibility for the welfare of its citizens; now she was in a position to pursue her goals as a progressive and a feminist. As historian Jacqueline R. Braitman has observed, Edson's challenge to traditional attitudes about the role of government "paralleled her belief that women's roles could no longer be determined by nineteenth-century proscriptions that allowed only men to be active in the public sphere while relegating women to the private domestic sphere."

In August 1913 the Wheatland riot suddenly and dramatically awakened public consciousness, and to some extent the public conscience, to the vile and disgraceful conditions in many farm labor camps. (See Chapter 20.) A state-sponsored investigation revealed that the conditions at Durst's hop ranch were typical of those inflicted on migratory workers by many other large agricultural employers throughout the state. The Commission of Immigration and Housing, created by the legislature a few months before, assumed the authority to inspect farm labor camps, and of the 641 that it investigated in 1914, only 195 met its minimum standards, and 188 were branded as dangerously unsanitary. The next year the legislature passed a new labor camp sanitation and housing act, to be enforced by the commission, but though it made admirable efforts at enforcement, its efforts were stubbornly resisted and were never fully effective. Another act, also a product of the Wheatland tragedy, required all employers to provide their workers with drinking water.

The progressives' concern for the welfare of working people produced few improvements in the status of the state's small but growing population of African Americans. Nor were black workers admitted to the ranks of organized labor; nearly all trade unions excluded blacks entirely until World War II. Black Californians responded by organizing their own self-help groups. Two chapters of the National Association for the Advancement of Colored People (NAACP) were formed in the state by 1915. Earlier an all-black town was established in Tulare County by Colonel Allen Allensworth, a former slave and retired army officer. By 1910 the town of Allensworth had several hundred residents, but it failed to achieve economic viability and eventually was abandoned.

THE ANTI-JAPANESE MOVEMENT

An important area of agreement between organized labor and the California progressives was their shared hostility toward the Japanese. The immigration of Japanese to California had been insignificant until the late 1890s, but it steadily increased in the early twentieth century, and in 1905 San Francisco labor union leaders formed an Asiatic Exclusion League to combat it. Under pressure from this league the Union Labor city government announced its intention of segregating Japanese public school children along with the Chinese.

California had almost completely excluded Chinese children from its public schools until a court ruling forbade this practice in 1885. In San Francisco, a separate public school had then been provided for them in Chinatown. When this Chinese school was rebuilt after the earthquake and fire, its name was changed to the Oriental School, and on October 11, 1906, the board of education adopted an order requiring Japanese public school children to attend it.

Protests from the Japanese government led to a diplomatic crisis between Japan and the United States, and President Roosevelt ordered an investigation by his secretary of commerce and labor, Victor H. Metcalf, a resident of Oakland and the only Californian in the cabinet. Metcalf reported that there had been only 93 Japanese pupils in the 23 public schools in San Francisco and that many of them had been born in the city. However, 27 had been alien teenagers placed in the elementary grades because of their lack of previous schooling in English. White racists, including Sacramento Assemblyman Grove L. Johnson, declaimed upon the menace to little American schoolgirls who were seated beside older boys with "evil oriental thoughts."

Early in 1907 President Roosevelt invited Mayor Schmitz and the members of the San Francisco Board of Education to Washington, D.C., where they agreed to a compromise. Only overage pupils and those not having facility in English might be placed in separate schools, and the new regulations would apply to all children of alien birth, not to Japanese as such.

In return President Roosevelt promised limits on Japanese immigration and negotiated the Gentlemen's Agreement in which Japan promised not to issue passports good for the continental United States to laborers, whether skilled or unskilled. But parents, wives, or children of Japanese already resident in the United States were not covered by this agreement, and through proxy marriages, arranged quite legally and in the traditional fashion by parents or other go-betweens in Japan, thousands of earlier Japanese immigrants brought "picture brides" to America. Many Californians denounced this as oriental duplicity, and demanded complete Japanese exclusion.

The arrival of the picture brides substantially increased the Japanese American population in California. Fewer than 500 married Japanese women were in California in 1900; 20 years later their number had increased to more than 20,000. Many Japanese American women worked alongside their husbands as farm laborers. Others were employed as domestics in middle-class homes, doing housework and laundering. They worked long hours and encouraged and supported one another. "If you don't talk to anyone," mused one Japanese American woman, "your heart gets heavy. So we told each other things right away."

Many Californians portrayed the Japanese with the same racial stereotypes that had been used against the Chinese in earlier decades, particularly the charges that they were unassimilable and that their low standard of living depressed wages. Soon, however, the Japanese became the object of a new complaint—that their standard of living rapidly became too high. Brought to California to replace the

Toki Okamoto, Japanese American picture bride, photographed about 1911. (*Courtesy of the National Archives, Pacific Sierra Region. Record group 85; Case file 10448/10-3.*)

Chinese as cheap farm laborers, some of them began acquiring farm land of their own. Much of this was land that they reclaimed in the Sacramento and San Joaquin valleys and in the San Joaquin delta. They were the first to demonstrate that rice could be grown successfully in California and that potatoes could be grown on a commercial scale. George Shima, known as the "potato king," produced the bulk of the state's crop on his large farm in the delta region.

Bills intended to halt the expansion of the Japanese in California agriculture began to be introduced in every legislative session, and were frequently protested by the Japanese ambassador in Washington. James D. Phelan, in a statement as near to tolerance of the Japanese as he ever came, once suggested that the United States should say "diplomatically" that it regarded "the Japanese as efficient human machines," but that "as such, they are a menace to our prosperity and happiness. Then the more sensitive citizens of Japan may find some consolation in our confession of economic inferiority." The small farmers of California, who feared the competition of Japanese, reacted with resentment and fury to the idea of making any such humiliating confession.

not break openly with Heney without a disastrous split in the Progressive party, but he solved the problem by running for governor himself, by backing Eshleman for lieutenant governor, and by giving Heney virtually no support in his campaign for senator. The result was that Heney lost the election while, in sharp contrast, the votes for Johnson for governor and Eshleman for lieutenant governor were overwhelming. Johnson became the first governor of California to be reelected since 1853. He planned to run for the other Senate seat in 1916 and then turn over the governorship to Eshleman.

In June 1916 Theodore Roosevelt declined the Progressives' nomination for the presidency, and thus virtually scuttled the national Progressive party. Returning to the Republican fold, he announced his support for Charles Evans Hughes. In California the old-guard Republicans headed by William H. Crocker, son of Charles Crocker, gleefully assumed that the influence of Hiram Johnson was dead. Hughes made the same miscalculation. In his campaign visit to California in August, Hughes permitted Crocker to plan all his speaking arrangements. They excluded Johnson from every platform where Hughes appeared and did not even arrange a meeting between the two. By chance, both stopped at the Virginia Hotel in Long Beach on the afternoon of August 20, but Hughes left for Los Angeles without being informed that Johnson was in the hotel.

The California primaries were held 9 days later. Johnson was still a registered Progressive, but he had cross-filed for the Republican nomination for United States senator. To the horror of the old guard, he won the Republican nomination over their candidate, and the Johnson progressives recaptured control of the Republican state organization.

Under the circumstances, Johnson could hardly have been expected to support Hughes very enthusiastically, and he did not. Hughes lost California, by less than 4000 votes, and the presidency of the United States by losing California. But Johnson, with both Republican and Progressive nominations, won the senatorship by a margin of nearly 300,000.

Once again the California Republican progressives seemed to have triumphed, but the untimely death of Lieutenant Governor Eshleman in February 1916 had reopened the problem of succession and created further disunity. Having the power to fill the vacant lieutenant governorship by appointment, Johnson wished to choose another man whose personal loyalty would be as complete as Eshleman's had been. The southern California leaders, however, insisted on the appointment of Congressman William D. Stephens, former president of the Los Angeles Chamber of Commerce. Johnson regarded Stephens as "a Taft" who would betray the cause of progressivism. Johnson was so reluctant to have Stephens succeed him that he delayed resigning the governorship until after the beginning of his term as senator and actually held both offices for 2 weeks in March 1917. He might have held them both for months longer if President Woodrow Wilson had not called Congress into special session in the war emergency.

Johnson had almost come to believe that he *was* the California progressive movement, and it was true that his personal leadership and popularity had been vital elements in its success. He had built up such a devoted personal following among California voters that they would keep him in the Senate until his death in 1945. But in doing everything he could to discredit Stephens, his successor as governor, he further weakened what remained of California progressivism.

Along with these personal and factional quarrels, larger and deeper forces were also contributing to the decline of the progressive movement. (See Chapter 23.) By 1916 many California progressives were satisfied that although they had accomplished little in the way of economic reform, their agenda of political and moral reform had largely been achieved.

SELECTED BIBLIOGRAPHY

A critical reevaluation of the California progressives is underway. For a sampling of the latest scholarship, see William Deverell and Tom Sitton (eds.), *California Progressivism: Revisited and Revised* (1994). Mowry's *California Progressives,* Olin's *California's Prodigal Sons,* Everett's "Chester Rowell," cited in Chapter 21, and the second volume of Franklin Hichborn's "California Politics," cited in Chapter 19, remain useful. Hichborn's *Story of the California Legislature of 1911,* and its counterparts for 1913 and 1915, analyze bills and votes. Michael Rogin and John L. Shover, *Political Change in California* (1970), analyze public reactions. On direct government, see David D. Schmidt, *Citizen Lawmakers: The Ballot Initiative Referendum* (1989). On regulation of railroads, other public utilities, banks, and other businesses, see Mansel G. Blackford, *The Politics of Business in California, 1890–1920* (1976), and Roger Charles Lister, "Bank Behavior, Regulation and Economic Development: California, 1860–1910," Ph.D. thesis, University of California, Davis (1982).

The role of California clubwomen is analyzed in two recent studies: Gayle Ann Gullett, "Feminism, Politics, and Voluntary Groups," Ph.D. thesis, University of California, Riverside (1983), and Sara Essa Gallaway, "Pioneering the Woman's Club Movement," Ph.D. thesis, Carnegie-Mellon University (1985). On woman suffrage see Susan Englander, *Class Conflict and Class Coalition in the California Woman Suffrage Movement, 1907–1911* (1992); Ronald Schaffer, "The Problem of Consciousness in the Woman Suffrage Movement," *Pacific Historical Review,* XLV (November 1976), pp. 469–494; and Donald W. Rodes, "The California Woman Suffrage Campaign of 1911," M.A. thesis, California State University, Hayward (1974). See also Jacqueline R. Braitman, "A California Stateswoman: The Public Career of Katherine Philips Edson," *California History,* LXV (June 1986), pp. 82–95; Gayle Gullett, "Women Progressives and the Politics of Americanization in California, 1915–1920," *Pacific Historical Review,* LXIV (February 1995), pp. 71–94; Judith Rosenberg Raftery, *Land of Fair Promise* (1992); and Sherry J. Katz, "Dual Commitments: Feminism, Socialism, and Women's Political Activism in California, 1890–1920," Ph.D. thesis, University of California, Los Angeles, 1991.

Labor measures are treated in Alexander P. Saxton, "San Francisco Labor and the Populist and Progressive Insurgencies," *Pacific Historical Review,* XXXIV (November 1965), pp. 421–438; Gerald D. Nash, "The Influence of Labor on State Policy, 1860–1920," *California Historical Society Quarterly,* XLII (September 1963), pp. 241–257; Norris C. Hundley, Jr.,"Katherine Philips Edson and the Fight for the California Minimum Wage, 1912–1923," *Pacific Historical Review,* XXIX (August 1960), pp. 271–286; and Thomas R. Clark, "Labor and Progressivism," *California History,* LXVI (September 1987), pp. 196–207.

Accounts of the anti-Japanese agitation include Frank W. Van Nuys, "A Progressive Confronts the Race Question," *California History,* LXXIII (Spring 1994), pp. 2–13; Roger Daniels, *The Politics of Prejudice* (1962); Herbert P. LePore, "Prelude to Prejudice: Hiram Johnson,

Woodrow Wilson, and the California Alien Land Law Controversy of 1913," *Southern California Quarterly,* LXI (Spring 1979), pp. 99–110; Madelon Berkowitz, "The California Progressives and Anti-Japanese Agitation," M.A. thesis, University of California, Berkeley (1966); and Yuji Ichioka, "Japanese Immigrant Response to the 1920 California Alien Land Law," *Agricultural History,* LVIII (April 1984), pp. 157–178. See also the special issue of *California History,* LXXIII (Spring 1994), devoted to Japanese Americans in California.

On state attempts at regulation of agriculture, see Grace H. Larsen, "A Progressive in Agriculture: Harris Weinstock," *Agricultural History,* XXXII (July 1958), pp. 187–193.

The confusion that progressivism brought to the two-party system is described in A. Lincoln, "Theodore Roosevelt, Hiram Johnson, and the Vice-Presidential Nomination of 1912," *Pacific Historical Review,* XXVIII (August 1959), pp. 267–284; Robert E. Hennings, *James D. Phelan and the Wilson Progressives of California* (1985); and Joseph P. Giovinco, "The California Career of Anthony Caminetti, Italian-American Politician," Ph.D. thesis, University of California, Berkeley (1973). The origins of cross-filing are discussed in Franklin Hichborn, "The Party, the Machine, and the Vote; the Story of Cross-Filing in California Politics," *California Historical Society Quarterly,* XXXVIII (December 1959), pp. 349–357, and XXXIX (March 1960), pp. 19–34; James C. Findley, "Cross-Filing and the Progressive Movement in California Politics," *Western Political Quarterly,* XXII (September 1959), pp. 699–711; and Robert E. Burke, "Cross-Filing in California Elections, 1914–1946," M.A. thesis, University of California, Berkeley (1947).

On the campaign of 1916, see Edward A. Dickson, "How Hughes Lost California in 1916," *Congressional Record* (August 19, 1954), and F. M. Davenport, "Did Hughes Snub Johnson?" *American Political Science Review,* XLIII (April 1949), pp. 321–332.

CHAPTER TWENTY-THREE

The Triumph of Conservatism

The coming of World War I ushered in an era of renewed conservatism in state and national affairs. During and after the war there was a strong reaction against radicalism and a further decline of organized labor and the progressive movement. The forces of conservatism were triumphant through the 1920s.

RISE AND FALL OF THE SOCIALIST MOVEMENT

In California, as well as in the United States as a whole, socialism reached its highest point during the progressive era. This not only alarmed conservatives but also gave them an opportunity to attack and weaken progressivism by linking it with socialism.

The beginning of the organized socialist movement in the state went back to the 1880s, when the eccentric millionaire H. Gaylord Wilshire developed a peculiarly American brand of socialism in Los Angeles. Wilshire was an irrepressible and almost incredible figure in the history of southern California. The son of a Cincinnati capitalist, he inherited and lost one fortune and then made and lost a series of others in real estate, orange groves, banks, gold mines, billboards, and even a cure-all electric belt of his own invention. In the boom of the 1880s he developed and subdivided the "Wilshire Tract" west of Los Angeles's Westlake Park. Harrison Gray Otis and Edwin T. Earl bought large adjoining lots and built their mansions in this subdivision, through the center of which ran a thoroughfare 120 feet wide named Wilshire Boulevard. But with the collapse of the boom in 1888 Gaylord Wilshire became an avowed socialist, and in 1890 he was the first socialist in the United States to run for Congress. Next he founded *Wilshire's Magazine,* which became the country's most widely circulated socialist journal. Its motto was "Let the Nation Own the Trusts," an idea that would also play a central part in Jack London's novel, *The Iron Heel.*

In later years Wilshire Boulevard would be to Los Angeles more or less what the Champs Elysees was to Paris, and more than 200 enterprises from a hotel and a country club to a cleaning and dyeing company would take the name of Wilshire because it signified impeccable commercial prestige. Few if any of the proprietors or patrons of these establishments knew the identity of the original bearer of the name.

In the 1890s the leadership of the California socialist movement passed from Wilshire to Job Harriman, a labor union lawyer who came to Los Angeles for his health. The extremely repressive tactics of Harrison Gray Otis and the Merchants' and Manufacturers' Association had driven so much of Los Angeles labor to socialism that Harriman repeatedly came close to being elected mayor of the city. He would almost certainly have been elected mayor in 1911 if he had not committed the socialist cause to the belief that the McNamara brothers were innocent victims of a capitalist frame-up and if the McNamaras had not shattered this faith by confessing their guilt a few days before the city election. (See Chapter 20.) Even after that great setback Harriman came within 800 votes of being elected mayor 2 years later, but after this final defeat he turned from political activity to the management of a socialist cooperative experiment at Llano del Rio in the Mojave Desert region north of Los Angeles.

In the state election of 1910 more than 12 percent of the vote went to the Socialist candidate for governor, J. Stitt Wilson, a Berkeley Methodist minister who described himself as a "social evangelist." In 1911 Wilson was elected mayor of Berkeley, although in his 2 years in that office he neither attempted nor accomplished anything radical. In 1912 he ran as the Socialist candidate for Congress against Joseph R. Knowland, the impregnable Republican leader of Oakland and dean of the California congressional delegation; although Knowland won 54 percent of the votes, Wilson drew a remarkable 40 percent. In 1912, Socialist congressional nominees in California won 18 percent of the votes, one Socialist assemblyman from Los Angeles was elected, and Eugene V. Debs won nearly 12 percent of the vote for president. The elections of 1914 produced two Socialist assemblymen and one state senator.

Though socialism called in theory for public ownership of all the means of production and distribution, the Socialists in the California Legislature pressed mainly for such limited measures as the 8-hour day. Most of the actual legislative proposals of the Socialists were so moderate that they were hardly distinguishable from those advocated by the more liberal of the progressives, but conservative forces formed a Sound Government League in order to fight them, and one of the league's bulletins denounced "creeping socialism," with which conservatives lumped most progressive measures.

The rising tide of socialism in the United States in the first 15 years of the century was a general humanitarian as well as working-class reaction to such prevailing conditions as poverty, long hours and low wages, and the abuse of child labor. The coming of World War I virtually shattered the socialist movement, not only by distracting the country's attention from these conditions but also by creating extreme disunity among the Socialists themselves. In California such prominent Socialists as Stitt Wilson and Jack London favored the Allied cause and resigned from the Socialist party in 1916 when it opposed American intervention.

THE MOONEY CASE

In northern California, the beginning of a long period of antilabor reaction coincided with the beginning of the war in Europe. In 1914, after several months of economic depression, an "army" of 1500 unemployed under "General" Charles T. Kelley was driven out of Sacramento by a force of deputized citizens armed with clubs. In Stockton, employers formed a merchants' and manufacturers' association in July 1914, imported professional strikebreakers and armed guards, and launched an open-shop drive that produced one of the bitterest labor wars in the state's history.

The San Francisco employers began their drive for the open shop in July 1916, in the midst of a growing national movement for military preparedness. Labor in general opposed the military preparedness movement, whereas most employers favored that movement and seized the opportunity to discredit labor as unpatriotic. San Francisco business and patriotic organizations planned a great Preparedness Day parade on Market Street, in which no labor union participated. The parade was held on July 22. In the midst of it, at 2:06 in the afternoon, a bomb explosion at the corner of Stewart and Market killed 10 persons and wounded 40. Suspicion soon fell upon a radical labor agitator named Thomas J. Mooney.

For several years before the Preparedness Day bombing, Mooney had been active in San Francisco as a left-wing trade union socialist with an aggressive personality and a genius for antagonizing people. An iron molder by trade, he was not a union official. The description of him as a "labor leader" came from opponents of organized labor. He was interested in strike activity for the purposes of social revolution.

In 1913 the electrical workers' union had conducted a long strike against the Pacific Gas and Electric Company (PG&E) throughout northern California during which there were hundreds of depredations against the company's property, 18 of them by dynamite explosions. Warren K. Billings, a young friend of Mooney, had been arrested at Sacramento for the illegal transportation of a suitcase full of dynamite and sentenced to 2 years in prison. Later in 1913 Mooney was arrested for illegal possession of explosives and charged with planning to use them to destroy the PG&E transmission line across Carquinez Straits. He was tried at Martinez, but the evidence was flimsy and he was acquitted.

In the summer of 1916 Mooney was trying unsuccessfully to organize a union among employees of the United Railroads in San Francisco. Within a few days after the Preparedness Day explosion the police arrested Mooney, Warren Billings, and three others. All five were arrested without evidence, warrants, or formal charges and were denied the right of legal counsel until after they were indicted. From the time of the arrests the police and the district attorney's office dropped all further search for evidence except that which could be made to point to the defendants' guilt. Billings was tried for murder in September, convicted, and sentenced to life imprisonment. Mooney was tried in January 1917, convicted, and sentenced to hang. The three others were acquitted or not brought to trial.

The main witnesses for the prosecution testified that they had seen Billings and Mooney at or near the scene of the crime and that Billings was carrying a suit-

Political activist Charlotte Anita Whitney (1867–1955) and her attorney John Francis Neylan (1885–1960). (*Courtesy of the Bancroft Library.*)

and also upheld the constitutionality of the California law as being within the state's police power. Neylan was more successful in his fight for a pardon, which Governor Clement C. Young finally granted in June 1927. In explaining his decision the governor argued that to imprison Whitney would "revive the waning spirits of radicalism" by making her a martyr. Besides, Young concluded, she was a "lifelong friend of the unfortunate," rather than "in any true sense a 'criminal,'" and "to condemn her at 60 years of age to a felon's cell" was "absolutely unthinkable."

Upton Sinclair and others, observing sardonically that a number of obscure men had been imprisoned for offenses identical in principle with Whitney's, charged that there was one law for the rich and another for the poor. Altogether, there had been 504 arrests and 264 trials under the California criminal syndicalism law, and 128 persons, mostly members of the IWW, had been sent to prison. Twenty-four states had adopted such laws, mostly in 1919, but in all these states except California they were dead letters after 1921. In California, active prosecutions continued until 1924, largely to discourage further attempts by the IWW to organize migratory farm workers. The law was eventually declared unconstitutional, in 1968, by the United States Supreme Court.

DECLINE OF ORGANIZED LABOR

In the 1920s the business community had considerable success in branding labor unions as unpatriotic. A large segment of American public opinion believed that the unions had at best been lukewarm in their support of the war and that they had been inclined to defend seditious radicals instead of joining in the national condemnation of them. Adding these widely held beliefs to their arsenal of weapons, employer organizations resumed their prewar battles for the open shop, and this time succeeded in establishing it even in what had previously been the union stronghold of San Francisco.

In the summer of 1921, after an unpopular and unsuccessful strike by the building trade unions, the San Francisco Chamber of Commerce created a new Industrial Association to establish and enforce "the American plan." This expression had recently received the approval of the National Association of Manufacturers as the official name for the open shop. The drive made such remarkable headway in San Francisco that for the rest of the decade the open shop predominated even in the construction of municipal buildings. The Industrial Association maintained a "permit system" under which it withheld building materials from employers who continued to "discriminate against nonunion men" by making closed-shop contracts with unions. An Impartial Wage Board, established by the association, nearly replaced collective bargaining in the building industry. Representatives of the Industrial Association of San Francisco often argued that it was not a "union-busting" organization, because it forbade employers to discriminate against union members—provided they were willing to work with nonunion people.

In Los Angeles, however, employers were often more candidly eager to destroy unions entirely. The Better America Federation, a new auxiliary of the Merchants' and Manufacturers' Association, was organized in Los Angeles in May 1920 to conduct a lobbying and propaganda battle against organized labor and progressivism. Its drive for members and money made the same sort of patriotic appeals that had been used to sell Liberty Bonds during the war. It lobbied against higher state taxes on banks and utilities and in favor of proposals to establish the open shop by law and to abolish all the state regulatory boards and commissions that the progressives had created. Its propaganda sought to associate with treason and subversion anyone who disagreed with its objectives.

Throughout the 1920s membership in labor unions steadily declined. In a period of prosperity and high employment, this was remarkable. The prestige of organized labor was low, and the prestige of employer organizations was correspondingly high. Many agreed with the Better America Federation in adopting as mottoes the slogan of President Warren Harding, "less government in business, more business in the government," and the aphorism of President Calvin Coolidge, "the business of America is business."

COLLAPSE OF THE DEMOCRATIC PARTY

During the last third of the nineteenth century the balance between the two major parties had been close in California, and Democratic candidates had won five gubernatorial elections to the Republicans' four. After 1900, however, a long series of defeats began to have a cumulative effect on the Democratic party's morale.

In the postwar decade the Republicans benefited from the general prosperity and from the wholesale migration to California of retired farmers and small business-people from the middle west. Throughout the 1920s the Democrats could win no more than 1 of California's 11 congressional seats. Cross-filing Republicans repeatedly won the Democratic nominations for 6 of the seats and were thus elected in the primaries, in which, in several cases, no Democrat even bothered to file. In 1922, of the 80 seats in the state assembly, the Democrats won only 3. Through most of the decade Republicans outnumbered Democrats in California by four to one in voter registration.

Democratic leadership was uninspiring. When William Gibbs McAdoo transferred his residence from New York to California in 1922, the California Democrats hoped that this acquisition of a leading contender for the presidency of the United States would revive their strength. But McAdoo, who favored strong enforcement of prohibition, made his home in Los Angeles and assumed the leadership of the dry Democrats of southern California, thus deepening the split with the northern California wing of the party, which was decidedly wet. William Randolph Hearst remained a nominal Democrat through the early 1920s, but later became a supporter and personal admirer of President Calvin Coolidge. The confused and weakened condition of the California Democratic party was reflected in a contemporary remark by the humorist Will Rogers: "I belong to no organized political party. I am a Democrat."

THE CONTINUING DECLINE OF REPUBLICAN PROGRESSIVISM

Senator Hiram Johnson had abandoned the remnants of the Progressive party by 1918, and he campaigned for the Republican presidential nomination in 1920 on a platform of narrowly nationalistic and isolationist "Americanism." His irreconcilable opposition to the League of Nations so far overshadowed his interest in domestic issues that he supported the conservative lawyer Samuel M. Shortridge for the Republican nomination for United States senator, against the distinguished progressive William Kent, largely because Shortridge opposed the League and Kent favored it.

Prohibition was another issue that confused the alignments among progressive and conservative Republicans, as well as among the Democrats. Many of the California progressives were "drys," and the disastrous failure of the prohibition experiment accelerated the general decline in the moral fervor of progressivism. Congress had submitted the Eighteenth Amendment to the states in December 1917, in the midst of the war, and California ratified it in the spring of 1919. It proved even less popular and less effective in California than in the rest of the country. Efforts to enforce it were concentrated against small cafés rather than against large distillers and bootleggers, and the Mexican border and long coastline made smuggling easy. The obvious breakdown of prohibition tended to weaken all respect for law and government. One jury had to be admonished for drinking up the liquor that was the chief evidence in the trial.

The continuing crusade against the Japanese, which had never had any genuine connection with progressivism, now became a part of the new wave of superheated patriotic antiforeignism that was aiding the conservative revival throughout the country. An initiative measure adopted by a vote of three to one in 1920 repealed the provision of the law of 1913 that had permitted Japanese aliens to lease land for 3 years. In the federal immigration act of 1924, California won its long fight for the complete exclusion of "aliens ineligible to citizenship." Without this clause, the quota system finally provided in the act would have permitted only 100 Japanese immigrants per year; but Johnson and Shortridge demanded and secured complete Japanese exclusion. The United States had never before offered Japan so gratuitous an insult. The Japanese ambassador's warning of "grave consequences" was interpreted in Congress as a threat, and for this reason it actually contributed to the passage of the exclusion clause.

An unexpected consequence of the exclusion of the Japanese and other Asians was an increase in the immigration of Filipinos. The Philippines were an American possession and thus Filipinos were not subject to the exclusionary provisions of the 1924 immigration act. Most of the Filipinos who immigrated to California were young and unskilled; they came to fill the farm-labor vacuum created by the exclusion of the Japanese. As their numbers increased, Filipino immigrants provoked a xenophobic reaction similar to the hostility that had greeted earlier newcomers from Asia.

The triumph of conservatism was most apparent in the election of Friend W. Richardson as governor in 1922. A former state treasurer and publisher of the *Berkeley Gazette,* Richardson promised and achieved a program of "sweeping retrenchment." His "economy budget" drastically reduced appropriations, particularly for regulatory boards, humanitarian agencies, and education. "The schools," he told the legislature, "must be put on a business basis. They must not only teach but practice thrift." As heads of the various regulatory commissions, he replaced the men appointed under Johnson and Stephens with conservatives, often representatives of the business interests that the commissions had been designed to regulate.

For the election of 1926, several leading California progressives formed a Progressive Voters' League and rallied behind the gubernatorial aspirations of Clement C. Young of Berkeley. Young had been speaker of the assembly during the progressive era and was now lieutenant governor. In his race for the governorship in 1926 he made his progressive followers uneasy by accepting the support of A. P. Giannini and his Bank of Italy. Giannini's swiftly growing institution, soon to be renamed the Bank of America, was well on the way toward its goal of a system of branches to cover the whole of California. Under Governor Richardson the state authorities had yielded to the complaints of independent bankers and had imposed restrictions on the statewide growth of branch banking. Shortly before the primary

On Hiram Johnson's drift away from progressivism, see Richard C. Lower, *A Bloc of One: The Political Career of Hiram Johnson* (1993); Richard D. Batman, "The Road to the Presidency: Hoover, Johnson, and the California Republican Party, 1920–1924," Ph.D. thesis, University of Southern California (1965); Robert E. Burke (ed.), *The Diary Letters of Hiram Johnson* (7 volumes, 1983); and Arlene Lazarowitz, "Hiram W. Johnson: The Old Progressive and New Deal Taxation," *California History,* LXIX (Winter 1990) pp. 342–353.

Political issues of the 1920s are also discussed in Jackson K. Putnam, *Modern California Politics, 1917–1980* (1980); Gilman M. Ostrander, *The Prohibition Movement in California, 1848–1933* (1957); Roger Daniels, *The Politics of Prejudice* (1962); Russell M. Posner, "The Progressive Voters' League, 1923–1926," *California Historical Society Quarterly,* XXXVI (September 1957), pp. 251–261; and Putnam, "The Persistence of Progressivism in the 1920s," *Pacific Historical Review,* XXXV (November 1966), pp. 395–411. See also Joseph Giovinco, "Democracy in Banking: The Bank of Italy and California's Italians," *California Historical Society Quarterly,* XLVII (September 1968), pp. 195–218; Gerald D. Nash, *A. P. Giannini and the Bank of America* (1992); and Felice A. Bonadio, *A. P. Giannini: Banker of America* (1994).

The story of the Filipino immigrants is told in Lorraine Jacobs Crouchett, *Filipinos in California* (1982), and Yen Le Espiritu, *Filipino American Lives* (1994).

On the adoption of the "Federal Plan," see George W. Bemis, "Sectionalism and Representation in the California State Legislature, 1911–1931," Ph.D. thesis, University of California, Berkeley (1935); Thomas S. Barclay, "Reapportionment in California," *Pacific Historical Review,* V (June 1936), pp. 93–129; and Bruce E. Cain, *The Reapportionment Puzzle* (1986).

CHAPTER TWENTY-FOUR

New Industries for Southern California

In the early twentieth century California's economy and population expanded with the growth of new industries. Most of the growth occurred in southern California, where the discovery of huge deposits of oil contributed not only to the rise of the petroleum industry, but also to the automobile revolution. At the same time, southern California was becoming the capital of the nation's new motion picture industry.

The significance of these changes was clear: the economic and political center of California was shifting southward. Whereas San Francisco had been the great city of the nineteenth century, Los Angeles was emerging as the city of the twentieth.

ORIGINS OF THE OIL INDUSTRY

California's oil industry had its first boom in the 1860s but did not begin to reach major proportions until the 1890s. Its great modern expansion came in the twentieth century.

The boom of the 1860s centered in the area near Ventura, along the southern California coast. In 1861 George S. Gilbert, a whale oil merchant, built a small refinery on the Ojai Ranch north of Ventura. From seepage oil, Gilbert manufactured small quantities of kerosene. In 1864 Thomas A. Scott, vice president of the Pennsylvania Railroad, sent a Yale University chemist, Benjamin Silliman, to evaluate some western mineral properties. In the course of his trip Silliman investigated the oil resources of the Ventura region. After absorbing the glib optimism of Gilbert, Silliman wrote a number of rosy reports. "California," he predicted, "will be found to have more oil in its soil than all the whales in the Pacific Ocean." In the Ojai region "the oil is struggling to the surface at every available point and is running away down the river for miles." The first 10 wells drilled on the Ojai property, he estimated, would yield an annual profit of more than $1 million.

From the late 1870s to the middle 1890s Standard had dominated the market in California with oil products imported by rail from its eastern fields and refineries. Standard moved into producing and refining operations in the far west in 1900 when it purchased control of the Pacific Coast Oil Company. This concern had been organized in 1878 by two of San Francisco's leading venture capitalists. In 1906 it was renamed the Standard Oil Company (California). In 1911 an antitrust decision of the United States Supreme Court forced the dissolution of the Standard network into its constituent companies, but Standard of California had already become by far the largest refinery on the Pacific coast.

Another California giant was the Associated Oil Company, originally formed by a number of small producers in the San Joaquin Valley in 1901. The Southern Pacific Railroad purchased control of Associated in 1909, mainly in order to develop its own burgeoning oil interests in the western San Joaquin Valley. By 1919 the Southern Pacific Land Company owned more than 19 percent of all the proved oil land in California, and through its controlling interest in the Associated Oil Company the railroad produced about 18 percent of the state's oil. During the next several years, however, the Southern Pacific gradually divested itself of its direct interests in oil production and refining.

In addition to Standard, Associated, and Union, the major California operators in this period included Shell, Richfield, the General Petroleum Corporation, which was later called the Mobil Oil Corporation, the Texas Company (Texaco), and Edward L. Doheny's Pan-American Petroleum Company.

THE OIL BOOM OF THE TWENTIES

Three tremendous discoveries in the early 1920s, all in the Los Angeles basin area, sur-passed all the earlier developments and launched a boom that put oil in the forefront of California's headlong economic expansion in the "prosperity decade." Standard opened the massive new field at Huntington Beach in 1920. The next year, Union brought in the great Santa Fe Springs field south of Whittier, and Shell tapped the still greater bonanza of Signal Hill at Long Beach—richest of all the world's oil deposits in terms of barrels per acre. The value of the California crude oil produced in the decade of the 1920s was more than $2\frac{1}{2}$ billion. This figure compares very strikingly with the value of all the gold ever mined in the state—about $2 billion. California ranked first among the states in crude oil production for several years in the 1920s.

In 1919 about two-thirds of California's oil came from the San Joaquin Valley, and the major refineries were concentrated in the San Francisco Bay area, but in the 1920s the predominance in all aspects of the oil industry quickly passed to the Los Angeles region. Exports of oil from Los Angeles harbor made it the largest oil port in the world. Petroleum refining became the state's largest manufacturing industry. In 1925 the value of oil refinery products was twice the value of the output of California's second-largest branch of manufacturing, the canning and preserving of fruits and vegetables.

The most infamous episode in the history of California's great oil boom of the postwar decade was the involvement of Edward L. Doheny in the scandal of the Elk

Hills naval oil reserve. Doheny and other oilmen persuaded the federal government that the best way to conserve the oil on western public lands, against the possibility of a future war in the Pacific, was to extract the oil and store it in tanks. With Secretary of the Interior Albert B. Fall, an old friend and a former fellow prospector, Doheny arranged to lease and develop the federal oil lands in the Elk Hills field in western Kern County. A large part of the oil was to be stored in tanks which Doheny agreed to build for the government on the west coast and at Pearl Harbor.

Fall received a payment of $100,000 in cash, which Doheny's son brought to him in a satchel. Later Fall was convicted of taking this money as a bribe, but Doheny was acquitted of having bribed him with it. Doheny insisted that in his own view the payment had been simply a loan to an old friend. To Fall $100,000 was a large sum but it was a trifling amount to Doheny, whose fortune exceeded $100 million. In spite of the legal determination that Doheny was innocent of criminal intent and Fall was guilty of it, the government in a civil suit won a cancellation of Doheny's leases on the ground that they had been obtained through a bribe.

By another irony, the whole Elk Hills affair was regarded at the time as less important than the scandal of the Teapot Dome reserve in Wyoming. For a similar leasing arrangement, operator Harry F. Sinclair paid Fall $300,000, presumably reflecting Teapot Dome's greater richness. But that field proved to be relatively unimportant, whereas Elk Hills proved to be the second-largest field in the nation.

THE AUTOMOBILE REVOLUTION

The vast, deep pools of oil that were discovered in the Los Angeles basin in the early 1920s proved extraordinarily rich in gasoline. Thus huge quantities of this great source of motive power became available at the very time and in the very region where the use of the automobile was spreading more rapidly than in any other time or place in history. In the early decades of the oil industry, gasoline had been a worse-than-useless by-product of the refineries, important only because of the difficult and dangerous problem of getting rid of it. But in the automobile age, gasoline became the most valuable ingredient in a barrel of oil, and the refineries were completely redesigned to extract as much of it as possible.

At the turn of the century there were only about 4000 horseless carriages in America, and they were toys of the rich, but a major turning point came when Henry Ford introduced his Model T in 1908 and when one of these remarkable cars set a new record for automobile travel a year later by crossing the continent in a mere 22 days, arriving in San Francisco with New York air still in its two front tires. This achievement proved that an inexpensive car could be a good one and that long-distance travel would soon be practical. At the same time, the reports of the primitive road conditions that the Ford had encountered dramatized the need for highways that would "get the country out of the mud."

In nineteenth-century America the counties were responsible for the building and maintenance of roads, but they had notoriously failed to perform this function either efficiently or honestly. In California the Southern Pacific used its control of county government to concentrate road building almost exclusively on feeders for its railroad lines. Some improvement came in the 1880s and 1890s, when bicycling became the rage and when the League of American Wheelmen became important as a better-roads lobby. Demands of farmers for passable roads increased with the establishment of rural free delivery of mail in 1894. Denunciations of glaring waste and corruption on the part of county road overseers led to the creation of a California state bureau of highways in 1895, but it had only research and advisory powers.

Two private organizations of motorists, the Automobile Club of Southern California with headquarters in Los Angeles and the California State Automobile Association with headquarters in San Francisco, were formed in 1900. With many wealthy and influential people on their boards of directors they soon became major forces in the battle for good roads. In 1909 the California Legislature authorized a bond issue of $18 million for the beginning of a system of paved state highways, and the voters approved the bonds in the general election the next year.

Financial support from the national government began with the federal Highway Aid Act of 1916, with dollar-matching grants to the states. Another major source of money was the state gasoline tax. First discovered by the Oregon Legislature in 1919, this form of revenue had several outstanding advantages. With obvious fairness, it apportioned the cost of highways among the users of them, and the tax was relatively painless because it was paid in driblets as a part of the price of the commodity. With funds for highways thus assured, the age of motorization was ready to come into full flower.

Mass motorization transformed California, and most of all, southern California, where climate, scenery, and boosterism combined with low gasoline prices and increasingly good roads to make the region a motorist's paradise. From 1920 to 1930 the population of Los Angeles County more than doubled, from less than a million to 2,208,492. The number of registered private automobiles quintupled, rising to 806,264. By 1925 the city of Los Angeles had one automobile for every three persons—more than twice the national average. Los Angeles became the most thoroughly motorized and motor-conscious city in the world.

It was also the first American metropolis whose major expansion occurred entirely within the automobile era, and the automobile intensified a process that Henry Huntington's Pacific Electric had begun—the freeing of the people of Los Angeles from the urban centralization that the limitations of the streetcar had enforced upon other great American cities. With their own cars people could live at a considerable distance from their work, and could own their homes, with lawns, flowers, and shrubbery. With the coming of the great construction boom of the 1920s Los Angeles soon had a larger ratio of single-family residences and a lower population density than any other large city in the United States. The modern supermarket, designed for customers who could provide their own transportation for large quantities of groceries, was born in Los Angeles. And Wilshire Boulevard's "Miracle Mile" was probably the first large business district in the world to be created especially for the automobile age.

The automobile spawned a remarkable tradition of roadside vernacu-
lar architecture. Shown here is an early drive-in restaurant in Santa
Monica Canyon featuring "service in your car." (*Courtesy of American Stock Photos, Los Angeles.*)

Tourism increased enormously in a great new wave of the American westward
movement, and "auto camps" and "tourist cabins" sprang up. Service stations
became a major new institution. The first of them has been credited to Earl B.
Gilmore, whose father had bought land for a dairy farm on a part of the Hancock
family's domain, once the Rancho La Brea. A substantial oil field had been opened
there in 1901, near the famous pits that had held the bones of prehistoric animals
mired in the tar. When Wilshire Boulevard was extended from Los Angeles to the
beach at Santa Monica in 1909, Earl Gilmore was just out of Stanford. He put a
tank on a farm wagon, painted it red and yellow, parked it at the corner of Wilshire
Boulevard at La Brea Avenue, and sold gasoline from his father's nearby refinery—
at 10 cents a gallon.

"Our forefathers," said the *Los Angeles Times* in 1926, "in their immortal
independence creed set forth 'the pursuit of happiness' as an inalienable right of
mankind. And how can one pursue happiness by any swifter and surer means . . .
than by the use of the automobile?" Such was the spirit that dominated the
prosperous twenties for better and sometimes for worse. The motorcar contributed
heavily, for example, to the deterioration of personal morals in the era of jazz, hip
flasks, and flappers, for an automobile was a reasonable facsimile of a private room,
readily transportable beyond the reach of chaperonage.

Quite as revolutionary as the effects of the internal combustion engine on the
cities were its effects on agriculture and on rural life. The automobile put an end to
the isolation of rural areas and reduced the differences in outlook between the
farmer and the city dweller, the truck brought much greater flexibility to
agricultural marketing, and the tractor was one of the most crucial laborsaving

cities, would flock to see even the crudest films at that modest price. Soon there were thousands of new movie houses called "nickelodeons"—a charming word formed by combining the price of admission and the Greek word for theater.

Thus, when the movies first came into mass production, they were the poor person's entertainment. Not only the audiences but also the distributors and producers of the early films were drawn very largely from the ranks of people who were struggling to rise from poverty. "Respectable" businesspeople and financiers shunned the infant movie industry as a possible investment. As Leo Rosten has put it, "The men who built the motion picture industry . . . were not drawn from the supposedly farsighted ranks of American business," but from "the marginal and shabby zones of enterprise, from vaudeville, nickelodeon parlors, theatrical agencies, flea circuses, petty trade." William Fox, born in Hungary, worked as a cloth sponger in New York before he opened a penny arcade and then a nickelodeon in Brooklyn. Jesse L. Lasky began his working life as a vaudeville cornet player in San Francisco. His brother-in-law, Samuel Goldwyn, was born Schmuel Gelbfisz in Poland, ran away from home in Warsaw, arrived in New York alone as a steerage passenger at 13, and began work as a glove salesman. Louis B. Mayer, born in Russia, spent part of his boyhood as a rag collector in Saint John, New Brunswick. Marcus Loew and Adolph Zukor were small fur dealers before they became partners in the theater business.

All these men were deeply sensitive about their origins. Only one member of the group, Lewis J. Selznick, took public pride in his humble beginnings. Hearing of the abdication of the Czar in March 1917, he sent him a famous and fascinating cablegram: "WHEN I WAS POOR BOY IN KIEV YOUR POLICEMEN WERE NOT KIND TO ME STOP I CAME TO AMERICA AND PROSPERED STOP NOW HEAR WITH REGRET YOU ARE OUT OF JOB OVER THERE STOP FEEL NO ILL WILL . . . SO IF YOU WILL COME NEW YORK CAN GIVE YOU FINE POSITION ACTING IN PICTURES STOP SALARY NO OBJECT STOP . . . SELZNICK."

In the early years the moviemakers, especially the members of the trust, were afraid that their mass audience was not intelligent enough to sit through any one picture longer than one reel (about 12 minutes) and too poor to afford the cost of longer and better pictures. But in 1913 the independent producer Jesse L. Lasky and his director Cecil B. deMille made the first American feature-length movie, *The Squaw Man*, in five reels and proved that longer films could be highly profitable.

Movie patrons had begun to favor certain players by 1910, but the companies in the trust would not advertise the names of actors and actresses lest they demand higher salaries. It was the independents who discovered the star system, through which they could achieve an unbroken succession of hits by featuring personalities so consistently attractive that the patrons would line up at the box office no matter what the quality of the films. Within a few years salaries of featured players leaped from a maximum of $15 a day to an average of $1500 a week. To the movie audiences the stars were figures of personified desire or symbols of the great moving forces of comedy or tragedy. Gladys Smith from Canada became better known as Mary Pickford, or America's Sweetheart, in which capacity she received $500,000 a year by 1915.

Movie audiences, centering their attention on the stars, have never developed an appreciation of the role of directors, but within the industry the vital importance of their function soon came to be recognized. Directors fuse the script, the performers, the camera operators, and the technicians into a single pattern, a motion picture. Ultimately their conception determines what the story is, what it means, and how it is told.

David Wark Griffith was the first great American director, and his film *The Birth of a Nation* was a remarkable motion picture, especially in such technological achievements as its filming of Civil War battle scenes. But it was also a racist distortion of American history, and because it was more widely shown and left a deeper emotional imprint on its audiences than almost any other film before or since, it stands as a classic example of both the enormous potential power of the art of the cinema and the possibilities for misuse of that power. Griffith was the son of a brigadier general in the Confederate Army, and his film, based on Thomas Dixon's novel *The Clansman,* glorified the role of the Ku Klux Klan in the reconstruction of the south and portrayed black people as an inferior race.

After a special showing of the film at the White House, President Wilson was reported to have said that "it is like writing history with lightning, and my one regret is that it is all so terribly true." Wilson was himself a southerner by birth and early education, and it was during his presidency that lunchrooms, drinking fountains, and lavatories in government buildings in the District of Columbia were racially segregated for the first time since the Civil War. But if President Wilson could see nothing wrong with *The Birth of a Nation,* there were many Americans who could; in the face of a great outcry from critics of the film, Wilson publicly disavowed his endorsement of it. The denunciations, however, merely gave it additional advertising. By 1930 more than 100 million people had seen *The Birth of a Nation,* and by 1948 it had grossed nearly $50 million. It did more to fasten racial stereotypes on the American mind than anything since *Uncle Tom's Cabin,* and it was partly responsible for the great revival of the Ku Klux Klan that reached its height in the 1920s.

A film of special significance in the cultural history of California was *Greed* (1923), based on Frank Norris's novel *McTeague, a Story of San Francisco* and directed by Erich von Stroheim. It was extravagantly produced and became a financial disaster that led to the decline of its director's career. The novel so fascinated von Stroheim that he filmed it not merely chapter by chapter but line by line, and not on artificial sets but in actual rooms and streets in San Francisco and actual places in Death Valley. After he had spent 6 months in reducing its enormous bulk, the film was still more than 4 hours long. When he refused to edit it further, the Metro-Goldwyn-Mayer executives took it out of his hands and turned it over to a cutter, who reduced it from 24 reels to 11. Von Stroheim refused to look at it again, though even in this mutilated form it was one of the greatest of all motion pictures.

Gradually the movies escaped from their earlier status as an essentially lower-class form of entertainment and began to make a very successful appeal to the

Suburbanization of Los Angeles, 1890–1930," *Journal of Urban Studies,* VIII (November 1981), pp. 3–26; R. M. Fogelson, *The Fragmented Metropolis: Los Angeles, 1850–1930* (1967); Ashleigh E. Brilliant, "Social Effects of the Automobile in Southern California during the Nineteen-Twenties," Ph.D. thesis, University of California, Berkeley (1964); and the same writer's article, "Some Aspects of Mass Motorization in Southern California, 1919–1929," *Southern California Quarterly,* XLVII (June 1965), pp. 191–208. On tourism see John F. Sears, *Sacred Places* (1989), and *Motoring Tourists and the Scenic West* (1989).

The coming of the film industry to California is described in Geoffrey Bell, *The Golden Gate and the Silver Screen* (1984), and Donald B. Parkhurst, "Broncho Billy and Niles, California," *Pacific Historian,* XXVI (Winter 1982), pp. 1–22. Major contributions to the history of motion pictures include Tom Gunning, *D. W. Griffith and the Origins of the American Narrative Film* (1991); Bernard F. Dick, *Columbia Pictures* (1991); Benjamin B. Hampton, *A History of the Movies* (1931); Richard Griffith and Arthur Mayer, *The Movies* (1957, 1971); Arthur Knight, *The Liveliest Art* (1957); and A. R. Fulton, *Motion Pictures* (1960). Leo C. Rosten's *Hollywood* (1939) is a survey of the industry as it was in the late 1930s, written with the aid of a team of social scientists. Hortense Powdermaker, *Hollywood, the Dream Factory* (1950), presents an anthropologist's view. On censorship, see Raymond Moley, *The Hays Office* (1945), and Ruth A. Inglis, *Freedom of the Movies* (1947).

CHAPTER TWENTY-FIVE

Controversies over Land and Water

Nineteenth-century Americans had regarded their country's natural resources as inexhaustible and had exploited them with the greatest recklessness. In the progressive era, however, interest in conservation greatly increased. California's natural resources were so spectacular and the controversies over their use and development were so complicated and intense that the issues and problems of conservation inevitably became a major theme in the state's history.

THE YOSEMITE AND JOHN MUIR

One of the many tributes to the incomparable beauty of the Yosemite Valley was the fact that it was the first area in the United States to be designated by the federal government as a park. This action was also one of the first historical landmarks in the growth of the modern sense of public responsibility for conservation in America.

The strongest impetus for creation of a Yosemite Park came from the country's leading landscape architect, Frederick Law Olmsted. In 1864, largely as a result of Olmsted's urging, Congress passed and President Lincoln signed an act granting the Yosemite Valley and the Mariposa Grove of Big Trees to the state of California. Olmsted was then appointed by the governor as the first chairman of the Yosemite State Park Commission. There was no precedent for the idea of a *national* park, but federal grants of land to the states for an assortment of other purposes were so frequent that the proposal for a park met little opposition.

Almost as important in the history of conservation as Yosemite Park itself was the personality of John Muir, who first came to the valley as a young man in 1868 and was never again entirely happy anywhere else. The valley and the mountains around it inspired him to a lifetime of writings and crusades which proclaimed his gospel of humanity's rebirth through the enjoyment of nature's beauty and of humanity's obligation to preserve that beauty as a sacred trust.

Muir had been born in Scotland—"with heather in him," as he said—and had spent his boyhood on a wilderness farm in Wisconsin. Almost from infancy his father forced him to a regimen of memorizing great parts of the Bible, an influence that was very apparent in his later thinking and writing. A good example was his famous description of the Sierra as he first saw it after he had landed at San Francisco and walked southward from Oakland to Gilroy and thence to the summit of Pacheco Pass. Across the Central Valley on a clear morning the great range "seemed not clothed with light but wholly composed of it, like the wall of some celestial city. . . . It seemed to me that the Sierra should be called, not the Nevada or Snowy Range, but the Range of Light."

After a short time in the Yosemite region, Muir wrote in his diary that "John the Baptist was not more eager to get all of his fellow sinners into the Jordan than I to baptize all of mine in the beauty of God's mountains." "Climb the mountains and get their good tidings," he wrote in his first book, *The Mountains of California.*

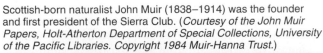

Scottish-born naturalist John Muir (1838–1914) was the founder and first president of the Sierra Club. (*Courtesy of the John Muir Papers, Holt-Atherton Department of Special Collections, University of the Pacific Libraries. Copyright 1984 Muir-Hanna Trust.*)

"Nature's peace will flow into you as sunshine flows into trees. The winds will blow their freshness into you and the storms their energy, while cares will drop off like autumn leaves."

Although Muir had studied geology and botany at the University of Wisconsin, he was not a scientist but rather a brilliant amateur naturalist. His essentially religious approach to nature was a blend of theism and pantheism. God, he felt, was "ensouled as a Principle in all forms of matter." Believing that evolution was not mere chance and survival of the fittest, Muir insisted that humanity, like nature in general, evolved by cooperation rather than competition. Thus Muir offered a philosophy of society as well as a philosophy of nature. Brought into their true relationship with the wilderness, humanity would see that they were not a separate entity but an integral part of a harmonious whole. Human beings had no right to subdue their fellow creatures or to appropriate and destroy their common heritage; to do so brought unbalance in nature and loss and poverty for all.

In 1889 Muir gained an important ally in Robert Underwood Johnson, one of the editors of the *Century* magazine. On a tour of the central Sierra, Muir convinced Johnson that the Yosemite was being poorly protected under state control and pointed out the devastation which sheep—those "hoofed locusts"—were being allowed to inflict on the mountain valleys of the region. Johnson urged Muir to carry his appeal to the people of the whole nation through articles in the *Century*.

For the next 15 years the California Legislature resisted the demands of Muir and his admirers that the state return the Yosemite Valley to the federal government, but in 1890 the eloquent writings of "great Nature's priest," as Johnson called Muir, aroused so much national emotion that Congress set aside a large area surrounding the valley as a national forest reserve administered by the secretary of the interior, who designated it as "Yosemite National Park." At the same time Congress created the Sequoia National Park and the General Grant, which was later incorporated in Kings Canyon. The creation of Sequoia incidentally ensured the final eviction of Burnette Haskell's socialistic Kaweah colony, and the biggest *Sequoiadendron giganteum,* which the Kaweahns had named the "Karl Marx tree," was hastily renamed the "General Sherman."

In 1892 Muir founded the Sierra Club, an organization as enthusiastically devoted to conservationist lobbying as it was to mountaineering.

With Theodore Roosevelt's accession to the presidency in September 1901, conservation gained another ally. Indeed Roosevelt was soon identifying the whole conservation movement as "my policy." Roosevelt's love of the outdoors was as deep and personal as that of John Muir, but the conservation philosophies of the two men were very different. Muir's views were part of a movement known as "aesthetic conservationism" or "preservationism." The preservationists believed that the true object of conservation was to preserve the beauty of the wilderness in its natural state. Roosevelt was more of a "utilitarian" conservationist, supporting the techniques of scientific forest management. In spite of their differences, Roosevelt in 1903 requested that Muir serve as his personal guide on a 4-day pack trip in the Yosemite region.

With such powerful allies, it was only a matter of time before Muir and his followers would prevail in their struggle to win federal protection for the Yosemite Valley. At last, in 1905, the California Legislature approved the recession of the Yosemite Valley to the federal government. A year later Congress approved the merging of the valley with the surrounding national park. Yosemite National Park today remains a monument to one of the great victories of the California conservation movement.

THE HETCH HETCHY CONTROVERSY

The city dweller, as well as the farmer, naturally attached great importance to an assured supply of water. San Francisco was worried by its dependence on the limited nearby resources of the Spring Valley Water Company. In 1900 a new city charter authorized a larger and municipally owned water system. The city engineer reported that the Hetch Hetchy Valley on the Tuolumne River in Yosemite National Park was the ideal site, superior to any of the possible alternatives. Mayor James D. Phelan applied to the secretary of the interior for permission to convert the Hetch Hetchy Valley into a reservoir, but the moment John Muir heard of the plan, he mobilized his forces for battle, and they fought so valiantly that the federal government delayed its final approval of the project for 13 years.

Hetch Hetchy was about 20 miles northwest of its "sister valley," the Yosemite. Though only about half as long and half as wide as its much more famous neighbor, it bore a striking and charming resemblance to it and was called by Muir the "other Yosemite." But Hetch Hetchy was so nearly inaccessible that very few people except Muir and some other members of the Sierra Club had ever seen it. Muir called the flooding of Hetch Hetchy as great a sacrilege as the destruction of a cathedral and denounced the proponents of it in the strongest terms he could think of.

James D. Phelan, an outstanding patron of the arts, was outraged at the accusation that he was callously indifferent to beauty. He denounced Muir in return and stoutly asserted that a lake, as well as a valley, could be beautiful.

Phelan and his supporters also argued that while the use of Hetch Hetchy would be granted free of charge, the possible alternative sites not only were inferior and inadequate, but also were all controlled by private interests who wished to sell them to the city at exorbitant prices. Considerable weight was given to this argument by sensational revelations concerning the designs of the Bay Cities Water Company. This corporation proposed to construct a water system, which it would sell to the city for $10.5 million, and in 1906 the Union Labor board of supervisors actually voted approval of the project. But this action was hastily reversed in the following year when the confessions of Boss Ruef and the supervisors revealed that the total estimated cost of the project was only $7.5 million; that of the $3 million of estimated profit, the company had promised $1 million as a fee to Ruef; and that Ruef had promised to divide half this money among the supervisors in return for their votes. This project, if it had been consummated, would have been by far the largest of all Ruef's corrupt transactions.

The federal government, sure of being denounced by someone for any action it might take in the Hetch Hetchy matter, vacillated and temporized. The settlement of the long struggle came at last in 1913, essentially because it happened that President Wilson's choice for secretary of the interior was Franklin K. Lane, who had been city attorney of San Francisco under Mayor Phelan and had written many of the city's briefs in the fight. With the weight of the new secretary thrown into the scales, Congress gave final permission for the Hetch Hetchy project. John Muir, defeated by this shift in the sands of politics, was brokenhearted and died a few months later.

THE OWENS VALLEY–LOS ANGELES AQUEDUCT

San Francisco's chief source of water, the Tuolumne River, begins its flow at the foot of a glacier on Mt. Lyell. Only 15 miles eastward across the Sierra divide are the headwaters of the Owens River, the stream to which Los Angeles reached out for the first of the great and distant new sources of water that its phenomenal twentieth-century growth would require. The story of the Owens Valley–Los Angeles Aqueduct involved controversies even more bitter than the struggle over Hetch Hetchy.

The man who conceived the Owens Valley Aqueduct project was Fred Eaton, city engineer of Los Angeles in the 1890s and its mayor from 1899 to 1901. Born in Los Angeles, Eaton had served as superintendent of the city's water system when it was a mere network of open ditches from the Los Angeles River, operated by a private company. For many years Eaton spent his vacations in prospecting for a new water supply. Choosing the Owens River, he recognized that the vital unit in its development would be a storage reservoir near its upper end, in Long Valley, above the main Owens Valley. Hoping for personal enrichment as the just reward of his concern for his native city, he quietly bought the land and the water rights in Long Valley and planned as a private enterprise to sell some of the Owens River water to farmers in Owens Valley and to sell the rest to the city of Los Angeles.

Between 1900 and 1905 the population of that city grew from 102,479 to more than 250,000. Moreover, the rainfall in these years was even less than usual, and in July 1904 Los Angeles came close to the stark terror of an actual water famine. The city engineer, William Mulholland, was a former protégé of Eaton's. For years he had responded with friendly ridicule to Eaton's confidential efforts to interest him in the remote Owens Valley. Now, however, Mulholland urgently begged Eaton to "show me this water supply."

In the meantime the United States Reclamation Service had formed a plan to irrigate the Owens Valley. When the federal agency refused to cooperate with Eaton as a private speculator and developer, he agreed to sell his interests to the city of Los Angeles. He also agreed to act as the city's confidential agent in purchasing further lands in Owens Valley necessary for an aqueduct. This he proceeded to do under the guise of buying lands for ranching purposes. The real purpose was to be kept secret as long as possible in order to prevent speculative increases in the price of the land.

The first public knowledge of the aqueduct project came in a long, detailed, and enthusiastic article in the *Los Angeles Times* on July 19, 1905. Not long afterward the *Los Angeles Examiner,* outraged that the *Times* had been permitted to scoop its rivals, published sensational charges of collusion and conspiracy.

Two years before, a syndicate including Harrison Gray Otis, Edwin T. Earl, Henry E. Huntington, and others had acquired options to buy extensive lands in the San Fernando Valley. Under the Owens Valley Aqueduct plan, now revealed, a reservoir just north of Los Angeles would be adjacent to these lands and would provide water for their irrigation as well as for the city's domestic supply. The whole aqueduct project, the *Examiner* charged, had been conceived by the members of this San Fernando land syndicate for their own speculative profit.

This charge, though periodically revived ever since, was based on an erroneous conclusion. The evidence is clear that in 1903 when this group of wealthy men had acquired the San Fernando land options, Eaton's dream of an aqueduct, if they had yet heard of it at all, was not the basis of their plan. Rather, they were acting on inside information from Henry E. Huntington that he was about to build a new line of the Pacific Electric into the San Fernando Valley. The same men were employing this highly profitable technique of group investment in several other prospective suburbs of Los Angeles at this same time.

In a special election in September 1905 the voters of the city overwhelmingly approved an issue of bonds for the beginning of the Owens Valley project. At the end of still another summer of frightening water shortage, the citizens of Los Angeles were in no mood to vote against a plan that promised them an adequate water supply.

The farmers and townspeople of the Owens Valley now began a bitter campaign of denunciation which they would continue for decades, charging that the aqueduct was a corrupt scheme to enrich a few of the leading capitalists of Los Angeles by seizing the water that would be needed for the agricultural development of the Owens Valley and using it to irrigate the San Fernando Valley instead. The federal government sided with the city. President Roosevelt was persuaded that the whole future growth of Los Angeles was more important than the interests of "a few settlers in Owens Valley." In 1908, to prevent homestead entries in the path of the proposed aqueduct, Roosevelt ordered the extension of the Sierra National Forest eastward to include the prospective right-of-way, even though the only trees in the region were those planted by the settlers themselves.

Under the direction of City Engineer Mulholland the construction of the 233-mile aqueduct began in 1908 and ended 5 years later, at a cost within his estimate of $25 million. Unfortunately the aqueduct took its water directly out of the lower Owens River. If a year-to-year storage reservoir in Long Valley had been built when the aqueduct was constructed, or soon afterward, enough water could have been provided to meet the needs of Owens Valley, along with those of the city, for some time to come, and much bitterness could have been avoided. But Fred Eaton had demanded a price of at least $1 million for his Long Valley land, and Mulholland, breaking his old friendship with Eaton, had denounced the price as too high and advised the city not to pay it. In the early 1920s a new cycle of dry years and the

Unidentified saboteurs dynamited the Owens Valley–Los Angeles Aqueduct 14 times in 1927.
(Courtesy of the Bancroft Library.)

continuing rapid growth of Los Angeles's population led the city to siphon off virtually the entire flow of the river, and in 1924 residents of Owens Valley began to dramatize their protests with a campaign of sabotage which later culminated in the dynamiting of several sections of the aqueduct.

Mulholland later succeeded in negotiating a compromise price for Long Valley, and a personal reconciliation with Fred Eaton. In 1941, several years after the deaths of Eaton and Mulholland, the dam in Long Valley was completed at last. The volume of water in the Owens River was also increased by extending a long tunnel northward to tap the streams flowing into Mono Lake.

THE BOULDER CANYON PROJECT

George Chaffey's Imperial Canal and William Mulholland's Owens Valley Aqueduct were temporary and inadequate answers to southern California's insatiable thirst. Seeking access to new sources of water, southern California turned its attention to a vast project for the development of the Colorado River.

Arthur Powell Davis, an engineer for the United States Reclamation Service, had first conceived in 1904 a broad proposal for the development of the lower Colorado under the unified control of the federal government, with a great dam to store the floods and to serve as the heart of the project. The first strong public support for this plan came from the people of the Imperial Valley, who lived in terror of floods. They had not forgotten the catastrophe that began in 1905 when the river burst into the Imperial Canal and created the Salton Sea before it was finally checked in 1907.

The settlers of the valley had many reasons to be dissatisfied with the Imperial Canal, particularly with the fact that its source and the first 50 miles of its flow were in Mexican territory. The Mexican government required that half the canal's water be reserved for the irrigation of Mexican lands, and it held down the price of the water used south of the border, so that a much higher price had to be charged on the American side. In 1911 the voters of the Imperial Valley formed the Imperial Irrigation District—the largest of its kind—and approved a bond issue to buy the Imperial Canal. Soon afterward they also began to agitate for an all-American canal, to be built north of the border.

Early in 1922, Secretary of the Interior Fall joined with Arthur Powell Davis, now director of the Reclamation Service, in recommending an extensive plan. Soon afterward their proposals were introduced in Congress in the form of the Swing-Johnson bill. Phil Swing, who had served for several years as chief counsel of the Imperial Irrigation District and had then been elected to Congress, sponsored the bill in the House, and Hiram Johnson gave it his powerful support in the Senate. Six years later it was finally approved as the Boulder Canyon Project Act, but only after a long and bitter struggle in both houses.

Under this plan the federal government was to construct a dam in or near Boulder Canyon, a plant for generating hydroelectric power, and an all-American canal just north of the Mexican border from the river to the Imperial Valley. Leasing of the power to public and private agencies in the region would repay the government for the cost of building the dam, and the Imperial Irrigation District would ultimately repay the cost of building the canal. The city of Los Angeles soon joined with the Imperial Valley in ardent support of the Boulder Canyon project. William Mulholland warned Los Angeles that its growth was outstripping its supply of water from the Owens Valley, and he called for the building of a much larger aqueduct as soon as possible, with the Colorado River as its source.

On the other hand, the federal project aroused tremendous opposition. The first difficulty to be surmounted was a wrangle among the seven states in the Colorado River area. The upper-basin states of Wyoming, Colorado, Utah, and New Mexico complained that all the benefits would go to the lower-basin states, Arizona, Nevada, and California, whose development would be so stimulated that they would gain an unfair share of the water under the laws of prior appropriation. In November 1922 Secretary of Commerce Herbert Hoover persuaded representatives of all seven states to agree to the Colorado River Compact, assuring the upper basin of a permanent claim to about half the flow of the river. Six of the state legislatures ratified the compact, but Arizona balked and began an opposition to the Boulder Canyon project that continued for years and a quarrel with California that continued for decades.

Further opposition came from the American owners of irrigated lands in Mexico, of whom the most notable was Harry Chandler, the son-in-law, heir, and successor of Harrison Gray Otis. Chandler headed a syndicate that owned 862,000 acres of land in Baja California, mainly in the region of the Imperial Canal. Not surprisingly, he and his *Los Angeles Times* denounced the Swing-Johnson bill as a socialistic menace to free American enterprise.

Of all the sources of opposition to the Boulder Canyon project, however, the most formidable were the private power companies. They were then engaged in a national struggle to prevent the federal government from "entering the power business." The Swing-Johnson bill provided that the federal government would not act as the distributor of the electric power from the Boulder Canyon project, but would lease it to private or municipal corporations, which would build their own transmission lines. Nevertheless the private companies fought the measure, largely for two reasons. The huge project would reduce the price of power in the southwest by increasing the supply of it, and much of the power would go to the municipally owned electric system of the city of Los Angeles, thus encouraging its growth at the expense of private companies.

That public ownership and distribution of electric power had come into existence in Los Angeles, a city as passionately committed to private enterprise as any community in the United States, is one of the many striking paradoxes of California history. It was even more remarkable in view of the fact that in northern California the private Pacific Gas and Electric Company (PG&E) achieved an almost complete monopoly over the distribution of power and light. In 1925, after a long controversy, the San Francisco board of supervisors turned over the power from Hetch Hetchy to PG&E. This arrangement was carried out even though Congress in 1913 had flatly forbidden the city to dispose of the power to any private company. Moreover, San Francisco made an almost incredibly bad bargain. PG&E paid the city $2.4 million a year for the Hetch Hetchy power, and then retailed the same power for $9 million a year. In sharp contrast, the City of Los Angeles Bureau of Power and Light gradually crowded out and bought out the distribution systems of several privately owned electric companies, in a process that those companies regarded as not merely creeping, but galloping, socialism.

Secretary of Commerce Herbert Hoover was deeply troubled by the charge that in building a great power plant the federal government would be dealing a heavy blow to a leading American private industry, but he could see no other way to pay for the dam. Hoover's election to the presidency, and the knowledge that he favored the project, finally ended the long battle over its adoption, and the Swing-Johnson bill became law on December 21, 1928.

During the long controversy over the Boulder Canyon project, the name "Boulder Dam" had been unofficially used by both sides of the debate. The official choice of a name for a federal dam, however, was a time-honored prerogative of the secretary of the interior. Dr. Ray Lyman Wilbur, who held that office under President Hoover, chose the name that seemed to him in every way most eminently suitable—Hoover Dam. When the mighty structure was about half finished, Franklin Roosevelt's secretary of the interior, Harold Ickes, declared his intention "to give Boulder dam its original and proper name, which my predecessor in office attempted feloniously to take from it." It was as "Boulder Dam" that President Roosevelt officially dedicated the structure, on September 30, 1935. In 1947 the Republican Eightieth Congress passed a bill to restore the name of "Hoover Dam," and President Truman signed the bill into law. Nevertheless, usage has sometimes continued to vary with partisan preference—or merely with confused recollection.

The building of the dam was a monumental accomplishment. To divert the river from the construction site, four bypass tunnels had to be built through the canyon walls, two on each side. Each of these tunnels was a mile long and 50 feet in diameter with a 3-foot concrete lining. Before any concrete could be poured for the foundation of the dam, the riverbed had to be cleaned down to the bare rock. Then it had to be kept clean and dry during the whole period of construction.

At the base of the dam was the world's largest powerhouse to date, containing the world's largest turbines and generators. They began to operate on September 11, 1936, when President Roosevelt pushed a golden key. Behind the dam was the world's largest reservoir, Lake Mead. Vast as the reservoir was, engineers soberly pointed out that it was doomed to impermanence. They warned that the Colorado would fill Lake Mead with silt within 300 years and that over the next 30 centuries the whole process would have to be repeated 10 times, at each of 10 other possible sites.

THE COLORADO RIVER AQUEDUCT

In 1923 Los Angeles and several neighboring communities had begun to plan the formation of a metropolitan water district for the purpose of building the world's longest and largest domestic water supply line from the Colorado River to the coastal basin. In the discussion of water projects in southern California it had become impossible to avoid the constant repetition of the phrase "the world's largest."

The Metropolitan Water District of Southern California, officially organized in 1928, originally included Los Angeles and 10 nearby cities. Many others later joined. A $220 million bond issue for the great aqueduct came before the district's voters on September 29, 1931. Though the concern of most of the voters was with water for domestic use, its role in the region's industrial development was equally vital. In 1919, for example, the Goodyear Tire and Rubber Company had become the first major industrial concern to locate a branch plant in Los Angeles because the city could promise the 8 million gallons of water a day that the plant would need. In the crucial petroleum industry, 77,000 gallons of water were needed to refine 100 barrels of oil. Later improvements in equipment would enable refineries to recover much of the water and use it repeatedly, but in 1930 the Union Oil Company plant at Long Beach was still using more water than all the rest of the city. With such compelling arguments in its favor, the huge bond issue passed by more than five to one. The aqueduct was finished on schedule in 1938, and in 1941 it began to deliver water to the coastal cities.

San Diego remained outside the Metropolitan Water District for several years, partly because it hoped to get water from a branch of the All-American Canal. The city had often shown desperate ingenuity in its long struggle with its water problem. In December 1915 in the midst of a particularly serious drought it had even signed a contract with a professional rainmaker, Charles M. Hatfield. Promising to fill the Morena reservoir for a fee of $10,000, Hatfield built a number of "evaporating tanks," presumably to send up fumes from some combination of chemicals that remained his professional secret. A few weeks later a cloudburst

MAJOR CALIFORNIA WATER PROJECTS
1900-1980

············· = municipal

―――― = federal

‑ ‑ ‑ ‑ = state

―┼―┼― = Central Valley
Project power lines

⌒ = dams

= Metropolitan Water
District of Southern
California

Shasta Lake

Shasta Dam

Keswick Dam

Tehama-Colusa Canal (1971)

Oroville

Lake Tahoe

Putah South Canal (1959)

Sacramento

Contra Costa Canal (1940)

Mokelumne Aq. (1929)

Mono Extension (1940)

Mono Lake

San Francisco

Tracy

Hetch Hetchy Aq. (1934)

South Bay Aq. (1962)

California Aqueduct (1968)

Delta-Mendota Canal (1951)

Madera Canal (1944)

Friant Dam

Friant-Kern Canal (1949)

Owens River

First Los Angeles Aq. (1913)

California Aq. (1971)

Bakersfield

Lake Mead

Hoover Dam

Davis Dam

Lake Havasu

Parker Dam

California Aq. (1973)

Colorado River Aq. (1941)

Los Angeles

First San Diego Aq. (1947)

Salton Sea

Imperial Dam

San Diego

All-American Canal (1941)

Second San Diego Aq. (1960)

overflowed the reservoir, washed out a smaller dam below it, and flooded a part of the town. The city council refused to pay Hatfield his fee; they pointed out that he had contracted to fill the reservoir, not to flood the community.

The growth of San Diego during World War II finally compelled the city and its neighbors to form a subgroup of the Metropolitan Water District of Southern California, and in 1945 construction work began on the first of two branch lines from the Colorado River Aqueduct to the San Diego region.

Congress repeatedly declined to repeal the 160-acre limitation, and the large Central Valley landholders sought relief in the courts. In 1958 the United States Supreme Court unanimously upheld the constitutionality of the acreage limitation. The purpose of the 160-acre limit, the court ruled, was to spread the benefits of federal water projects "in accordance with the greatest good of the greatest number of individuals. This limitation ensures that this enormous expenditure will not go in disproportionate share to a few individuals with large land holdings." The most significant effect of this decision was to convince most of the political leaders of California that any new water projects must be built with state rather than federal funds, so that the larger units of land could obtain cheap, publicly subsidized water.

After decades of controversy, California's large landowners scored a partial victory with congressional passage of the Reclamation Reform Act of 1982. This act repealed the 80-year-old 160-acre limit, increasing to 960 acres the amount of land that any one owner could irrigate with water from the federal projects. The act also called for rigorous enforcement of this new, more generous acreage limitation.

SELECTED BIBLIOGRAPHY

Michael Smith, in *Pacific Visions* (1988), gives a masterful account of an emerging environmental consciousness in California. Alfred Runte describes the long-standing struggle over Yosemite in *Yosemite: The Embattled Wilderness* (1990). John Muir is the subject of great and continuing interest. Major works include analyses of Muir and the conservation movement by Thurman Wilkins (1995), Frederick Turner (1985), Michael P. Cohen (1984), Stephen Fox (1981), Holway R. Jones (1965), and Linnie March Wolfe (1945); and an anthology edited by Sally M. Miller (1993) and a bibliography by William E. Kimes and Maymie B. Kimes (1984). See also Susan Schrepfer, *The Fight to Save the Redwoods* (1983), and special issues of *California History,* LXIX (Summer 1990) and LXXI (Summer 1992).

Norris Hundley, *The Great Thirst* (1992), presents a comprehensive survey of California water development. On the Hetch Hetchy controversy, see Kendrick A. Clements, "Politics and the Park," *Pacific Historical Review,* XLVII (May 1979), pp. 185–216, and "Engineers and Conservationists in the Progressive Era," *California History,* LVIII (Winter 1979–1980), pp. 282–303; Elmo R. Richardson, "The Struggle for the Valley," *California Historical Society Quarterly,* XXXVIII (September 1959), pp. 249–258; Stephen P. Sayles, "Hetch Hetchy Reversed," ibid., LXIV (Fall 1985), pp. 254–263; and Richard Lowitt, "The Hetch Hetchy Controversy," ibid., LXXIV (Summer 1995), pp. 190–203.

The best treatments of the Owens Valley–Los Angeles Aqueduct are in Robert A. Sauder, *Lost Frontier* (1994); Margaret Davis, *River in the Desert* (1993); John Walton, *Western Times and Water Wars* (1992); William L. Kahrl, *Water and Power* (1982); Abraham Hoffman, *Vision or Villainy* (1981); and Remi A. Nadeau, *The Water Seekers* (1950). Carey McWilliams, *Southern California Country* (1946), revived the syndicate conspiracy version of the Owens Valley project. W. W. Robinson disagreed in "Myth Making in the Los Angeles Area," *Southern California Quarterly,* XLV (March 1963), pp. 83–94.

The *Boulder Canyon Project* (1941) is a thorough study by economist Paul L. Kleinsorge. Norris Hundley, *Water in the West* (1975), and Beverly B. Moeller, *Phil Swing and Boulder Dam* (1971), discuss the national political problems. See also Joseph E. Stevens, *Hoover Dam*

(1988); Mark S. Foster, *Henry J. Kaiser* (1989); Andrew J. Dunar and Dennie McBride, *Building Hoover Dam* (1993); and Donald E. Wolf, *Big Dams and Other Dreams: The Six Companies Story* (1996).

Donald J. Pisani, *From the Family Farm to Agribusiness* (1984), is a seminal study, as are Donald Worster, *Rivers of Empire* (1985); Marc Reisner, *Cadillac Desert* (1986); Robert Kelley, *Battling the Inland Sea* (1990); and Philip L. Fradkin, *A River No More* (1996). See also the articles in "Water in California," a special issue of *Pacific Historian,* XXVII (Spring 1983), and "Water in the West," a special issue of *Journal of the West,* XXII (April 1983). Useful works on the Central Valley Project are Mary Montgomery and Marion Clawson, *History of Legislation . . . of the Central Valley Project* (1946); "The Central Valley Project and Related Problems," an edition of the *California Law Review,* XXXVIII (October 1950); and Hugh G. Hansen, *Central Valley Project: Federal or State?* (1955).

Charles M. Coleman, *P.G. and E. of California* (1952), refers to the company's political activities only in very general and favorable terms. A more critical view may be found in Carl D. Thompson, *Confessions of the Power Trust* (1932), based on the hearings of the Federal Trade Commission. See also William A. Myers, *Iron Men and Copper Wires: A Centennial History of the Southern California Edison Company* (1983).

Most of the arguments against the 160-acre limit were collected and elaborated in Sheridan Downey, *They Would Rule the Valley* (1947), "they" being the United States Bureau of Reclamation. The opposite viewpoint is well summarized in Paul S. Taylor, "Excess Land Law: Pressure versus Principle," *California Law Review,* XLVII (August 1959), pp. 499–541, and "Excess Land Law: Calculated Circumvention," ibid., LII (December 1964), pp. 978–1014. See also Clayton R. Koppes, "Public Water, Private Land: Origins of the Acreage Limitation Controversy, 1933–1953," *Pacific Historical Review,* XLVII (November 1978), pp. 607–636, and William D. Rowley, *Reclaiming the Arid West* (1996).

CHAPTER TWENTY-SIX

The Great Depression

The prosperity of the 1920s was not well-distributed. Proportionally, too much of the national income was in profits and too little in wages, and therefore America's capacity to produce exceeded its capacity to consume. During the 1920s American individualism had too often degenerated into irresponsibility and greed. One manifestation of this trend was the urge to get rich quickly and easily by gambling in the stock market. Millions of speculators bid up the prices of corporation stocks to levels that were further and further beyond any meaningful relation to their true value. The result was the great crash of October 1929, which marked the beginning of the worst and longest depression in American history.

The depression soon spread from Wall Street to San Francisco's Montgomery Street and then to many a small town's Main Street. California farm income sank in 1932 to scarcely more than half of what it had been in 1929, and there were thousands of mortgage foreclosures. The number of building permits in 1933 was less than one-ninth the peak figure of 1925. With the spread of mass unemployment in both city and country, the number of Californians dependent upon public relief in 1934 was more than 1,250,000—about one-fifth of the whole population of the state. But no mere statistics can convey the real meaning of the great depression. Its meaning was in the suffering, anxiety, and grief of the millions whose lives it blighted.

In California politics, reaction to this disaster came slowly at first. Then it became extreme and frantic. But through the whole decade of depression that followed the crash, politics and government in California remained confused, demoralized, and ineffectual.

"SUNNY JIM"

The choice of a governor in 1930, the first year of the depression, represented politics as worse than usual. James Rolph, Jr., had been mayor of San Francisco for 19 years, since his first election in 1911. His early career as mayor was quite creditable, but in 1918 he lost the fortune that he had made in the shipping business, and his health and efficiency began to decline. During the 1920s he still commanded great popular affection, mainly because of the convivial folksiness of his innumerable appearances as the city's official host, greeter, and master of ceremonies. In that "era of wonderful nonsense" he seemed a highly successful large-city mayor, but as governor, he was unable to cope with an emergency on the scale of the great depression.

Rolph's most important policy as governor was his opposition to tax reform. His views on taxation were those of the most conservative wing of the business community. Rolph was heavily in debt to one of San Francisco's leading bankers, who was also one of his closest political advisers. The legislature of 1933 adopted a sales tax, with Rolph's approval; but when the legislature also passed an income tax measure, Rolph vetoed it. The burden of the sales tax fell heavily on the poor, and the inclusion of food among the items subject to the tax was especially resented. Corner grocers, ringing up small sales, bitterly reminded their customers that they must add "a penny for Jimmy."

In a desperate and deluded attempt to regain his popularity, Rolph made the worst mistake of his career. He openly abetted and defended a lynching.

Throughout the country in the early 1930s there was a wave of kidnappings, including that of the Lindbergh baby in 1932. At San Jose, on November 26, 1933, two men who had confessed to the kidnapping and murder of the son of a wealthy local merchant were being held in the county jail. When there was talk of mob action, Governor Rolph made a public "promise" that he would never call out the National Guard "to protect those two fellows." A few hours later, with this open incitement from the governor, a mob broke into the jail, beat the sheriff unconscious, and hanged the two prisoners to trees in a nearby park.

Rolph then asserted in another public statement that "This is the best lesson California has ever given the country." He promised to pardon anyone who might be arrested for "the good job," and added that he would like to release all convicted kidnappers from the state prisons into the hands of "those fine, patriotic San Jose citizens who know how to handle such a situation." The lynchers, Rolph theorized, were men with "pioneer blood in their veins," who "were probably reminded of the metage of justice by the vigilantes in the early days of San Francisco's history." As the *New York Times* remarked in a scathing editorial, Judge Lynch had always been a shadowy, unidentified figure. Now there was an actual and visible Governor Lynch.

In 1934 Rolph began another of his picturesque election campaigns. In burnished leather boots and a red sash he inaugurated every fiesta, parade, and rodeo. But he collapsed during a precampaign tour and died on June 2. Lieutenant Governor Frank Merriam, a Long Beach real estate agent, succeeded him as governor.

SOCIAL MESSIAHS

Californians in the early 1930s were desperately searching for new leadership. It was increasingly clear that they could expect no help from the administrations of President Hoover and Governor Rolph, and the depression was growing steadily worse.

The sufferings of the elderly were especially severe. Thousands of them had come from other parts of the country to retire in Los Angeles or its suburbs. In the 1920s when they had been able to live fairly comfortably, before they lost their savings in the depression, most of them had been conservative in their economic and political ideas, and their interest in colorful leaders had been directed mainly toward religious evangelists. One of these was Sister Aimee Semple McPherson, who preached the "Four Square Gospel" with spectacular theatricality at her Angelus Temple and over her own radio station, KFSG. Sister Aimee also established a relief program for the needy, providing food and clothing for the homeless and destitute of Los Angeles. Another popular southern California evangelist was the Reverend Robert P. Shuler, who operated a rival radio station. In 1926 the Reverend Mr. Shuler had led the outcry against Sister Aimee when that somewhat tarnished angel was accused of having spent an illicit vacation in Carmel with the director of her radio station during the time when she claimed to have been kidnapped and held for ransom in Mexico. During the early 1930s Sister Aimee's following declined, not merely because of her personal indiscretions but because interest was shifting from religious to economic and political evangelism.

Technocracy, which advocated a new society based on scientific management, aroused so much enthusiasm in Los Angeles that chief technocrat Howard Scott moved his headquarters there from the east. In 1933 a group of unemployed businesspeople broke off from the technocratic persuasion to establish the Utopian Society. The utopians drew an overflow crowd for a pageant in the Hollywood Bowl, a spectacle that resembled some of Mrs. McPherson's productions at Angelus Temple except that it dramatized the triumph not of Good over Evil but of Abundance over Scarcity.

The founder of a much larger and more enduring new movement was Dr. Francis E. Townsend, an unemployed Long Beach physician. At the age of 66, having worked hard all his life, Dr. Townsend was facing destitution. In 1933 he formulated the Townsend Plan and backed it with an organization called Old Age Revolving Pensions, Ltd. All Americans over 60 were to receive pensions of $200 a month, all of which they must spend within 30 days. The money would come from a federal sales tax. This plan, according to Dr. Townsend and his followers, not only would provide a decent living for old people, but also would bring general prosperity by restoring "the proper circulation of money." Though the heart of the movement remained in southern California, Townsend Clubs sprang up all over the nation and soon had a membership of about one and half million "senior citizens." Their delegates assembled in regional and later in national conventions, where they sang "Onward Townsend Soldiers." The movement quickly became a powerful force in both state and national politics.

DEPRESSION AND DEPORTATION

The hard times of the 1930s also contributed to a resurgence of xenophobia and nativism. As in earlier times of crisis, California nativists eagerly sought scapegoats to blame for the state's economic difficulties.

Filipinos were among the first to feel the brunt of antiforeign hostility. White workers complained that recent immigrants from the Philippines were incapable of assimilation and posed an economic threat. Anti-Filipino riots broke out in several rural counties as well as in San Jose and San Francisco. The worst outbreak of violence occurred in 1930, in Watsonville, where one Filipino was killed and several others were badly beaten. "In many ways it was a crime to be a Filipino in California," recalled Carlos Bulosan.

The hostility culminated in a demand for the deportation of all Filipino workers. In 1935 Congress passed the Filipino Repatriation Act, offering to pay the transportation expenses of any Filipinos who wished to return to their homeland. The act also prohibited Filipinos thus repatriated from reentering the United States. More than 2000 persons left under terms of the act.

Far more effective was the move to repatriate aliens from Mexico. California nativists charged that Mexican immigrants were taking much-needed jobs away from American citizens. Nativists also alleged that most Mexicans in California were illegal immigrants and should be barred not only from employment, but also from all public assistance. The solution seemed obvious: deport the undesirable aliens.

The federal government responded with a program of mass repatriation. Between 1931 and 1933, more than 400,000 Spanish-speaking persons were removed from the United States and sent to Mexico; included were Mexican aliens and American citizens of Mexican ancestry. Federal, state, and local authorities at first encouraged a voluntary exodus, but forced deportations also occurred. In California, estimates of the number of deportees ranged from 75,000 to 100,000. The government of Mexico protested the indiscriminate apprehension and deportation of any person, regardless of citizenship, who "looked Mexican." And the *repatriados* and their families complained bitterly of mistreatment. As historian Albert Camarillo has observed, "The Chicano community did not passively accept the indignity heaped upon it by the governmental deportation drives." The pain of repatriation found expression in a poignant folk ballad:

Goodbye, my good friends,
You are all witnesses
Of the bad payment they give us.

LABOR STRIFE

In the agonies of the depression California's long tradition of social violence was reborn in new and bitter struggles between labor and employers.

California labor problems had always been at their worst in agriculture, partly because the growers had always been able to block the development of collective bargaining. When the depression turned most of the farm regions into economic disaster areas, labor relations became worse than ever before. Agricultural workers, ill fed or unfed, had to suffer the peculiar misery of watching food crops rot because they could not be sold for enough to pay the costs of harvesting and marketing.

Women performed much of the most arduous work in the canneries—peeling, cutting, and pitting the fruit. And it was women who often took the lead in mobilizing discontented workers to protest unfair and oppressive conditions. Excluded from the protection of existing labor laws, women in the canneries worked 16-hour days for 15 cents an hour. When women cannery workers struck in the Santa Clara Valley in 1931, police responded by breaking up a mass meeting with tear gas and fire hoses. About half the officers of the newly organized United Cannery, Agricultural, Packing, and Allied Workers of America (UCAPAWA) were women. Latinas were among the most effective leaders of the UCAPAWA, including the union's vice president Louisa Morena. In 1938 Morena also helped organize in Los Angeles a national Latino rights organization, the National Congress of Spanish Speaking People.

Again, as in the days of the IWW, the wretched conditions of the migratory agricultural workers and the general disinterest of conventional labor unions opened the door to the most extreme radicals, and the radicals played into the hands of the employers. The Cannery and Agricultural Workers' Industrial Union (CAWIU), which became active in 1933, was avowedly an arm of the Communist party and was openly eager to hasten the disintegration of the capitalist system in agriculture. It provided the leadership for the strikes of the grape pickers at Lodi and the cotton pickers in the southern San Joaquin Valley in 1933 and the vegetable pickers in the Imperial Valley in 1934. Employer vigilante groups, sometimes deputized by county sheriffs, did not hesitate to use violence in crushing these strikes, and the CAWIU was dissolved when its Communist leaders were arrested and convicted under the state criminal syndicalism law.

The National Industrial Recovery Act of 1933, in its famous section 7a, recognized the right of employees "to organize and bargain collectively through representatives of their own choosing." In the San Francisco Bay region, where organized labor had once been strong, the unions took courage from the new federal law and set out to regain the power they had lost in the 1920s. When the employers resisted, the struggle became even more violent than in the agricultural regions. Class conflict went to such extremes that police and the National Guard were used to break a strike on the San Francisco waterfront, and in retaliation nearly all the unions in the bay region joined in a general strike in sympathy with the demands of the maritime workers.

The employers in the San Francisco shipping industry had destroyed the power of the International Longshoremen's Association (ILA) in the Bay Area by breaking its strike in 1919. They had used the presence of radicals in several maritime unions as an excuse to destroy unionism itself. From 1919 until 1934 the only longshoremen's union in the San Francisco Bay area was the employer-controlled "Blue Book" union. Hiring was done under the "shape-up" system. The men gathered on the docks each day, and a hiring boss chose the ones who would get the day's work. The system was riddled with bribery, favoritism, and blacklisting.

A new local of the ILA was formed in San Francisco in the summer of 1933 and soon won practically all the workers away from the employer-controlled union. Within the new local of the ILA a working longshoreman named Harry R. Bridges led a militant group that persuaded the union to adopt its demands. These included union-controlled hiring halls, better wages and working conditions with extra pay for overtime, and coastwide bargaining so that the facilities in one port could not be used to break a strike or undercut wages in another.

To a group of employers who had enjoyed virtual freedom from any union demands at all for more than a decade, this program seemed "revolutionary." The employers charged that Bridges was a Communist. Bridges, a native of Australia, often said that his ideas were those of militant trade unionism and that he had held these opinions before the Communist party came into existence. In later years the United States government would make long and elaborate efforts to deport Bridges on the ground that he was a Communist, but he always denied the charge, and the government never proved it.

The dock workers in all the Pacific coast ports went on strike on May 9, 1934, and several seafaring unions struck soon afterward. The San Francisco Chamber of Commerce and the San Francisco Industrial Association held a joint meeting and made plans to support the Waterfront Employers' Union in an attempt to open the port with strikebreakers, on the ground that the longshoremen's union was "in the hands of a group of Communists." The business community was confident that

Strikers on the San Francisco waterfront flee from police through a cloud of tear gas on "bloody Thursday," July 5, 1934. *(Courtesy of the San Francisco Archives.)*

it could again break the longshore strike and destroy the union on the radicalism issue, as it had done in 1919.

⌐ On the morning of "bloody Thursday," July 5, 1934, 1000 San Francisco police officers tried to clear 5000 pickets from the Embarcadero, the main waterfront street, to enable strikebreakers to work. Pistols were fired on both sides. Sixty-four people were injured (thirty-one of them shot), and two strikers were killed. Governor Frank Merriam sent in the National Guard although Mayor Angelo Rossi had not asked for it. Seventeen hundred National Guard soldiers with fixed bayonets occupied the waterfront.

To this all-out attempt at "opening the port," organized labor responded by closing down most of the economic activity of most of the bay region. Virtually every union in San Francisco and Alameda counties joined in the general strike which began on the morning of Monday, July 16.

William Randolph Hearst, who was in England, sent instructions to John Francis Neylan, his chief counsel, to unite the major Bay Area newspaper publishers in a strategy of denouncing the general strike as Communist-inspired. News reports, as well as headlines and editorials, gave the impression that the strike was a part of a Communist conspiracy. Bands of vigilantes, with explicit encouragement from the newspapers and from Governor Merriam, broke into several Communist party offices in San Francisco and Oakland, smashed the furniture, and beat up anyone they found on the premises.

The general strike was called off at the end of its fourth day, Thursday, July 19. It had alienated majority public opinion to such a degree that American labor has never attempted a repetition of it. But if the general strike was largely a failure, so was the intransigent effort of the San Francisco employers to retain the open shop. Federal officials, including President Roosevelt, were now determined to settle the basic issues of the waterfront strike by federal arbitration. John Francis Neylan, who had always believed in collective bargaining, now used his influence in persuading the waterfront employers to accept unconditional arbitration. The federal board's ruling, announced on October 12, provided for hiring halls and gave the longshore union virtually complete control of them. This was the demand that the union had emphasized most. For years afterward the maritime employers were bitter at what they regarded as a triumph for radicalism, accomplished through federal intervention.

UPTON SINCLAIR AND EPIC

At the beginning of the state political campaigns of 1934 it seemed highly probable that California would elect its first Democratic governor in the twentieth century. The blame for the depression had fallen heavily on the Republicans. In the presidential election of 1932 President Hoover had lost not only his home state of California, but also his home county of Santa Clara, and Democrat William Gibbs McAdoo was elected United States senator from California in the Roosevelt avalanche. Almost any reasonably presentable New Dealer could probably have been elected governor of California in 1934, but Upton Sinclair, who had been the

Socialist candidate for the governorship in 1926 and 1930, threw the whole campaign into a turmoil by announcing in 1933 that he was changing his party registration and would run for governor as a Democrat.

Sinclair had been the country's best-known pamphleteer and propaganda novelist since 1906 when he had published *The Jungle,* a melodramatic story of the heartbreaking conditions of life among the immigrant packinghouse workers of Chicago. Sinclair moved to California in 1915 and made his home in Pasadena. In the middle of the waterfront strike at San Pedro in 1923 he was arrested for trying to read the Constitution of the United States to a meeting of strikers on a vacant lot, and this episode led him to found the southern California branch of the American Civil Liberties Union.

By 1933 he had written 47 books (about half his ultimate output), and there was hardly an aspect of capitalistic society in America that had not received unfavorable attention in one or another of his writings. On the other hand, he regarded Marx as a rigid doctrinaire. His own brand of socialism was of the romantic, Americanized sort that had produced the nineteenth-century utopian colonies.

It was characteristic of Sinclair that when he decided to run for governor as a Democrat, he began his campaign by writing a utopian novel about it. *I, Governor of California, and How I Ended Poverty: A True Story of the Future* (1933) was an imaginative history of California from 1933 to 1938. In lively fiction it told how Sinclair was elected governor after a campaign of unprecedented bitterness and how he then put all the unemployed to work in state-aided cooperative enterprises. Through this catchy, quasi-literary device Sinclair set forth his program to End Poverty in California (EPIC). If the voters should decide to let him make his novel come true, a California Authority for Land (CAL) would purchase all the farms that were sold for taxes and establish cooperative agricultural colonies on them, with cooperative stores for the members. A California Authority for Production (CAP) would acquire thousands of factories that had been idle or only partially in use, and a California Authority for Money (CAM) would issue bonds to finance the purchases of the lands and factories and scrip to serve as the medium of exchange among the members of the cooperatives.

The national Democratic administration regarded Sinclair's candidacy as extremely unfortunate and unwelcome. The goal of the New Deal was not to undermine the capitalist system but to save that system by reforming it. Yet not even a statement from President Roosevelt opposing Sinclair could have prevented him from winning the Democratic nomination. Under these circumstances the president adopted a policy of making no public comment whatever about the campaign in California.

The depression was still raging, and thousands of people still lived in terror of being unable to provide food for their families. Wherever Sinclair went, these people crowded around him to wring his hand and promise him their support. In August 1934 he won the nomination with the highest vote that a Democratic candidate for governor had ever received in a California primary. More than two-thirds of his total vote came from southern California. Fifty-four percent of it came from Los Angeles County, where unemployment and other forms of economic hardship were even worse than in the state as a whole.

Upton Sinclair's campaign weekly, the *EPIC News,* featured this editorial cartoon on June 9, 1934. *(Courtesy of the California Historical Society.)*

In the Republican primary the extremely conservative Governor Merriam won by a plurality over three relatively progressive candidates. As Democrat George Creel remarked, this left the voters of California with "a choice between epilepsy and catalepsy. Sinclair has a fantastic, impossible plan, and Merriam is as modern as the dinosaur age."

The California Republicans, now thoroughly frightened, organized an attack against Sinclair on a scale so elaborate and intensive that it marked the beginning of a whole new era in the history of American political campaign techniques. Louis B. Mayer, head of Metro-Goldwyn-Mayer studios and chairman of the Republican state central committee, mobilized the resources of the public relations, advertising, and movie industries.

Sinclair's own writings over the previous 30 years provided his opponents with much of their ammunition. He had denounced and antagonized a remarkable number of groups and institutions: the clergy, in his book *The Profits of Religion;* American colleges and universities, in *The Goose Step;* public schools and schoolteachers, in *The Goslings;* and the press, in *The Brass Check.* But his opponents did not content themselves with reprinting passages from these works; they also indulged in outright fabrications and distortions. In a faked newsreel a group of "tramps," who were actually movie extras made up for the part, were shown debarking from a freight train and telling an interviewer that they were the first of an army of hoboes from the east who were on their way to California because they had heard that as soon as Sinclair was elected there would be a general sharing of the wealth.

Sinclair's opponents falsely charged that he was an atheist, a believer in free love, and a Communist. The Communist party, in fact, denounced Sinclair as a

'On to California!'

Typical of the ridicule heaped on Upton Sinclair during his 1934 gubernatorial campaign was this political cartoon by Fred Korburg in the *San Francisco Call-Bulletin.* (*Courtesy of the* San Francisco Examiner.)

"social fascist"—its current term for anyone who advocated compromise with capitalism. Even the Socialist party of California repudiated him, although in somewhat milder language than the Communists. Sinclair also lost the support of Dr. Townsend and his followers by criticizing the Old Age Revolving Pensions plan as "a mere money scheme." Merriam, on the other hand, won an endorsement from Townsend by promising to recommend his plan to the national Congress.

In the November election Merriam won with a vote of 1,138,620 to 879,557 for Sinclair. A vote of 302,519 went to Raymond L. Haight, a Los Angeles Republican lawyer who had won the nominations of the Commonwealth and Progressive parties.

FROM MERRIAM TO OLSON

Governor Merriam realized and acknowledged that he could not have been elected without the support of many relatively conservative New Deal Democrats, and in 1935 he signed a number of bills that brought the state into conformity with some of the New Deal's policies and measures. The most active Democratic leader in the legislature was Culbert L. Olson, who had been elected state senator from Los Angeles County as a supporter of Sinclair. Though the senate was still predominantly conservative, Olson secured its approval of new laws which repealed the sales tax on food and established a moderate state income tax. Another measure slightly increased the provisions for assistance to the indigent aged.

In the New Deal's Social Security Act of 1935, and in the corresponding Old Age Security program which California adopted in the same year, the use of the word "security" was a gross exaggeration of the benefits actually provided for old people. For state-sponsored old-age pensions the federal government contributed four-fifths of the first $25 per month and half of any further amount up to $55. California set its maximum figure at $35, which was higher than in many other states, but to receive this maximum pension old people had to be not only without income, but also without relatives who could contribute to their support. These provisions were inadequate, and they required humiliating investigations of personal finances and family relationships.

The way was thus open for a new pension scheme for the state of California alone, and the result was the aberration known as "Ham 'n' Eggs." Robert Noble, a Los Angeles radio commentator, formed an organization called California Revolving Pensions and summarized its plan with the slogan "twenty-five dollars every Monday morning." Noble entrusted some of his advertising to an agency operated by the brothers Willis and Lawrence Allen, whose chief client up to that time had been the manufacturer of Grey-Gone, a hair tonic. The Allen brothers then formed their own pension organization, excluding Noble. They shifted his slogan to "thirty dollars every Thursday," and one of their campaign orators hit upon the motto "Ham 'n' Eggs for California," by which the plan came to be commonly known.

In the California elections of 1938, pensions were the most important single issue. William McAdoo's denunciation of the Ham 'n' Eggs movement cost him his seat in the United States Senate. Sheridan Downey, who had won an endorsement from the Allen brothers by enthusiastically endorsing their plan, defeated McAdoo in the Democratic primary. Downey, a Sacramento lawyer, had been the EPIC candidate for lieutenant governor as Upton Sinclair's running mate in 1934 (opponents had disparaged the ticket as "Uppey and Downey").

If Governor Merriam had flirted with the Ham 'n' Eggers in 1938 as he had flirted with the Townsendites in 1934, he would probably have been reelected. But he openly opposed Ham 'n' Eggs, while Culbert L. Olson won the Democratic nomination and the governorship largely by avoiding a clear stand on the issue. The Ham 'n' Eggs initiative was defeated in the 1938 election, but the vote in its favor, more than 1,143,000, was shockingly large. It might have passed had it not been for the exposure, during the last days of the campaign, of some of the corrupt practices of the Allen brothers, its cynical and irresponsible promoters.

One of Olson's first acts as governor was to carry out his campaign pledge of a pardon for Tom Mooney. Warren K. Billings, Mooney's codefendant, had also been convicted on perjured evidence, but because Billings had previously been convicted of a felony, his pardon would have required a recommendation by the state supreme court. The court recommended only a commutation of sentence to time served, and this Olson granted. Billings would ultimately receive his full pardon from another Democratic governor, Edmund G. Brown, in 1961.

At the end of his first week in office Governor Olson collapsed from exhaustion, and a month passed before he was able to resume his duties. This left the new administration without leadership at the most crucial time, and it never fully recovered from this demoralizing blow. But Olson could have accomplished little at best. Conservative Republicans still controlled the state senate, and although the Democrats had a small majority in the assembly, they were split into factions. Olson had almost no previous experience as an administrator. Tactless and quick-tempered, he often antagonized people whose support would have been essential to his success. The main accomplishments of his governorship were a few modest reforms in the state's penal system and in its provisions for the care of the mentally ill.

Throughout the country the reformist enthusiasm of the New Deal was waning. The number of liberal Democrats in Congress was sharply reduced in the 1938 elections, and as war clouds gathered in Europe and Asia, President Roosevelt turned most of his attention to the problems of foreign affairs and national defense. Olson's chance of bringing a New Deal to California was both too little and too late.

SELECTED BIBLIOGRAPHY

Kevin Starr, *Endangered Dreams: The Great Depression in California* (1995); Leonard Leader, *Los Angeles and the Great Depression* (1991); William H. Mullins, *The Depression and the Urban West Coast* (1991); and "The Great Depression and the West," a special issue of *Journal of the West,* XXIV (October 1985), offer general surveys of the period. Richard Lowitt, *The New Deal and the West* (1984), and Leonard J. Arrington, "The Sagebrush Resurrection," *Pacific Historical Review,* LII (February 1983), pp. 1–17, describe the effects of federal policy. See also Ronald L. Feinman, *Twilight of Progressivism* (1981).

Gubernatorial administrations during the depression are described in Jackson K. Putnam, *Modern California Politics* (1980), and H. Brett Melendy and Benjamin F. Gilbert, *The Governors of California* (1965). Brian McGinty, "Shadows in St. James Park," *California History,* LVII (Winter 1978–1979), pp. 290–307, describes the lynching in San Jose. Rolph's earlier and happier years are described in Morley Segal, "James Rolph, Jr., and the Early Days of the San Francisco Municipal Railway," *California Historical Society Quarterly,* XLIII (March 1964), pp. 3–18, and Moses Rischin, "Sunny Jim Rolph," ibid., LIII (Summer 1974), pp. 165–172. See also Royce D. Delmatier et al., *The Rumble of California Politics* (1970), and Michael P. Rogin and John L. Shover, *Political Change in California* (1970).

Arthur M. Schlesinger, Jr., *The Politics of Upheaval* (1960), includes excellent accounts of some of the major political developments in California in 1933 and 1934. Luther Whiteman and Samuel L. Lewis, *Glory Roads* (1936), describe technocracy, the Utopian Society, and other proposed roads to the millennium. William E. Akin, *Technocracy and the American Dream* (1977), is a thorough analysis. Biographies of Aimee Semple McPherson are by Nancy Barr Mavity (1931) and Lately Thomas (1959, 1970). On the Townsend Plan, see Abraham Holtzman, *The Townsend Movement* (1963), and J.D. Gaydowski, "The Genesis of the Townsend Plan," *Southern California Quarterly,* LII (December 1970), pp. 365–382.

For the resurgence of nativism in the 1930s, see Francisco E. Balderrama and Raymond Rodríguez, *Decade of Betrayal* (1995); Camille Guerin-Gonzales, *Mexican Workers and American Dreams* (1994); and Albert Camarillo, *Chicanos in California* (1984).

On the agricultural labor strikes, see Devra Weber, *Dark Sweat, White Gold* (1995); Vicki Ruiz, *Cannery Women, Cannery Lives* (1987); Clarke A. Chambers, *California Farm Organizations* (1952); and Glenna Matthews, "Fruit Workers of the Santa Clara Valley," *Pacific Historical Review,* LIV (February 1985), pp. 51–70. On the 1934 strike, see Frederic Claire Chiles, "War on the Waterfront," Ph.D. thesis. University of California, Santa Barbara (1981); John Kagel, "The Day the City Stopped," *California History,* LXIII (Summer 1984), pp. 212–223; Bruce

Nelson, *Workers on the Waterfront* (1988); and David F. Selvin, "An Excuse for Hysteria," *Pacific Historical Review,* LVIII (August 1989), pp. 361–374. On Bridges see Robert W. Cherny, "The Making of a Labor Radical," ibid., LXIV (August 1995), pp. 363–388; Harvey Schwartz, "Harry Bridges and the Scholars," *California History,* LIX (Spring 1980), pp. 66–79, and Charles P. Larrowe, *Harry Bridges* (1972).

Sinclair's temporary capture of the Democratic party is described in Gregg Mitchell, *The Campaign of the Century* (1992); Charles E. Larsen, "The Epic Campaign of 1934," *Pacific Historical Review,* XXVII (May 1958), pp. 127–148; Leon Harris, *Upton Sinclair, American Rebel* (1975); Leonard Leader. "Upton Sinclair's EPIC Switch: A Dilemma for American Socialists," *Southern California Quarterly,* LXII (Winter 1980), pp. 361–385; Judson A. Grenier, "Upton Sinclair: A Remembrance," *California Historical Society Quarterly,* XLVIII (June 1969), pp. 165–169; and Walton Bean, "Ideas of Reform in California," in George H. Knoles (ed.), *Essays and Assays: California History Reappraised* (1973), pp. 13–26.

An informal history of the rise of the Ham 'n' Eggs movement is Winston Moore and Marian Moore, *Out of the Frying Pan* (1939). See also Tom Zimmerman, "Ham and Eggs Everybody!" *Southern California Quarterly,* LXII (Spring 1980), pp. 1–48, and Carey McWilliams, "Pension Politics in California," in David Farrelly and Ivan Hinderaker (eds.), *The Politics of California* (1951). Jackson K. Putnam, *Old-Age Politics in California* (1970), is a major contribution.

An excellent study of the Olson administration is Robert E. Burke, *Olson's New Deal for California* (1953).

CHAPTER TWENTY-SEVEN

Cultural Trends

The cultural history of California during the early decades of the twentieth century was distinguished by several writers of great scope and power. As a cultural region, California was fast becoming one of the most dynamic and promising of any area in the United States.

ROBINSON JEFFERS

California's greatest poet was born in 1887 in Pittsburgh, Pennsylvania, where his father, William Hamilton Jeffers, was a distinguished professor of biblical literature in a Presbyterian theological seminary. At the age of 5 Robinson Jeffers began to learn Greek and Hebrew. His father was a liberal theologian who taught him to read the Bible as oriental literature rather than divine revelation.

When the boy was 16, the family moved to Pasadena. He attended Occidental College and then began graduate work at the University of Southern California, where he fell in love with Una Call Kuster, a student who was 2 years older than he, and who was the wife of another man. Eight years later Una Kuster finally obtained a divorce, and she and Jeffers were married. At about the same time, the young couple chanced to discover Carmel.

Jeffers immediately recognized the place where he would do his life's work. In the mountains of the Carmel coast he saw "people living amid magnificent unspoiled scenery essentially as they did in the Idyls or the Sagas, or in Homer's Ithaca. Here was life purged of its ephemeral accretions. Men were riding after cattle, or plowing the headland, hovered by white sea-gulls, as they have done for thousands of years." On the point of land between the lovely little bay and the mouth of the river, with granite carried up from the beach with his own hands, he built Tor House and Hawk Tower, a separate study.

In 1916 he published *Californians,* a volume of poems written in conventional poetic forms, but soon afterward, instead of rhyme and meter, Jeffers developed forms directly imitating nature. Also unconventional were the starkly tragic themes of the long narrative poems that began with *Tamar* (1924) and *Roan Stallion* (1925). Tamar Cauldwell, daughter of a rancher at Point Lobos, commits incest with her brother, and the whole family perishes when an insane aunt sets fire to the house. In *Roan Stallion* a part-Indian woman named California transfers her affections from her white husband to her horse. When her husband is being trampled by the stallion in the corral, though she could save his life by killing the horse with a rifle, she deliberately holds her fire until after her husband is dead.

With the publication of these poems in the middle of the 1920s, the work of Jeffers immediately found a place in the upper levels of American literary reputation. *The Women at Point Sur* (1927) was much less enthusiastically received, for its theme was even more shocking to most readers than the themes of the earlier narratives, though its story was told with equally compelling power and beauty of poetic form and metaphor. Barclay, a minister, after losing his son in the world war, denounces his church, becomes insane, goes to live as a boarder on an isolated ranch, and founds a new religion in which he is God. Then he rapes his own daughter. In addition, the plot includes episodes of child murder and suicide.

Jeffers described his own philosophy as "Inhumanism," though he used the term in his own very special sense. He rejected humanism because it overemphasized the rational, the urbane, and the civilized and because it attached too much importance to human consciousness—the characteristic of human beings that seemed to set them apart from nature. Jeffers's poems sought to explore the unconscious, the realm of humanity's "felt nature." But though he read Freud and Jung, Jeffers never sought the aid of a psychotherapist for himself, and both the poet and his wife denied that the circumstances of their own lives had anything to do with his choice of tragic themes.

It seemed, indeed, that no man could have asked more of fortune than to live with a beautiful, talented, and devoted wife in a place that looked north on Carmel Bay and south on Point Lobos, and there to write some of the most unforgettable of modern poetry. But if Jeffers had no conscious feeling of self-blame for loving the wife of another man and taking her to live in these isolated and beautiful surroundings, the subconscious fear of punishment was there nevertheless. It seems clear that the "imagined victims" in his poems suffered horrible punishments so that Jeffers and his wife need not suffer them.

During the depression of the 1930s, Jeffers's popularity and reputation sharply declined. The themes of his long poems, however, continued to be unrelentingly harsh. They dealt with adultery, murder, madness, and suicide. Jeffers had no sympathy with the complaint that his poems were full of tragedy and violence. These were the themes of Sophocles and Shakespeare, he pointed out, and they were not out of place in a century in which two world wars had killed 100 million people, and a third threatened to exterminate all the rest. "The Inquisitors," published in *The Double Axe and Other Poems* (1948), described three hills in the coast range, squatting like giant Indians to examine the pitiful remnants of human beings after an atomic holocaust.

Robinson Jeffers died in 1962, at 75. He has not had, and is not likely to have, any successful imitators.

JOHN STEINBECK

As clearly as Robinson Jeffers was California's most important poet, John Steinbeck might be said to be its most important novelist. Steinbeck's early writing had as distinctive a relation to the Salinas Valley and Monterey as did Jeffers's poems to the Carmel coast. Indeed Steinbeck portrayed the Salinas Valley with a thoroughness not given to any other American region in modern fiction, except perhaps William Faulkner's Mississippi.

Steinbeck was born in Salinas in 1902, the year Frank Norris died. He graduated from Salinas High School in 1919 and studied at Stanford University, but, like Norris at Berkeley, he never completed the requirements for a degree.

His first novel, *Cup of Gold* (1929), was an allegorical romance about Sir Henry Morgan, the pirate-governor of Jamaica. From this, Steinbeck turned to the California scene, which would provide the locales for most of his best writing. *The Pastures of Heaven* (1932) was set in a lovely, secluded, fictional valley somewhere near the Salinas Valley. Its unifying theme was the Munroe family, their thoughtless, vicious mediocrity, and the series of episodes in which they ruined the lives of their neighbors by trying to force them into conformity with the Munroes's notions of what was proper and respectable.

Steinbeck's satirizing of pretentious middle-class values was also apparent in *Tortilla Flat* (1935), which won him the beginnings of financial success and critical notice. Though several publishers had rejected this droll account of some Mexican American idlers in Monterey on the ground that it was too frivolous for the hard times of the depression, the book sold quite well to readers who enjoyed its supposed praise of a group of irresponsible people who were living on next to nothing. Steinbeck himself had been getting along on very little. His earlier novels had brought him only a few hundred dollars in royalties, and when he was writing *Tortilla Flat,* he would have been destitute if his father had not provided him with a small house in Pacific Grove and an allowance of $25 a month.

In Dubious Battle, published early in 1936, took its title from a line in Milton's *Paradise Lost* but dealt with the intensely contemporary and controversial theme of a strike of migratory agricultural laborers organized and led by Communists. The episodes were largely drawn from an actual strike in the cotton fields of the San Joaquin Valley 2 years earlier, though the "Torgas Valley" of the novel was a composite locale. It resembled the Pajaro Valley, north of Salinas, but there had been no strike there, and the crop in the novel was apples rather than cotton.

The main characters were also composites, partly drawn, like all of Steinbeck's characters, from persons he had known, including in this case two actual Communists. But the widespread charge that *In Dubious Battle* was communistic propaganda ignored the fact that its picture of the leading Communist organizer of the strike is extremely critical. Mac cares nothing for the fate of the workers and wishes only to use them for the destruction of private ownership. Steinbeck had as deep a dislike for communism as he had for any system that subordinated the spirit and dignity of the individual to a "Cause."

The strike is not yet over at the end of the novel, but it is obviously doomed, and the battle is "dubious" not in its outcome but in the merits of both sides. Steinbeck was equally critical of the radical leadership of the strike and the ruthlessness of the growers and their vigilante supporters. His most extreme contempt was reserved for the vigilantes. For once he was in full agreement with Mac: "They're the dirtiest guys in any town. . . . They like to hurt people, and they always give it a nice name, patriotism or protecting the constitution."

Steinbeck made an intensive personal investigation of migratory labor conditions in the middle 1930s and summarized his conclusions in a series of articles in the *San Francisco News* in October 1936, later reprinted as a pamphlet under the title *Their Blood Is Strong.* As background he sketched the history of California's importation of foreign labor, which he called "a disgraceful picture of greed and cruelty." Then he described the new agricultural labor supply, the impoverished native American migrants from the "Dust Bowl" area. For the solution of the desperate and dangerous problem he recommended that a new state agricultural labor board help to allot labor and determine fair wages and that the workers be helped to form union organizations. Finally, he insisted that vigilantism be drastically punished. It was, Steinbeck wrote, "a system of terrorism that would be unusual in the Fascist nations of the world," and its methods were being "more powerfully and more openly practiced in California than in any other place in the United States."

Of Mice and Men (1938) was a touching allegory of the life of California ranch hands. Made into a successful motion picture, it further increased Steinbeck's reputation. His masterpiece, however, was *The Grapes of Wrath,* published the following year and narrating the experiences of the Joad family, who were evicted from their farm in the Oklahoma Dust Bowl, journeyed to California in an ancient automobile, and suffered the miseries of migratory laborers in the San Joaquin Valley. It was "a crime . . . that goes beyond denunciation," Steinbeck wrote, that children were being allowed to die of starvation in the midst of rotting plenty.

The Kern County Board of Supervisors banned *The Grapes of Wrath* from the public schools and libraries under its jurisdiction, and the Associated Farmers launched an unsuccessful campaign to extend the ban to other counties, but the novel won the Pulitzer Prize and was a runaway best-seller. During the next 15 years it was reprinted nearly 50 times in 16 editions in English and translated into a dozen other languages. Darryl Zanuck of Twentieth Century-Fox made it into a film while it was still at the top of the national best-seller list. He had taken the precaution of sending private detectives to determine the accuracy of the novel, and they had reported that actual conditions were even worse than the ones Steinbeck described.

The financial success of *The Grapes of Wrath* enabled Steinbeck to take an extended vacation, which also served as the basis for his next book. He accompanied his friend Edward F. Ricketts, the proprietor of a laboratory of marine biology at

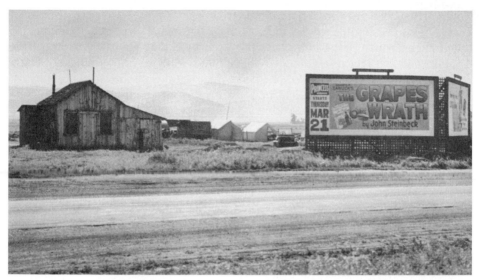

The Hollywood version of Steinbeck's *The Grapes of Wrath* was playing at theaters in towns across the Central Valley by 1940. (*Photograph by Dorothea Lange. Courtesy of the Oakland Museum.*)

Monterey, on an expedition to collect biological specimens in the Gulf of California and described this experience in *The Sea of Cortez* (1941). The mysteries of biology had always fascinated Steinbeck and had given him a love and respect for life in all its forms. Steinbeck immortalized Ed Ricketts, who deeply shared this feeling, in the character of Doc, the hero of *Cannery Row* (1945).

East of Eden (1952) was a powerful novel on which Steinbeck worked with intense labor for 4 years. He began it in order to record for the two small sons of his second marriage the story of his maternal ancestors, the Hamiltons, following their migration to the Salinas Valley after the Civil War. But the fictional family of Adam Trask entered the story and ultimately dominated it. As the final title suggests, the novel became an allegorical reworking of the story of Cain and Abel.

In 1962 Steinbeck's name was added to those of Sinclair Lewis, Ernest Hemingway, and William Faulkner among the very small group of American novelists to win the Nobel Prize for Literature. He died 6 years later.

WILLIAM SAROYAN AND OTHER WRITERS

Like Steinbeck's Salinas, William Saroyan's native town of Fresno provided much of the best material for his writing career. When Saroyan was 3 years old, his Armenian-born father died, leaving the family in poverty. From the age of 7 Saroyan sold newspapers on the streets of Fresno and later worked as a telegraph messenger and grape picker. He left school at 15, never received a high school diploma, and never went to college.

His first book, *The Daring Young Man on the Flying Trapeze,* consisted of 26 short stories, written at the rate of one a day in a furnished room in San Francisco in January 1934, when he was 25 years old. The title story describes the thoughts and fantasies of a young writer on a day when he has nothing to eat and is completely destitute except for one penny that he finds on the sidewalk.

To Saroyan the vital ingredient in literary style was creative spontaneity, and he worked to establish what he called a "tradition of carelessness," or a "jump in the river and start swimming immediately" style of writing. His most famous novel, and probably his best, was *The Human Comedy* (1943). It dealt mostly with the alternately touching and delightful experiences of two boys who were called Ulysses and Homer Macauley, but were obviously William Saroyan and his older brother, in a town that was called Ithaca, California, but was obviously Fresno.

He wrote several plays, including *My Heart's in the Highlands, The Time of Your Life,* and *Love's Old Sweet Song,* all produced in 1939. In *The Time of Your Life,* the characters are the habitués of a San Francisco waterfront bar, who are enabled to find their inherent virtue when a wealthy drunk gives them money to pursue their aspirations. This play won a Pulitzer Prize in 1940, but Saroyan declined to accept the $1000 award because he believed that "any material or official patronage . . . vitiates and embarrasses art at its source."

Louis B. Mayer brought Saroyan to Hollywood, but Saroyan detested Mayer and he disliked Hollywood. Nevertheless *The Human Comedy* and *The Time of Your Life* were made into successful films in 1943 and 1948. Following World War II Saroyan shunned the public limelight, saying that creativity required isolation. He divided his later years between Paris and Fresno and died in his hometown in 1981.

Saroyan was only one of several major novelists and playwrights who were attracted, however briefly, to southern California in the late 1930s and 1940s by the film industry. Two of the most important of these writers were Nathanael West, a native of New York who came to Hollywood as an aspiring scriptwriter, and the English novelist Aldous Huxley, who moved to Los Angeles in 1937. Both West and Huxley were powerfully struck by the contrast between the grim reality of depression-era southern California and the fanciful image of the region presented in the movies.

The Los Angeles of Nathanael West was a city built of illusion and artifice. In *The Day of the Locust* (1939), West describes the desperate quest of people who have been attracted by the California dream of opportunity and romance, but who find themselves impoverished and defeated. The dream becomes a nightmare, and in their desperation the people turn to violence. West's novel ends with an apocalyptic vision of Los Angeles in flames. Huxley shared West's distaste for southern California, regarding Los Angeles as a symbol for corrupt values and deception. In *After Many a Summer Dies the Swan* (1939) Huxley satirized the excesses of southern California's architecture and its religious and scientific cults. The major focus of the novel is a California tycoon, modeled on William Randolph Hearst, whose opulent mansion became for Huxley a bizarre Los Angeles in miniature.

WILLIAM RANDOLPH HEARST AND OTHER JOURNALISTS

Until his death in 1951, at 88, William Randolph Hearst continued to exert a powerful influence in California journalism and in several other aspects of California society and culture. His publishing empire, at its peak in 1932, included 26 newspapers in cities from Boston to Seattle and from Baltimore to Los Angeles. In California, he owned and controlled the *San Francisco Examiner* and *Call-Bulletin,* the *Los Angeles Examiner* and *Herald-Express,* and the *Oakland Post-Enquirer.* In total circulation of California newspapers in 1932, Hearst papers ranked first, second, third, and fifth, with Harry Chandler's *Los Angeles Times* ranking fourth. Thus a fantastic amount of power and influence was attached to the whims of one man who had never entirely ceased to be a spoiled child.

In 1919 Hearst had begun the building of his "castle" at San Simeon, which ultimately cost at least $30 million and was one of the most expensive and lavish residences, either private or royal, in the world. On one of his father's ranches was a 2000-foot eminence overlooking the Pacific. There during family camping trips and picnics in his childhood, Hearst had experienced the happiest moments of his life. He called it *La Cuesta Encantada,* The Enchanted Hill, and on its summit, with the aid of architect Julia Morgan of Berkeley, he built three palatial guest houses and a fourth and much larger structure called *La Casa*

Hearst Castle, the fabulous residence of William Randolph Hearst at San Simeon. *(Courtesy of the California Department of Transportation.)*

Grande. This central castle had 100 rooms, many of them transported from Europe with all their paneling, ceilings, and furniture. The rooms were filled with art objects and antiques, and the gardens and terraces with statuary. A huge, rocky hillside was planted with hundreds of full-grown trees at enormous expense because Hearst found its bareness unpleasant. The grounds were stocked with his own private zoo.

In his will Hearst expressed the wish that his castle should go to the University of California as a memorial to his mother, but the university felt that it lacked the funds to maintain the castle. Hearst's sons then persuaded the state of California to accept it as a gift in 1957. The fears that it would prove a massive and costly white elephant were not borne out. Half a million people visited it within the first 2 years after its opening as a state monument. Among the attractions of the place, along with its art treasures, was the chance to participate vicariously in the life of a man who had made such a determined attempt to have everything in the world that he wanted.

Even before his death, however, Hearst's newspaper chain had entered a gradual but steady decline, and by 1965 sales and consolidations had reduced the number of Hearst papers to about a third of what it had once been. In California's two principal cities the Hearst *Examiners,* after years of losing money, were forced to surrender the entire daily morning field to the *Los Angeles Times* and the *San Francisco Chronicle.* In the Sunday field, a new and strange alliance produced the *San Francisco Sunday Examiner & Chronicle,* with sections independently edited by the *Examiner* and by the *Chronicle.*

For newspapers, as well as for nations, hereditary monarchy has always been a notoriously risky method of choosing top-management personnel. Hearst's sons did not approach the journalistic pace that their father had set. The *Times* and the *Chronicle* were also family concerns. Their founders had no sons, but they were able to pass on their power effectively through the female line.

Harry Chandler, who succeeded his father-in-law Harrison Gray Otis as publisher of the *Times* in 1917, was even more energetic than Otis himself. Harry's son Norman, who became the publisher in 1945, improved the quality of the paper in some respects. And Norman's son Otis Chandler, who succeeded his father in 1960, improved it considerably more.

The *San Francisco Chronicle* passed from M. H. de Young to his son-in-law George T. Cameron in 1925, and to de Young's grandson Charles de Young Thieriot 30 years later. Under Cameron and his general manager Paul C. Smith the *Chronicle* made a valiant though generally thankless effort to be a west coast *New York Times.* But under Thieriot the *Chronicle* launched a much more successful drive to out-Hearst the *Examiner* in entertainment.

Meanwhile, big city newspapers throughout the state were challenged by several nationwide trends. From 1945 to 1965, the cost of newspaper production in large cities increased twice as fast as the income from advertising. At the same time there was an enormous increase in the number of suburban dailies. Both circulation and advertising followed the bulk of the population increase into the suburbs. Still further competition came from television advertising and newscasting.

THE ARTS

San Francisco maintained its reputation as the cultural capital of California without effective challenge until World War II, after which Los Angeles became a serious rival for cultural leadership.

For many years after its founding in the middle 1920s, the M. H. de Young Memorial Museum in San Francisco's Golden Gate Park remained the principal art gallery on the Pacific coast. By 1960 its attendance exceeded 1 million persons a year, and on Sundays it often had more visitors than even the Metropolitan Museum of Art in New York City. The California Palace of the Legion of Honor was established in 1924 in San Francisco's Lincoln Park. It attracted almost as large an attendance as the de Young. These two museums were heavily committed to the time-tested and accepted art of the past. The San Francisco Museum of Art, on the other hand, attempted the more difficult role of educating the public in the appreciation of contemporary painting and sculpture.

During the early decades of the twentieth century several public and private institutions for the promotion of the arts were established in southern California, laying the ground for the eventual preeminence of Los Angeles as a cultural center. In 1917 the Otis Art Institute was founded in the former home of Harrison Gray Otis, and 4 years later the Chouinard Art Institute, a school of art and design, was

Migrant Mother. Dorothea Lange took this famous photograph in 1936 at Nipomo, on Highway 101, south of San Luis Obispo. The family of Dust Bowl refugees had just sold the tires from its car to buy food. *(Courtesy of the Library of Congress.)*

Postcard view of an early twentieth-century bungalow in Los Angeles. *(Courtesy of the California State Library, Sacramento.)*

civil servants during short terms of residence. Pasadena attracted many wealthy people who also wanted fairly simple dwellings for part-time occupancy.

In 1903 the Greene brothers designed for Arturo Bandini a bungalow modeled on the plan of the early California adobes, though built of redwood. The rooms were grouped around three sides of a patio or central court, enclosed on the fourth side by a wooden, flower-covered pergola. The patio was an outdoor living room, and there was great freedom of movement between the indoor and outdoor parts of the house. The Greenes acquired so many wealthy clients that virtually all of their later houses were large and expensive, but their many imitators designed thousands of modest bungalows that were pleasant, practical, and enormously popular as homes, though they lacked the quality of the Greene brothers' fine woodcrafting.

The first California architect to be deeply committed to modernism was Irving Gill. Like Frank Lloyd Wright, Gill was trained as a drafter under Louis H. Sullivan in Chicago. Sullivan's motto was that "form follows function." Poor health brought Gill to San Diego in 1893, and there he developed a highly original style, using plaster-coated reinforced concrete walls, flat roofs, and simple windows, all with an austere complete absence of ornament.

When planning began for San Diego's Panama Pacific Exposition to be held in 1915, Gill was the city's best-known architect, but the local authorities entrusted the control of the building plans for the fair to Bertram Goodhue of New York, who had written a book on Spanish colonial architecture. Goodhue, in his buildings for the San Diego exposition, revived the extravagant and sometimes capricious ornamentation that had been the dominant style of architecture in Spain and Mexico in the late seventeenth and early eighteenth centuries. For many years after the San Diego fair there was a great vogue for elaborate Spanish ornamentation in California.

Nothing could have been in more extreme contrast with the work of Irving Gill. The San Diego exposition disheartened Gill and set back the public acceptance of modernism. Gill gave up his practice in San Diego and moved his office to Los Angeles, where he received only a few commissions.

When modernism finally began to achieve genuine acceptance in California, it was largely through the work of Richard Neutra, an Austrian architect who settled in Los Angeles in 1926. Neutra was one of the small international group, including Adolf Loos and Frank Lloyd Wright, who achieved an early realization that the machine was at the base of the new architecture, and not an evil spirit to be feared and exorcised. Neutra and other architects of the "international" style made use of many of the new materials and methods that machine production made possible. Examples were their uses of plate glass or prefabricated structural parts and of reinforced concrete as a self-supporting slab. Employing such modern materials and taking particular advantage of the mild climate to make the fullest use of sliding glass doors (or rather walls), Neutra designed some of the most delightful and beautiful homes, schools, and commercial buildings in southern California.

SELECTED BIBLIOGRAPHY

Robinson Jeffers is the subject of important studies by James Karman (1995), Louis Adamic (1983), Melba Berry Bennett (1966), Frederic I. Carpenter (1962), Radcliffe Squires (1956), Lawrence Clark Powell (1932, 1934, 1940), and George Sterling (1926). See also the bibliography compiled by S. S. Alberts (1933).

The best biography of John Steinbeck is Jackson J. Benson, *The True Adventures of John Steinbeck* (1984). More specialized is Brian St. Pierre, *John Steinbeck: The California Years* (1984). Other major works on Steinbeck are by David Wyatt (1990), Joseph J. Frontenrose (1964), Warren French (1961), and Peter Lisca (1958). Important articles include Tim Kappel, "Trampling Out the Vineyards: Kern County's Ban on *The Grapes of Wrath*," *California History*, LXI (Fall 1982), pp. 210–222, and Benson and Anne Loftis, "John Steinbeck and Farm Labor Unionization," *American Literature*, LII (May 1980), pp. 194–223.

Valuable commentaries on California writers are Edmund Wilson, *The Boys in the Back Room* (1941); Lawrence C. Powell's *Land of Fiction* (1952) and *California Classics* (1971); Gerald Haslam, "Literary California," *California History*, LXVIII (Winter 1989), pp. 188–195; and David Wyatt, *The Fall into Eden* (1987). General anthologies of California literature include Haslam (ed.), *Many Californias* (1991), John and LaRee Caughey (eds.), *California Heritage* (1971), and Robert Pearsall and Ursula S. Erickson (eds.), *The Californians* (2 volumes, 1960). Several hundred novels about California are listed and briefly described in Alice K. Melton, *California in Fiction* (1961). See also Newton D. Baird and Robert Greenwood, *An Annotated Bibliography of California Fiction, 1664–1970* (1971).

W. A. Swanberg's *Citizen Hearst* (1961) is the best biography. Several of the other works previously cited in Chapter 18 for the earlier part of Hearst's long career are relevant for the later part of it as well. See also Judith Robinson, *The Hearsts* (1991); Winifred Black Bonfils, *The Life and Personality of Phoebe Apperson Hearst* (1927, 1991); Lindsay Chaney, *The Hearsts* (1981); Richard H. Peterson, "Philanthropic Phoebe," *California History*, LXIV (Fall 1985), pp. 284–289; Oscar Lewis, *Fabulous San Simeon* (1958); Robert Gottlieb and Irene Wolt, *Thinking Big: The Story of the Los Angeles Times* (1977); and William Rivers and David Rubin, *A Region's Press: Anatomy of Newspapers in the San Francisco Bay Area* (1971).

On the arts, see Edan Milton Hughes, *Artists in California* (1986); Nancy D.W. Moure, *Painting and Sculpture in Los Angeles, 1900–1945* (1980); Stephen M. Fry (ed.), *California's Musical Wealth* (1988); Howard Swan, *History of Music in the Southwest 1825–1950* (1952); Ronald L. Davis, *A History of Opera in the American West* (1965); and José Rodriguez (ed.), *Music and Dance in California* (1940).

Harold Kirker, *Old Forms on a New Land* (1991), offers an interpretive survey of California architecture. Studies of individual architects include Ginger Wadsworth, *Julia Morgan* (1990); Taylor Coffman, *The Builders Behind the Castles* (1990); Richard Longstreth, *On the Edge of the World* (1982); Kenneth H. Cardwell, *Bernard Maybeck* (1977); Randell L. Makinson, *Greene and Greene* (1977); and Esther McCoy, *Five California Architects* (1960). On the architecture of southern California, see the studies by David Gebhard and Hariette Von Breton (1989), Paul Gleye (1981), Reyner Banham (1971), and Douglas Honnold (1956). The career of Richard Neutra can be traced in works by W. Dione Neutra (comp., 1986) and Esther McCoy (1960). Karen J. Weitze, *California's Mission Revival* (1984), describes the provincial forces opposed to modernism.

CHAPTER TWENTY-EIGHT

Wartime Growth and Problems

From 1919 to 1941 the strongest feeling of the majority of Americans toward world affairs was their determination that the United States must never be involved in another world war. Senator Hiram Johnson of California was in the forefront of those who were called "isolationists" in this sense. But the raid on Pearl Harbor on December 7, 1941, left the American people no further choice. The Japanese attack, which came without warning and destroyed or crippled most of the American Pacific fleet with bombs and aerial torpedoes, immediately produced more support for an all-out military and industrial effort than Americans had shown in any previous war.

THE IMPACT OF FEDERAL SPENDING

In the period including the fiscal years from 1940 to 1946 the federal government spent $360 billion within the continental United States. Of this sum, it spent about $35 billion in the state of California. It would be almost impossible to exaggerate and it is difficult even to comprehend the full effects of these unprecedented expenditures in stimulating economic expansion. Every previous element in the state's economic history was dwarfed in comparison. In the fiscal year ending June 30, 1930, the federal government's total expenditures had been less than $3 billion, of which it had spent only $191 million in California. In fiscal 1940, federal spending in the state had risen to $728 million, much of it for relief and old-age pensions. But in the single wartime fiscal year 1945 the federal government spent more than $8.5 billion in California.

When the Nazis began the war with their invasion of Poland in September 1939, neither California nor the rest of the country had fully recovered from the depression that had begun with the crash nearly 10 full years before. The state's population had increased 21.7 percent during the depressed 1930s (the lowest percentage increase recorded for any decade since American acquisition). But the total personal income of California in 1939 barely exceeded the 1930 figure of

$5 billion, and this meant that per capita income in 1939 had not yet climbed back to the level of 1930.

In 1945, however, the personal income of Californians was $15 billion. In other words, the war and the increase in federal spending raised total personal income in California to more than *three times* its prewar figure. This meant an enormous increase in per capita wealth, even allowing for inflation and for a state population growth of 30 percent between 1940 and 1945.

Federally financed activities took many forms, of which the most obvious were new or expanded military installations and new defense industries. In 1930 there had been only a handful of military installations in California, including the San Francisco Presidio, Fort Ord, the Mare Island Naval Shipyard, some naval facilities at San Diego, and March Field. By the end of the war all of these had been enormously expanded, and the list had grown to include camps Beale, Cooke, Pendleton, Roberts, and Stoneman; the Oakland Army Base and the Oakland Naval Supply Center; the Alameda Naval Air Station, the San Francisco Naval Shipyard, and the Treasure Island Naval Station; and several major Air Force bases—Castle, McClellan, Parks, and Travis.

Government money poured out through wage and salary payments to civilian and military personnel, investments in public and private facilities, purchases of supplies, and payments in the form of grants, subsidies, and interest. California received a disproportionate share of all these federal expenditures at a time when they had grown enormously.

The most apparent effect on California's economy, apart from the general increase in its size, was the wartime expansion of manufacturing. Under government contracts American private industry produced a great variety of the sinews of war. In California, almost overnight, ships and airplanes became the most important of all the state's products.

WARTIME SHIPYARDS

With the government providing the bulk of the capital, Henry J. Kaiser of Oakland became the chief private entrepreneur of California's wartime shipbuilding industry. Kaiser's reputation as an engineering and industrial genius had begun with the construction of Hoover and Parker dams and had continued to grow with his major role in the building of the San Francisco Bay Bridge and the dams at Bonneville and Grand Coulee. In order to produce his own cement, Kaiser had built Permanente, the largest cement plant in the world. Before the United States entered the war, he had projected the first steel mill on the Pacific coast, at Fontana 50 miles east of Los Angeles.

New shipyards sprang up in 1942 at Richmond, Oakland, Sausalito, Vallejo, and San Pedro. In full operation for 24 hours a day in three shifts, they were soon building "liberty ships" in 25 days, and in 1943 a new freighter was launched every 10 hours at one or another of the Kaiser shipyards.

At the peak of production in July 1943, civilian employment in the shipbuilding industry in California was nearly 300,000. Instead of the mass unemployment of the 1930s there was now a desperate shortage of labor. To one sign that said "Help Wanted!!! Male or Female, Young or Old, Experienced or Inexperienced," someone added "Dead or Alive!!!" Kaiser advertised for workers in every part of the country and, in addition to the climate, he offered such inducements as high wages, on-the-job training, a subsidized plan for group medical care, and exemption from the draft by virtue of employment in an essential war industry.

The mushroom growth of the shipyards put heavy strains on the surrounding communities, and every facility from schools to sewers was stretched to the breaking point or beyond it. Thousands of families lived in "temporary" wartime housing projects that would remain as slums for decades afterward. The most severe growing pains were probably those of the cities of Richmond and Vallejo. In each, the population increased from about 20,000 in 1940 to more than 100,000 in 1945, and the nonwhite population rose from less than 2 percent to nearly 14 percent.

Because the shipyards could not afford to exclude anyone from their desperately short supply of labor, they offered extraordinary opportunities for women

Workers at the Kaiser shipyard in San Pedro raise their hats in a victory salute during the spring of 1945. Note especially the presence of women in the workforce. *(Courtesy of Special Collections, San Francisco Public Library.)*

and members of minority races, whose previous chance for good pay in skilled occupations had been limited. Thousands of women were hired to work in the shipyards as electricians, steamfitters, and welders. But the disunity within American life was painfully evident in the intense prejudices of male shipyard workers against women and of whites against nonwhites. Black shipyard workers organized the United Negro Labor Committee to demand equal insurance benefits and voting privileges denied them by racially discriminatory unions. African American women were especially active in the fight for equal rights. When Frances Albrier completed twice the required number of hours of training as a welder and was denied employment at the Kaiser shipyards in Richmond, she successfully campaigned to change the company's hiring practices. Tarea Hall Pittman helped newly arrived southern blacks understand the urgency of the challenge they faced: "They could see the vestiges of discrimination here, that California was going to be exactly like Texas, Arkansas, Alabama, and Georgia and every place else if we didn't do something."

Racial divisions also were evident in the worst stateside disaster during the war. On July 17, 1944, two ammunition ships and a train exploded in a horrendous blast at the Port Chicago Naval Magazine on the south shore of Suisun Bay. Killed in the blast were 320 men, two-thirds of whom were African Americans serving in a segregated unit assigned the unenviable task of loading ammunition. After the disaster, 50 of the surviving members of the unit refused to return to duty, citing unsafe working conditions and a lack of proper training. All the sailors were convicted of mutiny and sentenced to military prison. Later efforts to have their convictions overturned failed, even though the Navy admitted "there can be no doubt that racial prejudice was responsible for the posting of African Americans to the loading divisions at Port Chicago." On the fiftieth anniversary of the incident, a memorial containing the names of the victims of the blast was dedicated at the site.

RISE OF THE AIRCRAFT INDUSTRY

The importance of shipbuilding was doomed to end with the war, but the wartime expansion in the manufacturing of aircraft and in the industries closely related to it became a much more enduring and ultimately a much larger factor in California's growth.

Before the 1930s, aircraft manufacturing in the United States was a small industry in which skilled artisans engaged in the leisurely production of custom-built planes. The more substantial factories were then in the east. Glenn L. Martin, who had established one of the first airplane factories in America in 1909, built some of his early planes in southern California, but he later moved his operations to Cleveland and then to Baltimore. In 1916 the brothers Allen and Malcolm Loughead set up a shop in Santa Barbara in association with John K. Northrop. During World War I they got a contract to build seaplanes for the Navy, but the war ended before they could begin production. Refusing to be discouraged, the three men moved their little factory to Burbank and dispelled the previously hopeless confusion over the pronunciation of "Loughead" by adopting "Lockheed" as their company name.

In 1920 young Donald Douglas left a job as chief engineer and vice president of Glenn L. Martin's company in Cleveland to go into business for himself in southern California. With an initial capital of $600 Douglas set up his drafting room in the rear half of a barber shop on Pico Boulevard in Los Angeles. No banker would lend him a cent, but he attracted the interest of Harry Chandler, publisher of the *Times* and perpetual booster of new industry for the Los Angeles area. On the strength of an order for three navy torpedo planes, Chandler and nine other southern California businesspeople lent Douglas a total of $15,000, enabling him to establish a factory in an abandoned motion picture studio in Santa Monica. That factory succeeded so well that in 1924 two Douglas-built Army planes made the first flight around the world, though they took several months to complete it.

T. Claude Ryan, a former Army flyer, established the first daily scheduled airline passenger service in the United States in 1922 between San Diego and Los Angeles, and the next year he began to manufacture planes at San Diego. There, his small company achieved a national reputation by building the *Spirit of St. Louis,* in which Charles A. Lindbergh made his spectacular flight from New York to Paris in 1927.

The depression was particularly hard on the aircraft industry. In 1932 Douglas went for 4 months without an order and kept his workers employed at gardening and plant maintenance, whereas the Lockheed company, whose general manager had mortgaged his house and car to meet a payroll during the previous Christmas week, went into bankruptcy.

Even in the period between the two world wars, more than half the country's airplane production was done under government contract, and no company survived without a share of military orders. Nevertheless, the military air forces of the United States in the late 1930s were alarmingly unprepared for war. As late as 1939, the entire output of the American aircraft industry was less than 6000 planes of all types—the full capacity of the factories then in existence. In May 1940, when the Nazis invaded France, President Roosevelt called for an output of 50,000 planes a year, and although this figure was then regarded as shocking and impossible, actual production would more than double it by 1944.

The wartime expansion of aircraft manufacturing compressed 40 years of normal industrial progress into 40 months. In 1933, all the airframe factories in southern California together employed only about 1000 people. In November 1943 they employed 280,300.

As in the shipyards, the airframe plants actively recruited women to fill jobs previously held by men. Women made up over 40 percent of the workforce of the aircraft industry in southern California and thus made a major contribution to the war effort. The new employment opportunities also had a significant impact on the attitudes of the women workers. One female airframe worker later recalled, "All my life, I sorta had an inferiority complex and that was gone—completely—'cause I found out I could do a lot of things that I didn't know I could do."

Women assembly workers rivet a gussett to a wing rib at the Long Beach plant of the Douglas Aircraft Company in October 1943. (*Courtesy of* "The Life and Times of Rosie the Riveter," *Clarity Productions.*)

Airframe plants, which made up the bulk of the aircraft industry in California, were only a part of the total process of aircraft production, but they were the largest part. They built the fuselage, wings, and tail; the engines, propellers, and other equipment were made in separate factories. During the war much of the automobile industry in Detroit was converted to making aircraft engines, but it was the airframe plants that assembled all the parts into the finished plane.

Aircraft accounted for nearly 60 percent of the money that the federal government spent under prime contracts for goods manufactured in California during World War II, but the profits of the aircraft companies were small. The great bulk of the expansion was accomplished with federal funds, through contracts under which the government guaranteed the entire cost and the companies received only a fixed fee in addition.

Four of the country's leading aircraft producers, Douglas, Lockheed, North American, and Northrop, had their main plants in the Los Angeles area, and two, Convair and Ryan, were in San Diego. Because clear, mild, and consistent weather offered great advantages for the production and testing of aircraft, climate became one of the principal factors in the location of airframe plants, and southern California therefore received a large share of the industry's wartime expansion. That share would have been even larger had it not been for the memory of Pearl Harbor and the fear that Japanese carrier-based bombers might attack the Pacific coast. The gigantic Douglas factory of Santa Monica was hidden under a camouflage cover, with dummy houses, streets, and trees, so that from the air and even from the ground it was almost impossible to distinguish the plant from its suburban residential surroundings.

THE "RELOCATION" OF THE JAPANESE AMERICANS

The elaborate and expensive camouflaging of southern California aircraft factories, though it proved unnecessary, did no great harm, but the fear of Japanese attack also led the government of the United States into a massive, tragic, and needless blunder. This was the evacuation from the west coast of all persons of Japanese ancestry and the imprisonment of most of them, citizens and aliens alike, without trial, behind barbed wire, under armed guard, in "relocation" camps in desert areas in the interior.

The attack on Pearl Harbor and false rumors of sabotage and other treasonable acts by Japanese Americans reactivated all the stereotyped racist delusions that had long formed the beliefs of many Californians about the Japanese. Since the early years of the century a number of the state's most influential newspapers, politicians, and organizations had frequently portrayed all persons of Japanese extraction as sly, sinister, ruthless, and incapable of loyalty to any country but Japan.

For the more effective dissemination of such ideas, Valentine S. McClatchy, publisher of the *Sacramento Bee,* had formed the California Joint Immigration Committee in 1921. This body coordinated the propaganda activities of four previous anti-Japanese organizations. Among its members were the secretary-treasurer of the state Federation of Labor, the master of the state Grange, the grand president of the Native Sons of the Golden West, the deputy adjutant of the California Department of the American Legion, and the attorney general of California. Attorney General Ulysses S. Webb, one of the principal authors of the state's alien land law, often asserted in public speeches that persons of Japanese origin had inherent racial traits that rendered them unassimilable and untrustworthy as Americans. Earl Warren, when he succeeded Webb as attorney general of California in 1939, held similar views.

Immediately after the raid on Pearl Harbor, rumors of treacherous acts by Japanese Americans in Hawaii began to circulate both in the islands and on the mainland. Rumormongers claimed to know on the best authority that Japanese vegetable trucks had blocked roads, or that one truck had rushed across Hickham Field and knocked the tails off a line of fighter planes, or that a huge arrow cut in a field of sugarcane the night before the raid had guided the Japanese bombers to this or that important target.

For the first several weeks after the Pearl Harbor raid the gradually increasing demands for some sort of mass action against the Japanese Americans on the west coast received little support from Lt. Gen. John L. DeWitt, head of the Western Defense Command. On December 26, DeWitt telephoned from his headquarters at the San Francisco Presidio to the provost marshal general in Washington to report that he had just received a visit from a representative of the Los Angeles Chamber of Commerce who demanded the internment of all the "Japanese" in the Los Angeles area, regardless of whether they were citizens of the United States. DeWitt was opposed. "I'm very doubtful that it would be a commonsense procedure," he told the provost marshal general. It would be "likely to alienate the loyal Japanese," and "an American citizen, after all, is an American citizen."

A month later, however, General DeWitt changed his mind, largely as a result of the sensational publicity given to the report of the Pearl Harbor investigating commission under Supreme Court Justice Owen J. Roberts. That report, published on January 25, 1942, laid the blame for the disaster mainly on the Army and Navy commanders in Hawaii, Lieutenant Gen. Walter C. Short and Admiral Husband E. Kimmel, respectively, and charged these two officers with "dereliction of duty" in having failed to take adequate precautions for the defense of the islands. Short and Kimmel had already been removed from their commands, but several congressional leaders now demanded that they suffer the further disgrace of being court-martialed. The Roberts Report also asserted that the "Japanese spies on the Island of Oahu" had included "persons having no open relations with the Japanese oreign Service." Many Americans interpreted this statement as new and official evidence of widespread Japanese American disloyalty.

The truth was that there was not a scrap of valid evidence to connect any Japanese American resident of Hawaii with any act of espionage or sabotage. But this would not be widely known until after the war. The Roberts Report, at the time it was published, had an enormous and inflammatory effect on public opinion, especially in California.

On January 27, DeWitt had a long conference with Governor Culbert L. Olson. A few weeks before, Olson had pleaded for tolerance of the Japanese Americans and for confidence in their loyalty, but now, DeWitt informed the War Department, the governor had joined those who were "bringing pressure to move all the Japanese out." Attorney General Earl Warren, Mayor Fletcher Bowron of Los Angeles, and many others were making this demand, DeWitt reported, and the agitation for it came from "the best people of California. Since the publication of the Roberts Report they feel that they are living in the midst of a lot of enemies." In a conference a few days later DeWitt remarked with intense emotion that "I am not going to be a second General Short."

DeWitt was now in a state of suppressed terror, brought on by fear of the disgrace that had befallen Short and Kimmel, and it was in this state of mind that he prepared a report to the secretary of war on the "Evacuation of Japanese and other Subversive Persons from the Pacific Coast." Among other remarkable statements, this document asserted that "the Japanese race is an enemy race" and that "along the vital Pacific Coast over 112,000 potential enemies, of Japanese extraction, are at large today. There are indications that these are organized and ready for concerted action at a favorable opportunity. The very fact that no sabotage has taken place to date is a disturbing and confirming indication that such action will be taken."

This fantastic line of reasoning was very widely accepted. On February 13 the entire west coast congressional delegation sent a letter to President Roosevelt demanding the "immediate evacuation of all persons of Japanese lineage . . . aliens and citizens alike" from "the entire strategic area" of California, Oregon, and Washington.

Secretary of War Henry L. Stimson and Assistant Secretary John J. McCloy, in a conference with President Roosevelt at the White House on February 11, had already asked the president for authorization to move Japanese American citizens as well as aliens from "restricted areas" on the west coast. There would "probably be repercussions," Roosevelt replied, but they must act from their judgment of military necessity. McCloy informed DeWitt by telephone that the president had given the War Department "carte blanche."

Meanwhile Attorney General Francis Biddle and his assistants in the Department of Justice had prepared a battery of arguments opposing the mass evacuation of American citizens as unconstitutional and the evacuation of the enemy aliens as unnecessary and unwise. Before they could present these arguments, the president informed Biddle that the question would be decided entirely on military grounds.

On February 19, President Roosevelt signed a most extraordinary document This was Executive Order 9066, authorizing the secretary of war "whenever he or any designated Commander deems such action necessary or desirable, to prescribe military areas . . . from which any or all persons may be excluded."

On March 2, the Western Defense Command issued its Public Proclamation No. 1. All persons of Japanese ancestry were, in effect, *ordered* to migrate *voluntarily* from "Military Area No. 1"—the western halves of California, Oregon, and Washington and the southern half of Arizona. But this led to bitter protests from communities and states in the interior against being "used as a dumping ground" for the presumably disloyal and dangerous Japanese, and on March 27 another proclamation ordered the coast Japanese to cease voluntary migration and instead to await controlled evacuation and internment. Soon afterward this order was extended to include Military Area No. 2—the other halves of the west coast states and Arizona.

There were then more than 93,000 Japanese Americans in California, 14,000 in Washington, and 4000 in Oregon, or a total of about 112,000 in the three coastal states. Of these more than 71,000 were *Nisei* and about 41,000 *Issei*. Nisei were American-born citizens, of whom only a few hundred were more than 35 years old; a large majority were under 21. *Issei* were Japanese immigrants, nearly all of whom were adults, because Japanese immigration had virtually ceased when Congress banned it in 1924. Because the Issei were Asians, they had never been eligible for naturalization, and their legal status was now that of enemy aliens. But in any case, the proclamations of the Western Defense Command generally used the word "Japanese" without making a distinction in the matter of citizenship.

During the spring of 1942, under Army supervision, nearly all the west coast Japanese Americans were confined in improvised "assembly centers" at racetracks, fairgrounds, or livestock exhibition halls. During the summer and fall they were evacuated to more permanent relocation camps. There were 10 of these, located in some of the bleakest parts of the continent. Two were in California—at Manzanar in the Owens Valley and at Tule Lake near the Oregon border. Most of the camps were in desert regions, intensely hot in summer and bitterly cold in winter. The buildings were made of wood frame and tar paper.

These barracks cities were called "relocation centers" rather than concentration camps, and they were under the control of a civilian agency, the War Relocation Authority (WRA). The administrators of the WRA were carefully chosen, mostly

A former landscape gardener from southern California demonstrated his skill and ingenuity by creating a rock garden alongside his tar paper–covered barracks at the Manzanar relocation center in 1942. *(Photograph by Dorothea Lange. Courtesy of the Bancroft Library.)*

from the permanent staffs of the federal departments of Agriculture and the Interior, and in general they were able and understanding persons who wished to allow the internees the maximum of self-government that was possible under the circumstances. But the camps were essentially prisons, surrounded by tall barbed wire fences and guarded by soldiers.

Relocation had a devastating effect on Japanese American families. The residents of the camps did their best to maintain traditional family structures, but disintegration was a constant threat. The stress hit many Japanese American women particularly hard. "Our family unit had been very strong until that time," Kimiko Kitamaya later recalled. "It broke down a little bit in the camps because the younger kids were running around and being very independent. So the family unit that we always considered as very strong, slowly disintegrated."

The evacuation was based upon the argument of "military necessity," but this argument was untenable. The Japanese never contemplated an invasion of the mainland of the United States, and moreover neither General DeWitt nor any other commander ever maintained that such a landing might be attempted. As for the possibility of air raids, the Japanese lost one of their carriers in the Battle of the Coral Sea, May 4–8, 1942; in the Battle of Midway, June 4–6, they lost four more—all the carriers they could have committed to any further action in the central Pacific, let alone in the eastern Pacific. Any possibility of an air attack on the American mainland ended with the Battle of Midway. Yet the movement of Japanese

American internees from the local assembly centers on the west coast to the relocation centers in the interior took place *after* that battle.

The logic behind the claim of military necessity becomes even more puzzling when the evacuation of Japanese Americans from the west coast is contrasted with the government's policy toward Italian Americans and German Americans. The United States was at war with Japan, Germany, and Italy, but only Americans of *Japanese* ancestry were subject to mass evacuation. Individual aliens from Germany and Italy—including some who were naturalized citizens—endured wartime internment and exclusion. But these actions affected only those aliens declared "dangerous" by various intelligence agencies. It was a small group. Out of the several hundred thousand German and Italian aliens living in the United States, only about 2000 were placed in wartime internment camps and 250 naturalized citizens were ordered to move from coastal states.

The argument of military necessity appears more curious still when one considers what happened to the Japanese Americans living in the Hawaiian Islands. There were about 160,000 persons of Japanese ancestry in the islands, one-third more than the number on the mainland. Not only did thousands of them live in close proximity to military and naval installations on Oahu, but they actually worked in them and continued to do so after Pearl Harbor, simply because they formed the bulk of the skilled labor on the island and could not have been replaced for months. Furthermore the military government that ruled the islands during most of the war argued that there was no need to relocate the Japanese Americans because they were already effectively controlled. All major "Japanese relocation" plans for Hawaii were thus abandoned. As an Army spokesman explained to the Honolulu press, "The shipping situation and the labor shortage make it a *military necessity* to keep most of the people of Japanese blood on the island." [The italics are inserted.]

It was not only the labor force of Hawaii that was dependent on the Japanese Americans at the outbreak of the war. The two Hawaiian National Guard regiments that shared in the task of guarding the islands included many men of Japanese descent. They were not withdrawn from the Guard regiments until May 1942, when sufficient replacements had finally arrived from the west coast. Then they were formed into the 100th Infantry Battalion. Later, mainland Japanese Americans recruited from relocation camps were enlisted in the all-Nisei 442d Regimental Combat Team. Their units distinguished themselves and suffered heavy losses in the invasion of Italy in the autumn of 1943. The 442d became the most decorated regiment in the annals of the American Army.

In the words of the official history of *The United States Army in World War II,* "little support for the argument that military necessity required a mass evacuation of the Japanese can be found in contemporary evidence." Instead, in defense of the Army, its official history makes the remarkable suggestion that "the cooperation of the white population of the Pacific states in the national defense effort could not have been . . . assured" if the government and the military had not bowed to "formidable pressure" from west coast civilians for Japanese American removal.

On the other hand, the United States Supreme Court in upholding the evacuation maintained that the Army had acted from military necessity and that in time of war it was not the prerogative of any civilians, even the members of that Court itself, to attempt to evaluate the decisions of the military on military matters.

In the Hirabayashi case in 1943 and the Korematsu and Endo cases in 1944, the Supreme Court drastically weakened the constitutional rights of all Americans in wartime by condoning a massive injustice that had been inflicted on a particular group of Americans because of their race. As Justice Frank Murphy put it in his dissent in the case of Korematsu, the majority of the Court upheld the government and the military in an action that went "over the . . . brink of constitutional power and . . . into the ugly abyss of racism." Justice Robert H. Jackson, in his separate dissent, pointed out that the principle approved by the majority decision would thereafter lie about "like a loaded weapon ready for the hand of any authority that can bring forward a plausible claim of an urgent need."

Most of the evacuees were held in the relocation camps for more than 2 years until after the War Department revoked the west coast exclusion orders in December 1944. About half of them returned to the west coast during 1945 and 1946. In many cases their return was greeted with threats and acts of terrorism, but strong voices were also raised in their behalf. General Joseph W. Stilwell, in particular, denounced the terrorists as "barfly commandos." Mary Masuda, a young woman who had spent 2½ years at the Gila River relocation center, received threats of violence from a group of vigilantes when she returned to her home near Santa Ana. Her brother, a war hero who had been killed in Italy, was posthumously awarded the Distinguished Service Cross. On December 8, 1945, General Stilwell presented Sergeant Masuda's medal to his sister in her home, and this sobering incident received wide publicity.

In the postwar years many Californians gradually came to realize the enormity of the mistake that had been made. Many could accept the view of the War Relocation Authority in its final report (1946): "Since we are continually striving, with the better part of our minds, to be a united people, it becomes important for us to understand and evaluate what we did, both officially and unofficially, to this particular racial segment of our population in time of global war."

SELECTED BIBLIOGRAPHY

The best general surveys of the period are Gerald D. Nash, *The American West Transformed* (1985) and *World War II and the West* (1990). Nash analyzes the impact of the war on California's economy, urban development, ethnic minorities, and cultural life. More localized studies include Marilynn S. Johnson, *The Second Gold Rush: Oakland and the East Bay in World War II* (1993), and Arthur C. Verge, *Paradise Transformed: Los Angeles during the Second World War* (1993).

On the relationship between urban development and defense spending, see Roger W. Lotchin, *Fortress California 1910–1961* (1992), and a special issue of the *Pacific Historical Review,* LXIII (August 1994), edited by Lotchin. See also Martin J. Schiesl, "City Planning and the Federal Government in World War II: The Los Angeles Experience," *California History,* LIX (Summer 1980), pp. 126–143; and Mark S. Foster, *Henry J. Kaiser* (1989).

Charles Wollenberg's *Marinship at War: Shipbuilding and Social Change in Wartime Sausalito* (1990) is a penetrating analysis. Dorothea Lange's wartime photos of the East Bay are available in Wollenberg (ed.), *Photographing the Second Gold Rush* (1995). See also Katherine Archibald, *Wartime Shipyard* (1947); "Richmond Took a Beating," *Fortune,* XXXI (February 1945), pp. 262–269; Joan M. Jensen and Gloria Ricci Lothrop, *California Women* (1987); Lawrence P. Crouchett, Lonnie G. Bunch, and Martha Kendall Winnacker, *Visions toward Tomorrow* (1989); and Sally M. Miller and Daniel A. Cornford (eds.), *American Labor in the Era of World War II* (1995).

John B. Rae's *Climb to Greatness: The American Aircraft Industry, 1920–1960* (1968) is the standard short account. Others are William A. Schoneberger and Paul Sonnenburg, *California Wings* (1987); Arlene Elliott, "The Rise of Aeronautics in California, 1849–1940," *Southern California Quarterly,* LII (March 1970), pp. 1–32; and Arthur P. Allen and Betty V. H. Schneider, *Industrial Relations in the California Aircraft Industry* (1956).

Jacobus tenBroek, Edward N. Barnhart, and Floyd W. Matson, *Prejudice, War, and the Constitution* (1954); U.S. Department of the Interior, War Relocation Authority, *WRA: A Story of Human Conservation* (1946); Allan R. Bosworth, *America's Concentration Camps* (1967); and Roger Daniels, *Concentration Camps* (1981), are general accounts of the causes, events, and historical and legal significance of the Japanese American evacuation.

Morton Grodzins, *Americans Betrayed* (1949), stresses the influence of California pressure groups and politicians on the making of the decision. U.S. Army, Western Defense Command, *Final Report: Japanese Evacuation from the West Coast, 1942* (1943), is a distressingly unreliable and misleading apologia, written largely by Colonel Karl R. Bendetsen and submitted over the signature of General DeWitt. U.S. Department of the Army, Office of Military History, *Command Decisions* (1959), edited by Kent R. Greenfield, includes a chapter by Stetson Conn, "The Decision to Evacuate the Japanese from the Pacific Coast." This adds much material drawn from the files of the War Department. An essentially similar chapter, revised in several important details, is in Conn et al., *Guarding the United States and Its Outposts* (1964), a volume in the official history of *The United States Army in World War II.* Roger Daniels, "The Decisions to Relocate the North American Japanese: Another Look," *Pacific Historical Review,* LI (February 1982), pp. 71–77, stresses the underlying racist motivations for relocation. See also Ward M. McAfee, "America's Two Japanese-American Policies during World War II," *Southern California Quarterly,* LXIX (Summer 1987), pp. 151–164. On the Supreme Court decisions see Peter Irons, *Justice at War* (1983) and *Justice Delayed* (1989). See also Rose D. Scherini, "Executive Order 9066 and Italian Americans," *California History,* LXX (Winter 1991/1992), pp. 366–377.

The impact of relocation on the Japanese Americans is described in Dorothy S. Thomas et al., *The Spoilage* (1946) and *The Salvage* (1952); Mine Okubo, *Citizen 13660* (1946), an enlightening memoir; *Impounded People,* written by Edward H. Spicer et al. for the War Relocation Authority in 1946 and published in 1969; Harry H. L. Kitano, *Japanese Americans* (1969); Bill Hosokawa, *Nisei* (1969); Audrie Girdner and Anne Loftis, *The Great Betrayal* (1969); Edison Uno, *Japanese Americans* (1971); and Maisie and Richard Conrat, *Executive Order 9066* (1972), with photographs by Dorothea Lange and others. Roger Daniels has compiled a documentary history in *American Concentration Camps* (1989) and a collection of interpretive essays in *Japanese Americans: From Relocation to Redress* (1986).

CHAPTER TWENTY-NINE

Politics California Style

The middle decades of the twentieth century were a crucial period in the political history of California. Both major parties remained extraordinarily weak, and new institutions emerged to fill the void. In the free-for-all of California politics, spurious issues and a galaxy of political exotics created an impression of political fervor. Pundits marveled ,at the anomalous spectacle of the state's Democratic majority consistently electing Republicans to office. The tide turned in 1958 when the Democrats at last managed to gain control of the state government.

Meanwhile California's political leaders were capturing the national limelight. The state was on its way to becoming the New York or Ohio of twentieth-century American politics, serving as a training ground for national leadership.

"NONPARTISANSHIP" FAVORS THE REPUBLICANS

The rolls of registered voters show that the great depression of the 1930s had converted California from an overwhelmingly Republican to a heavily Democratic state. In 1930 the number of Californians registered as Democrats had been only 22 percent of the two-party registration. In 1936 it had risen to 60 percent, and this three-to-two superiority of Democratic over Republican voters continued with little variation for decades afterward. Yet from 1942 until 1958 the preponderantly Democratic voters of California elected heavy majorities of Republicans to state offices.

More than ever before, the political conditions of the depressed 1930s had identified the Republicans as the party of the "haves" and the Democrats as the party of the "have-nots." A large majority of the business community continued to be Republican. So did a substantial proportion of white Anglo-Saxon protestants. The Democrats, on the other hand, drew the bulk of their following from labor, the unemployed, and ethnic and religious minority groups. Most of the huge increase in Democratic registration in the early 1930s was made up of citizens who had never taken the trouble to register before and who did so now out of a desire to vote for a government that would take a greater interest in the less advantaged members of society.

All this meant, however, that most Democratic voters were less educated and less informed than most Republican voters. In this situation California's peculiar cross-filing law tended to keep Republican incumbents in office. Under that law the party affiliations of candidates did not appear on the primary election ballot, but a candidate running for reelection was listed first and identified as "Incumbent." Hundreds of thousands of Democratic voters were quite unaware that the incumbent whose name appeared on the Democratic primary ballot could be and in fact usually was a Republican. Under this system, three-fourths of the elections to state offices were won in the primaries by incumbents who won the nominations of both major parties. In the legislative session of 1945, for example, 36 of the 40 state senators were elected in the primaries, and most of them were Republican incumbents.

In other respects, also, the Republicans were in a much better position than the Democrats to cope with the "nonpartisan" system (or rather the antiparty system), which the Republican progressives under Hiram Johnson had introduced. The Republicans not only had most of the experienced and successful candidates; they also had far more money for political campaigning, and they had the support of a great majority of the newspapers, including the three most influential ones, the *Los Angeles Times,* the *San Francisco Chronicle,* and the *Oakland Tribune.*

A newspaper is ordinarily a business enterprise, dependent for the bulk of its income on the advertising of other business enterprises. Consequently most newspaper publishers preferred the Republican party, with its orientation toward business interests, low taxes, and a minimum of governmental control. Remembering the preponderance of Democratic voters, however, California newspapers tended to support Republican candidates as individuals without overstressing their party affiliation.

FILLING THE VOID

Cross-filing and the other antiparty laws of the progressives had been designed to destroy the power of corrupt "political machines" in California. By weakening the traditional party organizations, these laws opened the way for alternative institutions to fill the power vacuum. These institutions included special-interest lobbyists, professional campaign-management firms, and informal party organizations.

Lobbying has often been known as "the fourth branch of government" or as "the third house" of a legislature. In fact, the lawmaking process in any democratic government would be crippled if the legislative body tried to operate without the constant flow of information from representatives of interested groups. But the corrupt use of power, and especially the power of money to influence legislation and the elections of legislators, has always been a menace to democracy.

Arthur H. Samish, king of the California lobbyists, represented a coalition of liquor, oil, bus, trucking, mining, banking, billboard, theatrical, racetrack, and other interests. He came to have almost as much power in the 1930s and 1940s as William F. Herrin had exercised at the turn of the century. Samish organized the state's brewers, distillers, and tavernkeepers into a kind of prosaloon league, and in 1935 he made a contract with the California State Brewers' Association providing an assessment of 5 cents on every barrel of beer for a political fund to be dispensed by Samish with no accounting. In later years he often reminded his clients in the liquor industry that as a result of his efforts California had the lowest liquor taxes in the nation. He also reminded the oil companies which retained him as a lobbyist that oil serverance taxes in Louisiana and Texas were about 100 times as high as in California.

In 1938 the Sacramento grand jury employed a private detective to investigate charges that Samish had attempted to bribe members of the state senate. The detective reported finding "ample evidence that corruption, direct and indirect, has influenced the course of legislation." Samish, it was discovered, had received from his clients about $500,000 during the previous 3 years. The basis of Samish's method was "to acquire influence with a group of Legislators through campaign contributions or other favors and then to sell that influence to industries concerned with legislation."

Ten years later, in 1949, *Collier's* magazine published an exposé called "The Secret Boss of California." Forgetting, for once, the importance of secrecy in his

Arthur H. Samish (1899–1974) and "Mr. Legislature." Taking pictures for *Collier's*, photographer Fred Lyon caught Samish in this remarkable pose in his suite at the Senator Hotel in Sacramento. *(Courtesy of The Bettmann Archive.)*

operations, and giving way to the most arrogant braggadocio, Samish posed for a color photograph in his hotel suite at the state capital. On his knee he held a ventriloquist's dummy which he addressed as "Mr. Legislature." The appearance of such an article and especially of such a picture in a national magazine finally compelled the California legislature to take some sort of action. It passed a law requiring lobbyists to register and to file monthly financial statements, but these statements usually proved to be so vague that they were meaningless.

The downfall of Samish finally resulted from his failure to report his income and expenditures to the federal government. In 1953 he was convicted of income tax evasion, and later served 2 years in a federal penitentiary. The state assembly reorganized its committee system in 1953 to eliminate Samish's influence. The next year one former speaker of the assembly was convicted of bribery in liquor license transactions and another was indicted, but released after two hung juries.

In addition to lobbying, which gained such a dangerous degree of influence over the legislature, another institution that emerged in California politics was the professional campaign-management firm—a distinctive contribution of California to American politics. In the 1930s an organization called Campaigns, Inc., founded by Californians Clem Whitaker and Leone Baxter, revolutionized political campaigning by making carefully planned use of the mass media and the commercial techniques of the advertising industry. It was natural that the first full-fledged professional campaign-management firm in the United States should have developed in California because of the state's lack of party organization, its constant influx of new voters, and its extraordinarily frequent use of the initiative and the referendum.

Clem Whitaker was a reporter in Sacramento at the age of 17. Within a few years he was operating his own Capitol News Bureau, furnishing syndicated news on state politics to more than 80 California papers. In 1933 he met Leone Baxter, an articulate young widow who worked for the Redding Chamber of Commerce. Joining forces, Whitaker and Baxter in 1934 managed the Republican campaign against Upton Sinclair, and though they later expressed regret at some of the shabbier devices they felt compelled to use against him, this campaign firmly established their reputation. The partners were married in 1938.

For the next 20 years their support decided many of the key issues of California politics. They usually managed the campaigns for or against five or six initiative or referendum propositions in every state election. Whitaker and Baxter would accept no campaign that was not in accord with their own political views, and as their financial success increased, their views became more and more conservative. The purposes of their clients, Baxter wrote, must be consistent with "individual initiative and personal responsibility; the free operation of our economic society; reasonable freedom from government control and direction." In 1945 Whitaker and Baxter took over the campaign of the California Medical Association to brand a state health plan as "socialized medicine." Their success led the American Medical Association (AMA) to employ them in 1949 for its drive to block President Truman's federal health insurance proposals. For the campaign against "medicare" they administered a multimillion-dollar fund drawn largely from special compulsory assessments upon the doctor members of the AMA. This was the largest cause that Whitaker and Baxter had ever served, but it was not the most meritorious. Their tactics created so much resentment that they ultimately did almost as much to advance as to retard the movement toward nationwide health insurance, which finally when into effect in 1966 in spite of their efforts.

Dozens of other professional campaign-management firms followed in the success of Whitaker and Baxter. Some firms specialized in boosting candidates, others in gathering the signatures needed to place propositions on the ballot. The influence of such firms in California politics was enormous. "If you give me $500,000," one professional campaign manager told author Gladwin Hill, "I'll guarantee to get on the ballot a measure to execute the governor by Christmas."

The third institution to emerge as a consequence of California's "nonpartisan politics" was the informal party organization. The Republicans had formed the first such body, the California Republican Assembly (CRA), at a low point in their party's fortunes in 1933, but the Democrats had been unable to follow suit because of the lack of comparable dedication and enthusiasm among their grassroots volunteer workers. In 1952, however, Adlai E. Stevenson became a kind of patron saint for liberal Democrats, and hundreds of new Democratic clubs sprang up in support of his presidential candidacy. Intense disappointment at his defeat played a part in bringing these clubs together in a statewide federation the next year, the California Democratic Council (CDC).

State conventions of the unofficial California Republican Assembly had contributed heavily to Republican successes by making preprimary endorsements of candidates. On the other hand, extreme confusion and division had continued to weaken the Democratic aspirants in the primaries until their party acquired its own informal nominating machinery in the state conventions of the California Democratic Council. For some years after this system was established, few candidates of either party could win nomination without the endorsement of the CRA or the CDC. Some protested that these endorsements defeated the whole purpose of the direct primary and virtually returned the nominating function to the party convention system, but the informal organizations were much more democratic and less subject to boss control than the old party conventions had been, and to the degree that they could unite each party behind one candidate, they reduced the costs of preprimary campaigning and the excessive role of money in elections.

THE GOVERNORSHIP OF EARL WARREN

The California Republicans found in Earl Warren a leader who was ideally qualified to turn the state's nonpartisan tradition to Republican advantage. Warren did this so successfully that when he was elected to his second term as governor in 1946, he won the Democratic as well as the Republican nomination and became the only California governor ever elected in the primary.

Warren was born in Los Angeles in 1891 and grew up in Kern City, a railroad town near Bakersfield. His father, who had come from Norway, was a master car mechanic for the Southern Pacific and later a real estate broker. Like Hiram Johnson, his political hero, Warren studied at the University of California in Berkeley and made his early political reputation as a public prosecutor. But the personalities of the two men were very different. Johnson was emotional and volatile; Warren was calm and almost stolid.

After a term as state attorney general, Warren easily defeated Culbert L. Olson for the governorship in 1942. During the war years when California enjoyed the unprecedented blessing of a large surplus of revenue from the wartime boom, Warren became a very popular governor. He sponsored reductions in taxes and still was able to preserve a surplus in the treasury for the postwar expansion of such services as highways and public higher education to keep up with the state's tremendous growth.

In 1945 Warren alarmed his conservative supporters by recommending a state compulsory health insurance law. Some of the more advanced Republican progressives had advocated state health insurance as early as 1916, but this, along with many other social reforms, had been a casualty of World War I. Governor Olson had revived the proposal, but the opposition of the California Medical Association and the private insurance companies, in alliance with conservative interests in general, had always defeated it. The same alliance now defeated Warren's proposals also, and the experience did much to disillusion him with the conservative elements in the Republican party.

The oil and trucking lobbies disillusioned him further by their resistance to an increase in the gasoline tax, which Warren requested in 1947 in order to pay for a great expansion of state highways and freeways. Sam Collins, speaker of the assembly, permitted an oil lobbyist to use the speaker's office as a command post for the battle against the tax bill, though a compromise increase was finally agreed upon. As Warren pointed out, the oil and trucking interests were remarkably shortsighted in their opposition to the measure, because it made possible a new statewide network of freeways that increased the sale of gasoline and greatly aided the growth of the trucking industry.

In Warren's election to an unprecedented third term as governor of California in 1950, he did not quite repeat his triumph of 1946 by winning the Democratic as well as the Republican nomination in the primary, but in the general election in November he received a million votes more than the Democratic nominee, Congressman James Roosevelt of Los Angeles.

Democrats often complained that Warren represented himself as nonpartisan whenever he ran for governor, but that in presidential years he was strictly a Republican. As temporary chairman and keynote speaker of the Republican national convention in 1944 he delivered an intensely partisan address. In 1948— the only election he ever lost—he was the Republican nominee for vice president, as the running mate of Governor Thomas E. Dewey of New York. In 1952 Warren was an important contender for the Republican presidential nomination, which he would probably have received as the compromise candidate if the convention had not managed to break the deadlock between Senator Robert A. Taft and Gen. Dwight D. Eisenhower.

In September 1953 President Eisenhower appointed Governor Warren as Chief Justice of the United States.

When Warren left the governorship, his successor was Lieutenant Governor Goodwin J. Knight, a Republican from Los Angeles. Though he strenuously opposed the liberal policies of Warren on such issues as state health insurance, Knight recognized that Warren's remarkable successes in gaining reelection as a Republican governor were based on his ability to capture Democratic votes, and particularly labor votes. Therefore Knight made and kept a promise that as governor he would veto all antilabor measures. Thus he received the formal endorsement of the California Federation of Labor, and in his campaign in 1954 he easily defeated his Democratic opponent, who had little political experience and was virtually unknown to most of the voters.

THE SPURIOUS ISSUE OF "LOYALTY"

The Republican ascendancy in state politics during the late 1940s and 1950s was aided by the anticommunist enthusiasm of the cold war. Cold war tensions also led to bitter division and recrimination in the state's film industry, and propelled the University of California into a storm of controversy that lasted for years.

Congress in 1938 created the House Un-American Activities Committee (HUAC), chaired by a conservative Democrat from Texas, Congressman Martin Dies. One of the early targets of HUAC's anticommunist investigations was the

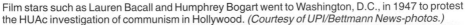

Film stars such as Lauren Bacall and Humphrey Bogart went to Washington, D.C., in 1947 to protest the HUAc investigation of communism in Hollywood. *(Courtesy of UPI/Bettmann News-photos.)*

film industry in Hollywood. In 1947 a list was issued of suspected Communists in the industry, and eventually 250 actors, writers, and directors were barred from further employment. Testimony against the "Red Menace in Hollywood" came from such industry leaders as Jack Warner, Louis B. Mayer, and Gary Cooper. Ronald Reagan, president of the Screen Actors Guild from 1947 to 1952, cooperated fully in the effort to rid the studios of suspected Communists. Walt Disney testified before Congress that the Screen Cartoonists Guild was Communist-controlled and had plotted to make Mickey Mouse follow the party line. Other film leaders—including Humphrey Bogart, Gene Kelly, Judy Garland, and Katharine Hepburn—risked their careers by speaking out against the anticommunist hysteria.

The impact of anticommunism was also soon apparent in state and national politics. With the defeat of Germany and Japan in World War II, the Soviet Union secured an enormous expansion of its military power, and of communist influence, in eastern Europe and eastern Asia. In the United States the Republican party had considerable success in blaming these menacing developments on the policies of the Democratic national administration. By charging that the liberal Democratic leadership was "soft on Communism," the Republicans had their revenge for all the years when they had been branded unfairly but effectively as the party of depression: They now branded the Democrats unfairly but effectively as the party of treason.

In the congressional elections of 1946 the Republicans gained control of both houses of Congress, and in California seven Democratic incumbents lost their seats in the House to Republicans. One of the victorious Republicans was Richard M. Nixon of Whittier, a political newcomer who defeated Jerry Voorhis, the liberal Democrat who had represented the district for 10 years and had been one of the most effective supporters of the New Deal.

Richard Nixon would later become the first native son of California to win the presidency of the United States. He was born in 1913 to Quaker parents at Yorba Linda in Orange County. In 1922 the family acquired a general store and gasoline station in Whittier, and there Richard and his brothers worked long hours after school. He worked his way through Whittier College, won a scholarship that enabled him to attend and graduate with honors from the law school of Duke University, practiced law in his hometown, and served during the war as a Naval Reserve officer.

In his campaign against Voorhis in 1946 Nixon followed a strategy of innuendo which the Republican National Committee had recommended to the party's candidates. He accused his Democratic opponent of disloyalty to America, not directly but through guilt by association. He charged that Voorhis was "one of those who front for un-American elements, wittingly or otherwise, by advocating increased federal controls over the lives of the people"; that Voorhis had the endorsement of the CIO Political Action Committee; and that the CIO-PAC was Communist-infiltrated. "Of course I knew that Jerry Voorhis wasn't a Communist," Nixon remarked afterward, "but I had to win. . . . Nice guys and sissies don't win many elections." Adlai Stevenson, a later victim of similar attacks, would describe them more harshly: "Nixonland, a land of slander and scare, of sly innuendo, of a poison pen, the anonymous phone call, and hustling, pushing, shoving—the land of smash and grab and anything to win."

As a member of HUAC during his first term in Congress, Nixon rendered a service of enormous practical value to his party. He discovered convincing evidence that Alger Hiss, a Democrat who had served in the State Department during the war, had been a secret Communist during the 1930s, when he had engaged in an espionage scheme to transmit government documents to the Russians. Eventually, on January 21, 1950, Hiss was convicted of perjury for denying these charges. Republicans now argued that under the Democrats a one-time Communist spy had been able to infiltrate the upper levels of the federal government, even the Department of State, and that therefore the Democratic party in general must be tainted with communism.

The nation's fear of world communism intensified with the explosion of the first Russian atomic bomb in 1949 and the outbreak of the Korean war in 1950. In this period many Americans were even willing to credit the wild charges of Senator Joseph McCarthy of Wisconsin, who made a series of speeches in which he "held in his hand a list" alleged to contain the names of "card-carrying Communists now employed in the State Department." McCarthy never uncovered a single person who was or ever had been a Communist in the government service. Nixon, on the other hand, had actually uncovered one such person, according to the verdict of a jury.

In 1950 Nixon won the election to the United States Senate over the Democratic nominee Congresswoman Helen Gahagan Douglas, a former Broadway actress. Nixon's most effective campaign weapon against Douglas was the charge that her voting record in the House of Representatives corresponded with the Communist party line. Nixon had chanced upon the most rapid political escalator that the times provided. In 1951, after his election as senator, and again in 1953 after his further elevation to the vice presidency, nearly every Republican member of the House of Representatives applied for a seat on the committee on un-American activities.

The California Legislature established its own joint "Fact-Finding Committee on Un-American Activities" in 1941, with Jack B. Tenney of Los Angeles as chairman. Tenney was a piano player and songwriter whose first widely known achievement was the composing of a popular song called "Mexicali Rose." As chairman of California's un-American activities committee Tenney set himself up as prosecutor, judge, and jury. He bullied witnesses and denied them the rights of due process that they would have had in a normal legal proceeding. He bracketed the innocent with the guilty, convicted by accusation, punished by publicity, and tried to silence criticism by directing these methods against every critic.

The reports of the Tenney committee often included charges of communist influence in the University of California. Early in 1949 Tenney introduced a proposal for a state constitutional amendment to take from the regents and give to the legislature the power to ensure the loyalty of the university's employees. The university's lobbyist and comptroller, James H. Corley, considered this a dangerous political interference in university affairs. He persuaded Tenney not to push his constitutional amendment in return for a promise that the university itself would take some sort of action. This led the regents to adopt the famous "loyalty oath," which embroiled the University of California in the bitterest controversy in the history of American higher education up to that time. The new oath required the professor or other university employee to swear that he or she did "not believe in," was "not a member of," and did "not support any party or organization that believes in, advocates, or teaches the overthrow of the United States Government, by force or by any illegal or unconstitutional methods." The faculty rebelled. Many distinguished scholars whose loyalty was beyond question refused to sign, and the university was thrown into an uproar that continued for nearly 3 years.

Ironically, the state supreme court eventually ruled that Tenney's proposed constitutional amendment would have been meaningless because the legislature had always had, and the regents had never had, the authority to ensure the loyalty of university employees. Another irony was that shortly after the proposed university oath was made public, Tenney was discredited and deprived of all his power in the legislature. In June 1949 he was forced to resign the chairmanship of the un-American activities committee because he had begun to accuse fellow members of the legislature of being Communist sympathizers.

In the face of the faculty rebellion against the special oath, University President Robert Gordon Sproul asked the regents to repeal it. But Regent John Francis Neylan led a majority of the board in refusing to do so, and in clinging to the refusal during a year of bitter debate. This was the same Neylan who had once accepted the case of Charlotte Anita Whitney and appealed her conviction for criminal syndicalism all the way to the United States Supreme Court–this fighting liberal of earlier years was still fighting but no longer liberal. He was, in fact, a strong admirer of Senator McCarthy.

Governor Warren, as an ex officio member of the board of regents, favored repeal of the special oath. It was, he argued, not only harmful to the university and to academic freedom; it was also completely worthless. A Communist, he pointed out, "would take the oath and laugh." No one who was plotting to commit treason would cavil at mere perjury. But these arguments did not prevail. Regent Lawrence Mario Giannini, son and successor of the founder of the Bank of America, said that if the board rescinded the oath, "flags would fly in the Kremlin" in celebration and he himself would feel compelled to "organize twentieth-century vigilantes" against the subsequent wave of communism in California. Other regents argued that "insubordination" not "disloyalty" was the issue. In August 1950, by a vote of 12 to 10 the board voted to dismiss 32 nonsigning professors. In September the academic senate at Berkeley voted to "condemn" this action of "a bare majority" of the regents. Thus for the first time in history an American university faculty adopted a formal resolution of censure against a university governing board.

Professor Edward C. Tolman, previously chair of the Berkeley psychology department, led the nonsigners in bringing suit against the board as represented by its secretary and treasurer, Robert M. Underhill. In 1951 a state district court of appeals ruled that the special oath violated the state constitutional provision protecting the freedom of the university against political influence. The state supreme court disagreed with this interpretation in its final ruling in *Tolman v. Underhill* in 1952, but it also invalidated the oath and ordered the professors reinstated, on the narrower ground that the requirement of a loyalty oath was within the power of the legislature and not of the regents. The legislature, in a special session called after the beginning of the Korean war in 1950, had adopted the Levering Act requiring an elaborate nondisloyalty oath of all state employees, including those of the university, and the state supreme court upheld this requirement. In doing so it was following the current doctrines of the United States Supreme Court; however, under Warren as Chief Justice that body became more liberal. In the 1960s, it struck down similar oath laws in several other states and thus enabled the supreme court of California to declare the Levering oath unconstitutional in 1967, largely on the ground that mere membership in an organization was not evidence of disloyalty.

The state committee on un-American activities went out of existence in 1971, after the senate's new president pro tem, James R. Mills, a liberal Democrat from San Diego, discovered that it had established "subversive" files on several senators because they had voted against its appropriations.

THE GOVERNORSHIP OF EDMUND G. BROWN

The year 1958 was a turning point in California politics. Before that year, the Republicans held five of the six statewide executive offices that were filled by partisan elections, both of the United States senatorships, nearly two-thirds of the seats in the House of Representatives, and more than two thirds of the seats in the state legislature. After 1958 these proportions were almost exactly reversed. Through a combination of Democratic efforts and Republican blunders, the latent Democratic majority was at last able to assert itself.

A key factor in the Democratic resurgence was the decision by Republican Senator William F. Knowland to run for governor in 1958 on a platform openly antagonistic to organized labor. Knowland's decision was based on a combination of personal and political factors, not the least of which was his desire to reverse Governor Knight's prolabor policies by securing passage of a state right-to-work law. The phrase "right to work," based on the idea that a worker should not have to join a union in order to hold a job, was a code name for an assault on the union shop. Following passage of the Taft-Hartley labor relations act of 1947, several states had adopted right-to-work laws forbidding union shop contracts. Knowland hoped to consolidate his position as a leader of American conservatism, lead the large California delegation to the Republican national convention in 1960, and thus secure for himself the presidential nomination.

Knowland succeeded in winning the Republican nomination for governor, and Edmund G. Brown emerged as the victor in the Democratic primary. Voters in the November election were thus faced with a sharp choice between candidates and philosophies. Knowland endorsed a right-to-work ballot proposal, Initiative Proposition 18, and Brown campaigned against it.

In the campaign of 1958 organized labor achieved the greatest degree of unity that it had shown in the whole history of California politics, in support of Brown and in opposition to Knowland and the open shop. There were about 1.5 million union members in California, and with their close relatives they constituted more than a third of the eligible voters. Against Proposition 18, labor collected a campaign fund in excess of $2.5 million, more than twice the total funds contributed in the proposition's favor. Labor also sponsored a huge campaign of billboard, television, and newspaper advertising, stressing the argument that the "so-called right to work means the right to work for less and less and less."

In the election of November 1958 Brown won nearly 60 percent of the votes, and Proposition 18 lost by almost exactly the same percentage. The vote for Brown was 3,140,176; for Knowland, 2,110,911. Brown carried 54 of the state's 58 counties. The Democrats won margins of 27 seats to 13 in the state senate and 47 to 33 in the assembly.

Edmund G. Brown, who now emerged as the leader of the California Democrats, was a native San Franciscan, born in 1905. When he was in the seventh grade at Fremont Grammar School, a ringing patriotic speech for the sale of liberty bonds had earned him the nickname of "Patrick Henry" Brown, and he continued to be known as Pat throughout his later career. He graduated from the San Francisco College of Law, became district attorney of San Francisco in 1944, and was elected state attorney general in 1950.

When Brown was inaugurated as governor in January 1959, the Democrats were in control of both houses of the California Legislature for the first time in 80 years. In his inaugural address, Governor Brown promised to follow "the path of responsible liberalism . . . , in the giant footsteps of such memorable governors as Hughes and Roosevelt in New York, Wilson in New Jersey, La Follette in Wisconsin, Altgeld and Stevenson in Illinois, and Johnson and Warren in California."

Brown proposed a number of liberal measures, and the legislature enacted most of them. He recommended a law against racial discrimination by employers and labor unions, and the legislature responded with a fair employment practices act. Maximum payments for unemployment insurance, disability, and workers' compensation were substantially increased. For the protection of consumers, a state office of consumer's counsel was created, with authority to act against false or misleading practices in labeling and packaging and deceptive carrying charges on installment credit purchases. A state economic development agency was established to attract new industries and aid long-range planning.

Tax increases were adopted to meet a deficit left over from the previous year and to enable the state government to keep up with the swift growth of the state's population by expanding its programs of highways, aid to local school districts, and crime control. At the governor's urging the legislature authorized studies that led to a Master Plan for Higher Education and to plans for the reorganization of many state offices under centralized departments. Cross-filing in elections was abolished. The legislature, however, in 1959 defeated Brown's request for a minimum wage of $1.25 an hour for workers not covered by federal law. Abolition of capital punishment, which he urged in 1960, was also rejected.

Probably Brown's greatest single achievement as governor was the adoption of the huge bond issue that enabled the state to proceed with its master plan for water development.

Most of California's water was in the northern half of the state, whereas most of the need for water was in the southern half. The Los Angeles basin, for example, had only 0.06 percent of California's natural stream flow of water. Under Governor Earl Warren, the legislature had authorized studies for a statewide water program that would ultimately be much larger than the federal Central Valley Project, but organized labor, conservative bankers, and majority opinion in northern California were strongly opposed to the state plan. Labor leaders argued that because the state program would not come under the federal limitation of 160 acres on the size of farms eligible to receive publicly subsidized water, the plan would result in the "unjust enrichment" of huge landowning corporations that were already too rich and too powerful. Major beneficiaries, labor pointed out, would include the Southern Pacific, Standard Oil, the Kern County Land Company, the Los Angeles Times Corporation, and other groups that held vast tracts in the southwestern San Joaquin Valley.

In the face of this opposition Governor Knight refused to become involved in the battle, but Governor Brown believed that the water plan was indispensable for California's future growth, and he threw all his political weight behind it. In 1959, at his insistence, the legislature authorized the submission to the voters of a bond issue of $1.75 billion. This was the largest issue of bonds ever adopted by any state for any purpose. Most of the money would be used for the Feather River Project, the first phase of a much larger long-range plan. The voters of California approved "Brown's water bonds" in November 1960 after he had urged them to do so in speeches throughout the state.

The heart of the Feather River Project was Oroville Dam, 735 feet high, the tallest in the United States, which assured a controlled flow of water to the San Joaquin Delta region. From the delta, as Brown said at the groundbreaking ceremonies in October 1961, "we are going to build a river 500 miles long" in order "to correct an accident of people and geography." He was referring to the aqueduct that would carry water along the western side of the San Joaquin Valley and into southern California.

EXTREMISTS, RIGHT AND LEFT

One of the key factors in California politics in the 1960s was the emergence of vividly colorful but startlingly eccentric new varieties of fanaticism at both ends of the political spectrum. On the far right, the John Birch Society became a ludicrous parody of the conservatism of the Republicans, and thus contributed substantially to their defeats in the state election of 1962 and the national election of 1964. At the other extreme, an anarchistic student wing of the "new left" parodied the liberalism of the Democrats and contributed to the defeat of Governor Brown in the election of 1966.

The tendency to polarization in philosophical and political opinions has always characterized the discussion of human affairs. Medieval philosophers asserted that every human being was born either a Platonist or an Aristotelian. Environment is a more probable explanation than heredity, though Gilbert and Sullivan, in the context of English party politics in the nineteenth century, maintained that:

Every boy and every gal
That's born into the world alive
Is either a little Liberal
Or else a little Conservative.

In twentieth-century American politics, especially after the 1930s, liberalism was the belief that government should take positive actions in the interests of the greater welfare and greater liberties of the whole people and that it should also take negative, regulatory actions to protect the public from abuses of freedom by private business. Most American conservatives, during the same period, regarded their doctrine as an alternative and superior theory of progress. They argued not merely for the need to conserve what was good in the past, but also for the related belief that the best way to ensure the continued progress and improvement of American society was to leave the fullest possible freedom to the operations of private enterprise. The mainstream of American politics was a constant process of compromise between these two philosophies. But to the extremists of both the radical right and the radical left, compromise was unendurable.

The John Birch Society was founded in 1958 by Robert Welch, a retired candy manufacturer who had been defeated for the Republican nomination for lieutenant governor of Massachusetts and who suspected that communist infiltration of the Republican party had been responsible for his defeat. Welch and many of his followers believed that the graduated income tax, social security, the United Nations, and racial integration in the public schools were communist plots; that the fluoridation of water was a communist conspiracy to weaken the American people by slow poison; and that President Harry S. Truman, President Dwight D. Eisenhower, and Chief Justice Earl Warren were communist agents.

Most Birchers concealed their membership, and the general public first became aware of the society's existence in January 1961, when Thomas M. Storke, veteran publisher of the *Santa Barbara News-Press,* exposed some of its activities in his newspaper. In 1962, Storke received a Pulitzer Prize for distinguished achievement in journalism "for calling public attention to the efforts of the semisecret John Birch Society to wage a campaign of hate and vilification." The *Los Angeles Times* published its own attack on the Birchers in March 1961. Nevertheless, the organization continued to grow in several parts of the country, and most of all in southern California. Wealthy businesspeople and retired military officers joined it in considerable numbers. Two Republican members of the House of Representatives from southern California avowed their membership in the Birch Society.

To Richard M. Nixon, who was planning to run for governor of California in 1962, the fantastic doctrines of Robert Welch and his followers were a serious embarrassment. Nixon felt that the Birch Society was "the monkey on the elephant's back" and that if he accepted its support, the result would be the best-financed but most disastrous campaign in the state's political history. Therefore he publicly repudiated the Birchers and stated that there was no place in the Republican party for anyone who charged that Dwight D. Eisenhower was a Communist. Nixon could hardly have done otherwise. He was indebted to Eisenhower for two terms as vice president and for the Republican presidential nomination in 1960. Nixon's attempt to dissociate himself from right-wing extremism cost him some of his right-wing support. Nixon then made a desperate effort to use his old issue of left-wing extremism against Governor Edmund G. Brown. But his campaign charge that Brown, a Roman Catholic, was "soft on communism" was absurdly unconvincing.

Another discreditable tactic backfired when Leone Baxter concocted a scheme, approved by Nixon and his campaign manager H. R. Haldeman, for a postcard poll pretending to come from an actually nonexistent group of Democrats and condemning the California Democratic Council as pro-Communist. Democratic leaders discovered and denounced this fraud, and 10 years later would recall it as a "warm-up for Watergate."

Throughout the 1962 campaign Nixon gave an irritating impression of arrogance and overconfidence that disenchanted many who had once voted for him. Many also disliked his apparent intention to serve only 2 years as governor and then use the office as a stepping-stone to the presidency in 1964. In the election on November 6, 1962, Brown defeated Nixon by nearly 300,000 votes. On the morning after the election, Nixon appeared at a press conference, unshaven and distraught, and delivered a rambling attack on the press, blaming his defeat on unfair reporting of his campaign. A few weeks later he announced that he would leave California to become a partner in a law firm in New York City.

The split between the moderates and the right-wing extremists continued to bedevil the Republicans in 1964. At the Republican national convention in San Francisco the large California delegation, headed by ex-Senator William F. Knowland, clinched the nomination for ultraconservative Senator Barry Goldwater of Arizona. It was widely reported that at least a hundred of Goldwater's delegates were Birchers. In an apparent reference to the Birch society, Goldwater included in his acceptance speech a statement that "extremism in the defense of liberty is no vice" and that "moderation in the pursuit of justice is not a virtue." His supporters at the convention cheered wildly, but the words had an opposite effect on millions of voters in the television audience. In the election in November, President Lyndon B. Johnson defeated Goldwater, both in California and in the nation, by the widest margins given to a presidential candidate since 1936.

Thus in 1964 the Democrats seemed firmly entrenched both in Washington and in Sacramento, but the political sands were soon to shift again. Lyndon Johnson was about to ruin his presidency with a disastrous war in Southeast Asia. And the screen and television actor Ronald Reagan had attracted considerable interest with a widely televised fund-raising address that was the highlight of the campaign for Goldwater.

SELECTED BIBLIOGRAPHY

Jackson K. Putnam, *Modern California Politics, 1917–1980* (1980), provides a useful overview of the gubernatorial administrations of the period. See also his interpretive article, "The Pattern of Modern California Politics," *Pacific Historical Review,* LXI (February 1992), pp. 23–52. Eugene C. Lee, *California Votes* (1963), gives a review and analysis of registration and voting from 1928 to 1962. William Buchanan, *Legislative Partisanship* (1963), includes a perceptive account of legislative politics from 1935 to 1960.

On the effects of cross-filing see Dean E. McHenry, "Cross Filing of Political Candidates in California," *Annals of the American Academy of Political and Social Science,* CCXLVIII (November 1946), pp. 226–231; Robert J. Pitchell, "The Electoral System and Voting Behavior: The Case of California's Cross-Filing," *Western Political Quarterly,* XII (June 1959), pp. 459–484; and Dean R. Cresap, *Party Politics in the Golden State* (1954).

The most detailed treatment of lobbying activities is Elmer R. Rusco, "Machine Politics, California Model: Arthur H. Samish and the Alcoholic Beverage Industry," Ph.D. thesis, University of California, Berkeley (1960). For the principal exposés, see Howard R. Philbrick, *Legislative Investigative Report* (1939), and Lester Velie, "The Secret Boss of California," *Collier's,* CXXIV (August 13 and 20, 1949). Arthur H. Samish and Bob Thomas, *The Secret Boss of California* (1971), present a lively memoir.

Important accounts of the rise of campaign management firms are Carey McWilliams, "Government by Whitaker and Baxter," *The Nation,* CLXXII (April 14 and 21 and May 5, 1951), and Robert J. Pitchell, "The Influence of Professional Campaign Management Firms in Partisan Elections in California," *Western Political Quarterly,* XI (June 1958), pp. 278–300. The rise of informal party organizations is described in Leonard C. Rowe, *Pre-primary Endorsements in California Politics* (1962); Markell C. Bear, *Story of the California Republican Assembly* (1955); Francis Carney, *The Rise of the Democratic Clubs in California* (1958); and James Q. Wilson, *The Amateur Democrat* (1962).

The career of Earl Warren is described in biographies by Irving Stone (1948), Luther A. Huston (1966), Leo Katcher (1967), John D. Weaver (1967), Bill Severn (1968), Richard B. Harvey (1969), Jack Harrison Pollack (1979), G. Edward White (1982), and Bernard Schwartz (1983). More specialized studies include Edward R. Long, "Earl Warren and the Politics of Anti-Communism," *Pacific Historical Review,* LI (February 1982), pp. 51–70. See also *The Memoirs of Earl Warren* (1977) and James J. Rawls, "The Earl Warren Oral History Project," *Pacific Historical Review,* LVI (February 1987), pp. 87–97.

On the loyalty issue in California, consult Larry Ceplair and Steven Englund, *The Inquisition in Hollywood* (1983); Jerold Simmons, "The Origin of the Campaign to Abolish HUAC," *Southern California Quarterly,* LXIV (Summer 1982), pp. 141–157; Edward L. Barrett, Jr., *The Tenney Committee* (1951); David P. Gardner, *The California Oath Controversy* (1967); George R. Stewart, *The Year of the Oath* (1950); and R. L. Pritchard, "California Un-American Activities Investigations," *California Historical Society Quarterly,* XLIX (December 1970), pp. 309–327. On Voorhis see his autobiography (1947) and Paul Bullock's biography (1978). Helen Gahagan Douglas is the subject of two articles in the *Southern California Quarterly:* Ingrid W. Scobie, LVIII (Spring 1976), and Colleen M. O'Connor, LXVII (Spring 1985). See also Scobie, *Center Stage: Helen Gahagan Douglas, A Life* (1992). The early career of Richard Nixon is covered in biographies by Earl Mazo (1960) and William Costello (1960). See also Richard M. Nixon, *Six Crises* (1962) and *RN: The Memoirs of Richard Nixon* (1978).

On the sweeping Democratic victory of 1958, see Kurt Schuparra, "Freedom vs. Tyranny," *Pacific Historical Review,* LXIII (November 1994), pp. 537–560, and Totton J. Anderson, "The 1958 Election in California," *Western Political Quarterly,* XII (March 1959), pp. 276–300. H. Brett Melendy and Benjamin F. Gilbert's *The Governors of California* includes a summary of Brown's governorship through 1964. See also Roger Rapoport, *California Dreaming: The Political Odyssey of Pat and Jerry Brown* (1982), and Gary G. Hamilton and Nicole W. Biggart, *Governor Reagan, Governor Brown* (1984). Thomas M. Storke describes his exposure of the Birch Society in *I Write for Freedom* (1963). On Brown's victory over Nixon, see Anderson and Eugene C. Lee, "The 1962 Election in California," *Western Political Quarterly,* XVI (June 1963), pp. 396–420.

CHAPTER THIRTY

Industrialized Agriculture and Disorganized Labor

The evolution of modern agriculture in California is a story of great complexity, marked by occasional moments of high drama. Through the middle of the twentieth century, agriculture remained California's largest single industry. The value of the state's farm products exceeded the value of the output of any branch of manufacturing in the state—or rather of any *other* branch of "manufacturing." California farms themselves, in the words of Carey McWilliams, had long been "factories in the field."

The structure of agriculture in the state was not only extraordinarily complex in itself; it was also closely interrelated with other industries, especially the canning, packing, processing, transportation, and marketing of food and kindred products.

GREEN GOLD

Among the states, California had ranked first in farm income since the 1930s, and its lead was steadily widening. Several of its climates permitted year-round growing and favored the production of fruit and truck crops for luxury markets at seasons when other states could offer little or no competition. California's unmatched level of farm capitalization permitted the greatest use of scientific techniques and resulted in the nation's highest level of farm productivity.

California's agriculture was not only the most prosperous in the country, but far and away the most diversified. Because of the variety of its soils and climates it had 118 different types of farms, according to the United States census classification, whereas Pennsylvania, which ranked second in this respect had only 25 types. Thanks in part to the genius of Luther Burbank of Santa Rosa, nearly 300 different agricultural commodities were produced in California, including all of the nation's commercial supply of almonds, artichokes, figs, nectarines, and olives; a third of the nation's fruit, including most of the apricots, grapes, pears, plums, and prunes; and more than a fourth of the nation's vegetables, including most of the asparagus, broccoli, carrots, celery, and lettuce.

Although California agriculture as a whole was remarkably diversified, the great majority of the farms were extremely specialized. Specialization even within a crop was common. For example, many farms produced peaches exclusively for canning or for drying, and many produced grapes only for the table or for raisins or for wine.

THE EMPIRE OF AGRIBUSINESS

Throughout the twentieth century successful farming in California was becoming a business organized in larger and larger units. This process of consolidation was occurring not only through "horizontal integration," or the merging of farm units into larger ones, but also through the still more revolutionary process of "vertical integration," in which a large company operated at every level from the field to the supermarket. The men who had pioneered in the formation of these vertically integrated agricultural corporations were two Italian immigrants, Mark J. Fontana and Joseph Di Giorgio.

Fontana had created the California Fruit Canner's Association in 1899 and in 1916 had been instrumental in merging four large packing concerns into the California Packing Corporation (CalPac), which became the world's largest canner of fruits and vegetables. CalPac was the grower as well as the packer of many of the goods that were sold under its Del Monte label. Joseph Di Giorgio had become a large grower in the southern San Joaquin Valley early in the century and had bought the marketing and shipping interests of the Earl Fruit Company in 1910. The canned goods produced by the Di Giorgio Corporation were known to consumers through its S&W label.

Another integrated "farmer" was Schenley Industries, which raised many of the grapes that went into its wines. Hunt Foods and Industries, headed by Norton Simon, did not operate as a grower but was important as the world's largest processor and distributor of tomato products and as a major producer of salad and cooking oils.

The backing of such large aggregations of capital facilitated the constant development of new technological advances in all of the complex operations of agribusiness. An indispensable ally in this process was the University of California's college of agriculture, an outgrowth of the Morrill Land Grant College Act, adopted a century earlier for the purpose of aiding the country's millions of small farmers. The federal and state funds that supported the college's tremendously successful research program were augmented by the funds of the Giannini Foundation of Agricultural Economics. A. P. Giannini, founder of the Bank of America, was also a regent of the university. His son, Lawrence Mario Giannini, succeeded him both as a regent and as head of the bank.

The impact of science and technology on California agriculture was astounding. In 1961 university agricultural engineers devised a mechanical tomato picker so efficient and gentle that when they ran a fresh egg through it, the egg was deposited in the box uncracked. Soon afterward they developed a mechanical thumb that could press down on the top of each head of lettuce, decide electronically whether

Cotton harvesting in San Joaquin Valley. The plants had been defoliated by aerial spraying. *(Courtesy of Agricultural Publications, University of California, Berkeley.)*

it was ready to be picked, and signal another part of the machine to pick it. Nine-tenths of California's cotton was being picked by machinery before the rate reached one-tenth in the southern states. Agricultural scientists developed mechanical tree shakers for fruits and nuts. For the more delicate fruits there were machines that could lift a human picker into the branches of the tree and swing him or her rapidly among them.

A major factor encouraging the further advance of a mechanized, highly capitalized agriculture, concentrated in high-income-per-acre crops, was the growth of the income of the average American family. With this increase came ever-greater demand for fruits, vegetables, dairy products, poultry, and eggs—all California specialties.

"FARM FASCISM" IN THE 1930s

California growers had discovered very early that the cost of labor was the only cost of production that they could usually keep down, and they had kept it down, with all the economic and political power at their command.

Since the early American period farmland values in California had been capitalized on the basis of the availability of cheap, unorganized migratory labor, much of it alien and nonwhite—Chinese, then Japanese, and later Mexican and Filipino. Thus the historic cheap-labor surplus, by helping to keep land prices high and farm mortgages heavy, had kept the small farmers' return on their own labor to a low level, while at the same time it had maintained the profits of the large farms that employed the bulk of the hired workers.

In 1933 and 1934, when the Communist party organized a series of agricultural strikes and made a determined effort to unionize migratory farm labor, the forces of agribusiness launched an all-out countercampaign through a new organization called the Associated Farmers of California. The funds for its support came largely from the California Packing Corporation; the Southern Pacific Railroad; the Industrial Association of San Francisco; Southern Californians, Inc., a group of industrial employers; the Holly Sugar Corporation; and the Spreckels Investment Company. The Pacific Gas and Electric Company also made common cause with the large growers because their needs for power to pump irrigation water made them some of its best customers. Most of these big-business concerns tried to keep their contributions to the Associated Farmers confidential in order to maintain the image of a "farmers' organization."

Throughout the state, units of the Associated Farmers worked in intimate cooperation with local law enforcement officials. Most county sheriffs were allied with agribusiness interests. In some counties, migratory workers could not be employed unless they were registered with the sheriff's office, and the Associated Farmers provided the sheriff with lists of "agitators" and "dangerous radicals," including all persons known to have been members of unions. Such people not only were denied employment but were often ordered out of the county.

When a strike threatened, growers or their managerial employees were often made special deputies, though they did not always wait for this legal authorization and often acted simply as armed vigilantes. In the strike of the AFL lettuce packers' union at Salinas in 1936, agribusiness groups recruited a "general staff" which supplanted the sheriff and the chief of police. Colonel Henry Sanborn, an Army Reserve officer and publisher of an anticommunist journal, was employed as "coordinator" of all antistrike forces, including the local law enforcement officers as well as a "citizens' army" armed with shotguns and pick handles. The chief of the state highway patrol and a representative of the state attorney general's office gave their approval to this arrangement.

The Associated Farmers also aided in many prosecutions not only of Communists but of almost any other agricultural strike leaders under the state criminal syndicalism law.

Among the justifications used by the embattled "farmers" in their extreme resistance to any form of labor unionism were two arguments that had some color of validity during the darkest years of the great depression in 1933 and 1934. At that time it was often true that growers could not have paid higher wages without raising the cost of production above the prices that the crops could be sold for; it was also true that the main attempts to organize migratory farm laborers were then in the hands of the Communist party. But agribusiness interests continued to repeat these arguments in later years when prices and profits had risen greatly and when radical influence was no longer substantially involved.

In the middle and later years of the 1930s, dispossessed families from the Dust Bowl region came into California at the rate of more than 100,000 persons a year, most of them to swell the supply of migratory farm labor. People of Anglo-American stock, working in family groups, now made up the bulk of the state's migratory labor force for the first time, and as a result, the public interest in the plight of farm laborers increased somewhat, though only temporarily. Carey McWilliams's *Factories in the Field* and John Steinbeck's *The Grapes of Wrath,* both published in 1939, helped to stimulate this interest. McWilliams's book included a chapter on the activities of the Associated Farmers and their allies entitled "The Rise of Farm Fascism."

distille agri business

In the administration of Gov. Culbert L. Olson, McWilliams was chief of the state division of immigration and housing, and in that capacity he made himself a thorn in the flesh of agribusiness by inspecting private farm-labor camps and denouncing their vile conditions. The annual convention of the Associated Farmers passed a resolution describing McWilliams as "California's Agricultural Pest Number One, outranking pear blight and the boll weevil." The state legislature, under agribusiness influence, passed a bill to abolish McWilliams's position, but Governor Olson pocket-vetoed this proposed "anti-McWilliams act."

In 1939 and 1940 the La Follette committee, a subcommittee of the United States Senate Committee on Education and Labor under the chairmanship of Sen. Robert M. La Follette, Jr., of Wisconsin, held extensive hearings in California to investigate "violations of free speech and rights of labor." But most of its recommendations for reform, introduced in 1942, produced no action in Congress. With the coming of World War II the "Okies" flocked to the shipyards; Mexicans and Mexican Americans again became the majority of the California farm labor force; and the public lost what interest it had had in the whole matter.

THE RISE AND FALL OF THE BRACERO PROGRAM

The demands of World War II produced a sudden, genuine, and desperate shortage of farm labor. A partial solution to the problem was provided by the use of German prisoners of war as farm laborers. Recent research by historian Bonnie Trask has found that more than 15,000 German prisoners were working in California cotton fields in 1945. President Truman halted the program the following year when all prisoners of war were repatriated.

Far more numerous were the wartime workers imported from Mexico. In 1942, under an act of Congress and an agreement with Mexico, the United States Department of Agriculture assumed the responsibility for recruiting, contracting, transporting, housing, and feeding these temporary immigrant farm workers. In a formal sense, this was the beginning of the "bracero program." The meaning of the Spanish word *braceros* ("the strong-armed ones") bore a striking resemblance to the meaning of the Tamil word *kuli*.

There had been an informal bracero program 25 years earlier during World War I, when private labor contractors had supplied California growers with seasonal workers from Mexico. Thousands of peons had been eager for the opportunity; the Mexican Revolution had turned many of them into displaced persons, much as the Taiping Rebellion had nudged thousands of destitute Chinese toward California in the 1850s.

The growers were able to persuade Congress not to include Mexico in the postwar quota system of immigration restrictions, and the surge of Mexicans into California had continued through the 1920s, but it had slowed in the depression years, and the Mexican government had then found itself forced to pay the costs of repatriating many of its impoverished nationals who could no longer obtain work in California and who were not eligible for relief there. In 1942 the Mexican government feared that this experience would be repeated, and it therefore demanded that the United States government, rather than private labor contractors, must take responsibility for the immigrant workers.

After World War II the bracero program continued in force with the enthusiastic support of California growers, though President Truman, to their irritation, removed the program from the grower-oriented Department of Agriculture and assigned it to the Department of Labor by executive order in 1948.

More numerous than the braceros in the years after the end of World War II were the illegal "undocumented workers." Although their exact numbers could not be known, it was estimated that more than half a million of these illegal immigrants crossed and recrossed the international boundary each year, most of them to work in the fields of California and other states in the southwest.

In 1951 Congress adopted the famous Public Law 78 and also gave special legislative recognition to a new agreement with Mexico. Together these measures provided the most elaborate plan of importing contract workers in which the United States had ever engaged, and although the plan was approved as a "Korean war emergency" measure, it ultimately provided the basis for continuing the bracero program until 1964, 11 years after the Korean war had ended.

Under this system, Mexican officials assembled the braceros, and the United States Department of Labor provided for their transportation to reception centers north of the border. There they were turned over to labor contractors representing the growers' associations. At the insistence of the Mexican government, there were standard contracts covering wages, hours, transportation, housing, and working conditions. The American government guaranteed the provision of emergency medical care, workers' compensation, disability and death benefits, and burial expenses. Though such provisions were minimal, they were far superior to the benefits available to American farm laborers, who enjoyed no legal protection at all.

In 1957, the peak year, California imported 192,438 braceros. In 1960 about 100,000 of them were at work in the state at the peak season in early September, and they formed about a quarter of the seasonal farm labor force. Most of them worked on the larger farms; about 5.2 percent of the farms in California employed 60 percent of the total number of seasonal hired workers—including more than 80 percent of the braceros.

As Congress continued to grant extensions of the program, it became increasingly hard to disguise the fact that the bracero system perpetuated the tragic poverty of the American migratory laborers. It depressed wages, destroyed the bargaining power of the domestic worker, and drove away local labor. There were many incidents in which braceros were used as strikebreakers with the connivance of government officials. Ostensibly, P.L. 78 allowed the importation of braceros only when it would "not adversely affect the wages and working conditions of domestic agricultural workers," when "sufficient domestic workers . . . [were] not available," and when "reasonable efforts [had] been made to attract domestic workers at wages . . . comparable to those offered foreign workers." This last provision would have tended to freeze farm wages at the wretched levels of the early 1950s, even if the rest of the provisions of P.L. 78 had been effectively was to represent all field-workers in future contracts with the growers, leaving all cannery workers and some truck drivers to the Teamsters.

"THE EQUAL PROTECTION OF THE LAWS"

Until 1966 agricultural labor was specifically excluded from the provisions of virtually every federal and state law that protected the rights of other workers. Minimum wages, unemployment insurance, social security, collective bargaining—all were guaranteed to others and specifically denied to farm labor. The rationalization for this was always that "farmers had special problems." The truth was that they had special political power. Agricultural employers were heavily overrepresented in Congress and in almost every state legislature, whereas the interests of farm workers were almost totally unrepresented until the 1960s.

The ending of the bracero program had been an important preliminary to reform, but only a negative one. At long last, in 1964, Congress made its first positive moves toward correcting a shameful set of conditions. The Economic Opportunity Act of 1964 included grants to agencies aiding migrant workers, and an amendment to the National Housing Act provided direct loans for construction of farm-labor housing. In September 1966, Congress took the historic step of extending the protection of a new federal minimum wage law to farm workers. This was only a token beginning. Whereas the minimum wage for most other workers was raised to $1.60 an hour, effective in 1968, the national minimum for farm labor was set at only $1, and not even this would apply to small employers.

These new federal laws were merely an entering wedge. More subsidies to help provide decent housing for migrant workers were essential in order to eradicate the rural slums that were far worse than anything in the cities. For migrant workers and their families the conditions of recruitment, transportation, health, sanitation, workers' compensation, child labor, education, and civil and political rights were disgracefully and incredibly substandard.

Of central importance was the right of collective bargaining and the guarantee of this right through extension to agriculture of laws governing union representation elections. At the federal level, attempts to extend the provisions of the National Labor Relations Act (NLRA) to farm workers remained deadlocked, partly because Chávez did not wish to give up the weapon of the secondary boycott, which was illegal for workers covered by the NLRA.

But in California the replacement of Gov. Ronald Reagan by Edmund G. Brown, Jr., made possible a landmark law providing for state-supervised secret-ballot elections in which California's 250,000 farm workers could pick a union to represent them, or reject unionization. Brown personally hammered out the compromise that was adopted in May 1975. The new law created a state Agricultural Labor Relations Board (ALRB) with quasi-judicial powers to oversee elections. The act allowed harvest-time strikes and permitted secondary boycotts in some limited circumstances.

In subsequent years, the makeup of the ALRB would become a matter of great controversy and remain subject to changes in the state's political leadership.

Nevertheless, it was clear that the passage of the new federal and state labor laws marked the beginning of a new era for California's agricultural workers.

SELECTED BIBLIOGRAPHY

Two works that analyze the rise of California agribusiness are Donald J. Pisani, *From the Family Farm to Agribusiness* (1984), which views the 1920s as the critical decade of transformation, and Theodore Saloutos, *The American Farm and the New Deal* (1982), which follows the story through the 1930s. On the role of public policy, see Dennis Nodín Valdés, "Machine Politics in California Agriculture," *Pacific Historical Review*, LXIII (May 1994), pp. 203–224; Ellen Liebman, *California Farmland* (1983); and Lawrence J. Jelinek, *Harvest Empire* (1979). Also useful are James H. Shideler (ed.), *Agriculture in the Development of the Far West* (1975), and Richard J. Orsi (comp.), *A List of References for the History of Agriculture in California* (1974).

Major works on the history of California's peculiar farm-labor problems are Cletus E. Daniel, *Bitter Harvest* (1981); Ernesto Galarza, *Farm Workers and Agri-Business in California* (1977); Varden Fuller, *Labor Relations in Agriculture* (1955); Lloyd S. Fisher, *The Harvest Labor Market in California* (1953); and Carey McWilliams, *Ill Fares the Land* (1942) and *Factories in the Field* (1939).

James N. Gregory has written the definitive study of migration to California during the great depression in *American Exodus: The Dust Bowl Migration and Okie Culture in California* (1989). See also Dorothea Lange and Paul S. Taylor, *An American Exodus* (1939), and Walter J. Stein, *California and the Dust Bowl Migration* (1973).

Bonnie Trask has illuminated an often overlooked part of the story. See her "German Prisoners of War in California Agriculture, 1943–1946," M.A. thesis (1971), and (with Mary Graham) "Agitation in the Fields," in Charles Clough (ed.), *Fresno County in the Twentieth Century* (1986).

On the use of Mexican and other immigrant labor, see Gilbert G. Gonzalez, *Labor and Community* (1992); Vicki Ruiz, *Cannery Women, Cannery Lives* (1987); George C. Kiser and Martha Woody Kiser, *Mexican Workers in the United States* (1979); Peter N. Kirstein, *Anglo over Bracero* (1977); Mark Reisler, *By the Sweat of Their Brow* (1976); Paul S. Taylor, *Mexican Labor in the United States* (1928); Charles Wollenberg, "*Huelga,* 1928 Style: The Imperial Valley Cantaloupe Workers' Strike," *Pacific Historical Review,* XXXVIII (February 1969), pp. 45–58; James F. Rooney, "The Effects of Imported Mexican Farm Labor in a California County," *American Journal of Economics and Sociology,* XX (October 1961), pp. 513–521; Leo Grebler, *Mexican Immigration to the United States* (1966); and R. K. Das, *Hindustani Workers on the Pacific Coast* (1923). On the Filipino farm laborers, see Craig Scharlin and Lilia V. Villanueva, *Philip Vera Cruz* (1992); Lorraine Jacobs Crouchett, *Filipinos in California* (1982); and Bruno Lasker, *Filipino Immigration to the United States* (1931).

Important studies of the bracero program are Henry P. Anderson, *The Bracero Program in California* (1976); Ernesto Galarza, *Merchants of Labor* (1964); Otey M. Scruggs, "The Evolution of the Mexican Farm Labor Agreement of 1942," *Agricultural History,* XXXIV (July 1960), pp. 140–149; Ellis W. Hawley, "The Politics of the Mexican Labor Issue, 1950–1965," ibid., XL (July 1966), pp. 157–176; N. Ray Gilmore and Gladys Gilmore, "The Bracero in California," *Pacific Historical Review,* XXXII (August 1963), pp. 265–282; and Truman E. Moore, *The Slaves We Rent* (1965).

On the movement led by César Chávez, see Richard Griswold del Castillo and Richard A. García, *César Chávez* (1995); García, "Dolores Huerta," *California History,* LXXII (Spring 1993), pp. 56–72; Peter Matthiessen, *Sal Si Puedes,* (1969); John G. Dunne, *Delano* (1971); Joan London and Henry Anderson, *So Shall Ye Reap* (1970); Ronald B. Taylor, *Chávez and the Farm Workers* (1975); and J. Craig Jenkins, *The Politics of Insurgency* (1985). Linda and Theodore Majka, *Farm Workers, Agribusiness, and the State* (1982), include a legislative history of the ALRB; while Rex L. Cottle et al., *Labor and Property Rights in California Agriculture* (1982), offers a highly critical view of the board.

CHAPTER THIRTY-ONE

Diversity and Conflict

One of the most deplorable aspects of the history of California has been the persistence of discrimination directed against the state's diverse ethnic and racial groups. During the twentieth century, progress was made in overcoming the burden of past discrimination, but the legacy of hostility and conflict remained.

CALIFORNIA INDIANS

All the nonwhite minorities in American California suffered from various kinds of unjust discrimination, but the mistreatment of the Indians began earliest and was by far the worst. In California, as in other parts of the United States, the history of American treatment of the Indians in the nineteenth century was too often a sickening record of racist murder and sanctimonious fraud.

The problems of the Indians in California were different from those of most other American Indian tribes in that only a minority of the California Indians were ever placed on reservations. The treaties of the early 1850s, providing for large reservations in California, were never ratified, and most of the attempts to provide small reservations were unsuccessful. The California Indians were left to survive as best they might on the fringes of white settlement; most of them did not survive. Of those who did, the majority became agricultural laborers.

Several idealistic individuals tried to improve the situation. In the early 1880s the New England author Helen Hunt Jackson sent copies of her critique of American Indian policy, *A Century of Dishonor* (1881), to all members of Congress. At Jackson's request Congress then made her a member of a special commission to report on the Indians of southern California. Although the commission's report had little effect on federal policy, Jackson's research for it aided the writing of *Ramona* (1884), a novel she intended to be the *Uncle Tom's Cabin* of Indian reform. *Ramona* powerfully portrayed the destitution of the homeless Indians of southern California and also, quite unintentionally, created a collection of regional myths that stimulated the tourist trade.

In 1901 Charles F. Lummis organized the Sequoya League with the aid of Thomas R. Bard, David Starr Jordan, and others. Its main object was better treatment of the Indians, and its main accomplishment was an act of Congress that provided money to purchase a tract of land near Pala for the Cupeño Indians who were evicted from Warner's Ranch in San Diego County.

During World War I, a number of Indians served in the armed forces, and in 1924, partly in recognition of that service, Congress gave American Indians the rights of citizenship in the United States and in the states of their residence. Congress also recognized that an injustice had been done to the California Indians, in particular, by the failure to ratify the reservation treaties of the early 1850s, which had promised them more than 7 million acres of land. In 1928 Congress authorized the attorney general of California to bring suit against the United States on behalf of the California Indians to determine what financial compensation should be made to them. A special census provided by the act of 1928 enumerated 23,585 persons as living descendants of California Indians, and thus entitled to compensation. But the case dragged on until 1944, and when the federal court of claims finally made its award, it was only for a little more than $5 million, or about $200 per person.

In the special case of the survivors of the Cahuilla tribe, also known as the Palm Springs Indians, the results of litigation were startlingly different. In the 1870s the federal government had granted the odd-numbered sections of desert land in the Palm Springs area to the Southern Pacific Railroad and the even-numbered sections, checkerboard-fashion, to the Cahuilla Indians. When Palm Springs became a booming resort town in the 1920s, the surviving Cahuilla, numbering about 100, tried to persuade the federal government to permit the leasing of some of their lands to the eager hotel promoters, but the government refused. Lee Arenas, one of the Cahuilla, managed to interest a former justice of the California Supreme Court, John W. Preston, in taking the case to the Supreme Court of the United States. In 1944 the Court ruled that each of the Cahuilla should receive the rental from $350,000 worth of individually allotted tribal land, as well as a share of the income from 30,000 acres of communal tribal land.

The contrast between the ridiculously inadequate award by the federal court of claims to the California Indians in 1944 and the lucrative award by the Supreme Court to the Palm Springs Indians in the same year was so striking that it helped persuade Congress to pass the Indian Claims Commission Act of 1946. This law entitled American Indians to payments from the federal government equivalent to the original value of the lands their ancestors had once occupied. The determination of the amounts was a fantastically complex matter, but in 1965, after many years of hearings, the descendants of the California Indians finally received and voted to accept an award of a little more than $29 million. This was about 45 cents an acre for 64 million acres of land, nearly two-thirds the total area of California.

The long and tragic decline in Indian population was reversed in the twentieth century, and the number of persons of Indian ancestry in the state began to rise steadily. The growth in population was due to natural increase and to migration to California of Indians from other states, who were aided by job training and relocation programs of the federal government. In 1965 the number of Indians living in California had risen to 75,000, less than 10 percent of whom were living on the 82 federal reservations. Only three reservations, at Hoopa Valley, Fort Yuma, and Bishop, had more than 500 residents, and only 18 reservations had more than 100. During the 1970s the Indian population in the state more than doubled, and in 1990 the Census Bureau reported that California, with more than 242,000 Indians, had the second largest Indian population of any state in the nation.

Throughout the twentieth century, both the United States and the state of California demonstrated awakenings of conscience in their treatment of Indian people. California abolished all legal distinctions between persons of Indian ancestry and other citizens and led the states in making Indians fully eligible to receive the benefits of the public schools, welfare assistance, old-age and survivors payments, and other public services. In spite of these gains, the Indians of California remained the state's most economically depressed minority group. The rate of unemployment among California Indians was more than three times as high as the rate for whites and somewhat above the rate for blacks. The California State Advisory Commission on Indian Affairs reported in 1966 that the median annual income for reservation Indians was $2268 per family. More than 40 percent of all rural and reservation Indians in the state had not gone beyond the eighth grade, and the school dropout rate for Indians was three times that of the general population.

During the 1960s California Indians increased their level of political involvement and established several pantribal organizations. The American Indian Historical Society, organized in 1964 by Cahuilla tribal chair Rupert Costo, established an active publication program and called for the revision of textbooks which contained negative stereotypes of Indians. In 1967, concern over the inadequacy of primary and secondary education for Indian youth led to the formation of the California Indian Education Association, and on many college campuses Native American Studies departments were formed.

The occupation of Alcatraz Island in San Francisco Bay by a group called Indians of All Tribes in 1969 to 1971 ushered in a period of increased activism among California Indians. In northeastern California, members of the Achumawi tribe engaged in sit-ins and took legal action to regain forest lands acquired by the Pacific Gas and Electric Company. In the northwestern part of the state, Yurok Indian fishermen clashed with law enforcement officers over fishing rights along the Klamath River. In 1978 and 1979 Indians in the Santa Barbara area occupied the site of a proposed supertanker terminal to protest the destruction of what they regarded as sacred land.

In recent years, California Indians also have demonstrated a growing interest in the preservation and revival of their native cultures. This resurgence of interest has produced some remarkable results. In 1974 the Cupeño, whose plight had spurred the Sequoya League to action in 1901, dedicated the Cupa Cultural Center at the Pala reservation and offered classes in Cupeño language, culture, and history. In neighboring Riverside County the Cahuilla founded the Malki Museum, offering native language classes and establishing a repository for Cahuilla artifacts and ethnographic information.

An important factor in turning the tide of public feeling in favor of the Japanese Americans was that they reacted to mistreatment in an extraordinary way—by establishing an unrivaled record of good citizenship. They ranked higher in education and lower in crime and juvenile delinquency than any other ethnic group in the United States, including the native whites. In 1960 they averaged 12 years of schooling, as against 11 for whites and 8.6 for blacks. By the 1970s the difference in educational attainment among the three groups had narrowed considerably, but the Japanese Americans retained a slight edge over the others. In impressive numbers they obtained advanced degrees and jobs in such professional fields as business administration, engineering, and optometry; by 1970 their median family income was $3000 higher than the national median. Their record of physical and mental health was almost incredible. The average longevity of Japanese Americans was 74.5 years for men and 81.2 years for women—nearly 7 years above the figures for California whites and well above the record of any other group in human history. Three Japanese traditions, the strength of the family, the belief in the value of education, and the belief in the virtue of hard work, did most to account for this unparalleled triumph over adversity.

The decline of anti-Japanese sentiment after World War II was foreshadowed during the war years by the federal government's removal of legal discrimination against the Chinese. Congress repealed the Chinese Exclusion Act in 1943 in order, as President Roosevelt put it, to "correct a historic mistake and silence the distorted Japanese propaganda." The results were more important in principle, however, than in practice. Although China was now permitted to have an immigration quota, it was so low that only about 10,000 Chinese were admitted under it in the next 20 years. In 1965, however, Congress abolished the national-origins quota system. Under the new law, total annual immigration remained about the same, but admission was on the basis of skills or family relationships. This permitted a substantial increase in Chinese immigration, much of it from Hong Kong to California.

Chinese Americans in the postwar period established a high rate of achievement grounded in traditional values similar to those underlying the success of the Japanese Americans. By the 1970s their average length of school attendance, for instance, surpassed that of whites but did not quite equal the record of the Japanese. For the Chinese Americans the educational picture was one of extremes: a very high proportion of them had gone to college, but also many had not gone beyond the eighth grade. The wartime shortages of engineers, scientists, doctors, and nurses opened thousands of professional jobs to educated Chinese Americans; this began to occur before the end of World War II, rather than after it, as in the case of the Japanese.

As with other minorities, Chinese and Japanese Americans in recent years also have increased their political activity. In 1974, March Fong Eu was elected secretary of state, becoming the first person of Asian ancestry to hold statewide office in California. She easily won reelection in four subsequent campaigns. In San Francisco, where Asian Americans made up nearly one-fourth the city's population, five Chinese Americans held elective office by 1980, whereas a decade earlier there had been none. Only about 6 percent of the population of Los Angeles was of Asian ancestry, and in 1985 Michael Woo became the first Asian American ever elected to the city council.

S. I. Hayakawa, the controversial president of San Francisco State University, became in 1976 the first Californian of Japanese ancestry to be elected to the United States Senate. He was defeated for reelection in 1982. In the 1980s Japanese Americans were elected to a host of local offices throughout the state, and Robert Matsui of Sacramento and Norman Mineta of Santa Clara were elected to the House of Representatives.

Filipino Americans in the years after World War II became one of the fastest-growing minority groups in the state. During the early decades of the twentieth century most Filipinos drawn to California were farm laborers, but under the 1965 immigration law the majority of Filipino immigrants were accountants, nurses, and other skilled professionals. By 1980 Filipino Americans were the largest Asian group in California and were expected to outnumber second-place Chinese Americans by almost two to one in the middle of the next century. A similar upsurge was also seen in the number of Korean Americans, especially in southern California. By 1980 there were some 200,000 Koreans in the Los Angeles area alone, a 500 percent increase since 1976.

Following the American withdrawal from Vietnam in the early 1970s, the escalating turmoil in southeast Asia led to a mass exodus of refugees. In desperation tens of thousands of Vietnamese, Laotians, and Cambodians fled to the sea, and eventually many of these "boat people" were resettled in the United States. California received about 40 percent of the nation's total Indo-Chinese refugee population, and state officials petitioned the federal government for additional aid in handling the influx. By the mid-1980s an estimated 200,000 refugees were in the state, the majority of whom were on public welfare. Volunteer agencies, including many church-related organizations, assisted in the resettlement effort by sponsoring individual refugee families.

AFRICAN AMERICANS

Of all the racial minorities, African Americans attracted the largest share of public attention in the decades after the end of World War II. They became more active than other groups in openly protesting against racial discrimination, and their protests, both peaceful and violent, received wide coverage in the national news media.

African Americans formed about 11 percent of the total population of the United States in 1940. Their major migration to California began in 1942 with the sudden demand for labor in the shipyards and other war industries, and thereafter the percentage of blacks in the state's population, which had been only 1.8 in 1940, rose to 4.3 in 1950 and 7.7 in 1980. But their presence was even more apparent because most of them became concentrated in all-black neighborhoods in the cities of Los Angeles, San Francisco, Oakland, Berkeley, and Richmond.

In the long struggle for equality, African Americans had to overcome major obstacles in three closely related areas: housing, employment, and education.

segregation, where it could be shown that a school district had deliberately segregated its schools in the past. The state court, however, ruled that busing was also a proper remedy for *de facto* or unintentional segregation, where segregated schools were the result of established residential patterns.

The greatest threat to the success of school desegregation in Los Angeles, as in cities around the country, was the decline of white enrollment. In the first year of court-ordered busing one-third of the white students assigned to new schools under the desegregation plan left the Los Angeles school district. Although the rate of "white flight" slowed the following year, the proportion of white students in the district declined from 56 percent in 1966 to 24 percent by 1980. The decline of white enrollment was part of a nationwide population shift from the central cities to the suburbs, a movement caused only partly by the controversy over deseg-regation. Nevertheless, the prospects for effective desegregation were considerably dimmed by the abandonment of the city schools by white students. As one school integration specialist commented, "There are simply not enough white children to go around."

At least as important as the political and social resistance to black penetration of white neighborhoods and schools was the economic discrimination that kept African Americans in menial jobs, or kept them from getting any jobs at all. In California, as in most other states, nearly all labor unions in fields involving skilled workers had excluded blacks entirely until World War II. As the number of blacks in the California workforce increased dramatically during the war, many unions established all-black "auxiliaries." Black workers in the auxiliaries were required to pay full union dues but were barred from voting in union elections and received unequal union benefits. In January 1945 the California Supreme Court ruled, in *James v. Marinship,* that the auxiliary practice was "contrary to public policy." This ruling produced important changes in union membership practices, but few blacks actually benefited from the decision. As the war ended, the number of blacks in the skilled workforce began to decline rapidly. In San Francisco, 75 percent of black heads of households had been skilled industrial workers during the war; by 1948, only 25 percent still held skilled jobs, and the black unemployment rate was nearly three times that for all other persons.

Thirty years after the end of World War II the unemployment rate for African Americans in the state was about twice that for the general population, and un-employment among black youths averaged nearly 40 percent. Almost a quarter of all black families in California lived in poverty in 1975, compared with less than 8 percent of whites. By 1980 the income of the typical black family was still less than 60 percent that of the average white family.

In spite of such continuing problems, a substantial black middle class was also emerging in the state. California in the 1980s led the nation in the number of busi-nesses owned by black entrepreneurs. For every 1000 blacks in the state, there were 25 black-owned firms, almost double the national average. By 1985 California had more than 44,000 black-owned businesses, with a total payroll of $217 million.

The number of blacks elected to political office also increased steadily in recent years. Wilson Riles in 1970 was elected superintendent of public instruction over the archconservative Max Rafferty, becoming the first African American to win statewide office. Three years later former police officer and city councilman Thomas Bradley was elected mayor of Los Angeles, receiving the largest white vote for a black candidate in any American city. Also, by 1973 California had three black representatives in Congress, Yvonne Brathwaite Burke, Ronald V. Dellums, and Augustus Hawkins, and the following year black state senator Mervyn Dymally was elected lieutenant governor. In 1978 Dymally failed to win reelection, and Burke was defeated in the race for attorney general by veteran Republican state senator George Deukmejian. Dymally and Maxine Waters of Los Angeles later joined Ron Dellums as members of California's congressional delegation. By 1992 two black senators and six black assembly members, including Assembly Speaker Willie L. Brown, Jr., of San Francisco, were serving in the state legislature. Probably the most popular black official holding partisan office was Los Angeles Mayor Bradley. He served an unprecedented five terms as chief executive of the state's largest city, and in both 1982 and 1986 he won the Democratic nomination for governor.

LATINOS

By far the largest ethnic minority in California in recent years has been the group that the census listed as of "Spanish origin," most of whom, in California, were Mexican Americans.

In 1910, the census had enumerated only 51,000 persons of Mexican ancestry in California, but the Mexican revolution of 1910–1920 combined with World War I to begin a long process of mass immigration from Mexico to the American southwest. By 1945, only Mexico City had a larger Mexican population than Los Angeles. The result, however, was what George I. Sánchez has called "cultural indigestion." Most of the immigrants were laborers. Barriers of prejudice and of language blocked their economic advancement and their social assimilation. In Los Angeles, they were concentrated in the eastern part of the city almost to the degree that blacks were concentrated in the southern part of it. World War II brought some limited progress. Paradoxically, some of this resulted from uneasy afterthoughts about two flagrant wartime episodes of Anglo-American bigotry—the "Sleepy Lagoon" murder trial and the "zoot suit" riots.

On August 2, 1942, on the east side of Los Angeles, the body of a Mexican American boy with a fractured skull was found beside a germ-infested old reservoir used as a swimming hole, which the newspapers dubbed the "Sleepy Lagoon." There had been some scuffling the night before between two juvenile gangs, but there was no direct evidence of murder, and no witness. Nevertheless, 300 young Latinos were arrested, 23 indicted, and 17 convicted. The defendants were brutally treated while in jail, and racial prejudice was apparent throughout the proceedings. In a pseudoscientific report to the grand jury, a police lieutenant explained violent crime by Mexicans as a racial characteristic, and the chief of police and the sheriff endorsed the report. The bias in the trial was so blatant and so clearly symptomatic of a larger social injustice that it ultimately led to some improvement in public attitudes. This came in part from the work of a defense committee headed by Carey McWilliams and in part from the verdict of the appellate court, which threw out all the convictions and strongly rebuked the trial judge.

During this period, some young Latinos were wearing the "zoot suit," originally as the proper costume for jitterbug dancing but later to attract attention, to show their emancipation from their elders, and to express their group solidarity. Much of the public believed that not only all zoot-suiters but virtually all young Latinos were *pachucos,* or juvenile hoodlums. On June 3, 1943, mobs of white sailors, soldiers, and civilians in downtown Los Angeles began to beat up zoot-suiters and tear off their clothes, and these race riots continued for 6 days until the Navy declared Los Angeles off limits.

The war and postwar periods brought a degree of occupational and geographical mobility that considerably weakened barriers against intermarriage, equality of employment, and housing opportunities. Mexican Americans were not segregated in the armed forces, and many acquired a new experience of integrated living. They volunteered in greater numbers and won more Congressional Medals of Honor, proportionately, than any other ethnic group. After the war, many improved their status by education under the "G.I. bill."

By the 1960s, Mexican Americans in California were more heterogeneous and much more urbanized than was commonly supposed. More than 85 percent of them lived in cities; less than 15 percent of those employed were agricultural laborers. During the 1960s many younger Mexican Americans joined a militant new crusade in search of ethnic identity. Reviving the belief of Mexican philosopher José Vasconcelos that people of mixed race would inherit the earth, many Mexican Americans began to call themselves *La Raza*—"the race" or "the people." Another appellation, also embraced with defiant pride, was *Chicano,* a shortened form of *Mexicano* with the first syllable dropped and the "x" pronounced as "ch" in the fashion of Mexico's Chihuahua Indians. The term "Chicano" was often used to embrace all Spanish-speaking people in the state, although a substantial portion of the Hispanic population was derived from places other than Mexico. In Los Angeles, for instance, 20 percent of all Latinos were descendant from Cuba, Puerto Rico, and Central and South America.

California's Spanish-speaking population was a deeply disadvantaged minority, caught in a vicious cycle of undereducation and underemployment. Of the Mexican Americans employed in California, about half were semiskilled or skilled workers, including those in the entrepreneurial and professional fields, but within almost every occupational group the earnings of the Mexican Americans were much lower than the average. In 1976 their median and annual income was slightly more than $10,000, compared with nearly $15,000 for Anglo-Americans. The percentage of families with annual incomes below the official poverty level was nearly twice the percentage for families in general. The school dropout rate for Latino students was twice that of Anglo students, and more than half of all Latinos in the job market lacked a high school diploma. Many children had grown up in households where only Spanish was spoken. In 1976 the state legislature adopted the most ambitious bilingual education program in the nation to help schools begin to deal more effectively with the language problem. By 1980 about 330,000 students were enrolled in special bilingual and bicultural classes. Voters in 1986, however, passed an initiative which declared English to be California's official language. Opponents of the measure feared that the new law would lead to a dismantling of the state's bilingual education program.

Although Latinos outnumbered blacks in the state by more than two to one, Mexican Americans had great difficulty in gaining political representation. The election of Edward R. Roybal to the Los Angeles city council in 1949 broke a long tradition of Anglo exclusiveness, but during the two decades following his election to Congress in 1962 no other Mexican American served on the council. No Latino has served as mayor of a major California city in modern history, and no Latino has been elected to statewide office. During the administration of Edmund G. Brown, Jr., Latinos were appointed in record numbers to the courts and state agencies but, by 1982, representation in the state legislature was limited to three senators and four members of the assembly.

Several factors contributed to the relative political weakness of the state's largest minority. Geographical diffusion of the Hispanic population drained off political strength, and in areas where their numbers were greatest, gerrymandering of election districts often prevented Latinos from exerting what strength they had. Anti-Latino prejudice remained a barrier. A disproportionate number of Hispanic judges, for instance, failed to win confirmation at the polls. Perhaps the biggest factor, however, was low voter participation by the Latino community. In Los Angeles, where Latinos constituted about 20 percent of the voting-age population, they accounted for only about 5 percent of the voter turnout in most citywide elections.

In the 1980s a major effort was made to arouse the "sleeping giant" of Latino political power. Voter registration drives were aimed at increasing the Hispanic presence at the polls. Registered Latino voters numbered about 1 million, but 700,000 eligible voters remained unregistered. Political action groups also encouraged Latino immigrants to apply for naturalization. About one-third of the 2.5 million adult Latinos in California were noncitizens. The number of Hispanic officeholders grew slowly during the 1980s, but mainly on the local level. By 1986 there were 450 Hispanic elected officials in the state, including city council members Richard Alatorre of Los Angeles and Blanca Alvarado of San Jose. Latinos suffered setbacks in state politics with the unsuccessful campaign of Mario Obledo for the Democratic gubernatorial nomination in 1982, and the 1986 defeat of Supreme Court Justice Cruz Reynoso.

Illegal immigration of "undocumented workers" from Mexico continued to swell the Latino population in California and remained an unsolved problem for state and federal officials. By crossing the border, Mexican immigrants could instantly increase their earning power 10 times or more. In the face of this powerful motive, all efforts to curb the flow of illegal immigrants proved ineffective. Estimates of the size of the illegal immigrant population in the state ranged from 750,000 to 1.5 million. Their impact on the state also remained unclear. Some studies indicated that the illegal aliens cost the state and federal government millions of dollars through their use of public services; other observers maintained that they contributed revenues far in excess of the cost of services they received. About 4 percent of the illegal aliens made claims on the welfare system in 1980, whereas nearly 75 percent paid income and social security taxes, and all paid sales taxes. In 1985 a Rand Corporation study termed "a myth" the belief that the large number of Mexican immigrants in California was hurting the state's economy. According to the Rand report, Mexican workers actually stimulated economic growth by keeping wage levels in the state competitive.

Employers throughout California wondered how their enterprises would manage under a new, more restrictive immigration law passed by Congress in 1986. The law imposed stiff penalties on employers who knowingly hire illegal aliens and provided for a substantial increase in the number of agents patrolling the nation's border with Mexico.

WOMEN

California has an ambiguous record in the history of thought, writing, and action relating to the place of women in society. The late-nineteenth-century feminist movement was well-represented in California by such energetic advocates of women's rights as Charlotte Perkins Gilman, author of *Women and Economics* (1898), and Laura De Force Gordon, the pioneer California journalist, lawyer, and suffragist. Following Gordon's successful campaign for the admission of women lawyers to the California bar, the state constitutional convention in 1879 approved the text she drafted for Article XX, section 18, of the new state constitution: "No person shall, on account of sex, be disqualified from entering upon or pursuing any lawful business, vocation or profession."

Gordon's views were shared by San Francisco novelist Gertrude Atherton who, both in her personal life and in her writing, was in constant rebellion against domesticity and the subjection to the male that she believed it involved. Born in 1857, Atherton had the misfortune of being widowed at an early age when her husband died at sea and his body was returned preserved in a barrel of rum. Her liberated fiction included local histories, sensational novels, treatises on women's rights, and an account of the sexual rejuvenation of older women.

In the next generation, the novelist Kathleen Norris, 23 years younger than Atherton, held opposite views about the social role of women and had far greater influence in spreading her views. Norris considered motherhood and the family the heart of any successful and happy woman's life, and this was the message of most of her nearly 80 books of phenomenally popular fiction, beginning in 1911 with *Mother,* an instant best-seller. In the 1930s her novels and short stories made her the highest-paid woman in the world. Her own success was implicit evidence that a woman could have both a career and a family, but she once wrote that "The whole basis of my entire life is Family. I don't care about anything else."

Although California had been one of the early states to grant women the vote, in 1911, California women were rarely successful in obtaining elective office. At first it appeared that it would be otherwise, for in 1918 four women were elected to the state assembly. Yet during the next 50 years only 10 other women were elected to the lower house, and none to the state senate. Women in the California congressional delegation usually numbered only one or two. Representative Florence Kahn was elected in 1925 to her late husband's seat in the House, where she continued to represent San Francisco and to maintain his vigorous advocacy of military preparedness until 1936, and Representative Helen Gahagan Douglas served in Congress from 1945 until her defeat by Richard Nixon in the senatorial election of 1950. As late as 1975, California ranked 48th among the states in the percentage of state elective offices held by women.

The nationwide women's movement of the 1960s and 1970s finally made itself felt in California state elections in 1976, when the number of women in the legislature doubled from three to six, including Rose A. Vuich of Dinuba, the first woman ever elected to the California Senate. By 1992, 22 of the legislature's 120 members were women, the highest number in state history. Also two women held statewide office—Secretary of State March Fong Eu and Treasurer Kathleen Brown—and Democrats Dianne Feinstein and Barbara Boxer were elected to the United States Senate.

On the local level, the number of women elected to public office increased remarkably during the 1970s and 1980s. Dianne Feinstein was president of the San Francisco Board of Supervisors in 1978 when Mayor George Moscone and Supervisor Harvey Milk were assassinated in their city hall offices. Feinstein was selected by her fellow supervisors to serve out the term of the slain mayor, and in 1979 she became the first woman to be elected the city's chief executive. The election attracted national attention because of the role of San Francisco's large homosexual population, estimated to constitute 20 percent of the city's electorate. Feinstein successfully appealed for support from homosexual voters, and the support they gave her was an important factor in her victory. San Jose city councilwoman Janet Gray Hayes became the first woman elected mayor of the state's fourth-largest city, and Anne Rudin was elected mayor of Sacramento. By 1986, 64 of the state's 296 county supervisors—22 percent—were women. Women were in the majority on boards in Fresno, Santa Clara, Riverside, and San Francisco counties.

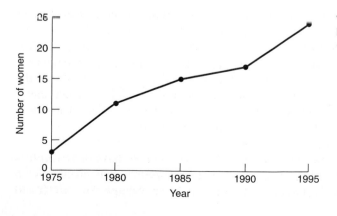

Women in the California legislature, 1975–1995. (*Based on data in the* California Journal.)

The number of women who have served in high appointive positions in state government has been nearly as meager as that of women who have held elective office. Katherine Philips Edson served as the first executive officer of the Industrial Welfare Commission under Governor Hiram Johnson, and Kate Richards O'Hare Cunningham, a nationally known crusader for prison reform, was appointed assistant director of the department of penology by Governor Culbert L. Olson in 1939. Phoebe Apperson Hearst became the first woman on the Board of Regents of the University of California in 1897 and served until her death in 1919. Others on the board included Dorothy Buffum Chandler, wife of *Los Angeles Times* publisher Norman Chandler, who served from 1954 to 1968 and was elected by her colleagues as vice chairwoman; Catherine Campbell Hearst, a regent from 1956 until her resignation in 1976; and Vilma S. Martinez, a founder and president of the Mexican-American Legal Defense and Educational Fund, who was appointed to the board in 1976.

It was in the administration of Governor Edmund G. Brown, Jr., that women for the first time were appointed to top positions of power throughout state government. In his two terms in office Brown appointed more than 1600 women to various boards and commissions and named women as directors of the departments of agriculture, finance, transportation, veterans affairs, motor vehicles, conservation, and corrections. In February 1977, Rose Elizabeth Bird became the first woman ever appointed to the California Supreme Court—and Governor Brown made her not merely a justice, but the *chief* justice. The following year Bird won confirmation at the polls by an extremely close margin.

Employment opportunities for women gradually expanded in the twentieth century, and an increasing proportion of women sought employment outside the home. World War II was a catalyst for change in the status of California women, just as it was for the state's racial minorities. Government and military officials and leaders of industry exhorted women to take jobs in factories and offices. "Rosie the Riveter" was the epitome of a woman doing her patriotic duty. About half the women who went to work in the wartime shipyards and aircraft plants had already been in the labor force, usually at lower-skilled and lower-paying jobs. At war's end most of the women workers wanted to continue in the work they were doing, but as male workers returned from the armed forces and as wartime industries cut back production, many women were displaced from their jobs. Nevertheless, the number of women in the workforce continued to increase. In 1950, 30 percent of all California women were working outside the home; by 1977 a majority of California women were in the labor force. Overwhelmingly women sought employment for economic reasons. Working was a necessity for the many widowed, divorced, and separated women who composed a major part of the female labor force. For other women, work was necessary to support their families or to provide better education or health care for their children. In the years following the war, relatively few California women sought employment merely for personal fulfillment.

In the early 1970s the National Organization for Women and other women's rights groups conducted a strong campaign for the equal rights amendment (ERA): "Equality of rights under the law shall not be denied or abridged by the United

States or by any state on account of sex." Congress approved the ERA by overwhelming votes in both houses in March 1972 and set a 7-year deadline for ratification of the amendment by three-fourths of the nation's state legislatures. In California the assembly approved the ERA less than a month after Congress had officially proposed it, and, following considerable debate, the state senate joined in ratifying it in November 1972. In the states as a whole, however, after an initial spurt of ratifications, strong opposition developed and stalled the process for several years. By the fall of 1978, 35 states had ratified the ERA, three short of the needed three-fourths majority. After a vigorous campaign by the amendment's supporters, Congress extended the deadline to June 30, 1982, but even with this extension the ERA failed to win the needed additional ratifications.

The issue which came to dominate the feminist movement in the 1980s was "comparable worth." Although women were making inroads into a few occupations with high status and high earnings, the majority of women continued to be employed as clerks and service workers. As more women moved into the labor force, the discrepancy between their wages and those of men actually increased in some fields. Most women in the workforce remained concentrated at the lower end of the pay scale, earning considerably less money than their male coworkers. Citing these economic inequities, feminists argued that women workers should receive equal pay for doing comparable, but not identical, work to that of men.

The California Legislature in 1981 declared that comparable worth should be considered when setting salaries for state employees in female-dominated jobs. Over the next 3 years, several additional comparable worth bills were passed by the legislature but were vetoed by Republican Governor George Deukmejian. The California Comparable Worth Task Force reported in 1985 that the state's labor force remained highly segregated by sex. It also found that for every $1 earned by a male worker in California, a female worker earned only 60 cents. The task force recommended that businesses in the state be required to close the gap by upgrading the pay scale for their women workers and by integrating them into traditionally male-dominated positions.

SELECTED BIBLIOGRAPHY

Several articles in Robert F. Heizer (ed.), *California* (1978), provide information on California Indians in the twentieth century. See also Diana Meyers Bahr, *From Mission to Metropolis* (1993); Adam Fortunate Eagle, *Alcatraz!* (1992); Joan Weibel-Orlando, *Indian Country, L.A.* (1993); George H. Phillips, *The Enduring Struggle* (1981); Jack D. Forbes, *Native Americans of California and Nevada* (1969); and Valerie Sherer Mathes, *Helen Hunt Jackson and Her Indian Reform Legacy* (1990). The larger context is provided in James J. Rawls, *Chief Red Fox Is Dead: A History of Native Americans since 1945* (1996), and Donald L. Parman, *Indians and the American West in the Twentieth Century* (1994). On population trends, see Sherburne F. Cook, *The Population of the California Indians, 1769–1970* (1976). Kenneth M. Johnson's monograph, *K-344, or The Indians of California v. the United States* (1966), also includes information on the broader history of California Indian problems. Heizer (ed.), *The California Indians v. The United States of America* (1978), contains documents from the 1959

Indian Claims Commission ruling. See also Ferdinand F. Fernandez, "Except a California Indian: A Study in Legal Discrimination," *Southern California Quarterly,* L (June 1968), pp. 161–175.

Sucheng Chan's *Asian Californians* (1991) and *Asian Americans* (1991) are useful surveys. The most thorough accounts of the continuing controversy over Japanese American relocation are Yasuko I. Takezawa, *Breaking the Silence* (1995); Leslie T. Hatamiya, *Righting a Wrong* (1993); and Roger Daniels et al., *Japanese Americans: From Relocation to Redress* (1986). General studies are David J. O'Brien and Stephen S. Fugita, *Japanese American Ethnicity* (1991), and Robert A. Wilson and Bill Hosokowa, *East to America* (1980). Works on the Chinese Americans include Shien Woo Kung, *Chinese in American Life* (1962); Rose Hum Lee, *The Chinese in the United States of America* (1960); and Betty Lee Sung, *The Story of the Chinese in America* (1971). See also H. Brett Melendy, *Asians in America: Filipinos, Koreans, and East Indians* (1977); Tricia Knoll, *Becoming Americans* (1982); Lorraine Crouchett, *Filipinos in California* (1982); Fred Cordova, *Filipinos* (1983); Eui-Young Yu et al. (eds.), *Koreans in Los Angeles* (1982); and Chan (ed.), *Hmong Means Free* (1994).

For historical background on the wartime and postwar black migration, see Rudolph Lapp, *Afro-Americans in California* (1987); Douglas Henry Daniels, *Pioneer Urbanites* (1980); Lawrence B. de Graaf, "The City of Black Angels: Emergence of the Los Angeles Ghetto, 1890–1930," *Pacific Historical Review,* XXXIX (August 1970), pp. 323–352; and Lawrence P. Crouchett et al., *Visions toward Tomorrow* (1989). On the migration and its problems see Gretchen Lemke-Santangelo, *Abiding Courage* (1996); Dolores Nason McBroome, *Parallel Communities* (1993); Albert S. Broussard, *Black San Francisco* (1993); and Charles Wollenberg, "Black vs. Navy Blue: The Mare Island Mutiny Court-Martial," *California History,* LVIII (Spring 1979), pp. 62–75 and *"James vs. Marinship:* Trouble on the New Black Frontier," ibid., LX (Fall 1981), pp. 262–279. On the housing issue, see Raymond E. Wolfinger and Fred E. Greenstein, "The Repeal of Fair Housing in California," *American Political Science Review,* LXII (September 1968), pp. 753–769; and Lawrence P. Crouchett, *William Byron Rumford* (1984).

Charles Wollenberg, *All Deliberate Speed* (1976); Irving G. Hendrick, *The Education of Non-whites in California* (1977); and Lillian Rubin, *Busing and Backlash* (1972) describe the controversy over school integration. On the Watts riot, see John A. McCone et al., *Violence in the City* (1965), and Nathan Cohen (ed.), *The Los Angeles Riots* (1970).

A useful guide to recent work on Mexican Americans is Armando Valdez et al., *The State of Chicano Research in Family, Labor and Migration Studies* (1983). General surveys of Chicano history include Mario T. Garcia, *Mexican Americans* (1991); Albert Camarillo, *Chicanos in California* (1984); Matt S. Meier and Feliciano Rivera, *The Chicanos* (1972); Leo Grebler et al., *The Mexican-American People* (1970); and Carey McWilliams, *North from Mexico* (1949). More specialized studies appear in Camarillo, *Chicanos in a Changing Society* (1979), which focuses on the Mexican American community in Santa Barbara; Richard Griswold del Castillo, *The Los Angeles Barrio, 1850–1890* (1980) and *La Familia* (1984); David G. Gutiérrez, *Walls and Mirrors* (1995); Ricardo Romo, *East Los Angeles* (1983); Maurice Mazón, *The Zoot-Suit Riots* (1984); Francisco Balderrama, *In Defense of La Raza* (1982); Rudolfo F. Acuña, *A Community under Siege* (1985); and Norris Hundley, Jr. (ed.), *The Chicano* (1975).

Anthologies on racial problems in California are Roger Daniels and Spencer C. Olin, Jr., (eds.), *Racism in California* (1972); George E. Frakes and Curtis B. Solberg (eds.), *Minorities in California History* (1971); and Charles Wollenberg (ed.), *Ethnic Conflict in California History* (1970). Thoughtful essays on the need for a multiethnic history of California include Wollenberg, "A Usable History for a Multicultural State," *California History,* LXIV (Summer

1985), pp. 202–209, and Martin Ridge, "Bilingualism, Biculturalism: California's New Past," *Southern California Quarterly,* LXVI (Spring 1984), pp. 47–60.

On the history of California women, see the special issues of *California History,* LXXII (Spring 1993); *Pacific Historical Review,* LXI (November 1992); *Pacific Historian,* XXVIII (Fall 1984); and *Journal of the West,* XXI (April 1982). The many biographies of California women include Emily Wortis Leider, *California's Daughter: Gertrude Atherton* (1991); Mary A. Hill, *Charlotte Perkins Gilman* (1980); and Charlotte S. McClure, *Gerturde Atherton* (1976). On political activity see Jacqueline R. Braitman, "Elizabeth Snyder and the Role of Women in the Postwar Resurgence of California's Democratic Party," *Pacific Historical Review,* LXII (May 1993), pp. 197–220, and Jean M. Smith, "The Voting Women of San Diego, 1920," *Journal of San Diego History,* XXVI (Spring 1980), pp. 133–154. On the status of women workers see Sheila Tropp Lichtman. "Women at Work, 1941–1945: Wartime Employment in the San Francisco Bay Area," Ph.D. thesis, University of California, Davis (1981); and *Women at Work in California* (1978), compiled by the California Employment Development Department. The battle over the ERA is described in Margaret I. Miller and Helene Linker, "Equal Rights Campaigns in California and Utah," *Society,* VI (May/June 1974), pp. 40–53. *California Women* is a monthly bulletin published by the California Commission on the Status of Women. Joan M. Jensen and Gloria Ricci Lothrop, *California Women: A History* (1987), provides a useful introduction to the subject.

CHAPTER THIRTY-TWO

A Season of Discontent

The social history of California in the 1960s is a study in contrasts. In the prosperous early years of the decade California became the most populous state in the union, culminating more than a century of phenomenal growth.

The 1960s were also years of unprecedented social ferment. Beginning at Berkeley in 1964, college campuses around the state were rocked by a series of student strikes and protest demonstrations. Many young people, alienated from a society they regarded as corrupt and decadent, turned to drugs and adopted unconventional styles of dress and behavior. The unpopular Vietnam war added immensely to the sense of youthful alienation and became the focus of a nationwide antiwar movement. The Watts riot of 1965 was evidence of another kind of discontent, and the following year the radical Black Panther party was organized in Oakland.

By the decade's end the population growth of California had sharply declined. Changed economic conditions, as well as a kind of malaise which affected the state and its image, contributed to a dramatic slowdown of migration to the state. In the 1970s the historic pattern of growth reasserted itself, but even then the rate of growth remained below that of previous decades.

THE GROWTH RATE: PEAK AND SLOWDOWN

Through the first half of the 1960s, economic opportunity continued to combine with the amenities of mild climate, scenic beauty, and California's romantic reputation to attract new residents from other states at the rate of almost 1000 a day. These newcomers made up nearly two-thirds of a total annual population increase of 600,000 at the peak in 1963. When California passed New York and became the most populous state late in 1962, Gov. Edmund G. Brown proclaimed a 4-day celebration—"California First Days"—and called for "the biggest party the state has ever seen." Communities across the state staged local celebrations, and at

Truckee an official delegation ceremoniously welcomed the latest carload of newcomers as they crossed the state line. Not everyone viewed California's rise to preeminence as an occasion for celebration. Californian Earl Warren, then United States Chief Justice, warned: "I would not celebrate with fireworks or dancing in the streets. Mere numbers do not mean happiness."

The growth of California's population was urban—or rather *suburban*—and was greatest in the southern part of the state. By the mid-1970s more than 90 percent of the people of California lived in the 17 areas that the Census Bureau listed as "metropolitan," and thus California was the nation's most urbanized as well as most

The 1970 census confirmed that California was the most populous state in the union. This prescient cartoon by Newton Pratt in the *Sacramento Bee* illustrates some of the problems of preeminence. (*Courtesy of the* Sacramento Bee.)

folksinger Malvina Reynolds composed a stirring protest song called "The Cement Octopus." Such intransigence made San Francisco the despair of both state and federal highway planners, who called the city the worst highway bottleneck in America.

The absence of another form of modernization, that of the port facilities of San Francisco, was more clearly disastrous for the city. In 1960 San Francisco still handled all the foreign imports of the Bay Area. By 1975 it had lost most of its seagoing traffic, largely to the port of Oakland, where the voters had approved bonds to build the massive cranes required for loading and unloading "containers." These were steel or aluminum boxes the size of a truck, lifted from a ship directly onto a truck chassis or railroad flatcar.

The railroads continued to prosper from the hauling of freight, but their passenger traffic steadily declined. They often begged the state public utilities commission to approve the discontinuance or drastic reduction of their passenger service, but the commission turned down most of these requests. The railroads were often accused of making their passenger trains and schedules as unattractive and inconvenient as possible, in the hope that they would eventually be permitted to discontinue entirely the unprofitable business of carrying passengers in competition with automobiles, buses, and airplanes. California's air transportation industry meanwhile doubled its volume in the 1960s, and the air lane between Los Angeles and San Francisco became the most traveled in the world.

While San Francisco was rebelling against freeways, it took the lead in planning an electrified rapid transit system that would have the great advantage of reducing not only traffic congestion but also air pollution from motor vehicle exhausts. In 1962 the voters of San Francisco, Alameda, and Contra Costa counties approved the formation of the Bay Area Rapid Transit (BART) District and the building of a rail network that would connect the cities and suburbs of the East Bay with the stations of a subway under Market Street in downtown San Francisco. BART carried its first passengers in 1972 using an automated, computerized operating system, no conductors, and only a single attendant on each train. It was the first all-new transit system to be built in the United States in 60 years, and in spite of many technical difficulties it was ultimately rated as one of the best.

In Los Angeles, on the other hand, most of the voters and taxpayers showed their determination to cling to the privilege of doing all their traveling throughout the sprawling metropolis in their private automobiles. Los Angeles had 1000 miles of freeways and 10,000 miles of cars. On an average day more than 350,000 cars and trucks passed one point near the civic center, at the junction of six freeways, where the interchange resembled the mechanism of a giant watch. Except for the very poor, nearly everyone between the ages of 15 and 85 had an automobile. The affluent majority repeatedly refused to subsidize a public rapid transit system, but it often showed considerable enthusiasm for elaborate transit studies and reports. A Southern California Rapid Transit District did come into existence, on paper, but for years it could do no more than operate a fleet of traffic-bound buses. It was not until 1980 that Los Angeles voters approved a sales tax increase to finance construction and operation of a new rail rapid transit system.

REAPPORTIONMENT

The population boom of the 1950s and early 1960s also led to increased demands for reform of the state's system of political representation. With the continued growth of the suburban parts of the metropolitan areas, especially those in southern California, the archaic "federal" system of representation in the California State Senate became more and more obviously inequitable. Los Angeles County, with a population of 6,036,771 in the 1960 census, was the most populous legislative district in the United States, yet it had the same number of votes in the state senate as the Alpine-Mono-Inyo district, with 14,294 people: one vote. A resident of Alpine, Mono, or Inyo County cast a vote worth 422 times as much as the vote of a resident of Los Angeles County. This was by far the widest disparity in any state. One-quarter of the population elected three-quarters of the California state senators. A majority of the senators could be elected by 10.7 percent of the California voters.

Initiative proposals to modify the "little federal" system and reapportion the California Senate were rejected at the polls in 1928, 1948, 1960, and 1962. Most voters clung to the hazy and misleading idea that what was appropriate for the federal government must be appropriate for the states. But the United States Supreme Court ruled in *Reynolds v. Sims,* on June 15, 1964, that one person's vote must be worth as much as another's in the election of state legislators. The equal protection clause of the Fourteenth Amendment, said the Court, required that seats in both houses of a state legislature be apportioned on a population basis. The so-called federal analogy was discarded as fallacious and inapplicable. Counties, the Court pointed out, were merely political subdivisions created by the state

The "one man, one vote" ruling of the Supreme Court and the consequent reapportionment of the state senate led to a revival in 1965 of the proposal to split California into two states. (*Courtesy of the* Sacramento Bee.)

'This'll Serve The Supreme Court And Its Reapportionment Right!'

governments, not sovereign entities like the states themselves. Chief Justice Earl Warren was one of the prime movers in the adoption of this "one man, one vote" doctrine, even though as governor of California he had been one of those who had opposed reapportionment of its state senate. The northern members of the California Senate, many of whom would lose their seats, engaged in a series of desperate maneuvers in the attempt to escape reapportionment. Senator Joseph A. Rattigan of Santa Rosa asked whether a proposal for armed insurrection would be in order, but in 1965 the legislature approved a new apportionment law that included no deviations of more than 15 percent in the populations of the new senatorial districts. Consequently, in the election of 1966, under the new plan of apportionment, the control of the state senate passed to southern California, which had elected a majority of the assembly members since the 1930s.

In 1965, the last year under the federal system, a large group of state senators from northern California revived a proposal that had been made periodically since the 1850s. This was a plan to divide the state at the Tehachapi Mountains, and this latest version of it would have included the counties of Santa Barbara and Kern within the northern state, giving only seven counties to the southern one. But polls showed that more than two-thirds of the voters, even in the north, were opposed to any plan for state division.

EDUCATION

In the years of headlong growth and general prosperity that followed World War II, California's public schools remained impoverished. The state spent more than 40 percent of its budget for education, and its per capita expenditures for public schools were among the highest in the country—but these figures were grossly misleading because California's school-age population grew twice as fast as its general population. Between 1950 and 1960, the total number of people in the state increased by roughly 50 percent, whereas public school enrollment grew by more than 100 percent. An unprecedentedly large proportion of the people who were migrating to California were young married couples, able and inclined to produce numerous children. The schools were chronically short of money, of classroom space, of teachers—of everything, in fact, except pupils.

The annual tidal waves of postwar babies that flooded into the public schools in the 1950s began to inundate the colleges and universities in the following decade, and the state responded by greatly expanding its system of public higher education. In 1960 the legislature adopted the Master Plan for Higher Education to prepare for the massive enrollment growth anticipated during the 1960s. The 1960s. The master plan defined the mission of the various "segments" of the state's system of higher education.

California's state college system traced its origin to 1862, when a 2-year normal school was established in San Francisco. This was moved to San Jose in 1870. Other such schools were later established elsewhere in the state. After their programs had been lengthened to 4 years, they were promoted to the rank of "teachers' colleges" in 1921, and designated as general "state colleges" in 1935.

After adding graduate instruction, most of them were renamed "state universities" in 1971. Later, the entire system became known as the California State University, or CSU. Its primary function was to provide undergraduate and graduate education through the master's degree.

The beginnings of 2-year junior colleges stemmed from the passage of a state law in 1907 authorizing the governing boards of city, district, or county high schools to establish post–high school courses. Fresno established the first public junior college in the United States in 1910, and California has since led all the states in the establishment and support of such institutions. By midcentury they had begun to be called "city colleges" or "community colleges," though state policy prevented them from expanding their programs to 4 years. The mission of the community colleges was to prepare students for transfer to a 4-year college, to award them an associate of arts or science degree, or to train them for employment in a vocational or technical program. The community colleges numbered more than 100 by 1980.

The general campuses of the University of California increased to eight. At Los Angeles, a "normal school" had become the University of California, Southern Branch, in 1919. This had become UCLA in 1931, and by the 1960s its student body was larger than the one at Berkeley. Santa Barbara State College became the University of California, Santa Barbara, in 1944. In the late 1940s, colleges of letters and science were established at Davis and at Riverside in connection with what had originally been branches of the universitywide college of agriculture. After 1960, new general campuses of the university were established at Santa Cruz, Irvine, and San Diego. Under the Master Plan, the university was entrusted with the responsibility of conducting advanced research and awarding doctoral degrees in addition to providing undergraduate education.

In the early 1970s it seemed as though higher education had overexpanded. The postwar baby boom continued through the 1950s, but the decline in birthrate following the introduction of oral contraceptives in 1960 and the decline in migration to the state in the late 1960s undercut earlier projections of growth in college enrollment. Funds for public education were slashed at all levels. The state's universities and 2-year community colleges were able to balance their budgets only by assigning a scandalously large share of their teaching loads to part-time teachers, to whom they paid low hourly wages. There was a surplus of trained teachers, as well as of many other people with college and university training, who suddenly found themselves overqualified and underemployed.

CAMPUS TURMOIL

American college students of the 1950s had been called "the silent generation." Those who reached college age in the 1950s had been born in the 1930s, and when these "depression babies" became young adults, they were too driven by anxiety about material success to be interested in any form of political or social dissent. Students took virtually no part, for example, in the University of California loyalty oath controversy.

The college students of the middle and later 1960s, on the other hand, were part of the great wave of postwar babies, born and reared in relative affluence, but in such numbers that they badly overcrowded the public schools and the colleges, and were often discontented with the crowding. Some of them discovered that their massive numbers could be a form of power.

Stirrings of student unrest in California had appeared as early as May 1960 when a crowd of college students, protesting their exclusion from a hearing of the House Un-American Activities Committee in the San Francisco city hall, jammed the rotunda by sitting down in the balcony. The police washed them down the stairs with fire hoses and drove them from the building with clubs. At about the same time, black college students in the southern states began to attack the racial segregation of lunch counters with the tactic of the sit-in. This tactic had been used for a short time in 1937, in a different context, by some of the relatively radical new CIO unions, in the form of the "sit-down strike" in which striking workers occupied the property of the employer, but organized labor had soon abandoned the sit-down, not only because it was ruled illegal but also because it alienated the public. In the early 1960s, however, the federal courts ruled that the racial segregation of lunch counters was unconstitutional and therefore that those who had participated in the lunch counter sit-ins were merely demanding their constitutional rights and could not be validly arrested.

Several students from the University of California at Berkeley had spent their summers in civil rights activities in the deep south, and when they returned to the campus in the fall of 1964, they organized sit-ins and other demonstrations to protest racial discrimination by Bay Area businesses. In September the university administration announced that a sidewalk area at the southern entrance to the campus—an area previously thought to belong to the city of Berkeley and thus to be beyond university control—was university property and ordered all student groups to stop using the area for setting up tables, recruiting members, or otherwise organizing for off-campus political activity. The groups affected by the university's order included student civil rights organizations, as well as groups ranging in their political philosophy from the far left to the far right. When the administration attempted to enforce its new order, students organized the Free Speech Movement (FSM), called a student strike, and used the civil rights tactics of mass civil disobedience against the university.

The university charter law of 1868 and the state constitution of 1879 (Article IX, section 9) had sought to keep the state university free from "political or sectarian influence," and the regents had long chosen to interpret that phrase as forbidding any political advocacy on a university campus. This had never been the true meaning of the provision. The full sentence forbade "political or sectarian influence *in the appointment of [the university's] regents and the administration of its affairs* [italics inserted]." Every governor of California with the possible exception of Earl Warren had flatly violated this provision by appointing regents for political reasons. But the regents, like the governors, preferred to ignore this aspect of the matter. Apparently they also chose to ignore the advice of their own attorney that their rules against political speech and advocacy on campus were in violation of the

United States Supreme Court's decision in *Edwards v. South Carolina* in 1963. This ruling stated that "student speakers may even advocate violations of the law provided such advocacy does not constitute a clear and present danger . . ." and that "much of the conduct that the public finds objectionable is constitutionally protected."

Thus the student rebellion at Berkeley in its beginnings was truly a free speech movement against unconstitutional restrictions, and in this particular sense it was successful. Following the disciplining of several students who defied the administration's order restricting political activity, crowds of students occupied the campus administration building. In December 1964 the largest sit-in occurred at Sproul Hall, and Governor Brown ordered state and local police to intervene. In the largest mass arrest in the state's history more than 700 persons, mostly students, were dragged or carried from the building. Later, in a mass trial, 578 of them were found guilty of trespassing, and many of resisting arrest. Less than a week after the Sproul Hall arrests, the Berkeley faculty passed resolutions that the university should not regulate the content of political advocacy, but should regulate only the time, place, and manner of it in order to prevent interference with normal university functions, and the university administration agreed to liberalize its rules governing student political activity.

At first the Berkeley student rebels relied on methods that were nonviolent, even though they did involve a kind of mass force, but the young radical leaders of the movement became overconfident. In a speech from the steps of Sproul Hall, FSM leader Mario Savio promised his followers that he could protect them from going to jail or from any other form of punishment. The apparent success of the tactics of sitting-in and going limp when arrested made the students feel invincible and invulnerable. The courts soon ruled, however, that occupying a university building was merely a form of illegal trespass and that going limp was merely a form of resisting arrest. When hundreds of students were sentenced to jail after their mass trial in Berkeley in 1965, many became disenchanted and embittered. The sense of newness and magic began to go out of the movement, and a sense of frustration and desperation took its place. The idea of nonviolence was soon lost in a welter of confrontation and disruption, and a drift toward violence and vandalism set in. Some student rebels made a mockery of the name of the Free Speech Movement and began to deny the right of free speech to anyone but themselves by shouting down any speaker who disagreed with them. This was a tragedy, not only for the young people themselves but for a society that cried out for improvement and that badly needed the freshness of youthful idealism.

The Free Speech Movement of 1964 gave Berkeley a considerable reputation as the cradle of student revolt in America, and in the subsequent years this reputation attracted many young radicals, some of them students and others former students, to the university campus and to parts of Berkeley and Oakland to the south of it. Protest against the escalation of the war in Vietnam and a continuing crusade against racism at home were now the major channels of youthful rebellion.

In October 1967 a major draft riot occurred after a crowd of antiwar demonstrators, trying to shut down the Oakland induction center, were routed by police who sprayed them with a temporarily blinding chemical known as Mace. The new vogue of student power spread across the country. In April 1968 hundreds of students staged a sit-in at Columbia University, and when it was broken up by police, many violently resisted arrest. In August, during the Democratic national convention in Chicago, there was a violent confrontation between police and the mass of young militants who had gathered in an effort to pressure the convention into taking a stand against the Vietnam war and into nominating Senator Eugene McCarthy. Prominent among the leaders of the Chicago demonstrations were two Californians: Tom Hayden, a leader of the radical Students for a Democratic Society, and Jerry Rubin, once a graduate student in sociology at Berkeley but now a full-time "revolutionary." Combining his political activities with the use of drugs, which he advocated as an aid to revolution, Rubin was addicted to the politics of absurdity. Earlier he had confronted the House Un-American Activities Committee dressed in a rented Revolutionary War uniform, and had made outrageous statements urging junior high school students to prepare to kill their parents and burn their school libraries.

Late in 1968 radical students at San Francisco State College demanded the creation of a black studies department run exclusively by blacks. This was the most important of a series of "non-negotiable demands," some of which had been drafted by a "Third World Liberation Front" including Latin American and Asian American radical students. To gain acceptance of their demands, the student leaders began a long strike characterized by Maoist rhetoric, violent disruption of classes, vandalism, and personal assault. The large tactical squad of the San Francisco police, specially trained for campus riot duty, finally broke the strike with mass maneuvers and arrests.

Before this uprising was over, a similar movement was launched at Berkeley, early in 1969, with a strike to demand an autonomous "third world college." Though this demand was not granted, the campus did establish a department of ethnic studies. Next came the disastrous affair of the "People's Park," in May 1969. This began when Berkeley's radical young "street people" tried to appropriate a block of university-owned land near Telegraph Avenue as a park for their own use. When the university fenced the block, a mob gathered to try to destroy the fence, and there was a riot in which sheriff's deputies responded to the throwing of rocks by firing shotguns. One young bystander, watching from a rooftop on Telegraph Avenue, was killed and another was blinded. This tragedy frightened, enraged, and "radicalized" thousands of young people throughout the region and produced such a massive movement to "take the park" that a force of the National Guard was sent to protect it. A National Guard helicopter broke up a disorderly crowd on the campus by spraying the whole area with tear gas, which drifted into dozens of classrooms and even into the campus hospital.

By this time, Berkeley was only one of many American university towns with large groups of rebellious and violence-prone young people. There was repeated violence and arson at Stanford. The University of California at Santa Barbara had long been thought of as a quietly conservative campus, but in February 1970 its student residential community of Isla Vista exploded in a series of riots in which

Helmeted members of the National Guard and the police stand guard before the ivy-covered walls of the chancellor's residence on the Berkeley campus during the 1969 "People's Park" controversy. *(Photograph by Lou de la Torre.)*

the branch of the Bank of America was burned and a student was killed when a deputy's gun discharged accidentally. Student rebellion reached a nationwide climax in May 1970 after a detachment of the Ohio National Guard shot and killed four young people on the campus of Kent State University, following the burning of the ROTC building in protest against the spreading of the war in southeast Asia to Cambodia. For the rest of the spring term many American campuses experienced various degrees of disruption. At Berkeley, thousands of students and a few faculty members tried to "reconstitute" the campus as a center for public argumentation against the war and tried to stop all other campus activity until the war was ended.

THE HIPPIE MOVEMENT

The college student radicalism of the 1960s was at first quite separate from the hippie movement, but gradually the two phenomena became interrelated. The word "hip" has been defined as "to be in the know, particularly about the drug underworld." The word "hippie" was derived from Norman Mailer's term "hipster." The appeal of the hippie mystique to young people in the 1960s had many aspects, including social protest and normal feelings of rebellion characteristic of adolescence. But many young adherents of the hippie movement were motivated by deep personal maladjustment and alienation. Craving love, joy, and self-realization many of them believed that such needs could be satisfied by certain drugs, especially when taken in the company of other young people with similar feelings. They often described their movement as a "subculture" or "counterculture," and sometimes quite candidly as a "drug culture." Its culture included electronically amplified rock music, psychedelic art, the doctrines of astrology and Krishna consciousness, and communal social relationships analogous with those of gypsies or of certain American Indian tribes.

An essential factor in the spread of the hippie movement was the popularization of the new drug lysergic acid diethylamide, or LSD. This drug was first synthesized by a Swiss chemist in 1938. In the early 1960s Dr. Timothy Leary, a lecturer on clinical psychology at Harvard and the holder of a Ph.D. in psychology from the University of California at Berkeley, was one of a group engaged in experiments with several drugs, including LSD, which they described as "psychedelic" or "consciousness-expanding." Their critics insisted that LSD was more accurately described as mind-distorting and hallucinogenic and that its effects on different individuals were dangerously unpredictable, a kind of "chemical Russian roulette." Colors intensified and changed, shape and spatial relations were distorted, and inanimate objects seemed to pulsate and to assume great emotional significance. To some the experience was deeply moving, exhilarating, and "self-revealing"—an experience of "cosmic oneness" or an "exploration of inner space." But to others it brought panic, bizarre and suicidal behavior, and temporary or even permanent psychosis. The frequency of the hippies' use of LSD varied considerably, but many of them used marijuana almost every day when they could obtain it.

In 1966 the news media began to give the hippies massive publicity and often described them as "flower children" or "the love generation." In 1967 when the movement reached its peak, there were probably about 200,000 hippies in the nation, and millions of other Americans, young and old, were sympathetic to the movement. The largest colony was in the Haight-Ashbury district of San Francisco, scene of the nationally publicized "summer of love" in 1967. Other large concentrations of hippies could be found in the Telegraph Avenue area south of the university campus in Berkeley; in Los Angeles on the Sunset Strip and along Fairfax Avenue in West Hollywood; and in Greenwich Village in New York. Smaller enclaves sprang up in almost every major American city, and there were various rural communes, notably in California, New Mexico, and Colorado.

Hippie leaders maintained that they were seeking to establish a new communal freedom from individual anxieties and to remove themselves from a decadent society full of war and oppression into a utopia of peace and love. It was more than coincidental that the years in which the hippie movement attracted its greatest following were also the years of the great expansion of American armed forces in Vietnam. Many young Americans believed that their country's participation in the war in southeast Asia was morally indefensible, and their hatred of the war was a major factor in their feelings of alienation from the whole prevailing system of society.

BLACK RADICALISM

About the time when student radicals had shifted their main attention to opposing the Vietnam war, and away from the black civil rights movement, that movement itself had taken a new and radical turn. In 1966, Stokley Carmichael became the new head of the Student Nonviolent Coordinating Committee. He soon turned it into a movement of violent nonstudents, ordered all whites to get out of it, and raised the cry of "black power." In the autumn of 1966, the Black Panther Party for Self-Defense was founded in Oakland by two young black militants, Huey P. Newton and Bobby G. Seale. They had met as students at the old Grove Street campus of Merritt College, a community college drawing many of its students from predominantly black areas in west and north Oakland. Newton and Seale were influenced by the writings of Malcolm X and Frantz Fanon, and later by those of Marx, Lenin, Mao Tse-tung, Ho Chi Minh, and Che Guevara. But their strongest feeling, growing out of their personal experience, was a hatred of the frequently prejudiced and cruel treatment of African Americans by white police. The black panther was originally the ballot emblem of a black civil rights party organized in Alabama in 1965. Newton liked the name and adopted it because, he said, the panther was reputed never to make an unprovoked attack, but to defend itself ferociously. Newton and Seale established a system of patrol cars; carrying law books and guns, they trailed police cars through the Oakland slums to protect the constitutional rights of African Americans.

One of the new party's first and most important converts was Eldridge Cleaver, a vigorously articulate black man who had twice been in prison. His first term, beginning when he was 18, had been spent in the California state prison at Soledad for possession of marijuana. After his release, according to his widely read memoir, *Soul on Ice,* he was burning with resentment and had turned to the raping of white women as a symbolic act of "insurrection," intended "to send waves of consternation throughout the white race." This brought him another and longer term in prison, during which he came to repudiate the act of rape and to regard his own resort to it as a symptom of the "dehumanization" that he had suffered; however, he resolved to fight by more effective means against the social system that he felt had brutalized and degraded black people like himself.

In prison Cleaver had become an admirer of the Black Muslim leader Malcolm X, who was assassinated in 1965. Early in 1967, the widow of Malcolm X made a visit to San Francisco, and Cleaver, recently released on parole, wanted to meet her. A squad of Black Panthers appeared at the airport and acted as her bodyguards while she was in the city. They wore paramilitary black uniforms and black berets and carried guns. The sight of them was an exhilarating experience for Cleaver, and he threw himself into the cause of the new party. He became its "minister of information." Seale was "chairman," and Newton was "minister of defense" and later "supreme commander."

Intense fear and hostility between police and Panthers soon led to many tragic shooting affrays. On October 28, 1967, gunfire erupted after an Oakland police car stopped an automobile driven by Huey Newton. One officer was killed; another policeman and Newton were wounded. On April 6, 1968, also in Oakland, there was more shooting in which two policemen were wounded, a young Panther was killed, and Eldridge Cleaver was wounded and arrested. Newton was tried in the summer of 1968 and convicted of manslaughter, but the conviction was reversed on

Pouarde, *City of the Dream: The History of San Diego* (1977); Christian L. Larsen, *Growth and Government in Sacramento* (1966); and Beth Bagwell, *Oakland* (1982). On reapportionment, see Bruce E. Cain, *The Reapportionment Puzzle* (1986).

Material on the history and problems of the public schools may be found in Irving G. Hendrick, *California Education* (1980); Roy W. Cloud, *Education in California* (1952); and Merton E. Hill, *The Junior College Movement in California, 1907–1948* (1949). The best of the institutional histories are Edith R. Mirrielees, *Stanford* (1959), and Verne A. Stadtman, *The University of California, 1868–1968* (1970).

Landon Y. Jones's *Great Expectations: America and the Baby Boom Generation* (1980) is a portrait of the generation which reached maturity in the 1960s. On campus radicalism, see Gerard J. DeGroot, "The Limits of Moral Protest," *Pacific Historical Review,* LXIV (February 1995), pp. 95–119; David Lance Goins, *The Free Speech Movement* (1993); W. J. Rorabaugh, *Berkeley at War* (1989); Seymour M. Lipset and Sheldon S. Wolin (eds.), *The Berkeley Student Revolt* (1965); Michael V. Miller and Susan Gilmore (eds.), *Revolution at Berkeley* (1965); and Irwin Unger, *The Movement* (1974). On the hippie phenomenon, See Timothy Miller, *The Hippies and American Values* (1991); Gene Anthony, *The Summer of Love* (1980); Theodore Roszak, *The Making of a Counter Culture* (1969); and Lewis Yablonsky, *The Hippie Trip* (1968), a sociological study.

Important works on black radicalism include Eldridge Cleaver, *Soul on Ice* (1968); Bobby Seale, *Seize the Time: The Story of the Black Panther Party and Huey P. Newton* (1970); Philip S. Foner (ed.), *The Black Panthers Speak* (1970); and Bruce Michael Taylor, "Black Radicalism in Southern California, 1950–1982," Ph.D. thesis, University of California, Los Angeles (1983).

CHAPTER THIRTY-THREE

Contemporary California Culture

In the years after World War II California emerged as a leading cultural region of the United States. Hollywood remained the nation's movie capital and soon became a center for the production of films, programs, and commercials for television. Works by California writers, artists, architects, and musicians achieved widespread recognition and often expressed values and attitudes distinctly Californian.

LITERATURE

A remarkable group of poets gathered in San Francisco in the late 1940s. Several of them, notably Robert Duncan and William Everson, had been conscientious objectors during the war and were attracted to San Francisco by the circle of pacifists and philosophical anarchists that formed there. The opposition of these poets to all government, and particularly to war, which they regarded as government at its worst, had an important influence on the intellectual atmosphere of the San Francisco Bay area for many years to come. Their poetry often manifested what Everson called "the repudiation of received forms," a conscious rejection of established literary standards of composition. In several articles in national magazines, the older poet Kenneth Rexroth did much to publicize "the San Francisco Renaissance" as a name for this regional movement of innovative and experimental poetry.

In the mid-1950s the cultural libertarianism of San Francisco attracted another group of writers, particularly from the New York area. Self-styled the "beat generation," they began to achieve notoriety in 1956 with the publication of Jack Kerouac's exuberant and formless novel *On the Road* and Allen Ginsberg's startling *Howl and Other Poems*. The beat writers were a somewhat different group from the poets of the San Francisco Renaissance, though they were often lumped together. They were even more extreme in rebelling against the prevailing norms of society and government and also against the established poetic and literary forms.

423

Kerouac announced in a television interview that "beat," a word of his own coinage, meant "beatific." When the Russians put the first Sputnik into orbit, the San Francisco columnist Herb Caen dubbed the beat generation the "beatniks," and the derisive nickname stuck.

Ginsberg's poems were first published in England, and much of their original fame resulted from their seizure by the San Francisco customs office on the ground that they were obscene. They were then published in San Francisco by Lawrence Ferlinghetti, poet and proprietor of the City Lights Bookshop, a center for many writers and artists. Ferlinghetti was tried and acquitted on a charge of publishing an obscene book, and the publicity of this trial did much to ensure popular interest in the beats and their writings. Kerouac's novels and Ferlinghetti's poems were relatively gentle and benevolent, but Ginsberg's poetry, though it had a kind of Whitmanesque power, was intensely morbid. His *Howl* consisted of one continuous sentence nearly 2000 words long and was filled with references to drugs, tragically unhappy sexual encounters, madness, and suicide, all blamed upon the corruption of the existing form of society. In many poems and speeches Ginsberg inveighed against materialism, technology, the war machine—"all the forces that have assaulted the individual human spirit."

In the 1960s a new generation of California writers established themselves as major figures in contemporary American literature. In some ways their work was an extension of the literary style and concerns of the beat generation, but it also reflected the turbulence of their own times. The impulse toward experimentalism, evident earlier in the poetry of Ginsberg and the runaway prose of Kerouac, was manifest in the complex layering of voices in the novels of Ken Kesey and the surreal imagery of Richard Brautigan. Kesey, born in Colorado in 1935, studied creative writing at Stanford University and worked briefly in the Veteran's Hospital at nearby Menlo Park. His comic, macabre first novel, *One Flew over the Cuckoo's Nest* (1962), is set in a mental ward and powerfully portrays the struggle of the individual against the overwhelming forces of conformity in modern society. Kesey adopted a lifestyle as unconventional as his prose, becoming a cult hero in the 1960s as he toured the country with a busload of followers known as the Merry Pranksters. Richard Brautigan moved to the San Francisco Bay area in the 1950s from his native Washington and first received widespread attention with his un-orthodox and disturbing book *Trout Fishing in America* (1967). Like some modern-day Leatherstocking, the narrator of *Trout Fishing* longs for the restoration of frontier innocence and agrarian simplicity, but finds that such qualities are beyond recall in the age of technology and commerce. In one memorable scene the narrator visits a wrecking yard in San Francisco and encounters, among the inventory of used doors and toilets, a "used trout stream," stacked in piles of various lengths and ready for sale. Brautigan produced 12 other works, of uneven quality, before his death in Bolinas in 1984.

Since the beginnings of the state's literature, serious California writers have provided a counterpoint to the prevailing myth of California as the land of boundless opportunity, success, and romance. The failure of this myth became a major preoccupation for the writers of the 1930s, finding its most powerful expression in the works of Nathanael West and John Steinbeck. The later generations of California writers also used the California dream as a background or a foil for their fiction. Much of the appeal of their work, as James D. Houston has pointed out, derived "from the fact that the dream is always there—if only to be betrayed— the ongoing western promise of the Big Romance, the Second Chance, which is a given in the environment, as potent and as insistent as the coastline."

One of the most important figures among the new California writers was novelist-essayist Joan Didion. Born and reared in Sacramento, Didion, in 1963, published her first novel, *Run River,* an evocative story of a rancher's daughter in California who, under the accumulation of a multitude of small pressures, goes insane. The novel is suffused with a pervasive sense of loss, the decline of a "certain pride," and the disappearance of old, familiar ways in the author's native Sacramento Valley. During the next several years Didion wrote a series of essays, collected as *Slouching towards Bethlehem* (1968), which expanded her vision of California in decline. In "Notes from a Native Daughter," Didion described the dramatic early history of Sacramento and its gradual evolution into the comfortable, rich farm town she knew as a girl. "In that gentle sleep Sacramento dreamed until perhaps 1950," she wrote, "when something happened. What happened was that Sacramento woke to the fact that the outside world was moving in, fast and hard. At the moment of its waking Sacramento lost, for better or for worse, its character. . . ." Didion made plain that she was talking about more than just her hometown, "for Sacramento *is* California, and California is a place in which a boom mentality and a sense of Chekhovian loss meet in uneasy suspension."

Didion also wrote about those who had come from "the outside world" to California, seeking and often not finding that which had eluded them somewhere

Joan Didion in the living room of her Malibu home in 1977. *(Photograph by Mary Lloyd Estrin. Courtesy of Simon & Schuster.)*

else. In "Some Dreamers of the Golden Dream" she told the pathetic story of a desperate woman, convicted of the murder of her husband, who lived in the San Bernardino Valley. "Of course she came from somewhere else, came off the prairie in search of something she had seen in a movie or heard on the radio, for this is a Southern California story." In the title essay, "Slouching towards Bethlehem," Didion provided a firsthand look at the Haight-Ashbury district of San Francisco in the spring of 1967. With an ear finely tuned to the rhetoric of the drug culture, she described with precision the sense of anomie and rootlessness of the young people drifting into San Francisco for the much heralded "summer of love." Didion's later essays and novels also conveyed a sense of loss, of disintegration, not just in California but in all of contemporary society.

An alternative vision of California informed the work of writer Gerald Haslam. Both Didion and Haslam were natives of the Central Valley, born just a year apart, but their sensibilities were radically different. Whereas Didion distanced herself from her California roots, Haslam celebrated his regional identity, making it the source of his greatest insight and power. Haslam became the leading spokesman for what he called "the other California," the small towns and rural areas of the state's interior. In half a dozen books of essays and short stories, Haslam wrote about the oil-rig workers, Mexican laborers, and poor white farmers of his native Kern County. His style, said Carey McWilliams, was "country music set to prose."

Haslam's first collection of short stories, *Okies* (1973), contained scenes that were reminiscent of John Steinbeck. There was a hint too of the naturalism of Frank Norris in Haslam's portrayal of the forces of poverty and hopelessness. Yet Haslam's vision was essentially optimistic. In an essay called "Writing about Home," published in *Coming of Age in California* (1990), Haslam acknowledged the disintegrating forces of modernism and offered the antidote of regionalism "for with it may come rootedness, tradition and values." When asked by critics why he continued to write about the region of his birth, Haslam replied: "In this site can be found all the great subjects, all the grand dramas, and they are not only themes of my stories and essays, but in a sense they are the settings, too: place and people and passion inseparable as the terrain of the heart. And the heart is our primary locale."

Poetry enjoyed a resurgence of popular interest during the latter decades of the twentieth century, and much of the best poetry written in California was suffused with influences both international and local. The landscape of northern California, for instance, was a powerful presence in the works of Berkeley poet Robert Haas. Yet Haas also translated into English the classics of Japanese *haiku* and the writings of his Lithuanian-born Berkeley colleague and Nobel Prize–winning poet Czeslaw Milosz. Haas himself was honored in 1995 by being named poet laureate of the United States. As for the recent renaissance of California poetry, Haas credited local pioneers. "If there's a flowering going on in poetry right now," he commented in 1996, "it's because there was this brilliant postwar generation, mostly symbolized here by Allen Ginsberg and the beats."

The new generation of California writers also included several African American, Latino, and Asian American authors whose work added a richness and distinctive texture to the recent literature of the state. In the early 1970s black novelists Al Young and Ishmael Reed began publishing in Berkeley the *Yardbird Reader,* a journal dedicated to the promotion of a diverse, multicultural American literature. Reed, a native of Tennessee, regarded California as the natural place for such an enterprise because here was America's first "truly world state," a state which had produced "a colorful gumbo culture." Reed called his own writing "neo-hoodooism," a blend of black magic, African imagery, and contemporary African American life. The complex, unrestrained style of his novels placed Reed squarely in the tradition of California's experimental literature. As the central character in Reed's *Yellow Back Radio Broke-Down* (1969) observes, "No one says a novel has to be one thing. It can be anything it wants to be, a vaudeville show, the six o'clock news, the mumblings of wild men saddled by demons." Like many other writings of his generation, Reed's work was a response to the dissension and chaos of recent California history. In *The Last Days of Louisiana Red* (1974), a novel set in Berkeley in the 1960s, Reed offered a thinly veiled parody of the Black Panther party and the once-fashionable rhetoric and violence of such organizations.

In 1959 José Antonio Villareal published *Pocho,* the first novel about Mexican American life written by a Mexican American. Son of immigrant parents, Villareal was born in the Imperial Valley and worked as a youth in California's orchards and fields. *Pocho* chronicled the hardships of Mexican immigrants who came to the United States following the revolution of 1910. It focused on the disintegration of the Rubio family in the Santa Clara Valley and on the dilemma of young Richard Rubio, torn between the traditional Mexican values of his parents and the new way of life he finds in California.

The most important figure in the emergence of a Mexican American literature was Luis Valdez, a playwright and director born in Delano in 1940. After graduation from San Jose State College, Valdez returned to Delano in 1965 and founded *El Teatro Campesino.* Combining ancient Mexican myths, bilingual dialogue, and a concern for contemporary political issues, *El Teatro* toured the state's agricultural labor camps and became the dramatic voice of the farm worker movement. The highly imaginative and inventive plays of Valdez had an appeal far beyond the farm workers for whom they were originally written. In 1978 Valdez's most ambitious work, *Zoot Suit,* premiered in Los Angeles and later made a brief run on Broadway. The play, inspired by the Los Angeles "Sleepy Lagoon" murder case of 1942, was made into a film in 1981 starring Edward James Olmos. Valdez's later works included *Bandido* (1981), a play about "Tiburcio Vasquez, Notorious California Bandit"; *Los Corridos* (1982), a series of playlets based on traditional Mexican folk ballads; and *I Don't Have to Show You No Stinkin' Badges* (1986), a comic-tragic view of an upwardly mobile Mexican American family in Los Angeles.

Reflecting the constant movement of people into California, a recurring theme in the state's literature has been the interplay of a character's present with a past lived somewhere else. This theme, evident in the work of the new Mexican American writers, was also a major concern of Maxine Hong Kingston, daughter of immigrants from China who came to the United States in the 1930s. Kingston was born in Stockton in 1940 and grew up with a keen interest in the stories and legends of her family's life in China. In *The Woman Warrior* (1976), a book

A scene from Luis Valdez's 1981 film *Zoot Suit,* starring Edward James Olmos as *El Pachuco. (Copyright © 1981 by Universal City Studios, Inc. Courtesy of MCA Publishing Rights, a Division of MCA Inc. All Rights Reserved.)*

subtitled *Memoirs of a Girlhood among Ghosts,* Kingston explained: "Those of us in the first American generations have had to figure out how the invisible world the emigrants built around our childhoods fit in solid America." Kingston's narrative explored both her childhood memories of growing up in the family laundry in Stockton and the customs, traditions, and fables of village life in China. In *China Men* (1980) Kingston took this exploration even further, contemplating the nature of exile and the effects of discrimination on earlier generations of Chinese immigrants. Her *Tripmaster Monkey* (1989) portrays the challenges facing Chinese Americans who attempt to balance the demands of assimilation with the imperatives of tradition. Likewise the theme of Amy Tan's *The Joy Luck Club* (1989), a collection of stories of four Chinese immigrant mothers and their American-born daughters, is the impact of past generations on the present. Tan was born in Oakland in 1952, the only daughter of Chinese immigrants, and recalled vividly the conflicting demands of her parents: "They wanted us to have American circumstances and Chinese character." Her second book, *The Kitchen God's Wife* (1991), was based on her mother's harrowing experiences in China and escape to the United States in 1949. In *The Hundred Secret Senses* (1995), Tan explores the world of nineteenth-century China and twentieth-century California through the all-seeing eyes of a young woman who navigates her way between cultures and epochs.

Similar concerns distinguished the work of Japanese American writers during this period. A common source of dramatic tension in their work was the contrast between contemporary California and a remembered or imagined life in Japan. Among the many books to deal with the experience of "relocation" during World War II, the most successful was *Farewell to Manzanar* (1973), written by Jeanne Wakatsuki Houston and her husband James D. Houston. *Farewell to Manzanar* tells the story of the Wakatsukis, an industrious southern California family resettled in 1942 at the Manzanar relocation camp in Owens Valley. The Wakatsukis face their hardships with dignity and resourcefulness, but disintegrate as a family unit. "I felt the miserable sense of loss," Jeanne Wakatsuki Houston recalled, "that comes when the center has collapsed and everything seems to be flying apart around you." David Mas Masumoto's *Silent Strength* (1985) and *Country Voices* (1987) present moving portraits of the effects of relocation on a small farming town in Fresno County. Masumoto, born after the war, recalled the silence that later surrounded the story of his own family's relocation: "A silence felt by my family and carried through the years; a silence that teaches yet I do not fully understand." The tension between acculturation and tradition, evident in Villareal's *Pocho* and Kingston's *Woman Warrior,* was thus heightened for Japanese Americans by the tragedy of relocation.

California has always been a fertile ground for the imagination. The latest generation of California writers, continuing in the tradition of Frank Norris and John Steinbeck, have created from California's recent past a literature redolent of the region but whose power and diversity are part of the larger American culture.

PAINTING AND SCULPTURE

Two of the most significant art movements in California since the end of World War II were abstract expressionism in the San Francisco Bay area in the late 1940s and the "L.A. look" of southern California in the 1960s. These two movements were part of larger currents in the development of modern art, but were also shaped by the distinct artistic environments of northern and southern California. Their order of occurrence was evidence of the growing importance of Los Angeles in the state's cultural history.

In the early 1930s the California art scene was vitalized by the visit of the German-born painter Hans Hofmann, often called the dean of abstract expressionism. Hofmann, whose abstract paintings exhibited bold thrusts of vibrant color, was a visiting instructor at the University of California at Berkeley and the Chouinard Art Institute in Los Angeles. His influence was especially strong in the Bay Area where in the late 1940s the California School of Fine Arts (later renamed the San Francisco Art Institute) invited Clyfford Still and Mark Rothko, two of the nation's leading abstract expressionists, to join the faculty. Still's paintings were characterized by large, ragged patches of dissonant color, while Rothko produced forceful rectangular shapes, blurred at the edges, painted in a more limited color range. The work of Still, Rothko, and the generation of artists they influenced marked the "golden age" of San Francisco painting.

By the middle 1950s abstract expressionism in the Bay Area had begun to decline. Many of the students of Clyfford Still followed him to New York where abstract expressionism was gaining acceptance, and the work of those left behind became increasingly imitative. Out of this decline came a movement away from total abstraction and back to a style of painting which represented figures or elements of the landscape. The most important of the so-called Bay Area figurative painters were David Park and Richard Diebenkorn, both of whom taught at the California School of Fine Arts. Park led the movement to representation with his richly colored paintings emphasizing the human form, whereas Diebenkorn remained essentially an abstract expressionist until 1955, after which he turned slowly to landscapes, figures, and still life. His colors, as one critic observed, were "essentially tonal, rooted in the California landscape."

It was also in the 1950s that the California beat generation made a distinct contribution to the evolution of modern art, the assemblage. The art of assemblage, a kind of sculpture created from bits of cast-off materials from everyday life, was a reaction against "high-brow" art just as the writing of Kerouac and Ginsberg represented a rejection of established literary standards. Constructed from old furniture, clothing, tin cans, license plates, store mannequins, wire, and string, the completed three-dimensional assemblages were often a statement of horror or anguish at the materialism and corruption of modern industrial society.

Out of the assemblage tradition came what was known as "funk art," a hybrid of painting and sculpture constructed from such materials as leather, clay, steel, and vinyl. The term "funk" apparently was borrowed from the vocabulary of jazz or blues musicians where "funky" meant a heavy beat, an earthy, sensual sound. Correspondingly, the constructions of such funk artists as Robert Arneson often were biomorphic forms with ribald or scatological connotations. Arneson's most controversial work was a ceramic bust of George Moscone, the mayor of San Francisco who was assassinated in 1978. The bust had an unnaturally long neck and was placed on a pedestal carved with graphic references to Moscone's life and death. Among the references was the word "Twinkies," a reminder of the defense argument that the judgment of Moscone's assassin had been impaired by his consumption of highly sugared cakes. The bust was unveiled at the George Moscone Convention Center in 1981 but was removed after heated protests. The *San Francisco Examiner* suggested that the bust should be "deposited out of public view—perhaps in the Bay, at the deepest place."

It was clear that the momentum in California art was shifting south. Abstract expressionism continued to be the dominant style of painting in Los Angeles in the 1950s, but by the end of the decade a distinctive regional variation had emerged. Among the paintings of Los Angeles artist Craig Kauffman in 1957 and 1958 were several works in which forms appeared sharply outlined in silhouette. Los Angeles painter Billy Al Bengston commented that Kauffman "was the first southern California artist *ever* to paint an original painting." In 1959 the Los Angeles County Museum opened an exhibition of four California painters whose work emphasized

Portrait of George. Robert Arneson's contro-versial ceramic bust of assassinated San Fran-cisco Mayor George Moscone. (*Courtesy of the artist. Photograph copyright Lee Fatherree, 1992.*)

an austere form of composition marked by geometric forms clearly, distinctly delineated. A Los Angeles critic christened the new style "hard edge," a term which accurately suggested the abrupt boundaries between shapes and colors in the new paintings. The exhibit at the county museum traveled to London, and hard edge abstraction provided Los Angeles with its first international success as a center for modern art.

One of the chief concerns of the hard edge painters was to achieve an immaculate finish to their work. By an extraordinarily even application of paint and by limiting their colors to two or three saturated hues, the hard edge abstractionists were able to create paintings with a remarkable optical shimmer. Critic Peter Plagens saw in these qualities a reflection of the aesthetic climate of Los Angeles. "Hard Edge arose out of Los Angeles's desert air, youthful cleanliness, spatial expanse, architectural tradition . . . and, most vaguely and most importantly, out of optimism."

In the middle 1960s a group of Los Angeles artists and sculptors, most notably Ed Ruscha, Billy Al Bengston, John McCracken, and Larry Bell, carried the con-cern for precision and impeccability of surface to an extreme. Their work achieved international recognition as the California finish fetish or, more commonly, the L.A. look. The objects they created were as lustrous as the glossy surface of a highly polished automobile or a new fiberglass surfboard. Among such sculptors the preferred materials were polyester resin or other new forms of plastic, neon, and stainless steel. Larry Bell, a sculptor born in Chicago in 1939 and educated at the Chouinard Art Institute, mastered the complicated procedures and expensive technology necessary to work the new materials and produced in the 1960s a series of mirrorlike cubes of chrome and glass. The inspiration for the cubes of Larry Bell seemed to be the "glass box" office buildings of downtown Los Angeles. Their materials were drawn from the local aerospace industry, and their concern with the surface of things, the facade, mirrored the influence of Hollywood. Even more than hard edge abstraction, the L.A. look was a product of the peculiar atmosphere of southern California.

One of the major international art movements of the 1960s was "pop art," a movement which both ridiculed and celebrated the affluent consumer society. Pop art flourished in southern California and, like abstract expressionism in the previous decade, took on there a distinctive regional quality. Los Angeles pop artists regarded impeccable craftmanship as crucial to their work, and they took great pains to produce art of a highly polished, finished quality. Pop art in Los Angeles, in other words, had the characteristic L.A. look. It was also distinguished by a mildness, subtlety, and benevolence that was lacking in the more strident pop art produced elsewhere.

Typical of the easygoing, nonmilitant pop artists working in southern California in the 1960s was Edward Ruscha. Born in Omaha in 1937 and reared in Oklahoma City, Ruscha moved to Los Angeles and attended Chouinard from 1956 to 1960. One of his best-known works was *Hollywood* (1968), a series of prints depicting the large sheet-metal letters in the Hollywood hills. The popular culture of Los Angeles was a major inspiration for the work of Ruscha, but his attitude toward that culture was ambiguous. One critic saw in the work of Ruscha a "mock worship of California's earthly paradise," and yet there was also in his work a kind of affectionate regard for Los Angeles and its environs. It remained for the viewer to decide whether the pastel sky of *Hollywood,* created by Ruscha out of Pepto-Bismal and caviar, was a tribute to the beauty of a Los Angeles sunset or a reminder of the unpleasant effects of smog.

Hollywood. A silk-screen print by Edward Ruscha. (*Gift of the Phoenix Collection of Graphic Art, San Francisco. Courtesy of the University Art Museum, University of California, Berkeley.*)

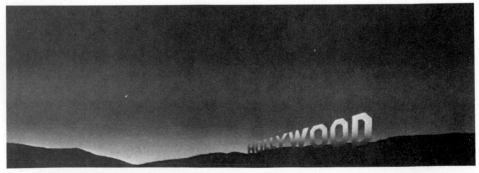

Less ambiguous were the so-called Chicano murals that appeared on the concrete walls of Los Angeles storm drains and freeway overpasses in the 1970s. The murals often featured crowded scenes of contemporary Latino life, painted on an imposing scale with bold lines and primary colors. Among the most successful muralists were "Los Four": Carlos Almaraz, Gilbert Luján, Frank Romero, and Beto de la Rocha. Almaraz traveled frequently to Mexico and saw firsthand the works of such master muralists as José Orozco and Diego Rivera. His intent was to adapt this grand tradition to the dramatization of such contemporary issues as the struggle of California's farm workers. "I paint and draw what I see and what I feel," Almaraz commented, "and reflect much of my Mexican background in this process." Similar concerns were evident in the work of Rupert Garcia. His series of dramatic posters illustrated a wide range of political and social issues. Each poster powerfully conveyed a specific mood, alternating between militant, melancholic, and majestic.

Among the important artists working in Los Angeles in the 1970s and 1980s was D. J. Hall. Her paintings often commented on the youth-obsessed middle-class women of southern California. Her style was akin to that of photo-realism, yet her canvases were marked by a tone at once more subtle and evocative. Her work presented a surface reality of youth and glamour, yet beneath that surface lurked the repressed dread of mortality and decay. In *Juice* (1982) Hall presents women of uncertain age in a blue-green swimming pool, their limbs grotesquely fore-shortened and foreshadowing the coming of shriveled skin and withered limbs. Her *Good and Plenty* (1985) suggests the superficiality of aging devotees of southern California's cult of youth.

Probing beneath the surface of things became an obsession of Los Angeles artists in the 1990s. Their thesis was a familiar one: just below the sunny facade of southern California lay a stratum of alienation, murder, and apocalyptic fantasies. Artist Chris Burden produced a work called *Medusa's Head* (1992) consisting of a 7-ton lump of dyed concrete and rocks hanging by a chain and symbolizing (perhaps) the degrading forces of modernization. Burden's work was included in a retrospective of 1990s art displayed at the Los Angeles Museum of Contemporary Art (MOCA). One bemused New York critic dismissed the entire collection as a monument to perpetual adolescence: "America invented it; Los Angeles glorifies it; and MOCA is its Louvre."

California art in recent decades has been dominated as much by institutions as by individuals. In 1968 the University Art Museum in Berkeley opened its new $3 million building, designed by Mario J. Ciampi, which included a special gallery for the large Hans Hofmann collection recently donated to the university by the artist. The following year the Oakland Museum opened its extraordinary new complex, a museum dedicated exclusively to the history, art, and natural history of California. Its art gallery included a retrospective of California art from the watercolors of visiting artists during the Spanish period, through the landscapes of William Keith and Albert Bierstadt, to the reflective cubes of Larry Bell. A splendid new home for the San Francisco Museum of Modern Art opened in 1995, a building hailed by one critic as "an extraordinary work of Modernist art in its own right."

Good and Plenty. A painting by D. J. Hall. In the full-size canvas a miniature California landscape is visible in the metallized sunglasses worn by the woman on the right. (*Courtesy of the artist and the Los Angeles Municipal Art Gallery.*)

The museum was part of Yerba Buena Gardens, an extravagant new 87-acre center for the visual and performing arts.

Meanwhile in southern California the Los Angeles County Museum of Art in 1965 was installed in magnificent new quarters on Wilshire Boulevard, adjacent to the La Brea tar pits, and in its first year it attracted a larger attendance than any other museum in the west. In 1971 the California Institute of the Arts, known popularly as Cal Arts, opened its new campus in the San Fernando Valley. Incorporating the Chouinard Art Institute and the Los Angeles Conservatory of Music, Cal Arts became a major educational institution for the visual and performing arts. Its new campus was in large part a monument to the generosity of the family of Walt Disney who contributed some $30 million to the institute.

Two other wealthy southern Californians made important contributions to the arts in recent years. In 1974 the Pasadena Art Museum, whose new buildings had opened in 1969 as a showcase for contemporary art, became the Norton Simon

Museum. Simon, a business executive with headquarters in Los Angeles, had created one of the largest collections of paintings and sculpture assembled by an individual in modern times. His collection included masterpieces by Rembrandt and Degas and became the permanent collection of the new Pasadena museum. The same year the J. Paul Getty Museum opened its new quarters near Pacific Palisades. The museum, modeled on a Roman villa, drew mixed reviews, for it included reproductions as well as authentic art among its displays of Greek and Roman antiquities, paintings, sculpture, and furniture. When Getty died in 1976, he left the bulk of his estate to the museum, making it the richest museum in the United States. The Getty Trust, valued at $4 billion, opened in 1997 its gleaming new Getty Center on a hilltop in the Brentwood section of Los Angeles.

ARCHITECTURE

The suburban growth of California's population following World War II spawned several distinctive forms of commercial and domestic architecture. At the center of the new suburban communities, dispersed widely by the spreading freeway system, were "shopping centers," clusters of stores designed exclusively for the automobile-borne shopper. The orientation of these stores toward their expansive parking lots, rather than toward the main street, was a major break with past traditions of commercial architecture. By the 1960s shopping centers had been transformed into "shopping malls," large self-contained units which centered on an enclosed mall and contained an array of small shops and one or more major department stores.

The houses that filled the new suburban tracts in the late 1940s and 1950s were almost all variations of a single style, the California ranch house. The roots of this ubiquitous style lay in the California bungalow of the early twentieth century, and like the bungalow the new ranch-style homes typically were single-floor dwellings, low in profile, with an informal arrangement of living spaces. Both styles were distinctly Californian in their emphasis on the close relation between indoor and outdoor living. The ranch-style homes were characterized by picture windows, sliding glass doors, terraces, patios, and, in the wealthier suburbs, swimming pools. Like the California bungalow, the "California ranch" was widely copied and came to be accepted as an important regional contribution to American domestic architecture.

Along the windswept cliffs of the Sonoma County coastline, a planned community of homes and condominiums known as Sea Ranch initiated in the 1960s yet another California style. Architects Charles Moore and William Turnbull in effect turned the California ranch house on end to create an elongated vertical box, sheathed in wooden siding and covered by a shedlike roof. Because the coastal winds were so strong, the Sea Ranch buildings were designed without overhanging eaves. The resulting "vertical shed-roof box" became the latest California export. As the cost of single-family homes rose to unbelievable heights, clusters of shed-roofed box apartments and condominiums began to dot the landscape from coast to coast. Roof gardens, balconies, and hot tubs succeeded terraces, patios, and pools, and the California ideal of the indoor-outdoor house lived on.

Whereas the suburbs of California proved to be centers of major architectural innovation in the twentieth century, California cities tended to follow rather than initiate trends in architectural design. The dominant style for commercial and institutional buildings since the end of World War II was the "international style," in which the structural skeleton of a building was often enclosed by a "curtain wall" of nonsupporting glass and metal panels. The impression of the typical international-style building was one of machinelike precision and anonymity, and skylines of cities across the state in the 1950s and 1960s came to be dominated by monuments to the high-rise aesthetic of internationalism.

Inevitably a reaction set in to the boring, unbearable monotony of the new buildings. California architects began to design structures such as Wurster Hall (1965) on the university campus at Berkeley and the civic center (1969) in Fremont which conformed to the tenets of "brutalism," bluntly exposing the building's concrete or steel frame as well as such "innards" as water pipes and air ducts. Also in the 1960s California shared in a movement known as the new formalism which reintroduced classical symmetry and such traditional materials as marble and granite. The Los Angeles Music Center (1964–1969) designed by Welton Becket, including the Dorothy Chandler Pavilion and the colonnade-enclosed Mark Taper Auditorium, was a striking example of the new style.

Most of the new commercial and institutional buildings in California cities were designed with an apparent disregard for their California setting. They could have been built anywhere. Architectural historian David Gebhard, however, has suggested that a distinctive "lack of intellectual intent" among California architects has given their work "a lightness and at times tinselly quality of make-believe which has more to do with Disneyland and Magic Mountain than it does with the traditional values of Modern architecture." Gebhard found a remarkable playfulness in the California architects' arbitrary use of such geometric shapes as circles, cones, and pyramids. San Francisco's Transamerica Pyramid (1972), designed by Los Angeles architect William Pereira, was a monumental and often unappreciated example of this whimsical quality of California design.

California architecture in recent years has also shown a strong interest in historicism. In some parts of the state the earlier mission revival and Spanish colonial revival never really ended. Since the mid-1920s new buildings in central Santa Barbara, by tradition and city ordinance, were Spanish in design. Thus in the mid-1970s new "Spanish-style" parking garages and overpasses for a crosstown freeway were proposed. In Sacramento a major restoration of the "old town" section of the city was completed, and more than $67 million was approved by the state legislature for renovation of the 1869 state capitol. The magnificently restored capitol was reopened in 1982. In communities around the state a rash of "Tudor" condominiums, "Norman" restaurants, and "medieval" motels suggested the breadth of interest in earlier styles. The most impressive manifestation of the new historicism was the J. Paul Getty Museum, modeled after the first-century Roman villa at Herculaneum.

The popularity of historicism constituted a fairly predictable, conservative response to the preceding years of innovation and experiment. The familiar standards of earlier styles of architectural design provided a sense of tradition and security, two qualities in short supply during the cultural and social upheavals of the 1960s.

MUSIC

By midcentury, California had become a world center for the composition and performance of the most advanced forms of contemporary music. In large measure the musical prominence of California was a product of the immigration to the state of leading European composers during the years before World War II.

The first and probably most influential of the Europeans to settle in California was Arnold Schoenberg, developer of the revolutionary twelve-tone technique of composition. Schoenberg had been a professor of music in Berlin until deposed by the Nazis because of his unconventional music and Jewish origins. In 1933 he immigrated to the United States and decided to settle permanently in Los Angeles, where he was appointed to the faculty of the University of Southern California in 1935 and later became a professor at UCLA. In 1940 Schoenberg was joined in southern California by Igor Stravinsky, the most important composer of the twentieth century. Stravinsky's music, like that of Schoenberg, was highly controversial and represented a radical departure from traditional forms of composition. He remained in Hollywood until 1969 and composed there major works for orchestra and chorus. Meanwhile in northern California Darius Milhaud, the foremost French composer since Ravel, joined the faculty of Mills College in Oakland after fleeing Nazi-occupied France. Following the war, Milhaud remained at Mills and also served as a professor of composition at the Paris Conservatory.

Schoenberg and Milhaud, through their teaching, directly influenced a generation of California composers and musicians. Most prominent among the twentieth-century composers born and educated in California was Los Angeles native John Cage. Like many of his contemporaries, Cage believed that the music of the western world was at a dead end and that composers henceforth must seek new sounds, new media, and indeed a new "language" of musical expression. In search of such a language, Cage studied composition under Schoenberg but soon moved beyond the twelve-tone technique to the use of electronic equipment, tape recordings, noisemakers, and assorted unconventional percussion instruments. His "Third Construction in Metal" (1941) was scored for rattles, drums, tin cans, cowbells, and a lion's roar.

The performance of contemporary music, often subject to skepticism and even hostility from concertgoers, was encouraged in California by several key individuals and institutions. In 1945 a group of young composers around Roger Sessions, then a professor of music at Berkeley, organized the Composers' Forum which for years sponsored a concert series featuring the work of Stravinsky, Schoenberg, and other contemporary composers. Under the direction of Pierre Monteux the San Francisco Symphony Orchestra in the 1940s also became a major force in popularizing the music of modern composers.

The San Francisco symphony continued to flourish under the leadership of the noted Austrian conductor Josef Krips during the 1960s and Seiji Ozawa in the early 1970s. Ozawa, born in China of Japanese parents, invariably conducted the classics as well as the most advanced contemporary music from memory—a remarkable feat. Replacing Ozawa in 1977 was the Dutch conductor Edo de Waart, under whose direction the San Francisco orchestra moved to its new quarters at the $31 million Louise M. Davies Symphony Hall in 1980. Davies Hall, together with the accompanying addition to the War Memorial Opera House and construction of the Zellerbach rehearsal hall, brought to completion the San Francisco Performing Arts Center begun nearly 50 years earlier.

As in all things cultural, the recent history of California music also reflected the rise of southern California. The traditional dominance of San Francisco had first been challenged by the creation of the Los Angeles Philharmonic Orchestra in 1919 which, under the direction of conductor Otto Klemperer in the 1930s, rose to first rank. From 1961 to 1978 the Los Angeles Philharmonic was under the direction of Zubin Mehta, a brilliant and glamorous conductor born in Bombay in 1936. During Mehta's tenure the Philharmonic finally obtained a permanent year-round home. Since the 1920s the summer concerts of the Los Angeles orchestra had been performed in the spectacular Hollywood Bowl, but the winter concerts were confined to an unsatisfactory leased auditorium. Los Angeles voters repeatedly had rejected bond issues for a municipally owned center for the performing arts. Dorothy Buffum Chandler worked almost single-handedly to secure enough private contributions to make possible a new complex of buildings for music and drama at the civic center. The largest of these structures, the Dorothy Chandler Pavilion, opened in 1964. A major counterpart to the Los Angeles center opened in 1986, the dramatic new Orange County Performing Arts Center in Costa Mesa.

In the years following World War II California also played a major role in the development of American popular music. In the 1940s much of the impetus for "traditionalist" jazz came from the state, and in the 1950s California was the center of the so-called west coast jazz movement. The band of Stan Kenton, a native of Kansas reared near Los Angeles, served as an important training ground for other California musicians. Pianist and composer Dave Brubeck organized a quartet in northern California which quickly rose to the top among modern jazz bands in the United States. Born in Concord in 1920, Brubeck had studied composition under Milhaud and Schoenberg.

If California can be said to have an indigenous music in the twentieth century, it would have to be rock. Although regarded by musicologists as being of little or no musical importance, rock music nevertheless was an important part of recent California history. During the 1960s California groups initiated several new rock styles and had an enormous impact on national and international popular music. Rock also was a galvanizing force for the "youth movement" of the 1960s, shaping and recording the social history of the period. Furthermore the new music from California often reinforced long-held popular conceptions about life in the Golden State and had a significant economic impact on the California economy. The recording industry generated thousands of new jobs and millions of dollars of income for Californians.

The emergence of rock in the late 1950s coincided with the onset of adolescence among the first wave of the postwar baby boom, the bulge in the American population caused by returning fathers at the end of World War II. The popularity of rock music and the strong sense of generational identity in the 1960s were rooted in this basic demographic fact. The so-called hard rock of the late 1950s was true teenage music, based on simple chords any adolescent could master on the guitar and celebrating in its lyrics the passions of teenage romance. By the end of the decade it appeared that rock music had exhausted its limited repertory.

California in the 1960s made three distinct contributions to popular music which revitalized rock. The "California sound" first appeared in the music of a group appropriately styled the Beach Boys, formed in 1961 in the suburbs of Los Angeles. Through their energetic melodies and cheerful repetitions, the Beach Boys effectively captured the bright simplicity of life on the southern California beaches in the early 1960s. The California sound not only reinvigorated American popular music, but also created a kind of modern legendry for California. Wholesome, tanned, and vigorous, the Beach Boys appeared in concert to be the very embodiment of California outdoor living; their lyrics were paeans to the climate of southern California. "Surfin' Safari" and "California Girls" insisted that life among the dunes and surf was carefree and that romantic opportunity was bountiful. A sense of easy mobility and love of speed was reflected in a score of recordings such as "Little Deuce Coupe" and "This Car of Mine."

Beginning in 1964 American young people were introduced to more sophisticated musical technique and melodic intricacy by a series of English rock bands. First, of course, came the Beatles, followed closely by Mick Jagger and the Rolling Stones. The first indications of an American response to the English invasion of popular music came from California. The new "Los Angeles sound," pioneered by a southern California group known as the Byrds, was essentially a combination of folk and rock music. The mix appealed to earlier devotees of hard rock and folk music and had the advantage of an American twang of country harmony. The popularity of Los Angeles folk rock was soon overshadowed by the appearance in San Francisco of the startling and highly controversial "acid rock." Originally intended to reproduce the distorted hearing of a person under the influence of LSD, acid rock was characterized by hyperamplification, bizarre electronic effects, and exotic imagery in its lyrics. When acid rock was performed at one of the city's auditoriums, such as the Fillmore or Avalon ballrooms, the illusion of an LSD experience was further heightened by "light shows" designed to reproduce the visual distortion induced by the drug.

The proliferation of rock bands in San Francisco in 1966 and 1967 was a measure of the tremendous influx of young people into the city. Some of the bands, such as the Quicksilver Messenger Service and the Grateful Dead, were immensely popular among residents of the Haight-Ashbury district, but did not achieve immediate commercial success. The first San Francisco band to establish a national following was the Jefferson Airplane, whose music was a blend of jazz, folk, blues, and "surrealistic tinkering." With the recording of such hits as "Embryonic Journey" and "White Rabbit," the band became a national sensation. Radio stations across the country broadcast the intonations of lead vocalist Grace Slick that "one pill makes you larger, and one pill makes you small."

In rapid succession California had spawned surf rock, folk rock, and acid rock. California was the center of the youth movement of the 1960s, and the music of the decade reflected this preeminence. It was appropriate, therefore, that a California musical event should become a symbol for the end of the decade and for the demise of "the movement." At the conclusion of their 1969 American tour, the Rolling Stones sought to hold a free concert in San Francisco's Golden Gate Park. The city refused to grant permission, and the concert was rescheduled for the Altamont Raceway in Alameda County. There, on December 6, 1969, more than 300,000 young people attended the performance, an event marred by violence. The Rolling Stones had recruited members of the Hell's Angels motorcycle gang to provide "security" for the band, and in the process the gang administered numerous beatings and stabbed one boy to death as he tried to reach the stage.

Altamont, combined with the death by drug overdose of rock superstars Jimi Hendrix and Janis Joplin the following year, triggered a change in the attitude of many young people toward drugs and signaled a sobering reevaluation of the future of the now-aging youth movement. One of the most popular rock lyrics of the early 1960s had celebrated the decade as "the dawning of the age of Aquarius," and one observer now remarked that the age of Aquarius had ended with the flash of a knife at Altamont. The student newspaper at the University of California at Berkeley described the tragedy of Altamont as "the end of a decade of dreams; the beginning of a decade of facing the realities of the human condition."

SELECTED BIBLIOGRAPHY

Anthologies of recent California literature include Gerald Haslam (ed.), *Many Californias* (1991); Haslam and James D. Houston (eds.), *California Heartland* (1979); Houston (ed.), *West Coast Fiction* (1979); and Ishmael Reed (ed.), *Calafia* (1979). Lawrence Ferlinghetti's *Literary California* (1980) is a lively survey by a central figure in the beat generation. See also Richard Candida Smith, *Utopia and Dissent* (1995); David Wyatt, *The Fall into Eden* (1986); Michael Davidson, *The San Francisco Renaissance* (1989); Houston, "The New Anatomy of California," *California History,* LXIII (Summer 1984), pp. 256–259; Houston, "Gerald Haslam's *The Other California,*" ibid., LXXII (Fall 1993), pp. 250–255; William Everson, *Archetype West* (1976); Thomas Parkinson (ed.), *A Casebook on the Beats* (1961); and Dennis McNally, *Desolate Angel: Jack Kerouac* (1980). Mark Royden Winchell, *Joan Didion* (1980), presents an analysis of the author's major works. On the work of Luis Valdez, see Yolanda Broyle Gonzalez, *El Teatro Campesino* (1994). Jeanne Wakatsuki Houston's sequel to *Farewell to Manzanar* (1973) is *Beyond Manzanar: Views of Asian-American Womanhood* (1985).

The best survey of modern California painting and sculpture is Peter Plagens, *Sunshine Muse* (1974). The northern California scene is described in Thomas Albright, *Art in the San Francisco Bay Area, 1945–1980* (1985), and Lawrence Ferlinghetti, "Bay Region Painting and Sculpture," *Art Digest* (August 1955), pp. 26 ff. On specific movements see Susan Landauer, *The San Francisco School of Abstract Expressionism* (1994); Peter Selz, *Funk* (1967); and Marcia Tucker, *"Bad" Painting* (1978). The emergence of Los Angeles is described in Anne

Bartlett Ayres, "Los Angeles Modernism and the Assemblage Tradition, 1948–1962," Ph.D. thesis, University of Southern California (1983); Barbara Rose, "Los Angeles: The Second City," *Art in America,* LIV (January 1966), pp. 110–115; and Nan R. Piene, "L.A. Trip," *Art in America,* LVIII (March 1970), pp. 138–141. Marcia R. McGrath's *Edward Ruscha, Books, Prints* (1972) is a catalog from an exhibition at the University of California, Santa Cruz.

The indispensable guides to contemporary California architecture are Sally Woodbridge, *California Architecture* (1988); David Gebhard et al., *A Guide to Architecture in San Francisco and Northern California* (1973); and Gebhard and Robert Winter, *A Guide to Architecture in Los Angeles and Southern California* (1977). Important interpretations include Gebhard and Susan King, *A View of California Architecture: 1960–1976* (1976), and Reyner Banham, *Los Angeles* (1971).

A valuable resource for the history of California music is Stephen M. Fry (ed.), *California's Musical Wealth* (1988). On the L.A. music scene, see Dorothy Lamb Crawford, *Evenings On and Off the Roof* (1995). Useful guides to recent popular music include Lillian Roxon, *Rock Encyclopedia* (1969); Jim Miller (ed.), *The Rolling Stone Illustrated History of Rock and Roll* (1976; rev. ed., 1980); Darby Slick, *Don't You Want Somebody to Love?* (1991); Jack McDonough, *San Francisco Rock* (1985); and Anthony Fawcett, *California Rock, California Sound* (1979). Richard Aquila, "Images of the American West in Rock Music," *Western Historical Quarterly,* XI (October 1980), pp. 415–432, includes an analysis of California imagery.

CHAPTER THIRTY-FOUR

Recent California Politics

The most visible result of the turmoil of the 1960s was a new wave of political conservatism in state and national affairs. Beset by rapid increases in the cost of living, voters became increasingly restive under the burden of taxation and resentful of the growth of government. Political candidates appealed to the conservative mood of the voters by offering to restore "law and order," cut welfare and other unwanted government programs, and lower taxes.

THE REAGAN YEARS

Ronald Reagan was among those who benefited most from the conservative revival. Reagan was a convert to conservatism. As a student at a small college in Illinois, the state of his birth, he had been one of the leaders of a strike against a drastic cut in the college's budget, a strike so successful that it forced the resignation of the president who had proposed the cut. Reagan came to Hollywood in 1937, where he not only became a successful actor, but also served as president of the Screen Actors Guild. In these early years his political views were those of a liberal Democrat. His name was once omitted from a list of supporters of Helen Gahagan Douglas because he was considered too far left. But later he became a Democrat for Eisenhower and a Democrat for Nixon, and finally changed his registration to Republican in 1962.

Reagan acquired a 305-acre ranch in the Malibu hills for the breeding of thoroughbred horses. The rise in the value of the land, and a series of large increases in the taxes on it, coincided with a change in Reagan's political philosophy. He became strongly hostile toward taxation and toward the growth of governmental activities that required tax support. During the same period, in the 1950s and early 1960s, the General Electric Company employed him to appear regularly on the television programs it sponsored and also to make speeches to its employees and to civic groups. These addresses lauded private enterprise and were increasingly critical of government.

During the presidential campaign of 1964, Reagan delivered a nationwide television speech in support of Barry Goldwater. Although the speech could not save Goldwater's doomed candidacy, it demonstrated beyond doubt the effectiveness of Reagan as a political campaigner. Following the Republican debacle in the November election, some conservatives expressed the wish that Reagan had been the candidate instead of Goldwater.

Among those attracted to Reagan were a group of wealthy southern California Republicans who formed the nucleus of a movement to make him the next governor of California. In 1965 Reagan met with members of this group, and after expressing some reluctance to become a candidate, he agreed to enter the Republican primary the following year. Reagan won the Republican nomination with considerable ease and faced in the general election Edmund G. Brown, the Democratic incumbent, who was seeking a third term.

During the gubernatorial campaign of 1966, the disorderly demonstrations at Berkeley and elsewhere continued to receive great attention from the news media. Although Governor Brown had taken a hard line in dealing with the Free Speech Movement, Reagan now used to his own advantage the issue of campus unrest and pledged that if elected he would clean up the "mess at Berkeley." Reagan also claimed that 8 years as governor was enough for any incumbent, and that Brown did not deserve a third term.

Another major factor in the gubernatorial campaign was the white backlash against black demands for residential desegregation and job equality. These issues shattered the coalition between organized labor and racial minority groups that had been essential to Brown's victories in 1958 and 1962. Reagan, in his campaign speeches, repeatedly expressed his opposition to the open-housing Rumford Act of 1963 but insisted that in doing so he was defending the right of private property, not indulging in racial bigotry. This stand won him the votes of many white Democrats, including many labor union members and their families. Reagan's attacks on the rising costs of government also won some defectors from the Democratic ranks. Many members of labor unions, and of the lower and middle classes in general, had been enjoying rising incomes and were experiencing a new resentment against taxation. In the election on November 8, 1966, Reagan defeated Brown by 3,742,913 to 2,749,174, a margin just short of a million votes.

In his inaugural address, delivered on January 5, 1967, Governor Ronald Reagan outlined the central idea of his administration: "The cost of California's government is too high. It adversely affects our business climate. . . . We are going to squeeze and cut and trim until we reduce the cost of government." Speaking as a self-styled "citizen-politician" who had never before held a public office, Reagan thus made a powerful appeal to the popular mood of hostility toward government and taxation. "The time has come," Reagan declared, "to run a check to see if all the services government provides were in answer to demands or were just goodies dreamed up for our supposed betterment."

Reagan's political and social philosophy was a stunning reversal of the ideas of such governors as Earl Warren and Edmund G. Brown, who had believed that government services should have a great, direct, and positive role in the state's devel-

Governor Ronald Reagan is sworn in by California Supreme Court Justice Marshall F. McComb in the specially decorated capitol rotunda shortly after midnight, January 2, 1967. Reagan's left hand is on the Bible of Father Junípero Serra, which is held by California Senate Chaplain Wilbur Choy. In the background are statues of Queen Isabella and Christopher Columbus. (*Courtesy of The Bettmann Archive.*)

opment. As governor, Reagan soon learned that an actual reduction in the total budget of a huge and growing state was virtually impossible. Most of the state government's annual expenditures were mandated by law. The largest of the state services whose budgets could be reduced at the governor's discretion were in the fields of mental health and higher education, and in these sensitive and vulnerable areas Reagan made drastic cuts. He slashed funding for the state department of mental health, cutting substantially its staff and effectiveness. Reagan also reduced funding for the state's colleges and universities, and proposed substantial increases in tuition to make up part of the difference. These measures, he said, "would help get rid of undesirables. Those there to agitate and not to study might think twice before they pay tuition." Reagan's cuts in mental health were generally regarded as the greatest mistake of his first year in office, but his hard-line education policies won him widespread approval.

In one of his campaign speeches, Reagan had said that he was "sick at what has happened at Berkeley. Sick at the sit-ins, the teach-ins, the walkouts. When I am elected governor I will organize a throw-out, and Clark Kerr will head that list."

Reagan was not, however, solely responsible for the dismissal of University of California President Kerr, although it occurred at the first regents' meeting that he attended as governor, early in 1967. Most of the regents had been dissatisfied with Kerr's handling of student disruptions since the Sproul Hall sit-in of December 1964. The dismissal of Kerr sent shock waves throughout the national academic community, where it was angrily denounced as an anti-intellectual assault on academic freedom.

Reagan's Democratic challenger in the 1970 gubernatorial election, Assembly Speaker Jesse Unruh, tried to blame Reagan for the continuation of campus disorders, but the voters doubted Unruh's claim that he could have dealt with unruly students more effectively. The hostile reaction of most California voters to the radicalism of the student new left contributed heavily to Reagan's reelection victory over Unruh.

Early in his second term Governor Reagan renewed and intensified his calls for "reform" of the welfare system, which to him meant primarily reduction of its cost. He called it "a cancer eating at our vitals." Democratic leaders in the legislature were skeptical that massive cuts in welfare could be achieved. They pointed out that Reagan's hopes of removing many people from the welfare rolls by requiring them to work would be limited by the fact that only about 1 percent of the recipients were able-bodied adult males, whereas the mass of them were mothers, children, the blind, the disabled, or the aged. Reagan and the Democratic legislators eventually worked out a compromise measure that was intended to reduce the cost of the state's welfare system by about $200 million.

When Reagan submitted his annual budget in January 1971, he insisted that the state's expenses for the next fiscal year could be met without increasing taxes, if welfare costs were further reduced, cost-of-living increases denied to state employees, and various other state expenses cut to the barest minimum. Yet in spite of these austerities Reagan was forced to sign a bill increasing state taxes by $500 million. The bulk of the new revenues came in the form of an income withholding tax, effective on January 1, 1972. Of the 38 states with income taxes, California had been the only one that did not provide for withholding; Reagan had long promised never to approve it, and after signing the bill he told reporters that he had had to be "dragged kicking and screaming" to the desk where he did so.

In 1973 Reagan sought to embody the essence of his conservative philosophy in a sweeping tax reduction measure. Reagan's proposal would have forced the gradual reduction of state spending over a period of years and required a two-thirds vote rather than a simple majority of the legislature to adopt a new tax or increase an existing one. Drafted by one of Reagan's special task forces, the measure was 5000 words long and very complex. In an unguarded moment Reagan confessed to a reporter that he himself did not fully understand the language of it. When the plan went to the voters as Proposition 1 in November 1973, it was decisively rejected. The voters thus handed the governor a stinging personal defeat.

All Reagan's promises of massive tax reductions proved impossible to carry out. The state budgets he signed increased every year, from $5 billion for 1967–1968 to $10.2 billion for 1974–1975.

In 1976 Ronald Reagan launched an all-out campaign for the Republican nomination for president. As Hiram Johnson had once dreamed of "Californianizing the nation" by taking to Washington the progressive program that he felt he had created in California, so Reagan hoped to take his conservative crusade all the way to the White House. The odds against him were heavy. The incumbent president, Gerald Ford, was also seeking the Republican nomination. Ford had assumed the presidency two years earlier, following the resignation of Richard Nixon during the Watergate scandal. At the 1976 Republican convention, Reagan came within about 100 delegate votes of winning the nomination away from the incumbent president who was seeking it—something that had not happened since 1884 when Chester A. Arthur lost to James G. Blaine.

Many observers concluded that Reagan's career in major public office was over, but Reagan and his advisers began at once laying the ground for yet another campaign for the presidency. Top Reagan aides formed the steering committee of a new political action committee, and its newsletter was mailed to former Reagan contributors and campaign workers. Reagan also kept in the public eye through a widely syndicated newspaper column and radio program. His message was the same as it had been 10 years earlier—cut taxes and government spending, balance the budget, and reduce government regulation of business.

JERRY BROWN AND THE ERA OF LIMITS

Ronald Reagan's effective use of the third-term issue in 1966 against Edmund G. Brown had made it practically impossible for Reagan himself to seek a third term as California governor in 1974. For the first time since 1958 the incumbent governor chose not to run for reelection, and the wide-open contest attracted 29 candidates, 18 in the Democratic primary alone, each of whom strove to achieve greater "name recognition." In this crowded field the Democrat whose name already had the highest statewide recognition was Edmund G. Brown, Jr., son of the former governor.

Known from youth as "Jerry," the younger Brown at first rejected his political inheritance and entered a Jesuit seminary to prepare for the priesthood. After 4 years he left the seminary, enrolled at the University of California at Berkeley, where he majored in Latin and Greek, and was graduated from Yale Law School in 1964. Moving to southern California, Brown launched his political career in 1969 with a successful campaign for a seat on the Los Angeles Community College District Board of Trustees. The following year, he was elected secretary of state. In his new office, Brown vigorously enforced campaign disclosure laws which had been ignored for decades and advocated stronger controls over campaign practices. In 1974 Brown became one of the principal sponsors of an initiative, known as the Political Reform Act, which called for imposition of tight limits on campaign contributions and spending, establishment of stricter disclosure requirements, and creation of a Fair Political Practices Commission.

During the 1974 gubernatorial campaign, the Watergate scandal dominated the headlines and Jerry Brown's name was linked with the most popular issue of

Governor Edmund G. Brown congratu-
lates his son (and future governor) Jerry
Brown at the 1960 commencement
exercises of the University of California,
Berkeley. *(Courtesy of the California
Historical Society.)*

the day, political reform. Brown won the Democratic primary, and the Political
Reform Act was overwhelmingly approved by the voters. Meanwhile in the
Republican primary, Reagan's heir apparent, Lt. Gov. Ed Reinecke, was indicted
for perjury by the Watergate grand jury and was defeated by State Controller
Houston Flournoy. Brown's margin of victory over Flournoy in the general election
was less than 178,000 votes out of more than 6 million cast, making the race the
closest gubernatorial contest in California since 1920.

Through largely symbolic actions Brown appealed to the strain of antigovern-
ment sentiment potent among voters in the aftermath of Watergate. He denounced
the new governor's mansion, built for Reagan with gifts of money from his wealthy
supporters, as "that Taj Mahal" and chose instead to live in a modest apartment. In
contrast to Reagan's official Cadillac, Brown went about in a blue Plymouth sedan.
On a more substantial level, Brown's policies toward government spending and
taxation were consistently conservative. At the beginning of his first term, he
pledged that he would approve no new taxes or general tax increases, and he recommended reducing proposed increases in state funds for higher education and
social welfare programs. "The first test of all of us," Brown counseled the legislature, "is to live within realistic limits."

The most important accomplishment of Brown's first term was enactment
of the landmark Agricultural Relations Act of 1975. The new law, which created
the Agricultural Labor Relations Board (ALRB) to oversee union elections by the
state's farm workers, was a personal triumph for the governor and his secretary of
agriculture, Rose Elizabeth Bird. Representatives from the state's agricultural
districts became angered when Brown appointed a majority of labor-oriented
members to the ALRB and the board adopted policies that the growers opposed. In

an effort to win farm support, Brown appointed a working farmer as director of the department of agriculture.

In late 1976 and early 1977 Brown's popularity encountered some setbacks. California public school finance was in serious difficulty, and there was shocking new evidence of scandalous conditions in several of the state's mental hospitals. Brown also came under powerful attack from business and labor groups which charged that he had created an "adverse business climate." Through his appointments to such agencies as the Air Resources Board and Energy Commission, Brown oversaw vigorous enforcement of environmental protection standards and withheld licensing of large-scale power plant facilities. Business leaders charged Brown was stifling economic development, and labor leaders complained of the loss of jobs. Stung by criticism that the "era of limits" was antibusiness, Brown began speaking of the "era of possibilities." He created an Office of Business Development to lure new industries to the state, traveled to Japan to encourage location of an automobile assembly plant in California, and supported legislation to streamline the regulatory process permitting new industrial construction.

The one very evident problem which Jerry Brown failed to solve during his first term was the need for tax reform. The overriding issue in the 1978 elections proved to be an initiative to reduce property taxes written by Howard Jarvis and Paul Gann and which appeared on the June primary ballot as Proposition 13. Brown campaigned vigorously against the initiative, while his chief Republican rival, Attorney General Evelle Younger, supported it. In the June election voters approved Proposition 13 by a landslide margin of nearly 2 million votes, and Brown and Younger each won their party's nomination for governor. Brown entered the general election campaign in serious trouble. For all his careful maneuvering to build support among major constituencies in the state, he had badly miscalculated the enormous popularity of the tax-cutting initiative. In June, he and Younger were about even in public opinion polls; one Los Angeles survey showed Brown trailing his opponent by 4 percentage points. Brown clearly had a choice. He could continue to oppose Proposition 13 and probably lose the election, or he could reverse his position and win.

Brown quickly became an enthusiastic supporter of the initiative. He imposed a freeze on all state hiring, banned pay raises for state employees, cut cost-of-living increases for welfare recipients, and worked with the legislature to distribute surplus state funds to local governments. "I've been talking about limits since I got here," Brown proudly announced, "and now Jarvis has given me new tools." Brown's enthusiasm following Proposition 13's passage was sufficient to convince voters that it was he, and not Younger, who would best be able to implement it. In November 1978 Brown defeated Younger by more than 1.3 million votes. Typical of the lack of party discipline in the state, Brown's lieutenant governor, Mervyn Dymally, was defeated by the Republican candidate, recording executive Mike Curb.

Brown began his second term in office with a call for further retrenchment in state government. He proposed a reduction of 5000 employees in the state workforce, a tax rebate of more than $1 billion, and an overall budget increase well

Garry Trudeau, creator of the syndicated cartoon strip *Doonesbury,*
lampooned Jerry Brown mercilessly for his rapid and frequent changes
in political positions. *(DOONESBURY. © 1980 by G. B. Trudeau.*
Reprinted with permission of UNIVERSAL PRESS SYNDICATE. All
rights reserved.)

below the rate of inflation. Brown defended his conservative economic policies
by reminding the legislature that his proposed budget "reflects the clear mandate of
the voters for a leaner government." His inaugural address in January was so
reminiscent of that of Reagan in 1967—"We are going to squeeze and cut and trim
until we reduce the cost of government"—that one political commentator saw it as
the beginning of "Ronald Reagan's Third Term."

   Brown's inaugural message also signaled his intention to challenge Jimmy
Carter for the presidency in 1980 by mounting a campaign to cut federal taxes and
goverment spending. From the beginning, Brown's campaign was beset by
financial problems, and his record in the 1980 presidential primaries was one of

dismal failure. After failing to win a single delegate in the early New England primaries, Brown withdrew from the race and returned to California where he faced the formidable task of rebuilding his sagging popularity. Brown's approval rating in the latest California Poll was the lowest of any governor in nearly two decades. His relations with the legislature had reached crisis proportions. By the time he withdrew from the presidential campaign, he had had more vetoes overridden by the legislature than had all other governors since 1942 combined.

In comparison with Brown's disastrous 1980 campaign for the presidency, Ronald Reagan's was a model of efficiency. Whereas Brown was never able to get his campaign off the ground, Reagan scored a landslide victory in the pivotal New Hampshire primary and eventually forced all other contenders for the Republican nomination to drop from the race. During the general election campaign against Jimmy Carter, Reagan emphasized his own conservative record as governor of California, claiming success in his battle to reform the welfare system, slash taxes, and reduce the size of government. Reagan's claims were widely accepted, in spite of his record of increased state taxes and expenditures while governor and the nearly unanimous judgment that his attempt at welfare reform was a failure. Repeated endlessly during the campaign was a television commercial that summarized Reagan's alleged accomplishments as California governor, presenting the image of a reliable, experienced government executive.

The size of the Republican victory in the November 1980 election was a surprise to most observers. Reagan won 489 electoral votes to Carter's 49, and for the first time in 26 years a Republican majority was elected to the United States Senate. Reagan defeated the incumbent president in California by more than 1.4 million votes.

In personnel and policy the new Reagan administration bore many similarities to Reagan's years as California governor. His efforts to reduce the state budget and cut taxes in California were duplicated on the national level when he won congressional approval of his "program for economic recovery." This sweeping program, which included the largest reduction in individual and business taxes ever enacted by Congress, called for a cut in personal income taxes of nearly 25 percent over 3 years. At the center of the Reagan program was a major reduction in virtually every area of the federal budget except defense. Reminiscent of Reagan's budgets in California, the heaviest cuts in federal spending were reserved for such areas as food stamps, Medicare, unemployment benefits, and student aid. Reagan also called for the reform or elimination of many federal regulations of business. Just as Reagan's philosophy as California governor had stood in sharp contrast to that of his predecessor, his federal economic policy marked a dramatic reversal of nearly half a century of expanding government involvement in the nation's social welfare.

THE TAX REVOLT

The reputation of a president or a governor is often defined in crisis. The nearest thing to a crisis during Jerry Brown's first term as governor was the onset of two winters of extraordinarily warm and dry weather in 1976 and 1977, when California faced the greatest danger of drought since the dry winters of the 1860s had wiped out the state's early cattle industry. Fortunately the rains returned and the crisis passed. The victory of Proposition 13 in the June 1978 primary marked the beginning of a different sort of drought, a massive reduction in government revenues, and presented Governor Brown, the legislature, and the people of California with a crisis of major proportions.

The roots of the tax revolt lay in several separate but related developments. First, inflation had deeply eroded the real income of California taxpayers. In the decade prior to the passage of Proposition 13 the cost of living in California had risen 79 percent. The cost of government was the one price that consumers had the power to vote down. Second, because state and local taxes were steadily increasing at rates greater than the general inflation rate, taxes were absorbing an increasing share of personal income. Property taxes in the decade before 1978 had increased nearly twice as much as the cost of living. Third, although the cost of government was steadily rising, the level of satisfaction with government services was declining. Dissatisfaction was especially strong among middle-income taxpayers who believed that in recent years government spending had shifted from programs that directly benefited them, such as those for streets and highways, to programs such as welfare that benefited only a few. Voters had become convinced that there was "fat" in state and local government—inefficiency, waste, unwanted services, high salaries, and fringe benefits for government workers—which could be cut without reducing such essential services as police and fire protection.

The sponsors of Proposition 13, Howard Jarvis and Paul Gann, needed about half a million signatures to qualify their measure for the June 1978 ballot. They soon gathered more than 1.2 million. The Jarvis-Gann constitutional amendment provided that property taxes should be limited to 1 percent of a property's assessed value. This meant an average reduction in property taxes of about 57 percent and a reduction in annual property tax revenues for cities, counties, school districts, and other units of local government of about $7 billion. The assessed value of all property would be rolled back to its 1975 level and could rise from that figure by only 2 percent per year. Property would be reassessed only when sold or improved. Furthermore, state and local governments were forbidden from increasing property taxes. The legislature or local voters could raise other taxes, but only by a two-thirds vote rather than by the previous simple majority.

The essence of Proposition 13, the restriction of property taxes to 1 percent of value, had appeared on the ballot in 1968 and again in 1972 but had been soundly defeated. By the latter half of the 1970s, however, property values in California were rising about 2 percent *per month*. Because several years often intervened between reassessments of a property's value, increases in property taxes of 40 or 50 percent were common and in some areas taxes had increased 90 percent between assessments. Local governments failed to reduce the tax rate and the governor and legislature failed to take effective action. Property owners were outraged, and many homeowners wondered whether the increased tax burden would force them to sell their homes.

islation, distributing state funds to local governments, permitted state intrusion into areas which previously had been local domain.

The distribution of bailout funds steadily depleted the surplus in the state treasury. After the enactment of Proposition 13 in 1978, the state began spending annually about a billion dollars more than it collected in tax revenues. Finally, in 1981, Governor Brown made the fateful announcement: "The surplus is gone. The cupboard is bare." The governor ordered immediate cuts in the budgets of most state departments, including the colleges and universities, and warned that California cities and counties would have "to tighten their belts in the face of a new fiscal austerity." With the surplus exhausted, California governments at last faced the awful dilemma of sharply reducing existing programs or raising new taxes.

THE GOVERNORSHIP OF GEORGE DEUKMEJIAN

In the midst of the state's worst fiscal crisis since the depression, Jerry Brown decided in 1982 to seek election to the United States Senate. Brown's prospects for victory were slim at best. He managed to win barely half the vote in the Democratic primary, hardly an impressive accomplishment for an incumbent governor. The Republican nominee was the 49-year-old mayor of San Diego, Pete Wilson, who was determined to make the election a referendum on the performance of Jerry Brown as governor. Wilson's strategy was successful; his margin of victory over Brown was more than 400,000 votes. "I shall return," the defeated governor told a post-election news conference, "but not for awhile."

The race for governor in 1982 also attracted widespread interest, in part because one of the major candidates was black. Tom Bradley, the popular mayor of Los Angeles, easily won the Democratic nomination. Attorney General George Deukmejian emerged as the Republican nominee and went on to defeat Bradley in one of the closest elections in California history. Deukmejian's plurality of 0.68 percent of the vote was the smallest of any incoming governor since 1886. The election was so close that an early morning edition of the *San Francisco Chronicle*—in a gaff reminiscent of the *Chicago Tribune*'s famous "Dewey Defeats Truman" headline of 1948—proclaimed "First Black Elected Governor."

Although interest in the election was high, neither candidate aroused much enthusiasm from the electorate. One political commentator labeled the race a contest between "Cautious Tom" and "Dull Duke."

George Deukmejian's 1982 victory was the result of several related factors. In spite of Tom Bradley's repeated efforts to distance himself from the discredited Brown administration, Bradley could not escape entirely the onus of the incumbent governor's unpopularity. "Tom Bradley's administration will be no different than Jerry Brown's," insisted Deukmejian. Both candidates denied that race was an issue in the election, and yet 6 percent of Californians polled during the campaign reported that they favored Deukmejian because Bradley was black or because they believed he would favor minorities. The racial issue proved doubly troubling for Bradley. Although he received strong support from minority leaders during the campaign, voter turnout in minority precincts on election day was lower than expected. Another important factor in the election was the impact of absentee voting. Bradley actually received more votes than Deukmejian from the Californians who went to the polls. It was the heavy response of absentee voters that gave Deukmejian his victory. For the first time in the state's history, the winner on election day was the loser.

The narrowness of Deukmejian's victory was reflected in the outcome of other contests in the 1982 election. In what seemed to be a new California tradition—that the governor and lieutenant governor be of different political parties—Democrat Leo McCarthy of San Francisco was elected to serve as the Republican governor's understudy. Democrats also won election to each of the remaining statewide partisan offices, and they strengthened their domination of the state's legislature and congressional delegation. The results of many of the races in 1982 were determined a year earlier by the Democratic-controlled legislature's redrawing of district lines. The most controversial part of the legislature's decennial reapportionment plan was its recarving of the state's 45 congressional districts. The new district lines enabled Democrats to increase their majority in the California congressional delegation by six seats, nearly a quarter of the party's gain across the nation. Republicans denounced the reapportionment plan as an "outrageous gerrymander."

During his 1982 campaign for governor, Deukmejian stressed his militant anticrime record and argued that crime was the major issue facing the people of California. As a state senator, Deukmejian had been a key figure in winning passage of a statute mandating a prison term for persons convicted of using a gun in the commission of a crime, and was the author of a new capital punishment law, passed by the legislature in 1977 over the veto of Governor Jerry Brown. Elected attorney general in 1978, Deukmejian reduced the justice department's environmental protection unit and focused his efforts instead on crime fighting. He attacked many of Brown's judicial appointees as "soft on crime," and conducted an ongoing feud with the liberal Supreme Court Chief Justice Rose Bird.

In his inaugural address on January 3, 1983, Governor Deukmejian offered a recapitulation of his conservative creed. He promised to appoint "common sense judges" to the state's courts, judges who were as concerned with the rights of victims as they were with the rights of criminals. He condemned the environmental policies of his Democratic predecessor, charging that they had "choked off growth and progress." In an explicit rejection of Brown's "era of limits" philosophy, the new governor proclaimed: "As far as I am concerned, there are no limits to what we can achieve."

The issue which soon came to dominate the Deukmejian administration was the state's worsening financial crisis. In the week after the election, the state controller announced that California had come "to the bottom of the barrel" and that it would have to borrow $400 million from private lenders to pay its current bills. Ever since the passage of Proposition 13 in 1978, the state had spent more each year than it had collected in taxes. After the surplus was exhausted in 1981, the state faced a projected deficit of $1.5 billion.

Deukmejian presented the legislature with a plan to make drastic cuts in state spending, including reductions in health and welfare programs and in aid to local governments. The Democratic-controlled legislature opposed the governor's plan and argued instead for a tax increase to protect existing programs. As the legislature debated the governor's plan, the financial crisis intensified. For the first time since the depression, the state was forced to pay some of its bills with "registered warrants" instead of cashable checks. The warrants in effect were IOUs from the state. Finally, after weeks of bitter controversy and growing public alarm, the legislature approved a compromise budget. The budget included most of the governor's proposals for spending cuts and called for a standby increase in the state sales tax if revenues in the year ahead were not sufficient to eliminate the remaining deficit.

California's financial crisis passed, temporarily, as the state and national economy boomed in the mid-1980s. Increased revenues poured into the state treasury, a tax increase was avoided, and the state once again began to accumulate a surplus. Deukmejian's popularity increased as the state's financial condition improved. By the middle of his first term in office, the California Poll found that he was more popular than Ronald Reagan had ever been during his 8 years as California governor. Deukmejian enjoyed moderate success in his dealings with the legislature, winning passage of at least a portion of his conservative agenda for the state. The legislature approved a revision of the state's welfare system, requiring some welfare recipients to work for their state checks, and authorized a speedup in the construction of new prisons.

The elections of 1984 provided an inconclusive measure of Deukmejian's strength. On the November ballot was an initiative to establish a state-run lottery. Major funding for the initiative campaign came from a subsidiary of a slot-machine company, the nation's largest manufacturer of lottery tickets and related parapher-nalia. Deukmejian opposed the initiative, as did most law-enforcement officials in the state, but it was enthusiastically approved by the voters. Half the lottery's revenues went to prizes, more than a third was allocated to education, and the remainder was for "administrative overhead." The biggest immediate winners were the companies that supplied the state with lottery tickets, computers, and other equipment. Although funds from the lottery for education surpassed early predic-tions, educators feared that the lottery bonanza would lead to a reduction in fund-ing from other sources. Critics of the lottery charged that it was a regressive tax, falling primarily on those who could least afford to pay.

Governor Deukmejian began his campaign for reelection in 1986 with a com-manding lead in public opinion polls. His Democratic opponent, once again, was Mayor Tom Bradley of Los Angeles. Bradley had scored an impressive victory in 1985, becoming the first mayor in the city's history to be elected to a fourth term. The glittering success of the 1984 Olympic Games, held in Los Angeles, bolstered the mayor's reputation as an able administrator. Yet Bradley's gubernatorial campaign was never able to make much of a dent in Deukmejian's support, nor could it match the Republican governor's ability to raise campaign funds. Even in the Democratic primary, Bradley fared poorly. Nearly half a million Democrats voted against him.

Overshadowing the other issues in the 1986 election was the battle over the reconfirmation of Supreme Court Chief Justice Rose Elizabeth Bird, a bitter contest that one political analyst called "the war of the Rose." Following her appointment to the court by Jerry Brown, Bird had been confirmed for an initial term in 1978 by the smallest margin in California judicial history. Her consistent opposition to the death penalty aroused vehement opposition from a host of conservative organizations, and she became a detested symbol for all those who believed that the courts had become too lenient on criminals. During the gubernatorial campaign, George Deukmejian reiterated his long-standing opposition to Bird, whereas Tom Bradley unsuccessfully tried to sidestep the issue.

Deukmejian easily defeated Bradley in the general election. The voters also overwhelmingly rejected the reconfirmation of Chief Justice Rose Bird, along with two other associate justices who had been appointed by Jerry Brown. The rejection of the three incumbent justices was the first such defeat since the state adopted the confirmation process more than 50 years earlier. Governor Deukmejian thus entered his second term not only with a strong vote of confidence, but also with the opportunity to mold a new, more conservative Supreme Court that could alter the direction of California law for years to come.

The impact of Deukmejian's judicial conservatism was soon apparent. Early in his second term he selected his longtime friend and former law partner Malcolm Lucas to be the new chief justice. Known as "Maximum Malcolm" for his sentencing policies while serving on the federal bench, Lucas was soon joined by other Deukmejian appointees to form a conservative majority on the high court. Under Lucas's direction, the state Supreme Court took a sharp turn to the right. Whereas death penalty cases had been routinely overturned by the Bird court, the Lucas court frequently upheld them.

The criminal justice system proved to be one of the few areas of state government in which George Deukmejian achieved substantial change. He appointed conservative judges to all levels of the state judiciary and signed dozens of laws that toughened the sentencing of convicted criminals. During his administration, 15 new prisons were constructed, the budget for the Department of Corrections more than quadrupled, and the number of Californians behind bars increased 250 percent.

Governor Deukmejian also took great pride in his improvement of the state's business climate. He believed that his predecessor had indulged in a "regulatory mania" that had burdened businesses with thousands of unnecessary rules and restrictions. Deukmejian modified or removed more than 25,000 state regulations and reduced the budget of state agencies such as the California Coastal Commission, the Agricultural Labor Relations Board, the Consumer Affairs Department, and the Public Employment Relations Board. Deukmejian filled such agencies with appointees who shared his probusiness ideology. Critics charged that the Republican governor had systematically neutered some of the state's toughest watchdog agencies, stripping workers and consumers of protections they had enjoyed for many years.

The impact of Deukmejian's economic policy was far from certain. The state's economy, like that of the nation, continued to expand during most of his tenure. As revenues flowed into the state treasury, Deukmejian boasted that he had "brought California from IOU to A-OK." But that assertion proved to be a vulnerable claim upon which to stake his legacy. Near the end of his second term, the national and state economy entered a prolonged recession. Deukmejian spent his last year in office scrambling to avoid blame for the state's sagging economy—an economy that he earlier claimed had benefited from his probusiness policies. In the end, Deukmejian left office with a state deficit twice as large as the one he had inherited from Jerry Brown.

THE PETE WILSON ADMINISTRATION

Californians grew increasingly disenchanted with George Deukmejian during his second term; polls showed a steady deterioration in his standing with voters. Deukmejian's blandness had been a welcome change following the activism of Jerry Brown, but after 8 years of "the duke," bland had become boring. Early in 1990 the voters seemed ready for a more dynamic style of political leadership. Former San Francisco Mayor Dianne Feinstein captured the mood of the electorate with her successful bid for the Democratic nomination for governor. Feinstein generated considerable excitement by being the first woman to become a serious contender for the state's highest office.

Republicans were especially eager to hold onto the governorship in 1990 in order to influence the vital reapportionment of state and congressional districts the following year. They were determined to prevent a repetition of the partisan gerrymandering that had created so many safe districts for Democrats following the 1980 census. "California reapportionment," declared the chair of the state Republican party, "is the most important political project short of the presidential race in the United States."

Many Republicans hoped that George Deukmejian, in spite of his declining popularity, could be persuaded to seek a third term in 1990. But Deukmejian declined to run, convinced that he had "kept his promises" and accomplished all that was on his limited agenda. Party leaders, including George Bush and Ronald Reagan, then urged United States Senator Pete Wilson to enter the race for governor. Wilson had been reelected in 1988 to a second term in the Senate and showed no enthusiasm for entering the fray of state politics. Eventually, however, Wilson consented to run. His sense of duty to his party, coupled with the attraction of enhancing his chances for a future run for the presidency, weighed heavily in his decision to enter the race.

Both Wilson and Feinstein campaigned in 1990 on a theme of "getting the state moving again." They each promised to be a more activist governor than Deukmejian had been, and they each took a remarkably similar stand on several key issues. Both favored the death penalty, abortion rights, and more vigorous protection of the environment. Wilson's great advantage in the general election was his access to superior financial resources. Unable to match the media blitz of Wilson, Feinstein failed to capitalize on the excitement she had generated during the early stage of the campaign. When the final ballots were counted, Wilson defeated Feinstein by a vote of 3,763,151 to 3,497,875.

In November 1990, the voters of California also approved one of the most far-reaching institutional changes ever adopted by the citizens of any state. Known as Proposition 140, the measure rivaled in importance Proposition 13, the tax-cutting initiative of 1978. Proposition 140 was a constitutional amendment that set limits on the number of terms state lawmakers could serve. Members of the assembly were limited to three terms or 6 years, whereas state senators and most other constitutional officers were limited to two terms or 8 years. The measure also cut the operating budget of the state legislature by nearly 40 percent. The passage of Proposition 140 sent shock waves through the nation; soon term-limit proposals were appearing on ballots in other states as well.

The support for Proposition 140 was a measure of widespread voter dissatisfaction with the workings of state government. Many Californians had become

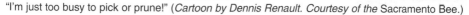

"I'm just too busy to pick or prune!" (*Cartoon by Dennis Renault. Courtesy of the* Sacramento Bee.)

convinced that the state legislature was dominated by powerful special interests and was hopelessly out of touch with the concerns of average citizens. Recent scandals in state and national government, such as the enormously costly collapse of the savings-and-loan industry, had further alienated voters from their elected officials. (Veteran Senator Alan Cranston and two California congressmen were direct casualties of the savings-and-loan scandal.) Convinced also that it was futile to try to defeat incumbents individually, voters decided that it was best to throw them out *en masse* through the passage of the term-limitation initiative. In upholding the constitutionality of the measure, Chief Justice Malcolm Lucas concurred that the electorate had a legitimate interest in protecting itself against "an entrenched, dynastic legislative bureaucracy."

Another sign of voter dissatisfaction with the political process was the dramatic decline in voter turnout. The number of Californians voting in the mid-1980s was actually *less* than the number who voted 20 years earlier, even though the state had gained 6 million eligible voters. Whereas in 1972 nearly 50 percent of all eligible voters cast a ballot, in 1990 voter participation had dropped to a mere 28 percent. Thus it was that a record low turnout of California voters approved term limits for their elected officials. Pollster Mervin Field sagely observed that the voters, as they left the political process, had tossed "a grenade back over their shoulders."

The enormity of the economic challenge facing the new governor in 1991 was soon apparent in the projections for the coming fiscal year. Whereas George Deukmejian had faced a projected deficit of $1.5 billion in his first year in office, Pete Wilson was confronted with a projected deficit of $14.3 billion. This was a staggering figure, an amount larger than the entire budgets of all but two of the other states.

The gap between revenues and expenditures was caused by a number of factors, chief of which was the deepening impact of the recession of the early 1990s. As major sectors of the California economy continued to slump, the flow of tax revenues into the state treasury slowed dramatically. Cutbacks in federal defense spending, triggered by the collapse of the Soviet Union, hit California especially hard. Many businesses, complaining of California's poor business climate, pulled up stakes and moved to other states. Compounding the problem further was the growth of what Wilson called California's "dependent population"—the illegal aliens, nonworking students, senior citizens, welfare recipients, prisoners, and Medi-Cal users who depended on state services. "We're experiencing something that's very troubling to me," Wilson explained, "and that is an outflow of those who are the producers— and a tremendous increase in the number of consumers of services."

In hammering out a new budget for California, Wilson and the legislature faced some difficult choices. It soon became apparent that the projected deficit could not be overcome by either raising revenues or curtailing expenditures. The solution lay in doing *both* at the same time. So it was that the state budget for 1991 included the largest tax increase in the history of California, totaling more than $7 billion in income and sales tax hikes, as well as increases in vehicle registration fees and the highest student fees ever. The budget also included a 4 percent reduction in monthly grants to recipients of Aid to Families with Dependent Children (AFDC), the first such cut in state history.

Governors Pete Wilson and George Deukmejian meet the press to discuss the gubernatorial transition in 1991. *(Courtesy of the Governor's Office.)*

California continued to face deficits of several billion dollars each year throughout the recession of the early 1990s. The workings of the state government often were imperiled by months of gridlock and partisan debate during what seemed like never-ending legislative battles over the budget. Ultimately the budget battles mellowed as California recovered from the recession. But, along the way, the state eased its financial burden by transferring property-tax revenues from local governments—especially from the counties—to school districts. This allowed the state to reduce, by a corresponding amount, its allocations for education.

County governments, already hard hit by Proposition 13, were left in a double bind. As their revenues diminished, they faced mounting expenses to pay for services mandated by the state. Anger over these "unfunded mandates" led voters in 27 northern counties to approve a nonbinding proposal to secede from California. Several counties were on the brink of insolvency, others ordered severe cutbacks in services. Losses from risky investment practices led Orange County to file for bankruptcy in what one observer called "the largest financial disaster that any county in the nation has ever faced."

Another issue that dominated much of Wilson's early first term was reapportionment of the California legislature and the state's congressional delegation.

Reapportionment was a matter of fundamental importance to both Republicans and Democrats because it would largely determine the balance of power between the two parties during the next decade. The Democratic-controlled legislature submitted to the governor three separate plans for redrawing the state's legislative and congressional districts. Wilson vetoed all three plans, accusing the legislature of drawing "contorted, misshapen districts" to preserve an unfair Democratic advantage. Wilson's veto sent the reapportionment issue to the state Supreme Court, a court firmly in the hands of jurists appointed by Republican governors. The court in turn appointed a three-member panel of "special masters" to redraw the district lines. When the panel unveiled its reapportionment plan, it appeared likely that Republicans would gain seats in both houses of the state legislature and in the state's congressional delegation.

The Republican gains, however, failed to materialize on schedule. The recession of the early 1990s proved to be the worst in 60 years and voters were looking for someone to blame. Incumbent officeholders across the nation bore the brunt of electoral discontent in the 1992 election. At the top of the ticket was incumbent Republican President George Bush. His bid for reelection was foiled by Bill Clinton, the first Democratic presidential candidate to carry California since the election of Lyndon Johnson in 1964. Anti-incumbent sentiment also helped defeat Republican John Seymour, Governor Wilson's hand-picked successor to fill his unexpired Senate term. Seymour was defeated by Democrat Dianne Feinstein, elected to what became known as the "short seat," because the winner would serve only 2 years before having to run again for a full 6-year term. Meanwhile, Democrat Barbara Boxer was elected to the "long seat" vacated by retiring Senator Alan Cranston. California thus became the first state in the nation to be represented simultaneously by two female Senators.

Pete Wilson entered the race for reelection in 1994 as the most unpopular governor in the history of California. His approval rating had fallen to an abysmal 15 percent. The Democratic nominee was Kathleen Brown, daughter of one former governor (Pat Brown) and brother of another (Jerry Brown). Brown's campaign was fraught with tactical errors and a muddled sense of direction, whereas Wilson ran the campaign of his life. The governor proved especially adept at turning discontent with the economy to his advantage. Aired repeatedly throughout the campaign was a television spot showing shadowy images of illegal aliens crossing the border into California from Mexico. The commercial's sound track was reminiscent of a 1950s horror movie. It intoned ominously, "They keep coming. . . ." Wilson's message was clear: Don't blame me for the state's economic problems, blame *them*.

On the ballot in 1994 were two initiatives that received Wilson's enthusiastic endorsement. Proposition 184, popularly known as the "three-strikes-and-you're-out" initiative, was similar to a recently enacted law aimed at putting repeat offenders in prison for life. The law provided that any felon convicted of a third offense, whether it was a violent crime or not, would be given a sentence of 25 years to life. With fear of crime ranking among the voters' top concerns, support for the initiative was overwhelming. The other hot-button issue on the ballot was Proposition 187, nicknamed the "save-our-state" initiative. It proposed denying nonemergency

The nomination and election of Dianne Feinstein and Barbara Boxer to the United States Senate prompted this ironic comment in 1992. (*Cartoon by Steve Greenberg. Courtesy of the* California Journal.)

medical care, public education, and other social services to undocumented residents. Kathleen Brown passionately denounced the measure as racist and xenophobic; Pete Wilson made it the centerpiece of his campaign. Opponents and supporters of the measure brandished authoritative reports, bolstered with an impressive array of statistics, that convincingly "proved" illegal aliens either boosted or undermined the economic well-being of the state. On election day, Propositions 184 and 187 were approved by a majority of California voters and Wilson scored the most impressive come-from-behind victory in state history. (A key provision of Proposition 184 later was declared unconstitutional by the state Supreme Court; Proposition 187 likewise was challenged in the courts and could not be implemented until its constitutionality was determined.) The final count in the governor's race was 4,357,713 votes for Wilson to 3,191,428 for Brown.

Proposition 187 also played a role in the race between Democratic Senator Dianne Feinstein and her Republican challenger Michael Huffington. The contest was one of the most negative in recent memory, with Huffington denouncing Feinstein as a "tax and spend liberal" and Feinstein responding by calling Huffington a "Texas oil millionaire." The outcome of the campaign was sealed when the *Los Angeles Times* reported that Huffington—a staunch supporter of Proposition 187—had employed an undocumented immigrant as a nanny for his two children. Huffington at first denied the charge and then blamed his wife.

Governor Pete Wilson fueled the growing opposition to illegal immigrants in his 1994 campaign for reelection. (*Cartoon © copyright 1993 by Paul Duginski.*)

"Nannygate" soon overwhelmed the campaign and Huffington went down to defeat by a narrow margin.

The 1994 election produced the long-expected Republican majority in the state assembly and brought to an end the reign of Democratic Assembly Speaker Willie L. Brown, Jr., but only after a tortuous melodrama of epic proportions. Following the election, Republicans held a 41 to 39 majority of the seats in the lower house. It appeared certain that Brown's tenure as speaker, the longest in state history, was over. But then, with unmatched political and parliamentary acumen, Brown managed to delay the inevitable. He convinced one Republican member of the assembly to defect and succeeded in expelling another. Brown thus was elected speaker once again, achieving what one political analyst called "the closest thing to a *coup d'état* in California since the Bear Flag Revolt." The Republicans were outraged; the defecting member of the assembly was recalled; and Brown stepped down as speaker to run for mayor of San Francisco. Brown then blocked the Republicans' choice for speaker by throwing the support of the Democratic caucus behind a maverick Republican who agreed to a power-sharing agreement with the Democrats. The maverick was Doris Allen, an Orange County Republican who became the first woman to serve as assembly speaker. Allen was regarded by her fellow Republicans as a traitor and soon was recalled. Only after more than a year of such political intrigue was the Republican majority able to elect its candidate of choice to the coveted speakership. Even this victory was short lived. Democrats regained control of the assembly in 1996 and promptly elected one of their own,

Cruz Bustamante, as the new speaker. Bustamante, a Fresno Democrat, was the first Latino to serve in the post.

The labyrinthine battle in the assembly confirmed the impression of many Californians that their state government was utterly ineffective and irrelevant. Editorial cartoonist Paul Duginski captured the cynical mood of the electorate with a cartoon showing a California-shaped canoe plummeting over a waterfall, while on board a Democratic donkey and Republican elephant flailed away at each other with paddles.

The departure of Willie Brown from the assembly, after 30 years in office, was the most visible sign of the impact of term limits. Proponents hoped that term limits would usher in an era of reform, making legislators more responsive to their constituents. As term limits steadily took their toll on veteran lawmakers, however, it became apparent that the legislature was losing much of its "institutional memory." The rapid turnover of officeholders increased, rather than diminished, the role of special interests and professional legislative staffs. Lobbyists had no term limits; they were now in a better position than ever before to supply the expertise needed by short-term lawmakers wrestling with a host of complex issues of public policy.

Governor Pete Wilson, buoyed by his reelection victory, made an unsuccessful bid for the Republican presidential nomination in 1996. Wilson hoped that his anti-illegal immigrant message would appeal to voters across the nation, but his campaign failed to catch fire. Following a tough speech denouncing undocumented aliens, delivered in front of the Statue of Liberty, Wilson was condemned by *The New York Times* in a scathing editorial entitled "An Insult to Miss Liberty." Back in his home state, Wilson was roundly criticized for breaking a pledge to serve out his second term as governor before seeking higher office.

In the midst of his ill-fated presidential campaign, Wilson launched a much-publicized attack on affirmative action. Affirmative action is the practice of taking race and gender into account in employment, education, and other areas of public life in order to counteract the effects of past discrimination. Defenders of the practice argued that to abandon affirmative action would reverse decades of progress in opening opportunities for minorities and women. Opponents argued that racial and gender preferences unfairly discriminated against white men and even worked against the individuals they were intended to help. "Almost every American can sense the tension and unfairness this system of racial spoils has produced," Wilson said in an open letter to the people of California in 1995. "The current system of special privilege based on race and gender is breeding resentment from those left standing on the sidelines."

Wilson took vigorous action to dismantle affirmative action in California. He signed an executive order eliminating 150 boards that advised state agencies on affirmative action and sued his own state government to overturn existing affirmative action laws. At a raucous meeting of the University of California board of regents in 1995, Wilson led the vote to end affirmative action in all university admissions, hiring, and contracting. He also gave his support to an anti-affirmative action initiative, approved by voters in November 1996 as Proposition 209. The initiative prohibited state and local governments from granting preferential treatment to any individual on the basis of race, sex, color, ethnicity, or national origin. Shortly after its passage, a federal judge issued an injunction blocking implementation until the courts determined if the initiative was constitutional.

As California approached the twenty-first century, a great deal had changed since the ascendancy of Ronald Reagan in the mid-1960s. Yet many of the fundamental issues and much of the rhetoric of politics remained the same. Californians still were wrestling with basic issues of identity and equity, trying to achieve stability in an era of rapid change—and the nation continued to look to California for political and social leadership. "It's not just that one-tenth of all Americans live in California, it's that California has a greater history of cultural and racial diversity than other states," observed civil rights leader Jesse Jackson. "Whether it's Proposition 13 or affirmative action, you can look to California to lead the nation."

SELECTED BIBLIOGRAPHY

A comprehensive history of recent California politics remains unwritten. A useful introduction, however, is provided by Jackson K. Putnam, *Modern California Politics, 1917–1980* (1980), and John C. Syer and John H. Culver, *Power and Politics in California* (1992). See also Gladwin Hill, *Dancing Bear* (1968), and Royce D. Delmatier et al., *The Rumble of California Politics* (1970). The *California Journal,* beginning in January 1970, is an indispensable digest of state government and politics.

The careers of Pat Brown and Ronald Reagan are analyzed in Gary G. Hamilton and Nicole Woolsey Biggart, *Governor Reagan, Governor Brown* (1984). Specialized studies include Gerard J. DeGroot, "Ronald Reagan and Student Unrest in California," *Pacific Historical Review,* LXV (February 1996), pp. 107–129; and Garin Burbank, "Governor Reagan's Only Defeat," *California History,* LXXII (Winter 1993/1994), pp. 360–373. Totton J. Anderson and Eugene C. Lee, in "The 1966 Election in California," *Western Political Quarterly,* XX (June 1967), pp. 535–554, deal with Reagan's first election. Ronald Reagan, *Where's the Rest of Me?* (1965), is an autobiography as told to Richard Hubler. Dissenting views may be found in Edmund G. Brown, Sr., *Reagan and Reality: The Two Californias* (1970) and *Ronald Reagan, the Political Chameleon* (1976). Biographical studies include Joseph Lewis (1968), Hedrick Smith et al. (1980), William Boyarsky (1981), Rowland Evans and Robert Novak (1981), and Lou Cannon (1982). Concerning welfare policies, see Garin Burbank, "Governor Reagan and California Welfare Reform," *California History,* LXX (Fall 1991), pp. 279–289, and Jackson K. Putnam, *Old-Age Politics in California from Richardson to Reagan* (1970).

Jerry Brown has been the subject of several books: Ed Salzman (1976), John C. Bollens and G. Robert Williams (1978), J. D. Lorenz (1978), Robert Pack (1978), and Orville Schell (1978). See especially Roger Rapoport, *California Dreaming: The Political Odyssey of Pat and Jerry Brown* (1982). For a survey of Brown's first term see Ed Salzman, "The Latest Jerry Brown," *California Journal,* VIII (June 1977), pp. 187–190, and "The Brown Record," ibid., IX (June 1978), pp. 173–176.

The *Tax Revolt Digest,* published monthly by the *California Journal* from November 1978 to October 1979, contains a wealth of information on the tax revolt in California and elsewhere. The best introduction to the subject is Jack Citrin, "The Legacy of Proposition 13," in Terry Schwadron (ed.), *California and the American Tax Revolt* (1984). For a view from the inside see Howard Jarvis, with Robert Pack, *I'm Mad as Hell* (1979). Among the many publications which assess the impact of Proposition 13 see especially John J. Kirlin, *The Impacts of Propo-*

sition 13 upon California Governments (1979); George G. Kaufman and Kenneth T. Roseus (eds.), *The Property Tax Revolt* (1981); and Valerie Raymond, *Surviving Proposition 13* (1988).

In contrast to his immediate predecessors, George Deukmejian has not attracted much attention from biographers. Analyses of the 1982 election include James R. Carroll, "Cautious Tom or Dull Duke," *California Journal,* XII (July 1982), pp. 229–231, and Tony Quinn, "Winning in the Mailbox," ibid., XIV (April 1983), pp. 148–150. See also J. Gregory Payne and Scott C. Ratzan, *Tom Bradley: The Impossible Dream* (1986). Larry Liebert offers a perceptive analysis of the Deukmejian governorship in "The Duke's Recipe for Success," *California Journal,* XVI (April 1985), pp. 141–144. Deukmejian offers his own views in an interview published in ibid., XV (January 1984), pp. 7–10. The story of the California lottery is told in Steve Wiegand, "Setting Up the California Lottery," ibid., XVI (March 1985), pp. 96–99. On the importance of the Rose Bird issue, see Preble Stolz, *Judging Judges: The Investigation of Rose Bird and the California Supreme Court* (1981), and Robert Fairbanks and Andrew Mann, "Rose Bird's Campaign," *California Journal,* XV (May 1984). The 1986 election is described in Richard Zeiger, "Bradley-Duke Rematch," ibid., XVII (October 1986), pp. 480–484.

Gerald C. Lubenow (ed.), *California Votes: The 1990 Governor's Race* (1991) and *California Votes: The 1994 Governor's Race* (1995) are invaluable resources on the campaigns of Pete Wilson. The beginnings of the Wilson administration are described in Richard Zeiger, "Pete Wilson Inherits a State in Disarray," *California Journal,* XXI (December 1990), pp. 560–563, and "Pete Wilson," ibid., XXII (December 1991), pp. 541–546. The later years are analyzed in Steve Scott, "Governor," ibid., XXV (December 1994), pp. 9–11; Scott and A. G. Block, "Pete Wilson's Second Term," ibid., XXVI (February 1995), pp. 13–16; Marc Sandalow, "Pete Blasts Off," ibid., XXVI (October 1995), p. 48; and Scott, "The Failed Campaign," ibid., XXVI (November 1995), pp. 16–21. On the intrigue in the assembly, see Scott, "Willie Brown's Magic Act," ibid., XXVI (February 1995), pp. 8–11; Scott, "Allen Wins, Willie Grins," ibid., XXVI (July 1995), pp. 14–15; Richard A Clucas, *The Speaker's Electoral Connection: Willie Brown and the California Assembly* (1995); and James Richardson, *Willie Brown: A Biography* (1996). Other important studies include Bruce E. Cain and Roger Noll, *Constitutional Reform in California* (1995); Eugene Smolensky, et al., *Welfare Reform in California* (1992); and Byran O. Jackson and Michael B. Preston, *Racial and Ethnic Politics in California* (1991). For an analysis of the controversies surrounding reapportionment, see A. G. Block, "The Reapportionment Failure," *California Journal.,* XXII (November 1991), pp. 503–505, and Bruce E. Cain, *The Reapportionment Puzzle* (1986). The pivotal role of ballot initiatives is the subject of Thomas E. Cronin, *Direct Democracy* (1989), and David D. Schmidt, *Citizen Lawmakers* (1989).

Among the best surveys of contemporary California politics are Charles M. Price and Charles G. Bell, *California Government Today* (1996); Michael J. Ross, *California: Its Government and Politics* (1996); and Larry N. Gerston and Terry Christensen, *California Politics and Government* (1995). Also valuable are the annual editions of *California Policy Choices,* edited by John J. Kirlin and David R. Winkler, containing essays identifying the "meaningful choices for Californians."

CHAPTER THIRTY-FIVE

The Environment and Energy

One of the major themes in California history since at least the progressive era has been controversy over the use and preservation of the state's natural resources. In recent years new groups have joined forces with older conservation organizations such as the Sierra Club to lobby for the protection of California's land, air, and water. The environmental protection movement scored a series of impressive victories, both in the state legislature and through the initiative process. The opponents of the environmentalists, however, marshaled their forces and began an effective counterattack. California business interests, allied often with organized labor, argued that environmental legislation retarded economic development by harming the state's "business climate." The struggle between the forces of economic development and environmental protection was waged on many fronts.

REGIONAL PROTECTION

The first important victory for the environmental protection movement came in 1965 with the establishment by the state legislature of the San Francisco Bay Conservation and Development Commission (BCDC). Uncontrolled filling of the bay during the previous century had reduced its size by 40 percent, and conservationists warned that without effective controls the bay would eventually become little more than a river. The new BCDC regulated all developments in a 100-foot-wide band around the bay shoreline and provided a useful model for the creation of other regional agencies in the state.

The commission was unable, however, to solve all of the bay's problems. Upstream diversions continued to diminish the flow of freshwater into the bay, and wastewater from irrigated lands in the interior carried huge loads of fertilizers, pesticides, and other toxic substances into the bay each year. As a result, the bay wildlife population continued to suffer a precipitous decline. The state Water Quality Control Board in 1995 found high levels of cancer-causing pollutants in the bay's resident harbor seal population and in eight species of fish. The survival of native plants and animals also was threatened by the invasion of exotic species introduced into the bay by the flushing of contaminated ballast water from visiting ships. In 1996 a federal report labeled San Francisco Bay "the most invaded aquatic ecosystem in North America."

More emotional fuel was added to the environmental movement early in 1969 when an offshore well of the Union Oil Company sprang a leak in the Santa Barbara Channel and smeared hundreds of square miles of ocean and 30 miles of beaches with oil. Dozens of species of shorebirds, marine mammals, and fish were adversely affected. In 1970 the state legislature, acting partly in response to the Santa Barbara oil spill, passed the California Endangered Species Act (CESA) to protect animal and plant species facing extinction, and the California Environmental Quality Act (CEQA). The CEQA required that an environmental impact report be submitted to appropriate public agencies for approval prior to the commencement of any project "which could have a significant effect on the environment." Under terms of the act, environmentalists brought suit to halt or modify scores of environmentally damaging projects. The California Chamber of Commerce denounced the act as harmful to the state's economy. The Santa Barbara oil spill also ignited a long-standing controversy over the further development of offshore oil resources. Whenever the federal government attempted to lease new offshore tracts to private companies to drill for oil and gas, California environmentalists argued that further development was a needless threat to the fragile ecosystem of the coast.

Californians in growing numbers were becoming convinced that the scenic regions of the state needed special protection from private development. In 1972 voters approved an initiative creating for 4 years a Coastal Zone Conservation Commission to govern development of California's coastline and to preserve reasonable public access to it. The legislature in 1976 established a permanent California Coastal Commission to serve as the final arbiter for the issuance of permits to build or develop property along the coast. The commission, which enjoyed the enthusiastic support of Democratic Governor Jerry Brown, denied permits for several large coastal developments and often required substantial modifications in the proposals it did approve. Business leaders soon charged that the commission was guilty of "bureaucratic and environmental zeal." Republican Governor George Deukmejian, an outspoken opponent of the commission, ordered substantial cuts in its budget and staff. Deukmejian's appointees to the commission generally voted as a prodevelopment bloc, approving several large hotel and housing projects.

The proponents of coastal protection scored a major victory in 1994 when Republican Governor Pete Wilson signed legislation permanently banning oil drilling along the California coast. The Sierra Club applauded Wilson for supporting the ban but criticized him for continuing the practice of his predecessor of making prodevelopment appointments to the coastal commission. The effectiveness of the commission was further weakened when one of its members was convicted of extortion and bribery for soliciting nearly a million dollars from landowners in exchange for permits to develop their properties.

The Tahoe Regional Planning Agency (TRPA), jointly operated by California and Nevada and authorized by Congress in 1967, tried to combat both the pollution of Lake Tahoe's pure, blue waters by sewage and the threatened destruction of the beauty of its surroundings by excessive and hasty construction, but for years the agency was unable to prevent the building of new gambling casinos on the Nevada shores. The effectiveness of the TRPA was further weakened in 1983 by the appointment of prodevelopment members to the agency board. Within 6 months of their appointment, the board approved developments on environmentally sensitive lands that previously had enjoyed TRPA protection.

Controversy also centered on measures to increase California's parklands and wilderness areas. Between 1950 and 1980 California parks doubled in size, whereas the number of annual visitors increased twentyfold. The National Park Service acquired additional lands in the state for the Point Reyes National Seashore, Redwood National Park, and the Golden Gate National Recreation Area. Environmentalists achieved one of their major goals in 1984 when Congress approved legislation granting federal wilderness protection to 3.2 million acres in California's national forests and national parks. The legislation was supported by a large coalition of environmental groups. It was opposed unsuccessfully by the California Chamber of Commerce and Governor Deukmejian.

Another important breakthrough came in 1994 when Congress passed the California Desert Protection Act, the largest wilderness protection measure in the history of the continental United States. Sponsored by Democratic Senator Dianne Feinstein, the act created two new national parks and extended federal protection over 7.6 million acres of desert lands. A Sierra Club spokesperson praised the act as "the sunrise for desert protection and the sunset for desert abuse."

Among the most spectacular lands under federal protection in California was the Yosemite Valley, which by the mid-1990s was being visited by more than 4 million people a year. On summer weekends the valley, only 1 mile wide and 7 miles long, was overburdened with visitors who trampled lush meadows and filled the roadways with bumper-to-bumper traffic. The National Park Service came under conflicting pressure from environmental organizations to "deurbanize" the valley and from the Yosemite Park and Curry Company, the park concessionaire, to maintain adequate services and conveniences for visitors. In 1980 the park service unveiled a master plan to remove most employee housing and offices to outlying areas of the park, to reduce overnight accommodations, and to restrict the number of private vehicles allowed into the valley. Congress failed, however, to appropriate adequate funding for the plan, and by 1990 it was evident that few of its provisions had been implemented. Traffic flow into the valley continued to rise, overnight lodging increased, and even a new video rental store and a pizza parlor were added. "They are turning Yosemite into a shopping mall," lamented a spokesperson for the Sierra Club. Prospects for the park brightened in 1995 when a new concessionaire embarked on a major cleanup and restoration program and banished the park's much-maligned video store.

One of the most intense environmental battles in recent years was fought over the few remaining stands of old-growth California redwoods. Environmental activists descended upon logging towns in the "Redwood Summer" of 1990 and attempted to block the cutting of the virgin trees, only 5 percent of which remained after a century and a half of virtually unrestricted timber harvesting. The disruptive tactics of the activists failed to slow the logging operations, but they succeeded in increasing public awareness of the issue. In November 1990 several initiatives appeared on the ballot to restrict or ban further old-growth logging. The most ambitious was Proposition 128, known as "Big Green," which would have significantly reduced timber harvesting and also established new standards regulating offshore oil development, pesticide usage, and air and water pollution. The initiative was supported by the Sierra Club and other environmental groups and opposed by a coalition of timber, chemical, and agricultural industries. The heavily financed campaign against "Big Green" contributed to its crushing defeat, with more than 63 percent of the public voting against it.

The defeat of Proposition 128 was a harbinger of further assaults on the environmental protection movement in the 1990s. Amid the worst economic recession since the great depression, business interests launched a concerted effort to dismantle or weaken a quarter century of environmental laws. Conservatives argued that the state's stringent environmental standards were retarding economic recovery. Governor Pete Wilson in 1993 called for the relaxation of a wide range of environmental regulations in order to foster the creation of "jobs, jobs, jobs." Two years later he supported legislation to weaken the state's landmark California Environmental Quality Act. The California League of Conservation Voters

A political cartoonist responds to the assault on environmental legislation. (*TOLES © 1995* The Buffalo News. *Reprinted with permission of UNIVERSAL PRESS SYNDICATE. All rights reserved.*)

successfully opposed the legislation, denouncing it as "by far the most dangerous attack ever mounted against the CEQA."

Also under assault in the 1990s was the California Endangered Species Act (CESA). In 1995 Governor Wilson announced his intention to drop all currently listed species within 5 years and to require more stringent standards of endangerment before relisting. The head of the Wilson administration's Resource Agency denounced the CESA for its "adverse economic consequences." Defenders of the act claimed that California had more endangered species than any other state. "We are losing species and habitats so fast it is almost mind-boggling," said Peter Moyle of the University of California, Davis. A lobbyist for the Sierra Club charged Wilson with caving in to the state's agribusiness and timber interests: "This provides opportunities for the governor's supporters to mow down more endangered species."

GROWTH CONTROL

The environmental movement, although its roots lay deep in California history, represented a radical reversal of traditional values. Throughout the state's history, growth had been thought of as the greatest good, but the environmentalists denounced unrestricted growth as a menace to the quality of life. Beginning with a Petaluma ordinance in 1973 limiting construction of new residential units within the city to 500 per year, communities across the state took steps to limit their population growth. Builders criticized the Petaluma measure as a "no-growth" plan and challenged its constitutionality, but in 1976 the United States Supreme Court upheld the ordinance. Within a decade, more than 130 slow-growth measures had appeared on local ballots, the majority of which were approved by the voters.

The growth-control movement was under constant attack from prodevelopment forces. Critics charged the movement was "elitist," dominated by wealthy residents who wanted to protect their own property values by stopping further construction. In the late 1980s, developers mounted a major counteroffensive against the movement to restrict growth. They amassed huge war chests and adopted sophisticated techniques to defeat local growth-control initiatives. Developers in Pasadena in 1986 easily defeated a slow-growth measure by outspending their opponents 50 to 1. Similar victories were scored by developers in Manhattan Beach and El Segundo. The prodevelopment forces in Orange County in 1988 spent $2.2 million to defeat a local growth-control initiative, overpowering their opponents who spent less than $100,000. It was the most expensive county initiative campaign in California history. "They bought themselves a landslide," commented the coauthor of the initiative. "It just shows you how much power that much money can generate."

Eventually, many Californians concluded that effective growth control could only be achieved by statewide or regional planning. It was apparent that such growth-related problems as urban sprawl, air pollution, and crowded freeways could never be solved by local governments. State leaders, during the Reagan and Deukmejian administrations, did little to try to manage growth. Governor Jerry

Brown addressed the issue, but was soon distracted by his presidential ambitions. "A lot of the problems we face today are the result of having three governors in a row who were not sensitive to the need for growth management," observed Ira Michael Heyman, chair of the influential Bay Vision 2020 Commission. In 1991 Governor Pete Wilson appointed a new Council on Growth Management to draft a comprehensive statewide plan for managing population growth.

The recession and attendant slowdown in population increase in the early 1990s temporarily reduced the intensity of the growth-control issue. As the California economy rebounded later in the decade, local communities became divided once again between progrowth and antigrowth forces. Affluent enclaves on the west side of Los Angeles, for instance, remained fiercely antigrowth, whereas poorer neighborhoods in the eastern and southern parts of the city were desperate for development. Said one Watts resident: "We would love to have a Sizzler. We all have to go to Compton for a nice meal on Saturday or Sunday. We want one here."

AIR POLLUTION

Air pollution was the most obvious menace to the quality of the California environment. "Smog" began to produce a sharp decrease in visibility and painful

Cartoon by Steve Greenberg in the *Daily News,* Los Angeles, September 16, 1979. The cartoon appeared following a prolonged bout of first- and second-stage smog alerts in the Los Angeles basin. (*Courtesy of the* Daily News, *Los Angeles.*)

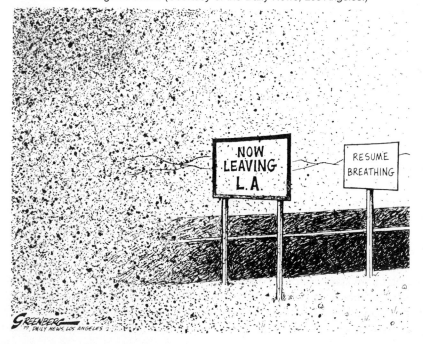

irritations of nose and eyes in Los Angeles in 1943, and by the 1960s this condition had become so chronic that on bad days the city vanished. When, as often happened, the air in and over the Los Angeles basin became stagnant and a temperature inversion occurred, the rays of the sun reacted photochemically with various waste products in the air to produce new and still more dangerous pollutants. The result was not merely a blight on the beauty of the region and a cause of sharp discomfort, but also a menace to health and a source of costly damage to several crops. The growing of leafy vegetables in the Los Angeles basin virtually ceased.

The San Francisco Bay area, like the Los Angeles basin, had a bowl-like shape, and smog began to be a severe problem in the bay region also. Los Angeles created an air pollution control district in 1947, and the San Francisco Bay counties formed a similar district in 1955. These agencies had some success in persuading or compelling industrial plants to reduce the emission of noxious wastes, often by installing expensive equipment. Yet the smog grew steadily worse. It became apparent that the chief offender was the automobile, with its output of hydrocarbons, oxides of nitrogen, and toxic carbon monoxide.

As the number of motor vehicles steadily increased, smog began to form in the interior valleys and threatened ultimately to spread over most of the state. When the toxins from vehicle emissions reached the upper atmosphere, they damaged the protective ozone layer that shielded the earth from the sun's harmful ultraviolet rays. Scientists feared that increased exposure to ultraviolet radiation could cause an elevated risk of skin cancer. The pollutants also created a blanket of gases over the earth, trapping the reflected heat from the sun and contributing to the problem of global warming. Excessive warming could lead to the melting of large portions of the polar ice caps, the flooding of low-lying coastal zones around the world, an increase in the spread of infectious diseases, and the death of some forests and agricultural crops.

The state legislature in 1960 passed the first automobile antismog law in the nation, requiring the installation of various smog-control devices in motor vehicle engines. Action by the federal government came 10 years later when Congress created the Environmental Protection Agency (EPA) and, in the Clean Air Act of 1970, provided that all new cars must be equipped with devices to reduce emissions of hydrocarbons, carbon monoxide, and nitrogen oxide. Congress amended the Clean Air Act in 1977 to provide economic sanctions against states that did not meet federal air quality standards. States such as California, where automobiles were significant sources of pollution, were required to establish vehicle inspection programs. After considerable delay the California legislature complied in 1982 and adopted a major new antismog law that required car owners to have their vehicles inspected every other year. Cars which met strict emission standards would be certified, whereas those that failed would have to be repaired or tuned up. The law applied to each of the state's populated air basins, including the San Francisco Bay area and much of southern California. By 1992 the biennial inspection program was costing California motorists over $400 million in fees, but had failed to catch many of the cars that caused the most air pollution. State officials estimated that

75 percent of the smog generated by California's automobiles was caused by 12 percent of the state's cars, many of which were older vehicles that either went undetected or were exempt from meeting the clean-air standards. Smog Check II, a controversial new program introduced in 1996, required that such "gross polluters" be junked, sold out of state, or repaired regardless of the cost.

Air quality improved steadily during the 1980s and 1990s in parts of California. The number of days of unhealthy smog in the Los Angeles basin fell by 25 percent between 1985 and 1995, yet air pollution in the area continued to exceed federal standards. The EPA announced in 1995 that the San Francisco Bay area had become the nation's largest metropolitan area to achieve federal air-quality standards. Air quality worsened, however, in inland communities that were even more vulnerable to smog than the coastal areas. Medium-sized cities in the Central Valley, such as Bakersfield and Fresno, had smog problems rivaling those of New York and Chicago. In 1987 the state Air Resources Board (ARB) estimated that air pollution was causing a 20 percent loss to the San Joaquin Valley's cotton and grape crops. Smog also continued to have a devastating impact on human health, contributing to 80,000 deaths a year in California.

State and federal agencies adopted stringent new air pollution regulations in the early 1990s. The state ARB in 1990 approved the most sweeping vehicle emissions standards in the world, including the first-ever requirement for mass production of electric cars. The new rules required automakers to start selling cleaner vehicles in the smoggy Los Angeles basin by 1994 and statewide 3 years later. Furthermore, 2 percent of all cars sold in California must produce *zero* emissions beginning in 1998, rising to 10 percent by 2003. Electric cars were the only vehicles that could meet this absolute standard. In 1991 the federal government once again revised the Clean Air Act, requiring automobile manufacturers to build thousands of cars that operated on clean-burning fuels such as natural gas or methanol. Also in 1991 the state ARB adopted the world's stiffest gasoline rules, intended to cut smog-forming emissions by an additional one-third within 5 years.

As the recession of the early 1990s worsened, California business interests lobbied to have the recently enacted air-quality regulations relaxed or suspended. The president of the Los Angeles Area Chamber of Commerce complained that the state's "mindless regulatory approach" was preventing economic recovery. The South Coast Air Quality Management District, announcing its intention to be more "business friendly," introduced a controversial "smog credit" program that permitted companies to buy and sell pollution credits. The oil industry and major automakers convinced the state ARB to drop its requirement that 2 percent of cars sold in the state be pollution-free by 1998. (The board held to its 10 percent goal for 2003.) General Motors, meanwhile, began marketing a sleek electric-powered sports car in southern California in the fall of 1996.

WATER RESOURCES

The long-standing controversy over the use and distribution of the state's water resources was renewed in the late 1970s as the legislature considered authorization of the Peripheral Canal, a 43-mile-long, 400-foot-wide channel around the periphery of San Francisco Bay which would connect the Sacramento River directly with the existing California Aqueduct. By being drawn from the Sacramento, rather than from the southern end of the Sacramento–San Joaquin River Delta, the annual supply of water delivered by the aqueduct to southern California could be increased by at least 700,000 acre-feet.

Support for the Peripheral Canal was virtually unanimous throughout southern California. The Metropolitan Water District (MWD) and the Kern County Water District, which together absorbed more than three-fourths of the supplies provided by the California Water Project, lobbied vigorously in support of the canal. Opposition to the canal was led by environmental groups such as the Planning and Conservation League and others in northern California who believed that the massive diversion of fresh water supplies from the delta would harm San Francisco Bay and delta water quality. As legislation authorizing the canal neared approval, opposition in northern California became strident. One Bay Area assemblyman warned: "Please, southerners, don't think you can rob our water and destroy our ecosystem, because there will be a civil war in this state if you do. The aqueduct will be blown up. National guardsmen will be shot."

In 1980 the legislature passed a bill which authorized construction of the Peripheral Canal and outlined environmental protections for the delta. A coalition of environmentalists, northern California public officials, and others remained opposed to the canal, however, and placed on the ballot a referendum to block its construction. When the referendum appeared on the ballot, in June 1982, the canal was rejected statewide by a vote of 62 percent.

An important step toward resolving the decades-long controversy between northern and southern California water interests was taken in 1986 when Congress approved a new policy of cooperation between federal and state water agencies. The federal government promised to use the huge resources of its Central Valley Project (CVP) to protect the water quality of the delta and San Francisco Bay. The state, for its part, agreed to allow up to 1 million acre-feet of surplus water from the federal system to flow through the California Aqueduct to southern California and the Central Valley. Representative George Miller of Contra Costa County called the agreement "a peace treaty that could end the California water wars."

A more basic water-policy issue was raised during the 1980s by the case of the Kesterson National Wildlife Refuge. The Kesterson refuge in 1980 began receiving thousands of acre-feet of drainage water from irrigated farmlands in the San Joaquin Valley. Within a few years gross abnormalities, deformities, and mutations were widespread among the refuge's wildlife population. Studies revealed that the wastewater flowing into the refuge contained high concentrations of salts from chemical fertilizers, pesticide residues, and the naturally occurring poison selenium. In 1985 the Interior Department ordered a halt to the flow of wastewater into Kesterson. Local growers unsuccessfully protested the order, arguing that it would take 42,000 acres of farmland out of production. Part of the refuge was ultimately declared a toxic dump, and hundreds of acres of poisoned ponds were filled with dirt. The manager of the refuge in 1991 declared the area "an environmental wasteland." The Kesterson disaster cast a pall over the future of large-scale irrigation projects throughout the valley.

Meanwhile other battles over the state's water resources continued unabated. A campaign to save Mono Lake pitted the National Audubon Society and a host of environmental groups against the city of Los Angeles. Described by Mark Twain as "one of the strangest freaks of nature to be found in any land," Mono Lake was the primary breeding ground for 90 percent of the California gull population and an important stopover for millions of migratory birds. Since the early 1940s Los Angeles had been tapping the streams flowing into Mono Lake, causing the water level in the lake to drop by more than 40 feet and its surface area to diminish by one-third. As the lake shrank, its chemical content began to change drastically, thus reducing the supply of brine shrimp necessary for the survival of the nesting gulls and their chicks. A University of California biologist reported in 1982 that only 5000 California gulls were hatched at Mono Lake that year, compared with more than 35,000 just 4 years earlier. In 1983 environmentalists scored a major victory when the state Supreme Court ruled that water could no longer be taken from a lake or other natural source without consideration of the possible harm to the source itself. The court's doctrine of "source protection" was a repudiation of Los Angeles's long-held exclusive right to take water from the Mono Lake Basin. The state legislature extended further protection to the lake in 1989 by agreeing to provide $60 million annually to Los Angeles to compensate the city for seeking alternative sources of water; 5 years later the California Water Resource Control Board ruled that the city must reduce its intake of the basin's waters. Over time, Mono Lake was expected to return to health.

A similar battle was waged over the preservation of the free-flowing waters of the rivers of northern California. Environmentalists lost their fight to protect a 9-mile stretch of white-water rapids along the upper Stanislaus River, but in 1984 Congress placed a similar portion of the Tuolumne under federal protection as a "wild and scenic" river. The following year, the Supreme Court upheld similar federal protection for large stretches of the Klamath, Trinity, Smith, and Eel rivers, all on the northwest coast, and the lower American River near Sacramento. The Court's ruling protected the rivers from dam building and logging. The Environmental Defense Fund hailed the Court's action as a "tremendous victory," whereas representatives of various water agencies and the state's timber industry complained that the ruling would have "dire economic consequences."

A prolonged drought began in 1987 that had a devastating impact on the California environment. By the early 1990s, the drought had contributed to the death of more than 10 million trees, including one-third of the forests on the slopes of the Sierra Nevada. Many of the drought-stricken trees no longer had enough sap or pitch to seal themselves against burrowing insects. The drought-weakened trees also contributed to several of the worst fire seasons in California history. The extremely low moisture content in the soil, and the accumulation of an unusually large amount of dry fuel, resulted in disastrous fires such as the conflagration in the Oakland Hills in 1991 that destroyed over 2600 homes and caused 25 deaths.

For decades the dumping of toxic substances from industrial and chemical plants in California went uncontrolled and largely unnoticed. By the mid-1980s 26.5 million truckloads of toxic wastes were being produced in California each year— about one truckload per person. As the wastes began to leach into the surrounding soil and water supply and to release noxious fumes into the atmosphere, they became serious health hazards. One such dump in Fullerton, site of a newly completed housing project, was found to be emitting toxic vapors from chemicals capable of causing cancer and damaging the liver, respiratory tract, and central nervous system. California environmentalists soon won legislation creating some of the nation's strictest regulations for the treating and disposing of toxic wastes. Consequently, California industries began shipping their wastes to nearby (and less regulated) states. Between 1986 and 1990, the number of tons of toxics exported from the Golden State increased by more than 900 percent.

The rate of progress in cleaning up the state's toxic-waste dump sites became a matter of controversy in the 1980s and 1990s. Federal and state agencies succeeded in cleaning up dozens of sites, but critics questioned the effectiveness of the cleanup operations and pointed out that many of the sites were small and insignif- icant. Los Angeles, Contra Costa, Alameda, Santa Clara, and Orange counties re- mained in the top 1 percent of the nation's hazardous waste counties. "I'm not im- pressed with California's performance," concluded one federal official. "We've discovered that even a progressive state like California is doing a worse job at toxic cleanup than the federal government." Meanwhile, the federal government's own "superfund" program to clean up the most seriously polluted sites was in nearly complete disarray by the late 1990s, a victim of political indecision and fiscal grid- lock. The major difficulties were the enormous costs involved and the uncertainty of who was to pay for the cleanup. Government researchers estimated that remov- ing all the toxic substances from the 10,000 known dump sites in the nation would cost in excess of $1 trillion.

California voters passed a major toxic-control initiative in 1986. Known as Proposition 65, the initiative required the state to maintain a list of chemicals known to cause cancer and birth defects. The initiative also required businesses to warn consumers of possible exposure to toxic chemicals and prohibited their discharge into potential supplies of drinking water. Many businesses throughout the state posted warning signs, and refineries and chemical plants changed their operating procedures to bring their discharges into compliance with the initiative. Within 5 years of the initiative's passage, the state's Environmental Protection Agency (EPA) reported that 85 percent of the companies surveyed had reduced or eliminated some form of toxic exposure. "In its first five years, Proposition 65 produced 100 years of progress," commented an attorney for the Environmental Defense Fund.

THE ENERGY CRISIS

One of the most volatile aspects of recent California history has been the fluctuation of the cost of energy. In the winter of 1973–1974 the Organization of Petroleum

Exporting Countries (OPEC) suddenly increased the price of a barrel of crude oil from $2.41 to $10.95. Over the next several years the price of oil continued to climb, reaching $35 a barrel by 1981. The most visible indicator of rising oil prices was at the gasoline pump, where the average price of a gallon of regular leaded rose from 68 cents in 1978 to a peak of $1.35 three years later. Prices for the more expensive unleaded and high-octane premium fuels rose even more dramatically.

The soaring price of petroleum had several major consequences. It helped propel inflation in the 1970s to the highest sustained levels in the peacetime history of the nation. The high cost of oil also led to the development of alternative energy sources and to dramatic improvements in energy efficiency. Worldwide oil demand fell by 6 million barrels per day between 1979 and 1983. Californians reduced their oil use by 17 percent.

Then, in the early 1980s, the OPEC cartel began to unravel and energy prices started to tumble downward. By 1984 the price of a barrel of crude oil had dropped to $25. Two years later oil was selling for less than $11 a barrel. The price of a gallon of regular gasoline fell below 80 cents in 1986. The decline in petroleum prices was accompanied by a reversal in the trend away from oil use. Between 1982 and 1984 the nation increased its oil consumption from 15 million barrels to 16.2 million. California's demand for oil rose by 8 percent.

The remarkable improvements made in energy efficiency during the 1970s and early 1980s, however, were of lasting importance. California adopted a sweeping program of energy conservation, and led the nation in the development of alternative energy sources.

The California Department of Transportation promoted a variety of projects—ride sharing, park-and-ride lots, exclusive bus and carpool lanes—to increase the energy efficiency of the state highway system. New cars sold in the state averaged 24 miles per gallon (mpg) in 1982, up from 13 mpg in 1974. The California Energy Commission, formed in 1975, set maximum energy consumption limits for new household appliances sold in the state and established the nation's most stringent energy conservation standards for new residential and commercial buildings. The new standards saved over $11 billion in energy costs between 1977 and 1994. The savings were expected to exceed $43 billion by 2011, supplying three-quarters of the state's increased electricity needs.

California's major alternative energy sources were solar, wind, geothermal, and cogeneration. With an average of 270 days of sunshine a year, the state had more than 40 percent of the total United States solar collector capacity. The winds off the Pacific coastline represented an enormous energy potential, and the volatile geology of the state provided California with the nation's largest geothermal resources. In 1996 renewable and alternative energy sources were supplying less than 8 percent of California's total energy needs, but the Energy Commission estimated that these sources could be providing more than 20 percent by the early twenty-first century.

The nation's first solar thermal power project began generating electricity in 1982. Called Solar One, the project was built for Southern California Edison in the Mojave Desert near Barstow. The power project consisted of 1800 heliostats, or

Solar One. This first-of-a-kind solar power plant produces enough electricity to meet the needs of approximately 6000 homes. *(Courtesy of Southern California Edison Company.)*

giant mirrors, which reflected sunlight onto a central boiler-receiver atop a 300-foot tower. The receiver produced superheated steam which was used to generate electricity. Farther north in the San Joaquin Valley, an even more ambitious solar project used huge photovoltaic collectors to convert sunlight directly into electricity.

The California legislature in 1977 enacted the nation's largest and most comprehensive tax incentive program for solar energy development. Over the next 5 years about 300,000 solar water-heating systems were installed in California homes. More solar equipment firms were established in California than in all the other states combined. In spite of these gains, the widespread acceptance of solar energy faced such barriers as initial high installation costs, financing, and consumer confidence. Critics of the solar tax credits called them "welfare for the wealthy," especially before the credit for solar-heated swimming pools was ended in 1980. All the solar tax credits expired at the end of 1986. Meanwhile "passive solar" construction, designed to allow buildings efficiently to collect and store heat from the sun, continued in importance in dozens of California communities.

The California legislature also encouraged the development of wind energy. Its wind energy bill of 1978 set a goal of meeting 10 percent of the state's electricity needs with wind power by the year 2000. During the early 1980s the world's largest collection of windmills was built near Livermore in eastern Alameda County. Nearly

2000 wind turbines were installed at Altamont Pass in 10 strikingly different designs. The windmills produced more than enough power to meet the electricity needs of all the households in the Livermore area. Over the next decade more than 16,000 wind turbine generators were installed throughout the state, in such places as San Gorgonio Pass near Palm Springs and in the Tehachapi Mountains, making California far and away the wind-power capital of the world. The wind power industry was plagued by design problems and unscrupulous developers in its formative years, but by the early 1990s the industry was moving ahead with a new generation of windmills that were more efficient and cost-effective. The California Energy Commission reported in 1996 that the state's windmills were producing 80 percent of the world's total supply of wind-generated electricity.

In 1960 the nation's first commercial geothermal power plant began operations at The Geysers in Sonoma County, where superheated steam released at the earth's surface was fed to turbines to generate electricity. By the early 1980s PG&E had 15 geothermal plants in operation with a total output of more than 900 megawatts of power, representing enough electricity to meet the needs of a city nearly the size of San Francisco. Geothermal resources elsewhere in California—notably in the Imperial Valley, along the eastern Sierra, and in the northeastern part of the state—boosted the total geothermal energy potential of the state to 15,000 megawatts. (One megawatt equals 1000 kilowatts, enough power to supply the electricity needs of about 1000 residential customers.)

Another important alternative source of energy was cogeneration, the use of waste heat, steam, or gases from an industrial plant for the generation of electricity. Used in Europe for decades, cogeneration only recently attracted much attention in the United States. In 1979 cogeneration represented only about 1 percent of the state's electric power production. The PUC, however, adopted an aggressive policy and ordered the state's utilities to offer incentives to their large industrial customers so that they could profitably produce their own electricity. The incentives proved to be phenomenally successful. Between 1983 and 1986, enough cogeneration projects were begun to produce over 15,000 megawatts of electricity.

California's commitment to the development of alternative sources of energy led to a remarkable change in the pattern of energy production. In 1977 California relied on petroleum for about 50 percent of its electricity generation. Three years later only 16 percent of the state's electricity came from this nonrenewable source, and by the late 1990s the proportion had been reduced to less than 1 percent. (The bulk of the supply came from hydro, coal, nuclear, natural gas, cogeneration, and a variety of renewable sources.)

NUCLEAR POWER

The most controversial new energy source was nuclear power. Energy planners in the early 1960s blithely predicted that by the end of the century nuclear power would be able to supply half the nation's energy needs and would be "too cheap to meter." Twenty years later that prospect had dimmed considerably.

The nation's first licensed commercial nuclear reactor began operations in 1957 at Vallecitos in Alameda County. The plant was shut down in 1977 by the federal Nuclear Regulatory Commission (NRC) after discovery of a nearby earthquake fault. In 1963 PG&E activated a second California reactor at Humboldt Bay. The Humboldt plant was plagued by malfunctions and frequent shutdowns after it was found to be releasing excessive amounts of radioactive vapors. The plant was closed in 1976 for failure to meet seismic safety standards, and 7 years later PG&E announced that it was shutting it down permanently. The first large-scale nuclear facility in California, the San Onofre plant located halfway between Los Angeles and San Diego, began operations in 1968 and by 1980 was providing Southern California Edison with 4 percent of its energy supply. In northern California the Rancho Seco plant near Sacramento went "on line" in 1975, but a series of breakdowns kept it from operating at full capacity. The Rancho Seco facility, owned by the Sacramento Municipal Utility District, earned a reputation for being the nation's least reliable nuclear plant and eventually was shut down by a vote of the people.

Opposition to nuclear power arose out of concern for the safe disposal of radioactive wastes produced by the plants, which remain potentially lethal for thou-

Concern over the safe disposal of radioactive wastes from nuclear power plants inspired this 1974 editorial cartoon by Dennis Renault in the *Sacramento Bee. (Courtesy of the* Sacramento Bee.)

'Someday, son, this will all be yours. And your son's. And your sons's son's. And your son's son's son's. And his son's. And his . . .'

The Diablo Canyon nuclear power plant. (*Courtesy of Pacific Gas and Electric Company.*)

sands of years. Opponents also feared the disastrous consequences of an accident at a nuclear plant. In 1976 the legislature prohibited the California Energy Commission from authorizing construction of any further nuclear plants until the federal government had approved "a documented technology for the disposal of high-level nuclear waste." Already authorized was the massive 2200-megawatt nuclear plant built for PG&E at Diablo Canyon near San Luis Obispo. Construction of the Diablo Canyon plant began in 1969 and was nearly complete when PG&E reported the discovery of a major offshore earthquake fault. After extensive new buttresses and other safeguards were added, the NRC in 1981 announced it was granting PG&E a permit to load fuel and begin low-power testing of the plant. Within days of the announcement, however, it was discovered that wrong diagrams had been used to design and build seismic safety supports in the reactor containment building. Additional design errors were uncovered in subsequent reviews, the testing permit was revoked, and the opening of the plant was further delayed.

Supporters of Diablo Canyon discounted the importance of the design errors and pointed to the need to get the plant on line as soon as possible. Power generated by the plant would offset the burning of 20 million barrels of oil a year. PG&E estimated that the $5.6 billion plant would add almost 20 percent to the company's total generating capacity and help provide the power necessary to meet future energy needs. The NRC in 1983 granted PG&E permission once again to load atomic fuel at the Diablo Canyon plant and to resume testing. The first unit of the facility began producing full power in 1985. The following year—more than 17 years after construction began—the entire plant went into full production.

PETROLEUM DEPENDENCY

California made great progress in the development of alternative sources of energy for the production of electricity, but still unsolved was the state's dependency on petroleum as a fuel for transportation. Petroleum, of course, was a finite resource. Once it was used up, it could not be replaced.

The proportion of California's total energy needs that were met by petroleum was one-fourth higher than that of the nation as a whole. California's higher level of oil dependency was due mainly to the state's huge transportation system, which was over 99 percent reliant on oil. During the energy crisis of the 1970s, California's use of oil for transportation fell. Gasoline consumption was reduced by the introduction of more fuel-efficient vehicles and by a reduction in the number of miles driven by the typical California motorist. By the mid-1980s, however, personal travel had returned to precrisis levels and gasoline usage was increasing once again.

The California Energy Commission in the 1980s and 1990s studied a variety of alternative transportation fuels, including methanol, ethanol, gasohol, natural gas, propane, and synthetic fuels. It found that methanol was the most promising alternative. Methanol was cleaner burning than other fuels and could be produced from biomass, natural gas, oil, or coal. The Energy Commission, in cooperation with private industry, put more than 6500 methanol-fueled vehicles into public and private transportation fleets. The commission also established 80 methanol fueling stations around the state. The Golden Gate Transit District, Yosemite National Park, and Federal Express introduced fleets of methanol-fueled vehicles for regular use. And major automakers—including Ford, General Motors, and Volkswagen—developed prototype methanol-powered cars.

In spite of such gains, California's dependence on petroleum for transportation remained undiminished, and its reliance on foreign sources steadily increased. The

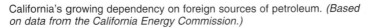

California's growing dependency on foreign sources of petroleum. *(Based on data from the California Energy Commission.)*

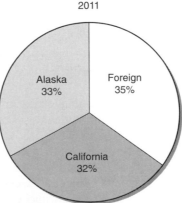

1990

Foreign 6%

Alaska 50%

California 44%

Demand in millions
of barrels of oil: 703

2011

Alaska 33%

Foreign 35%

California 32%

Projected demand in
millions of barrels of oil: 891

Persian Gulf crisis and the war against Iraq in 1991 demonstrated the importance of reducing the nation's reliance on a vital resource from such a volatile region as the Middle East. The California Energy Commission predicted that the state's reliance on foreign sources of petroleum would rise from 6 percent in 1990 to 35 percent by 2011.

The abundance of relatively inexpensive supplies of petroleum in the 1980s had lulled many Californians into assuming the energy crisis was over. "The general public doesn't realize the relatively precarious nature of the energy supplies we rely on," warned the chairperson of the energy commission. Governor Pete Wilson acknowledged the seriousness of the problem in 1991 by calling for a major expansion of California's energy research and development program, and in the same year the legislature issued its own "State Energy Strategy." Reducing the state's dependency on petroleum was one of the many challenges facing California as it neared the twenty-first century.

SELECTED BIBLIOGRAPHY

Two of the finest books on contemporary environmental issues are Carl G. Thelander (ed.), *California on the Edge* (1994), and Tim Palmer (ed.), *California's Threatened Environment* (1993). Also useful is Bern Kreissman, *California: An Environmental Atlas and Guide* (1991). An older collection of articles appears in Ed Salzmann (ed.), *California Environment and Energy* (1980). For historical background see Raymond F. Dasmann, *The Destruction of California* (1965), *California's Changing Environment* (1981), and "Environmental History," an edition of the *Pacific Historical Review*, XLI (August 1972). One of the best case studies is Alfred Runte, *Yosemite: The Embattled Wilderness* (1991). For a critique of the environmental movement see Bernard J. Frieden, *The Environmental Hustle* (1979).

The coastal issue is examined in Stanley Scott (ed.), *Coastal Conservation* (1981), and John Woolfenden, *Big Sur* (1981). On the issues of land use and conservation see Robert C. Fellmeth et al., *Politics of Land* (1973), produced by Ralph Nader's organization. Ted K. Bradshaw and Edward J. Blakeley, in *The Rural Community in the Advanced Industrial Society* (1980), examine California's changing rural communities as they are affected by new population growth. See also David E. Dowall, *The Suburban Squeeze* (1986), and Rob Kling, Spencer Olin, and Mark Poster (eds.), *Postsuburban California* (1991).

Competition for California Water (1982), edited by Ernest A. Englebert, is a symposium on alternative solutions to the state's future water needs. *The California Water Atlas* (1980), edited by William Kahrl, is a monumental collection of maps and text illustrating the development of state water resources; the definitive study is Norris Hundley, Jr., *The Great Thirst: Californians and Water* (1992). (See also the sources on California water cited in Chapter 25.) On the Peripheral Canal issue see Harry Dennis, *Water and Power* (1981); Elizabeth Johnson, "The Delta Canal, Anything but a Peripheral Issue," *California Journal*, XI (October 1980), pp. 376–378; and Michael DiLeo and Eleanor Smith, *Two Californias: The Truth about the Split-State Movement* (1983). The best account of the controversy over Lake Tahoe is Douglas Strong, *Tahoe: An Environmental History* (1984) and over Mono Lake is John Hart, *Storm over Mono* (1996). State and federal efforts to reduce smog may be followed in James E. Krier and Edmund Ursin, *Pollution and Policy* (1977).

James C. Williams provides historical background to the energy issue in "Energy Resources and Uses in Rural California: A Historical Overview," Ph.D. thesis, University of California,

Santa Barbara (1984). Raymond Vernon, *The Oil Crisis* (1976), contains a discussion of the national and international aspects of the escalation of OPEC prices. On the controversy over nuclear power, see Samuel J. Walker, "Reaction at the Fault," *Pacific Historical Review,* LIX (November 1990), pp. 323–348; Hal Rubin "Guide to Nuclear Power in California," *California Journal,* X (June 1979), pp. 200–207; and John W. Gofman and Arthur Tamplin, *Poisoned Power* (1971). The energy potential of conservation and alternative renewable resources is described in Robert W. Righter, "Wind Energy in California," *California History,* LXXIII (Summer 1994), pp. 142–155; Robert Stobaugh and Daniel Yergin (eds.), *Energy Future* (1979); Jennifer K. Hollon, *Solar Energy for California's Residential Sector* (1980); and Mary Ellen Leary, "Conserving Energy, California Style," *California Journal,* XI (June 1980), pp. 219–223. For a full assessment of public policy affecting California energy use, see the biennial report of the California Energy Commission.

CHAPTER THIRTY-SIX

An Advanced Industrial Economy

California's economic growth in recent decades has been phenomenal. California leads the nation in the most advanced industrial fields, including computers, electronics, aerospace, and biotechnology. It also remains the leading agricultural state and home to the nation's entertainment industry. If the state were an independent nation, it would be one of the world's major economic powers, ranking twelfth in the value of its international trade and seventh in gross domestic product.

THE SUNBELT SHIFT

The remarkable growth of the California economy has been a part of one of the greatest population shifts in American history. Since World War II, the southern and western regions of the country have grown much more rapidly than the northeast and midwest. The population of what came to be called the Sunbelt more than doubled between 1940 and 1980, whereas the population of the so-called Frostbelt increased by less than half.

The most commonly used indicators for economic growth are gross product, employment, and income. California's annual gross product, the value of all goods and services produced in the state, doubled between 1960 and 1985. A decade later, California was producing one-eighth of the nation's goods and services, exceeding the gross domestic product of both China and Canada. Employment in California also grew rapidly. Between 1950 and 1980, while older regions of the country were suffering from structural unemployment, California's labor force grew by 250 percent. The state lost more than half a million jobs during the recession of the early 1990s but gained them all back—and more—by middecade. Economic forecasters in 1995 predicted that California would post a 28 percent gain in jobs by 2005, compared to a national growth of just 19 percent. As California approached the turn of the century, its major metropolitan centers continued to generate more employment opportunities than those of any other state. "I don't think there's any question that New York simply isn't the dominant city," concluded an economist at Chase Manhattan Bank. "The whole point is there's a shift away from New York and to Los Angeles."

The economic indicator that best represented the welfare of the average Californian was personal income. Following the dramatic increase in per capita income during World War II, Californians continued to earn more than most of their fellow Americans. By 1959, California ranked third among the states in per capita income. In following years California's standing dropped steadily, but the state's per capita income remained 3 percent above the national average through the mid-1990s. Meanwhile the wages of the typical worker in the northeast fell farther below the national average.

A special presidential commission in 1980 issued a startling report on the Sunbelt shift. The report analyzed the growing regional disparities in the nation's economic growth and personal income, and concluded that many of the problems of the old industrial heartland were beyond solution. The commission recommended that the movement of people and resources to the Sunbelt should be positively encouraged by federal policy. The commission's report caused widespread dismay in the older sections of the country, but in California it was greeted with expressions of satisfaction and self-assurance.

THE PACIFIC RIM

Californians found themselves beneficiaries of another, even more far-reaching shift in the national economy. In 1977 the Pacific Rim overtook Europe as the leading trading partner of the United States. The 28 nations bordering the Pacific emerged as the most dynamic economic region in the world.

California had established itself as a major partner in trans-Pacific trade in the years before World War II. Standard Oil of California led the way by opening Japan as a market for the state's petroleum exports. This profitable trade was interrupted by the war, but was reestablished as part of the American postwar reconstruction of Japan. Even before the war's end, California entrepreneurs were looking to the rebuilding of the shattered economies of East Asia. Henry Kaiser, speaking before the San Francisco Chamber of Commerce, declared in July 1945: "I accept the judgment of the experts who proclaim that the Pacific Basin will be the theatre where civilization makes its next great advance. . . . I am ready to accept the forecast that the Orient will be one of our best customers, even as we will be one of theirs."

The driving force in the rise of the Pacific Rim was the economic vitality of the nations of East Asia. Japan, at the center of the emerging Asian industrial complex, developed the most productive workforce and industrial plant in the world. South Korea, Taiwan, and Hong Kong outperformed the economies of virtually every major European country.

This shift in the global economy was viewed with considerable apprehension in the world's traditional economic centers—from London and Paris to Boston and New York. In California, however, the view was much more sanguine. "Our future

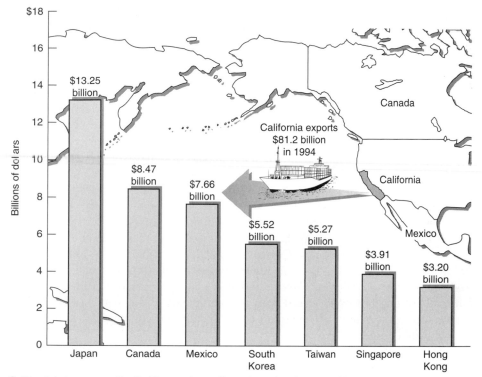

California's top seven Pacific Rim markets. *(Based on data from the Office of Economic Research, California Trade and Commerce Agency.)*

is with the Pacific Basin," observed the director of the California Office of International Trade. "Sixty percent of humanity lives there, over forty percent of all world trade. We're right in the middle of it. If the Basin prospers, we prosper." By 1984, California was doing more than $65 billion worth of business with the nations of the Pacific. Some 78 percent of the state's exports went to the Pacific Rim, and 85 percent of its imports came from Pacific nations. Overall, international trade represented 25 percent of the gross state product in 1995 and accounted for one out of every five jobs in California.

Pacific Rim capital as well as goods flowed into the state. "We're really becoming a financial center of the Asian community," observed a senior economist for the Bank of America. Asian investors spent millions of dollars for prime California properties, including banks, hotels, and luxury residences. Japanese interests succeeded in acquiring such cultural icons as Columbia Pictures and the Pebble Beach golf course on the Monterey Peninsula. Contrary to popular opinion, however, Japan was not the state's largest foreign investor. Japanese holdings amounted to only 15 percent of the total foreign investment in California, compared to Canada's 24 percent and Europe's combined total of 48 percent.

State and local officials in the late twentieth century took positive steps to encourage stronger commercial ties with the Pacific Rim. Delegations from San Francisco, Oakland, and Los Angeles visited Tokyo, Beijing, Manila, and other Asian cities. New trade links and "sister city" agreements were signed. The California Trade and Commerce Agency also sent missions to various Asian capitals to promote trade and investment, and in 1994 Governor Pete Wilson signed a memorandum of understanding to strengthen economic ties between Japan and California. Meanwhile, the University of California established at its San Diego campus a new teaching and degree program for Pacific Rim studies.

Californians also shared in the national debate over the North American Free Trade Agreement (NAFTA), approved by Congress in 1993. NAFTA allows the tariff-free exchange of goods, services, and investments among the United States, Canada, and Mexico. (An earlier free trade agreement between the United States and Canada was already in effect.) Supporters of NAFTA argued that it would boost California exports, benefiting especially the makers of the most technologically advanced products. Critics warned that it could lead to a lowering of environmental standards and to increased competition from Mexican agriculture and from cheap-labor *Maquiladora* industries along Mexico's northern border. Most observers, however, agreed with the sentiments of the state's official Mexican trade representative: "Having an economically vibrant neighbor is definitely in California's interest."

A major factor in the state's recovery from the recession of the early 1990s was the booming growth of its international trade. California accounted for 20 percent of the nation's total foreign trade in the mid-1990s, up from just 10 percent two decades earlier. Forty percent of all United States trade with Asia passed through California's ports and in 1994 Los Angeles overtook New York as America's premiere gateway for foreign trade. Near the end of the decade California's international trade was growing at a rate twice as fast as the overall economy. Chief among the state's exports were computers, electronic components, and telecommunications equipment, as well as advanced services such as engineering and financial consulting. The phenomenal growth of foreign trade, especially with the dynamic nations of the Pacific Rim, became one of the mainstays of the new California economy.

THE POST-INDUSTRIAL REVOLUTION

California's economy in the twentieth century not only expanded dramatically; it also underwent a basic transformation. There was a fundamental change in the kind of work people performed to earn their living.

Social scientists divide economies into three sectors or stages of development. The primary sector includes jobs which produce the basic raw materials needed for living. Jobs in agriculture, mining, forestry, and fishing are considered part of this sector. The primary sector is the basis of all pre-industrial societies. The secondary sector, which includes manufacturing and construction, is the mainstay of an industrial society. The third, or tertiary, sector of the economy is composed mainly of jobs in the "service" fields. Service jobs include healthcare, wholesale and retail trade, finance, insurance, real estate, government, transportation, communication, and utilities. The service fields expand as technological improvements in both the primary and secondary sectors increase productivity and enable workers to move on to other areas of employment. The rise of the service sector has been called the "post-industrial revolution," a twentieth-century phenomenon as fundamental as the nineteenth-century shift from an agricultural to an industrial economy.

The national economy became "post-industrial" sometime around 1956, when for the first time more than half the nation's workers were employed in service industries. California reached this crossover point far earlier. By the 1920s, over half of all Californians in the workforce were employed in the service sector. The tertiary sector grew to nearly 70 percent by 1970, far outdistancing the secondary sector, which accounted for only 27 percent of the labor force, and the primary sector, which had fallen to about 3 percent.

Changing business practices in the 1980s and 1990s contributed further to the rise of the service sector. Businesses began using outside firms for technical services previously provided by their own staff. Firms that offered services such as computer programming, engineering, and management consulting expanded rapidly to meet the demand. Economists predicted that providers of such professional services would become the state's largest employers in the early twenty-first century.

In spite of the predominance of the service industries, it would be premature to conclude that manufacturing was no longer an important part of the California economy. Ever since 1974, California has led the nation in manufacturing employment and has remained the number one industrial state, leading in almost every general manufacturing category. California's industrial base was threatened, however, by an exodus of manufacturers who complained that state taxes, environmental regulations, and high labor costs made it impossible for them to remain in California and stay competitive. Seeking lower operating costs and a more hospitable business climate, one-third of the state's manufacturing firms in the early 1990s announced plans to relocate some or all of their operations outside the state. Then, as California adopted more "business-friendly" policies in the mid-1990s, the exodus of manufacturers slowed. "We've definitely passed the period of net outward migration," observed the director of the Center for the Continuing Study of the California Economy. And Governor Pete Wilson proudly displayed new license plates for his official limousine. Underneath the state's name was the message "IS BACK."

HIGH TECHNOLOGY

The key factor in the economic transformation of California has been technological innovation. Technology was the driving force of the post-industrial revolution, just as it had been for the earlier transformation of the nation from an agricultural to an industrial society.

Technology in California has been boosted by successive waves of "foreign aid" from the federal government. The massive federal spending in the state during World War II continued after the war, and thus Washington helped finance the postwar economic expansion of California just as it did that of Japan and West Germany. The influx of federal aid tended to concentrate in California the most sophisticated technologies as well as a high level of technical expertise.

In the decades since the end of World War II, the center of much of California's high-technology industry has been the Santa Clara Valley. Once known as the Valley of Heart's Delight, this 25-mile stretch of the San Francisco peninsula was rechristened in the early 1970s as Silicon Valley. By 1980, the valley was generating 20 percent of all the high-technology jobs in the United States. Silicon Valley, home to more than 2000 high-technology companies, became the nation's ninth largest manufacturing region. Los Angeles, Orange, and San Diego counties also emerged as major centers of high-technology production.

The California electronics industry began early in the twentieth century. In 1909, Stanford University president David Starr Jordon invested $500 in a company sponsoring the pioneering work of a local Palo Alto engineer, Lee de Forest. Three years later, de Forest perfected the vacuum tube, a key invention in the evolution of modern electronics. The vacuum tube became the basis for future developments in radio, television, tape recorders, and early computers. Another local inventor, Philo Farnsworth, developed a technique for the electronic projection of pictures. Farnsworth achieved the first successful television transmission in 1927.

The person most responsible for the development of Silicon Valley was Frederick Terman, a professor of electrical engineering at Stanford. Terman became disturbed that his students often had to leave the state in order to find jobs as engineers. He began to encourage his graduates to form their own companies near the university. Two of Terman's brightest young students, William Hewlett and David Packard, acted upon his suggestion and formed an electronics company in a Palo Alto garage. From this humble beginning in 1938 came one of the world's largest and most successful electronics firms. In 1946 Frederick Terman became the dean of the Stanford engineering school. Terman proposed that the university lease some of its vast real estate holdings to local industries. The proposal was accepted, and in 1951 Stanford Industrial Park was created. The sleek, campuslike facilities of the park set a precedent for Silicon Valley industrial architecture. By 1980, fifty other industrial parks had been created on the San Francisco peninsula, most of them patterned on the Stanford model.

Another important step in the evolution of California's high-technology industry was the formation of the Shockley Transistor Company in Palo Alto in 1956. Stanford Professor William Shockley, whose discredited views on race and intelligence would later spark great controversy, discovered the principle that made possible the transistor. Transistors were far more efficient and long-lasting than vacuum tubes, and they represented a quantum leap forward in miniaturization. Transistors soon became the basis for a new generation of compact calculators, radios, televisions, and other electronic devices. The Shockley laboratories also experimented with the use of silicon as a semiconductor of electricity. Silicon, a common ingredient in beach sand, is the earth's most abundant element after oxygen. When mixed with minute bits of other chemicals, silicon could transmit on-off electrical signals—the basis of all modern computers—at incredible speeds. In a process that would repeat itself many times in the years ahead, eight of Shockley's top engineers left the company in 1957 to form their own firm. The new company, Fairchild Semiconductor, became the valley's first viable semiconductor company.

The most significant technological breakthrough in the history of electronics was the introduction in 1959 of the integrated circuit, commonly known as "the chip." Made of silicon and measuring a mere quarter inch on a side, a chip could hold over a million electronic components. The integrated circuit soon rendered the transistor obsolete. The microprocessor, or "computer on a chip," was a marvel of seemingly infinite capacity and application. It supplied the logic and the memory for a new generation of computers.

The success of California's high-technology industry rested on a unique combination of factors. Foremost was the contribution of the state's colleges and universities. California's leading institutions of higher education—including Stanford University, the University of California, and the California Institute of Technology—established themselves as centers for the most advanced work in the natural sciences, mathematics, chemistry, physics, and engineering. The universities provided the ideas and the technical knowledge necessary for technological innovation. California had more Nobel laureates than any other state, and Silicon Valley alone became the home of 6000 workers with advanced doctoral degrees.

A second factor in the rise of California high technology was the ready availability of capital. Not only was the federal government pumping billions of dollars into the state each year for research and development, but local financial institutions were also eager to invest in the high-technology boom.

The growth of high technology also depended upon the personal ambition of thousands of hard-driving California entrepreneurs. Often young and from modest backgrounds, the successful high-tech entrepreneurs combined sophisticated technical knowledge with sharp business skills. Steven Jobs and Stephen Wozniak, cofounders of Apple Computer, were typical of this new breed of business executive. Jobs and Wozniak built their first computer in a Los Altos garage in 1976. Within 5 years, Apple Computer occupied more than 20 buildings in Silicon Valley and had assembly plants around the world. Commenting on the wealth and lifestyle of California's new high-tech elite, *Fortune* magazine observed that Silicon Valley seemed to be "mass-producing millionaires."

High technology was not only producing California millionaires, it was also creating a new set of problems for the state. Electronics, especially the production of semiconductors, required a labor force that was markedly different from that of traditional manufacturing. At the top were highly skilled technical and professional workers. Compared with other industries, these workers were more numerous and better paid. The actual production work, however, required large numbers of low-skilled workers. Wages for these workers were below average for manufacturing. Many earned barely more than the minimum wage. Furthermore, the opportunity for advancement for these workers was less than in traditional industries. The high-tech workforce was also divided along ethnic and gender lines. Most of the production workers were women, about half of them Latinas and Asians.

For many years, the high-technology industry was viewed as a clean, light, "sunrise" industry as compared with the heavy, dirty "smokestack" industries of the past. This image was challenged in 1981 when officials in South San Jose discovered that more than 50,000 gallons of highly toxic solvents and other waste chemicals had leaked into the local water supply. The chemicals had come from an underground storage tank at a nearby manufacturing plant owned by Fairchild Semiconductor. Local residents blamed the leak for an unusually high incidence of birth defects, miscarriages, and liver and kidney diseases. In subsequent investigations, at least 120 other sites were identified where toxic solvents were leaking from underground tanks. One Silicon Valley investigator warned, "We're sitting on a toxic time-bomb." By 1986, Santa Clara County had earned the dubious honor of having more federal toxic cleanup sites than any other county in the nation.

High-technology companies also were identified as sources of air pollution. Although most of the smog was belched from the automobiles of electronics workers driving to and from their jobs, semiconductor firms were also emitting tons of fumes and toxic gases into the air each day through hidden vents. The air quality of Santa Clara County was consistently ranked as the worst in the Bay Area. More dangerous still, a rupture in a single cylinder of any of several commonly used gases at a high-tech plant could hospitalize or even kill hundreds of local residents.

The rapid growth of the high-technology industry exposed California to the danger of the "Detroit syndrome." Silicon Valley and other areas in the state became almost totally dependent on the electronics industry. The danger of such overreliance became apparent during the recession of the early 1990s as layoffs, plant closings, mandatory vacations, and salary cuts were announced almost daily at semiconductor and computer-related companies.

The economic downturn also affected the newest areas of high-tech wizardry, biotechnology, and genetic engineering. By the mid-1980s, about one-third of the nation's genetic engineering companies were headquartered in California, far more than in any other state. The "biotech" engineers developed a wide range of new products, including drugs for combating cancer and diabetes, and a popular artificial sweetener. During the early 1990s the staggering costs of drug development and the increased competition in the field spurred a wave of biotech alliances and mergers. The surviving firms remained competitive by reducing their production costs and laying off both top-level managers and highly skilled genetic engineers.

In an effort to lower costs further, many high-tech firms relocated their production facilities to remote areas. Hewlett-Packard, for example, opened a huge new plant near Roseville in Placer County where the costs of doing business were far lower than in the Bay Area. Other firms joined the exodus of businesses leaving the state altogether. Apple Computer in 1991 opened a new manufacturing plant in Colorado and relocated its customer service center from Silicon Valley to Texas. The state legislature responded by creating a Joint Committee on Science and Technology to increase the state's competitive edge.

Signs of a high-tech rebound were evident by the mid-1990s as employment opportunities expanded, exports boomed, and new products were introduced. After several years of layoffs, the high-tech workforce began growing again in 1994 and appeared likely to continue to experience modest growth into the new century. The state's improved business climate convinced dozens of high-tech firms that California wasn't such a bad place to do business after all. Intel, the world's largest maker of microchips, expanded its operations in Silicon Valley in 1995; 4 years earlier it had been part of the high-tech exodus. Especially encouraging was the growth in foreign markets for California's high-technology products. Leading the way were computers and computer components, including keyboards, disk drives, and specialized workstations.

The high-tech industry also was revitalized by the development of a new generation of innovative products for the home market. Multimedia, interactive video games, and CD-ROMs brought the world of high technology and entertainment into a mutually beneficial alliance. One of the most promising breakthroughs was virtual reality, a technology that created an illusion that the computer user was moving in a simulated three-dimensional space. Virtual reality had the potential for revolutionizing such fields as pilot training, architecture, and product design. American computer users in the 1990s also rushed to get on-line, linking their PCs through cyberspace to the Internet's World Wide Web. An estimated 35 percent of all American households were expected to be cruising the information superhighway by the year 2000, and California firms were well-positioned to handle the traffic. Silicon Valley's Netscape Communications, based in Mountain View, was producing 70 percent of the Web's software. Noting that the Internet was open to anyone with a computer and a modem, one inspired California journalist described cyberspace as "the new West" and credited Netscape with "laying down the railroad tracks to the future."

THE ARSENAL OF AMERICA

One of the most significant factors in the California economy since World War II has been the growth of the state's defense industry. At the war's end, many observers wondered if the California economy could adjust to peace. The state's industrial leaders, however, were determined not to lose the momentum generated by the wartime boom. The technological advances made during the war—in aerodynamics, electronics, radar, and other fields—provided the basis for California's domination of the postwar defense industry.

As tensions with the Soviet Union increased during the cold war, the United States entered into its first sustained peacetime defense boom. By the late 1940s, California's aircraft producers were benefiting from a new wave of military spending. California firms won 55 percent of all the Pentagon's airplane contracts in 1948, twice their percentage during the war. Defense spending accounted for more than half the state's economic growth between 1947 and 1957.

During the 1960s, the rivalry between the two superpowers led to a race to be the first nation to place a person on the moon. Each nation also sought to acquire a supply of missiles large enough to guarantee its security against the other. California's aircraft industry, transformed now into "aerospace," played a leading role in these new forms of international rivalry. In 1965 nearly 500,000 Californians— about one-third of the total number employed in manufacturing—were working in the various branches of the aerospace industry, including the production of aircraft, missiles, electronic equipment, and related instruments.

Southern California became the nation's leading center of aerodynamic research, partly because much of the aircraft industry was already concentrated there and partly because the empty spaces of the Mojave Desert to the north and east of Los Angeles were ideal for aerospace testing and experimentation. The concentration of scientific talent at the California Institute of Technology and the Jet Propulsion Laboratory, both in Pasadena, also played a major role in the region's burgeoning aerospace industry.

The first landing of American astronauts on the moon in July 1969 was a dazzling and historic event, breathlessly watched on television by millions. Public interest in the space program, however, did not remain high enough to keep expenditures for the National Aeronautics and Space Administration (NASA) from being cut in half between 1968 and 1971. Aerospace employment in California fell by 40 percent.

During the 1980s, under the Reagan presidency, the aerospace industry entered a new era of prosperity. Defense spending once again increased dramatically. Between 1980 and 1984, the value of prime contracts awarded by the Department of Defense to California firms more than doubled. The defense industry became the state's largest source of revenue, generating $28.5 billion in income. California firms in 1985 received about one-fifth of the nation's total defense budget—more than the combined total of the state's three nearest competitors.

Throughout the Reagan era of defense spending, southern California maintained its dominant position. Los Angeles County in 1984 received nearly $14 billion in military contracts, making it the nation's top location for weapons development. An additional $7 billion in contracts was awarded to firms in Orange, San Diego, Santa Barbara, and San Bernardino counties. In northern California, Santa Clara County received the lion's share of defense spending. Only six states in the country received more military dollars than Silicon Valley. The town of Sunnyvale, home of the Lockheed Missile and Space Company, won a larger portion of the national defense budget than 29 states.

The nation's defense came to be based on what was called the Triad, an interlocking network of three kinds of weapons: missiles launched from under the sea, strategic bombers, and ground-launched missiles. If California suddenly ended its defense-related work, two of the three legs of the Triad would be severely affected. Since the 1950s, the Lockheed Company has built all the submarine-launched ballistic missiles in the nation's arsenal. Missiles for the Polaris, Poseidon, and Trident submarines were all California products. Likewise, the latest generations of strategic bombers were developed in the state. Rockwell International, of El Segundo, was awarded a $20 billion contract in 1981 to build 100 B-1 bombers for the Strategic Air Command, and the Los Angeles–based Northrop Corporation became the prime contractor for developing the advanced-technology Stealth bomber. California also made a major contribution to the third leg of the Triad, missiles launched from the ground. Half of all the defense companies with contracts to build the MX missile—called by President Reagan the Peacekeeper—were California firms.

Not all of the federal money spent in California for weapons came from the Department of Defense. About a third of the research and development budget of the Department of Energy was allocated to the University of California for its operation of the Lawrence Livermore National Laboratory. This laboratory and its sister UC lab in New Mexico, the Los Alamos National Laboratory, were responsible for the development of all the nation's nuclear weapons. California also received more than a third of the funds distributed by NASA. Much of the NASA allocation was for the space shuttle program, about 30 percent of which was believed to be targeted for military purposes.

California led the nation as well in the variety of nuclear weapons located at the more than 100 military installations in the state. Strategic bombers were based at Mather, Castle, and March Air Force bases. San Diego, home to more military personnel than any other city in the nation, contained both a major naval base and an air station. In addition, California contained three important storage facilities for nuclear warheads. The largest of these, the Concord Naval Weapons Station, occupied a 12,000-acre site within a few miles of residential neighborhoods in suburban Contra Costa County. The weapons station contained hundreds of nuclear weapons, some of which had the explosive power of 1 million tons of TNT.

The role of California as the nation's arsenal aroused a growing controversy in the 1980s. Supporters of the defense industry emphasized the positive economic impact of military spending on California. Critics argued that the state was losing control over its own economy, becoming ever more subject to the boom and bust cycle of the defense contractors. Communities throughout the state expressed concern that they were becoming "defense junkies," so closely linked to the Pentagon's budget that cutbacks in defense spending could cause serious economic distress.

That distress came with unexpected suddenness following an astonishing series of international events in the late 1980s and early 1990s. The Berlin Wall, the most infamous symbol of the cold war division of Europe, came down in November of 1989 and was followed less than a year later by the reunification of West and East Germany. In early 1991 the Warsaw Pact was officially dissolved, and by year's end the Soviet Union had been transformed into a commonwealth of independent states. These monumental events had a profound effect on American defense policy because about 70 percent of United States defense spending had been aimed at protection against a Soviet threat. With that threat removed, or considerably reduced, cutbacks in defense spending were inevitable.

The most visible manifestation of the defense "build-down" was the closure or substantial reduction of more than 300 military bases across the country. Forty of the bases were in California, far more than in any other state. Included in four rounds of base closures between 1988 and 1995 were San Francisco's Presidio Army Base, Moffett Field Naval Air Station, Hunters Point Naval Shipyard,

Vallejo's Mare Island Naval Shipyard, Castle Air Force Base near Merced, Irvine's El Toro Marine Corps Air Station, and Monterey County's Fort Ord.

The base closures meant the loss of more than 50,000 civilian jobs in the state. Tens of thousands of other jobs were impacted. Senator Dianne Feinstein denounced the base closures as "a doomsday machine" for California, and Governor Pete Wilson complained that they were "savaging" the state's economy. Other observers pointed out that even after all the scheduled closures were completed, sometime around the year 2000, California still would have more than twice as many military installations as any other state. This was small comfort, however, to communities near the targeted bases. Contemplating the closure of Fort Ord, one Monterey businessperson warned: "When the military goes, businesses will collapse."

The base closures were part of an overall plan to reduce defense spending by 25 percent between 1990 and 1997. Ironically, President George Bush announced this sweeping proposal on August 2, 1990, the day Iraq invaded Kuwait. The long-range budget cuts were introduced to Congress in the midst of what the Bush administration called Operation Desert Storm, the most extensive use of military force by the United States in 20 years. In spite of the Persian Gulf crisis, Congress agreed to troop reductions that would bring American troop levels down to their lowest level since 1948. Production of major weapons systems, such as the MX missile and the Trident submarine program, was terminated; others were scaled back by one-third or more.

The defense cutbacks sent shock waves through the California economy. Major layoffs were announced by such stalwarts as McDonnell Douglas, Hughes, Lockheed, and Aerojet. Overall employment in the state's aerospace industry dropped from 370,000 in 1987 to an estimated 189,000 by 1994. Annual defense contracts awarded to California firms plummeted from $60 billion to less than $35 billion.

State and federal agencies encouraged defense contractors to convert their enormous productive capacities to peacetime use. "If you can build the best weapons in the world," Senator Barbara Boxer told a group of defense industry executives, "you can build the best buses in the world." Most observers believed, however, that it was unlikely that the defense industry would regain its dominant position in the California economy. "It's an unnatural act," one defense contractor concluded, "to instill a commercial mentality on a military business." The downsizing of the defense industry eventually came to be accepted as an economic fact of life. As a former executive at General Dynamics asked, "Who do you blame for the fact that peace broke out?"

The decline of defense spending was the single most important factor in the recession of the early 1990s. Ever since World War II, California's economy had relied on the steady infusion of defense dollars. Suddenly, that flow was drastically reduced.

California's recovery from the 1990s recession was extraordinary because it was achieved *without* a resumption of massive military spending. The growth in international trade, high technology, tourism, and the entertainment industry more than made up for the losses in aerospace and defense. "This is a recovery like no other," observed Joel Kotkin of Pepperdine University. "The fundamental economic mix has changed hugely and it's the kind of change that is positioning the state extremely well for the twenty-first century."

TOURISM

The only sector of the California economy able to rival the defense industry during the heyday of the cold war was tourism. And the continuing strength of the tourist industry helped pull the state out of the post-cold war recession of the early 1990s. California remained the nation's number one travel destination, ranking first among the 50 states in travel expenditures. Travelers in 1994 spent nearly $56 billion in the state, providing jobs for 691,000 Californians.

California had been a favorite vacation spot since the late nineteenth century. The term "tourism" was coined in the state to describe the growing travel industry spawned by the railroad and by the success of such resort hotels as the Del Monte near Monterey and San Diego's elegant Coronado. Tourist attractions in California were as various as the diverse interests of the visitors themselves. The five national parks—Yosemite, Sequoia, Redwood, Lassen, and Kings Canyon—remained perennial favorites, as did the countless other scenic attractions throughout the state.

California's top attractions in recent years were almost all commercial enterprises. Heading the list was Disneyland, the nation's premier amusement park,

Disneyland's Main Street. (*© The Walt Disney Company.*)

which opened amid the orange groves of Anaheim in 1955. Within a year nearly 4 million people had visited the park; by the mid-1990s annual attendance almost tripled. The success of Disneyland was due in part to its successful recreation of small-town America and its celebration of such traditional values as free enterprise and individual liberty. The other leading attractions in the state were Knotts Berry Farm, Universal Studios, the San Diego Zoo, and Sea World. Walter Knott opened his roadside fruit stand in Buena Park, southeast of Los Angeles in 1920. Knott later expanded his operations to include a restaurant, a gift shop, and an amusement park. Visitors to Universal Studios rode a Disneyesque tram through parting seas, past killer sharks, over a collapsing bridge, around space creatures, and into a roaring avalanche. The San Diego Zoo, ranked as the best in the nation, was an outgrowth of the city's Panama Pacific Exposition in 1915. The zoo eventually expanded to 125 acres and included some 1600 species of wildlife behind low walls and moats. Sea World opened at nearby Mission Bay Park in 1964, providing visitors a chance to see performing whales, dolphins, and sea lions.

Northern California also had its commercial attractions, most notably Santa Clara's Great America and Marine World/Africa USA in Vallejo, but the chief travel destination in the north was the city of San Francisco. Tourism became San Francisco's leading industry, prompting one critic to dub the city "Disneyland North." In addition to such long-standing favorites as Chinatown and North Beach, tourists flocked to the Cannery and the old Ghirardelli chocolate factory, two of the many structures in the city that were converted to tourist attractions. The appeal of Fisherman's Wharf was expanded southward to Pier 39 to include a collection of tourist-oriented shops constructed along the waterfront. The fishing industry itself, meanwhile, virtually disappeared from the wharf. "They are turning Fisherman's Wharf into a carnival," complained one of the area's few remaining fishermen.

Tourism flourished in California without any direct promotion by the state government. The state's Office of Visitor Services was dismantled in 1975; inquiries about tourism were returned to the senders unopened. Two years later a California Office of tourism was established, with a staff of one.

Following an unexpected decline in California's share of the national tourist market in the late 1970s, the state began an aggressive campaign to promote tourism. Governor George Deukmejian in 1983 announced the formation of the California Tourism Corporation, a nonprofit organization of state and industry representatives to plan a campaign to "sell California." The following year, the budget of the Office of Tourism was increased to $5 million and a marketing program was begun. The results of the promotional campaign were soon apparent. Travel spending in California rose by over 50 percent between 1982 and 1990.

Tourism in California—and the California economy in general—suffered temporary setbacks following two devastating earthquakes. The Loma Preita earthquake, measuring 7.1 on the Richter scale, hit northern California on October 17, 1989. It caused 63 deaths, destroyed over a thousand homes, collapsed freeways, and damaged a portion of the Bay Bridge. "Before when we thought of San Francisco, we thought of the 49ers," commented one frightened tourist. "Now we think earthquake." Southern California was hit by a 6.7 earthquake on

Major tourist attractions in California.

January 17, 1994. Centered in the Northridge area of the San Fernando Valley, the quake killed 57 people and caused more than $20 billion in damages.

Hoping to counteract the negative publicity generated by such disasters, the state Office of Tourism launched its first national television advertising campaign in 1994. The state also increased its participation in international forums to boost tourism from the United Kingdom, Germany, Japan, and Canada. Ecotourism within the state was encouraged by the identification of wildlife viewing areas. Increased concern about crimes against tourists prompted Governor Pete Wilson to establish the Governor's Workshop on Tourism Security.

Meanwhile, the proprietor of the state's leading tourist attraction in southern California announced plans to expand its operations. The Walt Disney Company began a major campaign to win approval from state and local regulatory agencies to build a new theme park and aquarium in Long Beach. The proposed development, to be called DisneySea, failed to win the needed approvals and was abandoned in 1991. Instead, the Disney company decided in 1996 to build a second theme park adjacent to Disneyland in Anaheim. The new park, called "Disney's California Adventure," represented a $1.4 billion investment and was scheduled to open in 2001. Barry Braverman, executive producer of Walt Disney Imagineering, explained that the new park would be a celebration of "the special magic of the California dream. Our goal is to immerse guests in compelling stories, evocative places and fantastic adventures that will bring the California dream to life."

ENTERTAINMENT

California has been the entertainment capital of the world since the golden age of Hollywood, and in recent years the entertainment industry has played an increasingly important role in the state's economy.

The number of Californians working in the motion picture industry doubled between 1984 and 1994. Indeed, the vigorous growth of the entertainment industry was one of the prime factors in California's recovery from the recession of the early 1990s. By middecade more than twice as many Californians were employed in the making of motion pictures than in the making of missiles, and the average entertainment worker was earning $10,000 more than a worker in the defense industry. Economists described this dramatic shift between defense and entertainment as an economic transformation comparable to the gold rush. *Fortune* magazine heralded the news with an article headlined "IT'S GLITZ NOT GUNS BEHIND CALIFORNIA'S COMEBACK."

Evidence of the transformation was not hard to find. San Francisco's Treasure Island Naval Station became a model for the conversion of surplus military bases into sound stages for the production of motion pictures. Several major films—including Disney's animated feature *James and the Giant Peach* and Warner Brother's thriller *Copycat*—were filmed at the base prior to its closure in 1997. San Bernardino's decommissioned Norton Air Force Base became the setting for Paramount's action film *Congo*. The perfect metaphor for the defense-to-entertainment metamorphosis was the transformation of an old hangar in Los Angeles into the first new film studio to be built in the city in nearly 60 years. The hangar once had been used to build military aircraft, including Howard Hughes's experimental seaplane the *Spruce Goose*. Now it was the home of DreamWorks SKG, a new high-tech entertainment complex founded by filmmaker Steven Spielberg, studio executive Jeffrey Katzenberg, and record producer David Geffen.

California's dominance of the entertainment industry was astounding. By the mid-1990s, the state's major studios and independent filmmakers were producing nearly three-quarters of all feature films made in the United States, pumping an estimated $16.3 billion into the state's economy. Likewise, almost 90 percent of all television series and other prime-time shows were being made in California. "Whether you want to be an actor, or a writer for films and television, or a producer—you still have to come to California," commented one award-winning Hollywood screenwriter.

Also flourishing in California were festivals celebrating the ethnic diversity of the entertainment industry. Best known was the international film and video festival sponsored by Oakland's Black Filmmakers Hall of Fame. Dedicated to "empowering future generations to excel in film, video, and television," the Hall of Fame offered year-round symposia, workshops, and lectures. The San Francisco International Asian American Film Festival, founded in 1982, soon became the largest of its kind in the world. "Much of what is happening in the Asian world is best expressed in video and film," said festival programmer Paul Yi. "These are the media that give people a chance to see commonalities around the world."

After decades of decentralization, the entertainment industry experienced a new burst of consolidation in the 1980s and 1990s. Typical was the expansion and revitalization of the Disney company. Under the direction of CEO Michael Eisner, Disney revived its animation and live-action production through the acquisition of Touchstone and Hollywood Pictures. It also captured a healthy share of the home video market by rationing the rerelease of Disney classics. Disney stores opened in malls across the nation and new Disney theme parks blossomed in Europe and Asia. In 1995 Disney acquired the ABC television network, thus becoming the largest entertainment conglomerate in America.

Not all the expansion of the entertainment industry was in southern California. Filmmakers George Lucas and Francis Ford Coppola established their Zoetroppe Studios in San Francisco in the late 1960s. A decade later, Lucas began building

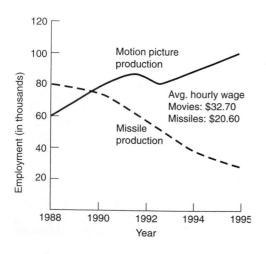

The number of Californians working in the film industry grew so rapidly that it far exceeded the number making missiles. *(Based on data in* Fortune *magazine.)*

Skywalker Ranch in the rolling hills of Marin County and opened his Industrial Light and Magic (ILM) special effects unit in nearby San Rafael. Skywalker Ranch became the most technically advanced filmmaking enterprise in the world, complete with state-of-the-art video editing equipment and other postproduction facilities. From the Lucas film studios came half a dozen of the highest-grossing movies ever made, including the fabulously successful *Star Wars* saga that ushered in a new era of special effects.

The most rapidly growing sector of the entertainment industry was what came to be called "Siliwood," the joining of the high-tech wizardry of Silicon Valley with the movie-making magic of Hollywood. The market for computerized special effects grew by more than 50 percent a year in the mid-1990s. The hottest new technology was digital imaging, first used by ILM designers in 1988 to create a shimmering, snakelike figure for an underwater movie called *The Abyss*. This first on-screen digital character was soon followed by computer-generated robots in *Terminator 2*, full-size dinosaurs in *Jurassic Park*, and dead presidents in *Forrest Gump*. In 1996 a computer graphics company, owned by Apple Computer co-

Computer artists at George Lucas's Industrial Light and Magic (ILM) studios used 3-D graphics to position a ferocious Tyrannosaurus Rex in *Jurassic Park* (1993). (*Copyright © by Universal City Studios, Inc. Courtesy of MCA Publishing Rights, a Division of MCA Inc. All Rights Reserved. Courtesy also of the* San Francisco Chronicle.)

founder Steven Jobs, won a special Academy Award for *Toy Story,* the first entirely computer-animated full-length feature film. "Computers are going to be as ubiquitous in the entertainment industry as they are in the business world," predicted the president of Silicon Graphics.

Local and state officials initiated a broad range of policies to support the burgeoning entertainment industry. In 1995 Los Angeles created the Entertainment Industry Development Corporation to speed the permit-granting process for local filmmakers and to assist them in gaining access to desired locations. Ten years earlier the state legislature created the California Film Commission (CFC) to retain, attract, and promote film production in the state. One of the CFC's most successful services was to collect and catalog more than 300,000 photographs of potential California locations for the shooting of films. The CFC began digitalizing its images in the 1990s with the help of NASA and the Jet Propulsion Laboratory in Pasadena. "The goal of the CFC," said the chair of the commission in 1993, "is to promote a better understanding that the motion picture industry provides a unique and significant contribution to the economy of California."

AGRICULTURE

Perhaps the most striking feature of California's contemporary economy was its diversity. Even as the state led the nation in such fields as high technology, tourism, and entertainment, it remained the nation's leading agricultural state. With less than 3 percent of United States farmland within its borders, California produced more than 50 percent of the country's fruits and vegetables. California led the nation in the production of beef cattle, sugar beets, strawberries, tomatoes, turkeys, and more than 60 other farm commodities, producing all of the nation's commercially grown almonds, artichokes, dates, figs, olives, pistachios, and prunes. California also gained the dubious distinction of being the nation's leading producer of marijuana, reckoned by some to be the state's largest cash crop. By the mid-1990s, California's agricultural cornucopia was pouring more than $20 billion worth of income into the state's economy, accounting for nearly 1 out of every 10 jobs in the state.

Modern California agriculture continued to be shaped by earlier trends, but it also faced some new and difficult challenges. Consolidation continued to reduce the number of farming units and to increase their average size. Between 1940 and 1980 the number of farms in the state was cut in half, and their average size more than doubled. Over 70 percent of California's farm income went to less than 15 percent of the farms, most of which were owned by large corporations. The state's leading owners of agricultural land were the Southern Pacific, J. G. Boswell Corporation, Salyer Land Company, and the Chevron and Getty oil companies.

Thousands of commmercial family farms continued to operate in California, but in the general trend toward consolidation and mechanization many small farmers were squeezed out. With production costs climbing and the value of their farmland plummeting, California's farmers staggered under a debt load that was five times their net income. Foreclosures on farm properties reached levels not seen since the 1930s.

Meanwhile, California's supply of prime agricultural land was threatened by urban development. By the mid-1990s, such land was being lost to housing developments, shopping centers, and freeways at the rate of more than 50,000 acres per year. The problem was especially evident in farm-rich Fresno County, the nation's leading agricultural county that also became one of its most rapidly urbanized. Most of the urban growth was caused by refugees from the coastal metropolitan areas who were attracted to the Central Valley by its relatively inexpensive housing and lower cost of living. The conversion of so much valuable farmland into tracts of suburban housing, in the words of a former Sierra Club president and Kern County resident, was "a crime and a tragedy."

Another unresolved problem in California agriculture was the status of the state's farm workers. The creation of the Agricultural Labor Relations Board (ALRB) in 1975 raised hopes that the status of California's agricultural workers would be permanently improved. Farm workers did make major gains during the late 1970s when Governor Jerry Brown appointed a prolabor majority to the ALRB. Many of these gains were reversed in the 1980s as Brown's Republican successor, George Deukmejian, staffed the board with representatives of the growers and reduced its funding. The influence of César Chávez and the United Farm Workers (UFW) also declined in the 1980s; union membership fell from more than 70,000 in the 1970s to less than 20,000 in 1993. The UFW experienced a modest renaissance in the mid-1990s, growing in membership to about 25,000. In 1996 the union signed a contract with one of the state's largest lettuce growers, ending a dispute nearly two decades old.

Employers of agricultural labor turned increasingly to the use of farm-labor contractors. The subsequent decline in wages, benefits, and working conditions for California's agricultural workers amounted to a counterrevolution in the fields. In 1990 a federal investigation revealed that only 40 percent of the harvesters in the San Joaquin Valley had toilets or hand-washing facilities available at the job sites. Incidents of hepatitis and related health problems were on the rise; compensation was rarely above the minimum wage. Conditions in some areas were comparable to what they had been during the depression a half century earlier.

California farmers also faced the challenge of increased foreign competition, as trade barriers around the world were reduced. Growers of specialty crops—such as broccoli, cauliflower, asparagus, and tomatoes—encountered particularly strong competition from Mexican farmers following Congressional approval of the North American Free Trade Agreement (NAFTA) in 1993. NAFTA tended to benefit, however, the state's beef and dairy industries as well as its growers of apples, pears, and nuts. Foreign ownership of key components of California's agricultural industry steadily increased. By the early 1990s, the state's only cotton mill was Japanese-owned, and some 64 of California's premium wineries were foreign-owned, mostly by Europeans. Almaden, Beaulieu, Inglenook, and Christian Brothers vineyards were all owned by British corporations. Beringer Brothers was owned by Switzerland's Nestlé Company, and the state's oldest premium winery, Buena Vista, was German-owned.

Exports of California agricultural products became increasingly important in recent decades. By the mid-1990s, more than half the state's cotton, rice, and wheat was being sold abroad. Annual exports of California food products exceeded $5 billion, with more than half the state's agricultural exports being shipped to the nations of the Pacific Rim.

As California neared the twenty-first century its economy had been transformed. Emerging from the worst recession in 60 years, Californians discovered that traditional industries, such as defense and aerospace, had declined and new ones had risen to take their place. In the words of one California economist: "While it's true that cutting-edge technologies, new-age film production, and expanding Pacific Rim trade were all present in California before the recession started, each of these industries happened to boom and come into its own in the middle of it. Now they're leading our way to the new future."

SELECTED BIBLIOGRAPHY

The literature on the Sunbelt is extensive. The term was coined by political strategist Kevin Phillips in his 1969 book *The Emerging Republican Majority.* More recent studies include Richard M. Bernard and Bradley Rice (eds.), *Sunbelt Cities* (1983); Peter Wiley and Robert Gottlieb, *Empires in the Sun* (1982); Carl Abbott, *The New Urban America* (1981); and Horace Sutton, "Sunbelt vs. Frostbelt," *Saturday Review,* V (April 1978), pp. 28–37. For a dissenting view, see Clyde E. Browning and Wil Gesler, "Sun Belt-Frost Belt: A Case of Sloppy Regionalizing," *Professional Geographer,* XXXI (February 1979), pp. 66–74.

The best available survey of California's contemporary economy is Joel Kotkin and Paul Grabowicz, *California, Inc.* (1982). Kotkin and Grabowicz analyze California's role in the Sunbelt shift and in the rise of the Pacific Rim. See also the excellent statewide survey in Dan Walters, *The New California* (1992). A useful compilation of statistics is available in *California: An Economic Profile* (1995) and *Facts on the Pacific Rim* (1985), publications of the California Department of Commerce, Office of Economic Research. For the larger context of the debate over NAFTA, see Abraham F. Lowenthal and Katrina Burgess (eds.), *The California-Mexico Connection* (1994).

The classic work on post-industrialism is Daniel Bell, *The Coming of Post-Industrial Society* (1973). On California see Todd R. LaPorte and C. Abrams, "Alternative Patterns of Postindustria: The California Experience," in Leon Lindberg (ed.), *Politics and the Future of Industrial Society* (1975); LaPorte and Ted K. Bradshaw, *Advanced Industrial California* (1977); and Michael B. Teitz, "The California Economy: Changing Structure and Policy Responses," in John J. Kirlin and Donald R. Winkler (eds.), *California Policy Choices* (1984). See also Rob Kling, Spencer Olin, and Mark Poster (eds.), *Postsuburban California* (1991).

On the rise of California's high-technology industry, see Dirk Hanson, *The New Alchemists: Silicon Valley and the Microelectronics Revolution* (1982), and T. R. Reid, *The Chip* (1985). Useful short histories of Silicon Valley appear in Charles Wollenberg, *Golden Gate Metropolis* (1985), and Moira Johnson, "Silicon Valley," *National Geographic* (October 1982), pp. 459–477. On the problems caused by the high-tech industries, see Bradley Cleveland, "A Polarization of the Workforce," *Bay Area Business* (August 1985), pp. 20–23, and Lenny Siegel, "High Tech Pollution," *Sierra Club Bulletin,* LXIX (December 1984), pp. 58–64.

Analyses of the defense industry in California appear in Ehud Yonay, "The Anatomy of U.S. Defense," *California,* X (October 1985), pp. 91, 146–148; David Phinney, "Deploying

Defense Dollars," *Bay Area Business Magazine* (March 1986), pp. 14–19, 50; J. S. Taub, "Defense Dollars," *California Journal,* XVIII (June 1987), pp. 274–277; and two publications from the California Department of Economic and Business Development, Office of Economic Policy: *The Aerospace Industry in California* (1981) and *The Effect of Increased Military Spending on California* (1982). Particularly useful is Patrick Lloyd Hatcher, *Economic Earthquakes: Converting Defense Cuts to Economic Opportunities* (1994).

Among the many articles on the state's recovery from the recession of the early 1990s, see especially those in *Fortune* (February 5, 1996), *The Washington Post* (January 20, 1996), *The New York Times* (December 18, 1995), *The Economist* (December 3, 1995), and *The Wall Street Journal* (February 3, 1995).

The California Department of Commerce, Office of Tourism, has compiled a statistical analysis of tourism in the state, *California Travel: Its Economic Impact* (1991). See also Michael Vinson, *Motoring Tourists and the Scenic West* (1989), and John F. Sears, *Sacred Places: American Tourist Attractions* (1989).

The literature on the entertainment industry is extensive. See, for instance, the "California Production Special Issue" of *The Hollywood Reporter* (November 3–5, 1995); Benedicte Raybaud and Danielle Starkey, "California's Film Industry Beats the Recession," *California Journal,* XXIV (January 1993), pp. 37–38; and the biographies of entertainment moguls in ibid., XXVI (December 1995), pp. 17–18.

Stephen Johnson, Gerald Haslam, and Robert Dawson, *The Great Central Valley* (1992), explores the natural and social history of California's agricultural heartland. Contemporary agricultural problems are analyzed in Jerome B. Siebert, "Agriculture," *California Journal,* XXI (January 1990), pp. 41–46, and Al Sokolow, "Urbanizing California's Farmlands," ibid., XXI (November 1990), pp. 535–538.

On the possible futures of California, see Richard W. Reinhardt, *California 2000: The Next Frontier* (1982), and John Hart (ed.), The *New Book of California Tomorrow: Reflections and Projections for the Golden State* (1985).

CHAPTER THIRTY-SEVEN

The New California Society

As California neared the twenty-first century, it remained the land of opportunity for an endless stream of newcomers from across the nation and around the world. Demographers predicted that the number of Californians would swell to more than 48 million by the year 2020. This burgeoning population put a tremendous strain on the state's infrastructure, including such basic services as transportation, education, health care, and the criminal justice system.

Coping with the problems of growth was especially difficult in an age when state and local governments were constrained by tight fiscal limits. Evidence mounted of a growing polarization of California society into a privileged "overclass" and an exploding "underclass" of frustrated Californians dependent on a system of inadequate and deteriorating public services.

TRANSPORTATION

One of the most visible and agonizing consequences of population growth was the growing congestion of the state's more than 160,000 miles of streets and highways. The problem was particularly severe in major metropolitan areas, where freeways filled daily with bumper-to-bumper traffic. At peak commute hours the average speed on urban freeways in 1990 was 23 miles per hour. The average speed was expected to drop to 15 miles per hour by the turn of the century. The psychological and economic consequences of such a calamity were awesome. "Traffic congestion is one of the most frustrating experiences people go through every day," observed a spokesperson for the California Chamber of Commerce.

The underlying cause of the congestion was readily apparent. During the 1980s the number of motor vehicles in California increased by more than 50 percent, whereas the capacity of the state highway system grew by only 4 percent.

The major barrier to achieving a solution to the state's transportation problem was the enormous cost involved. Building new freeways where they were needed most, in congested urban areas, had become prohibitively expensive. Construction of the Century Freeway in Los Angeles cost the state over $100 million a mile. While the expense of new construction soared, the willingness of Californians to pay for transportation improvements lagged far behind. The state gasoline tax, the main source of revenue for freeway construction, was among the lowest in the nation. In terms of per capita spending on highways, California slipped to dead last during the Deukmejian administration. "This state went from number 49 under Jerry Brown," observed a Republican Assemblyman from Newport Beach, "to number 50 under the Duke." By 1989 California actually ranked fifty-first in the nation, with less per capita spending on transportation than any other state or the District of Columbia.

In the late 1980s attitudes began to change. Faced with continued inaction by the state, local governments took the lead in financing transportation improvements. Voters in Santa Clara County approved a measure to raise the local sales tax to pay for better highways. Soon a dozen other counties followed. Encouraged by the actions of local governments, the state legislature in 1989 enacted an innovative plan to authorize private firms to build new highways and to collect tolls from the motorists who used them. Toll roads were really nothing new in California; more than 80 such roads had been in operation a century earlier. Supporters of the revived toll-road concept believed that it offered a unique opportunity for the private sector to help solve a critical problem. Critics charged that toll roads represented an unwelcome privatization of the state's infrastructure, leading eventually to "a two-tiered transit system with the affluent motoring along well-kept tollways and the poor bumping along from pothole to pothole." The first toll road built in California since the depression opened in the mid-1990s. Orange County's Foothill Tollway provided motorists with dashboard credit cards that were scanned as vehicles sped through toll plazas at freeway speeds. (Similar devices were at work collecting tolls on major bridges throughout California by the end of 1997.)

The resurgence of toll roads in the 1990s was just one manifestation of a new technology called Intelligent Vehicle Highway Systems (IVHS). Regarded as the core of the surface transportation system of the future, IVHS technology allowed traffic managers to operate existing freeways more efficiently by using integrated applications of electronics, computers, and communications technology. The first successful IVHS project encompassed one of the busiest commuter corridors in the nation, southern California's Santa Monica, Harbor, and San Diego freeways.

The most dramatic evidence of a growing willingness of voters to support needed improvements in the transportation system came in 1990 with the approval of a ballot initiative that doubled the state's gasoline tax. It was the largest single increase since the tax was first enacted in 1923. Revenue from the increased tax was to be used for an $18.5 billion program of new highway and railroad construction, the largest single transportation investment in state history. Voters also approved two bond measures that outlined specific road-building, mass transit, and railroad construction projects.

The new emphasis on rail transportation was reminiscent of an earlier era. Nearly all intercity travel in California had been by rail as late as 1920; 50 years later rail passenger service had virtually disappeared. The new rail system envisioned for the state included a high-speed rail corridor, linking each of the major urban areas. Once the corridor was in place, transit planners urged the state to adopt magnetic levitation technology that would enable passenger service at speeds approaching 300 miles per hour. The new generation of "California cars" speeding along the state's rail corridor would be ideally suited for business travel, equipped with fax machines, cellular telephones, and dining services complete with regional specialties, health foods, and fine California wines.

The bond measures approved in 1990 included funds for improving local commuter rail projects throughout the state. Improvements were slated for the Bay Area Rapid Transit system (BART) and the San Diego and San Jose trolleys, and construction was planned for two new commuter rail lines in the Los Angeles basin. BART announced plans to extend service to the San Francisco and Oakland airports and to cities in the outer East Bay. More ambitious plans included a second transbay tube connecting the San Francisco and Oakland airports and a line across the Golden Gate Bridge to Marin County. Bay Area residents were especially interested in a proposal to install an electric light-rail system across the San Francisco–Oakland Bay Bridge, a project that would double the bridge's carrying capacity. Electric commuter trains had occupied the lower deck of the bridge 30 years earlier, from its opening in 1936 until 1958.

The 1990 transportation bond measures also provided funds to subsidize the revival of an even older form of San Francisco commuter service—ferries across the bay. Regional planners in 1991 announced plans to establish a network of modern, high-tech passenger ferries to help relieve rush-hour pressures on the other transit systems in the Bay Area. Even at full capacity, however, the new system would not rival the huge fleet of ferries that once had carried 60 million passengers a year across the bay.

Southern California also witnessed the revival of an old idea for solving its transit problems. In 1993 a new 4-mile subway, dubbed the Metro Red Line, began carrying passengers in downtown Los Angeles. Meanwhile, nearly 200 miles of Metrolink commuter rail lines connected the city center with outlying communities in Orange, San Bernardino, and Riverside counties. The Metro Blue Line, an electric light-rail trolley, began operating between Los Angeles and Long Beach. The Blue Line was the first interurban rail line in the Los Angeles basin since 1961 when the last of the Pacific Electric's "Red Car" rail lines were torn up to make way for the freeways. The new light-rail line followed almost exactly the route of the last Pacific Electric line. Thus it was through the past that California seemed to be finding its way to the future.

EDUCATION

The relentless growth of California's population put enormous pressures on the state's already overburdened system of public education. Enrollment in elementary and secondary schools was expected to exceed 6 million students by the school year 2000–2001. Demographers predict the total school-age population of California

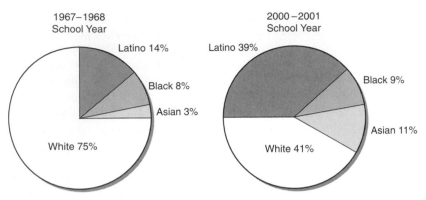

1967–1968
School Year

Latino 14%

Black 8%

Asian 3%

White 75%

2000–2001
School Year

Latino 39%

Black 9%

Asian 11%

White 41%

The changing ethnic makeup of California's public schools. *(Based on data from the California Department of Education.)*

would nearly double by the year 2020, meaning that the state would have to build 12 new classrooms *every day* to keep pace with the increase in students.

The need for more schools was just one of the many challenges facing Californians concerned with the welfare of the state's children. Michael W. Kirst, a professor in the School of Education at Stanford University, found that the number of California children living in poverty doubled between 1969 and 1989 to over 20 percent. By 1995 one out of every four children in California was living in poverty, a proportion that was expected to increase to one out of three by the year 2000. There was also a significant shift in the ethnicity of California's youth. Whereas one-quarter of the students in the state's schools were members of ethnic minorities in 1970, 25 years later over half were minority students and one out every four had only limited proficiency in English. "Increasingly, schools must meet the needs of children with backgrounds and experiences they were not set up to serve and historically have not served well," Kirst concluded. "Education must be part of a complete overhaul of the entire system for delivering children's services."

Particularly disturbing was the rise of violent crime in the public schools. Knifings, shootings, and membership in gangs were on the rise in districts throughout the state. "Gangs are so widespread in our schools that these kids aren't 'them' anymore," commented a parole agent for the California Youth Authority. "They are us." The problem was especially serious in the inner cities, but also was growing in rural and suburban schools. About 15 percent of all weapons violations in the nation's schools occurred in the Los Angeles area. By the late 1990s, California had the highest juvenile incarceration rate in the United States.

Educational reform was a major issue throughout the 1980s and 1990s. The legislature in 1983 passed the most comprehensive school reform law in state history, mandating over 80 separate changes. The law established tougher curriculum standards, disciplinary procedures, and new graduation requirements. The results of such reforms were far from clear. Student scores on standardized tests improved modestly, but the rate of improvement was agonizingly slow. In 1995 the reading comprehension scores of California's fourth graders were the lowest in the nation, tied with the fourth graders of Mississippi. Meanwhile, 80 percent of California's high school seniors scored lower than the national average on the Scholastic Aptitude Test (SAT). The president of the organization that sponsored the SAT warned of a growing division "between a small class of an educational elite and an underclass of students academically ill-prepared for the demands of college or the workplace."

The economic consequences of low student achievement were soon evident. In 1991 less than half of all job applicants in California were able to demonstrate satisfactory mathematical or verbal abilities on entry-level exams. Stephen Levy, director of the Center for the Continuing Study of the California Economy, warned in 1995 that the state's economic future was in peril unless dramatic improvements were made in public education. Levy argued that a highly skilled and well-educated workforce was absolutely essential if California was to remain competitive in the twenty-first century. The *Economist* agreed: "The state's shabby and dangerous schools look less and less like breeding grounds for the biotechnologists and virtual-reality script-writers of the future."

One of the most contentious areas of education reform in recent years was the adoption of state-approved textbooks. Under California law, textbooks used in the public schools were first subjected to an extensive review by the state Board of Education. Once the books were approved, state funds were available to local districts for their purchase. In 1987 the board adopted a new "framework" for the teaching of history and social studies in the public schools. The framework represented a radical departure from the way history and social studies were taught in the rest of the nation; as a consequence only one textbook publisher submitted an entire series to the board for approval. The new series won the board's approval, but became the subject of intense debate in districts across the state. Critics charged that the textbooks contained "egregious racial stereotyping." The superintendent of public instruction vigorously defended the series, denouncing its critics as "tribalists" who "make a livelihood of discrediting broader cultural values." One observer noted that the intensity of the textbook controversy revealed "how polarized we are, how much fear there is about diversity, and how the schools have become the battleground." Ultimately over 600 of the state's more than 1000 districts adopted the controversial new textbooks.

The fundamental issue facing many school districts was not whether they should adopt new textbooks, but whether they would have sufficient funds to pay their bills. By the mid-1990s, California's schools were in crisis. More than 120 districts were unable to meet current expenses, and several districts faced bankruptcy (including Richmond, Coachella, and Compton). Schools throughout the state were grossly underfunded and scandalously overcrowded. One of the most telling signs of decline was the decimation of the state's public school libraries. California schools in 1991 had only 1 librarian for every 4000 students, by far the worst ratio of any state in the nation. The passage of Proposition 98 in 1988 guaranteed the schools approximately 40 percent of the state's annual budget, yet California's per capita spending on education remained far below the national average. In 1995 California ranked forty-second among the 50 states in per pupil spending and by 40 percent between 1990 and the year 2005. When proposals to expand existing campuses met with resistance from local communities, President Gardner proposed in 1988 that three new campuses be added to the system. The legislature, however, failed to appropriate the necessary funds, and in 1993 the university abandoned its plans to build a new campus in Merced, Fresno, or Madera counties.

Fees at the University of California dramatically increased in the early 1990s, just as they had at CSU, leading to angry student protests on several campuses. Students at UC Davis occupied a university building; others held a boisterous rally on the steps of the state capitol in Sacramento. "We hope today is the beginning of a movement away from the death of higher education," declared one student leader. Defending the fee increase, the *San Francisco Chronicle* argued that California could no longer afford to be "the low-cost leader" in higher education.

One of the most promising trends in higher education in recent years was the increased enrollment of minority students at the University of California. The university's affirmative action recruitment policy led to a dramatic increase in the admission of "underrepresented minorities" throughout the 1980s. In the early 1990s, however, these gains were threatened by increased fees, enrollment caps, and reduced government support for minority recruitment. Minority enrollment was further threatened in 1995 by the decision of the university regents to end affirmative action in all admissions, hiring, and contracting. (See Chapter 34.)

Improving the quality of undergraduate education was another major challenge facing the state's colleges and universities. In 1990 the Carnegie Foundation for the Advancement of Teaching reported that undergraduate instruction was being short-changed at many institutions of higher education where instructors were evaluated almost entirely on the basis of their scholarly research and publication. Just 3 months later, President Donald Kennedy of Stanford University announced a bold new plan to improve undergraduate education. Kennedy's goal was to return the university's central focus to teaching undergraduates, rather than promoting faculty research. Support for improving undergraduate education also came from the University of California. Historian Page Smith, founding provost of the Santa Cruz campus, decried the emphasis on faculty research to the neglect of quality instruction. Smith added that most academic research was "pedestrian work" that was read only by a handful and "need not and should not be done." Meanwhile Berkeley sociologist Neil Smelser reported that the definition of scholarship was slowly expanding at several UC campuses to include increased recognition of the value of teaching.

HEALTH CARE

The health care system of California includes the most sophisticated technologies and advanced medical treatment programs in the world. Yet it also has left a large and growing number of Californians with limited access to even the most basic medical services. Dr. Kenneth Kizer, director of the California Department of Health Services, diagnosed the state's health care crisis as a "paradox of medical want amidst medical plenty."

California's system of health care was a complex mix of private and public institutions, and included a wide range of services funded by federal, state, and local governments. Ever since the mid-1960s, the federal government's Medicare program had provided aid to the elderly for medical care. Medicaid extended that assistance to those in need, such as the blind and disabled, who were too young to receive Medicare benefits. California's own Medi-Cal system administered the federal programs and contracted with doctors and hospitals to provide medical services to those who qualified for assistance.

The problems confronting the health care system were as complex as the system itself. First in importance was the rising cost of medical care. New hospital construction, the adoption of expensive new technologies, and escalating liability costs drove the cost of health care beyond the reach of many Californians. Likewise the price of medical insurance was rising at a rapid rate. Between 1987 and 1989 health insurance premiums rose over 30 percent; by 1992 they stood at more than $5500 per family. Employers were increasingly unable or unwilling to provide medical insurance benefits to their employees.

One of the most disturbing symptoms of the ailing health care system was the growing number of Californians without health insurance of any kind. By the early 1990s, six million Californians were uninsured, most of whom were working families with children. Many of the "medically poor" worked at low-paying jobs in the service sector. Their employers failed to provide them with private health insurance, and yet they failed to qualify for Medi-Cal. Unable to afford routine health care, they tended to seek medical treatment only when their conditions became acute. Hospital emergency rooms, required by state law to admit anyone with a medical emergency, became the primary health care providers for millions of Californians. "Emergency rooms are becoming the repository of the fact that we don't have a health-care system that is working," observed the chairperson of the California Assembly Health Committee.

Escalating medical costs and reduced levels of government support led many private hospitals to close their emergency rooms. Ten hospitals in Los Angeles County between 1985 and 1989 shut their trauma centers, emergency rooms fully staffed and equipped to treat critical injuries at all hours. Budget shortfalls threatened to close 4 additional county hospitals and more than 30 neighborhood clinics in 1995. The reductions in service more than doubled the response time required for a critically injured person to be taken by ambulance to a trauma center. The crisis in health care was thus a matter of life and death. "People who feel very comfortable and protected right now because they have insurance," warned one UCLA professor of public health, "could end up in the morgue because that hospital emergency room that they simply assumed would be there for them has its doors locked."

President Bill Clinton in 1993 proposed a comprehensive health care reform plan aimed at establishing "a guaranteed system of private insurance that will cover every American." Although the president's plan failed to win congressional approval, several of its key provisions already were in place in California. The state legislature in 1993 established the Health Insurance Plan of California (HIPC), an innovative experiment in "collective purchasing" that offered small businesses affordable insurance for their workers. Another element in the president's plan was to expand the availability of "managed care," systems of doctors and hospitals that provided health services to enrolled members for a predetermined annual fee. By 1995 about 40 percent of all Californians with private health insurance were receiving their medical services through managed-care health maintainance organizations (HMOs). President Clinton cited the Oakland-based Kaiser Permanente HMO as a model for the nation. Because such organizations generally provided medical services at lower rates, the state legislature required that all Medi-Cal patients be enrolled in managed-care systems by 1996. One health rights activist viewed the new require-ment as "a sea change in California's system of providing health-care services to the poor."

The most controversial health care issue in recent years was the acquired immuno-deficiency syndrome, better known as AIDS. The disease first appeared in California in June 1981, when five young homosexuals in Los Angeles were diagnosed as having a rare type of pneumonia found only in people with deficient immune systems. Almost simultaneously epidemiologists discovered the same disease among five homosexuals in San Francisco. Within weeks a rare type of skin cancer, known as Kaposi's sarcoma, was discovered among a group of sexually active young men in New York City. The federal Centers for Disease Control issued a preliminary warning: these phenomena appeared related and suggested "an association between some aspect of a homosexual lifestyle and disease."

The first breakthrough in treating the disease came 3 years later when scientists succeeded in isolating the human immunodeficiency virus (HIV) that caused AIDS. The virus attacked a person's immune system, leaving the body vulnerable to a host of opportunistic infections and cancers. Medical researchers soon developed a test for HIV and produced an antiviral compound (AZT) to treat the disease. The use of AZT proved effective in slowing, but not actually stopping, the development of AIDS among patients who were infected with HIV. Scientists also attempted to produce a vaccine that would prevent the spread of HIV, but the virus proved fiercely resistant to treatment, undergoing wide genetic mutations as it infected patient after patient. The virus was even able to change its genetic nature with uncanny speed as it spread within a single infected individual.

Shortly after the tenth anniversary of the onset of the AIDS epidemic, more than 200,000 Americans had been stricken with the disease and over 1 million others were infected with HIV. Homosexuals and intravenous drug users ac-counted for nearly 80 percent of all AIDS victims, but increasingly the disease was spreading among heterosexual men and women. The proportion of African Americans and Latinos stricken by the disease also was increasing. By the mid-1990s, AIDS was the leading cause of death among American males between the ages of 25 and 44. California had one-quarter of the nation's total AIDS cases, with 80 percent concentrated in San Francisco and Los Angeles. Thirty-three thousand San Franciscans were HIV-positive, more per capita than any other ma-jor American city. In southern California, only the seaside town of Laguna Beach had a higher rate of infection than San Francisco. Long fashionable as a gay tourist mecca, this popular resort community was hard hit by the disease. Randy Shilts, author of an early history of the AIDS epidemic, caught the irony of such devastation in an idyllic setting. "The reality of AIDS is so contrary," Shilts observed, "to the Southern California ethos of youth and beauty."

The federal government was slow at first to confront the seriousness of the epidemic. The Reagan administration's surgeon general, C. Everett Koop, favored a massive campaign of public education to prevent the spread of the disease. Koop specifically recommended that public schools teach that condoms were a crucial, if imperfect, method of prevention. Reagan's education secretary, William Bennett, denounced Koop's "condom-mania" and insisted that the nation's schools teach sexual abstinence as the only sure way of preventing the spread of the disease. Other conservative leaders argued that teaching about condoms would contribute to teenage promiscuity. President Reagan concurred, commenting in 1987 that sex should never be presented to schoolchildren as just "a physical thing, such as eating a ham sandwich." Meanwhile, the state of California led the nation in committing its resources to the fight against AIDS. The state developed a computerized AIDS registry, mandated universal blood-donor screening, and established a highly successful program for voluntary, anonymous HIV testing.

Prevention programs reduced the overall rate of HIV infection in the United States in the mid-1990s, but the rate continued to increase at an alarming rate among Americans between the ages of 13 and 19. "I don't think most young people really understand it," said a spokesperson for the National Association of People with AIDS. "We have to be clear: If you get HIV in your 20s, you will die by around 40 years old."

The AIDS epidemic, of course, was not limited to California or the United States. It soon became the fastest-growing disease in the world, taking an especially heavy toll in the developing countries of Africa. Twenty million people worldwide had been stricken by 1996, with 6000 new infections a day. The president of the World Health Organization declared that AIDS was "the world's first truly global epidemic, and it calls for a global response." He warned that the epidemic was "still gaining momentum and its major impact is yet to come."

CRIMINAL JUSTICE

Another issue of grave concern to Californians in recent decades was the rising crime rate. The rate of violent crime more than doubled in the 1960s and continued to spiral upward in the 1970s at an alarming rate. California voters demanded that their elected officials take vigorous action to ensure public safety.

The growing concern about crime led to several fundamental changes in California's criminal justice system. The most dramatic change came in 1977 when the state legislature reinstated the death penalty. The author of the new death penalty law was George Deukmejian, then a member of the state senate. Deukmejian's election as governor in 1982, and his appointment of a conservative majority to the state supreme court, cleared the way for the resumption of executions. Yet Deukmejian left office in 1991 without a single execution being carried out. It fell to his successor, Pete Wilson, in 1992 to oversee California's first execution in a quarter century. The process was already routine by 1996 as the fourth condemned inmate was put to death by lethal injection; more than 400 others awaited their turn on San Quentin's death row.

The legislature altered another important part of the criminal justice system in 1977 when it changed the way prison terms were set. Formerly, a state parole board had decided when prisoners were "rehabilitated" and ready to return to society. The legislature abandoned this practice in 1977 in favor of setting fixed sentences for specific crimes. Punishment, not rehabilitation, became the primary function of imprisonment. In subsequent years, the legislature regularly increased the length of prison terms and required mandatory sentences for a host of criminal offenses.

The results of the new sentencing policies were soon apparent. The state's prison population more than quadrupled between 1982 and 1996. To house this exploding population, the legislature authorized the building of 15 additional state prisons. New prison construction, however, was unable to keep pace with the growth in the number of inmates. By 1996 the state prisons were at 186 percent of capacity. Likewise, more than two-thirds of the state's county jails exceeded their capacity. California also incarcerated a higher percentage of its juveniles for longer periods of time than any other state in the nation. Barry Krisberg, president of the National

Political cartoonist Rob Wilson comments on the dramatic increase in the rate of incarceration and the construction of new prisons in California. (*Courtesy of the* California Journal.)

Council on Crime and Delinquency, reported that California's overall incarceration rate was the highest in the world.

Critics of the changes in the criminal justice system complained that a disproportionate share of the state's scarce resources was being spent on corrections. Between 1983 and 1995 more prison guards were hired in California than all other state employees combined, and the annual allocation for the Department of Corrections was the fastest-growing portion of the state budget. The superintendent of public instruction protested that California was building "Cadillac prisons and jalopy schools."

Whether the state's tougher sentencing policies and increased rate of incarceration caused a reduction in crime became a matter of widespread public debate. The overall crime rate in California decreased steadily since the peak year of 1980, proof to many that locking up more criminals had reduced crime. Others were not so sure. "It's quite impossible to authoritatively suggest what causes short-term changes in the crime rate," cautioned the former dean of the UC Berkeley School of Criminology. Another expert noted that demographic factors in California had a greater impact on the crime rate than did incarceration. The state's rate of violent crime followed more closely the declining proportion of young males in the population—those most likely to commit crimes—than it did the increasing rate of imprisonment. As California's overall population aged, its crime rate diminished.

Unfortunately all of the state did not share equally in the reduced crime rate. The state's tough new laws did little to slow the mayhem in the inner cities where many neighborhoods remained notoriously unsafe. The underlying causes of the continuing urban violence seemed all too obvious to the residents of the inner cities. One Oakland minister identified the chronic poverty and utter hopelessness of his parishioners as "a breeding ground of violence and hate." The head of Oakland's homicide unit agreed: "What you have here is year after year after year of low employment, poor schools, and the disintegration of the family."

Faced with the failure of imprisonment alone to solve the problem of violent crime, many experts concluded that new, long-term efforts at prevention were needed. Criminology professor Michael Rustigan of San Jose State University reported in 1992 that the vast majority of murderers came from broken homes and that they displayed symptoms of psychological disturbance at a very early age. The best way to reduce the rate of violent crime, he argued, was through early intervention. "We can go reactive, we can execute and stuff people in prison, but the murder rate still goes up," Rustigan pointed out. For a time, Governor Pete Wilson was among those who endorsed early intervention as the most cost-effective method of fighting crime. In his first state-of-the-state address in 1991, Wilson called for "a new vision of government, a vision based on the old adage that an ounce of prevention is worth a pound of cure." Three years later, however, Wilson ran for reelection in a campaign that stressed punishment over prevention. He supported in 1994 the enormously popular "three-strikes-and-you're-out" initiative that mandated stiffer sentences for repeat felons. When the state supreme court declared a key provision of the initiative to be unconstitutional, Wilson supported efforts to reinstate it.

Nowhere was the preventative approach needed more than in the fight against drug abuse. Drug-related crimes accounted for more than half of all the crimes committed in California. In Los Angeles, two out of three felons were under the influence of cocaine at the time of their arrest. In addition to crimes committed by those under the influence, drug-related offenses included crimes committed to finance the habit, crimes resulting from competition among drug dealers, and illicit drug manufacturing and trafficking. California led the nation in the number of clandestine drug labs producing methamphetamines and was the primary point of entry for cocaine from abroad. California drug gangs, centered in Los Angeles, distributed their deadly merchandise across the nation. One leading drug expert warned that California had became a "world-class" center for the manufacturing and distribution of drugs. "If California were a nation," he observed, "it would be the largest, most important polity among all the world's nations in terms of illicit drugs."

Efforts to combat the drug problem included a mix of federal and state programs, spending over a billion dollars a year. A highly successful antidrug education program in the schools and in the media contributed to a decline in drug use among young and middle-class users. There was no decline, however, among the growing underclass of Californians. The California Department of Justice reported that drug use among the state's poor was "intensifying at levels never seen before anywhere in the world." As with many other aspects of recent social history, California's pattern of drug abuse was divided along lines of social class. The outlook for the future was bleak. "The drug problem is expected to continue in rapacious severity at the poorer end of the social structure," observed Steven White, district attorney for Sacramento County. "What we're likely to see is an economic demarcation line. Those above the line will use drugs less; those below will continue as now, and may fall even farther into the chasm cut by drugs."

THE NEW CALIFORNIANS

In 1995 the United States Census Bureau released a report projecting California population trends to the year 2020. The report estimated that California's overall population would increase by more than 50 percent in the next quarter century, growing from 32 million to more than 48 million.

California's rate of population growth, in recent years, closely paralleled the health of the state's economy. During the boom of the 1980s, California's growth rate was more than twice that of the nation. In the early 1990s, during the state's worst recession since the 1930s, California actually grew more slowly than the nation. Then the rate of growth accelerated once again in the later 1990s as the state's economy rebounded. The fastest-growing areas within the state continued to be inland communities, from Escondido in the south to Redding in the north. Californians were moving in record numbers from crowded coastal enclaves, such as San Francisco and Los Angeles, to the interior valleys and hills. This migration from the cities was fueled in part by the development of portable jobs in the high-tech and services fields, as well as by the search for cheaper housing and a lower cost of living.

Substantial numbers of Californians also were moving out of the state altogether, complaining of such problems as traffic congestion, air pollution, and crime. During the recession of the early 1990s, more people left California than arrived from other states. About half of those leaving California settled in the nearby western states of Oregon, Arizona, and Nevada. The arrival of so many "California refugees" was not always welcomed by California's neighbors. They feared the Californians would bring their problems with them, contributing to a process derisively known as "creeping Californiazation."

The most striking quality of California's population was its increasing ethnic diversity. More than half the state's population growth in the 1980s and 1990s was from foreign immigration, primarily from Asia and Latin America. By 1995 one out of four Californians was foreign-born. Much of the remaining growth was due to the high birthrate among those who had recently arrived. Ethnic minorities made up only one-third of the state's population in 1980, but 10 years later they constituted 43 percent. Demographers predicted that California would have "a majority of minorities" by the early twenty-first century. Already no single ethnic group was in the majority in Imperial, Los Angeles, and San Francisco counties. David Reiff, author of *Los Angeles: Capital of the Third World* (1992), reported that the state's largest city was home not only to more Mexicans than any other city except Mexico City, but also to more Koreans than any other city except Seoul and to more Filipinos than any other city but Manila.

Los Angeles also had the distinction of being home to the nation's largest population of Native Americans. Although there were no distinct Indian neighborhoods in the city, a network of social and economic institutions provided the Indian people of Los Angeles with feelings of tradition and community. The 1990 census reported that more than 240,000 Indians lived throughout California, more than in any other state except Oklahoma. Projections to the year 2020 indicated that Native Americans would continue to make up less than 1 percent of California's overall population.

Economic development was a major concern of California Indians in the late twentieth century. The fastest-growing and most controversial sector of the Native American economy was legalized gambling; millions of dollars in gaming revenues revitalized tribal economies in California and across the nation. The California state government attempted to limit Indian-run gambling enterprises to low-stakes bingo and poker, but several tribes asserted their right to operate Nevada-style casinos. Marshall McKay (Wintun), chairman of the California-Nevada Indian Gambling Association, said in 1995 that "Indian gambling in the last ten years has had a more significant impact on Indian people than the last 150 years of government support."

Native people also remained active in a wide range of activities to revive and preserve traditional languages and cultures. Community-based groups flourished throughout the state, matching elders who were fluent in traditional languages with younger tribal members who were eager to learn. "The only way we'll stay alive as a people," observed Nancy Richardson Riley (Karuk), "is if we practice and live our culture."

The ethnic group experiencing the least growth in recent years was the category identified by the Census Bureau as "non-Hispanic whites." The Anglo population grew less than 14 percent during the 1980s, having the lowest birthrate and the highest rate of "out-migration." The Anglos' overall proportion in the population fell from two-thirds in 1980 to just 57 percent in 1990 and was expected to drop below 50 percent shortly after the turn of the century.

One of the most salient characteristics of the Anglo population was its relatively high rate of political participation. In the elections of the mid-1990s, Anglos composed less than 60 percent of the state's population, and yet they accounted for more than 80 percent of the voters. Likewise, non-Hispanic whites continued to hold the lion's share of elective offices in the state. Of the 120 members of the state legislature in 1996, only 11 were Latino, 6 African American, and 1 Asian. The 52 members of California's congressional delegation included 4 Latinos, 3 African Americans, and 2 Asians. As California's minority population approached majority status, it presented the state with a fundamental challenge. "It will test whether we can peacefully change," observed a spokeperson for California Tomorrow, "from a European dominated society with minorities to a world society where everybody is a minority."

This challenge was already being faced in the schools of California where no one ethnic group had been in the majority since 1988. Anglo students struggled to find ways to fit into a society increasingly defined in multicultural terms. Non-Hispanic whites at Anaheim High School stirred widespread controversy in 1992 by organizing a club for "European Americans." Critics feared that the club was racist, but the Anglo students argued successfully that the club was analogous to other campus organizations such as the Asian Club, the Black Students Union, and the Mexican American Engineering Society. Meanwhile in 1992 the Berkeley campus of the University of California began requiring all its first-year students to take a class on "American cultures." The requisite cultures to be included were Native American, African American, Latin American, Asian American, and European American.

The Census Bureau estimated in 1995 that African Americans would increase from 7.4 percent to about 8 percent of the state's population by the year 2020. The black population was expected to continue growing at a rate only moderately faster than that of non-Hispanic whites. The areas of greatest growth for African Americans were in the suburban neighborhoods of Riverside, Vallejo, Fresno, and Sacramento, rather than in the established black communities of Los Angeles, San Francisco, and Oakland. "Blacks are moving out of cities for the same reasons as whites," explained geographer James Johnson. "They want better housing and they want to get away from the negative things in the cities like gangs and poor schools." Blacks in growing numbers were also joining the exodus from California, moving to states in the deep south that their parents or grandparents had fled years ago.

As African Americans left the cities, their places were taken largely by Latinos and Asians. Racial tensions among the residents of the inner city intensified as competition for jobs and political power increased. Ishmael Reed, one of California's most talented African American writers, quoted approvingly the ironic comment that "in a multicultural environment, affirmative action may mean taking a job away from a black person and giving it to an Asian or Latino." Tensions erupted into violence in South Central Los Angeles in the early 1990s as black residents and Korean shopkeepers vented their mutual hostilities. One black resident of Compton explained the situation in terms of economic exploitation and competition: "It seems everybody's just trying to get over on the residents of Compton without giving anything back. That's where the hostility comes in. So the people out there resent these immigrants getting a leg up on them." Rapper Ice Cube put the matter more succinctly in the lyrics of his hit single "Black Korea." He warned "Oriental" shopkeepers that their stores would be burned down unless they paid respect to "the black fist."

The worst outbreak of violence occurred in the spring of 1992, following the acquittal of four white Los Angeles police officers accused of beating black motorist Rodney King. Five days of rioting, centered in South Central Los Angeles, left at least fifty people dead and nearly 4000 injured. In terms of loss of life and destruction of property, the riot was far more devastating than the Watts riot of 1965. Rioters touched off nearly 900 fires, destroying property valued at more than $1 billion. Especially hard hit was the business district known as Koreatown; more than 80 percent of the Korean-owned businesses were damaged or destroyed. Rioting also spread to neighboring communities such as Pasadena, Hollywood, and Beverly Hills. The violence ended only with a massive show of force by thousands of police, national guardsmen, and federal troops.

The underlying causes of the riot were the same as those that had led to the Watts riot more than a quarter of a century earlier. Conditions in South Central Los Angeles had actually gotten worse. Whereas 27 percent of the area's families lived in poverty in 1965, over 30 percent were impoverished in 1992. The major change was the ethnic identity of the residents. South Central Los Angeles was about 80 percent African American in 1965, whereas by 1992 more than half its residents were Latino. Of the more than 17,000 people arrested during the riot, two-thirds were unemployed. Some South Central community leaders described the violence as a "revolt of the poor" and pointed out that black and Latino Californians were twice as likely to live in poverty as Anglo Californians and their average income was one-third less. Jeffrey Lustig, director of the Center for California Studies, captured the larger significance of what was happening: "California is now a two-tiered society filled with rage."

Meanwhile, black Californians continued to exercise considerable political power within the state. African Americans held nearly 300 elective offices in the 1990s, an increase from just 200 a decade earlier. The most prominent black leader in the state remained Willie L. Brown, Jr., elected San Francisco's first African American mayor in 1995 after serving as assembly speaker longer than anyone in the history of California. Los Angeles Mayor Tom Bradley declined to seek reelection in 1993 after an unprecedented five terms as leader of the nation's second largest city.

Willie L. Brown, Jr., was elected mayor of San Francisco in 1995 after serving more than two decades as the speaker of the assembly. (*Courtesy of the Office of the Mayor.*)

Black leaders faced new challenges following such dramatic reversals as the University of California's decision to dismantle affirmative action in 1995 and passage the following year of the anti-affirmative action initiative, Proposition 209. "We must be more aggressive and we must be less patient," said the new leader of the Oakland branch of the National Association for the Advancement of Colored People (NAACP). "This rap generation is not going to be a patient group of people singing 'We Shall Overcome.'"

A remarkable diversity of opinion on contemporary social and political issues was evident within the African American community. Although the majority of black Californians continued to support affirmative action, an African American member of the University of California board of regents introduced the resolution to abandon the policy. Likewise, whereas most African Americans supported busing as a means of achieving integration and quality education in the public schools, others became outspoken opponents. Some black families even began supporting private "African-centered schools," hoping that they would better serve the needs of their children.

By far the fastest-growing ethnic group in California was the category described in the census as "Asian or Pacific Islander." California's Asian American population more than doubled during the 1980s, growing at a phenomenal rate of 127 percent. By 1990 nearly 1 out of every 10 Californians was of Asian descent, and 40 percent of all Asians in the United States lived in California. The Census Bureau in 1995 estimated that Asian Americans would make up 20 percent of the state's population by 2020. The influx of Asians was encouraged by the Immigration Reform Act of 1990 which substantially raised the annual number of immigrants allowed into the United States and tripled the number of openings for skilled workers. The composition of California's Asian American community was transformed by the continuing arrival of educated professionals with marketable skills from the Philippines, Korea, Hong Kong, and Taiwan.

The growing diversity within the Asian American community manifested itself in a variety of ways. By the 1990s nearly three-quarters of all Asian Americans were immigrants, whereas 20 years earlier less than half were foreign-born. Tensions increased between the native-born and those who were labeled "FOB," a pejorative acronym for immigrants "fresh off the boat." The newcomers to California came from more than 30 separate cultures. The single largest Asian group continued to be Filipinos, followed by Chinese, Japanese, Koreans, Vietnamese, Cambodians, and Laotians. To encompass also those who came from Guam, Tonga, and other islands of the Pacific, many came to prefer the term "Asian Pacific Americans."

Asian Americans continued to gain additional political power in California. Their role as lobbyists and campaign contributors was crucial in several recent California elections. Asian Americans tended to be considerably more conservative than other minorities, and they often supported candidates who appealed to their interests as homeowners and operators of small businesses. The highest ranking Asian American officeholder was Republican Matt Fong, elected state treasurer in 1994. Two years later Republican Ming Chin, son of a Chinese immigrant potato farmer, was appointed to the California State Supreme Court. In spite of their growing political power, Asian Americans lagged behind other citizens in their rate of voter registration and remained underrepresented in elected offices in both state and local government.

One of the areas where Asian Americans continued to excel was higher education. In the fall of 1991, Asian American students became the largest ethnic group among freshmen at the Berkeley and Los Angeles campuses of the University of California. Nearly all of the Asian Americans were admitted on the basis of their academic merit; half had straight-A averages in high school. "Asian success is a tribute to their hard work and the fact they took difficult courses and made an extra effort," commented one UC regent. Berkeley Chancellor Chang-Lin Tien agreed, pointing out that Asian American high school graduates were more than twice as likely as their white counterparts to meet UC's tough admissions requirements. The high level of educational and economic achievement of the Asian Americans led some demographers to see them as part of "an Anglo-Asian overclass that will dominate California's two-tier society of the 21st century."

The remarkable success of Asian Americans was clouded by an increase in ethnic hostilities during the prolonged recession of the early 1990s. "Fears of the old 'yellow peril' are still alive and well," warned Japanese American historian Nadine Hata, "as the preference for Asian high-technology products and automobiles is blamed for domestic unemployment and general economic malaise." Incidents of vandalism and violence directed against Asian Americans included cross burnings, fire bombings, beatings, and shootings. The director of the Japanese American Citizens League reported "a marked increase not just in the number of incidents of reported harassment but substantively in the viciousness of the harassment."

The largest number of new Californians in recent years were Latinos, most of whom were of Mexican origin. The state's Latino population grew by nearly 70 percent during the 1980s, reaching more than 25 percent of the state's total by 1990. Five years later the Census Bureau estimated that Latinos made up more than 30 percent of the state's population and that by the year 2020 they would exceed 36 percent, comprising the single largest ethnic group in California. Latino Californians tended to be younger than the general population, and their birthrate was nearly twice that of non-Latinos.

Los Angeles County continued to be the center of the state's Hispanic population; the number of Latinos living in the county was expected to more than double between 1990 and 2020, increasing from 3.3 million to 7.5 million. But Latino residents were also moving in record numbers from the crowded neighborhoods of East Los Angeles into the northern reaches of the San Fernando Valley. The Latino population in the Central Valley was also growing rapidly. More than 40 percent of the residents of Fresno, Merced, and Tulare counties were Latino and Asian. "This valley is the richest multiethnic rural environment in the nation, if not the world," observed Central Valley native Gerald Haslam.

Education remained one of the greatest challenges facing the state's Hispanic population. The dropout rate of Latino students continued to be far higher than that of non-Latinos. The state's landmark Bilingual Education Act expired in 1988, and the number of courses available for students with limited English skills remained inadequate. Latino Californians, however, were steadily overcoming the language barrier. "By the third generation, they have replaced Spanish with English," observed Arturo Vargas of the Mexican American Legal Defense and Educational Fund. "People are struggling to be part of this society, not be separate from it."

Latinos also made considerable progress in obtaining greater economic and political power. Although many Hispanic Californians continued to work as farm laborers, a substantial Latino middle class was emerging. The number of Latino-owned firms increased more than 80 percent in the 1980s, and many Hispanic entrepreneurs successfully bid for government contracts set aside for minority-owned companies. Latino business leaders were especially successful in the state's high-technology industry. Twelve of the top Hispanic high-tech firms in the country were in California, including a Santa Clara–based manufacturer of computer components called HispanTech. Despite their continuing low rates of voter registration, Latinos also were increasing in political influence. Helping mobilize the Latino community were Spanish-language newspapers such as *La Opinión*. Edited by Monica Lozano, whose grandfather founded the paper in Los Angeles during the 1920s, *La Opinión* had a readership of nearly half a million. Editor Lozano said that her goal was not just to report the news but to educate her Latino readership in the basics of the American political and economic system. Typical of the new generation of Hispanic leaders was Gloria Molina, the first Latina elected to the legislature in 1982 and the first to serve on the Los Angeles County Board of Supervisors. Molina interpreted her success as a sign that California's Latinos now "have a leadership that is willing to stand up and be counted." In 1996 Fresno Democrat Cruz Bustamante became the first Latino to serve as speaker of the assembly.

The spectacular growth of California's immigrant population became an intensely debated political issue in the 1990s. Republican Governor Pete Wilson in 1991 asserted that foreign immigration was a major reason for the state's economic

Monica Lozano, editor of Los Angeles–based *La Opinión,* the largest Spanish-language daily newspaper in the United States. (*Photograph courtesy of* La Opinion.)

problems. He argued that immigrants were heavy users of welfare and that their high birthrates dramatically increased the number of school-age children in the state. The governor's remarks ignited a firestorm of controversy, renewing a long and bitter debate about the place of immigrants in California society. Angry critics accused Wilson of "race-baiting and scapegoating." The controversy intensified in 1994 as California voters overwhelmingly approved Proposition 187, an initiative designed to deny public services to illegal aliens. (See Chapter 34.) Demographer Leo Estrada observed that the passage of Proposition 187 "was not the culmination of an anti-immigrant movement but rather the opening shot in a long battle to come." The growing Latino population, Estrada concluded, "makes it imperative that Californians confront the future of post-Anglo California."

A glimpse into that future was offered by the Census Bureau's projections in 1995. The bureau predicted that an additional 8 million immigrants would come to California in the next quarter century. By the year 2020, if current trends continued, non-Hispanic whites would number only about 34 percent of the state's population. Leon Bouvier, author of *Fifty Million Californians: Inevitable?* (1991), summed up the global significance of this demographic revolution: "No other industrial nation, let alone state, has ever experienced such a dramatic alteration of its ethnic composition."

The single most important challenge facing Californians in the years ahead was adjusting to the state's growing diversity. The challenge was to appreciate the strengths that came from diversity, to celebrate the differences as well as the shared experiences of this diverse population. "Let's put it this way," said Arturo Vargas. "If California cannot shape a true multicultural society, then the whole country is doomed." Or to put it in more positive terms, if California *can* meet the challenge of diversity, then the whole nation may be illumined by the brilliance of its example.

SELECTED BIBLIOGRAPHY

A good general introduction to the forces shaping contemporary California is Dan Walters, *The New California: Facing the 21st Century* (1992).

On transportation issues, see several publications from the California Department of Transportation: *Delivering on the Promise* (1992); *Travel and Related Factors in California* (1991); *California Transportation Directions: Mobility for 2010* (1991), a blueprint for future development; and *Going Places,* a bimonthly publication of contemporary issues. On the overburdened freeways and possible solutions, see Laura Mecoy, "Gridlock," *California Journal,* XVIII (July 1987), pp. 317–322; Steve Geissinger, "The Gas-Tax Gamble," ibid., XXI (April 1990), pp. 185–202; and Caren Bohan, "Stuck in Traffic," ibid., XXII (August 1991), pp. 349–352.

Useful guides to current issues in educational policy are the California Department of Education's *Fact Book: 1995–1996 Handbook of Education Information* (1996) and *Opening Doors: California Educational Reform* (1989). The critical survey of contemporary challenges is *The Conditions of Children in California* (1989), published by PACE (Policy Analysis for California Education). See also Robert K. Fullinwider, *Public Education in a Multicultural Society* (1996); Michael Kirst, "Education: The Solution to California's Problems," *California Journal,* XXI (January 1990), pp. 49–52; Dexter Waugh, "New Textbooks," ibid.,

XXII (March 1991), pp. 121–127; and William Trombley, "Higher Education for All," ibid., XXII (December 1991), pp. 557–562.

The crisis in health care is described in Kenneth Kizer, "Health: A Prescription for Equity," *California Journal,* XXI (January 1990), pp. 55–60; Lee Wallace, "Five Million Californians Can't Afford to Be Sick," ibid., XX (June 1989), pp. 261–264; and J. S. Taub, "An Ailing System," ibid., XVII (September 1987), pp. 427–434. On the AIDS epidemic see Taub, "The Politics of AIDS," ibid., XIX (February 1988), pp. 54–59; *California HIV/AIDS Update,* a monthly digest of statistical information published by the Department of Health Services, Office of AIDS; and Randy Shilts, *And the Band Played On: Politics, People, and the AIDS Epidemic* (1987).

On the soaring rate of incarceration and the construction of new prisons, see *Crime in California* (1994), published by the Office of the Legislative Analyst; Kristina Emanuels, "Prisons," *California Journal,* XX (December 1989), pp. 507–509; and Lee Romney, "Jail Money," ibid., XXII (August 1991), pp. 365–370. For a view from the inside, see *Corrections: Public Safety, Public Service* (1991) and *CDC Facts* (1992), publications of the California Department of Corrections. The problem of drug abuse is described in Steven White, "Law and Order," *California Journal,* XXI (January 1990), pp. 27–28, and Michaela Jarvis, "The War on Drugs," ibid., XXII (December 1991), pp. 553–566.

Major studies of the changing nature of California's population, in addition to those cited for Chapter 31, include Leon Bouvier, *Fifty Million Californians: Inevitable?* (1991); David Rieff, *Los Angeles: Capital of the Third World* (1992); Byran O. Jackson and Michael B. Preston (eds.), *Racial and Ethnic Politics in California* (1991); and John Horton, *The Politics of Diversity* (1995).

Author Index

Holliday, J. S., 103
Hollon, Jennifer K., 488
Holtzman, Abraham, 329
Honnold, Douglas, 344
Hornbeck, David, 9, 65
Horton, John, 533
Hosokawa, Bill, 357, 404
Houston, James D., 440
Houston, Jeanne Wakatsuki, 440
Howard, Robert West, 171
Hubler, Richard, 466
Hughes, Edna Milton, 225, 344
Hundley, Norris, Jr., 275, 316, 487
Hungerford, Edward, 162
Hunt, Aurora, 117
Hunt, Rockwell D., 77
Hurt, Peyton, 116
Hurtado, Albert L., 53, 144
Huston, Luther A., 373
Hutchinson, C. Alan, 65
Hutchinson, Ralph B., 207
Hutchinson, W. H., 301
Hutchison, Claude B., 162, 207
Hyslop, Richard S., 9

Ichioka, Yuji, 276
Igli, Ina Rae, 153
Inglis, Ruth A., 302
Irons, Peter, 357
Issel, William, 247, 260, 287, 421

Jackson, Byran O., 467, 533
Jackson, Donald, 90, 103
Jackson, Robert H., 52
Jackson, Sheldon G., 65
Jackson, W. Turrentine, 162
Jarvis, Howard, 466
Jarvis, Michaela, 533
Jelinek, Lawrence J., 162, 385
Jenkins, J. Craig, 386
Jensen, James M., 162
Jensen, Joan M., 357, 405
Johnson, David Alan, 116
Johnson, Elizabeth, 487
Johnson, Kenneth M., 90, 403
Johnson, Kristen, 77
Johnson, Marilynn S., 356
Johnson, Moira, 509
Johnson, Carolyn, 224
Johnson, Stephen, 510
Jones, Helen H., 171
Jones, Holway R., 316
Jones, Landon Y., 422

Kagel, John, 329
Kahrl, William L., 315, 487
Kappel, Tim, 343
Karman, James, 343

Katcher, Leo, 373
Katz, Sherry J., 275
Kauer, Ralph, 194
Kaufman, George G., 467
Kazin, Michael, 247
Kelley, Robert, 207, 317
Kelley, Robert L., 162, 317
Kelsey, Harry, 35
Kemble, Edward C., 153
Kemble, John H., 104, 183
Kimes, Maymie B., 316
Kimes, William E., 316
King, Gebhard, 441
King, Joseph, 77
King, Susan, 441
Kirker, Harold, 225, 344
Kirlin, John J., 46, 467, 509
Kirst, Michael, 532
Kirstein, Peter N., 385
Kiser, George C., 385
Kiser, Martha Woody, 385
Kitano, Harry H., 357
Kizer, Kenneth, 533
Kleinsorge, Paul L., 316
Kling, Rob, 487, 509
Knight, Arthur, 302
Knight, Robert E. L., 247
Knoles, George H., 330
Knoll, Tricia, 404
Koppes, Clayton R., 317
Kotkin, Joel, 509
Kreisman, Bern, 487
Krier, James E., 487
Kroeber, Theodora, 19, 143
Kroninger, Robert H., 235
Kung, Shien Woo, 404
Kurutz, Gary F., 103

Labor, Earle, 224
LaBotz, Dan, 301
Lambert, Paul F., 301
Landerer, Susan, 440
Lang, Julian, 9
Lange, Dorothea, 357, 385
Langum, David J., 76, 77, 89
La Pérouse, Jean François Galaup de, 53
LaPorte, Todd R., 509
Lapp, Rudolph M., 144, 404
Larimore, John A., 184
Larrowe, Charles E., 330
Larsen, Charles E., 330
Larsen, Christian L., 422
Larsen, Grace H., 276
Lasker, Bruno, 385
Lavender, David S., 171, 183, 184
Layne, J. Gregg, 260
Layton, Edwin, 287
Lazorowitz, Arlene, 288

Subject Index

Appendix

GOVERNORS OF CALIFORNIA	EVENTS IN CALIFORNIA HISTORY	
	Discovery of (Baja) California	1533
	Cabrillo's discovery of San Diego Bay	1542
	Drake's landing	1579
	Vizcaíno at the Bay of Monterey	1602
		1607
		1620
Gaspar de Portolá	Founding of San Diego	1769
	Discovery of San Francisco Bay	
Pedro Fages	Founding of Monterey	1770
Fernando Rivera y Moncada		1773
Felipe de Neve	Ayala's exploration of San Francisco Bay	1775
	Founding of San Francisco	1776
	Founding of Los Angeles	1781
Pedro Fages		1782
		1783
	Death of Serra	1784
	Visit of La Pérouse	1786
		1787
		1789
José Antonio Roméu	Visit of Malaspina	1791
José Joaquin de Arrillaga		1792
Diego De Borica		1794
		1797
José Joaquin de Arrillaga		1800
		1801
		1803
	Visit of Rezanov	1806
		1809
José Argüello		1814
Pablo Vincente de Solá		1815
		1817
Luis Argüello	End of Spanish rule	1822
José Maria Echeandia		1825
	Visit of Jedediah Smith	1826
		1829
Manuel Victoria		1831
Pío Pico		1832
José Maria Echeandía (South)		
Agustin V. Zamorano (North)		
José Figueroa		1833
	Secularization of the missions	1834
José Castro	Visit of Dana	1835
Nicholás Gutiérrez	Alvarado's "revolution" makes California	1836
Mariano Chico	autonomous	
Juan Bautista Alvarado		1837
	Arrival of Sutter	1839
	Bidwell-Bartleson party	1841
Manuel Micheltorena	Commodore Jones at Monterey	1842
Pío Pico		1845
José María Flores	American occupation	1846
MILITARY GOVERNORS: John D. Sloat,		
Robert F. Stockton, John C. Frémont,		
Stephen W. Kearny, Richard B. Mason,	Capitulation at Cahuenga	1847
	Discovery of gold	1848
Persifor F. Smith, Bennett Riley	Monterey Convention	1849
Peter H. Burnett, Ind. Dem.		
	Admission to statehood	1850
John McDougal, Ind. Dem.	1st Vigilance Committee in San Francisco	1851
John Bigler, Dem.	Wells Fargo founded	1852
		1853
J. Neely Johnson, Amer.	2nd Vigilance Committee in San Francisco	1856
		1857
John B. Weller, Dem.		1858
	Discovery of Comstock Lode	1859
Milton S. Latham, Lec. Dem.		1860
John G. Downey, Lec. Dem.		
		1861
Leland Stanford, Rep.		1862
Frederick F. Low, Union	Building of the Central Pacific	1863
	Mark Twain in San Francisco	1864
		1865
		1867
Henry H. Haight, Dem.		
	University of California chartered	1868
	Transcontinental railroad completed	1869

EVENTS IN AMERICAN HISTORY	PRESIDENTS OF THE UNITED STATES
Founding of Jamestown, Virginia Landing of Pilgrims at Plymouth	
Boston Massacre	
Battles of Lexington and Concord Declaration of Independence	
Treaty of Paris	
Constitutional Convention	
	George Washington
	John Adams
	Thomas Jefferson
Louisiana Purchase	
	James Madison
	James Monroe
	John Quincy Adams
	Andrew Jackson
Independence of Texas	
	Martin Van Buren
	William Henry Harrison, John Tyler
Annexation of Texas Mexican War	James K. Polk
	Zachary Taylor
	Millard Fillmore
	Franklin Pierce
	James Buchanan
Civil War Pacific Railroad Act	Abraham Lincoln
Pacific Railroad Act	
	Andrew Johnson
	Ulysses S. Grant

GOVERNORS OF CALIFORNIA

Newton Booth, Rep.

Romualdo Pacheco, Rep.
William Irwin, Dem.

George C. Perkins, Rep.

George Stoneman, Dem.

Washington Bartlett, Dem.
Robert W. Waterman, Rep.

Henry H. Markham, Rep.

James H. Budd, Dem.

Henry T. Gage, Rep.

George C. Pardee, Rep.

James N. Gillett, Rep.

Hiram W. Johnson, Rep.

Hiram W. Johnson (as Prog.)

William D. Stephens, Rep.

Friend W. Richardson, Rep.
Clement C. Young, Rep.

James Rolph, Jr., Rep.

Frank F. Merriam, Rep.
Culbert L. Olson, Dem.

Earl Warren, Rep.

Goodwin J. Knight, Rep.
Edmund G. Brown, Sr., Dem.

Ronald Reagan, Rep.

Edmund G. Brown, Jr., Dem.

George Deukmejian, Rep.

Pete Wilson, Rep.

EVENTS IN CALIFORNIA HISTORY

Event	Year
Los Angeles anti-Chinese riot	1871
Modoc Indian war	1873
	1875
Workingmen's Party formed	1877
New constitution	1879
Battle of Mussel Slough	1880
Los Angeles Times founded	1881
	1883
Santa Fe Railroad to L.A.	1885
	1887
	1889
Stanford University opened	1891
Sierra Club founded	1892
	1893
	1895
	1897
	1899
Ruef and Schmitz in power	1901
	1902
	1903
San Francisco graft prosecution	1906
Lincoln-Roosevelt League formed	1907
	1909
Progressives sweep elections	1910
Ishi "discovered"	1911
Los Angeles Aqueduct	1913
	1915
Preparedness Parade bombing	1916
	1917
Criminal syndicalism law	1919
	1921
	1923
	1927
First Academy Awards	1929
	1931
Central Valley Project Act	1933
Merriam defeats Sinclair	1934
Grapes of Wrath published	1939
	1941
Japanese American evacuation	1942
	1943
	1945
	1950
	1953
	1959
California water bonds	1960
	1961
Rumford Fair-Housing Act	1963
Berkeley Free Speech Movement	1964
Watts riot	1965
	1967
People's Park riot	1969
BART opened	1972
	1973
	1974
Agricultural Relations Act	1975
	1977
Proposition 13	1978
	1979
Medfly infestation	1981
	1983
Diablo Canyon at full power	1985
Chief Justice Bird rejected	1986
	1989
Term limits imposed	1990
Los Angeles riot	1992
	1993
Population exceeds 33 million	1996

EVENTS IN AMERICAN HISTORY	PRESIDENTS OF THE UNITED STATES
Panic of 1873	
	Rutherford B. Hayes
	James A. Garfield, Chester A. Arthur
	Grover Cleveland
	Benjamin Harrison
Panic of 1893	Grover Cleveland
	William McKinley
	Theodore Roosevelt
Newlands Reclamation Act	
	William H. Taft
	Woodrow Wilson
United States in World War I	
	Warren G. Harding
	Calvin Coolidge
Stock market crash Great Depression	Herbert C. Hoover
	Franklin D. Roosevelt
United States in World War II	
United Nations founded Korean War	Harry S. Truman
	Dwight D. Eisenhower
	John F. Kennedy
	Lyndon B. Johnson
Tonkin Gulf Resolution	
Moon landing Watergate incident Vietnam Peace Agreement OPEC oil price increases	Richard M. Nixon
	Gerald R. Ford
	Jimmy Carter
Three Mile Island nuclear accident	
	Ronald Reagan
Income tax reform	
	George Bush
Persian Gulf War	
	Bill Clinton